MANAGEMENT: THEORY, PROCESS AND PRACTICE

THIRD EDITION

RICHARD M. HODGETTS

FLORIDA INTERNATIONAL UNIVERSITY
MIAMI, FLORIDA

THE DRYDEN PRESS
CHICAGO
NEW YORK
PHILADELPHIA
SAN FRANCISCO
MONTREAL
TORONTO
LONDON
SYDNEY
TOKYO
MEXICO CITY
RIO DE JANEIRO
MADRID

MANAGEMENT:

THEORY, PROCESS AND PRACTICE

THIRD EDITION

This book is dedicated to Steven

Acquisitions Editor: Anne Smith
Developmental Editor: Pat Locke
Project Editor: Brian Link Weber
Design Director: William Seabright
Production Manager: Peter Coveney

Text and cover design by William Seabright
Copy editing by Wanda Giles

Address orders to:

383 Madison Avenue
New York, New York 10017

Address editorial correspondence to:

901 North Elm Street
Hinsdale, Illinois 60521

Library of Congress Catalog Card Number: 81-67234
ISBN: 0-03-059881-8
Printed in the United States of America
234-144-98765432

CBS College Publishing
The Dryden Press
Holt, Rinehart and Winston
Saunders College Publishing

THE DRYDEN PRESS SERIES IN MANAGEMENT

In this century human progress may be characterized by technical and scientific prowess, but it is accounted for by managerial expertise. Without the ability to formulate objectives, to devise plans, and to coordinate people and materials in a synergistic fashion, Henry Ford would never have built his production line and Neil Armstrong would never have walked on the moon. In many undertakings, management, the process of getting things done through people, is the key to success or failure.

The purpose of this book is to familiarize readers with basic modern management concepts and to acquaint them with the present status and the future of this growing field. I have assumed that readers of this text are newcomers to the study and practice of management. Therefore, the book can be used effectively in the first management course in undergraduate or junior colleges. In addition, it can be employed in professional training courses and is useful to practicing executives who wish to update their knowledge of the field.

I have attempted to present the concepts of modern management in a readable, interesting style through the use of the following special features.

DISTINGUISHING FEATURES

Organization

The book is divided into five major parts. Part 1 introduces and examines the challenge of management and the evolution of management thought. Part 2 examines the development of modern management theory, and emphasizes and explains the process school of management thought which is so important to today's practicing manager. Part 3 discusses the quantitative school of management thought; Part 4 views the behavioral school of management. Part 5 takes an overview of current management theory and practice.

After this overview, the concluding part looks at some critical dimensions on today's management scene, including business's social responsibilities, international business, and the growing professionalism of management. The part ends with some practical information on management as a career.

Exhibits

Numerous tables, charts, and illustrations are employed in this text to highlight important concepts and to present them in the clearest possible manner.

Historical Pictures and Biographical Sketches

Part 2 discusses a number of important contributors to early management thought. To provide the reader with a better understanding of these individuals, pictures and biographical sketches of a number of them are included.

Short Cases

Students too often learn theories without understanding their practical applications. For this reason, four short cases appear at the end of each chapter; they give readers many opportunities to apply the principles, processes, and practices presented in the individual chapters, and thus, reinforce the major concepts introduced.

Comprehensive Cases

The book contains four comprehensive cases, each located at the end of a major section or part. The purpose of these cases is to provide readers with an opportunity to integrate and apply many of the ideas contained in the preceding chapters to a realistic situation.

Glossary of Terms

At the end of the text is a glossary of terms that identifies or describes many of the concepts presented in the book. This glossary is more comprehensive than that contained in any other basic management text and provides a definition or explanation of the most important topics dealt with in the text.

SUPPLEMENTS AND TEACHING AIDS

The following supplements and teaching aids have been designed to accompany the text:

Study Guide and Readings—contains readings; fill-in, true/false, and multiple choice questions; work projects for each chapter; and selected readings.

Teacher's Manual—contains a synopsis of the goals and material in each chapter. In addition, it includes answers to the review and study questions at the end of each chapter, questions associated with the cases at the end of each chapter, and a large pool of true/false and multiple choice questions for testing purposes.

ACKNOWLEDGMENTS

Many individuals have played a decisive role in helping me write this book, although I accept full responsibility for all errors of omission and commission. In particular, I would like to thank Professor Fred Luthans, of the University of Nebraska, who provided me with many helpful suggestions and ideas. I would also like to thank those who have read, reviewed, and commented on portions of the text, in particular:

Gerald Bassford, Arizona State University; David Bateman, Southern Illinois University; Richard M. Conboy, University of North Carolina; Jagdish J. Danak, Eastern Michigan University; Ronald Greenwood, University of Wisconsin–LaCrosse; Richard M. Lewis, Central Michigan University; C. W. Millard, Iowa State University; Alfred Modica, Mercy College; Gerald L. Rossy, California State University–Northridge; Robert Rosen, University of South Carolina; Col. Robert L. Taylor, United States Air Force Academy; Edith Zoeber, Iowa State University.

I want to express special appreciation to my colleagues at Florida International University: Dean Leonardo Rodriguez of the School of Business; Professors Steve Altman, Karl Magnusen, and Enzo Valenzi. I am also grateful to Henry Albers, former Dean of The University of Petroleum and Minerals in Dhaharan, Saudi Arabia. Sincerest thanks to Anne Smith, Pat Locke, Brian Weber, Bill Seabright and Peter Coveney of The Dryden Press for their professional efforts. Finally, thanks go to Irene Young and Ruth Chapman for typing the manuscript.

Richard M. Hodgetts
Miami, 1982

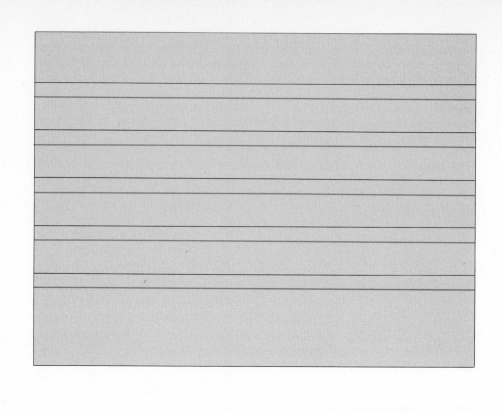

CONTENTS

PART 1

The first part of the book introduces the reader to the field of management. Particular attention is given to three objectives: (1) explaining what management is; (2) setting forth some of the challenges that will confront the manager during the 1980s and 1990s, and (3) studying the evolution of management thought from antiquity to the middle of the current century.

Chapter 1 explains the nature of management and where it is heading. Chapter 2 provides the background necessary for studying the field and determining how to meet the challenges that Chapter 1 describes. Chapter 3 focuses in some detail on particular modern management theories and practices.

The beginning of Chapter 1 discusses what management is and is not. It highlights the role of the manager as a person who works through other people. Then it examines the three waves of change that have altered management history. This discussion gives major emphasis to the third, and current, wave because of the large number of changes that it is setting in motion.

Chapter 2 traces the emergence of management thought from the Sumerians, the ancient Romans, and the Roman Catholic Church through the Industrial Revolution and finally up into the twentieth century. The foundations of modern management

DEVELOPMENT OF MANAGEMENT THEORY

were created by many contributors along this time continuum; this book will pay particular attention to the work of the scientific managers, the administrative management theorists, and the early behavioral researchers. After the contributions of these three groups are examined, they will be placed in a contemporary critical perspective by means of analyses of both their strong and weak points.

Chapter 3 reviews the development of modern management theory. Many people made contributions to early management thought. A few of the major examples are Frederick W. Taylor, who turned interest toward time-and-motion study; Henri Fayol, the early management theorist; and Elton Mayo, one of the early theorists in the sociopsychological aspects of working. The writing of these scholars continues today to exert influence on management theory; therefore, they and other significant early theorists appear in the chapter for historical and present-day reasons. Chapter 3 basically develops the concepts of three types of early modern management theory: scientific management, administrative management, and behavioral observation.

The overriding objective of Part 1 is to familiarize the reader with management by looking at both future challenges and past accomplishments in the field. The book then proceeds logically to the study of modern management theory and practice.

CHAPTER 1

THE CHALLENGE OF MANAGEMENT

GOALS OF THE CHAPTER

MANAGEMENT has been popularly defined as getting things done through people. In more complex terms, it is the process of setting objectives, organizing resources to attain these predetermined goals, and then evaluating the results for the purpose of determining future action. Whatever definition is used, management has for thousands of years been the key to success for individuals and civilizations alike. In this century effective management practices have helped raise the United States to a position of world power. Effective management has also played a key role in the success and development of giant corporations such as General Motors, American Telephone and Telegraph, and IBM. Today, as countries with opposing political theories seek détente, effective management will be needed to bring the sides together. Thus, whether one is examining the prerequisite for world prominence, corporate growth, or international peace, management must be considered.

The first goal of this chapter is to look at the nature of management by examining this process in action. The second goal is to study the waves of change in managerial theory and practice that have affected both employees and consumers. The third is to examine the specific challenges that are going to confront the modern manager because of the most recent wave of change.

When you are finished reading this chapter, you should be able to:

1. Define and describe what is meant by the term management.
2. Compare and contrast the first and second waves of change.
3. Explain the kinds of change the third wave is bringing and the types of challenges that will confront the manager of the 1980s and 1990s.
4. Explain why the study of management requires attention to the past and the future, as well as the present, for a solid grounding in the subject.

THE NATURE OF MANAGEMENT

The overall purpose of this book is to examine the field of management. In doing so, it is helpful to first discuss what a manager *is* and what a manager *is not.* The key characteristic which distinguishes managers from others is that managers get things done *through* other people. Consider the following individual, Sam Begley:

> Sam is the manager of a sales force for a medium-sized hardware manufacturer. Salaries for all salespeople are a direct percentage of sales. Sam's basic salary, however, is guaranteed although he also receives a 1 percent override on everything his people sell and a 15 percent commission on everything he personally sells. Except for Monday mornings, which he spends in the office answering correspondence and talking to his sales staff, Sam spends his entire week in the field, selling merchandise. "I don't have to motivate my people," says Sam. "They know what to do. My job is simply to take care of the office work and then get out and try to supplement my salary through sales activity."

Is Begley a manager? Not in the true sense of the word. There is very little he is doing *through* other people. Basically, he is an entrepreneur who is working for his own account. His job is very similar to that of the salespeople. Of course, he does carry out some managerial tasks, such as planning and organizing the office work, and undoubtedly he is responsible for controlling overall operations. However, these are really secondary to his sales efforts. In the final analysis, Begley does not represent the type of individual who would frequently use the information contained in this text. On the other hand, consider the case of Sharon Eaton:

> Sharon is in charge of the commercial loan department at a major bank. Her job is to maintain current commercial accounts while trying to obtain even more. There are sixteen people in the department, and her job requires her to spend a great deal of time in the office. However, she is also responsible for visiting with customers, entertaining them at lunches and dinners, helping them analyze their banking needs, and providing the services they require. Much of this activity is actually handled by her assistants in the department because she has other functions that also require time. Included in this group are discussing job-related matters with subordinates, assigning tasks to them, attending bank meetings, projecting departmental needs in terms of both personnel and budget and seeing that these are forwarded to higher management, and evaluating the overall performance of the personnel and offering suggestions for improvement.

Managers work through other people.

The job Eaton performs is much more managerial in nature than Begley's. It is certainly not the case that everything she does is through others; she performs many tasks herself. However, she is not entrepreneurial in the sense that Begley is.

When management in action is examined, it is important to remember that there are two parts to the picture. First is the work to be done. Second is the people who will be doing the work. An effective manager is work-oriented but also concerned with personnel. There is a *blend* of work and people. No effective manager can emphasize one to the exclusion of the other. In short, management is the process of getting things done through others, and this process puts emphasis on both the objectives to be attained and the people who will be pursuing them.

This book will undertake a close examination of the management process. Before getting to that, however, it is important to understand the kinds of challenges management is going to be facing in the decades ahead. Conditions will continue to change, and the manager must be prepared to respond to these new developments. What will the future look like? This question is best answered by first examining the past, present, and future waves of change.

THE WAVES OF CHANGE

In his recent book, *The Third Wave,* futurist Alvin Toffler makes some interesting predictions regarding what is likely to happen to the environment of the United States during the upcoming decades.[1] Toffler's analysis is particularly useful for the purposes of this text because it offers insights into the world of work during the 1980s and 1990s. A review of what has taken place during the previous two waves of change, however, is necessary for an understanding of this world.

The First Wave

Before the *first wave of change,* most people lived in small groups, which often migrated throughout a given area foraging for food. Fishing, hunting, and herding were basic to the survival process. The first wave began with the *agricultural revolution.* This revolution spread throughout the globe and dominated history from around 8000 B.C. to the beginning of the eighteenth century.

First came the agricultural revolution.

The Second Wave

Around 1700 A.D. the Industrial Revolution began. As industrialization started to dominate, the first wave lost its momentum. Except among tiny tribal populations in isolated remote areas, the world began to feel the effects of this industrialization. The *second wave of change* brought with it some important rules or principles that have actually programmed the behavior of people.

Then the Industrial Revolution.

One of these was *standardization.* Industrialization made it possible to produce identical goods in millions of units. The result was a general increase in volume and a corresponding decrease in price. People did not seem to mind standardization because they felt the convenience of it was worth the sacrifice of uniqueness.

When goods were standardized.

A second characteristic was *specialization.* In the workplace it became necessary to have large numbers of people performing a series of predetermined rote tasks. Each worker became a specialist at a particular job; their specialization in turn helped workers increase the number of units they could produce. The most famous early illustration of this was reported in the eighteenth century by Adam Smith. Smith noted that the average person could make perhaps one pin in an entire day but that in a factory setting, where there was specialization of labor, with one person drawing out the wire, another straightening it, a third cutting it, and so on, it was possible for a mere ten men to turn out twelve pounds of pins in a single day![2]

Jobs were specialized.

The basic idea was carried over to Henry Ford's assembly line, where sixty cars an hour were being produced by the mid-1920s. And this trend toward specialization was not restricted to manufacturing. It began to dominate many areas, including the professions. Specialists moved in to monopolize fields of knowledge, and these fields became specialized: There were now producers and consumers. The producers were those who provided the service; the consumers were those who used it. In the medical profession doctors provided health care, and the general public used it. In academia, teachers produced the education, and students consumed it.

A third basic characteristic of this revolution was *synchronization,* a coordination or

---

[1] Alvin Toffler, *The Third Wave* (New York: William Morrow, 1980).
[2] Adam Smith, *The Wealth of Nations* (1776; New York: Random House, Modern Library, 1937), pp. 4–5.

blending of all elements in the workplace. For example, since it made no sense for job orders to wait while machinery needed repair, schedules of preventive maintenance were set up so that the machinery was ready to operate and the orders could be quickly processed when the workers were on site. This characteristic even affected the work lives of the employees, for now there were set time periods during which they had to be on the job. Synchronization brought a new kind of time element into the workplace and, combined with standardization and specialization, resulted in the rise of an industrial complex.

Work elements were synchronized.

A fourth characteristic of the second wave was *concentration,* which took two forms. In the first type of concentration, people were taken off the farms and concentrated wherever the factories were located, often in the cities. In the second type, business began to concentrate when major companies started acquiring large inventories of the raw materials and other resources needed to dominate their respective industries. The giant corporations of today have resulted from such action. Consider the fact that as early as the mid-1960s there were only four large American manufacturers of automobiles still in existence. In Europe the situation was the same. Four German auto makers accounted for 91 percent of auto production; in France Renault, Citroen, Simca, and Peugeot turned out virtually all of the country's cars; and in Italy, Fiat alone accounted for over 90 percent of all auto production.

Resources were concentrated.

The situation was similar in many other industries. In America 80 percent or more of the aluminum, beer, cigarettes, and breakfast foods were produced by five or fewer firms in each field. In Germany 98 percent of the photo film, 92 percent of all the plasterboard and dyes, and 91 percent of the industrial sewing machines were being turned out by four or fewer firms in each of the respective categories. The same pattern held in education. At the turn of the century, major universities' student bodies were no larger than 5,000; most were much smaller. Today a university of this size is considered quite small. In fact, within many universities there are now colleges with more than 5,000 students!

A fifth characteristic of the second wave of change was *maximization.* Bigness began to be synonymous with efficiency. Business firms attempted to increase their market shares, their returns on investment, and their overall sales by annual increases of 10 to 15 percent. Any slippage was regarded as inefficient. In this race to maintain growth, acquisition and merger were used. Medium-sized firms combined their assets to become large. Larger firms often bought out smaller, more profitable ones in other industries, thus turning themselves into multi-industry conglomerates with high returns on capital.

Maximization was emphasized.

Finally, the second wave was characterized by *centralization.* Operational decisions were often pushed down the line while overall financial control was maintained at the top. Following the adage that the individual who controls the purse strings controls everything, large firms sought to hold a tight rein on operations. This particular characteristic was noticeable as early as a century ago in the railroads, when management carefully synchronized operations through centralized decision making. Railroad lines extending hundreds of miles from headquarters were run by home office managers.[3]

And operations were centralized.

These six principles have characterized the second wave. To a large degree they were responsible for the growth of the United States as an industrial power; and their use in other countries helped account for the rise of such industrial giants as Germany, England, France, Japan, and the Soviet Union.

If managers were going to operate solely within the framework of these six principles during the 1980s, the challenge of management would not be very great. There would

---

[3] Toffler, *Third Wave,* p. 50.

be basic guidelines to help, and the past would provide sufficient examples of what to expect in the future. However, it does not appear that such will be the case. Currently, a third wave of change is presenting new challenges and opportunities. No student of management can seriously study the field without having a fundamental understanding of what this latest wave promises to bring.

The Third Wave

The *third wave of change is* affecting much of the environment in which many modern organizations operate. New developments are taking place in many different areas, and while it is still too early to relate their overall impact on U.S. industry, it is possible to identify some of the changes that are occurring.

Dramatic new changes are occurring.

Before looking at them, one point requires emphasis: The future will *not* be a mere extension of the past. Dramatic changes are in sight. The management challenge for the upcoming decades will be one of anticipating what is likely to happen in the future and planning a proper response. For many businesses this is a new phenomenon because it strikes at the very heart of the traditional belief that things will remain about the same, a philosophy that has been fundamental to the thinking of many:

> Most people—to the extent that they bother to think about the future at all—assume the world they know will last indefinitely. They find it difficult to imagine a truly different way of life for themselves, let alone a totally new civilization. Of course they recognize that things are changing. But they assume today's changes will somehow pass them by and that nothing will shake the familiar economic framework and political structure. They confidently expect the future to continue the past.[4]

But the future appears very unlikely to replicate the past. Recent evidence suggests that managers of the future will have to cope with a great many changes and challenges, including the following seven: the technological environment, information handling, the world of work, organizational loyalty, organizational structures, redefinition of organizational purpose, and multinational corporations.

Technological Environment Technology will continue to advance. The result will be both opportunities and challenges for business. The management of energy is an excellent example. During the next few decades there will be the development of both renewable and exhaustible sources of energy.

New sources of energy are being discovered.

The result is going to be a large number of different energy sources, in contrast to the present small number. Besides the expansion of energy options, there will be less energy waste, since society will match the types and quality of energy being produced to its increasingly varied needs. The challenge for management will be one of determining how to most efficiently purchase and use this energy.

Genetic engineering is another example of technology that will affect business. Information on genetics is now doubling every two years, and major firms are currently using commercial applications of this "new biology." There is now talk of placing enzymes in automobiles; the enzymes would monitor exhausts and send data on pollution to microprocessors in the car, which would then adjust the engine. Other scientists are studying the possibility of using bacteria capable of converting sunlight into electrochemical energy. Some scientists are also considering whether life forms can be bred to replace nuclear power plants.

There is even a new agricultural revolution taking place. This bio-agricultural move-

---

[4] Ibid., p. 5.

ment is aimed at reducing the dependence on artificial fertilizer. The result will be high-yielding crops that will grow well in sandy or salty soil and also be able to fight off pests. It will be possible to create entirely new foods and fibers along with more effective energy conservation methods for sorting and processing foods. The result of all this should be the end of widespread famine anywhere on earth.

Of course, these are only speculative conclusions. However, scientists are convinced that technology is moving in these general directions. More importantly, technology is going to affect the way things are done in the workplace.

Information Handling The modern manager is a decision maker. As such, the individual requires up-to-date information from which to make choices. During the next few decades computer technology will provide managers with such information more efficiently than is common now. File cabinets and massive paperwork will give way to computer storage facilities. Terminals will link managerial offices, and memos will be sent electronically. Meanwhile, any information the manager wants from the file will be called up from storage in data banks.

At the secretarial level, speech recognition technology will make typing obsolete. Until then, companies will be content with machines that allow secretaries to erase mistakes right from the typewritten page and, for those who want to write long reports or memos and do editing at the same time, TV-like screens already exist that allow the writer to revise, rearrange, underline, insert, and delete before ordering the machine to type the page. These machines are of significant use now in major journalistic enterprises.

With these technological advances will come the inevitable fear of change. How will this new gadgetry affect people's jobs? There is a certain degree of calm and safety associated with being able to see and touch file copies of memos and papers. When information is stored in a data bank, however, many people feel that they are at the mercy of technology. It will be the manager's job to deal with this conflict and resolve it to the satisfaction of both workers and the organization.

The World of Work One of the first questions asked by those who study emerging technology is what effect all of this will have on the work force. Will computers eventually replace 50 percent of the people in every major accounting department? Will "thinking" machines take over the entire assembly line in Detroit? How will technology affect employees? While no final answer is clear yet, recent research shows that mechanization and automation do not bring unemployment. For example, as the blue-collar segment of the American work force has shrunk, the white-collar segment has increased dramatically. Table 1–1 provides some statistics on this development. Note that the percentage of the labor force accounted for by white-collar workers in 1968 was only 46.5, whereas in 1980 it stood at 50.5. Blue-collar workers, meanwhile, declined as a percentage of the labor force. In 1968 they represented 36.7 percent of the work force, but in 1980 they were down to 32.7. Similarly, service workers have increased in percentage while farm workers have declined.

Furthermore, research reveals that technology and employment seem to go hand in hand. For example, between 1963 and 1973, in a seven-nation study, Japan had the world's highest rate of investment in new technology as a percentage of value added. At the same time, Japan also had the highest growth in employment. Meanwhile, Britain, which had the lowest rate of investment, also had the greatest loss in jobs. The situation in the United States was similar to that in Japan.

As the United States continues to advance technologically, occupational jobs will

---

Table 1–1 Occupational Distribution of Workers: 1968 and 1980

Occupational Group	1968 (Actual)		1980 (Projected)	
	Number of Workers (in Thousands)	Percentage of Labor Force	Number of Workers (in Thousands)	Percentage of Labor Force
White-collar workers				
Professional and technical	10,300	13.6	15,500	16.3
Managers and officials	7,800	10.0	9,500	10.0
Clerical	12,800	16.9	17,300	18.2
Sales	4,600	6.0	6,000	6.0
Blue-collar workers				
Craftsmen and first-line supervisors	10,000	13.1	12,200	12.8
Operatives	14,000	18.4	15,400	16.2
Laborers	3,500	4.7	3,500	3.7
Service workers	9,400	12.4	13,100	13.8
Farm workers	3,500	4.6	2,600	2.7
Total	76,000	100.0	95,000	100.0

Note: Discrepancy in totals due to rounding. Source: U.S. Department of Labor.

change. There will be more room for professional, technical, and managerial people, while laborers, operatives, craftsmen, and first-line supervisors will decline in number. This new work force composition will present a variety of new challenges to the modern manager.

Specifically, life in the workplace will change—but not necessarily for the worse. Recent findings show that many people are dissatisfied with their current jobs. For example, consider the information in Table 1–2. At the lower levels of the hierarchy, most of the workers reporting to the surveyors believe they will be changing their occupation in the next five years. Notice, however, that as one goes up the hierarchy, this expectation diminishes. Only one in four professionals feel that they will change their occupation in the next five years.

How will the workplace change during the next couple of decades? One way, as has been noted, is through the introduction of still newer technology. New machinery and equipment will make the work easier to perform. Another trend will be toward a higher quality of work life. Many workers are demanding that they be allowed more control over their working schedules. With this *flexitime* approach they will be able to come to work at, say, 11:00 A.M. and leave at 7:00 P.M. rather than working the typical 9 to 5 schedule of earlier years. This means that people will be able to mesh their biological rhythms with their work demands. Someone who is basically an "afternoon" person will be able to show up around noon and work into the evening. If the person is a "night" person, and the work does not require daytime attendance, it is possible for the worker to come in at 6:00 P.M. and work until 2:00 A.M. Of course, there may be times when the individual has to coordinate activities with the manager or other workers, in which case it will be necessary to work certain times or days of the week. For the most part, however, individual workers will have increased control over their work time schedules.

So will the use of flexitime.

Surprisingly, this idea of a flexible schedule is new to many U.S. businesses, even though it has been employed for years in Europe. By the late 1970s, 25 percent of the

Table 1–2 *How Likely Is It That You Will Change Your Occupation in the Next Five Years?*

Occupation	Likely	Somewhat Likely	Not at All Likely
Semiskilled or unskilled worker	59.7%	24.8%	15.5%
Clerical worker	59.4	26.5	14.2
Other	52.5	27.7	19.8
Salesperson	50.6	21.6	27.8
First-line supervisor or skilled worker	38.7	31.4	30.0
Executive or manager	30.5	28.1	41.4
Professional	25.9	31.4	42.7

Source: Patricia A. Renwick, Edward E. Lawler, and the *Psychology Today* staff, "What You Really Want from Your Job." *Psychology Today,* May 1978, p. 55. Used by permission.

German work force (more than 5 million employees) were on one or another form of flexitime. In France, Finland, Denmark, Sweden, Italy, and Great Britain over 20,000 firms, with an estimated work force of 4 million, were also employing it, as were 15 percent of all Swiss industrial firms. Today, around 15 percent of the U.S. labor force is on flexitime, but the percentage is expected to continue increasing throughout the 1980s.

Additionally, time clocks will be eliminated in many cases, and people will not be confined to specific work locales. They will be allowed to move to other work locations during the day. This same type of freedom will extend to the way people dress and the pace at which they work. All of this may sound quite revolutionary and threatening to the authority of the manager. However, managers are already finding that the old days of bureaucratic control are starting to disappear. Employees are beginning to put up with less organizational control. They are demanding, and in most cases getting, more authority in their work lives.

Compensation packages will change.

This trend is also spreading to the area of employee compensation. In the past, most people were paid a fixed salary and a benefit package on top. In the future, workers will be given more control over what this compensation package looks like. Some employers, like TRW Inc., are now offering their employees a smorgasbord of such fringe benefits as medical benefits, pensions, optional holidays, and insurance. Individuals can tailor the package to their own personal needs. It is becoming evident that money alone does not motivate modern employees. They also want to feel important and to like their jobs. During the 1980s the workplace is going to become "a better place in which to live."

Organizational Loyalty Another development of the 1980s will be a continuing decline in organizational loyalty. Companies will find that their employees are well motivated and eager to pursue organizational objectives only if there is some personal payoff. Work which offers challenge, increased responsibility, and a feeling of accomplishment will

Loyalty will decline.

be vigorously pursued because these things attach a personal reward to the job. Rote, monotonous, boring tasks will be accepted only by those who badly need work or for whom the pay is better than what they could earn elsewhere. However, since no strong motivators are attached, those individuals who must do this kind of work will be likely to continue to see their work as "just a job."

Innovative redesign of the work will take place. People will once again become masters of the job rather than slaves to it. The workplace will evolve into an extension of the individual's social life. Thus, loyalty and camaraderie among employees will increase while organizational loyalty will decline. Interpersonal relations and commitment to objectives will replace blind organizational affiliation. The company as an economic entity will now become a socioeconomic institution. People will like and respect their organizations, but they will not fear them.

Organizational Structures Bureaucratic designs will continue to give way to more adaptive structures. The classical industrial bureaucracy, with its hierarchical, mechanistic designs, was well constructed for repetitive jobs and decision making in a stable environment. Today, however, these designs are being complemented by less top-heavy structures that are flatter and more flexible.

Many of these adaptive designs allow for the free flow of ideas up and down the line. A more democratic, participative approach is employed. Bureaucracy is giving way to *adhocracy,* or temporary structures. Rather than construct hierarchical arrangements that will last indefinitely, some firms now put departments, groups, or teams of employees together for the sole purpose of attaining one specific objective. Once this is done, the unit is disbanded and allowed to flow into other departments, groups, or teams which come together to pursue still other objectives.

Adaptive structures will increase in use.

Many of these adaptive structures make use of the matrix organization, in which employees often have two or more bosses. While representing a sharp break with earlier management practices, the matrix structure is being found a highly effective design for handling certain types of projects.

Redefinition of Organizational Purposes Many major corporations today are undergoing a kind of identity crisis. Top management is being forced to examine the organization's basic purposes. In particular, business firms are beginning to realize that there are many groups to which they have obligations.

In the late 1970s a research study revealed that almost half of all consumers who were polled believed they were getting worse treatment in the marketplace than they received ten years earlier. Additionally, 60 percent said that product quality had deteriorated, and most expressed a distrust of product guarantees. In short, public attention is now beginning to focus critically on the corporation's business activities, and the result is an increased cry for more responsiveness to its customers.

Public confidence in business is at a fifty-year low. Much of this can be traced to changes in personal values. People are making new demands on organizations, and the latter are finding it difficult to respond. Things have never been like this in the past. Until recently, for example, business firms focused their attention primarily on economic issues such as salaries, prices, and production efficiency, but today this is not enough. Corporate critics attack the organization for not providing equal opportunity to a full range of employees, not keeping the environment clean and safe, and not providing the safest and best-constructed products.

The result is that the modern corporation is no longer just a profit-making or goods and services producing institution. It is responsible for dealing with ecological, moral, political, and social problems as well. The corporation, responding both to external and internal pressure, is becoming a multipurpose institution. Examples are abundant. Amoco, the oil giant, in choosing a plant location, now supplements its economic evaluation with a detailed look at the impact of the plant on the physical environment, local employment conditions, and public facilities. Where alternative locations are similar in economic terms but different in social impact, the latter affects the final choice. Control Data has a similar approach. In fact, this firm has built its new plants in the inner-city areas of Minneapolis, St. Paul, and Washington, D.C., in order to help revive urban centers and provide employment to minorities. The corporation states its basic mission as improving the quality, equality, and potential of people's lives.

Social responsiveness will increase.

Other companies are rewarding their managers for meeting affirmative action targets, such as hiring the hardcore unemployed, minorities, and women. At Pillsbury, the giant food corporation, each of its three product groups now has to present not only the customary annual sales plan but a plan for hiring, training, and promoting women and minority group members. Social goals are as important as economic ones. AT&T also evaluates its employees on the attainment of social goals, and at the Chemical Bank in New York, 10 to 15 percent of a branch manager's performance appraisal is tied to such social performance areas as hiring and upgrading minorities, making loans to not-for-profit companies, and participating on community agency boards.

The challenge for the manager is clear. In a multipurpose organization, economic and noneconomic objectives have to be identified, weighted, and interrelated. How does one measure a noneconomic goal such as social responsibility? In the United States this is a question that still has no definitive answer. Many firms try to handle the situation by listing the "good works" they are performing. In Europe, however, there are companies which are very open and objective in this social self-evaluation:

> . . . a social report issued by the giant Swiss food firm, Migros—Genossenschafts—Bund, self-critically confesses that it pays women less than men, that many of its jobs are "extremely boring," and that its nitrous dioxide emissions have risen over a four-year period. Says the company's managing director, Pierre Arnold, "It takes courage for an enterprise to point out the differences between its goals and its actual results."[5]

In the future we are likely to see more attention paid to the area of social objectives. This will be reflected in company efforts to meet them and in reports of the results to stockholders and the general public.

Multinational Corporations Multinational corporations emerged in the post–World War II era, and today they are responsible for much of the trade that occurs between nations. A few examples of U.S. multinationals are IBM, GM, IT&T, Ford Motor, and Exxon. One noted writer remarked that, in contrast to a hundred years ago, the sun today does set on the British Empire—but it does not set on the scores of global corporate empires of the multinational corporations. Yet their impact on international trade cannot be measured solely in terms of geographic dispersion. Their economic size is astounding. The largest have annual sales revenues that are larger than the gross national product of all but about ten nations of the world! Their assets are also vast. For example, Exxon alone has a tanker fleet which is 50 percent larger than that of the Soviet Union.

Multinational management will be important.

The challenge of managing these giant corporations is as great as any that faces a chief executive of a country. Customs, language, culture, and values vary by nations. Managers in the United States may be making decisions that affect the firm's holdings in Brazil. Decisions by the branch manager in Amsterdam may affect the sales of the company's subsidiary in Belgium. In short, the multinational corporation is an interdependent, interactive body which transcends national boundaries. While the job of the overseas manager may appear to be the same as that of a colleague stationed stateside, the overseas job is more demanding because of the effects decisions can have on other overseas affiliates and branches. Additionally, there is the need to interact and fit in with the host country. For years IBM has done this in France by being one of the nation's largest exporters. Regardless of method, the multinational corporation must find ways to work within the framework of the country where it is doing business while also being responsive to the directives of the home office.

---

[5] Ibid., p. 227.

DEALING WITH MANAGEMENT CHALLENGES

The third wave of change thus presents new challenges to management. They can be grouped into ten categories:

1. Forecasting and planning for the future.
2. Designing effective organization structures.
3. Controlling operations.
4. Making effective decisions.
5. Communicating, motivating, and leading personnel.
6. Designing human resource programs for developing people's abilities and talents.
7. Understanding the role and impact of technology on the organization.
8. Being aware of and prepared to respond to social challenges.
9. Having basic understanding of management in the international arena.
10. Having basic knowledge of where the field of management is going and the new challenges that will complement or replace those noted here.

The challenges.

This book specifically addresses these ten challenges:

Challenge	Chapters
Planning	4
Organizing	5, 6
Controlling	7
Decision making	8, 9
Communicating, motivating, and leading	11, 12, 13
Designing human resource programs	14
Understanding the role and impact of technology	10, 15
Social challenges	16
International management	17
Future of management	18

And the response.

Of course, this study of management will do more than merely present the topics that constitute modern challenges. A comprehensive framework brings all these topics together in a unified composite in which the reader will see the relationships among the various functions the manager performs. And many topics not yet mentioned will be addressed by way of providing a comprehensive, up-to-date introduction to the field of modern management. While addressing the challenges of the third wave, this text also provides a great deal of additional practical management information.

AN INVITATION TO MANAGEMENT

Although they will require a well-thought-out approach, the managerial challenges of the 1980s are not beyond solution. This book will provide such an approach by means of a systematic analysis of the field.

From the Past

The foundations of modern management are to a large degree found in the past. The work of early civilizations and the experiences of managers in the Industrial Revolution were important in forming the basic foundations of modern management theory and practice.

The past provides foundation.

During the past century, contributions from individuals in the areas of factory management, administrative levels of the hierarchy, and behavioral sciences all helped mold modern management, and these contributions will be examined in Chapter 2.

To the Present

Management theory has three major lines of approach.

Management theory today has three major themes, or lines of approach, which need to be studied if one is to fully understand the field of management. These will be investigrated in Chapters 3 through 15 of this book, in which modern management theory is thoroughly explored. Such key areas as planning, organizing, controlling, decision making, quantitative methods, communication, motivation, leadership, and human resources development will all be studied. Attention will also be given to current management theory and where it appears to be heading.

To the Future

The future holds new challenges.

Finally, this text will direct attention to changes that will confront management throughout the remainder of this century. Particular focus will be placed on technology, the management of personnel and talent, social responsibility, international management, and corporate democracy. Consideration will also be given to the topic of careers in management. While some of this material will be covered in Chapters 5 through 15, most will be addressed in Chapters 16 through 18.

Readers who have finished this book will know where management has been, where it is today, and where it will be going. More importantly, they will have a basic understanding of the challenges that will be confronting the manager during this decade and will also know some of the tools, techniques, and approaches for dealing with these challenges.

In order to understand the present and predict the future, it is often best to begin with a review of the past. As the great historian Will Durant has noted, "The present is the past rolled up for action, and the past is the present unrolled for understanding."[6] To fully comprehend management theory, process, and practice, it is necessary to know how modern management thought evolved. The managerial challenges of tomorrow will be too important to be handled by expedient decisions. Sound fundamental concepts will have to serve as the basis for effective decision making. Accordingly, no student of modern management will be able to ignore the past. Nor should one wish to, for there is a wealth of basic information that can serve as knowledge that propels one forward to meet the challenges of tomorrow.

SUMMARY

Management is the process of getting things done through other people. Some individuals carry the title of manager but are not managers in the true sense of the word. They may have people reporting to them, but they tend to work alone, seeming to manage their subordinates as an afterthought. Such individuals are basically entrepreneurs, and

---

[6] Will Durant, *The Reformation* (New York: Simon and Schuster, 1957), p. viii.

---

it is likely that they will find themselves unable to cope with the dynamic changes now confronting modern organizations.

In studying these changes, it is possible to examine them in waves. The first wave started around 8000 B.C. and was characterized by the agricultural revolution. The second began in the early eighteenth century with industrialization. This wave was characterized by standardization, specialization, synchronization, concentration, maximization, and centralization.

The third wave, which is now beginning to strike the shores of industrial nations, promises to bring dramatic changes and challenges. Some of the major factors which will affect the modern manager's job are changes in the technological environment, new methods of information handling, new employee demands in the world of work, a decline in organizational loyalty, the evolution of adaptive organizational structures, a redefinition of organizational purpose, and the continued growth of multinational corporations. The impact of these events on the modern manager will be studied throughout this book, with attention directed toward explaining how these changes can be handled. A past-present-future framework will be used.

REVIEW AND STUDY QUESTIONS

1. In your own words, tell what is meant by the term *management*. Compare and contrast managers and nonmanagers. How do their roles differ?

2. How did the first wave of change affect civilization? What happened during this period?

3. When did the second wave of change begin? What changes did it bring?

4. What are the six characteristics of the second wave? Identify and explain each of them.

5. In your own words, explain what is meant by the following statement: Most people, to the extent that they bother to think about the future at all, assume the world they know will last indefinitely.

6. During the next decade, what kinds of changes can be expected in the technological environment? In information handling? How will these changes affect employment? What will their impact on the world of work be?

7. How content are modern workers with their jobs? Explain.

8. What is meant by the term *flexitime*? How likely is it that this concept will increase in use during the current decade? Defend your answer.

9. What is going to happen to organizational loyalty during this decade? Will it increase or decrease? Explain.

10. What will the changes in the bureaucratic designs of most organizations be?

11. How will businesses during the current decade go about redefining their organizational purposes?

12. How important is an understanding of the multinational corporation to the study of basic management? Why should these organizations be included in one's examination of the field? Support your answer.

SELECTED REFERENCES

Anthony, W. P. *Participative Management*. Reading, Mass.: Addison-Wesley, 1978.

Clarkson, S., ed. *Visions 2020*. Edmonton, Alberta, Canada: M. G. Hurtig, 1970.

Davis, Stanley M., and Lawrence, P. R. *Matrix*. Reading, Mass.: Addison-Wesley, 1977.

Drucker, Peter F. *The Concept of the Corporation.* New York: New American Library, Mentor, 1964.

Henderson, H. *Creating Alternative Futures: The End of Economics.* New York: Berkeley Windhover, 1978.

Janger, A. R. *Corporate Organization Structures: Service Companies.* New York: Conference Board, 1977.

Korda, Michael. *Power! How to Get It, How to Use It.* New York: Ballantine Books, 1975.

Loebl, E. *Humanomics: How We Can Make the Economy Serve Us—Not Destroy Us.* New York: Random House, 1976.

Luthans, Fred; Hodgetts, Richard M.; and Thompson, K. A. *Social Issues in Business,* 3d ed. New York: Macmillan, 1980.

Sampson, A. *The Seven Sisters: The Great Oil Companies and the World They Shaped.* New York: Bantam, 1976.

Sloan, A. P., Jr. *My Years with General Motors.* New York: MacFadden-Bartell, 1965.

Smith, Adam. *The Wealth of Nations.* 1776. New York: Random House, Modern Library, 1937.

Toffler, Alvin. *The Third Wave.* New York: William Morrow, 1980.

CASE: *Managerial Challenges*

When Roz Rovelle took a job with her present firm, she had two choices. One was to work on the road; the other was to work in the office, managing a department. On the road she would have been calling on business accounts, examining their needs, telling them about the company's products, and trying to make sales. She would have been given a sales quota and a specific number of accounts to cover each month. From that point on, she could have set her own pace just as long as she contacted and visited all the assigned accounts.

In the office Rovelle supervises eight subordinates. These individuals are responsible for seeing that orders from the salespeople are filled and any problems or complaints, from either the sales force or the customers, are handled.

Rovelle likes her job and feels she has made a wise choice of careers. "Sure," she told a friend, "I could have gone on the road and been my own boss. But the challenges of managerial work are more rewarding. I interact with lots of different people every day. I have met all the salespeople, and I have talked to most of our customers on the phone. So I know many of the same people I would have met had I been on the road. Additionally, I have authority over eight people and quite a bit of leeway in terms of how to resolve problems. This job is exciting! I love it. Oh, I'm sure I would have been happy as a salesperson, but I'm glad I chose management as a career instead."

Questions

1. What is meant by the term *management?* Is Roz Rovelle a manager?
2. What types of challenges does Rovelle face? What did she mean when she said "the challenges of managerial work are more rewarding"?
3. As she moves up the hierarchy, what new challenges do you think she will face? Use the chapter material to help in answering this question.

CASE: We Told You So

A large eastern insurance company recently brought in one of the nation's major computer firms to see if something could be done about the mass of paperwork confronting lower-level insurance personnel. After analyzing the needs of the company, the consulting firm recommended the purchase of a giant computer. The proposal was based on a cost-saving estimate of $3 million spread over the expected ten-year life of the machine.

After a series of top-level conferences, the insurance management decided to make the purchase. Managers then passed this information on to lower-level managers, who, with the help of their own people and some systems department staff, started revising job assignments. Most of the routine paper-processing tasks were to be reassigned to the computer. The rest of the work was to be handled by the regular clerical personnel. The problem, however, was that under this plan over 60 percent of the work was to be allocated to the computer. Not surprisingly, the staff was concerned about its continued employment.

Management tried to allay these fears by categorically stating that all efforts would be made to find work in other departments for any displaced employees. In making good on this promise, within the first month the firm transferred 30 percent of its personnel to other units. However, this move simply increased anxiety among the remaining workers. As one of them said, "You mark my words. There just aren't enough jobs in the company to absorb everyone. So it's just a matter of time before the company announces that it will be laying some of us off."

The statement seemed to reflect the sentiments of other employees because at just about this time, management noticed a decline in cooperation from these people. Both the managers and the systems engineers who were revising the work schedules found many of the workers unwilling to answer questions about their work assignments. Those who would answer provided only minimal information. One manager described the workers as "downright hostile." Another said, "They think they're going to be fired, so they're doing everything they can to screw us up." The result of this series of events was that it took three weeks longer than anticipated to get everything straightened out and transferred to the computer. Meanwhile, what about the clerical personnel? As it turned out, none of them was laid off. Work was found for all.

Questions

1. How common is it today to find technology having an effect on workers' jobs?

2. How much of a problem did the introduction of the computer present to the management team in this company?

3. If you had been in charge, how would you have tried to alleviate the fears of the employees who thought they would be replaced by the computer? Explain thoroughly.

CASE: Jack Dangrath's Evaluation

Jack Dangrath is the newly appointed head manager of an industrial complex located in the Northeast. He took over as head of operations two weeks ago, and his task is clear: Management wants more output and greater efficiency. The Northeast complex has been one of the organization's least efficient. It lost money for the five years preceding Dangrath's appointment.

Since arriving and analyzing the situation, Dangrath has learned a number of things about operations. Some of them follow:

1. The factory work force is inefficient because, among other things, it needs new equipment. The competition has better, more efficient machinery as a result of some key technological breakthroughs by machine manufacturers.
2. Some of the assembly jobs could be done more efficiently if each person assembled more parts—in other words, with less specialization of labor.
3. A recent in-house survey shows that most of the employees would like to try a flexitime working hours schedule.
4. A new computer has been installed in the accounting department, and there is a lot of talk about this department starting to lay people off.
5. Most department and unit managers, feeling that there is too much specialization, want more decision-making authority delegated to them.

Questions

1. Which of the characteristics of the second wave of change appear to be present in Jack Dangrath's new organization? Explain.
2. Which of the challenges of the third wave are now appearing in the organization? Describe them.
3. What would you recommend that Dangrath do in regard to each of the five listed developments? Make your answer as complete as possible.

CASE: Same Old Stuff

As part of honors convocation week, Bill Whitling, vice-president of a large bank, had been asked to talk to a group of graduating seniors in the college of business at State University. He was delighted to do so, as he wanted an opportunity to speak about the dynamic environment in which his firm operated. Whitling felt that the challenges facing his bank's managers typified those that new managers would soon meet. At one point in his talk, he said:

> Today, our management people are being confronted with new problems, and we have to come up with brand new solutions. Managers in our company certainly find that a business education is helpful. But there's a tremendous adjustment that has to be made in moving from the halls of academia to those of industry. Quite frankly, we've never before faced a similar situation; the challenges and problems are brand new.

During the question and answer session that followed, one student asked Whitling, "Aren't modern managers confronting the same basic problems that their counterparts in antiquity had to face? The way I see it, whether we're building the Great Pyramid or Chicago's Sears Tower, the management problems are virtually the same. Oh sure, the problems or issues may be more complex, but our forebears in the Roman Empire or other early civilizations probably wrestled with similar problems. After all, there's nothing new under the sun. Is there?"

Questions

1. Are modern managers facing totally new problems or the same old problems as always? Explain.

2. What problems do today's universities create for managers? Have these problems changed with time? Explain.

3. How can the study of management help modern managers do their jobs more effectively? Explain.

CHAPTER 2

THE EVOLUTION OF MANAGEMENT THOUGHT

GOALS OF THE CHAPTER

Management is not a new concept; it has been practiced for thousands of years. The primary goal of this chapter is to examine the evolution of management thought. The first part of the chapter illustrates some effective management practices from early organizations. Then the focus changes to more recent times and to the emergence of the factory system, the scientific management movement, early management theory, and behavioral beginnings. Finally, the chapter focuses on modern management thought in a comprehensive historical perspective. When you are finished reading this chapter, you should be able to:

1. *Discuss the contributions to management of the Sumerians, the Romans, and the Roman Catholic Church.*
2. *Relate the importance of the Industrial Revolution in the development of management thought.*
3. *Identify the contributions of Frederick Taylor, Frank Gilbreth, Lillian Moller Gilbreth, Henri Fayol, Elton Mayo, and Chester Barnard to the development of modern management thought.*
4. *Discuss the value of the Hawthorne studies to the behavioral approach to management.*
5. *Compare and contrast the contributions and shortcomings of the scientific managers, the administrative management theorists, and the behaviorists in modern management thought.*

MANAGEMENT IN ANTIQUITY

One of the earliest civilizations known is that of the Sumerians, whose culture is famous for the development of a written language. From 3000 B.C. onward, priests in the Sumerian city of Ur (the site of which is now in Iraq) kept business, legal, and historical records on clay tablets. Some of these tablets relate the management practices of Sumerian priests, the most influential class in the civilization. The priests were of such importance, in fact, that it appears highly likely that the Sumerians developed a written language in response to their need for a *managerial control process.*[1]

The ancient Romans also provided numerous illustrations of effective management. Perhaps the most famous is the emperor Diocletian's reorganization of his empire. Assuming his position in A.D. 284, Diocletian soon realized that the empire had acquired an unmanageable form. There were far too many people and matters of importance for the emperor to handle individually. Abandoning the old structure, in which all provincial governors reported directly to him, Diocletian established more levels in the hierarchy. The governors were pushed farther down the structure and, with the help of other administrators, the emperor was able to more effectively manage this vast empire.

The Roman Catholic Church also made important contributions to early management thought. One was the Church's wide use of job descriptions for its priests, bishops, presbyters, and other religious workers. Everyone's duties were clear, and a chain of command that extended from the pope to the laity was created. A second Roman Catholic contribution to management was that of *compulsory staff service,* the requirement that certain members of the church hierarchy seek the advice of other hierarchs before making particular kinds of decisions. A third was the use of *staff independence,* the assignment of certain advisors to key church officials. Since these advisors were not removable by the official they could give the advice they considered best, without fear of reprisals from superiors.[2]

THE INDUSTRIAL REVOLUTION

Although early civilizations and the Church provide illustrations of effective management practices, the technological innovations of the Industrial Revolution had a more dynamic impact on managerial thinking than anything that had occurred previously. This is clearly seen in the history of Great Britain between the years 1700 and 1785, when major changes occurred in the basic organization of production.

First in the century came the *domestic system,* in which people produced goods in their own homes. These were then taken to the local fair and sold. Soon, however, entrepreneurs entered the picture and offered to provide families with necessary production materials and pay them a fixed amount for each unit of output they provided. This was known as the *putting-out system,* and it was characterized by the entrepreneur's putting out the raw materials and then paying for the finished goods. Finally came the *factory system,* characterized by the placing of power-driven machinery under one roof. When significant numbers of people came to a central locale to work, the putting-out system was dead.

A managerial control process was developed.

Empire structure was reorganized

Administrative principles were developed.

The factory system eventually emerged.

---

[1] Will Durant, *The Story of Civilization, Part 1, Our Oriental Heritage* (New York: Simon and Schuster, 1954), p. 131.

[2] James D. Mooney and Alan C. Reiley, *Onward Industry!* (New York: Harper & Bros., 1931), p. 246.

Frederick W. Taylor, often referred to as the Father of Scientific Management, is the best known of all the scientific managers. Born in Germantown, Pennsylvania, in 1856, he spent many of his early years attending school in Germany and France and traveling on the European continent. In 1872 he enrolled in Phillips Exeter Academy to prepare for Harvard College. Although he passed the Harvard entrance exams with honors, poor eyesight prevented him from attending the college. In late 1874 Taylor entered the pattern making and machinist trades, in a small company owned by family friends. In 1878, employment in the machinist trade was difficult to obtain, so Taylor went to work as a laborer at the Midvale Steel Company. Within eight years he rose from ordinary laborer to chief engineer of the works. Meanwhile, continuing his education through correspondence courses and home study, he managed to complete all requirements for a mechanical engineering degree at Stevens Institute.[3]

*Frederick W. Taylor
(1856–1915)*

Management in the factory system was first characterized by strict control of operations. The owners of the enterprises were most concerned with making the greatest possible profit from their investment. A great deal of interest was therefore focused on streamlining operations, eliminating waste, and motivating workers to increase their output. (The motivation came in the form of money.) These developments led to the emergence of the scientific management movement.

THE SCIENTIFIC MANAGEMENT MOVEMENT

The factory system caused management to focus on developing the most scientific, rational principles for handling its people, machines, materials, and money. This challenge took two major forms: (1) how to increase *productivity* (output/input) by making work easier to perform, and (2) how to motivate workers to take advantage of new methods and techniques. The individuals who developed approaches for meeting these challenges helped lay the foundation for what is known as *scientific management.*

Frederick W. Taylor

The need to increase productivity followed the Industrial Revolution from Europe to the United States. The individuals who made scientific management a household word in the United States were, for the most part, trained mechanical engineers. Their major emphasis was on the management of *work,* and to a large degree they saw the worker as merely an adjunct of the machines. The most famous scientific manager in America was Frederick Winslow Taylor.

---

[3] Harlow S. Person, Foreword to *Principles of Scientific Management,* by Frederick W. Taylor, (New York: Harper & Bros., 1911), p. ix.

Bethlehem Steel Experiments In 1898 Frederick Taylor went to work for the Bethlehem Steel Company. While there, he conducted several important studies, the most significant in the area of pig-iron handling.

This experiment involved a group of about seventy-five men who loaded ingots (called pigs) of iron into open railroad cars. When Taylor arrived at Bethlehem Steel, each laborer was loading an average of 12.5 long tons a day. (A long ton is 2,240 pounds.) Taylor decided to experiment with the job to see whether he could increase the output. His research showed that a worker ought to be able to load 47 long tons a day, working 42 percent of the time and "free of load" for the other 58 percent. In order to test the validity of his theory, Taylor chose one of the workers, to whom he gave the pseudonym Schmidt, and began supervising the man very closely. Schmidt was told when and how to work, and Taylor wrote about this basic task concept:

Work instructions were provided.

> Perhaps the most prominent single element in modern scientific management is the task idea. The work of every workman is fully planned out by the management at least one day in advance, and each man receives in most cases complete written instructions, describing in detail the task which he is to accomplish, as well as the means to be used in doing the work. And the work planned in advance in this way constitutes a task which is to be solved . . . not by the workman alone, but in almost all cases by the joint effort of the work-man and the management. This task specifies not only what is to be done but how it is to be done and the exact time allowed for doing it.[4]

By early evening of the first day, Schmidt had loaded 47.5 long tons. Other men in the group were then gradually trained to load this amount.

Work tools were provided.

The experiment in pig-iron handling was only one such experiment by Taylor at Bethlehem Steel. Another dealt with the shoveling of iron ore and rice coal. After determining that an average scoop load of 21 pounds would result in maximum output, Taylor did away with the practice of workers bringing their own shovels. Instead, the company provided shovels, all designed to carry a 21-pound load. As a result of this experiment, the firm was able to reduce the number of yard laborers from 600 to 140, increase each laborer's average number of tons per day from 16 to 59, and cut the average cost of handling a ton of coal from 7.2 to 3.3 cents. At the same time, the average earnings per man per day rose from $1.15 to $1.88.

Taylor's Writings and Philosophy In 1885 Taylor joined the American Society of Mechanical Engineers (ASME). He eventually presented two papers before its membership. The first paper, presented in 1895, was entitled "A Piece Rate System." In it, Taylor expressed concern over some of the incentive payment schemes then being used in industry. As an alternative he recommended a differential piece-rate system. For each job in which it was to be employed, a time-and-motion study would first be conducted. On the basis of the results a standard for a fair day's work would be ascertained. A worker who produced less than standard would receive a certain price for each piece produced. A worker who reached or surpassed standard would be paid a higher per-unit piece rate. For example, if standard were 100 pieces a day, with the low rate being 1.1 cents per piece and the high rate being 1.8 cents per piece, a worker producing 90 pieces would receive 99 cents whereas a worker turning out 102 pieces would receive $1.84.

Wages were tied to output.

In 1903 Taylor presented a second paper, entitled "Shop Management," to the ASME. This time the emphasis was on his philosophy of management. Taylor pointed out the need to provide high wages and attain low per-unit production costs. This, he felt, would entail the scientific selection and training of workers coupled with management—*employee* cooperation.

---

[4] Taylor, *Principles of Scientific Management,* p. 39.

The audiences for both these papers failed to understand Taylor's emphases, thinking money to be of greater concern than systematic managerial work in scientific management. When Taylor put forth his ideas in his 1911 book, *Principles of Scientific Management*, he outlined four principles, the scope of which was greater than time-and-motion study. The *four principles of scientific management* represented a combination of mechanical, conceptual, and philosophical ideas:

First. *Develop a science for each element of a man's work, which replaces the old rule-of-thumb method.*

Second. *Scientifically select and then train, teach, and develop the workman, whereas in the past he chose his own work and trained himself as best he could.*

Third. *Heartily cooperate with the men so as to insure all of the work being done in accordance with the principles of the science which has been developed.*

Fourth. *There is an almost equal division of the work and the responsibility between the management and the workmen. The management take over all work for which they are better fitted than the workmen, while in the past almost all of the work and the greater part of the responsibility were thrown upon the men.*[5]

> Principles of scientific management were developed.

These principles help pinpoint Taylor's two major contributions to modern management. First, he separated the planning function from the operating function. Second, he pointed out the need for a complete change in attitude, almost a revolutionary shift, on the part of both workers and managers toward their jobs. Each had to work in harmony with the other.

Although his papers and writings brought him acclaim, Taylor's fame and his popular title, the father of scientific management, were probably accounted for more by his remarks to a congressional hearing in 1912 than by anything he had previously done. Scientific management and Frederick Taylor become synonymous terms. In some quarters, the system of shop management that he advocated became known as the Taylor system. However, as he stated in his testimony before the House, he was only one of many people instrumental in developing this system. Another, to whom he gave specific credit, was Frank Gilbreth

Frank and Lillian Gilbreth

Frank Gilbreth was a contractor who developed an early interest in the various motions used by bricklayers. Could any extraneous motions be eliminated, thereby reducing the time and effort necessary to lay bricks? After much experimentation, he was able to reduce the number of hand motions required to lay exterior brick from 18 to 4.5 and interior brick from 18 to 2. He also developed an adjustable stand to eliminate the need for stooping to pick up the bricks. Likewise, he had workers use mortar of proper consistency to eliminate "tapping." He was thus able to increase the number of bricks a worker could lay in an hour from 120 to 350.

> Bricklaying techniques were developed.

In 1904 Lillian Moller and Frank Gilbreth, who became known as the father of motion study, were married. Lillian Gilbreth had a strong background in management and psychology, and the two combined their talents for the purpose of developing better work methods. One of their most famous techniques was the use of motion pictures. By filming the individual at work and then playing back the film, they could analyze the person's motions *(motion study)* and determine which, if any, were extraneous.

Since the cameras in those days were hand cranked, Frank Gilbreth invented the *microchronometer*, a clock with a large sweeping hand that records time to 1/2000 of a

---

[5] Ibid., pp. 36–37.

Frank Gilbreth (1868–1924)

Lillian Gilbreth (1878–1972)

Frank Gilbreth, born in 1868, passed the entrance exams for the Mass-achusetts Institute of Technology but decided instead to go into the contracting business. Beginning as an apprentice bricklayer, he quickly became interested in the different sets of motions that were used in training bricklayers. First, the laborer was taught how to lay bricks; then he was taught how to work at a slow pace; finally, he was trained to work at a fast pace. Gilbreth wondered whether any of these three sets of motions could be eliminated in the interest of efficiency. From here he extended his time-and-motion study interests to many other areas of work. His wife Lillian was a constant companion and co-partner, in addition to becoming a renowned authority and inter-national lecturer in the field of management.

Standard hand motions were categorized.

minute, and placed it in the field of work being filmed. (Today, unless the camera contains constant-speed electric motors, the microchronometer is still used in photographing time-and-motion patterns.) Following its invention, the Gilbreths could analyze the individual's motions while determining precisely how long the work took *(time study.)* In addition, they went so far as to categorize all hand motions into only seventeen basic motions (such as "grasp," "hold," and "position"), which they called *therbligs*—Gilbreth spelled backward with the "t" and the "h" transposed.

EARLY MANAGEMENT THEORY

The scientific managers concentrated on the operational level of the organization. Their scope of activities encompassed the workers and the first-line supervisors, but little else. It was inevitable, however, that attention would gradually be focused farther up the hierarchy as the scientific management movement led to changes in the worker-manager ratio. Horace K. Hathaway, vice-president of the Tabor Manufacturing Company, explained:

> At the Tabor Manufacturing Company we have succeeded through the application of the Taylor principles of Scientific Management in increasing our production to about three times what it formerly was, with the total cost approximately the same and approximately the same total of men; of course with a very much smaller proportion of men in the shop, and a very much increased proportion of men in the planning department, or on the management side.[6]

With more and more people entering the management ranks, the study of management soon began to receive attention. These early observers were interested in such questions as what management is, what organizational principles are, and the methods by which managers could more effectively do their jobs. The people who devoted attention to answering these questions helped formulate the basis of modern management theory. The most important of them was Henri Fayol.

---

[6] *First Tuck School Conference on Scientific Management, October 12–14, 1911* (Hanover, N.H.: Amos Tuck School of Administration and Finance, Dartmouth College, 1912), p. 339.

*Henri Fayol
(1841–1925)*

Definition and Teaching of Administration

In 1916 Fayol wrote a monograph entitled *Industrial and General Administration,* attempting in it to synthesize his managerial experience and knowledge.[7] His overall goal was to elevate the status of administration by providing an analytical framework for management. One of the most important sections of this book dealt with the definition and teaching of administration.

Fayol wrote that all administrative activities and business undertakings could be divided into six groups:

1. *Technical operations (production, manufacture).*
2. *Commercial operations (purchases, sales, and exchanges).*
3. *Financial operations (finding and controlling capital).*
4. *Security operations (protection of goods and persons).*
5. *Accounting operations (stocktaking, balance sheet, costing, statistics).*
6. *Administrative operations (planning, organization, command, coordination, and control).*[8]

Fayol analyzed these six operations, noting that the worker's chief characteristic is technical ability, the relative importance of which declines while that of administrative ability increases as a laborer goes up the organizational hierarchy.

Managers need administrative ability.

Technical ability is the chief characteristic of the lower employees of a big undertaking and the heads of small industrial concerns; administrative ability is the chief characteristic of all the men in important positions. Technical ability is the most important quality at the bottom of the industrial ladder and administrative ability at the top.[9]

In contrasting Henri Fayol with Frederick W. Taylor, one sees Fayol was far less concerned than Taylor with the operational level and much more interested in approaching the subject from a general management point of view. In so doing, he made one of his greatest contributions to management—the identification of the administrator's activities

---

[7] Henri Fayol, *Industrial and General Administration,* trans. J. A. Coubrough (Geneva, Switzerland: International Management Institute, 1929).

[8] Ibid., p. 8.

[9] Ibid., p. 15.

or functions: planning, organizing, commanding, coordinating, and controlling. A manager who could carry out these functions properly would be effective. Fayol believed that insufficient attention was given to these functions. Many people recognized them as important but believed they could only be learned on the job, as technical skills are. Fayol disagreed, pointing out that administration could be taught in a scholastic setting, if only a theory of administration could be formulated.

Principles of Administration

Noting that the administrative function was concerned only with the human part of an undertaking, Fayol hastened to explain in his monograph that he employed the word *principles,* not *laws* or *rules,* because of the flexibility required in applying such concepts to people. Since these principles are hardly ever used twice in the same way because of changing conditions, individual administrators must adapt them to their particular needs. The fourteen principles that Fayol felt he had occasion to use most frequently were:

1. **Division of Work.** By employing the classic concept of specialization of labor, increases in efficiency can be achieved.
2. **Authority and Responsibility.** According to Fayol, authority and responsibility went hand in hand. *Authority* was "the right to command and the power to make oneself obeyed."[10] *Responsibility* was a reward or penalty accompanying the use of this power. In later years this principle would be called parity of authority and responsibility, indicating that the two should always be equal.
3. **Discipline.** The essence of discipline is "obedience, diligence, energy, correct attitude, and outward marks of respect, within the limits fixed by the agreement between a concern and its employees."[11]
4. **Unity of Command.** Everyone should have one and only one boss.
5. **Unity of Management.** Not to be confused with unity of command, unity of management calls for one manager and one plan for all operations having the same objective.
6. **Subordination of Individual Interests to the Common Good.** The goals of the organization must take precedence over those of individuals or groups of employees.
7. **Remuneration of the Staff.** Fayol believed that all employees should be paid for their work and that the payment plan should (a) ensure fair remuneration, (b) encourage keenness by rewarding successful effort, and (c) not lead to rewards beyond a reasonable limit.
8. **Centralization.** Fayol felt that centralization of authority was a natural tendency of organizations, since all major decisions were typically made by a few people at the top of the structure. In and of itself, this is neither good nor bad. It is, however, always present to some degree. The challenge is to ascertain what degree is best for the organization.
9. **The Hierarchy.** The hierarchy, or *scalar chain,* as it is often called, is the order of rank that runs through the organization from top to bottom. In order to preserve the integrity of the hierarchy and to ensure unity of command, communications should

---

[10] Ibid., p. 20.
[11] Ibid.

Figure 2–1 Fayol's Gangplank Principle

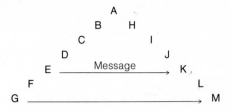

follow this formal channel. However, Fayol recognized the problem of red tape in a large organization and the resulting inadvisability of always taking the long, formal route. In Figure 2–1, for example, if one followed the scalar chain, E would have to ascend the hierarchy to A and then descend it to K in order to pass the lateral message.

To overcome this problem, Fayol prescribed his *gangplank principle*. People at the same level of the hierarchy should be allowed to communicate directly, provided that they have permission from their superiors to do so and that they tell their respective chiefs afterward what they have agreed to do. In this way, the integrity of the hierarchy is never threatened. Furthermore, Fayol remarked, if A made subordinates B and H use the gangplank principle and they did likewise for their subordinates, C and I, much greater efficiency would be introduced into the organization. Although it is an error to leave the hierarchical chain without a good reason, it would be a greater mistake to follow it when such a procedure would prove harmful to the undertaking.

10. **Order.** "A place for everything and everything in its place" was the way Fayol described the principle of order.
11. **Equity.** Equity results when friendliness is coupled with justice.
12. **Stability of Staff.** It takes time for an able employee to settle down to a job and perform satisfactorily. Thus, organizations should encourage the long-term commitment of their employees.
13. **Initiative.** Fayol defined *initiative* as the power to conceive and execute a plan of action.
14. **Esprit de Corps.** Esprit de corps, or morale, depends upon harmony and unity among an organization's staff.

In conclusion, Fayol also pointed out that he had made no attempt to be exhaustive in his coverage of principles. He had merely described some of those he had used most often.

Elements of Administration

The second part of Fayol's book was devoted to a description of the five functions, or "elements," as he called them, of administration: planning, organizing, commanding, coordinating, and controlling. He elaborated upon each as follows:

The functions
of management
are planning,
organizing,
commanding,
coordinating,
and controlling.

Planning requires a forecast of events and, based on the forecast, the construction of an operating program. Forecasts should extend as far into the future as the needs of the organization demand, although ten-year forecasts should be redrafted every five years.

Organizing entails the structuring of activities, materials, and personnel for accomplishing the assigned tasks. This calls for effective coordination of all the firm's resources.

Commanding encompasses the art of leadership coupled with the goal of putting the organization into motion. Setting a good example, making periodic examinations of the organization, eliminating incompetent personnel, and not getting bogged down with detail were some of the suggestions Fayol made for effectively carrying out this function.

Coordinating provides the requisite unity and harmony needed to attain organizational goals. One way of accomplishing this, Fayol believed, was through regular meetings of managers and subordinates. If this function were properly implemented, everything would flow smoothly.

Controlling entails seeing that everything is done in accord with the adopted plan. This function must be applied to all segments of an activity—workers, materials, and operations alike.

Fayol's Contribution

Fayol's contribution to management theory cannot be overstated. First, he provided a conceptual framework for analyzing the management process. In the post–World War II era, when colleges of business began to flourish in the United States, it was Fayol's conceptual framework that provided the guidelines along which many management texts were written. Writers would identify a number of managerial functions and then describe each in depth. Some even went so far as to provide specific principles of management at the end of each section—for example, principles of planning and principles of organizing. These scholars and writers became known as the *management process school,* and there is no doubt that the basic framework originated with Fayol.

Second, the attention Fayol focused on the need and possibility of teaching management via the development of a theory of administration put him in the forefront of classical management theoreticians. Much of what was to follow in the development of management theory and practice constituted an extension and development of his basic ideas.

BEHAVIORAL BEGINNINGS

At the time Henri Fayol and other administrative theorists were investigating the nature of management, interest in its behavioral aspects was generated, marking the beginning of the *human relations philosophy.* Three of the earliest contributors to behavioral and human relations studies were Elton Mayo, the Hawthorne studies researchers, and Chester Barnard.

MAYO'S MULE SPINNING INQUIRY

Mayo's most famous early experiment took place in a Philadelphia textile mill in 1923 and 1924. Its purpose was to identify the cause of high labor turnover in the mule spinning department, where workers made thread or yarn on mules, a type of spinning machine that was also called a mulejenny. Turnover in the company's other departments was between 5 and 6 percent a year, but in the mule spinning department it had risen as high as 250 percent.

Elton Mayo was an Australian who taught ethics, philosophy, and logic at Queensland University and later studied medicine in Edinburgh, Scotland. While in Edinburgh, he became a research associate in the study of psychopathology. Then, under a grant from the Laura Spelman Rockefeller Fund, he came to the United States and joined the faculty of the Wharton School of Finance and Commerce of the University of Pennsylvania. In 1926, he joined the Harvard University industrial research faculty.[12] While he was best known for his participation in the Hawthorne studies, Mayo's writings on the human and social problems of an industrial civilization helped provide important early insights into human behavior in the workplace.

Elton Mayo
(1880–1949)

Rest Periods

Mayo decided to make some changes in the work pattern to see whether the situation would improve. He introduced two ten-minute rest periods in the morning and two more in the afternoon for one of the groups in the department—with astounding results. Morale improved, high turnover ended, and production, despite the work breaks, remained the same. Soon the entire department was included in the rest-period experiment, and output increased tremendously. Monthly productivity, which had never been above 70 percent, rose over the next five months to an overall average of 80 percent; and with this increase came bonus pay, which was given for productivity over 75 percent.

With rest periods, productivity rose.

Analysis of the Results

What led to the high morale, high productivity, and virtual elimination of labor turnover? Mayo felt it was the systematic introduction of the rest periods, which not only helped overcome physical fatigue but reduced what he called pessimistic revery. Mayo extended the term *revery* to mean, basically, outlook on life. The reasoning was that a worker whose monotonous job led toward pessimistic revery would possibly be consumed by this attitude. The reduction of pessimism in the revery would therefore be presumed to increase energy and productivity.

Mayo and his associates drew some interesting physiological and psychological conclusions, but time and further research allowed for additional, more substantial, finds. The Hawthorne studies, which were done soon after Mayo's pioneering work, were notable among them.

HAWTHORNE STUDIES

The Hawthorne studies (1924–1932) had their roots in the logic of scientific management. The initial purpose of these experiments was to study the effect of illumination on output. Begun with that relatively simple goal, these studies at the Hawthorne Works

---

[12]   Daniel A. Wren, *The Evolution of Management Thought,* 2d ed. (New York: Ronald Press, 1979), pp. 299–300.

of Western Electric's plant near Cicero, Illinois, would have four major phases: the illumination experiments, the relay assembly test room study, the massive interviewing program, and the bank wiring observation room study.

Illumination Experiments

The illumination phase of the Hawthorne studies lasted two and a half years. During this period, three different experiments were conducted, with notable improvement in experimental design as the tests continued. However, the researchers were unable to ascertain the relationship between illumination and output.

Even so, the company did not feel that the experiments had been unsuccessful. On the contrary, Western Electric management believed that it had gained invaluable experience in the technique of conducting research and was eager to push forward. The result was phase two of the studies, the relay assembly test room experiment. Elton Mayo and a number of Harvard researchers entered at this stage in the program, though the Harvard group did not play a significant role until the third phase of the study.

Relay Assembly Test Room

In order to obtain more control over the factors affecting work performance, the researchers decided to isolate a small group of workers from the regular work force. Five assemblers and a layout operator (all women) were placed in a room with an observer who was to record everything that happened and maintain a friendly atmosphere. The six workers were told that the experiment was not designed to boost production but merely to study various types of working conditions so that the most suitable environment could be ascertained. They were instructed to keep working at the regular pace.

Once the impact of most of these new changes was noted, the researchers moved the experiment into its second stage. During this stage, rest pauses were introduced in order to determine what effect they would have on output. The result was an increase in productivity, leading to the initial hypothesis that the pauses reduced fatigue and thereby improved output. Applying this theory further, the researchers introduced shorter workdays and workweeks. Once again, output increased. However, when these changes were later terminated and original conditions re-established, output still remained high, indicating that the change in conditions was not the only reason for the increase in output. Some investigators hypothesized that the increases were related not to the rest pauses or shorter working hours but to the improved outlook that the workers had toward their work. But no one seemed able to answer the question of what the improved outlook could be related to.

After rejecting various hypotheses, the researchers concluded that the most likely cause was that changes in the social conditions and in the method of supervision brought about the improved attitudes and production rates. In order to gather information on this idea, management decided to investigate employee attitudes and the factors to which they could be traced. The result was a massive interviewing program. This program started simply as a plan for improving supervision, but it actually marked the turning point in the research and for a time overshadowed all other aspects of the project.

Massive Interviewing Program

Over 20,000 interviews were conducted in the third phase of the studies. The interviewers began by asking employees direct questions about supervision and the work environment in general. Although the interviewers made it clear that answers would be kept in strict confidence, the responses to questions were often guarded and stereotyped. The approach was therefore changed from direct to nondirect questioning. The employees were free to choose their own topics. A wealth of information about employee attitudes resulted. The researchers realized that an individual's work performance, position, and status in the organization were determined not by that person alone but also by the group members. Peers had an effect on individual performance. In order to study this more systematically, the research entered its fourth and final phase, that of the bank wiring observation room.

A nondirective interviewing technique was employed.

Bank Wiring Observation Room

In choosing a department to study, the investigators decided to concentrate on a small group engaged in one particular type of work rather than to encompass many groups with dissimilar jobs. The department chosen for the study was the bank wiring department, which had an all-male staff. For the next six months, the work and the behavior of this group were observed.

The Group's Output One significant finding was that most of the workers were restricting their output. Why did the workers restrict output? One told the interviewer that if they did too much work, the company would raise the expected amount. Another felt they might work themselves out of a job simply by working too hard and doing too much. Others felt that a slow pace protected the slower workers, preventing them from looking bad. It should also be noted that management seemed to accept this informal rate, though there was no official notice of it.

Some workers restricted their output.

The Supervisory Situation Study of the supervisory situation in the room also provided human behavioral insights, for the manner in which the men treated their superiors differed. Most of the employees regarded the group chief as one of themselves. As a result, they thought nothing of disobeying him. The section chief fared a little better. The assistant foreman, on the other hand, received much different treatment. The same pattern existed in the case of the foreman. In fact, when he was present, the workers refrained from any activity that was not strictly in accord with the rules. Thus, the workers' respect for, and apprehension in the presence of, others seemed to increase as these others progressed up the organizational hierarchy.

The workers treated the managers differently.

Group Dynamics Another aspect of the group that was closely observed was that of interpersonal relationships. The researchers gained a great deal of knowledge about the informal organization that existed in the room. For example, most of the workers engaged in various games, including baseball pools, shooting craps, sharing candy, and "binging." The latter, a device used to control individual behavior, consisted of hitting a worker as hard as possible on the upper arm. This person was then free to retaliate by striking back just as hard. Although the stated reason was to see who could hit the hardest, the underlying cause was often one of punishment for those who were accomplishing either too much or too little.

Interpersonal relations were studied.

Job trading and the helping of one another provided further bases for studying the group's behavior. Some individuals sought help while others gave it, although such action was in direct violation of company rules. This led to interest in the development of friendships and antagonisms. Who liked whom and who disliked whom?

Social Cliques By studying the types of games and other interactions of the participants, the investigators were able to divide the men into two groups, or cliques, which they labeled A and B. Several conclusions were drawn from the specification of these groups.

First, location in the room influenced the formation of a clique. The A group was located in the front of the room, the B group in the rear. Second, some men were accepted by neither clique. Third, each clique regarded itself as superior to the other, with the opinions based on either the things clique members did or the things they refrained from doing. For example, Clique A did not trade jobs and did not "bing" as often as did Clique B. Conversely, the members of Clique B did not argue among themselves or engage in games of chance as often as did Clique A. Fourth, each clique had certain *informal group norms* or sentiments which anyone wanting acceptance into the groups had to subscribe to. F. J. Roethlisberger and William J. Dickson identifed the first four of these, and George C. Homans later stated the fifth:

The researchers were able to identify social cliques.

1. *You should not turn out too much work. If you do, you are a "rate-buster."*
2. *You should not turn out too little work. If you do, you are a "chiseler."*
3. *You should not tell a superior anything that will react to the detriment of an associate. If you do, you are a "squealer."*
4. *You should not attempt to maintain social distance or act officious. If you are an inspector, for example, you should not act like one.*
5. *You should not be noisy, self-assertive, and anxious for leadership.*[13]

Norms of behavior were also identified.

Findings and Implications of Hawthorne

The Hawthorne studies constituted the single most important foundation for the behavioral approach to management. The conclusions drawn from them were many and varied.

Elimination of Mental Revery In Elton Mayo's opinion, one of the major explanations of the results rested with the elimination of what he had earlier called pessimistic revery. However, on the basis of the findings of the Hawthorne studies, Mayo now realized that rest pauses or changes in the work environment did not, of themselves, overcome this problem. Rather, the key was to be found in the reorganization of the workers. Thus, Mayo realized that the results were caused not by such scientific management practices as rest periods, but by sociopsychological phenomena, of which the restructuring of social networks is an example.

The restructuring of the social network was more important than rest periods.

Hawthorne Effect A second finding, and probably the most widely cited, is that of the *Hawthorne effect,* which is simply the observation that when people know they are being watched, they will act differently than when they are not aware of being observed. Applying this concept to the increase in productivity in the relay room, many modern psychologists contend that it was not the changes in the rest pauses that led to increased output but the fact that the workers liked the new situation, in which they were considered to be of some significance. The attention given them led them to increase their output. The Hawthorne effect thus seemed to lead to the decline in revery, but further investigation indicated that it was apparently not the only factor involved.

The novelty of the situation was important.

Supervisory Climate The relay assembly test room work force did more work than ever before, but the bank wiring room workers restricted their output. There had to be more than a Hawthorne effect and a resulting decline in pessimistic revery.

---

[13] F. J. Roethlisberger and William J. Dickson, *Management and the Worker* (Cambridge, Mass.: Harvard University Press, 1939), p. 522; and George C. Homans, *The Human Group* (New York: Harcourt, Brace & World, 1950), p. 79.

Chester I. Barnard (1886–1961)

What, then, accounted for the difference in output between the two rooms? The major difference may well have been the type of supervision. In the relay room the observer took over some of the supervisory functions, but in a supportive style. In the bank wiring room, however, the regular supervisors were used to maintain order and control. The observer was relegated to a minor role, having none of the authority of his relay room counterpart. This particular finding downplays the Hawthorne effect, which has probably received undue emphasis for far too long a time.

The style of supervision was another critical factor.

The Light from Hawthorne The illumination experiment at Hawthorne might be said to have lighted the way for the human relations research to follow. It was difficult for the original investigators of human relations studies to persevere in view of the various letdowns and surprises of the Hawthorne studies. But these researchers did continue and, as a result, reached two significant milestones.

First, the Hawthorne studies did yield insights into group and individual behavior. The researchers had laid important foundations, even though they realistically had to concede that they were further from the goals they had expected to achieve at Hawthorne than they might have hoped during the studies. Second, the Hawthorne studies had focused attention on the supervisory climate, providing an impetus for later research on leadership style.[14]

Chester I. Barnard (see biography above) was interested in making a logical analysis of organizational structure and applying sociological concepts to management, which he did in his book *The Functions of the Executive.* His work has proved so influential to the study of management that one writer has credited him with having had "a more profound impact on the thinking about the complex subject matter of human organization than has any other contributor to the continuum of management thought."[15] His theory has been of major importance in the development of management theory.

[14] For example, there were the pioneering studies conducted by Ronald Lippitt and Ralph K. White under Kurt Lewin at the University of Iowa. One of their best-known articles is "Patterns of Aggressive Behavior in Experimentally Created 'Social Climates,'" *Journal of Social Psychology,* May 1939, pp. 271–276.

[15] Claude S. George, Jr., *The History of Management Thought,* 2d ed. (Englewood Cliffs, N.J.: Prentice-Hall, 1972), p. 140.

Functions of the Executive

In *The Functions of the Executive,* Barnard pointed out that there had been no theory on the universal characteristics of organizations that seemed to correspond to his experience or to the implicit understanding shared by the leaders of any given organization. Much of what had been written, furthermore, seemed unrealistic and illogical. Using executive experience as his guide, Barnard sought to state two things: a description of the organizational process and a theory of cooperation.

He defined the formal organization as "a system of consciously coordinated activities of two or more persons."[16] Within this structure the executive is the most strategic factor, the person who must maintain a system of cooperative effort. The entire process is carried out through three essential executive functions.

There are three essential executive functions.

The first executive function is the establishment and maintenance of a communication system. It is the executive's primary job, and it is accomplished through careful employee selection, the use of positive and negative sanctions, and the securing of the informal organization.

The second executive function is the promotion and acquisition of essential effort from employees of the organization. It requires the recruiting of personnel and the development of an incentive program.

The third executive function is the formulation of the purpose and objectives of the organization. This calls for the skillful delegation of authority and development of a communication system for monitoring the overall plan.

The Theory of Authority

Throughout his book, Barnard emphasized the importance of inducing the subordinate to cooperate. Merely having the authority to give orders is insufficient, for the subordinate may refuse to obey. The result of this reasoning has become commonly known as the *acceptance theory of authority.* Authority, or the right to command, depends upon whether or not the subordinates obey. Naturally, one could reason that it is possible for the executive to bring sanctions, but this will not necessarily ensure acceptance of the orders, for the employee may be willing to accept any fate dealt out by management.

The acceptance theory of authority is explained.

The entire acceptance theory of authority would be quite threatening if this were all there was to it. Management might literally be at the mercy of the subordinates. However, Barnard realized that the consent and cooperation of subordinates are often easily obtained. First, the four conditions necessary for acceptance are generally present, so workers will regard a communication as authoritative. Second, each individual has what Barnard called a "zone of indifference." Orders falling within this zone are accepted without question. The others either fall on the neutral line or are conceived of as clearly unacceptable. The indifference zone tells the story, and it will be either wide or narrow, depending on the inducements being accorded the individual and the sacrifices the worker is making on behalf of the organization. The effective executive assures that all individuals feel they are receiving more from the organization than they are giving. This widens the indifference zone, and the subordinates agreeably accept most orders. Third, one person's refusal to obey will affect the efficiency of the organization. It will also threaten the other members. When this happens, co-workers will often pressure the individual to comply, and the result is general stability within the organization.

Zones of indifference are important.

---

[16] Chester I. Barnard, *The Functions of the Executive* (Cambridge, Mass.: Harvard University Press, 1938), p. 73.

Barnard's Contribution

Barnard made several important contributions to management theory. First, he described executive functions in analytic and dynamic terms, in contrast to the descriptive writers who had preceded him. Second, he stimulated interest in topics such as communication, motivation, decision making, objectives, and organizational relationships. Third, he advanced the work of Fayol and others who had been concerned with management from the standpoint of principles and functions. Barnard, drawing upon his interest in the psychological and sociological aspects of management, extended these ideas to include the interaction of people in the work force.

EARLY MANAGEMENT THOUGHT IN PERSPECTIVE

The scientific managers, early management theorists, and human relations researchers all made significant contributions to management, and all were complementary to one another. Frederick W. Taylor and his associates conducted important time-and-motion study research for forty years, 1880 to 1920. Then the early theorists in the years between 1915 and 1945 provided important information about the administrative side of management. From 1912 to 1955, the human relations researchers added a new level of sophistication to management thought. The objective of this part of the chapter is to place these three groups in perspective, first by examining some of the weaknesses and shortcomings of each group and then by reviewing the positive side of their contributions.

Scientific Management Shortcomings

Although the scientific managers made many important contributions to management, much of their work reflected a very limited understanding of the human element in the workplace. For example, most of the scientific management theorists seriously believed that money was the worker's prime motivation. This belief resulted in the development of various incentive payment plans such as Taylor's differential piece rate; if the employees worked harder, they would earn more money. Such thinking led these traditionalists to view the worker as an economic man.

Economic Man The term *economic man* refers to an individual who makes decisions that maximize economic objectives. In the case of the worker, it is the individual willing to stay on the job from dawn until dusk in order to take home the biggest paycheck possible. Wage incentive plans are very important to this type of person because they provide economic opportunity.

Lacking a solid understanding of human behavior, the scientific managers were unable to comprehend why not all employees took advantage of any chance to maximize their income. They failed to realize that some people might be happy merely to earn a satisfactory amount of money.[17]

Economic men maximize economic objectives.

The Irrationality of Rationalism A second shortcoming, complementary to the economic man theory, was the scientific managers' view of the worker as a totally rational human being who would weigh all alternatives and then choose the one that would give the greatest economic return. This thinking, of course, completely omitted any consideration of social factors. Furthermore, as noted by sociologist Peter M. Blau, "To administer a social organization according to purely technical criteria of rationality is irrational,

People are complex beings.

---

[17] Herbert A. Simon, *Administrative Behavior,* 3d ed. (New York: Free Press, 1976), p. xxix.

FIGURE 2–2 The Transformation Process

Incentive Payment Plan (Input) → Transformation Process (Black Box) → 10% Productivity Increase (Output)

because it ignores the nonrational aspects of social conduct."[18] The word *complex* would have been much more appropriate than *economic*, for many factors besides money motivate the worker.

The Black Box The scientific managers could have overcome these problems if they had concerned themselves with what is called the *black box concept*. For example, suppose that a company introduces a new incentive payment plan and productivity increases by 10 percent. Why does the increase in productivity occur? Is it brought about by the opportunity to earn more money? Is it caused by an increase in morale because the workers think management is interested in their well-being? Or is it caused by a third, as yet undemonstrated, reason? As Figure 2–2 shows, the answer rests in the black box, the transformation process that takes place between input and output.

The scientific managers did not analyze the transformation process.

To understand what goes on during this process, it is necessary to understand the importance of the human element. The Hawthorne researchers attempted to study this process by ascertaining, for example, why output increased in the relay room but did not increase in the bank wiring room. The scientific managers, however, were unconcerned with this line of thinking. They knew that workers produce more while working individually as opposed to working in groups, and they used this information to guide them in organizing the work force. Their basic approach to the management of people was simplistic, and this created limitations to their work.

Classical Management Deficiencies

The basic weakness of the classical theorists, especially Fayol, was that their statements on management principles were often too general to be of much help to the practicing manager. This problem is illustrated by the unity of command principle.

Unity of Command The unity of command principle states that everyone should have one, and only one, boss. Luther Gulick, a classical theorist in the 1930s, indicated quite clearly the importance that early management theorists assigned to this principle:

The significance of this principle in the process of co-ordination and organization must not be lost sight of. In building a structure of co-ordination, it is often tempting to set up more than one boss for a man who is doing work which has more than one relationship. Even as great a philosopher of management as Taylor fell into this error in setting up separate foremen to deal with machinery, with materials, with speed, etc., each with the power of giving orders directly to the individual workman. The rigid adherence to the principle

---

[18] Peter M. Blau, *Bureaucracy in Modern Society* (New York: Random House, 1956), p. 58.

of unity of command may have its absurdities; these are, however, unimportant in comparison with the certainty of confusion, inefficiency, and irresponsibility which arise from the violation of the principle [19]

The unity of command principle seems to contradict the principle of specialization (or division of labor), which states that efficiency will be increased if one task is divided among the members of a group. Herbert A. Simon, the American economist who was awarded the 1978 Nobel Prize in economic sciences for his research into the decision-making process in economic groups, has noted:

If unity of command, in Gulick's sense, is observed, the decisions of a person at any point in the administrative hierarchy are subject to influence through only one channel of authority; and if his decisions are of a kind that requires expertise in more than one field of knowledge, then advisory and informational services must be relied upon to supply those premises which lie in a field not recognized by the mode of specialization in the organization. For example, if an accountant in a school department is subordinate to an educator, and if unity of command is observed, then the finance department cannot issue direct orders to him regarding the technical, accounting aspects of his work. [20]

If unity of command were to be as vigorously enforced as Gulick suggested, specialization would be impeded. Realistically, it is necessary to introduce some flexibility into the interpretation of the principle. In so doing, however, other problems arise. The principle seems to lack some of its previous authority and may be less effective in solving administrative problems.

The Problem with Principles The classical theorists enumerated lists of principles in an attempt to make management more of a science and less of an art. This was an admirable objective, but in the process of implementing it, the theorists forced a rigidity into some principles, such as unity of command. In other cases, they were superficial in their attention.

Close analysis of classical principles reflects many shortcomings. Suffering the problems of both rigidity and vagueness, the theorists dealt with authority, responsibility, and other principles as concepts. However, when managers attempted to apply these ideas to the organizational structure, the outcome was far from satisfactory.

Unity of command is considered too inflexible a principle.

Inadequacy of the Human Relations Approach

The Hawthorne studies had a significant impact on management thought. One reason for this is that they complemented the work of the traditionalists. This is clearly seen in Figure 2–3, which applies the contributions of Taylor, Fayol, and Mayo to an organization chart. Taylor did the bulk of his work at the lower management–worker level; Fayol's contribution came at the administrative management level; the Hawthorne studies cut across the entire spectrum, providing information of value to all levels of management. Nonetheless, these studies and the resulting human relations movement had a number of problems.

The Scientific Method and Hawthorne One of the major criticisms of the human relations approach is directed at the very heart of the movement. Some researchers claim that the Hawthorne studies were not sufficiently scientific. These critics contend that the re-

[19] Luther Gulick, "Notes on the Theory of Organization," in *Papers on the Science of Administration,* ed. Luther Gulick and L. Urwick (New York: Institute of Public Administration, 1937), p. 9.

[20] Herbert A. Simon, *Administrative Behavior,* pp. 23–24.

Figure 2–3 Contributions to Management Thought

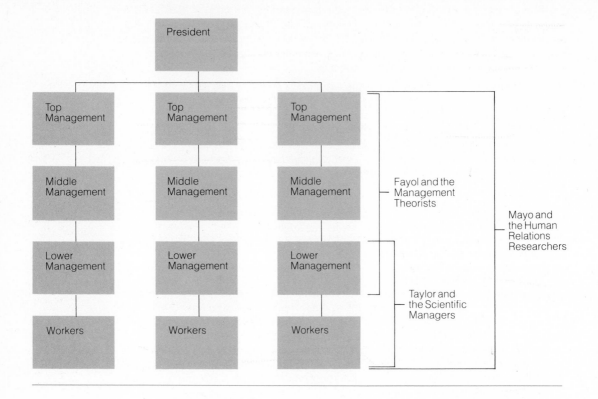

searchers held preconceived ideas and biases that affected their interpretation of the results. Others contend that the supporting evidence for the conclusions was just plain flimsy. Henry A. Landsberger, who made a systematic analysis of these studies in his book *Hawthorne Revisited,* criticized the studies further, challenging that the plant was not really typical because it was a thoroughly unpleasant place in which to work; that the researchers accepted management objectives, viewing the worker as a mere means of attaining these goals; and that the researchers gave inadequate attention to the personal attitudes people brought with them to the job, thus overlooking the effect of the unions and other extra-plant forces.[21]

The research procedure is criticized.

The Human Relations Philosophy Another criticism of the human relations movement is directed at one of its basic concepts, the idea that employee participation leads to job satisfaction and job satisfaction bring about increased productivity. Recent research challenges the assumption that happy workers are productive workers. Job satisfaction is a multidimensional variable, impossible to explain in such simplistic terms. Output depends not only on a person's morale but also on individual goals and motivation within

Happy workers are not necessarily productive workers.

---

[21]   Henry A. Landsberger, *Hawthorne Revisited* (Ithaca, N.Y.: Cornell University Press, 1958).

Human Relations	Human Resources
1. People need to be liked, to be respected, and to belong.	1. In addition to wanting to be liked, respected, and needed, most people want to contribute to the accomplishment of worthwhile objectives.
2. The manager's basic job is to make each employee believe that he or she is part of the departmental team.	2. The manager's basic job is to create an environment in which subordinates can contribute their full range of talents to the attainment of organizational goals. In so doing, he or she must attempt to uncover and tap their creative resources.
3. The manager should be willing to explain his or her plans to the subordinates and discuss any objections they might have. On routine matters, he or she should encourage participation by them in the planning and decision-making process.	3. The manager should allow participation in important matters as well as routine ones. In fact, the more important the decision, the more vigorously he or she should attempt to involve the subordinates.
4. Within narrow limits, individuals and groups should be permitted to exercise self-direction and self-control in carrying out plans.	4. The manager should continually try to expand the subordinates' use of self-control and self-direction, especially as they develop and demonstrate increased insight and ability.
5. Involving subordinates in the communication and decision-making process will help them in satisfying their needs for belonging and individual recognition.	5. As the manager makes use of the subordinates' experiences, insights, and creative abilities, the overall quality of decision making and performance will improve.
6. High morale and reduced resistance to formal authority may lead to improved performance. They should at least reduce intradepartmental friction and make the manager's job easier.	6. Employee satisfaction is brought about by improved performance and the chance to contribute creatively to this improvement.

the work force. In essence, the human relationists' philosophy was simplistic, and by the late 1950s it was fading from the scene. It was replaced by what some individuals call a *human resources philosophy,* which contains a more viable interpretation of the modern worker. Table 2–1 provides a comparison of the human relations and human resources theories.

The Positive Side of the Picture

It should be noted that only the shortcomings and deficiencies of the scientific managers, classical theorists, and human relationists have so far been mentioned in the chapter, for the positive accomplishments have been outlined earlier. It is, after all, impossible to view a school of thought in proper perspective if one examines only the strengths.

Yet it would be unfair not to give credit to these three groups for their accomplishments. They made mistakes, but they were breaking new ground; and many of the facts known to us today remained mysteries to them. Still they persisted, gathering information that proved useful. The scientific management pioneers helped industry reach new heights of efficiency. Contributions from the early management theorists have helped train executives in the principles of planning, organizing, and controlling. Human relations research provided important insights into human behavior in the work environment; and as they went along, these researchers improved their research design. Some of the early Hawthorne experiments, for example, were redone because the researchers realized they were not controlling some of the causal variables. Their concern with formulating an adequate research procedure has carried over to the present day, as reflected in the high degree of importance currently assigned to the scientific method as a research tool. Although there is no universally accepted method, there is general agreement as to the basic steps, which follow:

1. ***Identify the problem.*** Precisely what is the objective of the entire investigation?
2. ***Obtain preliminary information.*** Gather as many available facts as possible about the problem area. Obtain background information.
3. ***Pose a tentative solution to the problem.*** State a hypothesis, which can be tested and proved to be either right or wrong, that is most likely to solve the problem.
4. ***Investigate the problem area.*** Using both available data and, if possible, information gathered through experimentation, examine the problem in its entirety.
5. ***Classify the information.*** Take all the data that have been gathered and put them in an order that expedites their use and helps establish a relationship with the hypothesis.
6. ***State a tentative answer to the problem.*** Draw a conclusion regarding the right answer to the problem.
7. ***Test the answer.*** Implement the solution. If it works, the problem is solved. If not, go back to step 3 and continue through the process again.

Steps in the scientific method are listed.

This method is highly regarded by researchers. As Fred N. Kerlinger notes in his outstanding work, *Foundations of Behavioral Research:*

> The scientific method has one characteristic that no other method of attaining knowledge has: self-correction. There are built-in checks all along the way to scientific knowledge. These checks are so conceived and used that they control and verify the scientist's activities and conclusions to the end of attaining dependable knowledge outside himself.[22]

The refinement of this procedure has played a key role in modern management.

SUMMARY

Management is not a new concept. It has been employed for thousands of years, as seen in the practices of the Sumerians, the Romans, and the Roman Catholic Church. However, the emergence of the factory system presented management with a new challenge. With industrialization it became necessary to develop rational, scientific principles for handling workers, materials, money, and machinery. The scientific managers played a major role in helping attain this objective.

---

[22] Fred N. Kerlinger, *Foundations of Behavioral Research,* 2d ed. (New York: Holt, Rinehart and Winston, 1973), p. 6.

Figure 2–4 Changes in Managerial Philosophy

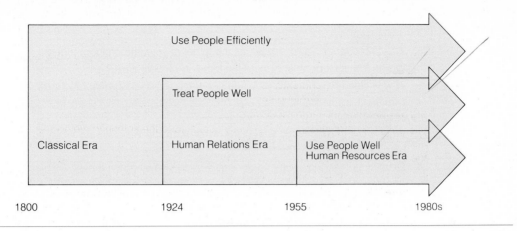

The primary goal of these managers was that of achieving the highest productivity possible by devising efficient work methods and encouraging employees to take advantage of these new techniques. In the United States, scientific management was made famous by people such as Frederick W. Taylor. His experiments at Bethlehem Steel illustrated the importance of time-and-motion study, and his differential piece-rate system provides students an insight into the types of wage incentive payment plans used during this period. Another important scientific manager of the day was Frank Gilbreth, renowned for his work in time-and-motion study and for a large body of work in management in which he collaborated with Lillian Gilbreth.

The success of the scientific managers brought about changes in the worker–manager ratio and moved the focus of attention farther up the hierarchy. The result was two distinct levels of inquiry about management. The first sought to identify generally the purview of management. The second sought to examine both individual and group behavior in organizations.

The most famous of the early management theorists was Henri Fayol. Fayol's outstanding contribution was the conceptual framework he provided for analyzing the management process. In the behavioral area, Elton Mayo studied group behavior in organizations. The Hawthorne studies, however, had an even greater impact on the field, and they became the single most important foundation for the behavioral approach to management. Meanwhile, Chester Barnard, whose acceptance theory of authority is still regarded as a major landmark in the development of management theory, made the most memorable contribution to early behavioral knowledge.

In perspective all three groups—the scientific managers, the classical theorists, and the human relationists—had shortcomings. Yet it must also be realized that they complemented each other, helping to form the basis for modern management theory and practice. The efficiency goals of the scientific managers and classical theorists led to the human relations philosophy of treating people well, which in turn has been replaced, as seen in Figure 2–4, by a human resources philosophy of using people well.

REVIEW AND STUDY QUESTIONS

1. What contributions did the Sumerians make to early management thought? Diocletian? The Roman Catholic Church? Put these contributions in your own words.
2. What was the domestic system? The putting-out system? The factory system? Explain each.
3. Why is Frederick Taylor known as the father of scientific management?
4. Why is Frank Gilbreth known as the father of motion study?
5. Why is Henri Fayol known as the father of modern management theory?
6. Did the Hawthorne researchers find any relationship between illumination and output? Explain.
7. What were the norms to which the workers in the bank wiring room subscribed? Identify and describe them.
8. Of what significance to management were the Hawthorne studies? Explain.
9. According to Chester Barnard, what are the three essential executive functions? Explain each.
10. What is the acceptance theory of authority? Do you agree with it? Explain your answer.
11. What is meant by the term *economic man*?
12. In understanding human behavior, what is meant by the term *irrationality of rationalism*?
13. What is the major argument raised against classical management principles? Be specific in your answer.
14. Summarize the major criticism directed toward the Hawthorne studies.
15. How does the human relations philosophy differ from the human resources philosophy?
16. What is the scientific method? Outline the steps in the process.

SELECTED REFERENCES

Anderson, B. F. *The Psychology Experiment: An Introduction to the Scientific Method.* Belmont, Calif.: Wadsworth Publishing, 1966.

Argyris, C. *Personality and Organization.* New York: Harper & Row, 1957.

Barnard, Chester I. *The Functions of the Executive.* Cambridge, Mass.: Harvard University Press, 1938.

Dubin, R. *Human Relations in Administration,* 2d ed. Englewood Cliffs, N.J.: Prentice-Hall, 1961.

Fayol, Henri. *General and Industrial Management.* Translated by Constance Starrs. London: Sir Isaac Pitman & Sons, 1949.

Gantt, Henry L. *Work, Wages, and Profits.* New York: Engineering Magazine, 1910.

Gilbreth, Frank B. *Motion Study.* New York: D. Van Nostrand, 1911.

Gilbreth, Lillian M. *The Psychology of Management.* New York: Sturgis and Walton, 1914.

Jay, Anthony. *Management and Machiavelli.* New York: Holt, Rinehart and Winston, 1967.

Kakar, S. *Frederick Taylor: A Study in Personality and Innovation.* Cambridge, Mass.: MIT Press, 1971.

Landsberger, Henry A. *Hawthorne Revisited.* Ithaca, N.Y.: State School of Industrial and Labor Relations, Cornell University Press, 1958.

Mayo, Elton. *The Human Problems of an Industrial Civilization.* Cambridge, Mass.: Harvard University Press, 1946.

Mee, J. F. *Management Thought in a Dynamic Economy.* New York: New York University Press, 1963.

Merrill, C. F., ed. *Classics in Management.* New York: American Management Association, 1960.

Milner, B. "Application of Scientific Methods to Management in the Soviet Union." *Academy of Management Review,* October 1977, pp. 554–560.

Mooney, J. D., and Reiley, A. C. *Onward Industry!* New York: Harper & Bros., 1931.

Munsterberg, H. *Business Psychology.* Chicago: LaSalle Extension University, 1915.

———. *Psychology and Industrial Efficiency.* Boston: Houghton Mifflin, 1913.

Roethlisberger, F. J. *Management and Morale.* Cambridge, Mass.: Harvard University Press, 1941.

Roethlisberger, F. J., and Dickson, W. J. *Management and the Worker.* Cambridge, Mass.: Harvard University Press, 1939.

Shepard, Jean M. "On Alex Carey's Radical Criticism of the Hawthorne Studies." *Academy of Management Journal,* March 1971, pp. 23–32.

Simon, H. A. *Administrative Behavior,* 3d ed. New York: Free Press, 1976.

Taylor, Frederick W. *Principles of Scientific Management.* New York: Harper & Bros., 1911.

Urwick, L. *The Elements of Administration.* New York: Harper & Bros., 1943.

Wrege, C. D., and Perroni, A. G. "Taylor's Pig-Tale: A Historical Analysis of Frederick W. Taylor's Pig-Iron Experiments." *Academy of Management Journal,* March 1974, pp. 6–27.

Wren, D. A. "Scientific Management in the U.S.S.R., with Particular Reference to the Contribution of Walter N. Polakov." *Academy of Management Review,* January 1980, pp. 1–11.

———. *The Evolution of Management Thought,* 2d ed. New York: Ronald Press, 1979.

CASE: *For a Few Dollars More*

A national manufacturing firm recently received a number of large orders for industrial equipment. Realizing that it would be unable to fill the orders unless a dramatic increase in output could be achieved, the company instituted an incentive plan to supplement the current hourly wage. Under this new program, all increases in productivity would result in direct pay increases of similar magnitude. For example:

Old Hourly Wage	Productivity Increase (in Percent)	Productivity Bonus	New Hourly Wage
$8.00	10%	$ .80	$ 8.80
8.00	20	1.60	9.60
8.00	30	2.40	10.40
8.00	40	3.20	11.20
8.00	50	4.00	12.00

In addition, the company was willing to apply the same incentive scheme for Saturday work, which paid time and a half, and Sunday work, which paid double time. Top management indicated that it was shooting for a 40 percent increase in productivity across the board.

Within sixty days, however, it became evident to management that the plan was not working. On the average, productivity was up only 17 percent, and despite all management efforts to promote weekend work only 23 percent of the workers were willing to work on Saturday and 14 percent on Sunday.

In giving his opinion of the situation, one manager said: "What more do the workers want? Under this new pay scheme they can increase their pay way above what they would ordinarily earn. However, most of the workers I talked to say they're not interested in the extra money. One of them told me he spent the whole weekend working in his garden. Another took his kids fishing for two days. I just don't understand guys like that. They'd rather loaf than work. I guess the Protestant Ethic is dead."

One of the workers, however, gave a different reason for the unexpectedly low productivity increases: "Who cares about the extra money? I'm making more than enough now. What am I going to do with an extra $2,000? Better that I stay home and enjoy my family and watch television on Sunday. I'm not going to knock myself out for a few dollars more."

Questions

1. Why is the incentive scheme having so little effect?

2. How would Frederick Taylor interpret the results?

3. What suggestions would you make to management? Incorporate the black box concept into your answer.

CASE: *My Boss Doesn't Understand Me*

Today, many workers feel that their superiors do not really understand them. Managers are accused of having very set, erroneous ideas about how to handle their employees. They assume that people dislike work, have to be threatened with punishment to get them to attain organizational objectives, lack ambition, dislike responsibility, and want to be told what to do. Does management really operate under these assumptions? Robert Townsend, former president of Avis Rent-a-Car, seems to think so. He summarizes the five assumptions above like this:

1. *Office hours nine to five for everybody except the fattest cats at the top. Just a giant cheap time clock. (Are we buying brains or hours?)*

2. *Unilateral promotions. For more money and a bigger title I'm expected to jump at the chance of moving my family to New York City. I run away from the friends and a lifestyle in Denver that have made me and my family happy and effective. (Organization comes first; individuals must sacrifice themselves to its demands.)*

3. *Hundreds of millions of dollars are spent annually "communicating" with employees. The message always boils down to: "Work hard, obey orders. We'll take care of you." (That message is obsolete by fifty years and wasn't very promising then.)*[23]

---

[23] Robert Townsend, *Up the Organization* (Greenwood, Conn.: Fawcett Publications, Inc., 1971), p. 120.

Questions

1. Did the scientific managers operate according to these five managerial assumptions? Explain.

2. What have we learned from the Hawthorne research that shows these assumptions to be wrong? Explain.

3. What can management do to overcome these erroneous assumptions?

CASE: **Technicians and Managers**

A management consulting firm in New York City received a phone call from a local industrial machine manufacturer. The company's board of directors had just concluded its quarterly meeting and had decided that something had to be done to improve operations. For the sixth consecutive quarter, profits had declined. Sales were higher than ever, but costs were apparently out of control.

The consultants spent ten weeks examining the firm's operations. Everyone in the company was interviewed, from the chief executive officer to the janitor. When the team finished its analysis, it submitted a 212 page report to the board. One of its key findings follows:

Since its inception, the company has had a policy of promoting from within. The prime criterion for these promotions appears to be technical competence. This is as true at the upper levels as at the lower ones. And it is not uncommon to find managers down on the machine floor examining and commenting on technical problems. Unfortunately, this leaves little time for managing. In fact, managerial functions such as planning, organizing and controlling are given almost no attention. What the company needs is an influx of outside management people who will place less attention on the technical side of the job and more on the management side.

Questions

1. How do these findings fit into Fayol's philosophy of management?

2. How common is it to find managers spending more time on the technical than on the managerial side of their job? Explain.

3. How can these problems be overcome?

CASE: **The Firefighter**

A fire broke out on the third floor of a machine shop on Long Island. According to the fire department, workers on the floor had apparently been throwing oily rags in the corner for three or four days. The maintenance crew had not picked up the rags. As a result, when someone flipped a lighted cigarette butt onto the rags, they immediately ignited.

As soon as the workers saw the blaze, most of them vacated the premises and gathered out in the parking lot. However, at least fifteen minutes passed before anyone turned in an alarm. This was done by Jaime Rodriguez, a new employee who was delivering some equipment to one of the work stations when he suddenly saw the blaze. Rodriguez pulled the fire alarm and then raced to the wall for a fire extinguisher. When the fire fighters arrived, they found Rodriguez vigorously fighting the blaze. Thanks to his assistance, the fire was quickly brought under control.

The first fire fighter on the scene told management: "Without that guy's quick thinking, you might have lost the whole building. He managed to confine the fire to one small area until we could get here and put it out." A thankful management gave Rodriguez a $10-a-week salary increase and a check for $500. Most of the workers, however, did not share management's point of view. Some of their remarks included:

"That guy Rodriguez is an idiot. He could have gotten his tail burned off. And for what? A crummy $500 and a piddly raise."

"My job around here is running a drill press. They don't pay me to fight fires or even to report them. It's not in my job description."

Six months later, Rodriguez quit the company. When asked why, he said: "I don't like working with these guys. Somehow we just don't get on."

Questions

1. Based on the information in this case, what conclusions can you draw about the norms and values of the workers? What is their code of expected behavior?

2. If you were told that there was a union in this shop, would that help explain the comments made by the workers? Would it be possible to draw any conclusions about worker–management relations? Explain.

3. Why do you think Rodriguez quit? Explain your opinion.

MODERN SCHOOLS OF MANAGEMENT THOUGHT

GOALS OF THE CHAPTER

Since World War II, management research has been a very busy and productive field. The concepts of Taylor, Fayol, Mayo, and their associates have expanded as scholars have increased past knowledge about management. The result has been that, at least at the present time, management theory is in what can be called a schools phase, and any student who approaches the field without a basic understanding of these schools does so at a considerable disadvantage.

The schools represent viewpoints on what management is and how it should be studied. Obviously, not everyone in management can be placed in a particular school; some defy such simple categorization. Nevertheless, the background and training of management theorists and practitioners are reflected in their beliefs about management and, in most cases, make them candidates for one of the three schools of thought that will be examined in this chapter: the management process school, the quantitative school, and the behavioral school. The goal of this chapter is to examine each of these schools in depth. When you have finished this chapter, you should be able to:

1. State the basic beliefs and tenets of the management process school.
2. Identify the ideas to which advocates of the quantitative school subscribe.
3. Understand the philosophy and composition of the behavioral school.
4. Describe the weaknesses present in each of the three schools.
5. Discuss the possibility of synthesizing the three schools into a unified composite.

Table 3–1 The Management Process as Seen by Various Authors

Functions	Fayol	Dessler	Haimann, Scott, and Connor	Hampton	Koontz, O'Donnell, and Weihrich	Sisk	Stoner	Wren and Voich
Planning	X	X	X	X	X	X	X	X
Organizing	X	X	X	X	X	X	X	X
Commanding	X							
Staffing		X	X		X			
Directing					X			
Influencing			X					
Actuating							X	
Coordinating	X							
Leading		X		X		X		
Controlling	X	X	X	X	X	X	X	X

Sources: Henri Fayol, *General and Industrial Management* (London: Sir Isaac Pitman and Sons, 1949); Gary Dessler, *Management Fundamentals: A Framework,* 2d ed. (Reston, Va.: Reston Publishing, 1979); Theo Haimann, William Scott, and Patrick E. Connor, *Managing the Modern Organization,* 3d ed. (Boston: Houghton Mifflin, 1978); David R. Hampton, *Contemporary Management* (New York: McGraw-Hill, 1981); Harold Koontz, Cyril O'Donnell, and Heinz Weihrich, *Management,* 7th ed. (New York: McGraw-Hill, 1980); Henry L. Sisk, *Management and Organization,* 3d ed. (Chicago: South-Western Publishing, 1977); James A. F. Stoner, *Management* (Englewood Cliffs, N.J.: Prentice-Hall, 1978); and Daniel A. Wren and Dan Voich, Jr., *Principles of Management: Process and Behavior,* 2d ed. (New York: Ronald Press, 1976).

MANAGEMENT PROCESS SCHOOL

The *management process school,* which is sometimes called the classical school, traces its ancestry to Henri Fayol. Its primary approach is to specify the *management functions* such as: planning, organizing, commanding, coordinating, and controlling. Its proponents continue to view these functions as a process that is, carried out by managers.

During the years immediately following World War II, the management process school flourished. The major reason for its acceptance can be traced to the outline it provides for the systematic study of management. A student who can identify management functions and then examine each in detail has a wealth of information about the field. Although modern management scientists (quantitative theorists) and behaviorists might take issue with this statement, some of the most prominent books in the field have been based on a process framework.

Table 3–1 presents the management process as seen by Fayol and seven current textbooks. As shown in the table, the scholars agree on the functions of planning, organizing, and controlling, but they appear to disagree about the others. However, many process school advocates place the blame for the seeming disagreement on semantics, or word choice. What one person calls directing, another includes in a definition of organizing. If the functions were spelled out in detail, everyone would have the same basic list of subfunctions or activities.

An Ongoing Framework

A major tenet of the process school is that the analysis of management along functional lines allows the construction of a framework into which all new management concepts can be placed. For example, a skeletal design of planning, organizing, and controlling emerges. Any new mathematical or behavioral technique that can improve managerial performance will fall into one of these three functional areas. The result is an enduring systematic design. Although this concept is now under attack, there is little doubt that the

Process approach provides a skeletal design.

Figure 3-1 Noninterrelated Management Functions

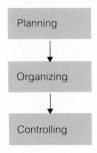

Figure 3-2 Interrelated Management Functions

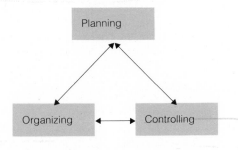

framework provided by the management process school has been the major reason for its acceptance by both students and practitioners.

Management as a Process

Management process proponents see the manager's job as a process of interrelated functions. Consider, for example, the case of planning, organizing, and controlling. Figure 3-1 does not represent management as a process because the functions follow in sequential order; only an indirect relationship exists between planning and controlling. Everything seems to be rigidly predetermined. Figure 3-2 more accurately represents the process concept of management as consisting of interrelated functions that are neither totally random nor rigidly predetermined. They are, instead, dynamic functions, each one playing an integral role in a larger picture in which all the functions are integrated. The total is thus greater than the sum of its parts.

Management is viewed as an interrelated functional process.

Management Principles

Another belief of process school advocates is that *principles of management* can be derived from an intellectual analysis of the managerial functions. Principles of each of the functions can therefore be extracted by dividing the manager's job into its components. For example, there is the *primacy of planning principle*, which states that planning precedes all other managerial functions. Managers must plan before they can organize and control. Under the organizing principle, called *absoluteness of responsibility*, a manager cannot escape responsibility for the activities of individual subordinates. The manager can delegate authority but not responsibility. If something goes wrong in delegated work, the subordinate has made the error and may be responsible for whatever penalties the manager exacts; but the error is, overall, the responsibility of the manager. The *exception principle*, a principle of control, holds that managers should concern themselves with exceptional cases, not routine results. Under this principle, significant deviations, such as very good or very bad profit performance, merit the manager's time far more than average or expected results.

The process principles are designed to improve organizational efficiency. They must not, however, be looked upon as rules, since a rule is supposed to be inflexible. For example, a sign that says "No Smoking" is a rule: It demands a certain kind of action and allows no deviations. Conversely, a principle, as used here, is merely a useful guideline that does not require rigid adherence. Advocates of the management process school, therefore, view principles simply as general guidelines that must be constant focal points for research. If a particular principle proves invalid or useless, it should be discarded. But it must not be assumed that a principle will be useful at all times or under all conditions or that a violation constitutes invalidation. Since management is an art as well as a science, the manager remains the final arbiter in choosing and applying principles.

Universality of Management Functions

Process school advocates also believe that basic management functions are performed by all managers, regardless of enterprise, activity, or hierarchical level. The manager of a manufacturing plant, the administrator of a hospital, and the local chief of police all carry out the same managerial functions. This is also true for their subordinate managers all the way down the hierarchy, although the percentage of time devoted to each function will, of course, vary according to the level. For example, again using planning, organizing, and controlling as illustrations, low-level managers, who are concerned with detailed and routine types of work, tend to do a great amount of controlling and less planning and organizing. However, as one progresses up the organizational chain, the work requires more creativity and administrative ability, resulting in an increase in the amount of time needed for planning and a decrease in that required for controlling. Figure 3–3 shows these proportional relationships.

Advocates believe that management process is universal.

A Philosophy of Management

The process school also stresses the development of a management philosophy. This requires answering such questions as: Precisely what does a manager do? What kinds of values are important to management? What values are important to workers? The development of a management philosophy results in helping the manager understand and establish relationships between material things and human beings. Process school advocates believe that managers can accomplish this feat more easily by following the management process theories, because then their activities revolve around certain functions. In carrying them out, managers employ the fundamental beliefs and attitudes to which they subscribe. The result is a modus operandi that links the management process with the fundamental ideals, basic concepts, and essential beliefs of the manager. The

A philosophy of management can be developed.

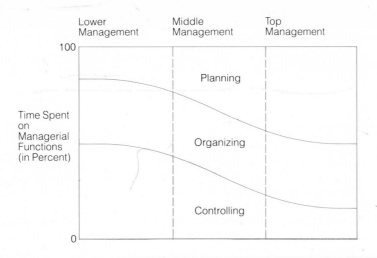

outcome is a philosophy that helps the manager win the support of subordinates in achieving organizational objectives. It also provides the groundwork for future action.

The process school has many advantages, the major one undoubtedly being the framework it offers for analyzing the field. Although viewed by many of its critics as simplistic and too static to be useful, it has been better received by practitioners and students than any of the other schools of management thought.

QUANTITATIVE SCHOOL

The *quantitative school,* which is also called the management science school, consists of those theorists who see management as a body of quantitative tools and methodologies designed to aid today's manager in making the complex decisions related to operations and production. Proponents of this school are concerned with decision making and, to a large degree, are modern-day adherents of Taylor's scientific management movement. They give a great deal of their attention to defining objectives and the problems that surround their achievement. This type of orderly, logical methodology is helpful in constructing problem-solving models. As will be seen later in the book, the approach has been effective in dealing with inventory, materials, and production control problems.

In the post–World War II era, many management scientists came onto the business scene. Today, they go by various and sundry titles, from management analysts to operations researchers to systems analysts. However, they share a number of common characteristics: (a) the application of scientific analysis to managerial problems, (b) the goal of improving the manager's decision-making ability, (c) a high regard for economic effectiveness criteria, (d) a reliance on mathematical models, and (e) the utilization of electronic computers. For purposes of this discussion, all individuals meeting these criteria are collectively placed in the quantitative school. Two topics that have been of major interest to these people are optimization and suboptimization.

Management scientists share some common characteristics.

Optimization and Suboptimization

It is a general managerial truth that most people do not maximize their goals. Instead, they satisfice them: For example, managers do not usually try to make all possible profit; they try instead to achieve a satisfactory level. However, it is possible sometimes, through the *optimization* of production (that is, the combining of all the resources in the right balance), to maximize profit. Maximization is a very difficult task, and to attain it, an approach called suboptimization is often used. *Suboptimization* means using less than the total of each input in order to maximize the total output, or profit. For example, consider a production setting in which materials are ordered, processed, and finished. A firm would try to suboptimize each of the three functions by using only the amount of each that would result in the greatest profit from each component. George R. Terry explains the process of achieving maximization through optimization and suboptimization in this way:

> Suppose our objective is to maximize production profits. To achieve this we consider the common portions of most enterprises to be (1) input, (2) process, and (3) output. Also, we optimize production, assuming all we can produce will be sold at a satisfactory market price. Since the totality—production—is to be optimized, its components of input, process, and output are optimized, as each relates to the totality. Common parlance for this is to suboptimize the components. Step No. 1: Input, or raw materials being received, are suboptimized. This will depend upon forecast demand, inventory carrying cost, and order processing cost. Likewise, Step No. 2: Process, or materials processed, are suboptimized by adequate consideration to production capacity, machine setup cost, and processing cost for each product. Last, Step No. 3: Suboptimization of output or products finished is obtained by considering product demand and transportation cost.[1]

Each step in the production process (ordering, processing, and finishing goods) is affected by suboptimization factors, as Figure 3–4 shows. The firm does not purchase all the raw materials it can; nor does it process or ship the total possible amount. Instead, it finds a balance that results in the ideal production level and the maximization of profit.

Mathematical Models

Optimization of resources is often achieved with the use of a mathematical model. The model can be a single equation or a series of equations, depending on the number of factors involved and the complexity of the situation. In the construction of these models, management scientists have found calculus to be one of the most useful branches of mathematics because it allows them to measure the rate of change in a dependent variable in relation to changes in an independent variable. For example, if a company increases the size of its plant and cost per unit declines, its management may want to learn the extent to which the production facilities can be expanded before the cost per unit will begin to increase. If the firm has a mathematical model constructed for this purpose, it merely has to determine at what point the cost per unit change moves from negative to either zero or positive, for at this point costs stop decreasing.

Problem solving via mathematical models is widely employed.

The same basic concept can also be used by many kinds of managers. For example, suppose an appliance store manager wants to know how many different product lines to carry. Assume that the individual then formulates the following mathematical equation:

$$Y = 16X - X^2,$$

where Y is equal to maximum profit and X is equal to the number of product lines carried. The equation states that maximum profit is equal to sixteen times the number of product

---

[1] George R. Terry, *Principles of Management,* 7th ed. (Homewood, Ill.: Richard D. Irwin, 1977), p. 30.

Figure 3–4 Optimization of Production and Maximization of Profit

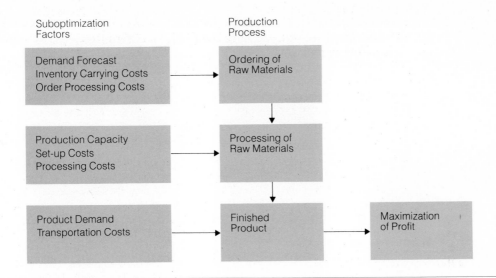

lines ($16X$) minus the number of product lines squared ($-X^2$). By increasing the value of X, the manager can attain the respective values of Y. For example:

When
$X = 0$
$Y = 16 \times 0 - 0^2$
$Y = 0$;
when
$X = 1$
$Y = 16 \times 1 - 1^2$
$Y = 15$.

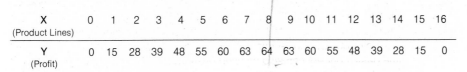

By constructing the entire table up to the point where Y again equals zero, it is possible to identify the entire range of positive profit values:

X (Product Lines)	0	1	2	3	4	5	6	7	8	9	10	11	12	13	14	15	16
Y (Profit)	0	15	28	39	48	55	60	63	64	63	60	55	48	39	28	15	0

Thus, the number of product lines that should be carried is eight, which will result in a maximization of profit.

Overview and Contributions

Although highly simplified, the above mathematical model is representative of the ones employed by management scientists. In fact, it is common to find adherents of this school relying strongly on such mathematical tools and techniques as linear programming,

Figure 3–5 Problem Solving via a Quantitative Approach

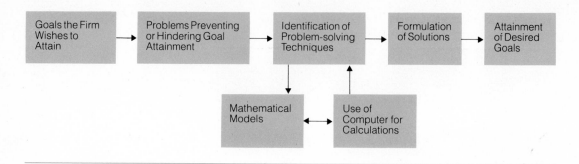

simulation, Monte Carlo theory, queuing theory, and game theory, topics that will be covered in Chapter 9. The quantitative school has gained many supporters in recent years. The increasing use of computers, accompanied by the development of more sophisticated mathematical models for solving business problems, accounts for many of the advances made by this school. In addition, the quantitative school has played an important role in the development of management thought by encouraging people to approach problem solving in an orderly fashion, looking more carefully at problem inputs and relationships. Figure 3–5 shows the ways in which this is accomplished. This school has also made clear the need for goal formulation and the measurement of performance.

BEHAVIORAL SCHOOL

The *behavioral school* grew out of the efforts of people who recognized the importance of the individual in the workplace and those who were interested in group processes. Today, it is common to find individuals in this school with training in the social sciences, including psychology, sociology, anthropology, social psychology, and industrial psychology, applying their skills to business problems.

As one would expect, behavioral school proponents are largely concerned with human behavior. They contend that because management entails getting things done through people, the effective manager must understand the importance of such factors as needs, drives, motivation, leadership, personality, behavior, work groups, and the management of change; for all these are going to have a direct effect on the manager's ability to manage. All members of the behavioral school share this philosophy, but some emphasize the individual and others the group. The behavioral school, therefore, consists of two branches: the interpersonal behavior branch and the group behavior branch.

Interpersonal Behavior

Some behaviorists are interested in interpersonal relations and are oriented toward individual and social psychology. They belong to the *interpersonal behavior branch* of the behavioral school.

The writers and scholars in this school are heavily oriented to individual psychology; and, indeed, most are trained as psychologists. Their focus is on the individual, and his or her motivations as a sociopsychological being. In this school are those who appear to emphasize human relations as an art that managers, even when foolishly trying to be amateur psychiatrists, can understand and practice. There are those who see the manager as a leader and may even equate managership and leadership—thus, in effect, treating all "led" activities as "managed." Others have concentrated on motivation or leadership and have cast important light on these subjects, which has been useful to managers.[2]

Members of this branch believe that the individual, not just the work group, must be understood if the manager is to do an effective job.

Group Behavior

The other branch of the behavioral school, often confused with its interpersonal behavior cousins, consists of individuals who see management as a social system, or collection of cultural interrelationships. Known collectively as the *group behavior branch,* they are highly sociological in nature, viewing human organizations as systems of interdependent groups, primary and secondary alike:

This approach varies all the way from the study of small groups, with their cultural and behavioral patterns, to the behavioral characteristics of large groups. It is often called a study of "organization behavior" and the term "organization" may be taken to mean the system, or pattern, of any set of group relationships in a company, a government agency, a hospital, or any other kind of undertaking.[3]

Advocates of the group behavior branch see the manager as an individual who must interact and deal with groups. For this reason, they place great emphasis on the need to understand both the formal and the informal organization.

Overview and Contributions

Although the interpersonal behavior branch stresses the importance of understanding the individual (psychology) and the group behavior branch places prime importance on the knowledge of group behavior (sociology), the two are actually interdependent. The group is made up of individuals, but the whole is actually greater than the sum of its parts. Both psychology and sociology are important to the behaviorists, regardless of the priorities assigned to each area in any given project.

Although the behavioral school lacks the type of framework used by management process advocates, it certainly does not lack structure. For example, communication, motivation, and leadership, a few of the school's basic concerns, are areas of major analysis. However, instead of working from functions to activities and principles, as do the management process advocates, the behaviorists work in the opposite direction; they start with human behavior research and build up to topics or functions. Thus, theirs is a much less rigid and more empirically based school of thought. Two prominent researchers in the field, Max S. Wortman and Fred Luthans, have enumerated several major contributions made by these behaviorists:

(1) **conceptual,** the formulation of concepts and explanations about individual and group behavior in the organization; (2) **methodological,** the empirical testing of these concepts in many different experimental and field settings; and (3) **operations,** the establishment of actual managerial policies and decisions

---

[2] Harold Koontz, "The Management Theory Jungle Revisited," *Academy of Management Review,* April 1980, pp. 177–178.
[3] Ibid., p. 178.

---

based on these conceptual and methodological frameworks. Since behavioral approaches have become widely disseminated throughout the management literature, there has been an increasing acceptance of the behavioral approach by management.[4]

TOWARD A UNIFIED THEORY?

There is still much disagreement.

Is there really a legitimate basis for these three schools of management thought, or should a synthesis be immediately undertaken? Many writers in the field believe a coalescence of the differing viewpoints can be achieved, but one of the key obstacles, in their view, is that of semantics. Everyone may say the same thing, but the use of different words can make it seem that the subjects are also different. One group of authors believes that "as is so often true when intelligent men differ in their interpretations of problems, some of the trouble lies in key words."[5]

Another major barrier is identified as differing definitions of management. If the field were clearly defined in terms of fairly specific content, differences among the various schools of management might be reduced to the point where synthesis would be possible. Although the idea sounds plausible, chances for its implementation are not good at present.[6] One of the reasons is the current lack of research:

> *The choice of a school or writer to follow presents a serious dilemma. . . . "I don't know" remains the appropriate answer. When sufficient research has been compiled, the schools will fade of their own accord. That they have not faded is good evidence that the quantity and quality of research to date is insufficient to render judgment.*
>
> *. . . No amount of argument between conflicting schools . . . is likely to achieve either consensus or truth.*[7]

Advocates of each of the three schools believe strongly in their own point of view and resist attempts at theory synthesis or integration. Unlike the process school theorists, who have been vigorous in their attempts to bring the quantitative and behavioral people into their domain, the latter groups consider that their own contribution to management is too significant to be relegated to the kind of secondary position being advocated for them by the process people. Nor are they necessarily wrong, for each of the three schools has its weaknesses as well as its strengths, and currently, none of them possesses the characteristics necessary for a successful and meaningful integration of management theory.

At present, a great deal of management research is in progress. However, this research is splintered: The focus of each effort is toward a specific topic or issue—for example, leadership styles in nonprofit organizations, strategic planning in a high technology industry, or testing of a motivation theory to see if earlier findings can be replicated. Little interest in trying to blend all available management information into an overall theory currently exists. Management scholars and practitioners seem content to go their own ways, investigating pieces of the giant management theory puzzle. For this reason, the schools of thought discussed here continue to remain valid points of departure in the study of modern management.

---

[4] Max S. Wortman, Jr., and Fred Luthans, eds., *Emerging Concepts in Management* (New York: Macmillan, 1975), p. 190.

[5] Harold Koontz and Cyril O'Donnell, *Management: A System and Contingency Analysis of Managerial Functions* (New York: McGraw-Hill, 1976), p. 66.

[6] W. Jack Duncan, "Transferring Management Theory to Practice," *Academy of Management Journal,* December 1974, pp. 724–738.

[7] John B. Miner, *Management Theory* (New York: Macmillan, 1971), p. 150.

THE WEAKNESSES OF THE SCHOOLS

All three schools have weaknesses. The following examines some of the shortcomings of each.

Process School Weaknesses

One of the foremost arguments against the process school is that it pays only lip service to the human element, regarding management as a static and dehumanized process. Although process advocates argue that this is not the case at all, behaviorists in particular remain unswayed.

A static approach?

Many also attack the school's foundation, claiming that management principles are not universally applicable. Such critics see the principles as most appropriate in stable production-line situations where unions are not very strong or where unemployment is high. When used in professional organizations, the principles often require modification, their application being contingent upon the specific situation. This is why Fayol and his associates, who operated under stable production-line situations, were able to use them effectively, whereas modern managers, operating under dynamic conditions, have trouble doing so.[8] In addition, principle proponents tend to formulate generalizations as principles even though they have not been empirically validated.

Are management principles universally applicable?

A third argument, along the same lines, questions the universality of the management process. Do all managers perform the same basic functions? There is considerable controversy on this point. Research has revealed that although similarities exist among various positions within firms, the same is not true among firms. When professional organizations (law firms, research and development laboratories, architectural firms, hospitals, universities) and administrative organizations (manufacturing companies, retailing firms, insurance agencies, transportation companies) are compared, the latter tend to be more bureaucratic, emphasizing rules, policies, procedures, and hierarchical authority.[9] Conversely, in professional organizations, power and authority tend to shift from the managerial jobs to those of the nonmanaging professions.[10] For example, doctors in hospitals sometimes have as much freedom to make decisions as do top administrators. Nurses often have more freedom of action or discretion in carrying out their tasks than do certain middle managers. Table 3–2 shows the results when Gerald Bell, in an eastern hospital, measured the amount of discretion employed by occupational groups in carrying out their work assignments. He found that the higher the degree of professional training, the greater the amount of discretion the employees exercised.[11]

Is the management process universal?

Results such as these have led John Miner, a leading management researcher, to conclude that "when decision-making authority is dispersed . . . some very sizeable changes in managerial functions must occur, relative to administrative organizations."[12]

---

[8] Ibid., p. 139–140.
[9] As used here, "professional organizations" are those which: (a) are recognized by society as having professional status, (b) are encouraged and influenced by a professional association or society, and (c) have a set of specialized techniques supported by a body of theory. For further information on this point, see John B. Miner, *The Management Process: Theory, Research and Practice,* 2d ed. (New York: Macmillan, 1978), p. 324.
[10] See Richard H. Hall, "Some Organizational Considerations in the Professional-Organizational Relationship," *Administrative Science Quarterly,* December 1967, pp. 461–478; and Gerald D. Bell, "Predictability of Work Demands and Professionalization as Determinants of Workers' Discretion," *Academy of Management Journal,* March 1966, pp. 20–28.
[11] Bell, "Predictability of Work Demands," p. 23.
[12] Miner, *Management Theory,* p. 88.

Table 3–2 Occupations and Their Average Discretion Scores in a Professional Organization

Occupation	Average Discretion Score
Administrator	5.7
Doctor	5.6
Department head (nursing)	5.2
Department head (others)	5.4
Assistant department head (nursing)	4.9
Assistant department head (others)	5.0
Nurse (staff)	4.5
Dietary supervisor	3.7
Plumber, carpenter (semi-skilled worker)	3.2
Secretary	3.1
Pharmacist	3.0
Laboratory technician	3.0
Orderly	3.0
X-ray technician	2.3
Nurses' aide	2.2
Cook	2.0
Dietary helper	1.4
Housekeeper, launderer, etc.	1.3

Source: Gerald D. Bell, "Predictability of Work Demands and Professionalization as Determinants of Workers' Discretion," *Academy of Management Journal,* March 1966, p. 23. Reprinted with permission.

He continues by noting that "analysis of professional versus administrative organizations once again leads to the conclusion that managerial functions are not universal. Not only do managerial jobs differ in their mix of functions depending on their level and the particular department involved, but they also differ from organization to organization. This interorganizational difference is particularly noticeable when administrative and professional types are compared."[13]

Quantitative School Weaknesses

Is it a tool or a school?

The quantitative school is attacked on the ground that it fails to see the complete picture. Is management a system of mathematical models and processes, or is this too narrow a view? Critics opt for the latter, calling management science a tool, not a school. They note that mathematics is used in physics, engineering, chemistry, and medicine, but it has never emerged as a separate school in these disciplines. Why should it do so in the field of management? There is no doubt that the management sciences have supplied very useful tools for the manager to employ in solving complex problems. Inventory, material, and production control have all been eased by these quantitative contributors. However, what about human behavior? How does one write an equation that solves people problems? Both the process and behavioral schools attack the quantitative theorists on this point, and the latter appear hard pressed to refute the argument.

---

[13] Ibid., p. 93.

Behavioral School Weaknesses

The major argument lodged against the behaviorists is that they, like the management science people, do not see the complete picture. Psychology, sociology, and related areas are all important in the study of management, but there is more to the field than just human behavior. Some forms of technical knowledge are also needed. The process school provides an important structural framework within which to study human behavior. The quantitative school offers an objective, quantifiable approach to decision making. Without these supplemental elements, managers cannot adequately apply their knowledge of behavior.

To be an effective manager, one must have more than a mere working knowledge of the human, dynamic model. True, the people in the workplace constitute a continually changing social system, but managers must supplement their ideas about their own and workers' rational behavior by a full understanding of the prevalence of nonrationality in human beings. Critics argue that the bheavioral school is only one segment, albeit an important one, of the total picture, and that in and of itself it is incomplete.

Is there failure to see the complete picture?

A CONCEPTUAL FRAMEWORK

As noted earlier, there is a need for further research if the three schools are ever to be synthesized. In addition, it should be realized that there are some who oppose any such action, contending that fundamental and inescapable differences among the various schools make a unified theory of management impossible.

Whether the three schools will ever come together is a matter of current debate. However, the student of management is well advised to travel all three roads—process, quantitative, and behavioral—for each makes important contributions to the study of management.

SUMMARY

Modern management theory is currently in the schools phase. Three schools of management thought are management process, quantitative, and behavioral.

The management process, or classical, school traces its ancestry to Fayol. One of its major tenets is that by analyzing management along functional lines, a framework can be constructed into which all new management concepts can be placed. This framework consists of a process of interrelated functions such as planning, organizing, and controlling. Another belief of the process school is that management principles can be derived through an analysis of managerial functions. A third tenet is that the basic management functions are performed by all managers, regardless of enterprise, activity, or hierarchical level. Additionally, the process school stresses the development of a management philosophy.

The quantitative, or management science, school consists of theorists who see management as a system of mathematical models and processes. Relying heavily on the application of scientific analysis to managerial problems, economic effectiveness criteria, and the use of computers, adherents of this school have promoted understanding of the need for goal formulation and the measurement of performance.

The behavioral school consists of two branches: interpersonal behavior and group behavior. The former is heavily psychological in orientation; the latter is heavily sociological. While this school lacks the type of framework used by management process advocates, it does not lack structure. However, there is a major difference in method. Instead of working from functions to activities and principles, as the management process advocates do, the behaviorists work in the opposite direction. They start with human behavior research and build up to topics or functions.

Today there is no unified theory of management. Several reasons can be cited, among them semantics, differing definitions of management, and lack of research. Advocates of each school claim that the others have serious flaws. The process school is seen as being too static; the quantitative school is seen as a series of useful tools but not a school; the behaviorists are attacked as failing to see the total picture.

It is still unclear whether the three schools will ever be synthesized. For this reason, the student of management is well advised to understand all three.

REVIEW AND STUDY QUESTIONS

1. What are the basic beliefs of management process school advocates?
2. How important are management principles to process school advocates?
3. Precisely what is meant by the term *universality of management functions?*
4. What background or training do management scientists have?
5. What is meant by the term *optimization? Suboptimization?*
6. What are some of the contributions made to management theory by the management scientists?
7. Identify and describe the two major branches of the behavioral school.
8. What contributions have the behaviorists made to management?
9. In your own words, what are the primary weaknesses of the process school? The quantitative school? The behavioral school?
10. Will the three schools of management ever be merged or synthesized? Give your reasoning as the main part of your answer.

SELECTED REFERENCES

Albers, H. H. *Principles of Management: A Modern Approach,* 4th ed. New York: Wiley, 1974.

Fayol, Henri. *General and Industrial Management.* Translated by Constance Starrs. London: Sir Isaac Pitman & Sons, 1949.

Gordon, P. J. "Management Territory: By Their Buzz Words Shall Ye Know Them." *Business Horizons,* February 1979, pp. 57–59.

Kelly, J. *Organizational Behaviour,* rev. ed. Homewood, Ill.: Richard D. Irwin, Dorsey Press, 1974.

Koontz, Harold, ed. *Toward a Unified Theory of Management.* New York: McGraw-Hill, 1964.

——. "The Management Theory Jungle." *Academy of Management Journal,* December 1961, pp. 174–188.

——. "The Management Theory Jungle Revisited." *Academy of Management Review,* April 1980, pp. 175–187.

Koontz, Harold; O'Donnell, Cyril; and Weihrich, Heinz. *Management,* 7th ed. New York: McGraw-Hill, 1980.

Miner, J. B. *Management Theory.* New York: Macmillan, 1971.

———. *The Management Process: Theory, Research, and Practice,* 2d ed. New York: Macmillan, 1978.

Woolf, D. A. "The Management Theory Jungle Revisited." *Advanced Management Journal,* October 1965, pp. 6–15.

Wortman, M. S., Jr., and Luthans, Fred, eds. *Emerging Concepts in Management,* 2d ed. New York: Macmillan, 1975.

CASE: The Manager's Job

In gathering data for a term paper on the functions of the manager, Sam Crocker, a junior at a large eastern business school, decided to interview five executives from different organizations. He asked the same question of each: "In your view, what are the functions of a manager?" Some of the executives explained their answers at great length; others merely listed managerial functions.

At the end of each interview Crocker would review the executive's comments, telling how he was going to summarize the answers. All agreed with his summations. The result of the five interviews follows:

Functions	Manager 1	Manager 2	Manager 3	Manager 4	Manager 5
Planning	X	X	X	X	X
Organizing	X	X	X	X	X
Staffing			X		
Communicating		X			
Coordinating	X				
Motivating	X			X	
Directing			X		
Controlling	X	X	X	X	X

Questions

1. How do you account for the apparent discrepancies in the replies of the managers? Explain.

2. If you were told that one of the managers was from an insurance company and the others were from manufacturing firms, which of the managers would you identify as an insurance manager? Give your reasoning.

3. If you were told that one of the five managers was a hospital administrator, which would you expect to be the administrator? Give your reasoning.

CASE: The Advertising Budget

The importance of advertising was always something that Jay Hallen, owner of a retail store, wondered about. In 1980 his store had an advertising budget of over $90,000, an increase of 17 percent from the previous year, but Hallen was really not sure how much of this money was being wisely spent. Nevertheless, he knew advertising was important, so he followed a simple guideline, spending 6 percent of estimated sales for advertising.

In mid-1980 Hallen received an announcement about a one-week management seminar being sponsored by a local university. Realizing that he had some middle-level managers who could profit from this training, he sent two of his up-and-coming people. When they returned, he learned that one of the speakers was a university professor who had talked about the need for constructing mathematical models for decision-making purposes. One of the professor's major points was that many companies spend more money on advertising than they should. Unaware of where to draw the line, they spend more and more each year. In fact, the speaker noted, a large percentage of firms tend to tie advertising to their sales forecast. If they estimate sales at $1 million, they spend $100,000; if they project sales at $2 million, they spend $200,000. "Actually," said the professor, "this is a very simple, and generally erroneous, approach. The only way to really ascertain how much to spend on advertising is to measure previous expenditures and results."

Hallen liked the basic idea, so he called the university and asked the professor to consider undertaking a consulting assignment. The professor agreed and for the next week examined the company's past sales figures and advertising expenditures and conducted some computer analysis. At the end of that time the professor concluded that advertising effectiveness could be determined with the following formula:

$$Y = 10X - X^2 + \$50,000,$$

where:

Y = Total sales.

X = Total advertising expenditures/$10,000.

Questions

1. Using just the above formula, how much sales income will the store obtain with advertising expenditures (per $10,000) from $10,000 to $110,000?

2. Based on the above answers, how much advertising should this company do? Explain.

3. How useful are management scientists in the field of management? Explain.

CASE: *A State of Confusion*

"Bill," said Anita Tuner, training director at Willowby Insurance, "how would you like to attend a training session in New York City this coming week?"

"What's it going to be about?" Bill Jarvis asked.

"Since when have you gotten so particular? Usually, when the company intends to send a few people to a training session, you jump at it. I can remember that winter you talked me into sending you to Miami Beach. You were sure interested in going to seminars then," responded Tuner.

"Yeah, but that was when I only had a little work to do. Now I've got work piled up on my desk and I don't want to run off to just any old training session."

Tuner spoke rather firmly as she said, "I wouldn't ask you to go to just any training session. Besides you know that I'm only asking you to repay a favor. Do you want to go or not?"

"Tell me what it's going to be about," Jarvis insisted.

"It's called 'Understanding Today's Worker,' " replied Tuner.

Jarvis answered, "Yeah, well, thanks, but I'm not interested." When asked why not, he said, "Because that last time you sent me to one of those behavioral seminars I came away more confused than before. Look, a lot of research being conducted in the behavioral sciences is great research, but it has no real applicability. I mean, there is just no way to take it back to the job and use it."

Tuner was skeptical. "You mean those people never tell you how you can apply it?"

"Oh no, they do that. The problem is that the way they explain it and the way it really works are two different things. The truth is, I really think I'm a lot better off just doing things my own way and not messing around with these new behavioral theories. They just leave me all confused."

Questions

1. Have the behaviorists really made any contribution to management? Explain.

2. How important is it to understand today's worker?

3. What does Jarvis mean by his statement that behavioral seminars leave him confused? Explain.

CASE: **One out of Three**

A midwestern insurance company recently had an opening in one of its lower-middle management positions. After evaluating a number of possible candidates, the selection committee narrowed its list to three people.

The first candidate was a newly hired management trainee who had only recently received a master's degree in business from a large eastern university. The man's major area of study at the undergraduate level had been general management, while at the graduate level he had concentrated on management theory and insurance. Although the company liked this applicant's general management background and felt his insurance courses provided him with some of the technical training he would need in supervising company personnel, some of the committee members were afraid that the young man's background was too general. "We need someone with a little more background and training in this business," said one committee member.

The second individual being considered for the position was a woman who, for the past two years, had been the leading salesperson in her regional office. She did not want to remain in sales for the rest of her life, so when she learned that the company was looking for a lower-level middle manager, she immediately applied for the job. On the positive side, the committee liked her track record. "This candidate has illustrated that she can deliver in the field," said one member. "This has seasoned her for the management ranks. After all, don't managers sell management's points of view to the employees?" On the negative side, however, some of the committee members were afraid that the woman might be too interested in personal selling and its behavioral aspects and fail to see the complete picture. One of them put it this way: "There's more to managing than just getting along with people."

The third person being considered for the job worked in the firm's actuarial department. She did fine technical work, and one committee member who felt this woman would be ideal for the job remarked: "The backbone of an insurance company is its actuarial department. This woman knows the ins and outs of insurance. This technical competence will help her do a good job." There was, however, concern that the woman might be too used to working with numbers and not accustomed to managing people. "Technical skill is important," said one member, "but it's no substitute for handling people."

After the committee discussed the three individuals for almost an hour, the convener called for action: "We have to make a decision on this matter today. We have a fair idea of the strong and weak points of each candidate. What do you say we choose one of the three and then adjourn for lunch?" Everyone agreed, and the undebatable motion to adjourn came as soon as the choice was recorded.

Questions

1. What characteristics of training would you look for in choosing from among the three candidates?

2. Which of the three candidates do you think would be most likely to be a management process advocate? A quantitative school supporter? A behavioral school advocate?

3. Based on your answer to the above question, which of the three would you choose for the job? Why?

Chapter 4 is devoted exclusively to the planning process, focusing particular attention on the need for comprehensive and strategic planning and the values of management in the planning process. The chapter also covers short-run (operational) planning.

Chapter 5 reviews the organizing process. This chapter presents the nuts-and-bolts ideas involved in integrating people with structure. Some of the major concepts covered are the various forms of departmentalization available to the manager, organization by committee, types of authority, and the need for understanding the informal organization.

THE MANAGEMENT PROCESS SCHOOL OF MANAGEMENT

Chapter 6 discusses adaptive organization structures. Many organizations are finding that because of advancing technology and other external factors, they must modify their structures to make them more responsive to the external environment. The chapter takes up some of the most common forms of modern organization design and the forces that help determine the "best" organization design.

Finally, Chapter 7 examines the control function, giving prime attention to the need for effective feedback and evaluation. Among the topics reviewed are the control process, budgeting, break-even analysis, key area control, and management audits.

CHAPTER 4

THE PLANNING PROCESS

GOALS OF THE CHAPTER

There is an adage in management: If you don't know where you are going, any path will get you there. However, when a person or a firm has objectives —and all businesses should— then planning is essential. This chapter will examine the planning process; define and observe comprehensive, strategic, and operational planning; and discuss the advantages and limitations of planning.

When you have finished reading this chapter, you should be able to:

1. Describe what is meant by the term comprehensive planning.
2. Define the term strategic planning.
3. Identify the three foundations of a strategic plan.
4. Relate some of the most common ways of conducting evaluations of external and internal environments.
5. Explain how a firm goes about developing a market niche.
6. Describe how a planning organization can help a business carry out comprehensive planning.
7. Outline some of the basic advantages of planning.
8. Explain why planning can help but still not be able to prevent or cure all future problems.

COMPREHENSIVE PLANNING

Modern businesses operate in a highly dynamic environment where change is a constant factor. As a result, it has become more and more necessary for companies to determine their objectives carefully and then systematically to construct plans for attaining them. This has become a continuous process throughout every organization. Naturally, managers at the upper levels should be concerned with long-range or strategic planning, whereas the attention of those managers at the lower levels ought to be focused mainly on operational planning. Yet research indicates that some top managers have not been devoting sufficient attention to long-range planning. Rather, they tend to spend most of their time worrying about short-run goals and performance results. In fact, it is not uncommon to find some chief executive officers who believe that comprehensive planning is something that can be delegated to their subordinates. When the overall plan is completed, they breathe a sigh of relief and think they can now get back to their real work.

Fortunately, however, there has been a marked trend in recent years toward *comprehensive planning,* a process in which all departments of the organization identify their objectives and determine how they will be attained. In this process, each department ties its objectives to those units above and below it in the hierarchy. The result is an integrated plan in which all groups work toward the same basic objectives. Today comprehensive planning is used not only by large organizations but by medium and small ones as well. In fact, smaller companies have begun to realize that, despite their limited resources, they have about the same fundamental planning requirements as larger companies.[1] This trend toward comprehensive planning on the part of large and small businesses alike will continue, and those firms that have not begun to take the requisite steps toward insuring well-coordinated overall plans will find themselves unable to maintain the pace.

Comprehensive planning involves all levels of the organization.

STRATEGIC PLANNING

George Steiner has defined *strategic planning* as "the process of determining the major objectives of an organization and the policies and strategies that will govern the acquisition, use, and disposition of resources to achieve those objectives."[2] Strategic plans provide a firm with long-range direction and growth from three foundations, the first of which is the *basic socioeconomic purpose* of the organization. Why is the business in existence? However it is stated, a socioeconomic purpose always entails a consideration of company survival (profits) and societal needs (social functions). The second foundation is the values and philosophy of the top management. This composite of values and ideals influences the strategic plan because it helps determine the manner in which management will treat its customers and employees. The third basic foundation is the assessment of the organization's strengths and weaknesses in the context of the external and internal environment. These three foundations of strategic planning are interdependent, as Figure 4–1 shows.

---

[1] For an excellent discussion of this area, see George A. Steiner, ed., *Managerial Long Range Planning* (New York: McGraw-Hill, 1963); and George A. Steiner, *Strategic Planning: What Every Manager Must Know* (New York: Free Press, 1979).

[2] George Steiner, *Top Management Planning* (New York: Macmillan, 1969), p. 34.

Figure 4–1 Basic Foundations of Strategic Plan

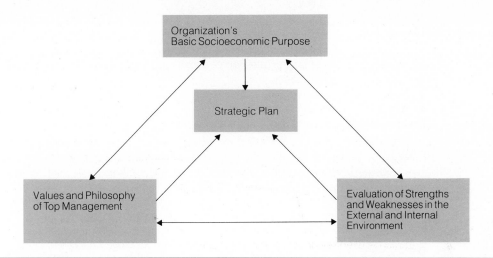

Basic Socioeconomic Purpose

More and more business firms are beginning to re-evaluate the purposes of their existence. For example, years ago, when Henry Ford entered the automobile business, he saw his basic mission as one of providing people with a basic necessity—a form of transportation. People needed cars for mobility; Ford could provide them. General Motors later broadened this idea, viewing the automobile as a luxury as well as a necessity. As a result, the firm offered the customer more extras and a wider line, albeit at a higher price, and replaced Ford as the number one automobile manufacturer. The nation's privately owned railroads have done the same, restating their purpose for existence so that they are no longer in the passenger-carrying business but in the transportation business. Today, almost all railway profits are derived from freight. The movie industry has also redefined its basic mission: It is no longer merely in the movie business; it is now in the business of informing as well as entertaining its audience.

The basic purpose for existence must be identified.

Furthermore, rather than talking about specific product lines, modern organizations tend to define their business in terms of *market definition*. The following lists of types of firms and market definitions provide some examples:

Type of Firm	Business It Is In (by Market Definition)
Copy machine	Office productivity
Oil	Energy
Cosmetic	Beauty
TV manufacturer	Entertainment
Computer	Information processing
Encyclopedia	Information development
Fertilizer	World hunger fighting

A critical fact about business, one which managers must remember, is that products change but basic markets remain. Autos may be replaced by electric bicycles, but the transportation market is still there. For this reason, the socioeconomic purpose is stated in terms of the market. From here, a basic mission statement can then be formulated. The following list illustrates this for some major firms:

1. Volkswagen's mission is to provide an economic means of private transportation.
2. American Telephone and Telegraph's mission is to provide quick and efficient communication capabilities.
3. IBM's mission is to meet the problem-solving needs of businesses.
4. Shell Oil's mission is to meet the energy needs of humanity.
5. International Minerals and Chemical Corporation's mission is to increase agricultural productivity to feed the world's hungry.[3]

Unless an organization can define its socioeconomic purpose and continuously redefine it as conditions change, it will lack a clear understanding of its basic mission and have great difficulty in constructing a strategic plan.

Management Values

In the 1970s, the idea of social responsibility received a tremendous amount of attention. Equal opportunity, ecology, and the various aspects of the consumer movement and its supporting legislation, which for convenience we can call consumerism, all became focal points for management consideration and action. Why did these issues rise to the fore? Part of the answer rests with external actions, such as government legislation. However, even more significant (and generally overlooked) have been the social action programs proposed by businesses themselves. What led to them? The answer rests in the values and beliefs of the top management.

Management values will influence the strategic plan.

In every organization all the managers bring a certain set of values to the workplace with them, and every generation tends to have differing values. Most of today's top managers are in the forty-five to sixty age group. This means that most of the managers of the 1980s will have been born during the years 1930 to 1945. The older ones will have some memory of the depression and World War II and, less importantly for them, the 1950s and the cold war, which form the first memories of today's younger managers. During the traumas of these early years, the values of the managers of the 1980s were formed. How do these values differ from those of the managers' parents and grandparents? Generally, 1980s managers are more socially conscious than earlier managers. They tend to be more concerned also with quality of life, and they have a more participative leadership style. These values predictably influence the managers' organizational strategic plans.

Evaluation of the Environment

Managers evaluate the external and internal environment to help identify organizational strengths and weaknesses. They can then formulate objectives based on the environmental studies. In evaluating the external environment, organizations rely most heavily on *forecasting,* the projection of future business conditions.

---

[3] Philip Kotler, *Marketing Management: Analysis, Planning, and Control,* 3d ed. (Englewood Cliffs, N.J.: Prentice-Hall, 1976), pp. 52–53.

External Environmental Forecasting Forecasting the external environment can be done in a number of ways, depending on what the management would like to know. But there is one paradoxically constant variable: The environment is always changing. The greater the change, the more important it is for the organization to gather data about it.

The dynamic environment of the business world can be seen through a sales comparison of the twenty largest industrials in the United States in 1969, when business conditions were very good, and in 1979, after the major recession of the early seventies. As Table 4–1 shows, eight of the top ten firms in _Fortune_'s 500 in 1969 had maintained their positions in this elite group in 1979, the other two having fallen into the second-ten category. Of the second group of ten, however, only five were still in the category, one having moved up to the top ten, one having been reclassified, and the other three having fallen out of the top twenty. The table illustrates that no firm is ever standing still: It must be moving forward, or it is actually falling behind. Table 4–2 shows this rather dramatically, comparing the last ten industrials in _Fortune_'s 500 in 1969 and 1979.

If the nation's top firms have to withstand such dynamics, it stands to reason that smaller businesses must undergo even more notable changes, simply because they lack the size and financial strength of their giant counterparts. Thus, their need for forecasting change is even greater. This chapter examines some of the ways of conducting forecasts. Those who study these approaches should keep in mind this statement by Robert C. Turner, a well-known economist:

> _Business forecasting is unavoidable. Every business decision involves a forecast, implicit or explicit, because every business decision pertains to the future. Although business decision makers should neither accept any forecast as infallible nor rely exclusively on it, they would be well advised to give forecasts . . . a significant weight in their own planning._[4]

1. **_Economic Forecasting._** The most common type of external forecasting is the economic forecast. If the economy is in an upswing, many businesses find their positions improved; sales rise and returns on investments increase. Conversely, a downturn has a dampening effect. Much depends on the current state of the economy as reflected by _gross national product (GNP),_ which is the value of goods and services produced in the country in a year.

   A. Extrapolation. The simplest form of economic forecast is that of _extrapolation,_ which is simply a projection of the current trend into the future. If a firm sold $100,000 worth of goods in 1979, $200,000 in 1980, and $300,000 in 1981, it might estimate continual $100,000 growth increments for the rest of the decade. Using extrapolation as a general method of business forecasting is, of course, dangerous, because it fails to take into account changing environmental conditions as reflected in economic cycles. However, in such cases as population growth or life expectancy, a long-term forecast based on extrapolation can be fairly accurate.

   B. Leads and Lags. The National Bureau of Economic Research (NBER) has discovered that when the economy turns up or down, some indicators seem to precede the change, some coincide with it, and still others follow it. There are thus a lead group, a coincident group, and a lag group.

   Of greatest importance to forecasters are the _lead indicators,_ for they tend to signal upcoming changes in the economic cycle. In all, there are twelve lead indicators on the NBER's short list, including average weekly hours worked, new business formations, new building permits, common stock prices, corporate profit

Various types of economic forecasts can be used to project developments in the external environment.

---

[4] Robert C. Turner, "Should You Take Business Forecasting Seriously?" _Business Horizons,_ April 1978, p. 72.

Table 4–1 Fortune's *Largest Industrials in 1969 and 1979 (on Basis of Sales)*

1969 Rank	Firm	1979 Rank
1	General Motors	2
2	Standard Oil (of New Jersey)	1
3	Ford Motor	4
4	General Electric	9
5	International Business Machines	8
6	Chrysler	17
7	Mobil Oil	3
8	Texaco	5
9	International Telephone & Telegraph	11
10	Gulf Oil	7
11	Western Electric	19
12	U.S. Steel	14
13	Standard Oil of California	6
14	Ling-Temco-Vought	31
15	Du Pont (E.I.) deNemours	16
16	Shell Oil	13
17	Westinghouse Electric	37
18	Standard Oil (Indiana)	10
19	General Telephone & Electronics[a]	—
20	Goodyear Tire & Rubber	28

[a]Now listed as a utility.

Source: *Fortune,* May 1970 and May 1980.

Table 4–2 *Change in Selected Firms in* Fortune's *500 between 1969 and 1979 (on Basis of Sales)*

1969 Rank	Firm	1979 Rank
491	National Presto Industries	—[a]
492	Peter Eckrich & Sons	—
493	Searle (G.D.)	288
494	Amerace Esna	—
495	Carpenter Technology	464
496	Knight Newspapers	291[b]
497	Olivetti Underwood	—
498	Lubrizol	351
499	Farmers Union Central Exchange[c]	—
500	Monfort of Colorado	381

[a]— = not ranked.
[b]Merged with Knight-Ridder newspapers.
[c]No longer listed as an industrial.

Source: *Fortune,* May 1970 and May 1980.

after taxes, new orders for durable goods, and changes in consumer installment credit. Many forecasters place great value on these indicators, feeling they provide the best clues as to what is likely to happen.

Lag indicators are important because they follow the economic cycle, making it possible to anticipate changes. The NBER has six indicators on its short list, including business expenditures for plant and equipment, unemployment rate, bank rates on short-term loans, manufacturers' inventories, and common and industrial loans outstanding. If the economy is beginning an upswing, banks can expect manufacturers to begin increasing their loans and investing money in plant and equipment. If the economy is beginning a downturn, there will be a reduction in business borrowing and plant and equipment expenditures, as well as a general increase in the unemployment rate.

Unfortunately, the lead and lag method of forecasting is more than a matter of merely plugging various values into a mathematical equation. Qualitative judgments must also be made to determine the impact of the indicators. For example, if the number of residential building permits increases, orders for durable goods rise, and the average number of weekly hours worked goes up, then the GNP may start to rise. Do these occurrences indicate that the company should float a new stock issue? Supposedly, the price of industrial stocks will begin to rise, but there is no certainty of this. In short, the lead and lag method helps the forecaster predict the future, but in so doing the individual is only making an educated guess. There is no guarantee that the guess is correct.

C. Econometrics. Another forecasting technique that is widely employed today is *econometrics,* a mathematical approach in which the main variables are brought together in a series of equations. GNP can then be forecast on the basis of various assumptions arrived at through these equations. The econometric technique provides the forecaster with a picture of what to expect under various conditions. Three such conditions—the most optimistic, the most likely, and the most pessimistic—exemplify some of the commonest types of sought-after answers.

The results can be further analyzed by applying them to specific industries and companies. For example, if a firm estimates that it will sell between 12 and 14 million units (pessimistic and optimistic) and further estimates that it will capture between 6 and 7 percent of the market, then sales will range from 720,000 to 980,000 units inclusive. These data can be used to construct initial income statements, illustrating profit and loss at various levels of sales. It is also possible to estimate production and marketing costs at these levels. If the forecasters like, they can make changes in one area while leaving everything else the same. For example, what impact would a 15 percent increase in advertising have on industry and company sales? The value of the econometric model is not only that it assists the company in forecasting the future; it also helps management predict results of various changes in strategy.

2. **Technological Forecasting.** Many firms must use technological forecasting. There are two ways of conducting such forecasts: exploratory and normative.

Exploratory forecasting begins with current knowledge and predicts the future on the basis of predictable technological progress. It is thus a rather passive process. Forecasters using this method tend to assume that current technological progress will continue at the same rate and that this advance will not be affected by external conditions. They can, if they wish, later speculate on how the forecast might be affected by the nontechnical environment.

Electronics development provides an illustration of how this method could be

Exploratory forecasting projects the future according to predictable technological progress.

used. Immediately after World War II, transistors were expensive and qualitatively unpredictable. Since then, however, their price has declined, their quality has improved, and their application has become widespread. If a business firm had decided to conduct an exploratory forecast right after World War II, it would have been possible to predict these events. Industrial firms in particular have found great value in this type of forecasting because the results can help companies in searching out clues as to market entry, potential competition, and ease of expansion into related product areas; and it has the added advantage of being rather easy to do.

Normative forecasting begins with an identification of some future technological objective—say, for example, the development of a space station by 1991. After the goal is set, the forecast works back to the present, identifying the obstacles to be surmounted along the way. Attention is devoted to both technical and nontechnical factors. For example, when will the technical know-how for a space station be available, and how will this time estimate be affected by government allocations? (That is, will the government put a lot of money into the project and develop it quickly, or will the project take a longer time because of reluctance or lack of enthusiasm in Washington?) Normative forecasting is a much more dynamic process than exploratory forecasting.

3. **Government Action.** Few companies escape government influence. Most businesses face a host of laws designed to prevent monopoly, promote competition, and encourage ethical practices. In addition, there is the ever-present concern with monetary action, whereby the federal government can regulate credit through the federal reserve banks and open market operations. This spurs the economy forward or, in the case of runaway inflation, helps put on the brakes. Likewise, the federal government can pump money into the economy or draw it out through such fiscal action as higher taxes or a refusal to spend what has been currently collected. For these reasons, the government has a direct impact on business strategy.

The effect of government action can be seen every day in the news. A January 1980 *Wall Street Journal,* for example, reported that Hughes Aircraft received an $8.9 million Air Force contract for radar spare parts, the Chamberlain Manufacturing Company was awarded a $6.8 million contract for high-explosive metal parts for artillery shells, and the United Technologies Corporation got a $4.4 million Air Force contract for jet engine parts.[5] When one considers that these types of contracts are awarded on an almost daily basis, the role and importance of government action in the planning process becomes clear.

4. **Sales Forecasting.** Businesses forecast the economy in general so as to set the stage for determining their own particular *sales forecasts.* Some use an econometric approach, but not all businesses have the expertise for employing such a sophisticated technique. For them, the questions of how many goods or services they will sell to whom, in which place, and by which methods, in light of economic projections, require a more down-to-earth sales forecast. In arriving at an answer, the first place a firm often turns to is its own sales records. A survey of current sales information will indicate what products are selling best in which areas and to what kinds of customers. Further sales forecast data can often be obtained from the United States Bureau of the Census, the Department of Commerce, local trade associations, and the Chamber of Commerce.

Another, and often supplemental, method of gauging sales is the *jury of execu-*

Normative forecasting works from the future back to the present.

The impact of government control must be evaluated.

Sales forecasting can be conducted in a number of ways.

---

[5] *Wall Street Journal,* January 4, 1980, p. 26.

tive opinion. In this approach, various executives in the organization are brought together for the purpose of constructing the sales forecast. Sometimes they work independently of each other; other times they form a joint opinion. In both cases, there is an input to the sales forecast based on what these executives believe will take place. Another version entails the review and modification of the executive forecast by the manager of marketing research. The value of the jury of executive opinion approach is that it allows input from executives who are in a position to make intelligent guesstimates about the future.

Another supplemental approach, often called the *grass-roots method,* entails a survey of the sales force. Since salespeople are in the field on a continuing basis, they should have some general ideas about what will and will not sell. Their ideas are obtained by the sales manager, who compiles the results and sends them up the line. In the process, the composites from salespeople in all the districts and regions are aggregated and sent to central headquarters, where they are compared with the forecast constructed by a home office staff. Finally, changes are made based on management decisions regarding advertising, product line, price, and other such considerations. Then the forecast is reviewed and approved. The major advantage of the grass-roots method is that it obtains sales information from the people who do the actual selling.

A third supplemental approach is that of *user expectation.* A firm that wants to know how the customer feels about a product can gain valuable information simply by going out and asking the consumer. Although some customers may say one thing and do another, if the firm obtains a large enough sample, it is possible to negate the impact of such responses.

Internal Environmental Evaluation A forecast of external environmental factors provides the organization with important planning information. However, these data must be supplemented with an evaluation of the internal environment, focusing particularly on the identification of the company's internal strengths and weaknesses. In making this evaluation, the manager must consider two factors:

1. **Material Resources.** The plant capacity plus the amount of cash, equipment, and inventory a company has on hand are important because they constitute the tools with which a strategic plan can be fashioned. Often these resources will help dictate a particular type of strategy. For example, a business with a large plant capacity will have a large fixed expense. However, if it can manufacture at capacity, the firm can spread these costs over many items, thereby reducing the cost per unit. This company will undoubtedly compete vigorously with a low price strategy. Conversely, a small manufacturer will not have so high a fixed expense but will also have fewer units among which to spread these costs. As a result, the small plant cannot meet the big manufacturer head-to-head in a price war. Therefore, it will devise a strategy that the larger competition cannot or will not effectively combat, such as high price coupled with a great degree of personal selling.

   Material resources such as cash, plant, and equipment must be evaluated.

   A second reason for evaluating material resources is to ascertain the financial strength of the firm. If a company has $1 million in cash and $9 million in other assets, it can often maintain a strategic posture far longer than a firm with only a tenth of these assets. This raises the question of how long a firm should remain with a particular strategic plan. The answer is to stick with it until it pays off or until it becomes evident that the results are not going to justify the costs. Unfortunately, many firms adopt strategic plans that are not in accord with their material resources and as a result find themselves continually revising and modifying their plan. A strategic plan should always be tempered by the available material resources.

2. ***Personnel Competence.*** In every organization workers will have a distinctive area of competence; there is something the work force does extremely well. For example, in a firm such as the *New York Times,* it is the ability to gather information from all over the world and compile it quickly, accurately, and in readable form. In contrast, many small papers use their people to gather local news happenings and rely upon wire sources to provide them with international news. Analogously, the "Big Three" auto manufacturers in America have the labor needed to mass produce and market cars, whereas Rolls Royce, in the same basic business, concentrates its efforts less on marketing and more on production quality. Because a strategic plan must draw upon the company's strengths, the competence of the workers is an important consideration.

Personnel competencies must be identified.

DEVELOPING A PROPITIOUS NICHE

On the basis of the external and internal environmental analysis, the philosophy of the management, and the socioeconomic mission of the organization, long-range objectives can be formulated. However, it should be noted that every strategic plan must be designed so as to develop or take advantage of a particular niche. Every organization must find a thing, or some things, it does best and build a strategy around this strength. For example, the *New York Times* has a specific market niche, selling its papers to thousands of people every day. It is not, however, the largest selling newspaper in New York City; this position is held by the *New York Daily News.* Anyone who has ever read the two papers knows that the *Daily News* is a picture newspaper written in a very easy-to-read style. It is much more appealing to the mass market than is the *Times.* Yet it would be foolish for the *Times* to copy the style of its competition. To do so would mean abandoning a niche in which its competencies are best employed. The basic mission, philosophy of management, and strength of the *Times* are all geared toward its current style of news coverage. This is what is known as *leading from strength.* Every well formulated plan draws upon the organization's strengths in fashioning the most successful strategy possible.

Surprising as it may seem, many businesses do not lead from strength. Instead, they tend to hold back and respond defensively to the environment. In fact, many managers spend an inordinate amount of time trying to straighten out little problem areas instead of boldly taking advantage of their strengths. They do not have a strategic, long-range plan. They spend most of their time on day-to-day matters, like chess players who seize poisoned pawns because the immediate capture of any enemy is given priority over the long-range development of their own pieces.

The firm must build a strategy that capitalizes on its strengths.

By identifying a niche in which its competencies can be effectively employed, an organization focuses on goals. In so doing, Peter Drucker, the world-famous management authority, has noted, the successful manager must never try to cover too much territory. Instead, the manager must milk a propitious niche for all it is worth, according to the following guidelines:

1. *Economic results require that managers concentrate their efforts on the smallest number of products, product lines, services, customers, markets, distribution channels, end uses, and so on which will produce the largest amount of revenue. Managers must minimize the attention devoted to products which produce primarily costs, because their value is too small or too splintered.*
2. *Economic results require also that staff efforts be concentrated on the very few activities that are capable of producing truly significant business results—with as little staff work and staff effort as possible spent on the others.*
3. *Effective cost control requires a similar concentration of work and efforts on those very few areas where improvement in cost performance will have significant impact on business performance and*

results—that is, on those areas where a relatively minor increase in efficiency will produce a major increase in economic effectiveness.

4. *Managers must allocate resources, especially high-grade human resources, to activities which provide opportunities for high economic results.*[6]

These basic ideas are employed by a number of firms that handle their strategic business plans like investment portfolios—pruning the losing lines and backing the successful ones through systematic analysis. In doing so, management first identifies the *strategic business units (SBUs)* which make up the firm. Each has the following characteristics:

1. *Is a single business or collection of related businesses.*
2. *Has a distinct mission.*
3. *Has its own competitors.*
4. *Has a responsible manager.*
5. *Consists of one or more program units and functional units.*
6. *Can benefit from strategic planning.*
7. *Can be planned independently of the other businesses.*[7]

SBUs share major characteristics.

Depending on the situation, an SBU can be an entire company division, a product line within a division, or a single product. Whatever it happens to be in a given company, the firm, on identifying the SBU, sets about evaluating its current and expected performance. While there are a number of ways of doing this, one of the most popular is that developed by General Electric, which has more than forty distinct businesses. Each must be rated on quantitative factors such as sales, profit, and return on investment, as well as hard-to-quantify factors such as market share, technology needs, employee loyalty in the industry, competitive stance, and social need. In conducting its annual planning review, GE has developed a strategic business planning grid, shown in Figure 4–2. On this grid are two dimensions, industry attractiveness and business strengths. Industry attractiveness takes into account such factors as market size, market growth rate, profit margin, and competitive intensity. Business strength includes relative market share, price competitiveness, product quality, and knowledge of the customer and the market.[8] Depending on the combination of each (high, medium, or low), the firm will decide to: (a) invest and grow, (b) get further information because the business might go either way, or (c) reduce the investment.[9]

In Figure 4–2A industry attractiveness is medium and business strengths are high. In this case the company would opt to invest and grow. In Figure 4–2B industry attractiveness is low and business strengths are medium. In this situation the company would not invest further and would start to reduce or consolidate its holdings. Finally, in Figure 4–2C industry attractiveness and business strengths are both medium. The company would wait for further information before making a final decision.

A similar approach, pioneered by the Boston Consulting Group, classifies the SBUs into a *business portfolio matrix* such as that shown in Figure 4–3. On the vertical axis is the annual market growth rate for each of the SBUs. Ten percent is the growth line dividing high and low growth. On the horizontal axis is the relative market share for each SBU in relation to the share held by the industry's largest competitor. The dividing line between low and high here is 1.5X, which means the SBU is 50 percent larger than its biggest competitor.

---

[6] Peter F. Drucker, "Managing for Business Effectiveness," *Harvard Business Review,* May–June 1963, p. 56.

[7] Philip Kotler, *Marketing Management: Analysis, Planning and Control,* 4th ed. (Englewood Cliffs, N.J.: Prentice-Hall, 1980), p. 76.

[8] For more on this subject, see Kotler, *Marketing Management,* chap. 4.

[9] See "General Electric's 'Spotlight Strategy' for Planning," *Business Week,* April 28, 1975, p. 49.

Figure 4–2 General Electric's Strategic Planning Grid

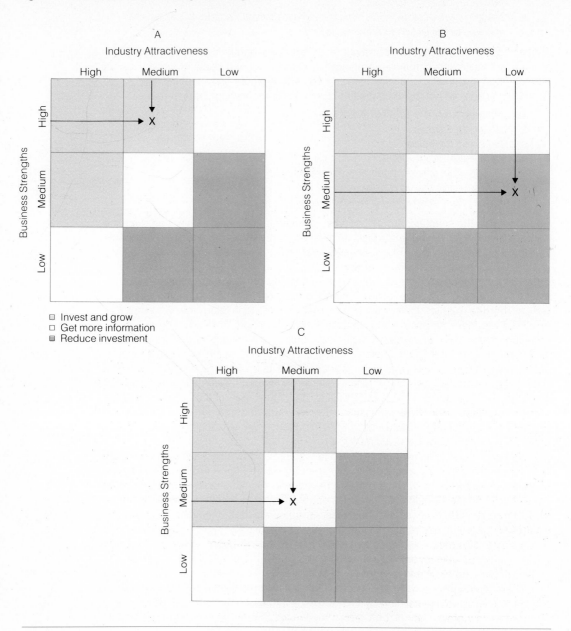

Source: Extrapolated from "General Electric's 'Stoplight Strategy' for Planning," *Business Week*, April 28, 1975, p. 49.

Figure 4–3 The Boston Consulting Group's Business Portfolio Matrix

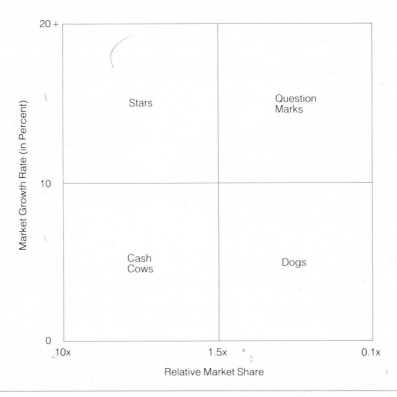

Source: Allan Gerald, "A Note on the Boston Consulting Group Concept of Competitive Analysis and Corporate Strategy," Intercollegiate Case Clearing House, ICCH 9–175–175 June 1976, p. 5.

Each of the quadrants represents a distinct type of cash flow situation. The four classifications follow:

Stars—high growth, high market share SBUs. These need a lot of cash to finance their rapid growth. When this growth slows down, they will become cash cows.

Cash cows—low growth, high market share SBUs. These throw off a lot of cash to support other SBUs and help the firm meet its bills.

Question marks—low share SBUs in high growth markets. These require a lot of cash in order to maintain their share, let alone increase it.

Dogs—low growth, low share SBUs. These may generate enough cash to maintain themselves but do not promise to be a large source of cash.[10]

The Boston Consulting Group made four business portfolio classifications.

---

[10] For more on this subject, see Charles W. Hofer and Dan Schendel, *Strategy Formulation: Analytical Concepts* (St. Paul, Minn.: West Publishing, 1978); George S. Day, "Diagnosing the Product Portfolio," *Journal of Marketing,* April 1977, pp. 29–38; and "Olin's Shift to Strategic Planning," *Business Week,* March 27, 1978, pp. 102–105.

After this evaluation, management must decide a strategy for each SBU. Typically, it will try to build those question marks which could become stars if their market share grew, hold on to the market of the cash cows, harvest weak cash cows or question marks whose futures look dim, and divest itself of dogs.

LONG- AND INTERMEDIATE-RANGE OBJECTIVES

A business formulates its long-range objectives on the basis of its socioeconomic purpose, the values of its top managers, and an analysis of its external and internal environments. For a manufacturing firm, as Figure 4–4 shows, some of the commonest goals have to do with manufacturing, finance, and marketing. However, in long-range perspective these goals are often insufficiently clear. For example, consider this goal: Open Nashville plant in third quarter 1984. Such statements of objectives need to be reduced to intermediate-range objectives, thereby increasing the amount of specificity and making the goals more action-oriented. In the example of the Nashville plant, some intermediate-range goals might be: (a) send site evaluators to view best location options, (b) select most favorable location, and (c) let bids for contractors.

From long-range goals, intermediate-range objectives can be formulated.

In Figure 4–4 the long-range objective is to increase sales by 15 percent a year. How can this be attained? First, the intermediate-range goals need to be clearly defined —in this case, to win a contract currently up for bid to sell widgets to a large West Coast manufacturer, to increase the size of the plant, and to establish in-house management training programs. In addition, all the long-range objectives convey the basic mission of manufacturing and selling widgets—that mission, in turn, being directly related to the socioeconomic purposes of the organization. The manufacture and sale of widgets will result in profits as well as the fulfillment of certain social functions, such as the satisfaction of demand for this particular good. There is thus an interrelated *hierarchy of objectives*, and the strategic plan assists the firm in identifying its long-range objectives and formulating the derivative intermediate-range goals.

OPERATIONAL PLANNING

The third type of planning is *operational planning*. Operational planning is short-range in contrast to strategic planning, and most low- and intermediate-level administrators spend a good deal of their time carrying out these short-range plans. Figure 4–5 shows the relationship between strategic and operational planning. Strategic planning can be viewed as the formulation of long-range objectives, whereas operational planning is the implementation of these decisions.

Operational planning is action-oriented.

The time-lapse between the formulation stage and the implementation stage may be as great as a decade, although firms most often opt for a five-year plan. For example, one survey of 420 companies revealed the following planning period distributions:

No corporate plan	16%
Under five years	6%
Five years only	53%
Five to ten years	8%
Ten years only	11%
Over ten years	6%[11]

---

[11] Reported in Steiner, *Top Management Planning*, p. 22.

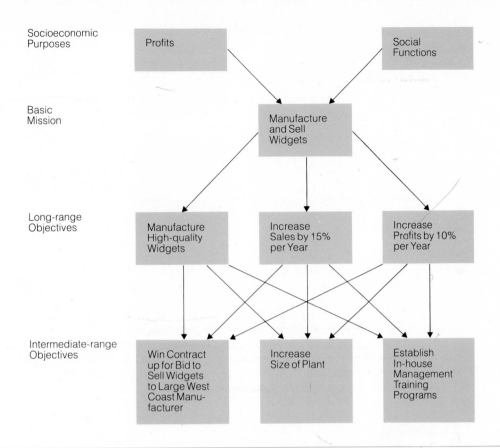

Socioeconomic Purposes

Basic Mission

Long-range Objectives

Intermediate-range Objectives

Figure 4–5 Planning Structure

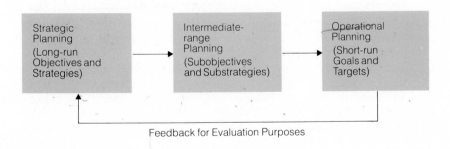

Feedback for Evaluation Purposes

Figure 4–6 Partial Elements of an Operational Plan

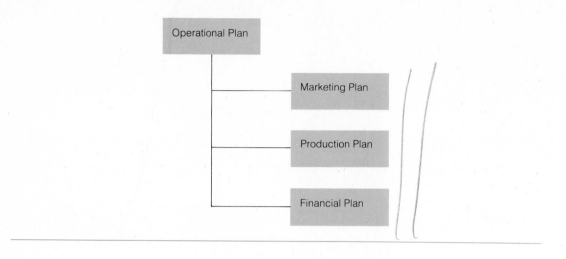

Most operational plans are divided into functional areas. In a manufacturing enterprise, for example, they would appear as in Figure 4–6. This plan is much more specific than its strategic counterpart, with goals and targets spelled out in great detail. As an operational plan comes down the chain of command, the level of abstraction decreases and the degree of specificity increases. Marketing plans, production plans, and financial plans are typical examples of operational planning.

Marketing Plan

Most marketing plans have two main objectives, selling current products and helping develop new ones. The former entails the setting of quotas and market shares for the various product lines. These objectives are translated into operational plans through advertising budgets, the maintenance of a sales force, the assignment of quotas, and the determination of product prices. Then at the end of the given period (for example, six months or a year), performance will be evaluated and goals or targets revised accordingly.

Selling current products and developing new ones are important marketing objectives.

Concurrently, the marketing plan will entail some consideration of new product development. Every business knows that each product has a limited life cycle, as Figure 4–7 illustrates. Some goods will maintain their market position for years while others may never get off the ground, and today's big sellers may have no market demand five years from now. For these reasons, product planning is necessary for generating new product ideas. Sometimes these will come from the research and development lab; other times they may be the result of suggestions from top management, salespeople, customers, or consultants. No matter where they come from, however, only about 2 of every 100 ideas will ever materialize in the form of profitable products. The rest will either be screened out for technical, economic, or market test reasons (95 percent) or will just plain fail to sell, despite all initial signs to the contrary (3 percent).

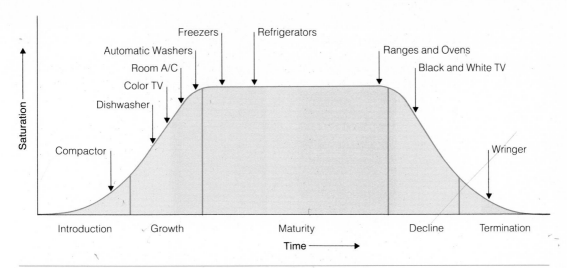

Figure 4–7 Life Cycle Stages of Various Products

Source: Adapted from John E. Smallwood, "The Product Life Cycle: A Key to Strategic Marketing Planning," *MSU Business Topics,* Winter 1973, p. 30. Reprinted by permission of the publisher, Division of Research, Graduate School of Business Administration, Michigan State University.

Production Plan

The production plan is designed to satisfy consumer demand by turning out the desired amount of goods. Sometimes production capability will be greater than estimated demand; other times it will be necessary for the manufacturing department to go to a second or third shift to meet this demand. Both instances illustrate that marketing and production planning are actually intertwined. This relationship is illustrated in Figure 4–8.

The basic objectives of a production plan will entail the purchase, coordination, and maintenance of factors of production—specifically machines, material, and people. How much will it cost to manufacture a particular good? The answer depends on the costs associated with raw materials, merchandise, supplies, labor, and equipment. For this reason, the production plan starts with the desired number of units (the objective) and works backward, determining the amount of equipment and the number of people needed to attain these goals.

The main production objective is to satisfy consumer demand.

Financial Plan

The financial plan, as seen in Figure 4–9, is also interrelated with the marketing and production plans; each of the three influences the others. However, it should be noted that the financial plan is often given more importance than the other plans because it provides a quantitative basis for decision making and control. In an operational plan, managers want to know how well they are doing; financial data tell them. For example, in the production plan the vice-president of production will follow cost per unit very closely; at the same time, the marketing vice-president will be watching the sales curve. Both managers know that if things do not go well, the results will be reflected in the financial feedback.

The financial plan provides a quantitative basis for decision making and control.

Figure 4–8   Interrelationship of Marketing and Production Planning

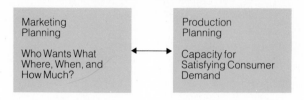

Figure 4–9   Interrelationships of Operational Planning Components

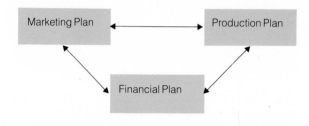

Harmonizing Functional Plans

Budgets are useful in harmonizing plans.

One way in which firms combine these three functional plans (marketing, production, finance) is through the use of the budget. Many managers believe the budget is only a control technique. Instead, it is equally a planning tool: It provides a basis for action. Expected results can be expressed in numerical terms, cash flows can be projected, number of hours to be worked in the current period can be calculated, and units of production can be determined. Furthermore, research shows that when plans are linked to budgets, overall accuracy tends to be greater than when they are not.[12]

Another way in which management draws operational plans together is by setting financial objectives, such as return on investment (profit/assets), market share, growth rate, and profit. In fact when marketing, production, and finance plans are harmonized, it is common to find the financial plan being the fulcrum upon which the other two are balanced. As Figure 4–10 shows, if the marketing or production plans are in disequilibrium, the imbalance will be reflected in the financial data, and corrective action will be taken to re-establish the necessary balance.

USE OF A PLANNING ORGANIZATION

As noted previously, managers in many firms are most concerned with day-to-day problems. They do not have time to construct strategic plans; their interest rests in carrying out operational plans. For this reason, it is common to find departments drawing up their own budgets—with supporting justifications for any proposed capital expenditures—

---

[12] Richard F. Vancil, "The Accuracy of Long-Range Planning," *Harvard Business Review*, September–October 1970, p. 100.

Figure 4–10   Functional Plan Fulcrum

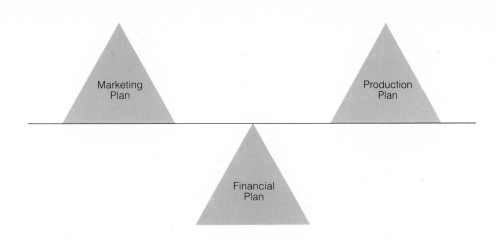

and forwarding these proposals to top management. The high level managers then combine departmental plans into divisional plans, which they in turn review, modify as indicated, and finally approve.

The development of a comprehensive plan is never simple. It requires a tremendous amount of coordination. For this reason many firms, especially large corporations, have begun to develop their own *planning organizations.* Often five to eight years pass before this structure functions smoothly. (Table 4–3 shows how this time is typically spent.) Even though the process is lengthy, there are two important advantages to be gleaned from it. First, some companies lack a complete appreciation for planning at the highest ranks of the organization. A planning organization can surmount this lack of complete commitment. Second, many managers within the structure have never really been taught the concept of planning. A planning organization helps overcome this deficiency.

A planning organization can help a firm design a comprehensive plan.

Organizational Metamorphosis

R. Hal Mason reports, as shown in the table, that a planning organization often begins at the top management level with the formation of a committee to identify and organize data on the firm and its industry position.[13] In Phase 1 attention is given to the development of a framework within which long-range planning can take place.

Phase 2 entails the formation of the first formal long-range plan. At best, it is often a rudimentary guide, lacking both depth and breadth. The plan is constructed by an executive planning staff at the upper divisions which acts as consultant to the rest of the organization.

In Phase 3, which occurs about three years after the plan's inception, the planning organization prepares its first comprehensive five-year plan. This is done through the coordination and integration of the plans prepared by the major operating units. It is a

---

[13] This five-phase metamorphosis comes from R. Hal Mason, "Developing a Planning Organization," *Business Horizons,* August 1969, pp. 61–69.

Table 4–3 Time Phases of a Planning Organization

Phase	Action	Time Span	Total Time Elapsed
1	Establish executive planning committee.	6–12 months	6–12 months
2	Select director of planning and provide *ad hoc* staff committee.	About 12 months	18–24 months
3	Director develops permanent planning staff at corporate level; division planning committees added.	12–36 months	30–60 months
4	Appoint vice-president of planning and corporate development reporting to president and executive planning committee; select division planning coordinator.	12–24 months	42–72 months
5	Specialize corporate development, planning, and evaluation functions; provide division planning staffs reporting to division heads but with relationship to corporate development and planning department.	12–36 months	60–108 months

Source: R. Hal Mason, "Developing a Planning, Organization," *Business Horizons*, August 1969, p. 62. Reprinted with permission.

Planning organizations often go through five phases.

"bottom-up" approach; the departments within each division or unit create plans and send them up the line. Thus the division carries the bulk of the total planning effort. During this phase, divisional planning committees will be added to the operating units to assist both the unit and the planning organization. These committees will assess reporting procedures and information generated about products, customers, and competitors. For its part, the planning organization will assist the committee in the design of the information and reporting systems.

By the time the committee reaches Phase 4, the annual preparation of a long-range plan will have become routine. Operating divisions have usually become attuned to developing plans that are in harmony with each other. At this stage it is also common to find that organizational planning takes on greater importance, and the head of the planning organization is often appointed to vice-presidential rank, reporting directly to the president.

In Phase 5, the final developmental step is reached. Mason describes the phase as follows:

The activities of planning groups at all levels tend to shift their attention increasingly toward corporate development activities, which include the matching of opportunity to corporate capabilities and the development of those capabilities. The formal development of planning information has become routine in certain ways, and each division is aware of the types of data it must generate for planning purposes. An integrated set of plans is put together within a format, and corporate action is evaluated relative to plan. The machinery for developing plans and updating the corporate plan exists and is functioning. This frees the planning group so that it can devote a growing share of its total resources to searching the environment, evaluating corporate strengths and weaknesses, and identifying opportunities for corporate growth and profit improvement.[14]

This type of organization is being employed by an increasing number of firms which realize that intelligent planning requires a concerted effort on the part of the management.

Figure 4–11 illustrates the steps involved in the overall planning process for large, diversified firms. Note in the figure that everyone, from the chief executive officer down to the functional department manager, is involved in the process. As the organization goes through these formal planning cycles, the emphasis shifts from formulation of objectives (strategic planning) to implementation of the plan (operational planning) through budget approval.

ADVANTAGES OF PLANNING

Planning gains a firm a number of important advantages. First, it forces a firm to forecast the environment. No longer does the management assume a wait-and-see attitude. Instead, the company begins evaluating conditions and formulating its own response. Passivity gives way to activity.

Second, planning gives the company direction in the form of objectives. Once the organization knows what it can and cannot do over the next one to five years, it can begin setting goals. Day-to-day operational thinking gives way to more long-run designs.

Third, planning provides a basis for teamwork. When the goals are clearly defined, work assignments can be determined and everyone can begin to contribute to the fulfillment of these objectives. This often leads to improvements in morale; it also helps develop management talent. The manager can now delegate authority to subordinates and begin to evaluate performance. Without planning, such coordination would be a dream; with planning, it is a reality.

Finally, planning helps management learn to live with ambiguity. This is especially true in long- and intermediate-range planning. Management must realize that vagueness has its virtues. If management demands perfect clarity beyond the point where such observations are possible, staff often refuse to do anything beyond operational planning.

PLANNING IS NO GUARANTEE

The development of the long-range plan and its integration with short-range plans are very useful. There is no guarantee, however, that a firm will be successful merely because it plans. Many things can go wrong, and they always, in one way or another, can be traced back to the premises on which the plan was formulated.

Sometimes information coming in from the field is erroneous. Salespeople may give strong endorsement to a particular modification of a current product, but the modified good may not sell very well. What potential customers say they are going to do and what they end up doing may be two different things, illustrating a problem inherent in marketing research.

---

[14] Ibid., pp. 68–69.

Figure 4-11 The Planning Process

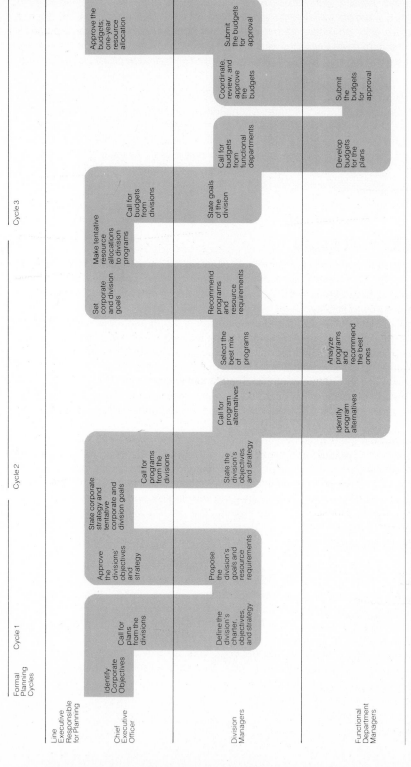

Formal Planning Cycles	Cycle 1	Cycle 2	Cycle 3
Line Executive Responsible for Planning	Identify Corporate Objectives	State corporate strategy and tentative corporate and division goals	Approve the budgets; one-year resource allocation
Chief Executive Officer	Call for plans from the divisions / Approve the divisions' objectives and strategy	Call for programs from the divisions / Set corporate and division goals / Make tentative resource allocations to division programs / Call for budgets from divisions	Coordinate, review, and approve the budgets / Submit the budgets for approval
Division Managers	Define the division's charter, objectives, and strategy / Propose the division's goals and resource requirements	State the division's objectives and strategy / Call for program alternatives / Select the best mix of programs / Recommend programs and resource requirements / State goals of the division / Call for budgets from functional departments	Submit the budgets for approval
Functional Department Managers		Identify program alternatives / Analyze programs and recommend the best ones	Develop budgets for the plans

Source: Adapted by permission of the *Harvard Business Review*. Exhibit from "Strategic Planning in Diversified Companies" by Richard F. Vancil and Peter Lorange, January–February 1975, pp. 84–85. Copyright © 1975 by the President and Fellows of Harvard College; all rights reserved.

A second basic problem is the economy. A plan predicated on a rising economy will run into trouble if a downturn is encountered. For example, during much of the ten-year period from 1970 to 1980, the economy expanded, and many organizational planners saw the future as more of the same. After all, it is far easier (and to many, more logical) to extrapolate the present than to wonder when the bloom will be off the rose. If a company has increased its sales by 25 percent a year for the last five years, it is very difficult for management to estimate the following year's increase at 15 percent. Psychologically, managers in this situation are taking a 10 percent cut. For this reason, many firms tend to extrapolate the economy during good times and estimate an upturn or leveling out during poor times. They design the economy to fit the plan instead of the proper reverse.

A third problem can be the company's financial position. A plan may rely heavily on strong advertising and personal promotion. If the company is then unable to finance this kind of campaign, the plan can fall flat. In fact, a downward spiral may occur with reduced promotional expenses leading to the nonmaterialization of sales, which results in the cutback of any further promotional effort. The publishing industry often faces this problem because of its small profit margin. For example, let us assume a textbook will be given an estimated sales price of $17.95 and an annual market potential of 5,000 copies. The advertising budget will be set at $10,000 for the first year and $5,000 for the second. However, if internal budgetary cuts require changes in the plan, the textbook price might be raised to $18.95 to help cover the publisher's in-house expenses. Yet such a move might also result in a decline in demand for the now-too-expensive book; perhaps only 3,500 copies would be bought. Revenue would then dip from an expected total of $89,750 to an actual total of $66,325. This, in turn, could lead the company to eliminate the follow-up advertising budget. Once the initial plan runs into trouble, everything goes awry because the plan is basically a sequence of cause–effect relationships that are supposed to work in particular ways. If the sequence of relationships is imperfect, every attempt to re-establish an equilibrium can lead to further problems.

A fourth common problem is lack of coordination. Even when the objectives are clear, the functional departments sometimes fail to synchronize their efforts. Sometimes this is caused by the staff's loss of enthusiasm for its own plan; more commonly, it results when the proposed plan is modified by higher authority. In either event, the human element comes into play, and plans are not implemented according to the previously determined schedule.

Planning does not lead to some future utopia in the life of any firm. Too many things can go wrong despite the most careful planning. Nevertheless, companies that plan do increase their chances for success, and it is that predictable benefit that leads intelligent managers to keep on planning.

SUMMARY

In this chapter comprehensive planning, which consists of strategic, intermediate, and operational plans, has been examined. Prime attention was given to long-run considerations, with the observation that most firms tend to be oriented too much toward the short run. The chapter also examined the roles played by the determination of the firm's basic socioeconomic mission, values of the top management, and analysis of the organization's strengths and weaknesses in the formulation of the strategic plan. The analysis of strengths requires accurate economic and sales forecasting coupled with a frank, honest evaluation of the company's material resources and personnel competencies. Only in this way can a firm identify a niche and formulate long-range objectives.

Although the long-range plan provides general direction, the intermediate-range and especially the operational plans are also important because they offer specific direction. The operational plan often consists of derivative functional plans such as marketing, production, and finance plans, designed to attain short-run objectives while harmonizing with the previously determined long-range goals. Such short-range plans provide management with a method for gauging progress, serving as a basis from which to adapt or modify current plans and construct future ones.

REVIEW AND STUDY QUESTIONS

1. Why has there been a marked trend toward comprehensive planning on the part of many business firms?
2. What is meant by the term *strategic planning?*
3. What are the three basic foundations of strategic planning? Describe each.
4. How do management values affect the planning process?
5. How does a firm conduct external environmental forecasting? Be specific.
6. How does a firm evaluate its internal environment?
7. Give an example of a firm developing a niche and explain what that has to do with planning?
8. What is meant by the term *operational planning?*
9. How can a planning organization be useful to management?
10. What are some of the advantages of planning? Explain.
11. What are some of the disadvantages of planning? Explain.
12. What are some of the common problems that can cause a plan to fail? Explain.

SELECTED REFERENCES

Ansoff, H. I. "Managing Strategic Surprise by Response to Weak Signals." *California Management Review,* Winter 1975, pp. 21–23.

Banks, L. "The Mission of Our Business Society." *Harvard Business Review,* May–June 1975, pp. 57–66.

Bracker, J. "The Historical Development of the Strategic Management Concept." *Academy of Management Journal,* January 1977, pp. 95–102.

Cohen, K. J., and Cyert, R. M. "Strategy: Formulation, Implementation and Monitoring." *Journal of Business,* July 1973, pp. 784–810.

Drucker, Peter F. *Management: Tasks, Responsibilities, Practices.* New York: Harper & Row, 1974, chaps. 5–10.

———. "Managing for Business Effectiveness." *Harvard Business Review,* May–June 1963, pp. 53–60.

Duncan, W. J. "Transferring Management Theory to Practice." *Academy of Management Journal,* December 1974, pp. 724–738.

Glueck, William F., and Willis, R. "Documentary Sources and Strategic Management Research." *Academy of Management Review,* January 1977, pp. 95–102.

Hall, W. K. "SBUs: Hot, New Topic in the Management of Diversification." *Business Horizons,* February 1978, pp. 17–25.

Hobbs, J. M., and Heany, D. F. "Coupling Strategy to Operating Plans." *Harvard Business Review,* May–June 1977, pp. 119–126.

Hofer, Charles W. "Toward a Contingency Theory of Business Strategy." *Harvard Business Review,* May–June 1977, pp. 119–126.

Kinnunen, R. M. "Hypotheses Related to Strategy Formulation in Large Divisionalized Companies." *Academy of Management Review,* October 1976, pp. 7–14.

Koontz, Harold. "Making Strategic Planning Work." *Business Horizons,* April 1976, pp. 37–47.

Kotler, Philip. *Marketing Management: Analysis, Planning, and Control,* 4th ed. (Englewood Cliffs, N.J.: Prentice-Hall, 1980), chap. 4.

Lebell, D., and Krasner, O. J. "Selecting Environmental Forecasting Techniques from Business Planning Requirements." *Academy of Management Review,* July 1977, pp. 373–383.

Linneman, R. E., and Kennell, J. D. "Shirt-Sleeve Approach to Long-Range Plans." *Harvard Business Review,* March–April 1977, pp. 141–150.

Lorange, Peter, and Vancil, Richard F. "How to Design a Strategic Planning System." *Harvard Business Review,* September–October 1976, pp. 75–81.

McCaskey, M. B. "A Contingency Approach to Planning: Planning with Goals and Planning without Goals." *Academy of Management Journal,* June 1974, pp. 281–291.

Mason, R. Hal. "Developing a Planning Organization." *Business Horizons,* August 1969, pp. 61–69.

Most, K. S. "Wanted: A Planning Model for the Firm." *Managerial Planning,* July–August 1973, pp. 1–6.

Paul, R. N.; Donovan, N. B.; and Taylor, J. W. "The Reality Gap in Strategic Planning." *Harvard Business Review,* May–June 1978, pp. 124–130.

Pekar, P. P., Jr., and Burack, E. H. "Management Control of Strategic Plans through Adaptive Techniques." *Academy of Management Journal,* March 1976, pp. 79–97.

Shanklin, W. L. "Strategic Business Planning: Yesterday, Today and Tomorrow." *Business Horizons,* October 1979, pp. 7–14.

Smallwood, J. E. "The Product Life Cycle: Key to Strategic Marketing Planning." *MSU Business Topics,* Winter 1973, pp. 29–35.

Steiner, G. A. *Strategic Planning: What Every Manager Must Know.* New York: Free Press, 1979.

———. *Top Management Planning.* New York: Macmillan, 1969.

Turner, Robert C. "Should You Take Business Forecasting Seriously?" *Business Horizons,* April 1978, pp. 64–73.

Van Dam, A. "The Future of Global Business Forecasting." *Business Horizons,* August 1977, pp. 46–50.

Wheelright, S. C., and Clarke, D. G. "Corporate Forecasting: Promise and Reality." *Harvard Business Review,* November–December 1976, pp. 40–42.

Woodward, H. N. "Management Strategies for Small Companies." *Harvard Business Review,* January–February 1976, pp. 113–121.

CASE: *Cleaning House*

During the 1970s the Colgate Palmolive Company acquired a great many firms. By the end of the decade, however, it had become apparent that some of these acquisitions had been poor choices. As 1980 rolled around, the company had sold a number of them and had others in line for sale. Some of those Colgate sold were: (a) Hebrew National Kosher Foods, a $5 million producer of processed meats; (b) Leach Industries, a $14 million maker of racquetball racquets; (c) the Ram Golf Corporation, a $20 million manufacturer of golf equipment; (d) Belle Sommers, a $10 million olive and pepper company; (e) fifty-eight Lum's and Ranch House restaurants in Georgia, Texas, and southern Florida, and (f) five sports equipment companies based in Britain. Remaining to be sold were the Bancroft Sporting Goods Company, a tennis manufacturing firm called Maui Divers of Hawaii Ltd., and a jewelry company. Analysts also forecasted that Colgate would divest itself of Pangburn Candy enterprises; Artex, a do-it-yourself hobby company; and Marissa Cristina, a women's apparel company. Helena Rubenstein, the cosmetics division, was also believed to be headed for the auctioneer's block.

Colgate found that its skill in marketing toothpaste and laundry soap did not extend to hot dogs, nail polish, and hockey sticks. By purchasing these companies, the firm found itself having to divert management attention from product introductions and brand maintenance to unrelated businesses about which it knew very little. Additionally, this cluster of firms accounted for losses that swelled from $4.5 million in 1978 to $26.5 million in 1979. After reviewing the company's long-range financial objectives, the Colgate president decided to discontinue those operations that were not attaining their objectives and concentrate the firm's resources where they could be put to better advantage.

Questions

1. How would you identify the basic mission of Colgate Palmolive?

2. Colgate had to sell many of its newly acquired companies. What mistakes resulted in the company's having to sell so much?

3. What does this case illustrate about the need for strategic planning? Be complete in your answer.

CASE: A Better Mousetrap

If you build a better mousetrap, it is said, the world will beat a path to your door. But will it really? The Woodstream Company had manufactured traps for catching all kinds of animals, from elephants to grizzly bears. One day, the firm decided to design and manufacture a streamlined mousetrap.

A product designer was brought in to design a trap that would look interesting enough for people to notice the change. The final product was made of plastic and looked like a sardine can with an arched doorway at floor level through which mice could enter. Any mouse coming through the doorway would trip a spring and be choked to death by a wire which, acting like an upside-down guillotine, would snap up from below.

The company called the new product "Little Champ" and priced it at 25 cents, in contrast to the wooden ones, which sold at two for 15 cents. Although the price was higher than average, the trap was easier to set, extremely efficient, and, perhaps best of all, could be cleaned and reused. It did not have to be thrown out with the mouse.

Looking forward to a booming demand, the company sent the traps out to hardware dealers across the nation. And the mousetraps just sat there on the hardware shelves, gathering expensive dust. Despite the changes in the traps' efficiency features, no one wanted them. Why? Apparently potential buyers, who thought nothing of throwing away the old wooden snap-trap, mouse and all, did not want to extract the dead mouse and clean the new plastic 25-cent trap.

The venture failed. Richard Woolworth, the company president, was unable to generate interest in the product, although he certainly tried. For example, during a New York City garbage strike, Woolworth wired the governor of New York, offering to ship a million rat traps for $144,000. But the governor, a man, was not interested; and the Woodstream Company finally gave up on the product.

Questions

1. What kind of planning should the Woodstream Company have done before manufacturing these traps?

2. Why was the company unable to sell the traps? Do you agree with the above analysis, or are there other reasons for the failure? Explain.

3. Is there anything the company can now do with the traps, or is the venture a total loss?

Source: Adapted from Stephen J. Fansweet, "Dick Woolworth Builds a Better Mousetrap—and Falls on His Face," *Wall Street Journal,* September 24, 1970, p. 1.

CASE: *Milking the Cow*

Marie Newsom had been president of Newsom Printing for five years, having left a high-paying job in sales for an eastern publishing firm to return to the family business. "We were on the verge of selling out," she told Willy Chishilm, her management consultant. "My dad, who started the business, had died, and the other members of the family didn't want anything to do with it. That was when I began to look into the possibility of taking over and seeing what I could do. Well, you know the story. You've been here for a week now looking over operations and examining our financial statements. You know better than anyone how well we've done over the last four years."

Chishilm moved his chair closer to the desk and placed some papers on top of it. "Marie, you look just great on paper. I have absolutely no arguments with your technical operations. Some of the new machinery you purchased is going to save you a lot of money in the long run. And your staff morale is sky high. My management team has been talking to your people since Wednesday, and there hasn't been one negative comment about anything."

"Somehow, Willy, I don't think this is your way of telling me that everything is perfect."

"Right. It's my way of leading up to a plan of action that I want to recommend to you. You do have a problem here. You're too short-run oriented. You have no real idea of where you are going. You've got a couple of banks that you are supplying with printed material and a lot of walk-in business and that's all."

"Oh, I don't know about that. You can't forget that seventeen firms in town send all their printing orders to us also."

"Okay, them too. However, that's all you've got. You are tied directly into the orders you get from your local captive businesses and anyone coming in off the streets and that's it."

"So what's so wrong with that? Look at our sales. In 1980 we did over $1.5 million of business. In 1981 we had sales of $1.75 million. This year we're anticipating $2.0 million, but at the rate we're going, it's going to be closer to $2.2 million. It seems to me we're in great shape."

"Financially speaking, you are. However, have you any idea where Newsom Printing is going to be in 1985? Or how about 1995? What are your long-range plans?"

"Willy, you know I don't mess with long-range planning. I don't need it. In this town there are two large banks. They send all their business to us. They always have. Besides them, we have those other seventeen companies, most of which are insurance firms that need an awful lot of printing done. All I have to do is keep worrying about the next three months. That's my long-range plan, ninety days into the future. As long as I know I have enough financing at the bank and my collections are taking place on time, I have a good cash flow. What else is there to running a successful business?"

"Marie, do you think the banks you print for got to be as large as they are by planning ninety days into the future?"

"No, but then I'm not a bank. My business has a number of companies that rely upon it exclusively for their printing. There is no company in town that can match my price on any job because I've got the best equipment and can offer higher quality and lower prices than any of them. So tell me why I need to worry about long-range planning. My whole plan consists of keeping the machines in working order and not letting the competition get any technological jumps on me. That's the only way I can get beaten out of a job, and it's just not going to happen. In a manner of speaking, I've carved a niche for myself. This niche is a very fat, profitable cow, and my job is to sit here and milk that cow for all it's worth. The last thing on my mind is long-range or, as you call it, strategic planning. Who needs it? When you've got a good thing going, enjoy it. What can long-range planning do for a business like mine?"

Questions

1. What are the advantages of long-range planning? Be specific.

2. What arguments should Chishilm raise in defense of his long-range planning proposal?

3. Can long-range planning really be of any value to Newsom Printing, or is the firm better off sticking with its current short-range planning approach? Defend your opinion.

CASE: Just Leave Us Alone

The Johnson Corporation was founded by Buzz Johnson in 1959. The going was rough in the early years, but by 1965 things had started to improve, and in the late 1960s, while the economy was dipping, Johnson's business was at its best. Sales and profits set new highs between 1976 and 1981, as seen in the listed company data:

Year	Sales	Net Profit
1976	$4,600,000	$ 400,000
1977	4,900,000	510,000
1978	5,300,000	636,000
1979	6,000,000	720,000
1980	7,850,000	1,020,000
1981	9,000,000	1,350,000

The firm's record was so outstanding, in fact, that a number of large corporations made offers to buy it. Finally, after careful consideration, Johnson accepted the offer of a large Eastern conglomerate. In addition to a very lucrative financial settlement, the conglomerate agreed that Johnson and his management team would remain at the helm, with business continuing as usual. The only major change was that all long-range and short-range performance goals (profitability, return on investment, sales, and the like) would have to be cleared with the planning organization at the conglomerate's headquarters so as to ensure overall organizational coordination.

Initially everything went smoothly, but by the end of the first year it was apparent things were not going well at all. Johnson called a meeting of his top people to see if things could be ironed out. He also persuaded the vice-president of corporate planning and his two staff assistants to fly in for the conference. Johnson sensed bad feelings between his people and the central planning group and decided it was time for both to air their gripes. The basic points of view presented by the two groups follow:

Johnson Group

Before we were purchased by the Eastern conglomerate, we used to run our own show around here. After all, who knows more about how to manufacture and sell our product than we do? But now we're asked to coordinate our plans with those of seven other companies. And sometimes our suggested plans apparently don't fit in because they're rejected or modified by the corporate planning department. We've had it with being told how to run our own end of the business. This concept of overall coordinated planning is having a drastic effect on the morale of our management team. Why don't you Easterners just leave us alone?

Corporate Planning Group

We have eight major companies in our conglomerate. The only way we can make these eight work as one is to coordinate their long- and short-range planning. We know people don't like to be told how to do their own job. And we don't mean to do that. But there has to be some harmony if we're to work as one big team. We can understand that managers don't like having their plans modified or revised, but this just can't be helped. And until the management of the Johnson Corporation realizes that it's part of a team, we're going to continue to have this problem. Big companies can't offer the personal touch that small ones can. When you become the member of a conglomerate, you have to be willing to give up a little autonomy. Perhaps the Johnson management should try seeing things from our point of view.

Questions

1. Can a conglomerate operate as what the planners called "one big team" without running into the kind of problems seen in this case?

2. Is the Johnson management right? Is the central planning organization indifferent to its problems?

3. How can this problem be solved? Present a feasible solution.

CHAPTER 5

THE ORGANIZING PROCESS

GOALS OF THE CHAPTER

Organizing entails the assignment of duties and the coordination of efforts among all organizational staff to ensure maximum efficiency in the attainment of predetermined objectives. The goals of this chapter are to examine the nature, purpose, and function of organizing.
When you have finished reading the chapter, you should be able to do the following:

1. Identify and describe the most commonly used forms of departmentalization.

2. Discuss the advantages and limitations of the committee form of organization.

3. Define the concept of span of control and relate its importance to effective organization design.

4. Describe the three types of authority used in organizational settings —line, staff, and functional —and relate their value in effective organizing.

5. Identify the determinants of decentralization and explain why some organizations are basically decentralized while others are basically centralized.

6. Describe the informal organization and discuss its importance to the modern manager.

FROM STRATEGY TO STRUCTURE

Strategy is a prerequisite for structure.

It has already been noted that the planning process encompasses strategic, intermediate, and operational plans. Our model can now be expanded, as in Figure 5–1, to include the organization structure, hence the often used phrase from strategy to structure, which research has shown to be an accurate statement. Alfred D. Chandler, Jr., after conducting intensive studies of General Motors, DuPont, Standard Oil of New Jersey, and Sears, Roebuck and Company, showed that strategy is a prerequisite for structure.[1] If an organization has no sense of where it is going, it also has no intelligent basis for organizing human effort and material resources. This chapter will be devoted to the various structures and concepts that can assist the manager in this process.

COMMON FORMS OF DEPARTMENTALIZATION

Perhaps the easiest way to grasp the function of organizing is to examine the mechanics of the process. By dividing the work and the work force into group activities, managers can form departments for the purpose of specialization. The three most widely used types of departmentalization are functional, product, and territorial.

Functional Departmentalization

Functional departmentalization, the most widely used departmentalization form, occurs when an enterprise organizes itself around the firm's major activities. In a manufacturing enterprise, in which the *organic functions*—those activities which are vital to the continued existence of a firm—are marketing, production, and finance, a typical functional organization chart is that shown in Figure 5–2. The figure shows also what an *organization chart* basically is—a diagram of an organization's departments and their relationships to each other.

Functional departmentalization is the most widely used.

In nonmanufacturing firms these functions differ. For example, in a large bank they often include comptroller, operations, legal, and public relations. In an insurance company it would be common to find actuarial, underwriting, agency, and claim adjustment. In a public utility organic functions would include accounting, sales, engineering, and personnel. All these are illustrations of major functional departments, which, in turn, can have *derivative departments.* For example, expanding Figure 5–2 to include second-level functional departments might result in the organization chart shown in Figure 5–3.

Similar charts could be drawn for all functionally organized enterprises, but the structure need not stop at the second level. Third-, fourth-, and even fifth-level departments may evolve, depending on the size of the enterprise.

Perhaps the major reason that functional departmentalization is so widely employed is the emphasis it places on basic activities, providing a logic and framework for specialization. However, functional departmentalization also has some drawbacks. It can create a form of mental tunnel vision, in which functional specialists see nothing but their own areas of interest. Also, in some instances, firms adopt functional departmentalization because other companies are doing it. They decide to follow that kind of lead even if another form—departmentalization by product, for example—would actually be more beneficial for them.

---

[1] Alfred D. Chandler, Jr., *Strategy and Structure* (Garden City, N.Y.: Anchor Books, Doubleday, 1966).

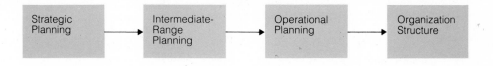

Figure 5 –1   From Strategy to Structure

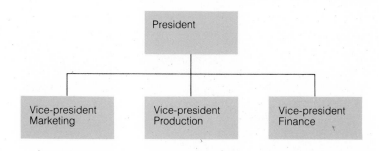

Figure 5 –2   Typical Functional Organization Chart in Manufacturing

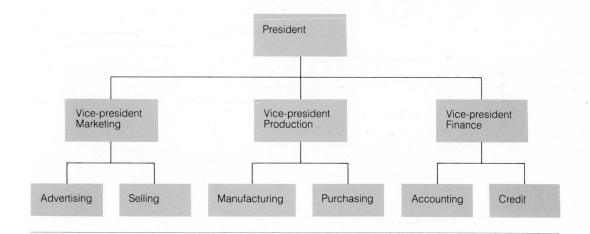

Figure 5 –3   Derivative Functional Departments

Product Departmentalization

Product departmentalization has had increasing importance in recent years, especially among multi-line, large-scale enterprises. General Motors, DuPont, RCA, and General Electric all employ it. Many firms now organized by product were originally functional organizations which, as they grew, developed a need for a reorganization along product lines. Figure 5–4 is a simple illustration of a manufacturing firm reorganized along product lines. The organic functions of marketing, production, and finance can still be found in

Product departmentalization is employed by many multi-line, large-scale companies.

Figure 5–4 *Product Organization Chart for a Manufacturing Firm*

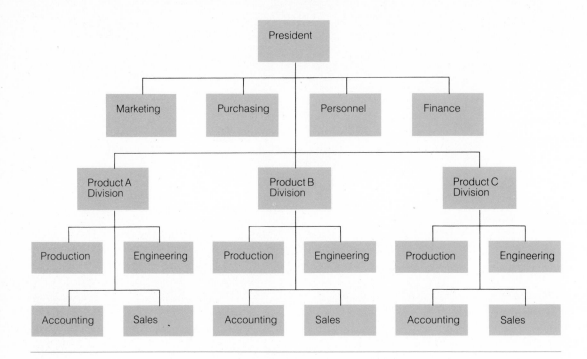

the structure, but prime attention now goes to the product lines, with all activities that relate to a particular product brought together.

Perhaps the main value of product departmentalization is that it facilitates coordination and allows for specialization. If the firm is large, this can be especially beneficial. For example, General Electric in 1980 had five major operating groups, each containing no fewer than eight—and in some cases as many as eleven—divisions. Figure 5–5 shows the consumer products and industrial groups. Had GE opted for functional departmentalization, the kind of massive coordination necessary in running such an enterprise would have proved impossible.

The product form of departmentalization can also aid in the measurement and control of operating performance. Since all revenues and costs can be differentiated and assigned to a particular product line, cost centers can be established, high profit areas can be cultivated, and unprofitable product lines can be dropped.

Product departmentalization also provides an excellent opportunity for training executive personnel. Since the department or division is multifunctional, it often operates like a complete company, providing executives with a wealth of diversified functional experience that is useful in overcoming narrowness of interest and seasoning them for the future. This can be very important to a manager who will one day be chief executive charged with coordinating marketing, finance, and production activities. To overemphasize any one of these areas to the detriment of the others can have catastrophic results.

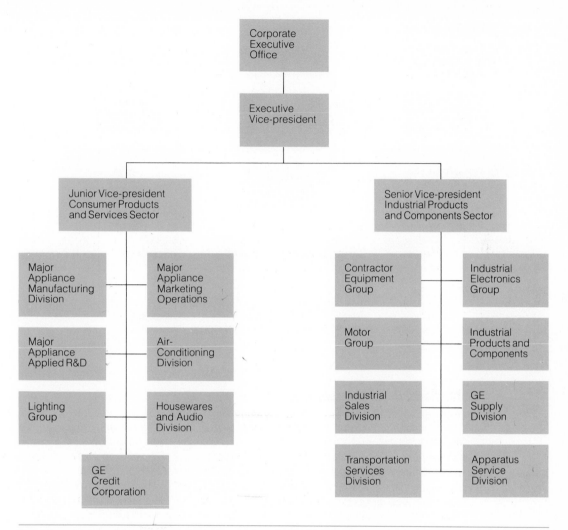

Source: General Electric's 1979 Annual Report.

On the other hand, this form also has potential problem areas. First, the product divisions may try to become too autonomous, thereby presenting top management with a control problem. Second, because of its emphasis on semi-autonomism, product departmentalization works well only in those organizations that have a sufficient number of employees with general management ability. Third, it is common to find product divisions duplicating some of the facilities found at the top levels of the structure, making product departmentalization an expensive organizational form.

Figure 5–6 Territorial Organization Chart for a Manufacturing Firm

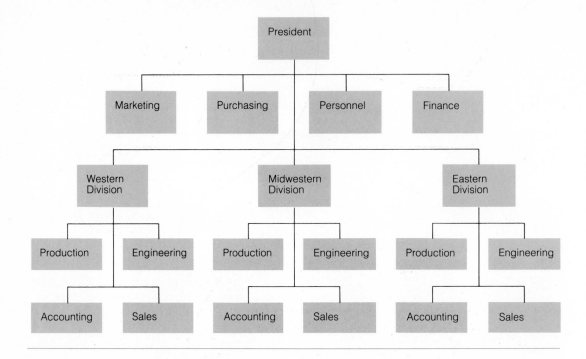

Territorial Departmentalization

When an enterprise is physically dispersed, as in the case of a large-scale organization, it is not uncommon to find *territorial departmentalization,* as seen in Figure 5–6. Contrasting this figure with that of product departmentalization (Figure 5–4) illustrates how similar the two forms really are.

Geographically dispersed organizations often employ territorial departmentalization.

The major advantage of a territorial organization is that of local operation. For example, a firm that manufactures close to the supply of raw materials can produce its product at a lower cost per unit. Furthermore, employees in local sales departments can get to know their customers and markets much better than salespeople who live far away from their territories.

The disadvantages of territorial departmentalization are the same as those found in product departmentalization. It is often difficult for top management to control operations, and there is a tendency to duplicate services.

Other Types of Departmentalization

Functional, product, and territorial are only three types of departmentalization. There are numerous other forms, some of the most common being departmentalization by simple numbers, by time, by customer, and by equipment or process.

Departmentalization by simple numbers is used when the success of the undertaking depends exclusively on the amount of available labor. In community chest drives, for example, each manager is given a number of volunteers and a section of the city to canvass. Success depends to a great extent on the number of people available to ring doorbells. The U.S. military, in which portions of the infantry are still organized on the basis of numbers of people, provides another illustration. In the business setting, common labor crews are also organized this way.

Departmentalization by time is one of the oldest ways of grouping activities. For example, the division of the work force into three shifts—day, swing, and graveyard—is a common application of this form. Police and fire departments, hospitals, and other such emergency services all over the world still use this approach, as do industrial firms facing great demand for their goods.

Departmentalization by customer is used by organizations such as meat packers, retail stores, and container manufacturers. The meat packer's major departments are frequently dairy, poultry, beef, lamb, veal, and by-products; those of the retail store are often men's clothing, women's clothing, and children's clothing; and the container company's major departments are likely to be drug and chemical, closure and plastics, and beverage industries. Educational institutions that offer both regular day courses on campus and extension courses at night or off campus in order to cater to the needs of different groups of students are another example. Departmentalization by customer helps organizations meet the special and widely varying needs of the customers they depend on.

Departmentalization by equipment (process departmentalization) is often used in manufacturing organizations—for example, in the establishment of an electronic data processing department. Similarly, it is common in many plants to find lathe presses or automatic screw machines arranged in one locale. The basic value of this organizational form is the economic advantages that such groupings bring about. By placing the machines together, the company can obtain greater efficiency.

All the basic departmentalization patterns examined thus far are common organizational forms. It should be noted, however, that every enterprise employs its own particular variation. Most organizations have some form of hybridization in their designs—for example, a basically functional organization with traces of product, equipment, process, customer, and territorial departmentalization. Organization charts are rarely specimens of pure functional, product, or territorial departmentalization.

In addition, there are a number of other forms of departmentalization.

COMMITTEE ORGANIZATIONS

Another common organizational form, often used in conjunction with departmentalization, is the committee. Research indicates that committees are increasingly used in business. In general, there are two types. The most common is the *ad hoc committee,* a committee that is appointed for a particular purpose and then disbanded after it has analyzed a problem or conducted some research in order to give its recommendations. The other type, which does not disband, is often called the *standing committee;* many of these are also advisory, like the ad hoc committees. If a committee has the authority to order implementation of its recommendations, however, its members are working in a *plural executive* capacity. The most common illustration of a plural executive is a board of directors, but in large corporations it is not uncommon to find the high-level policy committees—for example, executive or finance—also serving in the plural executive capacity.

Another common organization form is the committee.

Advantages of Committees

Committees have some important advantages to offer. Three of the most commonly cited are group deliberation, motivation, and coordination.

Group Deliberation Two heads being better than one, a committee would be expected to have more knowledge, experience, and judgment than any lone individual. When an organization focuses the attention of a committee on a particular problem, the result is often a solution superior to that which could have been obtained from any one member working independently.

Motivation Research has shown that when subordinates are permitted to participate in the decision-making process, enthusiasm for accepting and implementing the recommendations often increases. The work force supports the probem because its members had a hand in fashioning it. Committees can provide the basis for such action.

Coordination Committees are also useful in coordinating plans and transmitting information. The implementation of a major program, for example, often involves many departments, and a committee can help each to see where it fits in the overall plan. It can also obtain agreement on what each is going to do and when, thereby coordinating overall efforts.

Disadvantages of Committees

Despite all their advantages, committees are the butt of many jokes (for example, the one about a camel being a horse designed by a committee) because the drawbacks to using committees in the organizational design often outweigh the returns. Three of the most commonly cited disadvantages are waste of time, compromise, and lack of individual action.

Waste of Time The adage that time is money can be well considered in evaluating the costs and worth of committees. Many of them are far too large, and many spend an excessive amount of time discussing trivial matters. On the issue of size, C. Northcote Parkinson has remarked that there is constant pressure to increase the number of people on a committee if for no other reason than to include more individuals with specialized knowledge.[2]

On the issue of time spent on trivial matters, Parkinson notes that complex issues often confound people, who, because they are unwilling to admit ignorance, adopt a policy of silence. The result is the dispatching of crucial decisions, such as the allocation of $1.2 billion for an atomic reactor, within a matter of minutes. However on simple issues that are understandable to all, such as the construction of a $5,000 bicycle shed for use by the clerical staff, committee members come alive. Comprehending both the issue and expenses (and realizing they were lax in their participation in the atomic reactor topic), they spring into action with newfound vigor.[3] Parkinson attributes this phenomenon to the *law of triviality,* which states that "the time spent on any item of the agenda will be in inverse proportion to the sum involved."[4] If this is true, many committees may indeed not be worth the cost.

Compromise Committees always pose the danger of inappropriate compromise. After haggling over an issue for a long time, the group may decide to mediate the matter. No one gets what anyone started out for, but the ultimate decision is one everybody can live with. Unfortunately, the result is often a mediocre decision, truly representing the least common denominator.

---

[2] C. Northcote Parkinson, *Parkinson's Law* (Boston: Houghton Mifflin, 1957), chap. 3.
[3] Ibid.
[4] Ibid., p. 24.

Lack of Individual Action There are some things that are better accomplished by individuals than by committees. For example, one very famous American Management Association report found that although committees were considered useful in handling jurisdictional questions, such as interdepartmental disputes, many executives regarded them as ineffective in carrying out such functions as decision making, organizing, executing, and leading.[5] Instead, the respondents preferred individual action. People in management must recognize the times when committees do not perform as well as the individual manager.

How to Use Committees Effectively

In view of their drawbacks, a manager working with committees should adhere to some important guidelines if committees are to be effectively employed. First, the objective of the group must be clearly stated. Second, participants must be carefully chosen so that they provide the expertise needed to attain the objective. Third, the size must be manageable, allowing for discussion and healthy disagreement without becoming too unwieldy in the process. Fourth, an agenda indicating the topics for discussion and analysis must be sent out beforehand so that everyone can be prepared to begin immediately. Fifth, the chair must be able to encourage participation while keeping the group headed toward the objective. Although these guidelines cannot ensure success, they have been found to improve committee performance markedly because they are designed to overcome specific common pitfalls.

There are five important guidelines for using committees effectively.

SPAN OF CONTROL

Span of control, which refers to the number of people reporting to a given superior, is another important organizing concept. Many of the classical theorists believed the ideal span to be between three and six workers. Although this number is open to dispute, the span will certainly have a great deal of influence on the organizational design. For example, taking two companies with approximately the same number of employees, Figure 5–7 illustrates how the structure would appear if a narrow span of control were employed, while Figure 5–8 shows a company with a wide span of control.

A narrow span of control requires that the organization have more levels in the hierarchy, and the structure therefore looks very much like a pyramid. Conversely, the organization with the wide span of control has fewer levels and a rectangular shape; it is shallow and wide. The organization chart for the firm with the narrow span of control is called a tall structure; the one for the firm with the wide span is called a flat structure.

Flat and Tall Structures

Classical bureaucratic organizations typically have very *tall organization structures,* characterized by narrow spans that allow the manager to exercise tight control. The manager has only a few subordinates and can therefore be aware of everything the subordinates are doing.

The most famous departure from the narrow span was made by Sears, Roebuck and Company and is often attributed to James C. Worthy, a management consultant and

---

[5] Ernest Dale, *Planning and Developing the Company Organization Structure,* Research Report No. 20 (New York: American Management Association, 1952), p. 92.

Figure 5–7   Narrow Span of Control

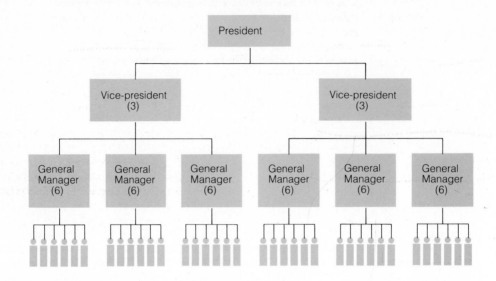

Figure 5–8   Wide Span of Control

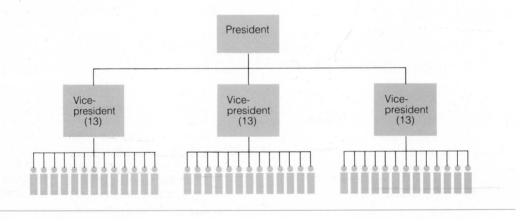

former vice-president of the company.[6] After experimenting with both conventional and flat structures, the Sears management concluded that on the basis of sales volume, profit, morale, and management competence, the flat design was superior. Several factors accounted for the results. First, having a large number of subordinate managers, the superiors found they had to delegate important decisions; they did not have the time

---

[6]   James C. Worthy, "Organizational Structure and Employee Morale," *American Sociological Review,* April 1950, pp. 169–179; and "Factors Influencing Employee Morale," *Harvard Business Review,* January 1950, pp. 61–73.

to do everything themselves. In turn, by being forced to manage, the subordinates became better at their jobs. This led to increased morale and higher quality performance. It also made store managers more selective in choosing subordinates, because they knew they would have to delegate considerable authority to the people they hired. In addition, reducing the number of hierarchical levels improved communication. Such a structure helped overcome what Peter Drucker, one of the best known and most highly regarded authorities on management today, calls the major malorganization symptom, which he states this way:

> The most common and most serious symptom of malorganization is multiplication of the number of management levels. A basic rule of organization is to build the least possible number of management levels and forge the shortest possible chain of command.[7]

This does not mean, however, that flat structures are always superior. Research by Rocco Carzo, Jr., and John N. Yanouzas, for example, has shown that groups operating under a basically tall structure had significantly better results than those operating under a flat structure.[8] There are arguments to be made for each structure, indicating that the right span is a function of the situation, the manager, the subordinates, and the work itself.[9] Perhaps Robert J. House and John B. Miner have summarized this entire area best:

There are benefits to both flat and tall structures.

> The implications for the span of control seem to be that (1) under most circumstances the optimal span is likely to be in the range 5 through 10; (2) the larger spans, say 8 through 10, are most often appropriate at the highest policy-making levels of an organization, where greater resources for diversified problem-solving appear to be needed (although diversified problem-solving without larger spans may well be possible); (3) the breadth of effective spans of first line supervisors is contingent on the technology of the organization; and (4) in prescribing the span of control for specific situations consideration must be given to a host of local factors such as the desirability of high group cohesiveness, the performance demands of the task, the degree of stress in the environment, task interdependencies, the need for member satisfaction, and the leadership skills available to the organization.[10]

AUTHORITY-RESPONSIBILITY RELATIONSHIPS

Concurrent with the formation of an organization structure exists the need for assigning specific duties to the employees. Often companies will construct position descriptions which outline the functions each individual is to perform, the authority and responsibility associated with the position, and the inherent organizational relationships attached to the position. (Such items as to whom the employee reports and is responsible and a statement of necessary employee interactions that the job sets up would be dealt with in this third part of the description.)

---

[7] Peter F. Drucker, *Management: Tasks, Responsibilities, Practices* (New York: Harper & Row, 1974), p. 546.

[8] Rocco Carzo, Jr., and John N. Yanouzas, "Effects of Flat and Tall Organization Structure," *Administrative Science Quarterly*, June 1969, pp. 178–191.

[9] For more on this topic, see Dan R. Dalton, William D. Todor, Michael J. Spendolini, Gordon J. Fielding, and Lyman W. Porter, "Organization Structure and Performance: A Critical Review," *Academy of Management Review,* January 1980, pp. 49–64.

[10] Robert J. House and John B. Miner, "Merging Management and Behavioral Theory: The Interaction between Span of Control and Group Size," *Administrative Science Quarterly,* September 1969, pp. 461–462.

Figure 5–9 *Formal Theory of Authority*

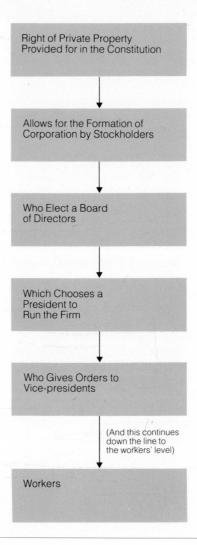

Right of Private Property
Provided for in the Constitution

Allows for the Formation of
Corporation by Stockholders

Who Elect a Board
of Directors

Which Chooses a
President to
Run the Firm

Who Gives Orders to
Vice-presidents

(And this continues
down the line to
the workers' level)

Workers

Sources of Authority

It has already been noted that authority is the right to command. The *formal theory of authority*, which supports the organizational hierarchy, contends that authority comes from the top, as seen in Figure 5–9. Chester I. Barnard, however, argued that authority actually comes from the bottom because no one has authority unless subordinates accept directives; this is the basis of Barnard's famous *acceptance theory of authority*.

There are several other theories of authority. One is the *authority of the situation*. For example, if a person hands a bank teller a note demanding all the money, the teller, by pressing the silent burglar alarm which calls the police for bank emergencies, has exercised the authority of the situation. This authority is limited to an occasion, but there is no doubt that the person who seizes it has the right to command. Crisis situations, which usually call for instant action, often impel those present to assume authority whether or not it has been formally delegated to them.

Another theory of authority is known as the *authority of knowledge.* The person who knows the most about the situation simply becomes the person in charge of the operation. For example, if the president of the United States is flying to Paris for an urgent summit conference and the plane encounters engine trouble twenty minutes into flight from Dulles International, the pilot will tell the president that they are turning back. As commander in chief, the U.S. president has the authority to countermand this order. However, none has ever done such a thing because the presidents have realized that their pilots know far more about this type of situation than they do. Superior knowledge gives the pilot the requisite authority.

Another exercise of this type of authority involved a particular president on a plane filled with confusion over whether city, county, state, or federal law allowed the plane carrying the body of President John F. Kennedy and also carrying the newly-sworn president, Lyndon B. Johnson, could leave Dallas's Love Field for its flight back to Washington on November 22, 1963. Johnson's decision to get the plane airborne resolved the arguments over jurisdiction; he did not, however, make a practice of ordering his jet to take off. His decision on this day was based on his knowledge of all four governments and of their rights and powers in addition to his awareness of the need for the president to be close to the seat of national power. He was the person on the plane with the greatest relevant knowledge; therefore, he made the accepted decision.

It is evident that there is more than one source of authority. The acceptance theory in particular illustrates that the concept is dynamic, pointing the way to consideration of such topics as power and the role of the informal organization. Before taking up these subjects, however, this chapter will assess the three major types of authority: line authority, staff authority, and functional authority. Line authority and staff authority come from the departments that bear their names. *Line departments* carry out activities directly related to the accomplishment of the firm's major objectives, whereas *staff departments* carry out activities that are indirectly related to these objectives. For reasons that will develop clearly, it is necessary to defer the discussion of functional authority. But each of the three types of authority is an essential part of the basic framework of an organization's structure. Although they are always modified in practice, as were the forms of departmentalization just examined, the three types are and will continue to be of central importance to an understanding of the organizing process.

There are three major types of authority.

TYPES OF AUTHORITY

Line Authority

Line authority, the most fundamental type of authority, is often referred to as direct authority because it encompasses the right to give orders and to have decisions implemented. All superiors have line authority over their subordinates. The military provides a classic illustration. The general has line authority over the colonel, who has line authority over the major, and so on down the hierarchy. Analogously, as seen in Figure 5–10, the president of a company has line authority over the vice-presidents. In turn, the vice-president of production can give direct orders to the heads of manufacturing and purchasing, who are the immediate subordinates of the vice-president, and they, in turn, have direct

Line authority is direct authority.

Figure 5–10   Line Authority

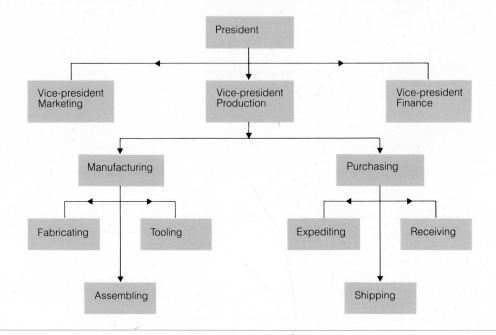

authority over their respective subordinates. Line authority results in a chain of command, often called the scalar chain, which runs from the top to the bottom of the organization and establishes an authority-responsibility relationship throughout.

Staff Authority

Staff authority is auxiliary authority. Its scope is limited in one significant way: It does not provide the right to command. Rather, the nature of the staff relationship is supportive. Individuals with staff authority assist, advise, recommend, and facilitate organizational activities. As an organization grows in size, executives face increasingly complex problems. Line authority alone is inadequate, and as a result, staff relationships are created.

One of the most common examples of staff authority is the subordinate manager who provides auxiliary services for a superior in the form of recommendations or advice. Another example is the assistant to the president whose job is to counsel the chief executive. A third illustration is the lawyer charged with providing legal advice to the president of a company. Figure 5–11 provides an illustration of a line-staff chart.

Staff authority is auxiliary authority.

Line-Staff Problems

It may well be considered that the line-staff authority relationship virtually created the need for functional authority. Therefore, before discussing the third fundamental type of authority, it will be necessary to discuss the line-staff relationship in some detail. Many firms have found that staff authority can be advantageous and can also lead to authority

Figure 5–11 Line-Staff Organization

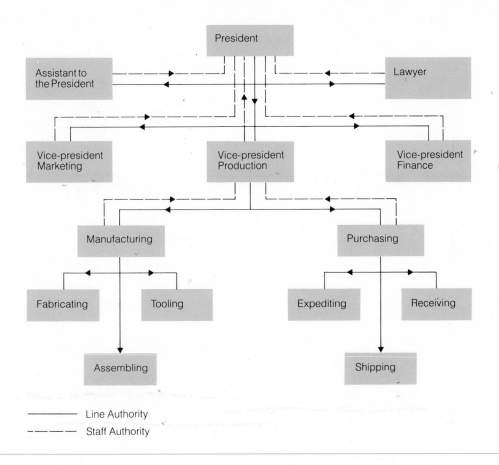

Line Authority
Staff Authority

conflicts between line and staff executives. One of the major causes rests in the attitudes of the two groups. For example, it is common to find that a line executive is an older person who came up the hard way. If this executive has a college degree (many do not), it may have been earned primarily through correspondence study or night classes. Conversely, the staff counterpart is often a younger person, perhaps with a master's degree in business, who may be bursting with bright ideas about how to improve operations. The line executive sees the young person as lacking in practical experience. The staff executive sees the older person as unwilling to try new ideas.

A second problem arises from the fact that line executives have ultimate responsibility for the decisions they make. If they accept a staff recommendation and the results are poor, they cannot pass the buck back upstairs. This makes them wary of staff advice. Conversely, staff people see hesitancy or refusal on the part of the line executives as indecisiveness and inability to recognize substantive recommendations. They feel the line should accept their expertise outright instead of having to be diplomatically persuaded to accept staff recommendations.

Some of the other common reasons for line-staff conflicts are brought about by the following attitudes and philosophies:

Line	Staff
1. Highly action-oriented.	1. Concerned with studying a problem in depth before making recommendations.
2. Highly intuitive, in contrast to analytical staff.	2. Highly analytical, in contrast to intuitive line.
3. Often shortsighted.	3. Often too long-range-oriented.
4. Often ask the wrong kinds of questions.	4. Have answers and therefore spend time looking for questions.
5. Want simple, easy-to-use solutions.	5. Complicate the situation by providing esoteric data.
6. Accustomed to examining some of the available alternatives and choosing one of them.	6. Interested in examining all possible alternatives, weighing and analyzing them, then choosing the best, regardless of time or cost restraints.
7. Highly protective of the organization.	7. Highly critical of the organization.

Various causes of line-staff conflicts have been identified.

When line and staff attitudes and philosophies are in conflict, the organization will not achieve maximum benefit from the work force. However, it is not necessary for these conditions to exist. Various approaches can be used to improve line-staff relations.

Improving Line-Staff Relations

One of the most effective ways to bring about and foster line-staff cooperation is to get everyone to understand the nature of the authority relationships. If the line people realize that they are responsible for making operating decisions and that staff people are there to assist them, the line may obtain a greater appreciation of the staff. Likewise, staff people must understand that theirs is only an auxiliary function; they must sell their ideas to line supervisors. They cannot order implementation of their recommendations; they must persuade line managers to adopt them. That often means that staff presentations to line executives must be sufficiently persuasive to help the line supervisor sell the idea to line workers.

There are a number of steps for improving line-staff relations.

A second approach, which may seem obvious but unfortunately is not, is to encourage the line to listen to the staff. Chapter 2 showed how the Roman Catholic Church has used the concept of compulsory staff service for centuries, thus requiring the solicitation of staff advice. Although such a mandatory approach can have serious drawbacks in a business setting, line managers should at least be encouraged to listen to their staff. Many line executives have found that their proposals and plans are more readily accepted if they consult with the staff before submitting them. Such an approach ensures a united front when top management then asks the staff how they feel about the proposal.

A third method of forestalling line-staff relationship problems is keeping staff specialists informed about matters that fall within their province. It is impossible for assistants to help line managers who fail to relate the kind of information they need or to explain the types of decisions confronting them. A line manager who does keep an information flow open, however, paves the way for effective staff work.

Another useful method of dealing with line-staff relations is that of *completed staff work*. This concept involves studying the problem and presenting a solution or recommendation in such a way that the line executive can either approve or disapprove the action.

Figure 5–12 Line Departments with Functional Authority

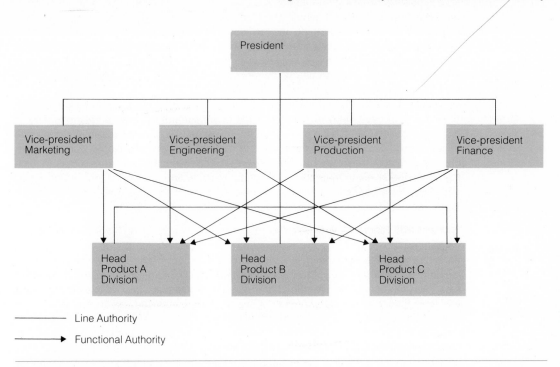

Prior to presentation, the staff works out all details of a planned project. Although the approach can involve a tremendous amount of time on the part of staff people, it saves the line manager from being subjected to continual meetings and discussions. The entire project is assumed by the staff specialists, and the line people are not bothered with details until the entire issue is presented to them. This technique not only provides a basis for justifying the existence of staff; it also gives them an opportunity to sell their ideas to the line.

Functional Authority

As an organization grows in size, specialization increases. In addition to the use of line and staff authority, many firms also employ *functional authority,* authority in a department other than one's own. This authority is delegated to an individual or a department concerned with a specified policy, practice, or process being carried out by individuals in other units, and it can be exercised by managers in both line and staff departments. For example, as shown in Figure 5–12, in a product departmentalization structure, certain line managers can have functional authority over the product division managers. In such a case, a vice-president of finance may be able to require the divisions to keep particular kinds of accounting records. At the same time, the vice-president of marketing may be able to request from the departments the presentation of the weekly sales data in tabular form. In a manner of speaking, the vice-presidents in this sort of situation have a slice of line authority in the divisions. It should be stressed, however, that this is limited

Functional authority is the right to give orders in a department other than one's own.

authority based on expertise and designed to improve organizational efficiency. For this reason, it is common to find functional authority limited to telling people how they are to do something and when it should be done. It seldom involves where, what, or who, for this would seriously undermine the divisional manager's own line authority. Furthermore, the president will almost always tell the division heads that functional authority is going to be delegated to the vice-presidents of marketing, engineering, production, and finance, asking the division heads' opinions in the process. This method is used to ensure that power grabbing stays at a minimum.

Functional authority can also be delegated to staff specialists. For example, the president may have many auxiliary staff members, including a public relations director and legal counsel. In a pure staff situation, these people offer advice only in their own areas of expertise. However, the president may find it more efficient to delegate functional authority to these people. The president who works this way allows staff to issue their own directives, in their own areas of authority, to line managers, thus making it unnecessary for all communication to be cleared through the president. This situation is illustrated in Figure 5–13. A pure staff relationship no longer exists.

Problems with Functional Authority The major problem in employing functional authority is the danger of undermining the integrity of managerial positions. For this reason, it is important to indicate precisely who has functional authority and in what matters. Unfortunately, many organizations fail to do this. As a result, managers take wide latitude in their interpretation of the breadth of their functional authority, and confusion and anger ensue. In theory, functional authority is supposed to be limited, but in practice the reverse is often more accurate. Written definitions of functional authority are one means of reducing this problem. Another way is to limit the scope of such authority whenever possible, so that it does not extend more than one hierarchical level below that of the manager holding the functional authority. Such a rule prevents a top executive from undermining other managers in the structure by giving orders directly to their subordinates. Functional authority certainly has advantages for the organization; however, it should be employed with prudence.

DECENTRALIZATION OF AUTHORITY

For some time now many firms, especially large ones, have followed a policy of decentralizing authority. The term *decentralization* should not be confused with that of delegation. Although the two are closely related, *decentralization* is much more encompassing in nature, reflecting a management philosophy regarding which decisions to send down the line and which to maintain near the top for purposes of organizational control. All organizations have some degree of decentralization, since absolute centralization is virtually impossible. For this reason, decentralization must be viewed as a relative concept, not as an absolute. Ernest Dale, a well-known management writer, has described some conditions when decentralization is greater:

1. *The greater the number of decisions made lower down the management hierarchy.*
2. *The more important the decisions made lower down the management hierarchy. For example, the greater the sum of capital expenditure that can be approved by the plant manager without consulting anyone else, the greater the degree of decentralization in this field.*
3. *The more functions affected by decisions made at lower levels. Thus companies which permit only operational decisions to be made at separate branch plants are less decentralized than those which also permit financial and personnel decisions at branch plants.*
4. *The less checking required on the decision. Decentralization is greatest when no check at all must be*

Functional authority can undermine a manager's authority.

Decentralization is a relative concept.

Figure 5 –13 Staff Departments with Functional Authority

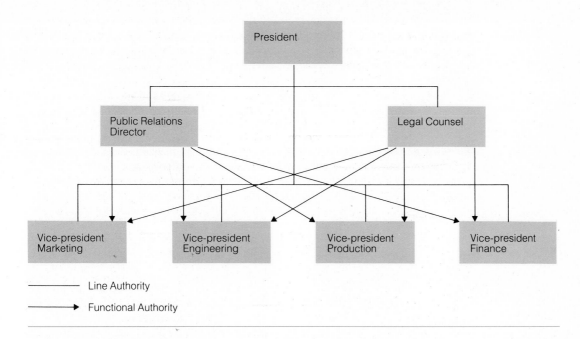

—————— Line Authority

———▶ Functional Authority

made; less when superiors have to be informed of the decision after it has been made; still less if superiors have to be consulted before the decision is made. The fewer people to be consulted, and the lower they are on the management hierarchy, the greater the degree of decentralization.[11]

Determinants of Decentralization

Many factors influence the decentralization of authority. Most are beyond control of the individual manager, hence the previous statement distinguishing this term from delegation, whereby the manager decides which duties to assign to a subordinate. Some of the most important determinants of the degree of decentralization follow.

Cost Factors As a rule of thumb, the greater the cost involved, the more likely it is that the decision will be made at the upper levels. It is not uncommon to find a firm with a policy permitting all expenditures of $500 or less to be approved by an operating department while all others are decided upon by a centralized purchasing or finance committee. In this way top management is able to control major expenditures for such items as capital equipment. Many organizations, including General Motors, employ highly centralized controls in the financial area.

The degree of decentralization depends on a number of factors.

Uniform Policy A desire for uniform policies is another cause for centralization of authority. Standardization of quality, price, credit, and delivery can be beneficial because it ensures that everyone will be treated alike. Similarly, standardization of financial and

[11] Dale, *Planning and Developing the Company Organization Structure,* p. 107.

accounting records makes it easier to compare the performance of various units and analyze their overall efficiency. When the firm wants everything done in a particular, uniform way, centralization of policy is desirable.

Company Size As a firm gets larger, it is impossible to maintain the old degree of centralization; top management cannot continue to hold such a tight grip on the reins. It is common to find such firms reorganizing and assigning more authority to the various departments and operating units. In this way, the company reduces the expenses that often accompany growth. The units operate on a more autonomous basis, the top management concerning itself with tasks such as planning, financing, evaluating, and controlling the overall operations of the firm. Day-to-day activities are handled at the lower levels.

Philosophy of Top Management Many firms are highly centralized, whereas others are highly decentralized simply because of the character and philosophy of their top management. Henry Ford's firm was highly centralized because that was the way he wanted it; Ford decided matters for the entire company. Conversely, General Motors has been highly decentralized for years because in 1920 A. P. Sloan was able to get his reorganization plan accepted by the board of directors. In essence, it called for decentralization of operating authority to the divisions while maintaining centralized control at the top levels. Ernest Dale described the two principles on which the recommendations rested in this way:

1. *The responsibility attached to the chief executive of each operation shall in no way be limited. Each such organization headed by its chief executive shall be complete in every necessary function and enabled to exercise its full initiative in a logical development. (Decentralization of operations.)*
2. *Certain central organization functions are absolutely essential to the logical development and proper coordination of the Corporation's activities. (Centralized staff services to advise the line of specialized phases of the work, and central measurement of results to check the exercise of delegated responsibility.)* [12]

Philosophy of Subordinate Managers The philosophy of subordinate managers affects decentralization because these people can either encourage or discourage such a policy. If subordinates want decentralization, top management may feel there is little to be gained by maintaining all important decision making at the upper levels. The desire by the subordinates for independence and the willingness to assume increased responsibility may convince them to become more decentralized. Conversely, a shortage of lower-level managers that leaves the current group of subordinates with an excessive amount of work sometimes encourages top management to maintain a more centralized approach.

Functional Area Some functional areas of enterprise will be more decentralized than others. For example, in a manufacturing firm, production will often be highly decentralized. As the size of the facilities increases, authority will be decentralized so that it rests at the operating level. This is so because the people who do production operations tend to know them better than anyone else. Sales also will often be decentralized for this same reason. Of course, budgets and controls will still have a great deal of centralization, as will other areas in which overall control is necessary: pricing, advertising, and market research, for example. Finance will be highly centralized; top management will

---

[12] Ernest Dale, *The Great Organizers* (New York: McGraw-Hill, 1960), p. 87.

maintain that control over the entire organization. Although decisions on small expenditures may be made at the lower levels, those that seriously affect the company's profit or financial stability will be made at the top.

THE ART OF DELEGATION

Delegation is a process the manager uses in distributing work to the subordinates. The process encompasses three basic steps: the assigning of duties to the subordinates; the granting of authority to carry out these duties; and the creation of an obligation whereby the subordinate assumes responsibility to the superior to complete the task satisfactorily.[13]

Delegation, like decentralization, is often a matter of personal preference on the part of the manager. However, while some will delegate so much work to their subordinates that they virtually abdicate their role as manager, it is far more common to find the reverse. Many managers hang on to everything, refusing to allow their subordinates to try their hands at anything. This unwillingness to let go is based on the assumption that the manager can do the job better than the subordinate. Delegation, to a manager like this, is at best a bother and at worst a personal threat. Unfortunately, this attitude is often self-defeating. It leads subordinates to the conclusion that they are not trusted by their superior. It also results in a failure to develop effective management talent. How can a junior executive ever be expected to fill the boss's shoes if the subordinate never gets the opportunity to try and to be observed?

These deficiencies can be overcome if the manager is willing to follow certain key steps. First, the manager must agree to try delegating authority and to do so in explicit terms. The subordinates must know exactly what they are to do and what kinds of results are going to be expected. Second, the person and the job must be carefully matched. Third, if there is a problem, the manager should have some form of open-door policy that encourages the subordinate to seek assistance. Fourth, broad, not narrow, controls should be established so that the manager knows when things are going well. At least initially, the manager should overlook minor problems and pay attention to significant deviations. The manager thus controls the situation without appearing to try to monitor everything. The subordinate should be expected to make some mistakes; beginners do, however great their potential. Fifth, when the job is done, the manager should praise the subordinate's performance in the areas in which good results were obtained and express a willingness to work with the individual in improving the other areas. The manager can best do this by continuing to delegate tasks to the subordinate, indicating trust and confidence in the less experienced person.

The manager must take steps to improve delegation.

THE INFORMAL ORGANIZATION

Attention has thus far been focused exclusively on the formal organization as designed and implemented by management. No organization, however, actually operates solely along formal lines. The individuals in any structure tend to remake it, changing things to meet their own needs and strengths. Functional design theorists contend that an organization should initially be developed without regard for the human element, but it is

---

[13] William H. Newman and E. Kirby Warren, *The Process of Management: Concepts, Behavior, and Practice,* 4th ed. (Englewood Cliffs, N.J.: Prentice-Hall, 1977), pp. 39–42.

never long before this theoretic ideal gives way to some more practical structure created by the actual firm within its various environments and with its individual assets and deficiencies. E. Wight Bakke called this a *fusion process,* stating that:

> *When an individual and an organization come together in such way that the individual is a participant in, and a member of, the organization and the two are mutually dependent on each other, both are reconstructed in the process. The organization to some degree remakes the individual and the individual to some degree remakes the organization.* [14]

Consideration of this informal structure introduces a more dynamic view of the organization than is available from a mere analysis of the formal design. To obtain a mental picture of the *informal organization,* it is helpful to regard it as a structure superimposed on the formal one.

The informal organization is not shown on the organization chart.

The organization chart cannot show all the informal relationships that exist in the organization. Just an attempt to depict functional authority, for example, would lead to a mass of lines running all over the page. It is probably impossible to draw the informal organization. Not only are the relationships varied, but they are continually changing. Sometimes an informal organization consists of members of the same work group. Other times it involves intergroup membership, as when formal lines are abandoned in the name of expediency and managers turn to unofficial channels in order to get things done.

For example, if the head of a production unit has a personal friend in the purchasing department and it appears that the new order of raw materials ordered by production will not arrive on time, a friendly phone call will activate the friend in purchasing, who will check on and expedite the shipment. Or say that an assembly-line supervisor has outstanding rapport with the union. When the labor contract comes up for renegotiation, the industrial relations department may call in this supervisor to get a realistic idea of what to include in the new contract. The supervisor, while not a member of the industrial relations department, still has input into the contract. A production supervisor with a knack for developing new methods can, similarly, end up with de facto jurisdiction over the methods department, even though methods is part of engineering, not production.

Power and Authority

Informal relationships supplement formal authority. Realistically speaking, authority consists of two things: formal authority delegated by one's superior (authority of the position) and *personal power* (authority of the individual). Although what creates personal power is less clear than what creates invested power, numerous factors can be cited.

---

[14] E. Wight Bakke, *The Fusion Process* (New Haven: Labor and Management Center, Yale University, 1953), pp. 12–13.

Association with what can be considered the right groups is helpful. The manager who belongs to the same country club as the company president may strike up a social friendship with the top executive. Once other members of the organization are aware of this relationship, the manager may find individuals, including immediate superiors, much more willing to comply with the requests of the boss's friend. The same can often be true of a shop steward in a powerful union. The line supervisor may feel there is far more to be gained than lost by keeping this steward happy. The last thing a first-line supervisor wants is a union-management rift, and the shop steward may be useful in preventing one.

The sources of informal power can be identified.

Experience and drive are still other power factors. People who know their jobs and do them well find others willing to cooperate and assist them; interdepartmental doors open to them. In addition, their superiors tend to rely on them and back them up if they run into some kind of problem. No manager can afford to have productive subordinates stymied. Research shows that an individual with such sociopsychological factors as drive, decisiveness, and determination not only is positively viewed by others but often establishes credibility as someone who can be relied on. The individual's real power may increase as a result.

Education can also be helpful; some companies view it as a major criterion for promotion. When one group of researchers conducted a massive computer analysis of over three thousand employees in the marketing department of a major petroleum corporation, they found education to be one of the most important variables in the promotion process.[15] In addition, their research revealed that not all those persons on their way up (called promotables) had high job performance ranking, indicating that there is more than one route to securing power.[16]

Other power factors include religion, politics, race, sex, and national origin. In some firms, especially at top management levels, a white Republican Protestant man named Adams or Hancock or Randolph may have more power than a Catholic Democrat named O'Hara, essentially because the people at the top belong to the former category, those white Anglo-Saxon Protestants sometimes known as WASPS. On the other hand, the WASP hold on corporate power is not universal. In Boston or San Antonio, for example, the Catholic Democrat may be at a decided advantage over the WASP. Similarly, despite legislation to the contrary, race, sex, and national origin are still bases for the establishment of power relationships.[17]

Formal and Informal Organizational Relationships

The informal organization is an inevitable product of human social processes. Unfortunately, too many organizations view it as a destructive element that needs to be weeded out. Actually, the informal organization can offer some very important advantages. Primarily, it is a source of satisfaction for the members, often bringing about much higher morale than would otherwise be the case.

The informal organization can be very helpful to the company.

Early writings in the field pictured the informal organization as disruptive and the role of management as one of manipulating the group into accepting formal goals. Today, it is evident that such manipulation is seldom necessary. The goals of the formal

---

[15] James W. Walker, Fred Luthans, and Richard M. Hodgetts, "Who Really Are the Promotables?" *Personnel Journal,* February 1970, pp. 123–127.

[16] Fred Luthans, James W. Walker, and Richard M. Hodgetts, "Evidence on the Validity of Management Education," *Academy of Management Journal,* December 1969, pp. 451–457.

[17] For more on power, see Rosabeth Moss Kanter, "Power Failure in Management Circuits," *Harvard Business Review,* July–August 1977, pp. 65–75.

and informal organizations are often mutually reinforcing. Of course, this has not always been true, but until management is quite certain that the informal organization is in irreparable conflict with the formal, all attempts should be made to nurture the relationship. It does management no good to try to form a clear-cut distinction between the two. They are interrelated parts of a complex system, and management's job must be that of creating an organizational climate in which the goals and expectations of both groups can be attained.

There is now an increasing need for more adaptive, less bureaucratic organizational structures that help organizations meet the varied demands of their environments. A great amount of new organization design research and the evolution of modern organization structures which often radically modify or extend the concepts presented in this chapter have resulted from this need. Management in the 1980s will continue to respond to this vast and dynamic need.

SUMMARY

This chapter examined the nature, purpose, and function of organizing. Organizing involves the assignment of duties and the coordination of efforts among all organizational personnel to ensure maximum efficiency in the attainment of predetermined objectives. The process covers a broad area and offers the manager many alternatives in both routine and critical situations. The numerous forms of departmentalization include functional, product, territorial, simple numbers, time, customer, and equipment or process. Another common organizational form, often used in conjunction with departmentalization, is committees. The two general types of committees are ad hoc and standing. The chapter showed that committees can be effectively used to complement the basic organizational structure.

Span of control is the phrase used to refer to the number of people reporting to a given superior. A wide span of control results in a flat organization chart, while a narrow span results in a tall organization chart.

There are three basic types of authority: line, staff, and functional. Line authority is direct authority, as illustrated by a manager who gives orders directly to a subordinate. Staff authority is auxiliary authority that is supportive in nature, as in the case of the lawyer who has authority to advise the president on legal matters. Functional authority is authority in a department other than one's own, as in the case of the vice-president of finance who can give orders to the head of a product division in regard to financial matters.

The chapter devoted particular attention to problem areas such as line-staff conflicts, which show that organizing is certainly no mechanical function. For example, line people tend to be highly action-oriented, while staff people are concerned with studying problems in depth before making recommendations.

The last part of the chapter examined the topics of decentralization and the informal organization. Decentralization is influenced by a number of factors, including cost, uniform policy, company size, philosophy of top management, philosophy of subordinate managers, and the functional area in which one works. The informal organization is the organizational arrangement created by the individuals who work in the structure. Their informal relationships supplement formal authority. Authority thus consists of two factors: formal authority, which is delegated by one's superior, and personal power, which can be attained in a number of different ways, including experience, drive, and education.

With the introduction of the informal organization, it becomes obvious that organizing is a dynamic process. While this chapter has set forth some of the basic ideas every manager must know about organizing, new organization structures are now emerging.

Drawing upon the ideas presented here, modern structures are now adapting these concepts to meet the demands of the external environment. The result has been the emergence of adaptive structures, the focus of attention in the next chapter.

REVIEW AND STUDY QUESTIONS

1. What is meant by the phrase *from strategy to structure?* Include in your answer a discussion of the planning process.
2. List the most widely used forms of departmentalization.
3. How does functional departmentalization differ from product departmentalization? How does it differ from territorial departmentalization? What are the advantages associated with each?
4. What are the common advantages and disadvantages of committees?
5. How does a tall organizational structure differ from a flat one?
6. What impact does the span of control have on the structure?
7. What is meant by the term *authority?* Where does authority come from?
8. What is line authority? Staff authority? Functional authority? Explain by using an illustration of each.
9. What are some common line-staff conflicts? What gives rise to them? How can they be prevented or overcome?
10. How does decentralization differ from delegation? Give an illustration of each.
11. What are some of the factors that influence the degree of delegation that takes place in an organization? Differentiate between those that encourage it and those that discourage it.
12. List and discuss some of the key steps used to improve a manager's ability to delegate authority.
13. How does the formal organization differ from the informal? What role does personal power play? Explain.
14. Are the objectives of the formal and informal organization always in conflict? Defend your answer.

SELECTED REFERENCES

Chandler, Alfred D., Jr. *Strategy and Structure.* Garden City, N.Y.: Anchor Books, Doubleday, 1966.

Clark, P. A. *Organizational Design: Theory and Practice.* Research Report No. 20. New York: American Management Association, 1952.

Dale, Ernest. *The Great Organizers.* New York: McGraw-Hill, 1960.

Dalton, Dan R.; Todor, William D.; Spendolini, Michael J.; Fielding, Gordon J.; and Porter, Lyman W. "Organizational Structure and Performance: A Critical Review." *Academy of Management Review,* January 1980, pp. 49–64.

Drucker, Peter F. *Management: Tasks, Responsibilities, Practices.* New York: Harper & Row, 1974, chaps. 41–48.

Harrell, Thomas, and Alpert, Bernard. "The Need for Autonomy among Managers." *Academy of Management Review,* April 1979, pp. 259–267.

House, Robert J., and Miner, John B. "Merging Management and Behavioral Theory: The Interaction between Span of Control and Group Size." *Administrative Science Quarterly,* September 1969, pp. 451–464.

Figure 5–14 Fun-For-All, Inc., Organization Chart, September 1978

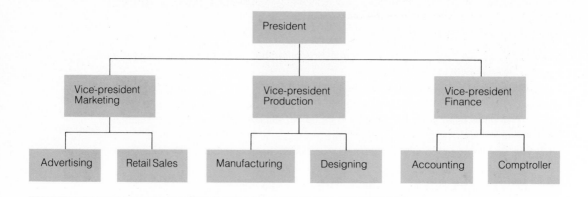

Kanter, Rosabeth Moss. "Power Failure in Management Circuits." *Harvard Business Review,* July–August 1978, pp. 65–75.

Parkinson, C. Northcote. *Parkinson's Law.* Boston: Houghton Mifflin, 1957.

Urwick, Lt. Col. L. F. "V.A. Graicunas and the Span of Control." *Academy of Management Journal,* June 1974, pp. 349–464.

———. "That Word 'Organization.'" *Academy of Management Review,* January 1976, pp. 89–91.

Van Fleet, D. D., and Bedeian, Arthur G. "A History of the Span of Management." *Academy of Management Review,* July 1977, pp. 356–372.

CASE: A New Switch

Fun-For-All is a national manufacturing firm that produces and sells toys and games. Prior to 1975, the company specialized in children's toys, but in the late seventies adult games began to gain acceptance, and Fun-For-All followed that market trend. The basic feature of the adult games is that they have no single, correct strategy and as a result require a great deal of thought on the part of the participant. For example, Monopoly, from Parker Brothers, has a basic strategy that often depends upon chance rather than skill. Players who are wise buy as much land as they can and start putting houses, and eventually hotels, on the property. However, true adult games, such as chess, are much more complex. There is no one right way to win a chess match; the outcome depends on what one's opponent does and also on one's own skill. The same is true for backgammon.

In 1980 Fun-For-All decided to market an expensive ($100) backgammon set. The company was convinced that despite the sluggish economy, demand for such a high-priced game would be sufficient to justify a 25 percent return on investment. By Christmas, thanks to timing and a strong advertising program, the firm had sold four times the number of sets it had initially forecast.

In 1981, because of growing sales, the management of Fun-For-All was considering reorganization. At the time, the firm was organized along functional lines, as in Figure 5–14. However, the president thought the company might be wiser to change to product departmentalization, and some of the people in marketing also seemed to think that it would be a good idea. The production department, however, felt more was to be gained from functional departmentalization. The finance people seemed indifferent about the matter, but indicated they would make an analysis of the two structures if the president desired.

The president's reorganization plan was to set up three product divisions: boys' toys, girls' toys, and adult games. The first two divisions accounted for over 75 percent of the firm's sales, but the latter was growing rapidly and would, according to marketing estimates, account for over 50 percent of all sales by 1985.

Questions

1. Draw the proposed reorganization chart. Be as complete as possible.

2. In this company's situation, what are the advantages of product departmentalization over functional departmentalization?

3. What recommendations would you make to the president before deciding to switch from functional to product departmentalization? Explain.

CASE: A Matter of Opinion

Julian Bacal had been a production manager for over thirty years, and he knew virtually everything about production. Bacal's new assistant, Catherine Knowles, had great admiration for him. She felt she had learned more about how to handle workers and obtain increased output in her first four weeks on the job with Bacal than in her four years of undergraduate business school.

During this initial period, Knowles tried to keep her eyes and ears open; she was determined to learn as much about the job as possible. For example, she knew that Charles Jackson, another production manager, was a good friend of Bacal, and she had instructions that she should take care of any favors Jackson needed from Bacal if Bacal was not there to handle the request himself. Gradually, she also began to learn the names and positions of other people with whom the production department came in contact on a rather regular basis. One of these was Eileen Menger from the personnel department, who often visited Bacal. Knowles knew Bacal was interested in hiring some production supervisors and had asked Menger to take out some ads and to keep scouting the local colleges and universities when she went out recruiting.

About six months after Knowles had started, she knew her way around pretty well. At least she thought she did, until she walked into Bacal's office and was horrified to see that her boss and Eileen Menger were yelling angrily at one another. When they heard the door open, they immediately lowered their voices, but the situation was clearly tense. Knowles backed out the door. A few minutes later she noticed Menger leaving and went back in:

"I'm sorry, Mr. Bacal. I didn't realize you had anyone in here with you."

"That's okay. Come on in Miss Knowles. I think it's about time you realized that not everyone around here agrees with everyone else all the time."

"But what conflict can you be having with Miss Menger? Isn't she in personnel?"

"Yes, but she screens all incoming people. Remember those tests you took as part of your application process?"

"Sure."

"Well, they're designed to find out something about your management potential. At least that's what Menger says. Supposedly, eight out of ten people who do well on them become good supervisory managers and the other two do not. Now our Miss Menger wants us to use that test as a screening device."

"And you don't want to?"

"Let's put it this way. I want to see an applicant face-to-face and talk. I know what to look for in a good supervisor; I don't need any test to tell me how a guy can handle himself. Two young fellows interviewed and tested for that job we have open. I want to hire the one that did poorly on the exam. He's going to work out. Miss Menger disagrees."

"Can she force you to use the test as a screening device?"

"No. Her entire job is to evaluate the applicants and give me her recommendations. I decide who gets hired in this department. The truth is, Menger's getting just too damn smart. She's supposed to be advising me and she winds up giving me orders. Imagine telling me that that young fellow I interviewed last week did poorly on the exam and I should forget about hiring him. Well, until the president decides that Menger has more savvy about how to run this department than I do, I'm going to make all the hiring decisions."

Questions

1. What kind of authority does Menger have? How do you know?

2. What kind of line-staff conflict is represented here? Explain.

3. How can these problems be prevented in the future? Make your answer specific.

CASE: *I Did It My Way*

Anyone who ever mentioned Shayling, Inc., was actually talking about a man more than a business—Peter Shayling, founder, owner, president, and chairman of the board. Shayling, Inc., was one of the largest television retail and repair stores in the city, with gross sales of over $5 million. Shayling delighted in telling customers how he had started out in a small shop on the outskirts of town and gradually increased the size of his business to where he could afford to move into his current modern, midtown facilities.

When his store was very small, Shayling and his wife, Linda, did everything, including keeping the books. The only outside assistance they had was an accountant who came in every three months to balance the ledgers and compute the taxes. Gradually, as volume increased, Shayling began hiring paid help. First, he brought in a television repairman; then he hired a salesman. In midyear 1981, fifteen people were working for Shayling, nine in the repair and delivery shop, six on the sales floor.

Although things appeared to be going well, Shayling admitted to his wife that he was disturbed by the large turnover in his sales staff; on an average, he was losing one salesperson a month. He was also losing an average of one repairer every other month. About this time Shayling received a call from a group of MBA candidates in a nearby college of business who were taking an upper division management course that required them to analyze a local concern. They wanted to know if Shayling would let them write their paper on his company. Although initially reluctant, he decided to take advantage of the students' offer of a list of recommendations, so he agreed. "It's like getting free consulting," he told his wife.

Six weeks later the team sent him a copy of its paper. The analysis and recommendations were of great interest to Shayling. He felt the team had done an admirable job, and he intended to implement many of the suggested changes. However, he disagreed strenuously with the following segment of the report:

> The high sales turnover can be directly attributed to the owner's failure to delegate authority. No salesperson is ever able to introduce a product to a customer or close a sale without Mr. Shayling getting into the act; he is everywhere. The result is a decline in morale brought about by the fact that the owner seems to lack faith in his own personnel. An analogous situation exists in the repair shop, although not to the same degree. In summary, Mr. Shayling should spend more time managing and less time looking over people's shoulders.

In defense of his actions, Shayling noted to his wife that the students undoubtedly lacked an understanding of the television repair business. "You've got to be on top of everything all the time," he said. "And far from getting in the way, I am really quite helpful to the sales force. After all, who knows more about how to sell than me? I built this store from nothing and I did it my way, which, it so happens, is the *right* way! And there's no substitute for success. In fact, if I change anything at all about the way I handle my sales crew, I'll get in there and mix it up with them a little more. They'd do an even better job if I spent more time helping them out. Why wouldn't they? After all, one of them is always new."

Questions

1. Is failure to delegate a cause of poor morale? Explain.

2. How is Shayling's action typical of many owner-managers? Explain.

3. How can Shayling overcome his problem? Be specific in your recommendations.

4. Could the report have been worded differently so as to sell the recommendation to Shayling? Explain, giving reasons for your opinion and methods for implementing it.

CASE: A Matter of Autonomy

One of the latest research issues in organizing is that of autonomy. How much independence, freedom, and self-direction should a manager allow subordinates? While many needs, from power to achievement, have been studied in depth, rather little attention has been paid to the need for autonomy among subordinate managers.

In one recent article on the subject, Thomas Harrell and Bernard Alpert recommended balancing an individual's need for autonomy with the degrees of such autonomy that are available. Using government bureaucrats, tenured full professors at private universities, and business entrepreneurs as examples, they constructed the material in Figure 5–15.

The figure shows that an individual who has a need for more or less autonomy than the organization allows will not achieve a best "fit" between person and organization. The reverse is also true; if the organization allows for more or less autonomy than the individual needs, things will be less than ideal.

Questions

1. What degrees of autonomy would be best for government bureaucrats? Tenured full professors at private universities? Business entrepreneurs? (Use Figure 5–15 as the basis for your answers.)

Figure 5–15 An Individual and Organizational Autonomy Grid

		Individual Need for Autonomy	
	Low	Medium	High
Business Entrepreneur (High)	Perfect miss. Misses chances to invest and expand.	Moderately successful small business owner/operator.	Perfect fit. High job satisfaction; high activity; long hours of work.
Private University Tenured Full Professor (Medium)	Retires, but still accepts paycheck after getting tenure.	Perfect fit. Productive scholar.	Moderate fit. Abuses consulting privileges but meets classes.
Government Bureaucrat (Low)	Perfect fit. High job satisfaction. Low activity. Watches the clock.	Does job. Plays organizational politics to expand number of subordinates to get higher pay.	Perfect miss. Low job satisfaction, high tension troublemaker. Looks for another job.

Degrees of Organizational Autonomy Possible

Source: Reprinted by permission from Thomas Harrell and Bernard Alpert, "The Need for Autonomy among Managers," *Academy of Management Review*, April 1979, p. 264.

2. Would a successful bureaucrat do well in a business enterprise? Would a successful business entrepreneur do well as a professor at a private university? Defend your answers.

3. What does this case relate about the importance of autonomy in the organizing process? Explain.

CHAPTER 6

ADAPTIVE ORGANIZATION STRUCTURES

GOALS OF THE CHAPTER

Change—and adapting to and coping with it—is one of the greatest challenges facing the modern manager. Some change is brought on by conditions in the external environment; some is internally generated. In either case, the organization must be capable of meeting the demands of the situation. One way in which organizations are meeting this demand is through the use of adaptive organization structures. Organizations find that with new, flexible designs, they are better able to interact with their external environment. These structures also encourage the use of effective motivation and leadership techniques. The goals of this chapter are to examine the impact of technology on organization structure, to study some of the adaptive organization designs, and to learn what is meant by the term contingency organization design. When you have completed this chapter, you should be able to:

1. Define the characteristics of an ideal bureaucracy.
2. Explain why bureaucratic structures are declining in importance.
3. Examine the effect of technology on the personnel and structure of organizations.
4. Describe what a project organization is and how it functions.
5. Compare and contrast project and matrix structures.
6. Discuss the differences between a free-form organization and a bureaucratic design.
7. Explain what contingency organization design is.
8. Identify and describe those forces that help determine the "best" organization structure.

THE DECLINE OF BUREAUCRATIC STRUCTURES

Bureaucratic and adaptive organization designs represent two logical extremes. On a continuum, they would appear as shown in Figure 6–1.

A highly structured organization, the *bureaucracy* in its ideal form has five main characteristics. Max Weber, a German sociologist, made one of the earliest and best known studies of bureaucratic organizational design. Peter Blau has identified the Weber characteristics in this way:

These are the characteristics of an ideal bureaucracy.

1. *A clear-cut division of labor resulting in a host of specialized experts in each position.*
2. *A hierarchy of offices, with each lower one being controlled and supervised by a higher one.*
3. *A consistent system of abstract rules and standards which assures uniformity in the performance of all duties and the coordination of various tasks.*
4. *A spirit of formalistic impersonality in which officials carry out the duties of their office.*
5. *Employment based on technical qualifications and protected from arbitrary dismissal.*[1]

Of course, no modern organization employs the bureaucracy in its ideal form; however, many use some version of it. The problem with these total organization structures is that, to a degree, they have proved unworkable. Quite simply, many of them lack the ability to cope with the stress, change, and tension of today's complex environment. This is particularly true in the case of organizations facing technological change.

TECHNOLOGY AND PERSONNEL

Many modern organizations must keep up with technological developments. However, it is also important for management to keep in mind that these technological changes have an effect on both the personnel and the structure of an organization.

---

[1] Peter M. Blau, *Bureaucracy in Modern Society* (New York: Random House, 1956), pp. 28–33.

Figure 6–1   An Organization Structure Continuum

Bureaucratic Structures	——————	Adaptive Structures

Technology, Tension, and Effectiveness

Bringing people and technology together can cause tension. For example, Figure 6–2 shows a relationship between effectiveness and tension. Up to Point B in the figure, some degree of pressure, accountability, responsibility, pride, and obligation is necessary. However, if tension is increased beyond this point (to Point C, for example), effectiveness can decline.[2]

The same is true in the case of technological capability and effectiveness, as seen in Figure 6–3. In this figure, the field to the left of Point E shows insufficient technological capacity for getting the job done; to the right of this point there is too much.

Figures 6–2 and 6–3 can be brought together and overlapped in three-dimensional style. As Henry M. Boettinger notes:

If a brilliant technologist makes optimal provision of tools (Point E) to an inept manager who operates at Points A or C, he has wasted his time. If an ideal manager, carrying his people to Point B, has been furnished the wrong processes or equipment (points D or F), his people cannot catch rivals who have skilled technologists looking after their interests.

One can compensate for bad technology, to some extent, with greater leadership, and for poor leadership with superb technology. But peak performance can never be achieved without peaks in both domains — the human and the technical.[3]

The challenge is thus one of introducing neither too much nor too little tension or technology, and this is not an easy task.

Technology can cause tension and impair effectiveness.

Effect of Technology on the People

At the worker level, for example, technology can affect the social relationships among the people by bringing about changes in such human elements as the size and composition of the work group or the frequency of contact with other workers. E. L. Trist and K. W. Bamforth discovered this when they conducted research among post–World War I coal miners. The miners initially worked in small, independent, cohesive groups. However, advances in technology and equipment led to changes in the composition of these work groups, and the result was a decline in productivity. Only when management restored many of the social and small group relationships did output again increase.[4]

---

[2] For more on this topic, see Henry M. Boettinger, "Technology in the Manager's Future," *Harvard Business Review,* November–December 1970, pp. 4–14, 165.

[3] Ibid., p. 14.

[4] E. L. Trist and K. W. Bamforth, "Some Social and Psychological Consequences of the Longwall Method of Coal-getting," *Human Relations,* February 1951, pp. 3–38.

Figure 6–2 *Relationship between Effectiveness and Tension*

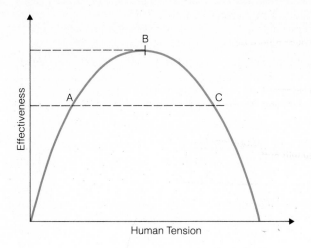

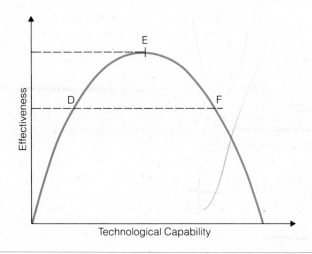

Technology can affect the psychosocial system.

It is perhaps the greatest fear of workers faced with new technology that the machinery will lead to the abolition of jobs or to the reduction of tasks to such simplistic levels that workers can hardly endure the stress of their new, extremely dull functions. Since the human being must be able to support one or more persons by means of work and since the mind resists its own belittling, such changes, brought about by advancing technology, have a profound effect on the psychosocial system. In order to prevent intolerable upheaval, management must be simultaneously and equally aware of the social (human) and the technical (operational) aspects and needs of the organization.

One of the most important studies in this area was conducted by Floyd C. Mann, Lawrence K. Williams, and their associates at the Institute for Social Research.[5] They analyzed the effect on personnel of a changeover to electronic data processing equipment in a major utility over a five-year period and reported:

> One of the most pressing problems during this period was the maintenance of a high level of group morale and individual job satisfaction. Every attempt was made to arrive at solutions that would be satisfactory to each individual. While the general policy of reassignment served as guidelines, many unique solutions had to be invented in individual cases. The old problem remained of devising a solution that would meet the employee's personal needs, the company objectives, and still be perceived as appropriate publicly.[6]

Unless the impact of technology on the worker is considered, organizational effectiveness and efficiency will suffer.

Technology affects the managerial as well as the production staffs. Managers today are more specialized than ever before, as seen through the ever-growing number of public relations people, operations researchers, and other staff personnel in organizations. Previously, major consideration was given to breaking jobs into their component parts. Now, however, the emphasis is on integrating the work of the managers, especially in those industries in which technology plays a major role.

Tom Burns and G. M. Stalker, for example, undertook a study of a number of British and Scottish firms. The companies, which had operated in stable technologies and environments, were trying to move into the electronics field, which is characterized by rapidly changing technology.[7] The researchers found that as the companies made this transition, they underwent significant changes in their management systems. Initially, they had had *mechanistic organization structures*, characterized by formal job descriptions and a rigid overall structure. It was quite clear to everyone what all workers did and to whom they reported.

In the new environment, however, another managerial system developed—the *organic organization structure*. (See Table 6–1 for a comparison of some of the key dimensions of mechanistic and organic organization structures.) Management had to adapt to changing conditions, and the old mechanistic structure gave way to a more flexible one. Managers found themselves in more frequent interaction with each other; they also placed greater emphasis on lateral, rather than vertical, communication. In order to survive in this new, highly dynamic environment, the managers began to restructure the old line-staff relationships in favor of more flexible ones.

Technology can also lead to the replacement of mechanistic structures by organic ones.

TECHNOLOGY AND STRUCTURE

Technology has been seen to have profound effects on people within a workplace. Its effects on organizational structure are equally powerful. One of the most significant studies evaluating the impact of technology on structure was conducted by Joan Wood-

---

[5] Floyd C. Mann and Lawrence K. Williams, "Observations on the Dynamics of a Change to Electronic Data-Processing Equipment," *Administrative Science Quarterly,* September 1960, pp. 217–256.

[6] Ibid., pp. 244–245.

[7] Tom Burns and G. M. Stalker, *The Management of Innovation* (London: Tavistock Publications, 1961).

Table 6–1 A Comparison of Some of the Key Dimensions of Mechanistic and Organic Organization Structures

	Characteristics of Organization Systems	
Systems and Their Key Dimensions	Closed/Stable/ Mechanistic	Open/Adaptive/ Organic
Environmental Suprasystem		
General nature	Peaceful	Turbulent
Predictability	High certainty	High uncertainty
Technology	Stable	Dynamic
Degree of environmental influence on organization	Low	High
Overall Organizational System		
Emphasis of organization	On performance	On problem solving
Predictability of actions	Relatively certain	Relatively uncertain
Decision-making process	Programmable	Nonprogrammable
Goals and Values		
Overall values	Efficiency, predictability, security, risk averting	Effectiveness, adaptability, responsiveness, risk taking
Involvement in setting objectives	Primarily from the top down	Wide participation, including people from the bottom as well as from the top
Technical System		
Knowledge	Highly specialized	Highly generalized
Time perspective	Short-term	Long-term
Interdependency of tasks	Low	High

ward.[8] Her research, which covered a hundred firms in a London suburb, was designed to determine how structural variables affected economic success. She found the answer by analyzing the types of technology the firms were employing. There were three types in all:

1. ***Mass and large batch production.*** This type of technology is used for mass-production items. Automobiles and television sets are illustrations.
2. ***Continuous process production*** This type of technology is employed in producing continuous-flow production items. The manufacture of chemicals or the processing of oils are illustrations.

---

[8] Joan Woodward, *Industrial Organization: Theory and Practice* (London: Oxford University Press, 1965).

Table 6 – 1 Continued

Systems and Their Key Dimensions	Characteristics of Organization Systems	
	Closed/Stable/ Mechanistic	*Open/Adaptive/ Organic*
Structural System		
Procedures and rules	Many, often formal and written	Few, often informal and unwritten
Levels of the hierarchy	Many	Few
Source of authority	Position in organization	Knowledge of individual
Responsibility	Attached to position	Assumed by individual
Psychosocial System		
Interpersonal relationships	Formal	Informal
Personal involvement	Low	High
Motivation factors	Emphasis on lower-level needs	Emphasis on upper-level needs
Leadership Style	Autocratic	Democratic
Managerial System		
Content of communications	Decisions and instructions	Advice and information
Control process	Impersonal use of devices such as rules and regulations	Interpersonal contacts, persuasion, and suggestions
Means of resolving conflict	Superior uses the "book" in handling the matter	Group resolves issue with situational ethics

3. ***Unit and small batch production*** This type of technology is used for "one-of-a-kind" products or those built to customer specifications. Lunar modules and locomotives are illustrations.

The appropriateness of the organizational structure, Woodward found, was dependent on the type of technology the firm used. If the company employed mass-production techniques, a mechanistic structure seemed to work best. Conversely, if the firm used continuous-process or unit production, in which technology plays a more significant role, an organic structure seemed to work best. Table 6–2 illustrates these findings.

In addition, Woodward found that the organic structures tended to be oriented more toward human relations than were the mechanistic ones.

Since Joan Woodward's initial study, other researchers have also attempted to eval-

Table 6–2 *Woodward's Research Findings*

Mechanistic	Organic
Mass production	Continuous process Unit production

Table 6–3 *Research Findings Relating Technology and Organization Structure*

	Organization Structure		
Researcher	Mechanistic	Intermediate	Organic
Woodward	Mass production		Continuous process Unit production
Zwerman	Mass production		Unit production
Lawrence and Lorsch	Stable environment	Intermediate degree of stability	Dynamic environment
Meyer	Low degree of interdependency		High degree of interdependency

uate the importance of technology on the organization. Perhaps the most widely known of these is William L. Zwerman, who, using fifty-five firms from the Minneapolis area, replicated Woodward's research in the United States.[9] In essence, he corroborated her basic findings,[10] concluding that the "type of production technology was most closely and consistently related to variations in the organizational characteristics of the firms."[11]

In a related study, Paul R. Lawrence and Jay W. Lorsch posed the question of which form of management is best under which conditions. Employing a sample of ten industrial organizations, they grouped them by degree of market and technological change.[12] The six in the plastics industry were categorized as operating in a highly dynamic environment; the two in the consumer foods industry were seen as being in an environment with an intermediate degree of change; the two in the standardized container industry were identified as being in a relatively stable environment. The researchers found that to be successful, those in the dynamic environment needed a flexible structure, whereas those in the stable environment were most effective with a mechanistic management system, and those in the intermediate environment needed to operate somewhere between the two extremes.

---

[9] William L. Zwerman, *New Perspectives on Organization Theory* (Westport, Conn.: Greenwood Publishing, 1970).

[10] Because of a lack of firms in continuous-process operations, however, he was unable to make any inferences about this particular group.

[11] Zwerman, *New Perspectives on Organization Theory,* p. 148.

[12] Paul R. Lawrence and Jay W. Lorsch, *Organization and Environment* (Boston: Harvard Graduate School of Business Administration, 1967).

Figure 6—4 Impact of Technology on Structure

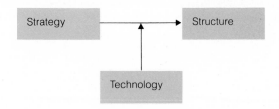

Marshall W. Meyer, studying the impact of automation on the formal structure, investigated 254 state and local government departments of finance.[13] He found that automation creates interdependency in the organization, and nonhierarchical (organic) structures are better able to deal with the situation than are rigid, hierarchical (mechanical) ones.

Numerous research studies have been conducted on the effect of technology on structure.

Other research further substantiates these findings.[14] The general pattern is already clear: Technology has a definite impact on organizational structure (see Table 6–3). It is thus possible to extend Chandler's thesis of "from strategy to structure"[15] by incorporating the technological factor in Figure 6–4.

One final point merits attention. Technology is not the only factor affecting structure; nor is it always the most critical. David J. Hickson's research team, in fact, found it to be of significant importance only for small organizations.[16] Where it does play a role, it is the effect on such variables as span of control and manager-manager and manager-subordinate relationships that is important. As Joan Woodward has noted:

> *Among the organizational characteristics showing a direct relationship with technical advance were: the length of the line of command; the span of control of the chief executive; the percentage of total turnover allocated to the payment of wages and salaries; and the ratios of managers to total personnel, of clerical and administrative staff to manual workers, of direct to indirect labour, and of graduate to non-graduate supervision in production departments.*[17]

Thus, for reasons having to do with technology and other variables, new organization designs have been created. What forms are these new designs taking? There are many answers to this question. Some of the most common include the project organization, the matrix structure, and free-form organization designs, which will now be examined.

---

13 Marshall W. Meyer, "Automation and Bureaucratic Structure," *American Journal of Sociology*, November 1968, pp. 256–264.

14 For example, see Edward Harvey, "Technology and the Structure of Organizations," *American Sociological Review*, April 1968, pp. 256–264.

15 Alfred D. Chandler, *Strategy and Structure* (Garden City, N.Y.: Anchor Books, Doubleday, 1966).

16 David J. Hickson, D. S. Pugh, and Diana C. Pheysey, "Operations Technology and Organization Structure: An Empirical Reappraisal," *Administrative Science Quarterly*, September 1969, pp. 378–397.

17 Woodward, *Industrial Organization*, p. 51.

THE PROJECT ORGANIZATION

The use of the project organization has increased throughout the last decade. It is currently being employed in numerous and diverse undertakings from building dams and weapon systems to conducting research and development, choosing distribution center sites, and redesigning bank credit-card systems. The *project organization* can take various forms, but one overriding characteristic distinguishes it from the usual line and staff departments: Once the project has been completed, the organization is phased out. This is made clear by its very definition. Project management is "the gathering of the best available talent to accomplish a specific and complex undertaking within time, cost and/or quality parameters, followed by the disbanding of the team upon completion of the undertaking."[18] In a manner of speaking, the project manager and project staff work themselves out of a job. The group members then go on to another project, are given jobs elsewhere in the organization, or, in some cases, are phased entirely out of a firm.

The major advantage of the project form of organization is that it allows a project manager and team to concentrate their attention on one specific undertaking. The manager makes sure that the project does not get lost in the shuffle of organizational activities. In short, project managers act as focal points for their project activities.

Criteria for using a project structure are set forth.

Although the project structure has many advantages, its application is limited. For example, one writer has recommended criteria for the use of a project structure, stating that it should be: (a) definable in terms of a specific goal, (b) somewhat unique and unfamiliar to the existing organization, (c) complex with respect to interdependence of activities necessary to accomplishment, (d) critical with respect to possible gain or loss, and (e) temporary with respect to duration of need.[19]

Planning the Project

Once it has been determined that a project organization will be used, the objectives must be set, the personnel drawn together, the structure formulated, and a control system designed for obtaining feedback. Although the organization will be more fluid than its conventional line-staff counterpart, there will still be the assignment of authority and responsibility. The structure is thus formalized to a degree. A project manager will be appointed to oversee the proceedings, and employees will report to this individual. Some of the workers will remain through the duration of the project while others may be involved for only a short period of time. The duties of the project group vary, naturally, with the objectives and the organizational structure. In the development and production of a ballistic missile, for example, many people would be assigned to the project. Collectively, they would have responsibility for the following activities:

1. Ascertaining the overall organizational strategic plan.
2. Determining both the technical specifications of the missile and the desires of the customers, i.e., the federal government.
3. Building, testing, and evaluating the prototype.
4. Establishing reliability, maintainability, and supportability requirements of the project.
5. Determining supply sources for the project items that must be purchased.
6. Negotiating and managing all contracts associated with the project.

---

[18] Richard M. Hodgetts, "An Interindustry Analysis of Certain Aspects of Project Management" (Ph.D. dissertation, University of Oklahoma, 1968), p. 7.

[19] John M. Stewart, "Making Project Management Work," *Business Horizons,* Fall 1965, pp. 54–68.

7. Developing and maintaining all schedules designed to produce the missile on time.
8. Seeing that technical manuals and reports required for the project are drawn up and distributed.
9. Planning, installing, operating, and maintaining the completed project.
10. Providing supportability for the missile after it is produced, i.e., spare parts, support equipment, and trained personnel.
11. Continually monitoring all costs associated with the project.
12. Establishing project design and performance characteristics.
13. Providing the most up to date technology within time and cost parameters.
14. Identifying and developing the personnel skills that will be required in using the product.[20]

Designing the Project Structure

Once project objectives have been ascertained, the project structure can be designed. The structure can take numerous forms, from simple to complex. In the simple project structure, shown in Figure 6–5, the project manager is put in charge of an undertaking and is also given direct authority over the team members. The project manager has all the resources needed for getting the job done, and the project structure departments are exact duplicates of the permanent functional organization. This type of design is often referred to as a pure, or aggregate, project structure. However, because of its duplication of facilities, the aggregate structure is one of the most expensive ways to organize a project, and its use is generally reserved for very large undertakings. More common is the structure in which a project manager occupies the role of advisor to the general manager, who in turn administers the entire project within a functional organization hierarchy (see Figure 6–6 for an illustration of this). A third variation, the matrix structure, is the most common of all.

Pure project structure is reserved for large undertakings.

THE MATRIX STRUCTURE

A *matrix structure* is a hybrid organizational form, containing characteristics of both project and functional structures. Unfortunately, it is common to find the terms *matrix organization* and *project organization* used interchangeably, although there are very distinct differences between the two. The major difference is that project employees in the matrix structure are only lent to the project manager for a specific undertaking, rather than being purely responsible only to the project manager for some period of time. Thus, project staff members in a matrix structure have a dual responsibility. First, they are responsible to the head of their functional department, the person who has assigned them to the project. The functional department head is their line superior and will, despite the added matrix structure, continue to be so. But aside from that, the matrix project manager exercises what is called *project authority* over the project staff. Thus, these employees report to two executives, one permanent, the other for the matrix project only. Figure 6–7 describes three project managers, each with project authority over personnel from departments supporting their respective undertakings.

Matrix structure is a functional and project organization hybrid.

When the concepts of functional and project authority are brought together, the result is an organization structure that is both vertical and horizontal. The vertical pattern is brought about by the typical line authority flowing down from superior to subordinate.

---

[20] Adapted from David I. Cleland and William R. King, *Systems Analysis and Project Management,* 2d ed. (New York: McGraw-Hill, 1975), pp. 243–244.

Figure 6–5 Pure Project Organization

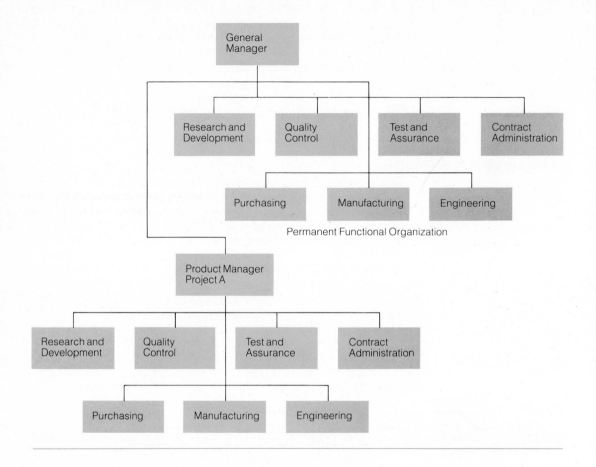

The horizontal authority flow is caused by the fact that both the scalar principle and unity of command principle are violated, and in their place comes the need for close cooperation between the project manager and the respective functional managers (see Figure 6–8). All this is clearer following a detailed examination of the concept of project authority.

*Project
authority flows
horizontally.*

Project Authority

Project authority can be identified and described as follows:

*Project authority
is defined.*

> *One major problem has been cited consistently in studies made of the project [matrix] organization: while the functional managers have line or direct authority over their subordinates, the project managers must work through the respective functional managers, who supply the team personnel, in running their projects. The project managers have an "authority-gap" because they do not possess authority to reward or promote their personnel. They lack complete authority over the team and thus possess what is called "project author-*

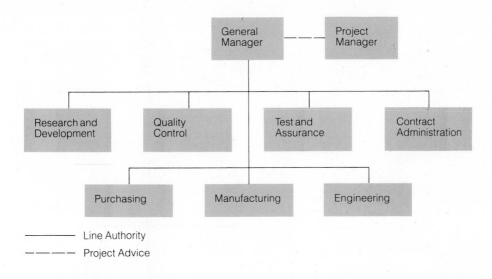

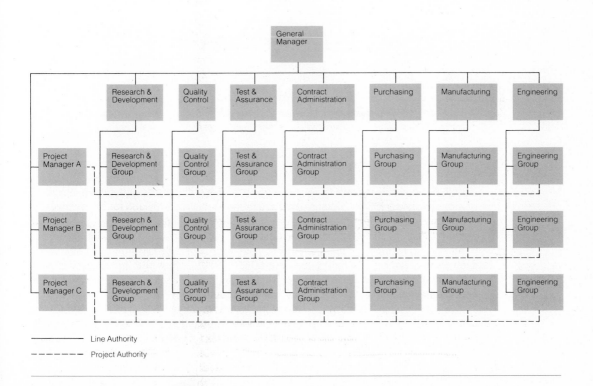

Figure 6–7 Matrix Organization

Figure 6–8 Authority in the Matrix Organization

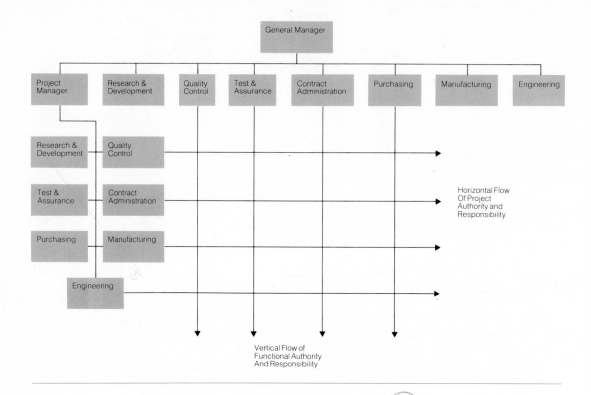

ity." Because their responsibility outweighs their authority, the project managers must find ways of increasing their authority and thus minimizing their "authority-gap."[21]

This lack of complete authority means that the project manager cannot rely exclusively upon conventional line authority. Instead, this individual must work with the functional managers, convincing them that they should support the project by giving its manager the assistance needed to finish the undertaking within the assigned time, cost, and quality parameters. This persuasive bargaining calls for a horizontal relationship in which one manager coordinates activities with another. What is sometimes called legal authority, such as the hierarchical flow, position descriptions, and policy documents, is of little value to most project managers. Instead, they must rely upon reality authority, such as negotiation with their peers, the building of alliances with the functional managers, and the effective use of the informal organization. (See Table 6–4, which compares the functional and project organizations in detail.)

In investigating leadership techniques used by project managers to supplement their project authority and overcome their authority gap, the author discovered a general pattern. All project managers in the study indicated that personality and persuasive

---

[21] Richard M. Hodgetts, "Leadership Techniques in the Project Organization," *Academy of Management Journal,* June 1968, p. 211.

ability were important. In addition, some of them relied upon negotiation, competence, and reciprocal favors. The use of these approaches illustrates the importance that project managers assign to reality authority.

Each project manager's need for these techniques varies. On those projects where the manager is given little formal authority, the horizontal relationships will be of great importance. Conversely, in those cases where a great deal of authority has been delegated to the project manager, the structure is less a matrix organization and more a pure project organization. Research shows that smaller projects (those with less dollar size) tend to be more common than do larger ones, and their project managers tend to have less formal authority than do those who are overseeing larger undertakings.[22] This means that they have to rely more on a human relations than on a formal authority approach. For example, in forty-one of the firms surveyed, the author found that there was a continuum ranging from small project organizations to large ones. As an examiner progresses across the continuum, project authority declines in importance and formal authority replaces it. Informal leadership techniques such as negotiation, personality, persuasive ability, competence, and reciprocal favors are not as useful to the manager of a large project as they are to the manager of a small one. One project manager, involved in a multibillion-dollar undertaking, explained this phenomenon as follows:

> It would appear to be vital . . . that the organizational environment, into which the project manager is placed, be such that he need not depend entirely on negotiating ability, a dynamic personality, etc., to perform his most important job. For this reason the organization of a project, in a manner to give the project manager the control he needs over the area of budgeting, planning, and scheduling becomes a basic consideration. The organization must be so designed that the project manager indeed does control the people assigned to the project, in the sense they are responsible to him. Thus, the organization gives the project manager his authority so he can devote more of his time to obtaining the schedule, cost, and technical performance goals of the project.[23]

Additional research in these areas confirms the need of most project managers to rely on influence sources other than formal authority. For example, Edward J. Dunne, Jr., Michael J. Stahl, and Leonard J. Melhart, Jr., asked project managers why project personnel complied with their requests, asked project personnel why they complied with the project manager's request, and asked project personnel why they complied with orders from their immediate functional manager.[24] (The parenthetic phrases name the kind of authority source described in the individual items.) The list of resources from which the respondents were to choose follows:

1. *I feel he has formal authority to direct me. (Formal authority)*
2. *I feel he can directly influence my performance rating. (Direct rating)*
3. *I feel he can indirectly influence my performance rating. (Indirect rating)*
4. *I feel he can influence my future work assignment. (Future work)*
5. *I feel he can apply pressure or penalize me in some way. (Pressure/penalize)*
6. *I respect him and place confidence in his special knowledge and advice. (Expertise)*
7. *He has established a personal friendship with me. (Friendship)*
8. *I feel the things he asks me to do are professionally challenging. (Challenge)*
9. *I recognize his position and responsibilities. (Position/responsibility)*[25]

---

[22] Ibid., pp. 211–219.
[23] Ibid., p. 218.
[24] Edward J. Dunne, Jr., Michael J. Stahl, and Leonard J. Melhart, Jr., "Influence Sources of Project and Functional Managers in Matrix Organizations," *Academy of Management Journal,* March 1978, pp. 135–140.
[25] Ibid., p. 137.

Table 6-4 *Comparison of the Functional and the Project Viewpoints*

Phenomena	Functional Viewpoint	Project Viewpoint
Line-staff organizational dichotomy	Line functions have direct responsibility for accomplishing the objectives: line commands, staff advises.	Vestiges of the hierarchical model remain, but line functions are placed in a support position. A web of authority and responsibility relationships exists.
Scalar principle	The chain of authority relationships is from superior to subordinate throughout the organization. Central, crucial, and important business is conducted up and down the vertical hierarchy.	Elements of the vertical chain exist, but prime emphasis is placed on horizontal and diagonal work flow. Important business is conducted as the legitimacy of the task requires.
Superior-subordinate relationship	This is the most important relationship; if kept healthy, success will follow. All important business is conducted through a pyramiding structure of superiors-subordinates.	Peer to peer, manager to technical expert, associate to associate relationships are used to conduct much of the salient business.
Organizational objectives	Organizational objectives are sought by the parent unit (an assembly of	Management of a project becomes a joint venture of many relatively

The responses are presented in Table 6-5. Notice in the case of both the project manager and the project group members that formal authority ranked in the bottom half, but when it came to responding to the functional manager, formal authority ranked close to the top. In short, influence sources are more important in project organization matters, and formal authority is more important in nonproject matters.

Advantages of Matrix Organizations

Although the manager of a matrix organization faces many challenges, there are also numerous advantages to employing such a structure. David I. Cleland and William R. King identify the advantages as follows:

Certain benefits are associated with the use of a matrix structure.

1. *The project is emphasized by designating one individual as the focal point for all matters pertaining to it.*
2. *Utilization of manpower can be flexible because a reservoir of specialists is maintained in functional organizations.*

Table 6–4 Continued

Phenomena	Functional Viewpoint	Project Viewpoint
	suborganizations) working within its environment. The objective is unilateral.	independent organizations. Thus, the objective becomes multilateral.
Unity of direction	The general manager acts as the head for a group of activities having the same plan.	The project manager manages across functional and organizational lines to accomplish a common interorganizational objective.
Parity of authority and responsibility	Consistent with functional management, the integrity of the superior-subordinate relationship is maintained through functional authority and advisory staff services.	Considerable opportunity exists for the project manager's responsibility to exceed his or her authority. Support people are often responsible to other managers (functional) for pay, performance reports, promotions, and so forth.
Time duration	Tends to perpetuate itself to provide continuing facilitative support.	The project (and hence the organization) is finite in duration.

Source: David I. Cleland, ''Understanding Project Authority,'' *Business Horizons*, Spring 1966, p. 66. Copyright, 1966, by the Foundation for the School of Business at Indiana University. Reprinted by permission.

3. *Specialized knowledge is available to all programs on an equal basis; knowledge and experience can be transferred from one project to another.*

4. *Project people have a functional home when they are no longer needed on a given project.*

5. *Responsiveness to project needs and customer desires is generally faster because lines of communication are established and decision points are centralized.*

6. *Management consistency between projects can be maintained through the deliberate conflict operating in the project-functional environment.*

7. *A better balance between time, cost and performance can be obtained through the built-in checks and balances (the deliberate conflict) and the continuous negotiations carried on between the project and the functional organizations.*[26]

In recent years others have also sung the praises of matrix organizations. For example, Stanley M. Davis and Paul R. Lawrence, while noting that corporations such as Bech-

---

[26] Cleland and King, *Systems Analysis*, pp. 251–252.

Table 6-5 *Influence Scores*

Why Project Managers Believe Employees Comply with Project Requests		Why Project Staff Members Comply with Requests from Project Managers		Why Project Staff Members Comply with Orders from Immediate Functional Managers	
Source	Score[a]	Source	Score	Source	Score
Expertise	80	Position/ responsibility	79	Position/ responsibility	88
Position/ responsibility	74	Expertise	75	Formal authority	85
Friendship	65	Challenge	62	Expertise	81
Challenge	56	Friendship	54	Direct rating	80
Pressure/penalize	30	Indirect rating	35	Challenge	74
Indirect rating	26	Formal authority	25	Indirect rating	62
Future work	25	Future work	22	Friendship	58
Formal authority	18	Pressure/penalize	22	Pressure/penalize	56
Direct rating	9	Direct rating	14	Future work	55

[a]The score range was 1–100, with higher ratings indicating higher importance.
Source: Reprinted by permission from Edward J. Dunne, Jr., Michael J. Stahl, and Leonard J. Melhart, Jr., "Influence Sources of Project and Functional Managers in Matrix Organizations," *Academy of Management Journal,* March 1978, p. 137.

tel, Citibank, Dow Chemical, Shell Oil, and Texas Instruments all use matrix designs, have concluded that the biggest advantage of this structure is that "it facilitates a rapid management response to changing market and technical requirements."[27] On the other hand, they also note that there are drawbacks to the matrix organization and that managers should be aware of them.

Disadvantages of Matrix Organizations

Numerous drawbacks to the matrix organization could be cited, but the following five are probably the most significant. An examiner of these disadvantages must keep in mind that most of them are built into the use of the matrix. Managers cannot avoid them; they can only learn to deal more effectively with them.

One of the primary disadvantages relates to power struggles. Since use of the matrix means use of dual command, managers often end up jockeying for power. Many project managers spend a lot of their time trying to get preferential treatment for their projects—even when it is unnecessary. The only way to deal with this problem is for the top functional manager to balance project needs with organizational resources and for project managers to place the overall organization ahead of the personal satisfaction associated with project completion.

There may be power struggles.

Second, the matrix entails wide use of group decision making because group cooperation is required for project success. However, if the project manager is not careful, a syndrome called groupitis will develop, in which case every decision will be hammered out in large numbers of contentious meetings. The waste of time is obviously expensive. Moreover, such meetings can negatively affect the morale of project participants. The

Groupitis may develop.

[27] Stanley M. Davis and Paul R. Lawrence, "Problems of Matrix Organizations," *Harvard Business Review,* May–June 1978, p. 132.

best way to overcome this problem is to make it a personal managerial policy to use group decision making as often as necessary and as little as possible.

Third, if an organization has many ongoing projects, the result may be a severe layering of matrixes. Matrix projects mushroom everywhere, with some large matrix structures creating their own internal matrixes. As Davis and Lawrence note: "When this occurs, organization charts begin to resemble blueprints for a complex electronic machine, relationships become unnecessarily complex, and the matrix form may become more of a burden that it is worth."[28] The best remedy is for the functional manager to whom the project head reports to insist that the structure be kept as simple as possible. Uncontrolled growth of matrix structures often results in power struggles between the managers; during such conflict, organizational efficiency suffers badly.

There may be a severe layering of matrixes.

Fourth, a matrix structure can be expensive. The dual chain of command may cause management costs to double. This is particularly true when the structure is being set up. As the matrix matures, these added costs should be offset by efficiency increases. Therefore, as long as the organization keeps its eye on cost control and carefully monitors the matrix through its growth period, things should turn out all right.

Matrix structures can be expensive.

Fifth, when there is an economic crunch and the organization has to cut back, matrix structures are often the first to go. This is often as it should be. In a weak economy, some projects may experience drastic turnabouts in customer demand and so have to be terminated. However, the drawback is that some companies blame the matrix for the decline in business. In these cases, the matrix is abandoned forever—an unfortunate outcome, since the matrix is not responsible for the economic setback. Management should have plans for handling economic declines. The matrix should not become a scapegoat for poor management. The way to avoid this pitfall is for top management to realize that while the matrix can help achieve new levels of efficiency, it is not a substitute for effective management. In summing up their analysis of matrix organization pitfalls, Davis and Lawrence write:

The matrix may be quickly abandoned.

> We do not recommend that every company adopt the matrix form. But where it is relevant, it can become an important part of an effective managerial process. Like any new method it may develop serious bugs, but the experience that many new companies are acquiring with this organization form can now help others realize its benefits and avoid its pitfalls.[29]

Both the matrix and project organizations represent effective modern organizing structures. Another such design that is being employed by more and more firms is the free-form, or organic, organization structure.

FREE-FORM ORGANIZATIONS

The free-form organization structure (also called organic) has proved very useful in large-scale organizations, which suffer most severely from the negative effects of the bureaucratic process. The essence of this structure is in its name. The organization can take any form, but the objective is always the same: The design must help the executive manage change. For this reason, firms using a free-form structure tend to play down the organizational hierarchy, with its emphasis on departmentalization and job descriptions. Instead, all reasonable attempts are made to free workers from petty controls. In fact, some individuals have even suggested doing away with the traditional worker-boss relationship.

Free-form structure discourages petty controls.

---

[28] Ibid., p. 139.
[29] Ibid., p. 142.

With rigid bureaucratic rules discarded, the manager is given freedom that is necessary to do a particular job. Many times the only controls top management employs are those related to profits or the allocation of scarce resources. In turn, it is common to find managers in these free-form organizations handling their subordinates with similar latitude. Reliance on consensus plays a major role, and two-way communication is encouraged. The organization operates as a team, as opposed to a department with a structured superior-subordinate relationship. In fact, at the upper levels there is sometimes *multiple* top management. The president alone does not make the final decisions on major matters; instead, decisions are made by a group of three or four key executives. The result is an "office of the president," staffed by more than one individual. A manager must remember, however, that this team approach at the top level has not worked well for every form. It should be used only after careful managerial consideration has been given to its advantages and disadvantages.

Synergy and Strategic Planning

Another common characteristic of free-form structures is the emphasis on getting all departments, units, and subsidiaries to work together. Although some organizational forms (holding companies, for example) will have many separate, unrelated, semi-autonomous firms operating under one banner, free-form companies tend to have fewer such holdings, and they try to blend them in harmonious fashion. As a result of this cooperative action, or synergism, the total effect is greater than the sum of the individual parts working independently. To a large extent, this synergy is accomplished at the top level of the organization.

Cooperative action is attained via strategic planning.

What happens is that the central management will draw up a strategic plan that is designed to obtain the greatest synergistic effect from its units. Resources are then allocated on the basis of the potential synergism. Although the units are encouraged to plan, top management makes the final decision on all strategic plans. In this way, the master plan for each division can be revised in light of overall enterprise commitments and objectives.

The main synergistic ingredient is centralized control with decentralized operation. Additionally, strong emphasis is placed on organizing along the lines of profit centers. Further, managers are urged to take risks and to operate their units more from a human-behavior standpoint than ever before. Perhaps this is the reason why firms using free-form structures tend to stress the need for young, dynamic managers unshackled by outmoded assumptions. It also accounts for the fact that free-form organizations are most widely used by firms whose operations are "highly adaptive to products or services on the frontier of public use (e.g., air pollution devices) and those meeting an essential and high-demand industrial, consumer, or military need (e.g., electronic devices, lenses and frames, space-age hardware)."[30] Still another characteristic of these structures is their use of computerized performance evaluations, which determine whether a division or department is contributing to overall profitability. Units which do not do this are likely to be pruned from the organization.

Emphasis is given to decentralized operation with centralized control.

Free-form Organizations in Action

Numerous firms have employed free-form structures. One of them is the Polaroid Corporation, which uses the free form within the formal organizational pattern. Company managers have dubbed it a "sun-satellite system":

---

[30] John H. Pascucci, "The Emergence of Free-form Management," *Personnel Administration*, September–October 1968, pp. 37–38.

Every individual in the overall structure . . . plays two roles. On the primary job assigned to him, he is literally the sun of his own solar system. He is the expert. He is the boss. He is it. In this role, he is surrounded by satellites. These satellites serve him. They feed him ideas, back him up, listen to him when he needs listening to, do chores and perform feats for him.[31]

Polaroid uses sun-satellite systems.

Polaroid's management cites a number of advantages to this free-form structure. First, the individual is secure, since people are "suns" in their own systems. Therefore, employees do not feel at risk in cooperating with colleagues and they freely give their help. A second advantage is that it is possible to form task groups quickly when new or difficult tasks come along. The structure naturally requires rapid communication; it also calls for a considerable degree of self-discipline on the part of all employees. However, these needs were seen earlier to be prerequisites for the effective use of any free-form structure.

Another company using the free-form structure is the International Minerals & Chemical Corporation (IMC), which has done pioneering work in the industrial marketing of chemicals, fertilizers, and food additives. In the mid-sixties, IMC established a new function—organization planning—and brought in a consultant to direct the activity. A specialist in free-form management, the consultant found that his job, put at its most basic function, became one of suggesting change. Soon the firm started using a concept called "cross-hatching." Teams literally flowed in and out of the organizational structure, much in the same way as Polaroid's sun satellites were superimposed on its formal structure. Managers began talking more and more in terms of teamwork. In reference to the new structure, the director of organization planning pointed out that the unity of command concept was inaccurate and that "a man has as many bosses as there are demands upon him, as in life."[32] In short, the IMC structure was designed to fit the job and not vice versa.

IMC employs "cross-hatching."

A third firm that has turned to the free-form structure is the Insurance Company of North America (INA). In an industry that had seen companies increase their fields of specialization from fire to property, casualty, and life insurance, structures suddenly mushroomed, haphazardly and on a crisis-development plan. Corporations consisted of many small companies with no overall direction. It was common to find managerial duplication, organizational overlap, and inefficiency throughout insurance company structures, INA's among them. Underwriting was fragmented by the major line of insurance. Field service and production activities serving primary customers contained areas of overlap. Leadership was divided. Policy holder services were handled by separate management so that functions such as audit, inspection, and claims were all going separate, sometimes inharmonious ways.

INA reorganized, using a free-form structure.

To rectify the situation, INA reorganized according to a free-form structure. The company scrapped the old authoritarian concept of management based on strict obedience in order to tap the full potential of each individual. The INA president described the result, saying: "Each member of management joins with all the others in a united effort to achieve the objectives sought. And each member of management reaches up to share with his superior or superiors their responsibilities and their objectives."[33]

Polaroid, IMC, and INA are not alone in using free-form structures. IBM, American Standard, Xerox, Litton Industries, and Textron are other major organizations that have employed free-form structure. Litton, for example, currently makes use of task teams in

---

[31] Jack B. Weiner, "The New Art of Free-Form Management," *Dun's Review and Modern Industry,* December 1964, p. 32.

[32] Ibid., p. 54.

[33] Ibid., p. 56.

order to organize itself for rapid growth in the microwave industry.[34] And Textron, following the free-form concept of evaluating performance and terminating unprofitable units, has given up its textiles mills and has added metal products, precision machines, and other consumer and industrial products to its manufacturing lines.

The Challenges of Free-Form Structures

Despite the successes free-form structures have led to, they are not without their drawbacks and challenges. The major challenge of the free-form structure is that it discards or deemphasizes such management principles as unity of command and the scalar chain. In their place is a form of situational management in which individuals are encouraged to interact and work rather unpredictably with other members of the organization. Operating within the profit-center concept, they are encouraged to carry out their strategic plans in an environment designed to deal with change. New technology may alter the nature of their work, but the organizational structure is able to take advantage of these changes. For the dynamic, mature manager, the new environment is a welcome relief; for the middle-of-the-road traditionalist, it is a nightmare that brings on tension, anxiety, and fear. The lack of rigidity disrupts the average individual's orientation, and many managers are unable to adapt to the new system.

Management principles are de-emphasized.

Second, free-form structures are designed to incorporate change. This is why they are found in firms operating in highly technical industries. Not all organizations, however, operate in this kind of environment. Thus, the structure can have limited value for some firms.

Structures help manage change.

Third, free-form structures encourage excellence. Managers are on their own and allowed to use the approach they feel works best in attaining the objective. And questions must arise:

Free-form design encourages excellence.

> But if free-form management can bestow such benefits, why don't more companies adopt it? Perhaps the major reason is that time-worn management methods and structures are also protective devices for assigning responsibility for failure. The point is sharply emphasized by Robert H. Schaffer: . . . "The easiest place to camouflage failures in obtaining goals," insists Schaffer, "is the well-fractioned organization where, as any veteran can testify, stalled performance almost always is attributable to 'the system,' to other departments or to forces that lie outside the control of any department."[35]

For a variety of reasons, the use of free-form structures appears to be increasing. First, managers are demanding more flexible organizations to meet the changes and challenges of the eighties. Second, managers are more competent than ever before, so they can effectively utilize these new organizational structures. Third, new technological developments are putting pressure on companies to modernize their organizational designs. Fourth, bureaucratic super-structures will no longer do the job; too much dependence on organization charts and job descriptions stunts the growth of the enterprise. For many, free-form structures will prove to be the answer to a large number of old problems.

CONTINGENCY ORGANIZATION DESIGN

The right organization structure will depend on the situation.

The key word currently characterizing organization design is *contingency*. This word, and the theory it designates, means simply using whatever approach is most effective. Today, the development of structures in which minimum attention is given to the formal

---

[34] William W. George, "Task Teams for Rapid Growth," *Harvard Business Review,* March–April 1977, pp. 71–80.
[35] Ibid.

division of duties is resulting in increasingly flexible designs. Mechanistic structures are, in many cases, being replaced by organic ones. Of course, each company has to evaluate its own situation, but as Jay W. Lorsch and Paul R. Lawrence note, a trend toward *contingency organization design* now seems important:

> During the past few years there has been evident a new trend in the study of organizational phenomena. Underlying this new approach is the idea that the internal functioning of organizations must be consistent with the demands of the organization task, technology, or external environment, and the needs of its members if the organization is to be effective. Rather than searching for the panacea of the one best way to organize under all conditions, investigators have more and more tended to examine the functioning of organizations in relation to the needs of their particular members and the external pressures facing them. Basically, this approach seems to be leading to the development of a "contingency" theory of organization with the appropriate internal states and processes of the organization contingent upon external requirements and member needs.[36]

William F. Glueck, after conducting a review of the literature, offered the following guidelines for contingency organization design:

1. When low cost and efficiency are the keys to successful goal achievement, the effective organization should use functional departmentalization.
2. When the environment is complex and the critical variable is exact meshing of output times, matrix structuring is effective.
3. If it is large and operates in a stable technological and market environment, an enterprise will tend to formalize its organization structure.
4. The greater the intensity of competition, the greater the degree of decentralization.
5. The greater the volatility of the environment, the more decentralized and flexible the organization is likely to be.
6. Organizations that implement the organizational style appropriate to their strategy will be more effective than those that use an inappropriate style.[37]

Influencing Forces

Y. K. Shetty and Howard M. Carlisle echo statements by Lawrence and Lorsch and by Glueck about the need for contingency design, noting that the "best" organization structure must vary according to situation. In essence, structure is a function of forces in the managers, the subordinates, the task, and the environment.[38] Forces in the managers are readily evident. A superior who feels that the work force is basically lazy will design a structure that reflects these views and will refuse to delegate much authority. Conversely, a manager who believes that the best method of managing depends on putting faith in the workers and sharing information and responsibility with them will be more prone to using a design that facilitates decentralization and delegation of authority. Forces in the subordinates would include motives such as a desire for autonomy and an opportunity to participate in decision making. If these factors are present, they will have an impact on the structure. Forces in the task are often reflected in technology. Shetty and Carlisle note: "Technology may determine the extent to which the job may be pro-

---

[36] Jay W. Lorsch and Paul R. Lawrence, *Studies in Organization Design* (Homewood, Ill.: Richard D. Irwin, Dorsey Press, 1970), p. 1.

[37] William F. Glueck, *Management,* 2d ed. (Hinsdale, Ill.: Dryden Press, 1980), chaps. 11 and 12. For more on this topic see also John Child, "What Determines Organization: The Universals vs. the It-All-Depends," *Organizational Dynamics,* Summer 1974, pp. 2–18.

[38] Y. K. Shetty and Howard M. Carlisle, "A Contingency Model of Organization Design," *California Management Review,* Fall 1972, pp. 38–45.

Figure 6–9   Forces Affecting Organization Structure

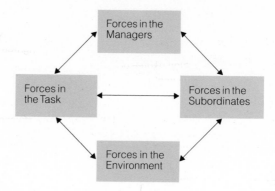

Source: Adapted by permission from Y. K. Shetty and Howard M. Carlisle, "A Contingency Model of Organization Design," *California Management Review*, Fall 1972, p. 44.

grammed, that is, employee behaviors may be precisely specified. The kind of organization required in a low task structure is not the same as that required in a high task structure."[39] Environmental forces include the availability of resources, the nature of the competition, the predictability of demand, and the type of products or services being provided by the company.

These four interacting factors influence the type of organizational design that will evolve, as Figure 6–9 shows. By employing this framework, a company can identify the conditions enhancing or impeding a particular structure. Sometimes it needs a more flexible design, other times a more structured one:

> *The organization appropriate in one market-technology environment may be irrelevant or even dysfunctional in another environment. A firm producing a standardized product sold in a stable market may require a pattern of organization altogether different from a company manufacturing a highly technical product for a more dynamic market. There is no one pattern of organization style that is universally appropriate.*[40]

A Matter of "Fit"

In essence, then, management must look for what is essentially the right "fit" among personnel, organizational characteristics, and task requirement. John J. Morse and Jay W. Lorsch illustrated this when they made an analysis of four business firms, two highly effective and two less effective. One of the highly effective firms was an Akron container manufacturing plant in which formal relationships were highly structured, rules were specific and comprehensive, and the time orientation was short-term. The other was a Stockton research lab where formal relations were less well defined, rules were minimal and flexible, and the time orientation was long-term. Table 6–6 shows Morse and

---

[39] Ibid., p. 42.
[40] Ibid., p. 44.

Characteristics	Akron	Stockton
1. Structural orientation	Perceptions of tightly controlled behavior and a high degree of structure	Perceptions of a low degree of structure
2. Distribution of influence	Perceptions of low total influence, concentrated at upper levels in the organization	Perceptions of high total influence, more evenly spread out among all levels
3. Character of superior-subordinate relations	Low freedom vis-à-vis superiors to choose and handle jobs, directive type of supervision	High freedom vis-à-vis superiors to choose and handle projects, participatory type of supervision
4. Character of colleague relations	Perceptions of many similarities among colleagues, high degree of coordination of colleague effort	Perceptions of many differences among colleagues, relatively low degree of coordination of colleague effort
5. Time orientation	Short-term	Long-term
6. Goal orientation	Manufacturing	Scientific
7. Top executive's "managerial style"	More concerned with task than people	More concerned with task than people

Lorsch's comparison of the two. Both firms, despite these differences, were successful because their structures brought the task and the people together in the right way. Conversely, in the two less effective plants they studied, these researchers found that the formal and informal organizational characteristics did not fit the task requirements as well as in the successful counterparts in Akron and Stockton. This indicates the importance of a correct task-organization-people fit.

> *In arguing for an approach which emphasizes the fit among task, organization, and people, we are putting to rest the question of which organizational approach — the classical or the participative — is best. In its place we are raising a new question: What organizational approach is most appropriate given the task and the people involved?*
>
> *For many enterprises, given the new needs of younger employees for more autonomy, and the rapid rates of social and technological change, it may well be that the more participative approach is the most*

appropriate. But there will still be many situations in which the more controlled and formalized organization is desirable. Such an organization need not be coercive or punitive. If it makes sense to the individuals involved, given their needs and their jobs, they will find it rewarding and motivating.[41]

SUMMARY

The use of bureaucratic structures has begun to decline. One reason for this decline is that the inherent assumptions underlying bureaucracy are unrealistic. The organization cannot function with mechanical rules and regulations that have limited value in motivating and leading the modern worker.

In overcoming bureaucratic deficiencies, many firms are turning to adaptive organization structures, new designs based on a number of assumptions. One such assumption is that the organization operates in a dynamic environment. A second is that personnel, task, and environment are related and must be fit together properly for the best structure and output. This chapter initially directed attention to the impact of technology and its effect on organizational personnel, from the workers right up to the managers. At the worker level, technology affects social relationships as well as job content. At the managerial level, it encourages greater integration of colleagues and of planning effort.

Technology also affects the organization structure by causing changes in such factors as the length of the line of command, the span of control of the chief executive, and the ratio of managers to total personnel. In addition, mechanistic designs tend to give way to organic ones, as has been seen in the research of Woodward, Zwerman, Lawrence and Lorsch, and Meyer, to name only five prominent researchers in the organization-study boom of recent times.

What do these new organic structures look like? How do they work? Exactly when are they used? These questions are answered through examinations of project, matrix, and free-form designs. The project organization form entails "the gathering of the best available talent to accomplish a specific and complex understanding within time, cost and/or quality parameters, followed by the disbanding of the team upon completion of the undertaking."[42] Project organization has been employed in numerous and diverse ways, from building dams and weapon systems to conducting research and development and designing bank credit-card systems. The major advantage of this organizational form is that it allows the project manager and team to concentrate their attention on one specific undertaking.

The matrix structure is a hybrid form of organization, containing characteristics of both project and functional structures. In a matrix design, employees are in a sense on partial loan to the matrix project manager. These employees, therefore, have a dual responsibility—to the line manager who lent them to the project and to the project manager for whom they work for the life of the project. The result is a uniquely horizontal and vertical flow of authority. Since the project manager has only project authority, this individual must rely on human relations assets and skills—for example, negotiation, personality, persuasive ability, the aura of competence, and the brokerage of reciprocal favors. While the matrix structure has advantages, the organization con-

---

[41] John J. Morse and Jay W. Lorsch, "Beyond Theory Y," *Harvard Business Review*, May–June 1970. p. 68.

[42] Hodgetts, "Interindustry Analysis of Certain Aspects of Project Management," p. 7.

sidering its use must also weigh the disadvantages inherent in it. Only after considering both aspects of the matrix can an organization make an intelligent decision regarding its overall value.

Another adaptive organization design is the free-form, or organic, structure. This design can take any shape, but it always has two prime characteristics: the downplay of rigid bureaucratic rules and an emphasis on self-regulation. A number of conglomerates have adopted this organization form; they include Polaroid, International Minerals & Chemical Corporation, Insurance Company of North America, IBM, Litton Industries, American Standard, Xerox, and Textron. Perhaps the greatest advantage of a free-form structure is its value to the manager who must cope with change.

What kind of structure is best? The question has no single right answer. "Best" depends on the situation. For that reason, the area of contingency organization design is currently very important. Some firms need a mechanistic structure; others work better with an organic one. The answer to the question thus depends on forces operating on managers, subordinates, task, and environment.

This chapter has examined the ways in which organizations are redesigning their structures in order to adapt more effectively to their environments. However, the organizing process only helps bring together the workers and the work. Management still needs a basis for comparing the plan and the results.

REVIEW AND STUDY QUESTIONS

1. What are the characteristics of an ideal bureaucracy?
2. Why is the bureaucratic form of organization declining today?
3. What impact can technology have on workers? On managers?
4. What is a mechanistic organization structure? Give an example, and explain how your example fits the structure definition.
5. What is an organic organization structure? Give an example, including in your discussion of it the aspects of the example that make it organic.
6. What effect does technology have on organization structure? Base your answer on recent research, particularly Joan Woodward's research in the London suburbs.
7. What is a project organization?
8. When can a project organization be used most effectively? Explain.
9. Explain this statement: A matrix structure is a hybrid form of organization, containing characteristics of both project and functional structures.
10. What is project authority?
11. Describe in your own words some of the advantages of a matrix structure. What are some of its disadvantages?
12. How is the free-form organization useful to large-scale organizations?
13. How do free-form organizations employ synergy in their strategic planning?
14. What is a contingency organization design?
15. What are some common guidelines for contingency organization designs? Explain the guidelines that you cite.
16. The research team of Y. K. Shetty and Howard M. Carlisle noted that the "best" organization structure is a function of four forces. Identify and explain all four.
17. Explain what John J. Morse and Jay W. Lorsch meant when they discussed the need for "fit" among task, organization, and personnel.

SELECTED REFERENCES

Bell, D. "Communications Technology—For Better or for Worse." *Harvard Business Review,* May–June 1979, pp. 20–22, 26.

Boettinger, Henry M. "Technology in the Manager's Future." *Harvard Business Review,* November–December 1970, pp. 4–14, 165.

Butler, A. G., Jr. "Project Management: A Study in Organizational Conflict." *Academy of Management Journal,* March 1973, pp. 84–101.

Burns, Tom, and Stalker, G. M. *The Management of Innovation.* London: Tavistock Publications, 1961.

Child, John. "Predicting and Understanding Organization Structure." *Administrative Science Quarterly,* June 1973, pp. 168–185.

Cleland, David I. "Understanding Project Authority." *Business Horizons,* Spring 1967, pp. 63–70.

Cleland, David I., and King, William R. *Systems Analysis and Project Management,* 2d ed. New York: McGraw-Hill, 1975.

Davis, Stanley, and Lawrence, Paul R. "Problems of Matrix Organizations." *Harvard Business Review,* May–June 1978, pp. 131–142.

Dunne, Edward J., Jr.; Stahl, Michael J.; and Melhart, Leonard J., Jr. "Influence Sources of Project and Functional Managers in Matrix Organizations." *Academy of Management Journal,* March 1978, pp. 135–140.

George, W. W. "Task Teams for Rapid Growth." *Harvard Business Review,* March–April 1977, pp. 71–80.

Gerwin, D. "The Comparative Analysis of Structure and Technology: A Critical Appraisal." *Academy of Management Review,* January 1979, pp. 41–51.

Gross, A. C., and Ware, W. W. "Energy Prospects to 1990." *Business Horizons,* June 1975, pp. 5–18.

Hickson, David J.; Pugh, D. J.; and Pheysey, Diana C. "Operations Technology and Organization Structure: An Empirical Reappraisal." *Administrative Science Quarterly,* September 1969, pp. 378–397.

Hodgetts, Richard M. "Leadership Techniques in the Project Organization." *Academy of Management Journal,* June 1968, pp. 211–219.

Hunt, R. G. "Technology and Organization." *Academy of Management Journal,* September 1970, pp. 235–252.

Kast, F. E., and Rosenzweig, J. E. *Contingency Views of Organization and Management.* Chicago: Science Research Associates, 1973.

———. *Organization and Management: A Systems Approach,* 3d ed. New York: McGraw-Hill, 1980, chap. 9.

Kolodny, Harvey F. "Evolution to a Matrix Organization." *Academy of Management Review,* October 1979, pp. 543–554.

Lawrence, Paul R., and Lorsch, Jay W. *Organization and Environment.* Boston: Harvard Graduate School of Business Administration, 1967.

Likert, Rensis. *The Human Organization.* New York: McGraw-Hill, 1967.

McFarland, D. E. *Management: Foundations and Practices,* 5th ed. New York: Macmillan, 1979, chap. 14.

Morse, John J., and Lorsch, Jay W. "Beyond Theory Y." *Harvard Business Review,* May–June 1970, pp. 61–68.

Peters, T. J. "Beyond the Matrix Organization." *Business Horizons,* October 1979, pp. 15–27.

Rhodes, R. "80 Ways the Eighties Will Change Your Life." *Playboy,* January 1980, pp. 149, 156, 200, 263–264, 266–267.

"Robots Join the Labor Force." *Business Week,* June 9, 1980, pp. 72–76.

Shetty, Y. K., and Carlisle, Howard M. "A Contingency Model of Organization Design." *California Management Review,* Fall 1972, pp. 38–45.

Swager, W. L. "Technological Forecasting in Planning: A Method of Using Relevance Trees." *Business Horizons,* February 1973, pp. 37–44.

"Technology Gives the U.S. a Big Edge." *Business Week,* June 30, 1980, pp. 102–106.

Toren, N. "Bureaucracy and Professional Professionalism: A Reconsideration of Weber's Thesis." *Academy of Management Review,* July 1976, pp. 36–46.

CASE: New Challenges, New Structures

Bureaucratic structures employ calculable rules and operate with little, if any, regard for people. Although the bureaucracy has precision in much of what it does, it also strictly subordinates individual interest to that of the organization. Some of the major criticisms of bureaucracies include the following:

1. There is inadequate allowance for personal growth.
2. There is too much emphasis on conformity.
3. The informal organization is not adequately addressed.
4. The authority system, with its strict superior-subordinate structure, is outdated.
5. There is no adequate means for resolving intergroup conflict.
6. Group-think, the social conformity to group ideas by members of the group, is encouraged.
7. The development of mature personalities is discouraged.
8. Innovation is thwarted.
9. Human resources are not fully utilized.
10. People are encouraged to become "organization people."

Furthermore, point out critics of the bureaucratic structure, great changes are taking place in the environment. Some of the changes that will affect organizations during the 1980s follow:

1. Organization size will increase.
2. The organization will heavily stress intellectual activities.
3. Managers will place greater emphasis on suggestion and persuasion than on coercion and the use of authoritarian power.
4. Organizational complexity will increase.
5. People throughout the organization will influence company matters, even planning and decision making.
6. Computerized information decision systems will increasingly affect organizations.

7. Interorganizational coordination and problem solving will increase.

8. The number of scientists and professionals in business organizations will rise.

9. Organizational goals will increase, with the intent that all will be achieved. Maximizing any one particular goal will no longer be common practice.

10. The external environment will continue to change dramatically.

As a result, there will be a movement in many firms away from the mechanistic-bureaucratic structure and toward a flexible-organic system.

Questions

1. Do you think that many organizations have already begun to move toward more flexible organic systems? Explain.

2. Can you think of reasons in addition to those cited in the case that might cause business firms to abandon their old bureaucratic structures?

3. In what industries would you expect to find organic structures widely used? In what industries would you expect to find firms staying with a basically mechanistic-bureaucratic structure? Explain your opinions.

CASE: More Order, Not Less

When Sousa Incorporated started business in 1950, its three founders stated the firm's basic mission as one of "inventing and manufacturing sophisticated telecommunication equipment." Over the next thirty years the company prospered, thanks to the high degree of technical expertise possessed by the owners and the staff they hired. In 1981, however, the founders decided that they had had enough. They wished to retire and spend the rest of their years in leisure. They therefore sold Sousa for $60 million to a large national conglomerate. This was the conglomerate's first venture into the communications industry; its initial success had come in manufacturing. Nevertheless, the board of directors liked Sousa's profitability picture and felt that the company was making an excellent acquisition.

Soon after the takeover, the Sousa work force was told that the conglomerate would make no radical changes; everything was to be "business as usual." But there was one exception: The conglomerate would be reorganizing the structure of the firm. The new owners preferred a line-staff organization. When asked about this, the new president of the firm said: "We feel Sousa is too disorganized. We want to create more formal lines of communication and authority-responsibility relationships. This way everyone will know what to do and to whom activities are to be reported. At present, this is not the case."

Within six months after the reorganization, however, Sousa's financial statements indicated that something was quite wrong. Instead of obtaining high profitability, the newly acquired company was reporting its first loss in years. The president and his advisors were unable to explain why. One of the board members put it this way: "We tried to straighten out the firm's chaotic nature by introducing some order into the structure. But instead of becoming more profitable, Sousa is now losing money. The president has talked it over with us and decided to call in a management consulting firm. Perhaps we need an even more formalized structure than we thought. In any event, something has to be done."

Questions

1. Explain why the new organization structure is not working.

2. Do you agree with the new president's comment about Sousa being too disorganized?

3. What recommendations would you make to this firm? Explain, bringing the topics of mechanistic and organic structures into your discussion.

CASE: *The Glorified Coordinator*

William Uyesugi, a graduate student of business at State University, was writing a paper on modern organization structures. As part of his research he interviewed project, matrix, and free-form organization managers in ten major corporations throughout the city. One of the managers worked in a consumer products firm. She explained her job as follows:

I'm responsible for developing a consumer product. In order to get the job done, I've had people assigned to me from the various functional departments: research, design, manufacturing, and test. Of course, these people will stay within their own departments; but when I need them, they will work for me.

I spent most of last week figuring out exactly when I'd need these people. I'm going to need the R&D people starting next week. Then, when they're finished with the project, I'll have it manufactured and tested. This will come in about two months. The reason I know the schedule so well is that this week I have to go around to the functional managers and ask them to assign people to me for the project. They'll want to see the time schedule and then they'll figure out who can work on my project. Of course, these people will continue to report to their functional boss, but they will be working on my project. Nevertheless, I suppose you'd be right if you called me a glorified project coordinator or an expediter. After all, my only goal is to get everyone together and make sure the product is manufactured on time. Then it will be tested in various sections of the country; and if it catches on, the company will set up a new product department to handle it. Meanwhile, I'll go on to another project.

Questions

1. What kind of authority does the project manager have over the project personnel in this case?

2. Is this a project, matrix, or free-form organization? Give your reasoning.

CASE: *Fly Me to the Moon*

In his second State of the Union address to the Congress in May 1961, President John F. Kennedy stated, "I believe that this nation should commit itself to achieving the goal, before this decade is out, of landing a man on the moon and returning him safely to earth." The race to the moon was on.

The United States undertook three distinct projects: Mercury, Gemini, and Apollo. Mercury's primary objectives included investigating human capabilities in the space environment and developing manned space flight technology. Gemini's primary goals entailed subjecting two men and supporting equipment to long duration flights, effecting rendezvous and docking maneuvers with other orbiting vehicles, and perfecting methods of re-entry and landing. Apollo had three primary goals: to put two men on the moon, to allow them to carry out limited exploration, and then to return them safely to earth.

To achieve Apollo's goals, the United States needed a spacecraft to get the astronauts into and out of the moon's orbit and a lunar excursion module (LEM) to take them down to the moon's surface and return them to the spacecraft. In order to build these two pieces of equipment, the National Aeronautics and Space Administration (NASA) solicited contracts. The award for the spacecraft was given to North American Aviation while Grumman Aircraft received the LEM contract. In addition, NASA set up a project organization, known as the Apollo Spacecraft Program Office (ASPO), to monitor the contractors and see that the hardware was built on time and within cost and quality parameters. As the contractors built the spacecraft and the LEM, ASPO personnel would check to see that everything was going according to schedule. If there was a problem, for example, and the contractor wanted to change the design of the hardware, ASPO had to clear the change. In short, the Apollo program people were charged with seeing that contractors did their jobs correctly. ASPO headquarters were located in Houston, but the ASPO people were continually flying out to see contractors on site. They also had frequent reports made to them so they could ascertain that progress was being made and that the work quality was appropriate.

Questions

1. What kind of authority did the Apollo Spacecraft Program Office have over contractors? Explain your answer.

2. Was the ASPO a project, matrix, or free-form organization? Why do you think so?

3. Could NASA have gotten the moonshot launched and landed as efficiently as it did if it had used a different organization structure? Defend your opinion.

CHAPTER 7

THE CONTROLLING PROCESS

GOALS OF THE CHAPTER

An organization that attains its objectives can formulate more ambitious ones. A firm that falls short of its goals must develop a revised plan. In both cases, the firms must conduct evaluations to assess their performance; the controlling process is the means whereby businesses evaluate plans and experiences.

The goals of this chapter are to examine the nature and process of control, with prime focus on traditional, specialized, and overall control techniques. This chapter shows a strong link between planning and controlling. The two are so entwined that it is sometimes difficult to determine where one leaves off and the other begins. And so it is within the chapter.

When you have finished this chapter, you should be able to:

1. Describe the three basic steps in the controlling process.
2. Discuss the requirements for an effective control system.
3. Relate how comprehensive budgeting and zero-base budgeting work.
4. Explain how the break-even point can be used for control purposes.
5. Present a brief description of the Gantt chart, PERT, and milestone budgeting, noting how they can help an organization control its operations.
6. Describe some of the most commonly used techniques for controlling an organization's overall performance.

THE BASIC CONTROLLING PROCESS

As Henri Fayol noted: "The control of an undertaking consists of seeing that everything is being carried out in accordance with the plan which has been adopted, the orders which have been given, and the principles which have been laid down. Its object is to point out mistakes in order that they may be rectified and prevented from occurring again."[1]

The controlling process has three basic steps: the establishment of standards, the comparison of performance against these standards, and the correction of deviations that have occurred. The latter two, of course, can only be attained through the establishment of effective feedback. This section will examine these three basic steps and the role of feedback in the controlling process.

Establishing Standards

Standards provide a basis against which performance can be measured. They are often a result of the goals the organization formulates during its planning phase. Sometimes they are very specific, expressed in terms of costs, revenues, products, or hours worked. Other times they are more qualitative in nature—for example, a desire to maintain high morale among the employees or to design a public relations program for gaining community goodwill.

Comparing Performance with Standards

Ideally, management should design a control system that permits it to identify major problems before they occur. For example, research shows that workers' attitudes toward their jobs decline before their productivity goes down. If management could identify the lead factor, it could began taking steps to prevent the impending decline in output. However, since this is more often an idealistic wish than a practical solution, the next best step is to identify such deviations as early as possible. Most competent managers do so through use of the exception principle, which holds that attention should be focused on especially good or especially bad situations. Managers who work on this principle avoid the major danger of trying to control every deviation, great or small; they do not spread themselves so thin that they are inert when managerial attention and action are clearly indicated.

The major problem most managers encounter is how to measure actual performance. Some standards are easily measurable, but others require custom-made appraisals. Still others seem actually to defy objective evaluation. For example, how does one really measure worker motivation, since motivation is an intervening variable (that is, an internal psychological process unavailable for direct observation and accessible for judgment only through inference)? If Georgia appears interested in her work, she is motivated; if she looks uninterested, she is unmotivated, even though this appraisal may well be inaccurate. Another common performance measurement dilemma occurs when a firm tries to evaluate a top-level manager—for example, the vice-president of marketing. The further up the organization one goes, the more difficult it is to develop precise, measurable standards. Whatever criteria are selected, they will be vague. Management has found that as work becomes less technical, standards become

Some standards are not easily measured.

---

[1] Henri Fayol, *Industrial and General Administration,* trans. J. A. Coubrough (Geneva, Switzerland: International Management Institute, 1929), p. 77.

more difficult to develop; appraisals are exceedingly hard to make. For this reason, a trend has developed in recent years toward evaluating workers almost exclusively on objective bases. If a standard is not measurable, it is not employed. This approach, the flaws of which are obvious, still has the major asset of greatly reducing subjective, biased evaluations. It also provides direction for subordinates, who know the bases on which their performance will be judged.

Correcting Deviations

The correction of deviations should begin with an investigation of why the errors occurred. Sometimes a planning premise may have been wrong. Sales may have been lower than anticipated because of an overly optimistic forecast. Or a strike in the plant may have caused unexpected delays in production. The cause of the deviation will help determine the appropriate action. But a key point to be noted here is that some problems are no one's fault. From time to time even the best market forecasts will be wrong. For example, a few years ago a large distiller marketed a dry white whiskey that, despite an extensive market research program, failed to achieve widespread acceptance. And in the case of a union strike, the walkout may be more a function of union demands than of management offers. The company may be able to give a maximum offer of 12 percent in salary and 7.2 percent in fringe benefits over a two-year period. If the union refuses to settle for less than 20 percent and 12.8 percent respectively, a strike may occur. In short, not all deviations are directly attributable to any single individual or group, and if management tries to assess blame for every error, employee attitudes toward work may suffer, in which case the short-term success in appraisal could lead to a long-term productivity decline.

Of course, there are times when a manager will make an error in judgment or a worker will handle an order improperly. When this occurs, if the errors are grave or habitual, corrective action may require the replacement of the individual or the assignment of additional training. However, the action can be determined only after the specific causes of the deviation have been evaluated.

After the cause is identified, problem-solving measures can be enacted.

Establishing Effective Feedback

An ideal control system provides timely feedback that can be used to monitor and correct deviations. A basic illustration is provided by the human body. If something happens that causes the body to leave its "normal" state, basic control mechanisms will attempt to reestablish the status quo. This self-regulating, or control, property is known as homeostasis. For example, if a man cuts his finger, his body will begin working to coagulate the blood and close the wound. The feedback mechanism in the human system can perform phenomenal feats if conditions are somehow bearable: Some people who suffer massive heart attacks or are hit by Mack trucks survive.

The same basic concept of feedback is present in the thermostat system of a house. The desired temperature is programmed when the resident sets an indicator that communicates the setting to the system that controls the furnace. If a family desires 68°F, the heating unit will maintain the temperature at this level, turning on and off as necessary.

An organization also requires a feedback system. With the information provided by such a system, the company can monitor activities, identifying those that are not in accord with plans and taking the necessary corrective action. Figure 7–1 depicts the establishment of such a system.

It should be noted, however, that organizational control systems differ from those

Figure 7–1 *Simple Feedback Process*

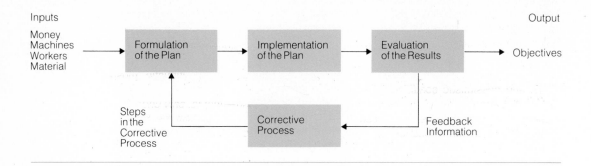

found in the human body and the home thermostat: The body and the thermostat are essentially automatic and employ, at least in the short-run, only data from within the system. Organizational control, on the other hand, is seldom automatic. Usually, by the time feedback results are evaluated, other errors have occurred, and the organization is in a "catch-up" situation. In addition, organizational control employs data from outside the system. This occurs in the corrective process when the manager decides how to handle deviations, thereby introducing new decisions or inputs into the process. For this reason, mechanical control systems are often known as *closed-loop* systems, whereas organizational control systems are often called *open-loop* systems. Naturally, the latter must be viewed on a spectrum. If most organizational decisions are handled via established policies or procedures, the system is more nearly automatic than one requiring managers to formulate their own action. Nevertheless, even with feedback, organizational control presents a challenge to the manager.

Organizations must develop effective feedback control systems.

REQUIREMENTS FOR AN EFFECTIVE CONTROL SYSTEM

The process of control is not automatic. If the organization wants an effective control system, it has to tailor one to its own specifications. In addition to the two previously mentioned requirements—that controls be objective and that the manager employ the exception—the five following assets are common to many effective control systems.

Providing Useful, Understandable Information

Control systems will differ from organization to organization and from manager to manager. Information that is valuable to one individual may be useless to another. The key question each must ask is, what information do I need to control the activities within my jurisdiction? This approach is valuable for two reasons. First, it forces individual managers to decide what they need to know and in what form. This definition and selection process is known as information design and results in useful, understandable data; it will be discussed in more detail later in the chapter. Second, the approach provides a basis for screening out irrelevant reports and information that the individual may be receiving.

Timeliness

Controls should quickly report deviations. In addition, a well-designed system should be capable of identifying potential problem areas before they manifest themselves. For example, forecasting a cash flow for the next ninety days based on optimistic, most likely, and pessimistic conditions can provide management with a short-run financial picture. If it appears likely that the company will run out of cash—that is, only under the most optimistic conditions will it remain in the black—there may still be time to negotiate a loan with a local bank. In this way, controls become lead rather than lag factors.

Flexibility

Most plans will deviate from expectations, and some will be outright failures. Unless a control system is flexible, it will be unable to maintain control of operations during such events. The value of flexible control can be readily seen in the use of flexible budgets, which increase or contract on the basis of the volume of business. Flexibility helps management control operations regardless of economic conditions.

Economy

A control system must be worth the expense. However, it is often difficult to determine when the marginal costs associated with the system equal the marginal revenues obtained from it. Naturally, a small company cannot afford to install the expensive systems employed by a large corporation, but often it must consider a minor control expenditure, such as a time clock. The company will want to know whether the clock will reduce tardiness and whether it will cause work output to increase. Perhaps the clock will reduce tardiness. But perhaps the output will decrease. (The reverse outcomes might also occur.) Even assuming that tardiness is reduced, it is still possible that people will not do more work. They may just sit around waiting to clock out at 5:00 P.M. On the other hand, productivity may rise, and although a large firm may be able to absorb low productivity, a small one may not; so the system could prove useful to the latter. In either event, if a firm decides to put in a time clock, it must be willing to compare productivity (and the related issue of morale) both before and after the installation. Only in this way can it be sure that the control mechanism has been economical. This guideline also applies to revenues and expenses associated with control systems that are much more difficult to evaluate. For example, what is the cost-benefit ratio attached to a new monthly progress report that must be submitted by all unit managers? This kind of question will be difficult to answer in many cases, as it requires a highly subjective estimate. Nevertheless, some attempt must be made to do so.

Leading to Corrective Action

An effective control system must lead to corrective action; merely uncovering deviations from plans is not enough. The system must also disclose where the problem areas are and who or what is responsible for them. From here management can evaluate the situation and decide upon the appropriate action.

TRADITIONAL CONTROL TECHNIQUES

Management can employ its choice from among a large number of control techniques. Some of the more traditional ones include budgeting, break-even analysis, and personal observation.

Budgeting

In the Chapter 5 discussion of budgets, it was noted that organizations often use them to harmonize functional plans. Used in this way, the budget is a type of plan, specifying anticipated results in numerical terms. However, the *budget* is also a control device that provides a basis for feedback, evaluation, and follow-up.

Comprehensive Budgeting Many organizations use *comprehensive budgeting* when all phases of operations are covered by budgets. This often begins with the submission of budget proposals by subordinate managers. After the proposals are discussed with the superiors to whatever extent is necessary, they are next forwarded to higher management. The result is a bottom-up approach, which ensures consideration of the needs and desires of, and participation by, lower management in the budgeting process. However, the process does not stop here. At the top of the organization there is often a budget committee whose purpose is to review the entire program. In a manufacturing firm, for example, this committee may consist of the president and the vice-presidents of finance, marketing, and production, who have line authority to make whatever final budget revisions are necessary. In other cases, the committee may be staffed by lower ranking personnel who have advisory authority only. In either case, the result is an integration of the individual budgets into a comprehensive one and the paring away of excessive requests. Thus, although everyone has an input into the budget, top management maintains the authority to make necessary adjustments. This power is very important, for some departments will request 130 percent of what they need and hope to be cut back no more than 20 percent. Of course, the challenge is in knowing where to cut. An overall 30 percent reduction in budget requests is harmful to those units that are not padding their estimates and helpful to those that are. For this reason, top management must impress on its employees the importance of submitting reasonable budgets and must also try to ensure that they do.

A "from-the-bottom-up" approach is used.

Zero-base Budgeting At the present time *zero-base budgeting (ZBB)* is being used by a half-dozen states, a score of cities, and several hundred companies, including Texas Instruments, Southern California Edison, Union Carbide, Westinghouse, and Playboy Enterprises.[2] The concept of ZBB, which is often applied to support services, is rather simple:

> Managers, starting at the lowest "cost centers" of an organization, must justify everything they do as if they were building their operation from scratch. Every manager isolates basic services and overhead items he controls—a typing pool, a computer, or a mailroom, for example—and then writes a brief outline of why each exists and how much it costs. This outline—or "decision package" in ZBB jargon—usually identifies a minimum expenditure level below the current outlay, plus an expanded service level if more money were available. It also examines alternative ways of performing a task, such as hiring temporary help or outside contractors. Finally, managers rank all their decision packages by priority and pass them on to their superiors, who go through the same exercise at a higher plane.[3]

---

[2] Burton V. Dean and Scott S. Cowen, "Zero-Base Budgeting in the Private Sector," *Business Horizons,* August 1979, p. 78.

[3] "What It Means to Build a Budget from Zero," *Business Week,* April 18, 1977, p. 160.

When it comes to actual production areas such as product lines, however, ZBB is applied somewhat differently. In these cases the company decides how much profit it wants to make on its investment. Then each unit or division submits a budget requesting a given amount of money and stating the amount of profit that can be expected from this investment. By carefully reviewing each budget proposal and the expected return, the top management can prune the marginal lines and put its money behind the most promising winners.

Proponents of ZBB cite many advantages, some of which follow:

1. ZBB focuses the budgeting process; it directs the firm toward a comprehensive analysis of its needs and goals.
2. ZBB is efficient, as it combines planning and budgeting into one process instead of the two somewhat related functions they have been under traditional systems.
3. ZBB ensures that all managers, whatever their level in the firm, evaluate in detail the cost-effectiveness of their units' activities.
4. ZBB, because it involves every manager, gives firms the benefit of much expanded management participation in planning and budgeting at all organizational levels.

Opponents of ZBB, meanwhile, note that it requires a great deal more time, work, people, and money than more standard approaches to budgeting. Many business firms that have used ZBB, however, think that it saves more money than it costs. For example, Southern California Edison claims savings of over $300,000 annually thanks to ZBB; Westinghouse Electric saved $4.2 million in overhead costs in just one year with ZBB; and Ford Motor once said that its savings ran into "the millions."[4] In fact, ZBB is catching on so fast around the country that consulting companies now hold ZBB seminars for business firms, and the major accounting firms advise their clients on zero-base budgeting.[5] In the seventies, such consultation and advice was very rare.

Avoiding Inflexibility in Budgeting Budgets are useful planning and control tools, but they can prove cumbersome in the event of overbudgeting. It is not sound practice to spell out all expenses in such detail as to deprive the manager of freedom of action. Some managers become so committed to carved-in-stone dollar amounts that they assign higher priorities to the budget than to organizational objectives. This is counterproductive management that can even cause a firm a profit loss, though the penny-wise manager certainly does not want or expect that to happen. But such a manager does make it possible.

Problems caused by such inflexibility have led to alternative budgeting forms, and one which has received a great deal of attention is the *variable expense budget*. This budget is used to complement different levels of activity. When a budget period ends, calculations are made as to what the expenses for each unit should, by projections, have been. If activity was as expected, departments almost certainly will be within their budgets. However, if volume was much higher than expected, many departments will have overspent. With the variable expense budget, the firm in such a position can at this point, computing from a predetermined formula, adjust departmental budgets according to current reality. But it is necessary to recall that the variable budget is not a substitute for a comprehensive budgetary program. Rather, it is a supplement to it.

---

[4] Ibid.

[5] For more on this topic, see Mark W. Dirsmith and Stephen F. Jablonsky, "Zero-Base Budgeting as a Management Technique and Political Strategy," *Academy of Management Review*, October 1979, pp. 555–565; and James D. Suver and Ray L. Brown, "Where Does Zero-Base Budgeting Work?" *Harvard Business Review*, November–December 1977, pp. 76–84.

Some companies use a *supplemental monthly budget,* a variation of the variable budget. Under this plan, the firm determines a minimum operational budget. Just prior to the beginning of each month, a supplemental budget that provides the units with additional funds is drawn up. This approach differs from the variable budget in that adjustments are made before the period begins rather than when it is over.

The *alternative budget* is another version of the flexible budget. Under this approach, the company establishes budgets for high, medium, and low levels of operations. Then, at the beginning of the particular period, managers are told under which budget they will be operating.

All these approaches indicate the need for flexibility in the budgeting process. As sources of information feedback, they can perform a useful function for the manager. However, a manager must not become too reliant on them. It is essential that a manager regard budgets only as tools for attaining organizational control.

Break-even Point

Break-even analysis is another common control technique. At the end of any given period of operation, an organization hopes to make a profit. In order for this to happen, total revenue must exceed total costs. For purposes of analysis, costs can be divided into two categories: fixed and variable. *Fixed costs* are those that will remain constant (at least in the short-run) regardless of operations. Some examples are property insurance, property taxes, depreciation, and administrative salaries. *Variable costs* are those that will change in relation to output. Labor salaries and cost of materials are examples.

*The break-even
point occurs
when total
fixed and
variable
expenses are
covered.*

In computing the *break-even point (BEP),* the manager uses three cost-revenue components: total fixed cost, selling price per unit, and variable cost per unit. By subtracting the variable cost associated with the unit from its selling price, a margin-above-cost is obtained. This margin can then be applied to the total fixed cost, with the BEP occurring when the total of these margins equals total fixed cost. In simple mathematical terms:

$$BEP = \frac{TFC}{P - VC}$$

where:
BEP = Break-even point in units
TFC = Total fixed cost
P = Price per unit
VC = Variable cost per unit.

Consider the following example. Company A has conducted market research on a new product and has determined that it can sell 25,000 units at $10 each. The firm's total fixed costs are $120,000, and its variable cost per unit is $4. Given this information, will the venture be profitable? The answer is going to depend on the BEP. Applying the relevant data to the formula results in the following:

$$BEP = \frac{\$120,000}{\$10 - \$4}$$

$$= \frac{\$120,000}{\$6}$$

$$= 20,000 \text{ units.}$$

The firm's BEP is 20,000 units. Figure 7–2 illustrates this solution graphically. Sales are projected at 25,000 units; therefore, the venture should prove profitable. However, if

Figure 7–2 Break-even Point Computation

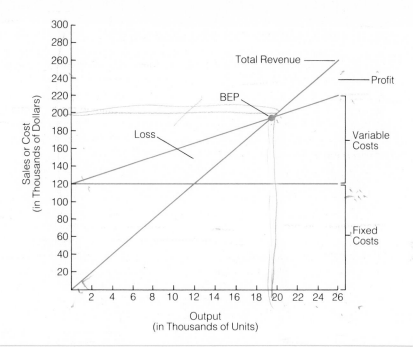

market research showed a demand of anything under 20,000 units, the company could not break even on the project.

BEP analysis is a useful control device because of its emphasis on the marginal concept. In addition, it helps establish initial guidelines for control. In the example of Company A, fixed costs should remain at $120,000, variable cost per unit should be $4, and profits should occur after 20,000 units are sold. If costs or expected sales change, management has a basis for evaluating the impact and taking any necessary corrective action.

Personal Observation

Personal observation is another common control technique. Although it is employed in virtually every organization, it is especially common in small and medium-sized firms. Nonprofit organizations that are under little pressure to show results on a time-cost basis also make wide use of it.

Although personal observation alone is an incomplete form of control, it is an excellent supplement to budgets and break-even analysis. Despite all the information reported to modern managers, they still find that they can learn some things only by such means as a walk through the firm. There is no substitute for a firsthand view of operations, and personal observation provides just this.

A firsthand view can be useful.

SPECIALIZED CONTROL TECHNIQUES

In addition to traditional control techniques, management has developed many specialized tools to improve the quality of control. Space does not allow discussion of all of them, but two will be examined: information design and time-event analyses.

Information Design

Information design is critical to an organization, especially since the advent of modern computers that can provide a wealth of data on virtually any area the manager would like to examine. Without some system for filtering out relevant from irrelevant information, managers can find themselves swamped with reports and numbers, most of which are meaningless to them.

The result has been the development of specialized organizational systems and procedures designed to provide useful information to the operating manager; the data can be presented in whatever form is needed for control purposes. In some large corporations, managers simply have to determine what they need, when they need it, and the format in which they would like it. Often, managers ask for the automatic transmission of periodic reports. A spin-off of this concept is seen in corporations whose service departments keep executives informed by forwarding copies of articles and reports appearing in newspapers and journals on topics that the managers have indicated are of interest to them. In this way, individual managers can keep up on their specialized areas without personally having to spend a lot of time searching journals for useful information.

Time-event Analyses

Some of the most successful approaches to control have been attained through *time-event analysis*, which is a number of techniques that permit the manager to see how all the segments of the project interrelate, evaluate overall progress, and identify and take early corrective action on problem areas. One of the earliest techniques, still in use, is the chart developed by Henry Gantt. The principles contained in it have served as the basis for both Program Evaluation and Review Technique (PERT) and milestone scheduling.

Gantt Chart The *Gantt chart* has proved to be a useful planning and control technique. The basic concept involves the graphic depiction of work progress over a period of time. Figure 7–3 provides an illustration.

The Gantt chart is a control technique that is easy to read and understand.

An examination of the figure reveals that three orders are being filled, each requiring the performance of certain operations. For the week illustrated in the chart, Order 1 is scheduled for manufacturing on Monday and Tuesday, assembling on Wednesday, painting on Thursday, and testing on Friday. Order 2 is scheduled for manufacturing on Monday, Tuesday, and Wednesday, assembling on Thursday, and painting on Friday. Order 3 is scheduled for manufacturing on Monday and Tuesday, assembling on Wednesday and Thursday, and painting on Friday. The solid vertical lines in the figure indicate the time required for each operation; the dotted horizontal lines denote progress. The "V" after Thursday indicates that the chart reflects the situation as of the close of business on that day. Based on this information, it is evident that Order 1 is on time, Order 2 is a day ahead of schedule, and Order 3 is a day behind. With this information, the manager is in a position to control the situation—for example, by transferring those working on Order 2 to Order 3 and making up the lost day. This concept of identifying the work to be done and plotting it on a time axis has provided the foundation for PERT.

Figure 7–3 Simplified Gantt Chart

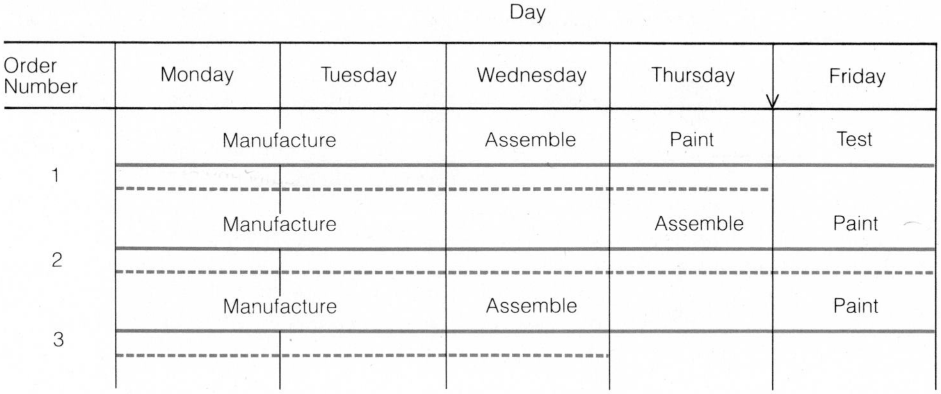

Day

Order Number	Monday	Tuesday	Wednesday	Thursday	Friday
1	Manufacture		Assemble	Paint	Test
2	Manufacture			Assemble	Paint
3	Manufacture		Assemble		Paint

Program Evaluation and Review Technique PERT was developed by the Special Projects Office of the United States Navy and applied to the planning and control of the Polaris Weapon System in 1958. The technique has proved very useful in managing complex projects. It is too elaborate for sensible use in lesser projects.

The manager receives only pertinent data.

PERT employs what is called a time-event network. In building the network, events and activities are first identified. An *event* is a point in time when an activity is begun or finished; it is generally represented in the network by a circle. An *activity* is an operation required to accomplish a particular goal; it is represented in the network by an arrow. Figure 7–4 illustrates a simple PERT network that might be used for such a project as building a house. Although an actual PERT network would normally be far too complex and unwieldy for such a small project, this figure provides an example of the network. The events are numbered for purposes of identification. The network not only identifies all events but also establishes a relationship among them. For example, Event 3 in Figure 7–4 cannot be completed before Event 2; and Event 8 must be finished before Event 10 can be started.

Relationships among the events are determined.

Once the PERT network is constructed, attention is focused on time estimates. Quite often the people responsible for each activity assist in determining optimistic, most likely, and pessimistic time estimates for accomplishing their respective activities. These estimates are then used to compute the *expected time* for each activity. The equation for this is:

Expected time can be calculated.

$$t_E = \frac{t_o + 4t_m + t_p}{6},$$

where: t_E = Expected time
t_o = Optimistic time
t_m = Most likely time
t_p = Pessimistic time.

Figure 7–5 illustrates a PERT network with the three estimates for each activity and the expected time (expressed in weeks, directly below each activity estimate in parentheses). For example, the expected time between Events 1 and 2 is:

Figure 7–4 Simple PERT Network

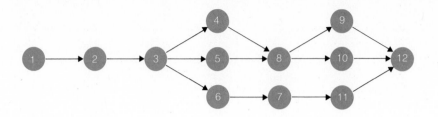

1. Begin House
2. Install Basement
3. Erect Frame
4. Put in Floors
5. Put on Roof
6. Put Brick around Bottom of House
7. Finish Upper Outside Part of House
8. Wire Inside
9. Install Electric Heating Unit
10. Install Electric Kitchen Appliances
11. Put in Doors and Cabinets
12. Complete House

$$t_E = \frac{8 + 4(10) + 12}{6}$$

$$t_E = 10 \text{ weeks.}$$

The critical path is the longest path.

For control purposes, it is now possible to determine the *critical path,* which is the sequence of activities and events that is longer than any other. In Figure 7–5, only five possible paths through the network exist. Along with their expected times, they are:

Path	Expected Times	Total
1–2–3–6–11–14	10.0 + 5.0 + 6.0 + 13.8 + 12.0	46.8
1–2–3–7–11–14	10.0 + 5.0 + 5.2 + 14.8 + 12.0	47.0
1–2–4–8–12–14	10.0 + 2.0 + 15.0 + 8.0 + 6.0	41.0
1–2–4–9–12–14	10.0 + 2.0 + 10.3 + 7.0 + 6.0	35.3
1–2–5–10–13–14	10.0 + 2.2 + 18.0 + 10.0 + 4.0	44.2

Path 1–2–3–7–11–14 is the critical path, since it is longer than any other.

The final component that must be considered is *slack,* the time difference between scheduled completion and each of the paths. If, for example, the project in Figure 7–5 had to be completed within fifty-two weeks, all the paths would have slack. On the other hand, if the completion date were forty weeks, four of the paths would have negative slack and would have to be shortened if the schedule were to be met. There are a number of ways of doing this. Richard J. Hopeman lists these as follows:

Figure 7–5 PERT Network with Time

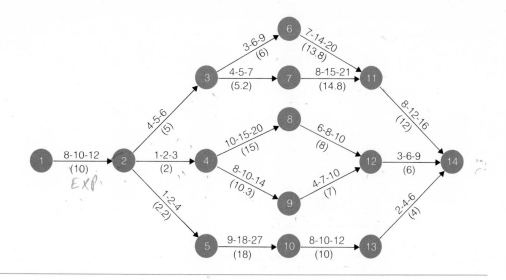

1. *The expected time for particular activities may be reduced, if possible.*
2. *Men, machines, materials, and money can be transferred from slack paths to the critical path or near-critical paths.*
3. *Some activities may be eliminated from the project.*
4. *Additional men, machines, materials, and money may be allocated to the critical path or near-critical paths.*
5. *Some of the activities which are normally sequential may be done in parallel.*[6]

Perhaps the major advantage of PERT is that it forces managers to plan. In addition, because of the times assigned to each activity, it provides a basis for identifying critical areas and correcting or monitoring them. PERT's disadvantages are also clear: PERT is practical only for nonrecurring undertakings, and it must be possible to assign times to the events despite the fact that the entire project is new to the company. In addition, some managers criticize PERT's emphasis on time without consideration to cost. As a result, in recent years there has been the development of PERT/COST, in which costs are applied to activities in the network.

Milestone Scheduling Although PERT is useful for sophisticated projects, it is often abandoned as the undertaking comes to a close and complexity declines. Since PERT can help integrate and simultaneously analyze thousands of activities, it is not surprising that less complex control techniques can be more economically employed as a project winds down. One of these is milestone scheduling, an approach used by the

Milestone scheduling is a useful technique for less complex projects.

---

[6] Richard J. Hopeman, *Production: Concepts, Analysis, Control,* 3d ed. (Columbus, Ohio: Charles E. Merrill Publishing, 1976), p. 343.

Figure 7–6 Simplified Milestone Schedule

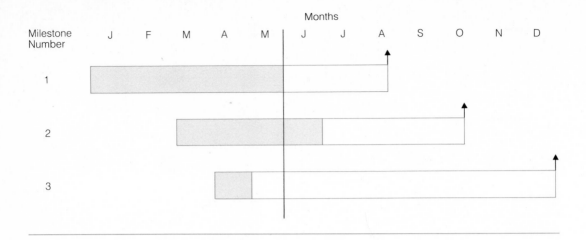

National Aeronautics and Space Administration (NASA) in the management of the Apollo Program.[7]

Milestone scheduling, a schedule and control procedure, employs bar charts to monitor progress. In this way, the manager can determine which segments of the undertaking are ahead of schedule, on time, or behind schedule. The technique is very similar to that of the Gantt chart, but the Gantt chart is used exclusively for production activities. Milestone scheduling, on the other hand, can be employed for virtually any undertaking.

Figure 7–6 shows three milestones. The first was begun in January, is scheduled for completion at the end of August, and is on time. The second was begun in March, is scheduled for completion in October, and is currently a month ahead of expectations. The third was begun in April, is scheduled for completion in December, and is currently running a month behind expectations. Milestone scheduling allows the manager to see a program in its simpler parts, thereby providing more effective control than sophisticated techniques.

CONTROLLING OVERALL PERFORMANCE

Most of the techniques discussed thus far are useful in controlling specific activities, but they do not measure overall performance. Several tools are used for evaluating total accomplishments. Among them are profit and loss, return on investment, key area control, and auditing.

---

[7] *Program Scheduling and Review Handbook,* NHB2330.1 (Washington, D.C.: National Aeronautics and Space Administration, October 1965).

Figure 7–7 Computation of Return on Investment

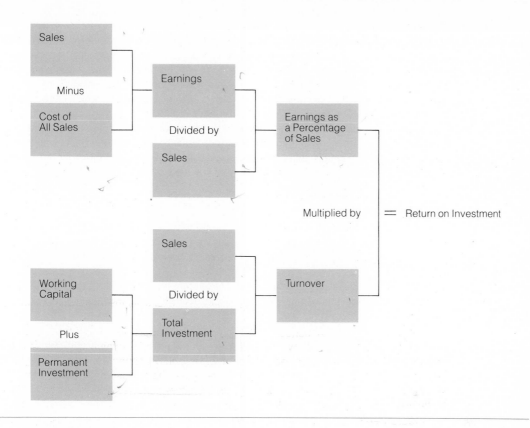

Profit and Loss

Perhaps the most commonly employed overall control is the income statement, which shows all revenues and expenses for the particular period of operation and provides a basis for comparing actual and expected results. Primary concern naturally goes to the basic question of whether or not the firm finished in the black, but it is also possible to ascertain whether and where the firm went wrong during the period, thereby establishing a basis for corrective action. In particular, the company can analyze the income statement in detail, noting how much each unit's operating expense has increased over the last year and determining whether the expenditures of each were justified or are in need of control during the next fiscal period. Similarly, it is possible to compare the profits (and losses) of operating divisions to see which was the most successful and why.

Return on Investment

Another widely used control technique is that of *return on investment (ROI),* which measures how well a firm is performing with the assets at its command. The method for computing ROI is presented in Figure 7–7.

The ROI technique is favorably viewed by many companies because it answers a basic question: How well are we doing with what we have? After all, a firm with $4 million in profits is far ahead of one with $10,000 in profits. However, if the former company has a total investment of $10 billion but the latter has one of only $10,000, the smaller firm is doing far better than the larger in terms of overall performance. According to the ROI approach, profits are relative and efficiency is of major importance.

The ROI concept need not be restricted to overall company results. It can be brought down to the divisional product level by way of measuring how well each division is doing. By comparing results with expectations, problem areas can be pinpointed for control purposes. The important thing to remember about ROI is that a good return will vary by industry. Therefore, results should be judged only in comparison with the competition. Also, exclusive reliance on this technique can lead to preoccupation with financial factors.[8] For this reason, it is advantageous to supplement profit and/or ROI with other overall control techniques, such as key area control.

Key Area Control

General Electric provides a good illustration of a firm employing *key area control*. For more than twenty years, this company has measured results in eight areas: profitability, market position, productivity, product leadership, personnel development, employee attitudes, public responsibility, and integration of short- and long-range goals. GE has not been able to develop the desired measurements for all of these areas, but by concentrating attention on them it has been able to obtain an appraisal of overall performance.

It is interesting to note that GE prefers to use profitability rather than ROI. In recent years, some financial experts have supported this approach, arguing that the final criterion of success is always profit, whatever the firm's efficiency. It is certainly true that only one of General Electric's eight key areas relates directly to profit. The remainder are related to environmental factors (political, economic, and social) vital to overall control, as the following descriptions illustrate:

Profitability. Total profits after all expenses, including cost of capital, are deducted.

Market Position. Share of the market is one of the key criteria here. In addition, the company attempts to measure customer satisfaction and to discover what the consumer wants but is not getting.

Productivity. Goods and services produced and sold are compared with the inputs necessary to arrive at some measure of productivity.

Product Leadership. Includes market position, innovation, and the ability to take advantage of new ideas in producing successful new products.

Personnel Development. The key criterion employed here is whether or not people are available when needed. Is there an adequate supply of manpower for meeting new and complex assignments in addition to filling vacancies?

Employee Attitudes. Absenteeism, labor turnover, and safety records are some of the criteria employed to evaluate attitudes. Another is the use of employee surveys.

---

[8] For example, for years Du Pont would not approve a new product program yielding less than a 20 percent ROI. As a result, Du Pont passed up xerography and the Land (Polaroid) camera. See "Lighting a Fire under the Sleeping Giant," *Business Week,* September 12, 1970, pp. 40–41.

Public Responsibility. Attention in this area is focused on many groups, including employees, customers, and the local community. In each case, indices have been developed to evaluate how well the company is doing.

Integration of Short- and Long-Range Goals. By encouraging formulation of long-range planning, the company ensures that short-run goals reflect these long-range objectives.

The GE approach is only one of many that can be employed for key area control. However, it emphasizes the importance of determining major criteria and monitoring performance in accord with the results obtained. No organization can maintain control of every aspect of operation. Instead, it must identify those that provide a basic picture of how well things are going and abide by the feedback obtained. Some organizations rely upon various forms of auditing to help perform this function.

Auditing

Hearing the word *audit,* an individual may immediately think of a public accounting firm. However, three basic types of audits are useful for overall control: external audits, internal audits, and management audits.

External Audit An *external audit* is conducted by accountants from outside the firm. It entails the examination and evaluation of the firm's financial transactions and accounts. This audit is generally performed by a certified public accounting firm, which expresses its opinion of the hiring company's financial statements in the areas of fairness, consistency, and conformity with the accepted principles of accounting. Usually this audit entails a detailed verification of all important balance sheet items with a view toward ascertaining whether the major assets, liabilities, and capital accounts are being accurately reported. The CPA firm does not delve into such nonfinancial areas as evaluating plans, policies, and procedures. However, when one realizes that the auditors will only certify accounts that are in order, it is evident that they provide an indirect control over all operations.

External audits are conducted by outside accounting people

Internal Audit An *internal audit* is conducted by the organization's own staff specialists. In essence, the auditing team examines and evaluates the firm's operations, determining where things have gone well and where corrective action is needed. Generally, much of the auditors' work is restricted to the financial area, but this need not be the case. They can also be useful in evaluating nonquantitative areas. In this kind of review, the internal audit goes further than its external counterpart and approaches what is commonly known as the management audit. Many firms have found in recent years that these staff specialists often can be quicker, cheaper, and more effective than external auditors.[9]

Internal audits are conducted by company personnel.

Management Audit A *management audit* picks up where a financial audit leaves off. Sometimes the audit is conducted by the firm itself, in which case it is known as a *self-audit,* an approach first advocated back in the 1930s.[10]

The purpose of the self-audit is to examine the company's position on a periodic basis, often every two, three, or five years. By studying the market trends, technological changes, and political and social factors affecting the industry, the company can construct a forecast of the external environment.

Some management audits are carried out by the firm itself.

---

[9] Robert E. Kelley, "Should You Have an Internal Consultant?" *Harvard Business Review,* November–December 1977, pp. 110–120.

[10] Billy E. Goetz, *Management Planning and Control* (New York: McGraw-Hill, 1949), p. 167.

Next, the audit turns to the firm itself. How well has it maintained its industry position? What is the competitive outlook? How do the customers feel about the firm's products? Answers to these questions help relate the company to its industry.

On the basis of the results, the firm can examine overall objectives and policies; and future and continuing programs, procedures, personnel, management, and financial positions can be put into clearer focus. If the self-audit is continued, the auditors' attention moves from the macro- to the micro-level; eventually all segments and activities of the company are analyzed. But this concept of continuation points toward the biggest problem of the self-audit: Many firms simply do not or cannot find time to conduct one. Furthermore, those who do have found very real dangers associated with using their own employees, from whatever level or levels. Bias, lack of competence to judge, inability to gain information from noncooperating individuals, intrafirm politics that lead to contradictory information, and stresses exerted on the auditors are among the common hazards self-auditors experience.

Others are conducted by outside organizations.

One way of overcoming this problem is to employ an external management audit such as that conducted by the American Institute of Management. Founded a number of years ago by Jackson Martindell, the institute uses a list of 301 questions to rate companies in the areas of fiscal policies, health of earnings, fairness to stockholders, research and development, sales vigor, economic function, directors, corporate structure, executive ability, and production efficiency.[11] Each of the ten areas is assigned a point value, with 3,500 of the 10,000 possible points allotted to managerial elements. To obtain a rating of "excellent," a company must receive 7,500 points.

The AIM audit is only one technique for conducting a management audit. Many others are available, from the approach recommended by W. T. Greenwood[12] for evaluating the overall firm to the one employed by the United States Department of Defense in evaluating companies bidding on major defense contracts. It appears that the future will see even greater interest in this area, for management consulting and accounting audit firms have found management audits to be an attractive area for expansion for a number of years now.[13] This is not surprising, though it is a rather new phenomenon. But these consulting firms are taking what is actually a small step from their current activities to management auditing. Perhaps the future will see the development of a certified management audit analogous to the current independent certified accounting audit.

SUMMARY

In this chapter the controlling process has been examined. The three basic steps in this process are the establishment of standards, the comparison of performance with these standards, and the correction of deviations. The key to the entire process rests on effective feedback.

In attaining feedback, the manager can use various control techniques. Some of the more traditional include budgeting, break-even analysis, and personal observation. Some of the more specialized entail information design and time-event analyses, such as PERT and milestone scheduling. Since these analytic techniques are not designed to

---

[11] Jackson Martindell, *The Scientific Appraisal of Management* (New York: Harper & Bros., 1950), and *The Appraisal of Management* (New York: Harper & Bros., 1962).

[12] W. T. Greenwood, *A Management Audit System,* rev. ed. (Carbondale, Ill.: School of Business, Southern Illinois University, 1967).

[13] See "Should CPAs Be Management Consultants?" *Business Week,* April 18, 1977, pp. 70, 73.

control overall performance, the manager needing overall performance control can simply turn to such other techniques as profit and loss, return on investment, key area control, and auditing.

REVIEW AND STUDY QUESTIONS

1. What are the three basic steps in the controlling process? Describe each.
2. Why is feedback so important for effective control?
3. What are the requirements for an effective control system? List and explain some of them in your own words.
4. Of what value is budgeting in the controlling process? Does budgeting lead to inflexibility? Explain.
5. How can the break-even point assist the manager in controlling operations? Explain, incorporating the following terms into your discussion: unit price, total fixed cost, and variable cost per unit.
6. What is information design? How is it of value to the manager?
7. Why is PERT a useful control technique? As you explain, incorporate the following terms into your discussion: events, activities, expected time, and critical path.
8. Why is return on investment so widely used as an overall control technique? Is it better than a profit and loss approach? Explain.
9. What is key area control? What are some of the areas used by General Electric in controlling its operations? Explain the importance of each as you would expect it to be used by GE.
10. How useful are external audits in the control process? Internal audits? Management audits? Which do you think is best? Why?

SELECTED REFERENCES

Barrett, M. E., and Fraser, L. B. III. "Conflicting Roles in Budgeting for Operations." *Harvard Business Review,* July–August 1977, pp. 137–146.

Buchele, R. B. "How to Evaluate a Firm." *California Management Review,* Fall 1962, pp. 5–17.

"Consultants Move to the Executive Suite." *Business Week,* November 7, 1977, pp. 76, 79.

Cowen, S. S.; Dean, B. V.; and Lohrasbi, A. "Zero Base Budgeting as a Management Tool." *MSU Business Topics,* Spring 1978, pp. 29–39.

Dean, B. V., and Cowen, S. S. "Zero-Base Budgeting in the Private Sector." *Business Horizons,* August 1979, pp. 73–83.

Dirsmith, M. W., and Jablonsky, S. F. "Zero-Base Budgeting as a Management Technique and Political Strategy." *Academy of Management Journal,* October 1979, pp. 555–565.

Drucker, Peter F. *Management: Tasks, Responsibilities, Practices.* New York: Harper & Row, 1974, chap. 39.

Farney, D. "Zero-Base Budgeting, a Pet Carter Project, Is Off to a Slow Start." *Wall Street Journal,* December 19, 1977, p. 16.

Gibbons, C. C. "The Psychology of Budgeting." *Business Horizons,* June 1972, pp. 47–58.

Giglioni, G. B., and Bedeian, Arthur G. "A Conspectus of Management Control Theory: 1900–1972." *Academy of Management Journal,* June 1974, pp. 292–305.

Kelley, R. E. "Should You Have an Internal Consultant?" *Harvard Business Review,* November–December 1978, pp. 110–120.

Koontz, Harold, and Bradspies, R. W. "Managing through Feedforward Control." *Business Horizons,* June 1972, pp. 25–36.

Marcus, S., and Walters, K. D. "Assault on Managerial Autonomy." *Harvard Business Review,* January–February 1978, pp. 58–65.

Martindell, Jackson. *The Appraisal of Management.* New York: Harper & Row, 1962.

Schonberger, R. J. "Custom-Tailored PERT/CPM Systems." *Business Horizons,* December 1972, pp. 64–66.

Searby, F. W. "Return to Return on Investment." *Harvard Business Review,* March–April 1975, pp. 113–119.

"Should CPAs Be Management Consultants?" *Business Week,* April 18, 1977, pp. 70, 73.

Suver, J. D., and Brown, R. D. "Where Does Zero-Base Budgeting Work?" *Harvard Business Review,* November–December 1977, pp. 76–84.

Tannenbaum, A. S. *Control in Organizations.* New York: McGraw-Hill, 1968.

CASE: Safety Margins

Anne Marie Mosolini had been with the Widget Works Company for only a couple of months, but already she could tell that the job was to her liking. One of the things she enjoyed most was the rapid responsibility increases that came her way. For example, she had been told to make up a departmental budget for the next fiscal year. After poring over past budgetary requests and talking to her subordinates, Mosolini submitted her proposal. The next step in the process was to meet with her superior and defend the requests. Then her proposal would be sent up the line. Her staff had told Mosolini that top management seldom cut back any requests. The key hurdle was getting one's superior to approve a recommended budget.

As a result, Mosolini spent most of the morning preparing herself for this meeting. She felt that everything in her request was essential, and she wanted to be able to defend each item. The meeting, however, did not go according to her expectations. Her superior, Blake Cotton, began:

"Anne Marie, I've examined your budget request and would like to talk to you about a few items. For example, you estimate $77,612 under administrative expenses."

"Yes sir. I can show you the worksheet I used, if you'd like."

"Oh, that's not necessary. The only reason the figure caught my eye was that it was such an odd amount. Look, let's round it off to $80,000."

"Okay."

"And there are a few other budget estimates I see here that are also in need of rounding, so I'll just change them also."

"How much of an estimate does that make it?"

"Exactly $240,000."

"Well, that's a little bit higher than what I need. Are you sure it's okay?"

"Sure, don't worry about it. You can never tell when something is going to cost a little bit more than you initially thought."

"Okay, Blake. It's all right with me if it's all right with you."

"Fine. And, oh, by the way, how did you arrive at these other estimates?"

"Well, I worked back from what I thought my department would be doing this fiscal year to how much it would cost to get this work done. There's a manual that was sent around to me, and I took my basic format from it."

"That certainly is one way to get a handle on it. But I'd suggest that you be sure to add some safety margins to each of your requests."

"Safety margins?"

"Sure, you know. A little something extra just in case things go wrong. Besides, you never know when management is going to cut around here, and it always pays to have asked for a little more than you need when that happens. Do you know what I mean?"

"I think so."

"Fine. Well here's your budget back. Besides the figure rounding, add in 10 percent across the board, and send it back in to me. I'll forward it from here."

Questions

1. Is Cotton right or wrong in suggesting that Mosolini change her budget requests? Explain.

2. How common do you think this kind of action is?

3. What are the dangers in overestimating budget requests? Be specific.

4. Why do you think this conversation occurred? Explain.

CASE: Efficiency vs. Profitability

Samuel Frenz was a product division manager at Darby Inc., a midwestern manufacturing firm. In the late 1960s, the Darby management decided to abandon its profitability control guideline and begin evaluating product divisions on the basis of return on investment. Management hoped to measure overall efficiency in this way.

The idea was fine with Frenz, and for the next decade his division's ROI rose from 12.3 percent to 15.7 percent. However, during the late 1970s the division began to encounter vigorous competition, and although the market for its product increased, Frenz had to spend more and more money on advertising and personal selling to maintain market share. The result was an eventual decline in his division's ROI, which had fallen to 13.7 percent by 1981. This in turn prompted comments from the top management, and Frenz was called into his boss's office:

"Sam, the board of directors has been reviewing product division ROI's, and yours is the only one that has declined. Quite frankly, the board is concerned."

"Well, I am too, but if that board thinks you can improve ROI in such a competitive industry, it is sitting up nights waiting for the tooth fairy. We have had to spend a lot of money on advertising and personal selling. I'd like to know one company with a better ROI than ours. Or one competitive division that can match mine."

"I understand. But the questions is, what are you going to do to improve your division's ROI?"

"I'd like to pose a different question. Why is the board evaluating my ROI? Don't those people know that when you get as large as we are, in as competitive an industry as this, ROI slips? Why don't they evaluate me on profitability? My profits are up over last year, but I can't hold my ROI performance at an all-time high."

"Do you want to write the board a letter outlining your proposal?"

"Well, I'm not in a position to tell you what to do. I'm the one on the carpet. What do you think would help me and the board get together on how we look at things?"

Questions

1. What are the advantages of using ROI as an overall control technique? What are the disadvantages?

2. Should the board switch back from ROI to profits? Give your reasoning.

3. How would you answer Frenz's last question? Explain, indicating why you would recommend switching to profitability or sticking with ROI.

CASE: *Doing It Yourself?*

The Canteran Corporation has a number of control problems. One is the continual increase in the cost of goods. During each of the last ten months the cost of scrap waste has increased by 3 to 4 percent. This is having a dampening effect on profits. Some of the first-line supervisors claim that the company needs more efficient machinery, but others feel that the workers are not cooperating in holding down scrap waste.

A second problem has to do with the computer, which was installed only nine months ago. Since the installation, more and more control reports have been computerized. Despite this information system improvement, many of the middle managers report that the weekly computer printouts they receive are not helping them understand how to better control departmental operations.

A third problem is the reorganization plan top management has been working on for the last six months. The company feels that if it can reorganize operations, greater internal efficiency will result. However, there are currently so many suggestions as to how to reorganize that the committee responsible for developing the plan is having trouble deciding how to process them to a point where they can be used and a decision made.

In an effort to resolve these three problems, the president of the company has been thinking about using a team of management consultants. This idea has won approval from everyone with whom the president has discussed it. However, some feel the firm should use in-house consultants, and others believe that management experts from outside should be employed. The three main arguments for the use of internal consultants are: (a) they know the operations of the firm, (b) it will cost less to employ them, and (c) if things do not work out well, in-house consultants will still be around and can do additional consultation. The arguments for the outside consultants are: (a) they can provide fresh insights to solving problems, (b) they will bring with them a wealth of experience from other firms, and (c) because this is what they do for a living, they are going to be more cost-effective than the in-house people.

The president has not made up his mind yet. He is certain that consultants are needed. But he must now decide whether to bring them in from the outside or have the company do the job itself.

Questions

1. What advantages are to be gained from a management audit? Explain.

2. Compare and contrast the value of inside and outside consultants to the Canteran Corporation, stating in your answer when and why each could be preferable.

3. What would you recommend that the president of Canteran do? Defend your answer.

CASE: The Dean's Dilemma

Things had certainly changed at State University. When Dean Williams had first come to the College of Business, life seemed much simpler. However, as inflation spiraled upward, the taxpayers of the state gave every indication that they were through pouring money into the university. As a result, the university administration announced a general tightening up. Departmental lines would be cut and hiring determined on a need basis. As if this were not enough, legislators began raising the question of faculty evaluations. How do we know we are getting our money's worth, they asked, if there is no evaluation process?

In response to the question, the university administration announced that it was going to look into the matter. Thereupon, all deans were asked to poll their colleges for the purpose of deciding what form of evaluation they felt was fair for judging performance. Two camps sprang up in the College of Business. The first wanted to evaluate teaching as the first criterion, with community affairs and research secondary. The other group wanted research as the primary judgment criterion and teaching and community affairs as secondary criteria. The positions could be summarized as follows:

Teaching as Primary

Position for: The university has been established by the people of this state to perform a specific service, namely the dissemination of knowledge to the students. This is the primary basis on which teachers should be evaluated. The evaluation process should take two paths: evaluations by the students in the classroom and evaluation by the department chairpersons on the basis of classroom observation.

Position against: Teaching is certainly important, but there is no way to judge truly effective performance. The students are going to be biased in their opinion, those receiving the highest grades being more positive in their comments about the instructors than those receiving the lowest grades. Thus the system encourages an easy grading policy. In addition, the chairpersons are incapable of judging all the people because they are not experts in all areas. For example, how can a management chairperson with an emphasis in organizational behavior judge a colleague teaching mathematical decision making? Teaching is valuable, but because it cannot be quantified, it should be discarded as a basis for evaluation.

Research as Primary

Position for: The only objective criterion available for judging teaching ability is research. A professor who conducts research is going to be better prepared than one who does not. In addition, the instructor has a responsibility to not only teach but enhance the reputation of the university, and this can be done most effectively through research. In short, "publish or perish" is the only way to improve the quality of education, and it should be the basis for all evaluations.

Position against: To engage in a policy of "publish or perish" is to get into the numbers game. In addition, how is one to evaluate the contribution of each article? And in the case of books, is not remuneration in the form of royalties sufficient? Why should people be promoted or receive high evaluation when all they are doing is enhancing their own financial positions? Research is important, but it must not be allowed to occupy a primary position.

Questions

1. How should faculty performance be evaluated? Explain.

2. In light of your answer to the above question, what kinds of measuring tools should a dean employ to ensure that a faculty is doing a good job? Explain in detail.

For a long time after World War II, the Swiss dominated the watch business. However, in the mid 1970s, after U.S. semiconductor technology helped usher in the era of the digital watch, this began to change. U.S. watchmakers were convinced that their technological edge would allow them to dominate the digital watch business, but they were wrong. Digitals have indeed captured a large share of the watch market, and analysts predict that by 1990 they will account for almost two-thirds of all watches sold in the world. But U.S. firms have found themselves unable to keep up. Some of the U.S. manufacturing firms have had trouble mastering the new technology required to produce these watches, and others have run into problems marketing the watches. Japanese and Hong Kong manufacturers have a lead in the market, and the Swiss are fighting to keep up. Americans are now running a distant fourth. The following sections examine each of these countries in an effort to discover their relative strengths.

The Japanese

The Japanese are on the verge of becoming the world's leading watch manufacturers. In fact, a battle is shaping up, but it appears to be among Japanese firms themselves, not between Japan and the rest of the world. A price war has sprung up, with Hattori, Citizen, and Casio, the big three in watchmaking, as combatants. The 1979 Japanese market share accounted for by the three was as follows: Hattori, 39 percent; Citizen, 32 percent; and Casio, 12 percent. During 1979 the Japanese watchmakers boosted their share of the electronic quartz watch worldwide market to almost 21 percent, pulling just about even with the Swiss in this category.

Casio is the most dynamic of the big three. Lowering the price of its digitals, the company forced its two larger rivals to cut their prices in an effort to maintain market share. Casio's strategy appears clear-cut: Concentrate on the lower-priced end of the market and make profits through large-volume sales. Additionally, the firm feels that its capability in designing integrated circuits, the brains of the quartz electronic watch, will allow it to add new features which customers now seem to want—calendars, calculators, and alarms. Over 25 percent of Casio's watch sales are accounted for by the multifunctional models.

Hattori, famous for its Seiko brand watches, is also getting into lower-priced offerings, as is Citizen. Using its existing watch modules, the company has changed the cases, bands, and packaging and has cut its profit margins in order to lower the retail price. As Hattori and Citizen begin invading this lower-priced market niche, and Casio fights back, the world may find non-Japanese firms unable to compete.

The Swiss

In the late 1940s the Swiss watchmaking industry held 80 percent of the world market; that market had shrunk by the early 1980s to around 20 percent. Three factors have helped bring about this decline: revolutionary technology, an aggressive Japanese watchmaking industry, and a rise in the value of the Swiss franc. The Swiss franc, for example, rose from a U.S. value of 23 cents in 1971 to a high of 70 cents later in the decade before dropping back to 58 cents in the early 1980s. The rise in value has more than doubled the price of Swiss products in the dollar markets, including North and South America, the Middle East, and Southeast Asia. This price increase was devastating to the Swiss watchmakers, for these areas of the world account for around two-thirds of Swiss exports.

According to the experts, however, technology has been the biggest problem in the case of Switzerland. Many of today's customers want quartz electronic watches, in which the Swiss had the initial lead. In 1967 Swiss laboratories turned out a quartz analog watch whose electronics module surpassed the accuracy of the Bulova Accutron, then the most precise watch on the market. But Japan's Hattori took the market with its Seiko brand.

A similar situation occurred with the other type of quartz watch, the all-electronic version which used an electronic display to give the time in digits. The Swiss had one of these watches developed before any other models were on the market, but the marketers did not take the product seriously. As a result, they lost out first to the U.S. semiconductor manufacturers and then to the low-cost producers in Japan and Hong Kong.

The Swiss argue that they have not lost that great a segment of the market. In addition to the 53 million watches they manufactured at home in 1979, they also made 7 million watches in Swiss-owned factories abroad and exported movements and components to foreign companies to account for 21 million more. Their share is thus close to an actual 30 percent of the world's 275 million wristwatch market demand. Yet market-line problems seem to bode ill for the Swiss. For example, in 1976 only 4 percent of Swiss-produced watches were electronic. By 1979 the figure had risen only to 13 percent. Furthermore, in 1979 only one-quarter of the electronic modules were digital. The Swiss continue to state publicly that the market wants the traditional styling of quartz analog watches. Privately, however, the industry admits that the digital watch shows the greatest promise.

The Swiss realize that price will continue to be an important consideration. For this reason, despite the long Swiss resistance toward making watches with low-cost labor, Switzerland has moved some of its production to low-priced labor areas. Given the increase in demand for low-priced watches, Swiss watchmakers have had to realize that some manufacturing processes must be carried out in other countries. However, they intend to continue making elegant and expensive watches in Switzerland.

Hong Kong

In the early 1980s, the British Crown Colony of Hong Kong shipped more finished watches than any other country in the world; and analysts were uncertain whether or for how long that would continue to be so. Hong Kong companies are sometimes considered by the world business community to specialize in jumping from one business to another. For example, at the height of the Hong Kong market lead in watches in the early 1980s, some companies began building their own watch modules while others started converting their operations to the manufacture of home computers and handheld games.

The clear late-1970s and early-1980s fad was digital watches, and in 1979 British Crown Colony assemblers turned out 43 million of them. But while Hong Kong did export millions of mechanical and electronic watches (one-quarter of the world's output, in fact), most of the exports were inexpensive models, assembled simply from imported parts. As a result, some of these watches were claimed by Japanese, Swiss, or U.S. firms which either owned the operations outright or which held an interest in them via joint ventures with Hong Kong entrepreneurs. For example, Hattori assembles 25 percent of its Seiko watches in Hong Kong.

The biggest problem Hong Kong assemblers faced in the early 1980s was their eroding profit margin. In the late 1970s simple models that sold for $8 to $9 returned a profit of $2. But only a few years later, because of aggressive sales techniques and loft factories with low overhead, margins were down to 50 cents per watch. Market observers anticipated, if events continued on this course, a price war similar to the one that hit handheld calculators in the early to mid 1980s.

Hong Kong watchmakers prepared to handle this problem in several ways. Some began to import equipment that would enable them to make watch modules themselves. Others looked for opportunities to establish ties with Japanese, Swiss, or U.S. firms. Some began to set up their own after-sales service firms.

One of the most integrated manufacturers in Hong Kong is Unik Time Ltd., the largest digital watch producer in the colony and a subsidiary of Micro-Electronics Ltd. The latter owns a company in Santa Clara, California, where design and high technology work is done; it also has an arrangement for the assembly of its semiconductors in Canton and Shanghai in China. Micro-Electronics thus designs its watches in California, assembles the components in China, and mass produces the watches in Hong Kong.

One of the reasons analysts believe Hong Kong could survive in the watch business is because of its ability to produce straps, dials, and cases. While the easily assembled electronic works cost under $20, Hong Kong's support skills protect the colony from other cheap labor competitors like Taiwan and South Korea. However, even Hong Kong watchmakers have had to admit that there will always be a market for expensive Swiss watches. As one watch company official has noted, "Many people still feel that a watch has to have a 'Swiss' stamp in order for it to be good."

The Americans

Low-cost mechanical watches took a tremendous toll on such well-known U.S. watch firms as Benrus, Elgin, Hamilton, and Waltham. Digital imports drove U.S. electronics firms like Fairchild Camera & Instrument, Intel, Litronix, and Motorola right out of the watch business. And by the early 1980s, Texas Instruments (TI) and Timex Corporation were losing money in it. To put the situation bluntly, the entire U.S. watch industry was in the dumps as the 1980s began.

TI has had difficulty marketing its technology. In the beginning, its watch strategy was based on its ability to lead the downward price spiral of the digital. Following this approach, it undercut the price of Timex's mechanical watch line. The Texas firm developed a digital watch that could be made from TI-built parts on highly mechanized equipment and sold at a lower price than anything else on the market. By 1976 TI had introduced a $20 plastic-cased watch with a red digital display activated by push-buttons; a few months later it cut the price to $10. Unfortunately, while millions of customers did buy the watch, many were dissatisfied because of poor or unavailable service, malfunctioning pushbuttons, and displays that could not be read in bright sunlight.

Pushbutton watches began to be replaced by digitals that showed time continuously on liquid crystal displays (LCDs). TI had the basic patent for LCD watches, but it was not ready to mass produce the display or the necessary semiconductor device. Furthermore, advancing technology in large-scale integrated (LSI) circuits gave watchmakers the ability to add more and more features to digitals. TI, not believing that consumers wanted watches with alarms, stopwatches, or dual time-zone functions, fell behind.

TI was saying by 1981 that it was on a comeback trail. Seven of its thirteen basic watch models and more than half the watches it now sells come from offshore assemblers. Included in this product group are multiple-function watches, the fastest growing segment of the market. TI believes that its problems can be traced to poor forecasting of technology trends. But analysts think the problems went deeper; they argue that TI got out of touch with the consumer. Boardroom goals and directives were not in line with each other. The Texas Instruments of the early 1980s wanted to become a world leader in watches, but it had neither broadened nor updated its product line.

At the same time, Timex appeared to have another kind of problem—its shaky electronics technology. When the company was turning out 50 percent of all watches sold in the United States, Timex believed that the digital watch was an expensive gimmick which would never threaten the mechanical watch line. Even by the early 1970s, Timex was doing very little new-product work; nor did it have the machinery to tool up for change.

When Timex finally realized the role that digitals were going to play in the market, it had to rely exclusively on outside suppliers for the new technology. The company's hurry-up strategy showed through, and its digitals did not sell well. However, the firm kept on trying. In 1979, thanks to Timex's old reputation for quality and service, a 25 percent increase in TV advertising, and a strong consumer following, the company sold 10 percent of the 60 million digitals that were purchased worldwide. Other Timex lines, however, did not sell well; and the company's overall sales in units from 1975 through 1979 stayed at around 36 million. In the United States, Timex's market share has dropped to less than 33 percent—a far cry from the 50+ percent of the late 1960s.

In early 1980 the majority stockholder of this private company took over the reins of leadership, banking heavily at the outset on a new quartz analog watch line that would sell in the $40 to $60 range. At the same time, Timex began to diversify. In 1979 the company paid $8 million for General Electric's Telechron Division, reintroducing in 1980 GE's line of clocks and timers, redesigned and promoted under the Timex label. The firm also introduced a line of pocket watches and planned to lend its name to a line of watchbands. It intended to develop or acquire a higher-priced watch brand that would carve a niche for Timex in the upper end of the market. Another early-1980s development was the company's decision to manufacture 35-millimeter cameras for a tiny Atlanta company, Nimslo Technology, Inc., which developed the 3–D camera. Timex insiders further reported that the company had begun again to take defense contracts; and by 1981 Timex was producing gyroscopes and inertial navigation platforms for military aircraft.

Will the Timex strategy succeed? Will TI make a successful comeback? These questions are difficult to answer. However, one thing is certain. The two U.S. companies have their work cut out for them if they intend to stop the Japanese, the Swiss, and the Hong Kong assemblers from wresting the remainder of the market from their grip.

Questions

1. In your own words, describe the conditions that currently exist in the watchmaking business.

2. If Texas Instruments and Timex hope to come back, how important will strategic planning be for them? Make your answer as complete as you can.

3. How can the organizing and controlling concepts discussed in Chapters 5, 6, and 7 of this text be of value to the two firms in their efforts? Explain.

PART   *3*

The goal of Part 3 is to familiarize the reader with some of the basic ideas and concepts of the quantitative, or management science, school. As with the management process and the behavioral schools, the quantitative school has not reached universal agreement regarding its domain. One can argue with all but the most purely quantitative subjects in this section simply by raising the question of whether the material fits into one of the other schools' parameters. A good example is the topic of decision making. Both the process and the behavioral schools would claim that this area is within their domain, and there can be no argument with that contention: Decision making knows no bounds. It is an integral part of every manager's job. However, decision making is discussed in Part 3 because the entire area of modern quantitative decision making is of major importance to an understanding of the management sciences.

Chapter 8 examines the quantitative decision-making process, with emphasis on the

THE QUANTITATIVE SCHOOL OF MANAGEMENT

point that this process is certainly not a mere mechanical function. Personal values are involved in choosing among alternatives, and to picture management scientists as cold, calculating mathematicians is erroneous. Chapter 9 extends the concept of choosing among alternatives by examining some of the important tools and techniques of operations research that are currently being employed by modern managers.

Finally, Chapter 10 discusses information systems and decision making. Once information is analyzed, it must be transmitted to the appropriate manager for action. This requires a well designed information system, often complemented by a computer; and the chapter examines the relationship of the information system; the computer, and the quantitative school of management. Chapter 10 also views the link between the quantitative school and the behavioral school. In fact, the closing segment of this chapter is dedicated to an analysis of some behavioral effects of information systems.

FUNDAMENTALS OF DECISION MAKING

GOALS OF THE CHAPTER

The goal of this chapter is to examine the fundamentals of decision making. A review of the steps in the process will be followed first by an analysis of the impact of personal values on the decision-making process. Next, the types of decisions and the conditions under which they are made —that is, certainty, risk, and uncertainty —will be scrutinized. Finally, three of the more common decision-making techniques —marginal analysis, financial analysis, and the Delphi technique —will be reviewed in detail.

When you have finished this chapter, you should be able to:

1. Define the steps in the decision-making process.
2. Discuss what is meant by the term rationality and relate its importance in understanding the decision-making process.
3. Explain how values affect decision making.
4. Outline a classification system for examining all decisions, including organizational and personal decisions, basic and routine decisions, and programmed and nonprogrammed decisions.
5. Relate the three basic conditions under which decisions are made.
6. Discuss the role of objective and subjective probability in decision making.
7. Describe the benefit of marginal analysis.
8. Explain the importance of financial analysis in decision making.
9. Describe how the Delphi technique works.

DECISION-MAKING PROCESS

Decision making
involves
choosing
from among
alternatives.

Decision making is commonly defined as choosing from among alternatives. Herbert A. Simon has identified the process as searching the environment for conditions calling for a decision; inventing, developing, and analyzing the available courses of action; and choosing one of the particular courses of action.[1] However, this three-step process, consisting of intelligence, design, and choice activities, is only one of many decision-making methods.

A second and more detailed method is the following:

1. *Identify the problem.*
2. *Diagnose the situation.*
3. *Collect and analyze data relevant to the issue.*
4. *Ascertain solutions that may be used in solving the problem.*
5. *Analyze these alternative solutions.*
6. *Select the approach that appears most likely to solve the problem.*
7. *Implement it.*

Regardless of the specific process employed by the manager, some formal diagnosis must be conducted, alternative solutions formulated and analyzed, and a decision made regarding the approach to take. This is as true in the development of strategic, intermediate, and operational plans as it is in solving simple job problems.

One of the primary characteristics of this entire process is its dynamism, the steps being implemented within a time framework. The past is the time dimension in which the problem is identified and diagnosed. The present is the point at which the alternatives are formulated and a choice made regarding the plan of action. The future is the time period during which the decision will be implemented and an evaluation made regarding the outcome.

RATIONALITY AND THE MEANS-END HIERARCHY

There are
degrees of
rationality
in decision
making.

Not all decisions made by workers are rational. Some are nonrational; others are irrational. The same is true of managers. In addition, degrees of rationality exist. A man lost in the desert may wander in circles. His solution may be wrong, but is it not rational? Virtually everyone in this situation walks around in circles. This raises the question of precisely what is meant by the term *rational*. Some people assign the term to actions that attain a given end. In this case, the man in the desert is not acting rationally because his actions are not leading him out of his dilemma. Other individuals feel that *rational* refers to a choice of the best alternative of those available. In this case, the man is probably acting rationally because of the alternatives facing him. He may conclude that no one knows he is lost, so he cannot rely on a search party's finding him. His only salvation rests in saving himself by, for example, finding the nearest oasis. The only way to do this is to start walking and hope to locate one before too long.

It is
difficult to
separate
means
from ends.

Some decision theorists believe that rational decisions are forthcoming if appropriate means for reaching desired goals are chosen. However, it is often difficult to separate means from ends, for every end is really just a means to another end. This is what is known as the *means-end hierarchy*. When the man in the desert finds the oasis, he will remain there, using it as his base of operations (means) until he can establish contact with the

---

[1] Herbert A. Simon, *The New Science of Management Decision* (New York: Harper & Row, 1960), p. 2.

---

outside world and have help sent to him (end). The plane that takes him out (means) will allow him to return to his old way of life (end).

Rationality, within the decision-making framework, is a relative term—dependent upon the situation and the individuals involved. An objectively rational *organizational* decision designed to ensure the company a profitable year may be welcomed by the employees until they learn that it calls for the elimination of all Christmas bonuses; then it is seen as a nonrational or irrational decision. Likewise, *personally* rational decisions such as the establishment of thirty-minute coffee breaks to eliminate escessive fatigue may be favorably viewed by the workers but seen by the management as disastrous to overall company efficiency. One reason for the imprecision in decision making is the personal values of the people involved.

PERSONAL VALUES AND DECISION MAKING

All managers bring a certain set of values to the workplace. These values can be broken down and applied to managers on an individual basis. Edward Spranger identified six such values: theoretical, economic, aesthetic, social, political, and religious. The description of each is presented in Table 8–1. When William D. Guth and Renato Tagiuri employed this classification scheme with high-level United States executives attending the Advanced Management Program of the Harvard Business School Seminar, they obtained the following average profile:[2]

Value	Score
Economic	45
Theoretical	44
Political	44
Religious	39
Aesthetic	35
Social	33
	240

The scores represent the importance of the values as seen by the average manager in the study.

The economic, theoretical, and political scores seem justifiably high, for the top manager must be interested in efficiency and profit (economic), possess conceptual skills required for endeavors such as long-range planning (theoretical), and be able to get along with people and convince them to work together as a team (political). However, the researchers also found that the profiles varied considerably in regard to religious, aesthetic, and social values, indicating that one must not be too hasty in trying to construct a stereotype of the typical executive.

The personal values of each manager can have a significant effect on the decision-making process. This is one reason that social action programs, for example, internally generated and heavily funded by the company itself, have been undertaken by many

---

[2] William D. Guth and Renato Tagiuri, "Personal Values and Corporate Strategy," *Harvard Business Review,* September–October 1965, p. 126. The questionnaire was designed to yield 240 points distributed over the six values.

Table 8-1 Spranger's Value Orientations

1. The *theoretical* man is primarily interested in the discovery of truth, in the systematic ordering of his knowledge. In pursuing this goal he typically takes a "cognitive" approach, looking for identities and differences, with relative disregard for the beauty or utility of objects, seeking only to observe and to reason. His interests are empirical, critical, and rational. He is an intellectual. Scientists or philosophers are often of this type (but they are not the only ones).

2. The *economic* man is primarily oriented toward what is useful. He is interested in the practical affairs of the business world; in the production, marketing, and consumption of goods; in the use of economic resources; and in the accumulation of tangible wealth. He is thoroughly "practical" and fits well the stereotype of the American businessman.

3. The *aesthetic* man finds his chief interest in the artistic aspects of life, although he need not be a creative artist. He values form and harmony. He views experience in terms of grace, symmetry, or harmony. Each single event is savored for its own sake.

4. The essential value for the *social* man is love of people—the altruistic or philanthropic aspect of love. The social man values people as ends, and tends to be kind, sympathetic, unselfish. He finds those who have strong theoretical, economic, and aesthetic orientations rather cold. Unlike the political type, the social man regards love as the most important component of human relationships. In its purest form the social orientation is selfless and approaches the religious attitude.

5. The *political* man is characteristically oriented toward power, not necessarily in politics, but in whatever area he functions. Most leaders have a high power orientation. Competition plays a large role in all life, and many writers have regarded power as the most universal motive. For some men, this motive is uppermost, driving them to seek personal power, influence, and recognition.

6. The *religious* man is one "whose mental structure is permanently directed to the creation of the highest and absolutely satisfying value experience." The dominant value for him is unity. He seeks to relate himself to the universe in a meaningful way and has a mystical orientation.

Source: Adapted by permission of the *Harvard Business Review*. Excerpt from "Personal Values and Corporate Strategy" by William D. Guth and Renato Tagiuri, September–October 1965, p. 126. Copyright © 1965 by the President and Fellows of Harvard College, all rights reserved.

Managers' personal values influence their decision making.

business firms in recent years.[3] Managers are much more oriented toward social responsibility than they were a decade ago. However, no one should think this means the firm is going to expend all its energies on such programs. In fact, when researchers in one study asked chief executive officers to rank their responsibilities to society, stockholders, employees, customers, and creditors, they received the results shown in Table 8-2.

Business executives reported an interest in fulfilling their social responsibility, but they were not going to put such programs ahead of their obligations to the stockholders. Again, personal values play an important role in the decision-making process.

[3] See, for example, Fred Luthans, Richard M. Hodgetts, and Kenneth R. Thompson, *Social Issues in Business,* 3d ed. (New York: Macmillan, 1980), chaps. 6, 8, and 10.

Table –2 *Response by Top Company Executive to the Question:*
To Whom Do You Owe Your Greatest Responsibility?

Interest Group	Relative Ranking
Stockholders	1
Employees	2
Customers	3
Society	4
Creditors	5

Source: Reprinted by permission from Charles P. Edmonds III and John H. Hand, "What Are the Real Long-run Objectives of Business?" *Business Horizons,* December 1976, p. 77.

TYPES OF DECISIONS

Managers make many decisions, and in order to obtain a clear understanding of the decision-making process, a classification system is useful. Three such systems are available, each based on different types of decisions. They are organizational and personal decisions, basic and routine decisions, and programmed and nonprogrammed decisions.

Organizational and Personal Decisions

Organizational decisions are those made by executives in their official managerial roles. The adoption of strategies, the setting of objectives, and the approval of plans are a few examples. The implementation of such decisions is often delegated to others; thus, the decisions require the support of many people throughout the organization if they are to be properly implemented.

Personal decisions relate to the manager as an individual, not as a member of the organization. Such decisions are not delegated to others because their implementation does not require the support of organizational personnel. Deciding to retire, taking a job offer from a competitive firm, or slipping out and spending the afternoon on the golf course are all personal decisions.

Although it is possible to distinguish between organizational and personal decisions according to definition, in practice it is not. For example, when a company president who believes in social activism decides to make a concerted effort to hire the hardcore unemployed, a personal decision is translated into an organizational one. Many decisions made by managers have both organizational and personal elements in them.

Organizational decisions can be delegated to others.

Personal decisions are not delegated.

Basic and Routine Decisions

A second approach is to classify decisions into basic and routine categories. *Basic decisions* can be viewed as much more important than routine ones. They involve long-range commitments, large expenditures of funds, and such a degree of importance that a serious mistake might well jeopardize the well-being of the company. Selection of a product line, the choice of a new plant site, or a decision to integrate vertically by purchasing sources of raw materials to complement the current production facilities are all basic decisions.

Routine decisions are often repetitive in nature, having only a minor impact on the firm.

Basic decisions can have major organizational effects.

For this reason, most organizations have formulated a host of procedures to guide the manager in handling them. Some individuals in the organization, who spend most of their time making routine decisions, find these guidelines very useful.

At this point it may be helpful to define procedures and policies. *Procedures* are guides to action. Often referred to as types of plans, they relate the chronological steps entailed in attaining some objective. Sometimes procedures are drawn up for use in a particular department. In a retail store, for example, five steps may be involved in the return of faulty merchandise; the first would involve making sure that the goods were not damaged by the buyer, and the last would be the department manager's approval. Other procedures, such as a discrepancy in a paycheck, are organizational. The employee must tell the payroll department to have the pay recalculated and, if there has been an error, must return the incorrect check for a revised one. Procedures are useful in helping with routine decisions because they break processes down into steps.

Policies, often confused with procedures, are also types of plans, but they are guides to thinking as well as to action. As a result, they do not tell a manager how to do something; they merely channel the decision making along a particular line by delimiting the span of consideration. For example, a department may have a policy of hiring only those with a college education. However, how does one define a college education? If the manager is willing to accept one year of job experience and three years of formal college as the equivalent of a four-year diploma, more than mere action is involved; the manager has had to think to determine the equivalency line. The manager knows no one without a college degree or its equivalent (action) is acceptable and can confine all energies to evaluating the latter cases (thinking). In this case, a policy is helpful to the manager because it limits the number of people eligible for a job in the department. Policies are also useful at the organizational level. For example, a firm may have a policy of setting up new plants in cities with a population of at least 100,000. This is a guide to action because it limits the number of eligible cities. It is also a guide to thinking because now the executive must decide in which particular city to build the new plant. Policies play an important role in handling basic decisions.

Programmed and Nonprogrammed Decisions

Herbert A. Simon, borrowing from computer technology, has proposed the classification of decisions into the areas of programmed and nonprogrammed. These two types can be viewed on a continuum, programmed being at one end and nonprogrammed at the other. *Programmed decisions* correspond roughly to the routine decisions, with procedures playing a key role. *Nonprogrammed decisions* are similar to the category of basic decisions, being highly novel, important, and unstructured in nature. Policies play an important role in making these decisions. The value of viewing decision making in this manner is that it permits a clearer understanding of the methods that accompany each type.

DECISION-MAKING CONDITIONS

There are three possible conditions under which decisions can be made: certainty, risk, and uncertainty.

Certainty

Certainty is present when the manager knows exactly what will happen. Although *certainty decisions* constitute only a small percentage of managerial decisions, they do occur. For example, $10,000 invested in a government note for one year at 6 percent will return

$600 in interest. Although it can be argued that there is a degree of risk in everything, including government notes, for all practical purposes this investment can be labeled as a sure thing.

Likewise, the allocation of resources to various product lines often constitutes decision making under conditions of certainty. The manager knows what physical resources are on hand and the amount of time it will take to process them into finished goods. If there are two or three processes available, the manager can conduct a cost-contribution study to determine which is most profitable (if profit is the decision guideline) or which will produce the good most quickly (if speed is of the essence). In dealing with fixed quantities such as raw materials and machines, the manager is often making decisions under certainty, the prime goal being that of determining the desired objective. Once this is accomplished, the manager can simply evaluate the alternatives and choose the best one.

Certainty is present when the manager knows the outcome of each alternative.

Risk

Most of the manager's decisions are *risk decisions;* that is, some information is available, but it is insufficient to answer all questions about the outcome. One method often used to assist the decision maker is that of probability estimates.

Risk is present if the manager has only partial information for evaluating the outcome of each alternative.

"So, there's unpaid tax, penalty on the tax, interest on the penalty, tax on the interest. . . ."

Probability Estimates Although the manager may not know with a high degree of certainty the outcome of each decision, it may still be possible to estimate some level of probability for each of the alternatives. Such estimates are often based on experience. The manager draws on past occurrences in determining the likelihood of particular events. Naturally, no situation is ever identical to a previous one, but it may be sufficiently similar to justify using experience as a guide. Probability assignments permit a determination of the expected values of all events. For example, consider the case of the firm with four available strategies: A, B, C, and D. Each has a *conditional value,* which is the profit that will be returned to the firm if it is implemented and proves successful; a *probability,* which is a likelihood of success; and an *expected value,* which is the result of the conditional value multiplied by the probability. These data can be arranged as in Table 8–3.

Table 8–3 illustrates that the manager should opt for Strategy D because it promises the greatest expected value. Although it has the lowest conditional value of all four, the probability of success is far higher, resulting in the large expected value.

Table 8-3 *Expected Values for Strategies A-D*

Available Strategies	Conditional Value	Success Probability	Expected Value
A	$1,000,000	0.05	$ 50,000
B	800,000	0.10	80,000
C	750,000	0.20	150,000
D	400,000	0.65	260,000

Objective probability can be assigned on the basis of past experience.

Objective and Subjective Probabilities If a probability can be determined on the basis of past experience, it is known as an objective probability. What is the probability of obtaining a head in the toss of a fair coin? It is 0.5. Over the long run, there will be just as many heads as tails. Likewise, many companies are able, on the basis of past experience, to assign objective probabilities to events such as predicting success on a particular psychological test. Persons whose test scores are in the top 20 percent may have an 0.8 probability of success as a amanger. This would indicate that eight out of every ten in this category have done well as managers.

Subjective probability is often assigned on the basis of gut feel.

Sometimes, however, it is not possible to determine a suitable objective probability estimate. The manager may not feel there is sufficient information to determine whether the success probability is 0.5 or 0.8. In this case, the individual must make a subjective estimate, employing what is commonly called gut feel.

Although not as precise as an objective probability, subjective probability is nevertheless better than completely ignoring the probabilities of occurrence associated with the various alternatives. It also provides a basis for sharpening one's judgment since subjective probability assignments will occur again.

Risk Preference The assignment of probabilities is never as simple as it might appear. The decision maker who finalizes the assignment is the ultimate arbiter, and different managers will assign varying estimates to identical alternatives for various reasons.

For example, most managers are greater risk takers when investing or spending company funds than when they have their own money at stake. Furthermore, in making a decision on plant and equipment, some will demand a higher success probability than if the same amount were being invested in advertising, while others will do just the opposite. In short, attitudes toward risk vary. Why? Part of the answer is found in the fact that some people have a high dislike for risk while others have a low dislike for it. Another part of the answer is found in the fact that managers who are risk averters in some situations are gamblers in others.

Some managers take risks; others avert risk.

Regardless of the reason, managers' risk preferences will play a key role in determining their probability assignments. Figure 8-1 presents the preference curves of high, average, and low risk-takers. The S-curve illustrates the risk preferences of people in their personal lives. When the stakes are low, most individuals tend to be more willing to gamble than when they are high. For example, the author has asked businessmen if they would be willing to accept an outright gift of $5 or would prefer to take a chance on winning $15 or nothing against the correct call of the flip of a fair coin. Most have taken the latter alternative, being willing to gamble for $15 or nothing. Conversely, when the stakes are raised to $50,000 and $150,000 respectively, most managers choose the cer-

Figure 8–1 Risk-Preference Curves

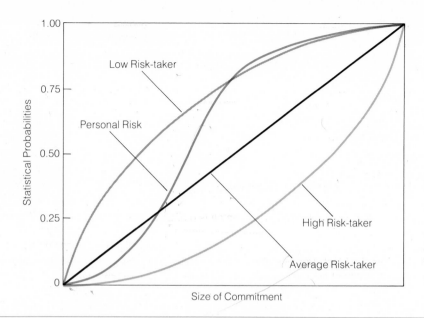

tain $50,000 sum. Objectively speaking, they are unwise, for the expected value of the $150,000 is $75,000 ($150,000 × 0.5), since the odds are fifty-fifty that they will call the flip of the coin correctly. However, the managers prefer the guaranteed $50,000.

Uncertainty

Uncertainty decisions are those for which managers feel they cannot develop probability estimates because they have no way of gauging the likelihood of the various alternatives. It is very difficult to say precisely when this occurs. Many individuals contend that experience and the ability to generalize from similar situations make uncertainty impossible; the manager can always assign some probability estimates to a decision matter. Yet there are times when executives feel they are indeed dealing with uncertainty. Nevertheless, research shows that they are wise to construct conditional values for each alternative under each state of nature. For example, an airplane manufacturer is considering the production of a giant helicopter for the military, and three basic design versions are under serious consideration: A, B, and C. The first is the most sophisticated and expensive of the three, while the last is the least sophisticated and expensive. The two basic states of nature are seen as being either a generation of peace or continual fighting of brushfire wars. Furthermore, the manufacturer has assigned conditional values to the respective strategies and states of nature, as shown in Table 8–4. Additionally, if peace prevails, the military will buy the least expensive helicopter, but if brushfire wars continue, it will purchase the most expensive.

What decision should the manager make? If there is no reason for believing that one event is more likely to occur than any other, the manager can employ what is called the *Laplace criterion,* which applies equal probabilities to all states of nature. If this approach is

Probability estimates should be developed even if the manager must make a decision under uncertainty.

Table 8–4 Conditional Values Associated with Manufacturing Giant Helicopter

	States of Nature	
Strategies	Generation of Peace	Continual Brushfire Wars
Helicopter A	−$ 250,000	$5,000,000
Helicopter B	1,000,000	1,000,000
Helicopter C	4,500,000	500,000

Table 8–5 Expected Values for Manufacturing Giant Helicopter Using Laplace Criterion (Equal Probability)

	States of Nature	
Strategies	Generation of Peace	Continual Brushfire Wars
Helicopter A	−$ 125,000	$2,500,000
Helicopter B	500,000	500,000
Helicopter C	2,250,000	250,000

Equal probability can be applied to all events.

followed, the firm should manufacture Helicopter C, because it offers an expected value of $2,500,000 ($4,500,000 × 0.5 + $500,000 × .05), which is greater than the value from either of the other strategies, as Table 8–5 shows. Helicopter A has an expected value of $2,375,000 (− $250,000 × 0.5 + $5,000,000 × 0.5); Helicopter B has an expected value of $1,000,000 ($1,000,000 × 0.5 + $1,000,000 × 0.5).

A pessimistic approach can be used.

A second approach is the use of the *maximin,* or pessimism, *criterion,* which holds that the manager should ascertain the worst conditions for each strategy. As Table 8–4 shows, the figures in this case are − $250,000 for A, $1,000,000 for B, and $500,000 for C. The strategy that offers the best payoff under these conditions should be implemented; in this case Helicopter B should be manufactured. By using this approach, the manager maximizes the minimum gain; hence the term *maximin.*

An optimistic approach can be taken.

A third approach is the use of the criterion of optimism, commonly called the *maximax criterion.* Since the manager is unsure of the outcome, it is just as rational to be optimistic as pessimistic. The manager can logically look on the bright side and assign a probability of, for example, 0.8 to the likelihood of the most favorable outcomes of each strategy and 0.2 to the least favorable outcomes of each. Then the best and worst conditional values associated with these three strategies can be multiplied by their respective probabilities to obtain weighted values, as seen in Table 8–6. Finally, these values can be added. In this instance, Helicopter A is the best choice.

Dealing with decisions under uncertainty is no easy task. In the three approaches used here, a different strategy emerged as the most favorable each time. The assumptions the manager makes regarding conditional values and probability estimates and the methods employed in evaluating the alternatives will all influence the outcome.

	Conditional Values		Weighted Values		
Strategy	Best Condition	Worst Condition	Best Condition	Worst Condition	Sum of Weighted Values
Helicopter A	$5,000,000	−$ 250,000	$4,000,000	−$ 50,000	$3,950,000
Helicopter B	1,000,000	1,000,000	800,000	200,000	1,000,000
Helicopter C	4,500,000	500,000	3,600,000	100,000	3,700,000

DECISION-MAKING TECHNIQUES

Attention has thus far been focused mainly on the environment in which the manager makes decisions—certainty, risk, and uncertainty. However, it is also useful to examine some of the specific techniques that have proved valuable in the decision-making process. Three of these techniques are marginal analysis, financial analysis, and the Delphi technique.

Marginal Analysis

Marginal analysis has been of interest to economists for years. In its essence, *marginal analysis* is concerned with the extra output that can be attained by adding an extra unit of input. For example, if one more machine is added to the assembly line and 200 more widgets are produced each day, the daily marginal product from that machine is 200. If a new air-conditioning system is installed, making the environment more pleasant, and if 500 more widgets are subsequently produced each week, the weekly marginal product from the air conditioner is 500.

The manager can use the concept of the margin to answer such questions as how much more output will result if one more worker is hired. The answer, often called *marginal physical product,* provides a basis for determining whether or not one new worker will bring about profitable additional output.

Marginal Physical Product Consider the case of the new shipping manager who has five workers loading five trucks. After pondering the matter, the manager hires five new workers; two people are now loading each truck. The result, as seen in Table 8–7, is that the total number of boxes loaded each day rises from 800 to 2,000. Two employees working as a team are able to do more than they could if working independently. With a third team worker, the daily total rises to 2,900.

Output may be increased if one worker is added.

As the table shows, the total mounts to 4,000 and then drops off to 3,700 when the number of workers per truck reaches seven. Why? Various causes can be cited. On the physical side, there may simply be too many people; they may be getting in each other's way. A behaviorist might wonder whether the seven are horsing around more or whether they may have an informal agreement to hold down output. In either event, seven workers per truck are too many.

If the manager's decision must rest solely on output, six is the ideal team size. However, there is a diminishing marginal physical product after the second worker is

Table 8-7 *Units of Marginal Physical Product*

Number of Workers per Truck	Total Boxes Loaded	Marginal Physical Product
0	0	0
1	800	800
2	2,000	1,200
3	2,900	900
4	3,500	600
5	3,900	400
6	4,000	100
7	3,700	(300)

Figure 8-2 *Total Output*

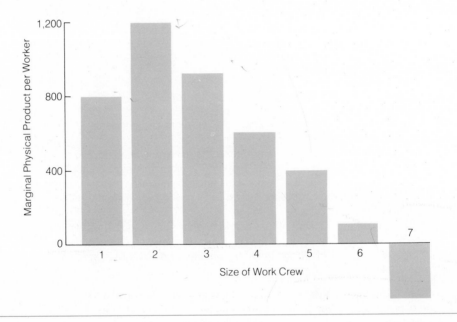

hired. The contributions from the third through the sixth increase the total but reduce the average from 1,000 boxes when there are two workers to 967, 875, 780, and 667 respectively as the next four workers are added. This rise in the total output with the accompanying decline in the marginal physical product is seen in Figures 8-2 and 8-3 respectively.

Profit Consideration The decline in marginal output will limit the size of the work crew. More realistically, however, the manager will refine the decision further with a consideration of profit. How much money will the company make at each work crew size? Table

Figure 8–3 Bar Graph of Physical Product

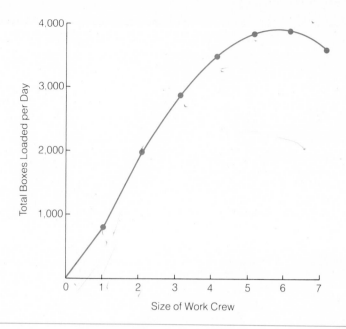

8–8 shows total profits under the premise that there is a ten-cent profit for every box loaded if all costs except work crew wages are considered. It is evident from the data that the company stands to make $240 a day if there are five people on the work crew. Any other size will result in a decline in this profit. In making such decisions, managers must consider profit as well as productivity.

However, profit is of more importance than mere physical output.

It was noted earlier that most managers are satisficers (administrative people) and not maximizers (economic people). However, in some cases, especially production, the manager will often be far closer to the end of the spectrum represented by economic people than to that represented by administrative people. For example, consider the case of the aerospace firm that is pondering the acceptance of a subcontract to build communication satellite subsystems. The major contractor wants eight of them built and would like to know whether the company is willing to undertake the contract. The purchase price of each subsystem will be $18,000. In order to determine the profitability of the venture, the firm must first construct its cost and revenue data, as seen in Table 8–9. The information reveals that if the company manufactures all eight subsystems, it will lose $26,000. The ideal production is six, for at this point the firm will net $32,000. This is also seen in Figure 8–4, where the data are presented graphically. The profit point at which the distance between total revenue and total cost is greatest is that corresponding to six units. The company should therefore refuse the contract.

The solution can be verified further if the *marginal revenue* and *marginal cost* data in Table 8–9 are examined. For every unit manufactured, the company obtains marginal revenue of $18,000. However, it also has an accompanying marginal cost associated with the

Table 8–8   Profit per Truck

Number of Workers	Salary Cost per Day	Profit per Box before Loading Salaries	Boxes Loaded	Total Profit before Loading Salaries	Total Profit
1	$ 30	$.10	800	$ 80	$ 50
2	60	.10	2,000	200	140
3	90	.10	2,900	290	200
4	120	.10	3,500	350	230
5	150	.10	3,900	390	240
6	180	.10	4,000	400	220
7	210	.10	3,700	370	160

Table 8–9   Costs and Revenues Associated with Manufacture of Communications Subsystems

Number Manufactured	Total Revenue	Total Cost	Total Profit	Marginal Revenue	Marginal Cost
1	$ 18,000	$ 30,000	($12,000)	$18,000	$30,000
2	36,000	35,000	1,000	18,000	5,000
3	54,000	40,000	14,000	18,000	5,000
4	72,000	50,000	22,000	18,000	10,000
5	90,000	60,000	30,000	18,000	10,000
6	108,000	76,000	32,000	18,000	16,000
7	126,000	110,000	16,000	18,000	34,000
8	144,000	170,000	(26,000)	18,000	60,000

production. A scrutiny of this marginal revenue (MR) and marginal cost (MC) data shows that for the sixth unit the firm will increase overall profit by $2,000 ($18,000 − $16,000). At seven units, overall profits will decline by $16,000; this is so because the marginal revenue is still only $18,000, but the marginal cost now associated with this unit is $34,000. Obviously, the company should agree to manufacture no more than six units. The profit maximization rule is to manufacture to the point where MC equals MR or, if they do not equalize, to the last point where MR is larger than MC (as in this case). Such an analysis can prove a useful decision-making technique for the manager. It not only helps identify the maximum profit point; it also prevents the undertaking of unprofitable ventures.

Marginal revenue and marginal cost must be computed.

Financial Analysis

Although marginal analysis is useful to the manager, it is nonetheless a specialized technique that considers situations only one at a time. It is therefore not a particularly helpful long-range guide to action. To provide a dynamic view of the future, many managers have turned to financial analytical techniques, which can be used for such functions as estimating the profitability of an investment, calculating the payback period, and/or analyzing discounted cash inflows and outflows.

Figure 8–4 *Maximum Profit Determination*

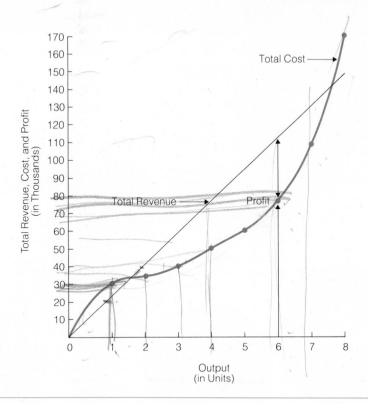

Consider the situation of the manager who is evaluating the purchase of two machines, A and B, solely on the basis of after-tax profitability. Which machine will provide more net profit for the firm? Machine A costs $150,000 and has an estimated useful life of five years. Machine B costs $200,000 and also has a five-year useful life. As seen in Table 8–10, when depreciation and taxes are deducted, Machine A will return $55,000 in net income, whereas Machine B will net the firm $60,000. Therefore, on the basis of after-tax profitability, Machine B will be the manager's choice.

After-tax profitability is one guideline.

It should be noted, however, that although the B alternative is more profitable, it also entails an added investment of $50,000. This raises the question of whether the manager has made a wise choice by allowing net profit to be the sole guide? After all, should the company not expect to obtain more profit from the larger investment? Sometimes a manager is on sound ground when opting for the alternative returning the greatest net profit; other times, however, one may forego the consideration of profit and concentrate on the *payback period,* which is the length of time it will take the company to recover its investment. Table 8–11 presents the cumulative cash recovery period. Estimating weekly recovery as 1/52 of the annual total, it will require approximately 3 years, 33 weeks to recover the $150,000 invested for Machine A and 3 years, 37 weeks to recover the $200,000 invested for Machine B. On the basis of the payback period, the manager would opt for Machine A.

Payback period is another guideline.

A third approach, even more useful than the previous two, is that of *net present value.* With this method the manager evaluates the expected return from each investment, using

Table 8–10 *Evaluating an Investment on the Basis of Net Profit*

Machine A

Year	Added Income before Taxes	Depreciation	Taxable Income	After-tax Income (Assuming 50 Percent Tax Rate)
1	$ 30,000	$30,000	$ 0	$ 0
2	50,000	30,000	20,000	10,000
3	60,000	30,000	30,000	15,000
4	80,000	30,000	50,000	25,000
5	40,000	30,000	10,000	5,000
			$110,000	$55,000

Machine B

Year	Added Income before Taxes	Depreciation	Taxable Income	After-tax Income (Assuming 50 Percent Tax Rate)
1	$ 40,000	$40,000	$ 0	$ 0
2	60,000	40,000	20,000	10,000
3	80,000	40,000	40,000	20,000
4	100,000	40,000	60,000	30,000
5	40,000	40,000	0	0
			$120,000	$60,000

Notes: Investment for Machine A is $150,000; Machine B, $200,000. Both machines have an estimated life of five years. Depreciation is on a straight-line basis.

a discounted dollar analysis of cash inflows. Such an analysis presents future cash inflows in terms of current dollars. The longer the manager has to wait for the inflows, the less they are worth in current dollars. For purposes of illustration, assume that the manager chooses to discount the future inflows of funds by 10 percent. In this case the annual cash flow recovery in Table 8–12 has to be multiplied by the appropriate discount factor. For example, a dollar returned a year from today is worth 0.909 cents using a 10 percent discount, while a dollar returned two years from today is worth 0.826 cents in current dollars. By multiplying the cash inflows by their respective discount factors, as seen in Table 8–12, discounted dollars can be calculated for the five-year investment. Then, to obtain the net present value, the manager must merely subtract the initial investment from the discounted dollar total and opt for that alternative which returns the greatest amount. Machine A will return $22,035 ($172,035 minus $150,000), whereas Machine B will return $20,210 ($220,210 minus $200,000). The manager should, therefore, choose alternative A.

Net present value is a third guideline.

The Delphi Technique

The *Delphi technique* uses a combination quantitative and qualitative approach to decision making, and it has become very popular for technological forecasting. Developed by the Rand Corporation, the Delphi at present is used by fifty to one-hundred major corporations. In essence, the approach pools the opinions of experts and calls for:

Table 8–11 Evaluating an Investment on the Basis of Payback Period

Machine A

Year	After-tax Income	Depreciation	Annual Cash Recovery	Cumulative Cash Recovery
1	$ 0	$30,000	$30,000	$ 30,000
2	10,000	30,000	40,000	70,000
3	15,000	30,000	45,000	115,000
4	25,000	30,000	55,000	170,000
5	5,000	30,000	35,000	205,000

Machine B

Year	After-tax Income	Depreciation	Annual Cash Recovery	Cumulative Cash Recovery
1	$ 0	$40,000	$40,000	$ 40,000
2	10,000	40,000	50,000	90,000
3	20,000	40,000	60,000	150,000
4	30,000	40,000	70,000	220,000
5	0	40,000	40,000	260,000

Table 8–12 Discounted Cash Flows for Machines A and B

Machine A

Year	Outflows of Cash	Inflows of Cash	Discount Factor	Discounted Dollars
0	$150,000	$ 0	1.000	$150,000
1	0	30,000	0.909	27,270
2	0	40,000	0.826	33,040
3	0	45,000	0.751	33,795
4	0	55,000	0.683	37,565
5	0	35,000	0.621	21,735
Scrap value (20%)		30,000	0.621	18,630
				$172,035

Machine B

Year	Outflows of Cash	Inflows of Cash	Discount Factor	Discounted Dollars
0	$200,000	$ 0	1.000	$200,000
1	0	40,000	0.909	36,360
2	0	50,000	0.826	41,300
3	0	60,000	0.751	45,060
4	0	70,000	0.683	47,810
5	0	40,000	0.621	24,840
Scrap value (20%)		40,000	0.621	24,840
				$220,210

Figure 8–5   Delphi Technique, Round One

Desirability			Feasibility			Timing (Year by Which Probable Event Will Have Occurred)		
High	Average	Low	High	Likely	Unlikely	10 Percent Probability	50 Percent Probability	90 Percent Probability

1. An anonymous prediction of important events in the area in question, from each expert in a group, in the form of brief statements.
2. A clarification of these statements by the investigator.
3. The successive, individual requestioning of each of the experts, combined with feedback supplied from the other experts *via* the investigator.[4]

In the first round of questioning, the experts might be asked individually to list, for example, the developments they believe will occur in their fields within the next twenty years that will have a significant effect on the company. Each may also be asked to comment on the desirability, feasibility, and timing of these developments. Figure 8–5 provides an illustration of the format that might be used.

Then, in a second round, the investigator gives each expert a composite of the predictions made by the others and the opportunity to modify his or her original estimates. This process is usually followed by still further rounds, often a total of five. The result is generally a consensus among the participants regarding the most significant events that will affect the company (Events, A, E, H, and I), the likelihood of their eventual development (90 percent, 70 percent, 60 percent, and 40 percent), and the time period in which they can be expected to occur (1985, 1987, 1990, and 1995). Table 8–13 illustrates the results of some Delphi forecasts.

Despite its apparent lack of scientific rigor, Delphi has proved very successful. In fact, the Rand Corporation has validated the technique through controlled experimentation. Its use has not been confined exclusively to technological forecasting. It has also been successfully employed, for example, to help participants formulate responses to questions whose answers are already known—for example, how many votes were cast for Lincoln in 1860, or how many Texas oil wells were there in 1960? In most cases, after a few rounds of questioning, the consensus has moved close to the actual answer, and it is thus easy to see why Delphi is so popular.[5]

Delphi allows the participants to revise their estimates.

---

[4] "The Basic Delphi Method," *Harvard Business Review,* May–June 1969, p. 81.
[5] For an in-depth review of this area, see Richard M. Hodgetts, *The Business Enterprise: Social Challenge, Social Response* (Philadelphia: W. B. Saunders, 1977), pp. 295–318.

Table 8–13 Examples of Delphi Forecasts

Description of Event	Year Selected by Percentage of Respondents as Date of Probable Occurrence		
	25%	*50%*	*75%*
There will be a single national building code.	1975	1977	1980
Polymers will be created by molecular tailoring, with service temperature ranges in excess of 1000°F.	1971	1976	2000
SST aircraft will be in regular service over land areas.	1980	1982	1985
Hydrocarbon/air fuel cell will be commercially available.	1974	1983	1990
A source of transplant organs for humans will be developed through selective breeding of animals that are tissue compatible.	1990	2015	2015

Sources: Alan R. Fusfeld and Richard N. Foster, "The Delphi Technique: Survey and Comment," *Business Horizons,* June 1971, p. 65. Fusfeld and Foster show the following sources. First two examples from "McGraw-Hill Survey of Technological Break-throughs and Widespread Applications of Significant Technical Developments" (New York: McGraw-Hill, 1968); third example from "Delphi Studies as an Aid to Corporate Planning" (Austin, Texas: Industrial Management Center, 1970); fourth example from James R. Bright, ed., *Technological Forecasting for Industry and Government,* particularly, "The Delphi Method—An Illustration"; last example from T. J. Gordon and Robert H. Ament, "Forecasts of Some Technological and Scientific Developments and Their Societal Consequences," Report No. 6. The Institute for the Future.

Technical and Nontechnical Factors The major problem confronting many forecasters is that of evaluating technical and nontechnical factors. In the technical area, for example, a pharmaceutical company might estimate that chemical control of hereditary defects will be made practicable through molecular engineering by 1995. However, what if by chance occurrence someone stumbles onto a discovery and makes a major break-through in this field in 1988? How can such developments be forecast?

> *Technical factors such as chance occurrence can undermine a forecast.*

Meanwhile, on the nontechnical side, there is the problem of lack of public accept-ance. The American supersonic transport (SST) is an illustration. In 1963, when the United States learned that the British and French were going to combine their efforts to build the Concorde, an SST, President Kennedy urged the Congress to allocate funds for a feasibility study. By 1970, the plane was already in the mock-up stage, but by this time the entire project had become a political issue. The Nixon administration stood squarely behind the development and production of the craft, but the public apparently did not; and this was reflected in the vote of the Congress. One reason was undoubtedly studies—for example one at Columbia University, which showed that the government and the contractors stood to lose large sums of money if the plane was built. People were just not going to pay the extra money to get, for example, from New York to London a few

> *Nontechnical factors such as lack of public acceptance can also undermine a forecast.*

Figure 8–6 Process of Technical Knowledge

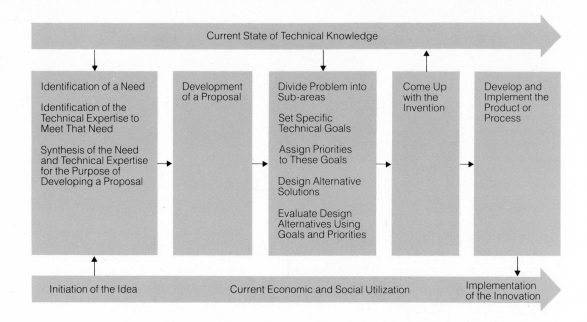

Source: Adapted by permission from James M. Utterback. "The Process of Technological Innovation within the Firm," *Academy of Management Journal*, March, 1971, p. 78.

hours earlier. Nontechnical factors (lack of demand for the aircraft, lack of profit for all parties involved) proved to be more important than the technical ones.[6]

The case of the SST is only one that shows why the forecaster must evaluate technical progress and nontechnical constraints. These two concepts can be brought together, as seen in Figure 8–6, which illustrates the process of technical innovation. Since the forecast must incorporate changes in the social, political, economic, and technical environments, it is evident that formal forecasting techniques are by nature incomplete. The manager must also employ an informal scanning process, always alert to variables that can, even nonrationally or irrationally, affect the forecast. Sometimes such a problem can be so obvious that it is overlooked. Consider the following case of a technology manager in a large company:

Several years ago he initiated a technological forecasting effort on one-shot basis, using a morphological technique with some Delphi inputs. Over 100 fields of technology were selected for study, with the objective of identifying broad areas of expertise where the company should develop or maintain a capability in the future. After an extensive forecasting procedure, 12 areas of potential importance were selected and

---

[6] For more on the application of the Delphi technique, see Richard J. Tersine and Walter E. Riggs, "The Delphi Technique: A Long-Range Planning Tool," *Business Horizons*, April 1976, pp. 51–56; and Richard M. Hodgetts, "Applying the Delphi Technique to Management Gaming," *Simulation*, July 1977, pp. 209–212.

recommended to the planning committee. Yet, as the manager of technology later noted, even after this rigorous search, one of the most significant areas —environmental control —was not identified.[7]

A Strategic Criteria Approach In recent years some firms have developed a strategic criteria approach to use in determining whether a potentially radical technological innovation will be successful. Using this approach, these firms feel they can better identify a technological winner.[8]

The approach is rather simple. First, the organization examines whether the technological innovation has "inventive merit." George R. White and Margaret B. W. Graham have described the process of determining whether an inventive concept really has such merit:

> *A truly significant inventive concept will use its new combination of scientific principles to relieve or avoid major constraints inherent in the previous art. In the case of the transistor, elimination of the heated cathode of a vacuum tube allowed portable radio size and weight to be reduced while offering longer battery life and greater reliability. Similarly, for the jet transport case, the Pratt & Whitney J57 engine used the key invention of twin spool geometry to overmatch all existing jets in power and fuel economy as well as to surpass all piston and turboprop engines in power and speed.[9]*

Second, the firm examines the innovation's "embodiment merit." How much information and technology is currently available and how many new breakthroughs must take place in order to make the innovation a reality?

Third is "operational merit." Can the innovation be handled by the company's current organization structure and business practices, or will operations have to be drastically changed? For example, a firm that is already manufacturing and retailing stereo equipment may have no trouble handling new stereo innovation. It has the basic manufacturing know-how and the outlets for selling it. On the other hand, if the company developed a radically new product but had no sales or marketing organization, it would be at a disadvantage. A new type of hearing aid is an example. Competitors with a less efficient hearing aid will probably have the right structure and business practices already in operation; for this reason, they are likely to continue to dominate the market.

Fourth, "market merit" must be considered. In so doing, the manager must give attention to two factors: (1) Is there a sufficient demand for the product? (2) Can total revenue be increased by reducing price and/or increasing the attractiveness of the product?

> *The market effect of radical product innovations is best gauged by comparing them with their less radical product competitors. Miniature transistor radios owed their popularity to one attractive feature —mobility. The light weight and small size of the Japanese pocket radio provided play-as-you-go rather than carry-and-set-down portability. Pocket radios needed no substantial price concessions to have major competitive advantage over their bulky U.S. competitors. When in subsequent years Japanese manufacturers reduced their prices to reflect their by-then lower costs, they were able to extend their revenue opportunity still further via market elasticity.[10]*

---

[7] John P. Dory and Robert J. Lord, "Does TF Really Work?" *Harvard Business Review,* November–December 1970, p. 22.

[8] The information in this section is based on George R. White and Margaret B. W. Graham, "How to Spot a Technological Winner," *Harvard Business Review,* March–April 1978, pp. 146–152.

[9] Ibid., p. 147.

[10] Ibid., p. 149.

Table 8—4 Assessing Technological Winners

Product: Computerized Cars

Inventive merit	A digital microprocessor control of engines will decrease pollution and improve fuel consumption.
Embodiment merit	Sensors and actuator components, not computer chips, will be required.
Operational merit	The expansion of car manufacturers and their suppliers into on-board computerized activities will result in major new design, manufacturing, and marketing opportunities.
Market merit	This innovation will help the manufacturer maintain old market share.

Product: The SST

Inventive merit	The plane will reduce air travel time but cause sonic boom and require high fuel consumption.
Embodiment merit	Major advances will be required in engines, controls, structures, and pollution analysis.
Operational merit	The U.S. transcontinental market will be unable to support the SST fleet.
Market merit	The value of customer time saved is, at best, unclear.

The inventive merit and embodiment merit combine to give potency to technology. The operational merit and market merit help the organization identify its business advantage. In turn, technology potency and business advantage bring about innovation success. Table 8–14 provides an example of how these four kinds of merit can be used in assessing various types of products. In the case of the SST it is the market value that defeats the project's prospects.

SUMMARY

This chapter has examined the fundamentals of decision making. The decision-making process consists of: (a) identifying the problem, (b) diagnosing the situation, (c) collecting and analyzing data relevant to the issue, (d) ascertaining solutions that may be used in solving the problem, (e) analyzing these alternative solutions, (f) selecting the one that appears most likely to solve the problem, and (g) implementing it. Yet the decision-making process is much more than simply following a list of steps; a great deal of subjective as well as objective evaluation must take place. For example, the personal values of the top manager will play a significant role in the assignment of risk and uncertainty probabilities. In many cases even modern managerial decision making may well be 75 percent subjective, 25 percent objective.

Nevertheless, the manager must be as rational as possible, drawing upon all available techniques and guidelines in choosing among the various alternatives. Some of the techniques that are most useful in this process include the Laplace criterion, the maximin criterion, the maximax criterion, marginal analysis, financial analysis, and the Delphi technique. And these represent only a few of the techniques available to the modern manager. Modern decision making is notable for the great variety of decision-making aids it has discovered.

REVIEW AND STUDY QUESTIONS

1. What is meant by the term *decision making?*
2. What are the steps in the decision-making process? Explain each.
3. What is meant by the term *rationality?* Are all decisions rational ones? Defend your answer.
4. How does value orientation affect the decision-making process? Give an illustration.
5. What are organizational decisions and personal decisions? Basic and routine decisions? Programmed and nonprogrammed decisions? Give an illustration of each.
6. How does a procedure differ from a policy?
7. What are the three basic conditions under which decisions are made? Explain each.
8. What roles do objective and subjective probability play in the decision-making process?
9. How does risk preference affect the decision-making process?
10. Of what benefit is marginal analysis to the manager in the decision-making process? Give an illustration.
11. Of what value is financial analysis to the manager in the decision-making process? Give an illustration.
12. How can a manager use the Delphi technique in making a technological forecast? Explain by discussing the steps in the process.
13. How can a strategic criteria approach help a business forecast the success of a technological innovation? Explain.

SELECTED REFERENCES

Bonoma, T. V., and Slevin, D. P. "Management and the Type II Error." *Business Horizons,* August 1979, pp. 61–67.

Drucker, Peter F. *Management: Tasks, Responsibilities, Practices.* New York: Harper & Row, 1974, chap. 37.

Greiner, Larry E.; Leitch, D. P.; and Barnes, Leroy B. "Putting Judgment Back into Decisions." *Harvard Business Review,* March–April 1970, pp. 59–66.

Guth, William D., and Tagiuri, Renato. "Personal Values and Corporate Strategy." *Harvard Business Review,* September–October 1965, pp. 123–132.

Hodgetts, Richard M. "Applying the Delphi Technique to Management Gaming." *Simulation,* July 1977, pp. 209–212.

Ives, B. D. "Decisions Theory and the Practicing Manager." *Business Horizons,* June 1973, pp. 38–40.

Kabus, I. "You Can Bank on Uncertainty." *Harvard Business Review,* May–June 1976, pp. 95–105.

Neumann, S., and Segev, E. "Human Resources and Corporate Risk Management." *Personnel Journal,* February 1978, pp. 76–79.

Roman, D. D. "Technological Forecasting in the Decision Process." *Academy of Management Journal,* June 1970, pp. 127–138.

Sihler, W. W. "Framework for Financial Decisions." *Harvard Business Review,* March–April 1971, pp. 123–135.

Simon, Herbert I. *The New Science of Management Decision.* New York: Harper & Bros., 1960.

White, George R., and Graham, Margaret B. W. "How to Spot a Technological Winner." *Harvard Business Review,* March–April 1978, pp. 146–152.

Williams, L. K. "Some Correlates of Risk Taking." *Personnel Psychology,* Autumn 1965, pp. 297–310.

CASE: The New Entrepreneurs

Perhaps no decision is more difficult for people than that of going into business for themselves. Yet in the stock brokerage industry, more and more individuals are beginning to do just this, setting up their own small companies and carving out a market niche. What makes this development so interesting is that in recent years the overall securities industry has become increasingly dominated by a handful of big firms, the largest of which is Merrill Lynch, Pierce, Fenner & Smith. Yet statistics show that by the early 1980s small firms were entering at an annual rate of 7 percent, quite a large number for an industry that has seen scores of medium-sized and even large firms merge or fold in recent years.

One of the main reasons that small firms have been able to secure a foothold in this market is that security legislation passed in 1975 made it relatively cheap and easy for a small company to get started. In 1976 further changes, this time in the rates small companies paid larger ones to execute their market orders and handle their bookkeeping, were made; and it became even easier to start a small-scale securities firm.

Many of the new companies provide their customers with individualized services at lower rates than the big brokerage houses, and the big houses either cannot or will not compete at these rates. Basically, the small brokerage houses do one or both of the following: (a) prepare research and act as a broker for individuals and financial institutions, and (b) sell research to large firms interested in the brokerage firm's study of their industry. (In this kind of situation General Motors might buy auto industry research, just as Dow might buy chemical business research and Delta airline-industry research.)

Can these small brokerage houses survive? Only time will tell. However, one thing is certain. Their owners are determined to fight the big firms for a share of the industry.

Questions

1. Using Spranger's values (theoretical, economic, aesthetic, social, political, religious) as your guide, state which values you believe are most important to the small business entrepreneurs and explain your reasoning.

2. Do you think the small firms are risk seekers, risk avoiders, or something between these two poles? Why?

3. How will the values of these small entrepreneurs affect their decision making? Be complete in your answer.

CASE: One, Two, or Three

Lawrence Sims had fought the proposed increase in plant facilities. "It's a poor idea," he told the board of directors, "because there just isn't enough demand to sustain this increased supply. Four major firms have entered our industry in the last year, and three more are knocking on the door; they know a profitable venture when they see one. The days of high prices and high profits are over. We are in for at least a decade of severe competition. Instead of increasing our capacity, we ought to be considering a new industry to invest funds in, one that might make us a 15 percent return on investment. Right now we have all our eggs in one basket, and we are jeopardizing them by increasing our commitment with a 25 percent increase in plant. We may even be endangering the basket. This is irresponsible!"

The board listened attentively but outvoted the president. Plant expansion was ordered for completion within eighteen months. Sims decided that the only way to salvage the company was to find some way of increasing demand for the product. After ten months of investigation and research, the president and his top executives agreed that three basic strategies were available. First, they could increase the amount of advertising from $300,000 to $400,000. This would result in total sales of $30 million. Second, they could lower the price of the product by 20 percent. Market research data indicated that this would lead to sales of $60,000,000. Finally, they could opt for a strong research and development program. If the firm invested $1 million in R&D, sales for the upcoming year would be $25 million. In terms of success probability, the executives estimated that the first of these strategies had a 60 percent chance of succeeding, the second had a 20 percent chance, and the third had a 70 percent success probability. In addition, the tax rates associated with the three were 48, 50, and 46 percent respectively.

Questions

1. Is this a case of decision making under certainty, risk, or uncertainty? Explain.

2. What are the expected values associated with each of the three strategies? Show all your calculations. In light of your work, which of the three strategies should the management choose?

3. Will the net profit margin before taxes associated with each of the three strategies have any bearing on the final decision? Explain why or why not.

CASE: The Profitable Pen

Nomathemba Jackson, president of Wilten Manufacturing, and her staff of planning advisors had spent the morning discussing the manufacture of a new felt tip pen. The process for the pen had been discovered in the company's R&D lab. The plan was to blanket the New York City area with an advertising campaign announcing the new product. Although the pen would be priced higher than those of the competition, its estimated life was four times that of the average felt tip pen currently on the market.

Through the use of market research and all acquirable information about the success of competitive firms, Wilten compiled the following demand schedule and total cost figures for the first year of operations:

Price	Felt Pens Demanded	Total Cost
$1.20	Virtually 0	$ 80,000
1.10	100,000	90,000
1.00	115,000	100,000
.90	130,000	105,000
.80	140,000	115,000
.70	150,000	130,000
.60	155,000	145,000
.50	160,000	170,000

Realizing that this was probably the most accurate information they would be able to obtain, the president and her advisors decided to push ahead with the production and sale of the new pen if the figures indicated the venture would be profitable. Then, if they were successful in the New York City area, they would expand to a national market. However, if the current data indicated that the product could not be successfully marketed because of lack of demand and/or excessive costs, Wilten would sell the process to one of their competitors. Jackson saw little problem with this latter alternative, since the company had applied for a patent on the process and company attorneys indicated that there would be no trouble getting one. Initial estimates placed the value of the felt pen process at $60,000.

Questions

1. Given the data in the case, do you think the pen can be manufactured and marketed successfully? Explain in detail.

2. Would the firm be better off marketing the pen or selling the process? Show your calculations.

CASE: The Car Dealer's Dilemma

A local car dealer has been making an estimate of the number of cars his agency will sell with three strategies—low price, increased advertising, and improved service—under two states of nature—average or dynamic growth of the gross national product (GNP). His data are shown in the table:

	States of Nature	
Strategies	Average Growth of GNP	Dynamic Growth of GNP
Low price	1,300 cars	1,400 cars
Increased advertising	1,200 cars	1,600 cars
Improved service	1,250 cars	1,500 cars

Questions

1. Using the Laplace criterion, which applies equal probability to all states of nature, which of the above three strategies should the dealer implement? Give your reasoning.

2. If the dealer uses the maximin approach, which of the above three strategies should he implement? Explain.

3. If the dealer employs a maximax criterion and assigns a 0.8 probability to dynamic growth and a 0.2 probability to average growth, which of the above alternatives should he implement? Explain.

CHAPTER 9

MODERN QUANTITATIVE DECISION-MAKING TOOLS AND PROCESSES

GOALS OF THE CHAPTER

Mathematical decision making has been given increased emphasis in recent years. The goal of this chapter is to examine some of the mathematical tools and processes currently being employed by managers, especially those in the area of operations management. However, the quantitative approach has both advantages and disadvantages. On the positive side, for example, quantitative techniques make it possible to screen out many of the subjective processes that often cause a decision to go awry. Also, quantitative processes sometimes allow faster and more accurate solutions to complex problems.

On the other hand, quantitative tools cannot guarantee effective decision making; they have numerous limitations. For example, if the mathematical expression or model does not properly represent reality, the answer will be wrong. If, say, a manager estimates that Decision A will produce either $1 million or nothing and that it has a success probability of 10 percent, whereas Decision B will produce either $200,000 or nothing and it has a success probability of 90 percent, it will be wiser to choose Decision B. The former has an expected payoff if only $100,000 [($1,000,000)(0.10) + ($0)(0.90)], but the latter has an expected payoff of $180,000 [($200,000)(0.90) + ($0)(0.10)].

But what if the manager is wrong in these estimates? What if Decision A's probability for success is really 0.90 and Decision B's is only 0.10? Then, because of erroneous probability assignments, the manager has made a serious mistake. Decision A's expected payoff of $900,000 [($1,000,000)(0.90) + ($0)(0.10)] will be much larger than Decision B's payoff of $20,000 [($200,000)(0.10) + ($0)(0.90)]. Second, sometimes the costs associated with a quantitative solution do not justify the returns: A mathematical approach may be much more expensive than a nonmathematical one. Third, it is often difficult to quantify all the necessary variables associated with a problem, and in such cases it may not be possible to use a quantitative approach.

Nevertheless, many managers find mathematical tools and techniques very helpful in the decision-making process. These tools, for the most part, come out of operations research (OR), and this chapter examines some of them. In certain cases in the chapter, a mathematical explanation is given, whereas in others, because of time and space limitations, only a qualitative description is offered.

When you have finished this chapter, you should be able to:

1. Describe the characteristics of operations management and some of the primary areas of concern for operations managers.
2. Define the term operations research.
3. Discuss the value of linear programming in the decision-making process.
4. State the importance of the economic order quantity formula in solving inventory control problems.
5. Solve simple game theory problems.
6. Explain how both queuing theory and the Monte Carlo method can help the manager in decision making.
7. Describe a decision tree and state its value in handling both short- and long-run problems.
8. Provide some illustrations of the kinds of problems managers often solve with heuristic programming.

OPERATIONS MANAGEMENT

Many people who are greatly interested in decision making and quantitative tools and techniques are also concerned with operations management. Operations Management takes into account the design, operation, and control of organizational systems; it is heavily concerned with such functions as work flow, production planning, purchasing, material requirements, inventory control, and quality control. Operations management people work, among other places, in factories and production settings. Many of the quantitative tools that this chapter examines were designed to help them resolve problems that arise in these surroundings.

Distinguishing Characteristics

Emphasis is placed on an interdisciplinary approach.

Three characteristics distinguish operations management. One is that an interdisciplinary approach is used in problem solving. If a statistician or mathematician is required to solve the problem, such a person is used. If the situation is more broadly based and calls for expertise in human physiology or psychological stress, such experts are brought in.

The scientific method is important.

Second, operations research gives strong emphasis to the scientific method. OR managers use hypothesis testing and analysis in finding practical solutions to the problem at hand.

Overall perspective is considered necessary.

Third, operations management takes a holistic (overall) perspective, looking at each problem in terms of the total organization. For example, in order to increase output by 5 percent, it may be necessary to increase machine speed by 5 percent. How much of an effect will this speedup have on the machine? How much will it cost in terms of repair or replacement expenses? By looking at the overall effect of the decision, operations management people can weigh the value of the increased output against the cost of this action.

Areas of Concern

Operations managers have many areas of concern. One is work flow layout. In order to obtain the most efficient work flow, how should the factory or office be designed? Virtually every business in the United States has sought to determine an ideal layout, whether for the purpose of decreasing production time, utilizing existing space more effectively, or providing for employee convenience, safety, and comfort.

One is work flow layout.

Another operations management concern is inventory control. How can the organization ensure that it has neither too much nor too little inventory on hand?

Another is inventory control.

A third area of concern is production planning and control. This process matches facilities, equipment, personnel, and materials against sales forecasts in determining which goes to production and in what quantities. It is common to find operations managers using such techniques as PERT and milestone budgeting, which were discussed in Chapter 7, as well as others that will be examined later in this chapter, to control the various operations.

A third is production planning and control.

Purchasing is a fourth concern. Should the organization make or buy the materials and parts used in its products? When it purchases, from whom should it buy? How does the firm select a vendor? How can the vendor's reliability, service performance, product quality, and price be checked out and compared to those of competitive sellers?

A fourth is purchasing.

Still another area of concern is that of quality control. This process of ensuring that goods conform to design specifications is a vital function. A typical quality control approach used by modern organizations is that of random sampling, in which a small number of goods are examined and a conclusion is drawn on the basis of the sample results. For example, instead of testing every ballpoint pen, the researcher tests ten of every thousand. If more than five of the ten are defective, the organization will examine the production process and find out what is wrong. If five or fewer are defective, this is an acceptable standard, and the firm will ship the pens to its dealers. The cost of having to give the dealer a credit for five out of a thousand pens is much smaller than that of examining the overall production process in an effort to find out why the five were defective. It is, of course, possible that the sample could have been a poor one and that fifty pens per thousand might be defective. In such an event, there might indeed be a problem with the production process. However, the firm accepts the risk associated with making a decision on the basis of a random sample when it chooses this testing method.

A fifth is quality control.

Work flow layout, inventory control, production planning and control, purchasing, and quality control are only five of the areas of concern for operations management people. However, they are representative. The remainder of this chapter examines some of the tools and processes used in operations management. The best place to begin this examination is with the topic of operations research.

OPERATIONS RESEARCH

The application of quantitative methods to decision making began in earnest during World War II. The approach has been termed *operations research,* or management science. Herbert A. Simon tersely summed up its history when he wrote:

> Operations research is a movement that, emerging out of the military needs of World War II, has brought the decision-making problems of management within the range of interests of large numbers of natural scientists and, particularly, of mathematicians and statisticians. The operations researchers soon joined forces with mathematical economists who had come into the same area—to the mutual benefit of both

groups. And by now there has been widespread fraternization between these exponents of the "new" scientific management and . . . industrial engineering. No meaningful line can be drawn any more to demarcate operations research from scientific management or scientific management from management science.[1]

Since it is so difficult to specify the domain of operations research, there has been considerable confusion over the use of the term. Some attach it to any new mathematical approach to decision making. Others (for example, mathematicians, physicists, and engineers) claim that an interdisciplinary approach must be involved. Still others contend that the process or technique must be sophisticated before it falls under the heading of OR. In an attempt to make the area understandable, Harold Koontz, Cyril O'Donnell, and Heinz Weihrich have identified the essential OR decision-making methods as follows:

Here are the essential methods of OR.

1. An emphasis on models that symbolize the relationship among the variables that are involved.
2. An emphasis on goals and the development of techniques for measuring effectiveness.
3. The incorporation of at least the most important variables into the model.
4. The design of a mathematical model.
5. The quantification of all variables to the greatest degree possible.
6. The supplementation of quantifiable data with the use of probability.[2]

Using these essentials, operations research has developed a number of problem-solving tools and techniques, including linear programming, inventory control, game theory, queuing theory, and Monte Carlo simulation.

LINEAR PROGRAMMING

One of the most widely used techniques of operations research is that of *linear programming.* Robert O. Ferguson and Lauren F. Sargent have described it as:

What is linear programming?

> *A technique for specifying how to use limited resources or capacities of a business to obtain a particular objective, such as least cost, highest margin, or least time, when those resources have alternative uses. It is a technique that systematizes for certain conditions the process of selecting the most desirable course of action from a number of available courses of action, thereby giving management information for making a more effective decision about the resources under its control.*[3]

Here are characteristics of linear programming problems.

All linear programming problems must have two basic characteristics. First, two or more activities must be competing for limited resources. Second, all relationships in the problem must be linear. If these two conditions exist, the technique can be employed. One of the best ways to grasp the fundamentals of the approach is to use it to solve a particular problem. Following is a simple illustration of an allocation problem, using one of the most common linear programming approaches, the graphic method.

---

[1] Herbert A. Simon, *The New Science of Management Decision* (New York: Harper & Bros., 1960), p. 15.
[2] Adapted from Harold Koontz, Cyril O'Donnell, and Heinz Weihrich, *Management,* 7th ed. (New York: McGraw-Hill, 1980), p. 250.
[3] Robert O. Ferguson and Lauren F. Sargent, *Linear Programming* (New York: McGraw-Hill, 1958), p. 3.

Table 9–1 Company A's Resources

Product	Hours Required per Unit				
	Manufacture	*Paint*	*Assembly*	*Test*	*Profit per Unit*
Model A	15.0	1.0	3.0	3.0	$400
Model B	10.0	1.0	2.0	—	$300
Hours available during next 30 days	21,000	1,200	3,000	2,400	

The Graphic Method

Company A wishes to maximize its profit by manufacturing two products: Model A and Model B. A wholesaler has signed a contract promising to take off the company's hands at a predetermined price all the goods it can manufacture over the next thirty days. The basic question, therefore, is how many units of each to manufacture. Analysis reveals the information in Table 9–1.

Taking into account the information in the table, how many Model A and Model B units should be manufactured? Merely looking at the data will not provide an answer. However, the analyst can draw certain conclusions in regard to constraints. For example, no more than 21,000 hours of manufacturing time are available to produce the two models. The constraint can be written in this way:

Here is a mathematical expression of the constraints.

$$15A + 10B \leq 21,000 \text{ hours.}$$

Likewise, the other three constraints (painting, assembly, and test) can be expressed as follows:

$$1A + 1B \leq 1200 \text{ hours.}$$
$$3A + 2B \leq 3000 \text{ hours.}$$
$$3A \leq 2400 \text{ hours.}$$

In addition, maximization of the profit objective can be expressed by the statement:

$$\text{Profit maximization} = \$400A + \$300B,$$

subject, of course, to the initial four constraints and to the fact that A and B cannot be negative. Since there is no such thing as negative production, $A \geq 0$ and $B \geq 0$.

Having identified the constraints and the profit maximization function, the maximum number of units that can be manufactured can now be determined. That is:

$$15A + 10B \leq 21,000 \text{ hours.}$$

If

$$B = 0,$$

then

$$15A \leq 21,000$$
$$A \leq 1,400.$$

Conversely, if

$$A = 0,$$

then

$$10B \leq 21,000$$
$$B \leq 2,100.$$

Thus, if only one model is produced, the greatest number of Model A and Model B units that can be manufactured is 1,400 and 2,100 respectively. This can be graphed as in Figure 9–1.

The maximum number of units of A and B respectively that can be painted is:

$$1A + 1B \leq 1,200 \text{ hours.}$$

If

$$B = 0,$$

then

$$1A \leq 1,200$$
$$A \leq 1,200.$$

Conversely, if

$$A = 0,$$

then

$$1B \leq 1,200$$
$$B \leq 1,200.$$

This can be graphed as in Figure 9–2.

In terms of the assembly constraint, the number of Model A and Model B units that it is possible to assemble can be determined as follows:

$$3A + 2B = 3,000.$$

If

$$B = 0,$$

then

$$3A = 3,000$$
$$A = 1,000.$$

Conversely, if

$$A = 0,$$

then

$$2B \leq 3,000$$
$$B \leq 1,500.$$

This can be graphed as in Figure 9–3.

Finally, although Model B requires no testing, the number of Model A units that it is possible to test can be determined as follows:

$$3A \leq 2,400.$$
$$A \leq 800.$$

This can be graphed as in Figure 9–4.

The feasibility area represents all possible production combinations.

All four graphs can then be consolidated; what emerges is Figure 9–5. The area that is shaded is the feasibility area; that is, any combination of Model A and Model B can be produced as long as it falls within this area. Everything outside the area is infeasible because those particular combinations will require more manufacturing, painting, assembling, and/or testing hours than are available.

The next question is, what combination of those that are feasible should be manufactured? It has already been ascertained that:

$$\text{Profit maximization} = \$400A + \$300B.$$

Therefore, for every three units of A or four units of B sold, the profit will be identical: $1,200. The ratio of A to B will be 3 to 4. If this ratio is maintained, starting as close to the origin as possible and gradually working outward, all combinations of

Figure 9–1 *Manufacturing Constraints*

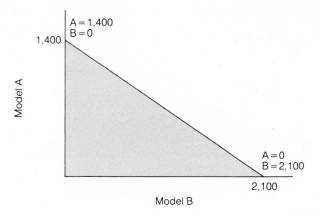

Figure 9–2 *Painting Constraints*

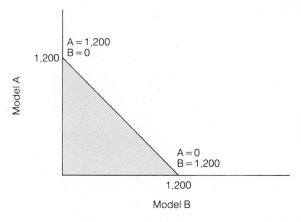

Figure 9–3 *Assembly Constraints*

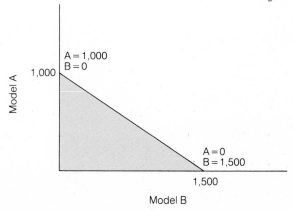

Figure 9–4 *Testing Constraint*

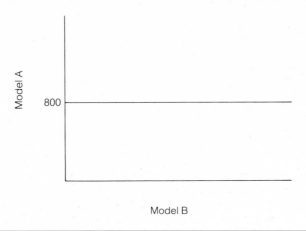

Figure 9–5 *Feasibility Area (in Hundreds of Units)*

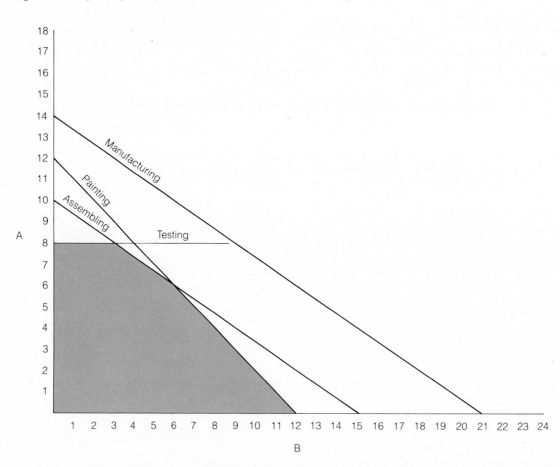

Figure 9–6 $1,200 Isoprofit Line (in Hundreds of Units)

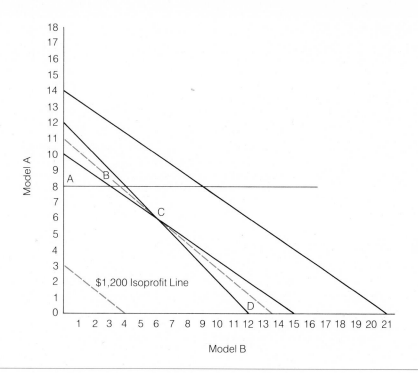

feasible production can eventually be analyzed. Figure 9–6 shows this, the isoprofit line, for $1,200. If this line is continued out to its furthest point from the origin, it will either come to rest on one of the lines forming the feasibility boundary area, or it will nick one of the four points labeled A, B, C, and D respectively in the figure. The slope of the isoprofit line shows that it will probably touch one of the four points before continuing out into the infeasible area, and this is precisely what happens. The isoprofit line will touch Point C, and it is here that profit is maximized at 600 units of Model A and 600 units of Model B. This can be verified by examining all four points—A, B, C, and D.

The computation of the isoprofit line is explained.

Point A: $400 (800) + $300 (0)   = $320,000.
Point B: $400 (800) + $300 (300) = $410,000.
Point C: $400 (600) + $300 (600) = $420,000.
Point D: $400 (0)   + $300 (1,200) = $360,000.

No other combination will result in as much profit as that obtained at Point C. This statement can be tested. The verifier simply has to remember the constraints that are present—for example, that one unit of A cannot be traded for one unit of B because it takes more time to manufacture a unit of A than to manufacture a unit of B.

Linear programming can be used in the solution of many kinds of allocation decision problems, but its application is certainly limited. The first limitation is that the decision problem must be formulated in quantitative terms for linear programming to be employed effectively. In many instances, the costs associated with gathering these

These are the limitations of linear programming.

Figure 9–7 *Constant Depletion Rate*

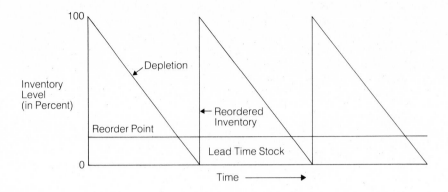

Table 9–2 *Trial-and-Error Approach*

Number of Orders Placed	Size of Each Order	Order Cost	Carrying Cost $\left(\dfrac{Inventory/2}{\times \$20 \times 0.05}\right)$	Total Cost
1	5,000	$ 100	$2,500.00	$2,600.00
2	2,500	200	1,250.00	1,450.00
3	1,667	300	833.50	1,133.50
6	833	600	416.50	1,016.50
10	500	1,000	250.00	1,250.00
20	250	2,000	125.00	2,125.00

data outweigh the savings obtained from the use of the technique. Likewise, many allocation problems do not lend themselves to this approach because the relationship between the variables is not linear. Approximate solutions are sometimes possible in such cases. Finally, unless all variables are known with certainty, in which case the model is deterministic, it is sometimes impossible to use the technique. Nevertheless, the approach has many advantages, and its application in the area of business decision making is increasing.

INVENTORY CONTROL

Another common problem faced by some managers is that of maintaining adequate inventories. No one wants to have too many units available because there are costs associated with carrying these goods. On the other hand, a store that runs out of inventory risks losing a customer's future business. To resolve this dilemma, the manager must analyze costs and formulate some assumptions about supply and demand.

Two types of costs merit the manager's consideration. The first are *clerical and adminis-trative costs,* expenses associated with ordering inventory. Every time an order for more goods is placed, time and effort are expended. Naturally, if a firm wished to reduce these particular costs to their lowest possible level, it could place one order covering all the goods that would be needed for the entire year. However, that is a very unrealistic solution in view of the second type of costs, popularly known as carrying costs. *Carry-ing costs* are the amount of money invested in the inventory and other sundry expenses covering storage space, taxes, and obsolesence. The greater the inventory the firm carries, the greater its carrying costs will be.

Solving the Problem

One way for the manager to solve the inventory problem is to make certain assumptions regarding future demand and then attempt a solution. Three of the most common assumptions made in determining optimal inventory size are that (a) demand is known with certainty, (b) the lead time necessary for reordering goods is also known with cer-tainty, and (c) the inventory will be depleted at a constant rate. These assumptions can be diagrammed as in Figure 9–7.

Three assumptions are often made in determining optimal inventory size.

These three assumptions are obviously not realistic at all times, but they do provide a basis from which the manager can make a decision. Now the manager has to decide whether to use what can be labeled a trial-and-error approach or an OR tool known as the *economic order quantity (EOQ)* formula.

The EOQ formula is important. To show how this is so, one can solve a problem us-ing two methods: trial and error and EOQ. Assume that Guy Smith is the manager of an appliance department for a large eastern discount store. He has estimated annual de-mand for blenders for the upcoming year to be 5,000. Further, he has calculated the or-der costs (clerical and administrative) as $100 per order and has broken down carrying costs into component parts as follows: (a) the value of a blender is $20; (b) insurance, taxes, storage, and other expenses are 5 percent per year; and (c) average inventory carried at any one time is equal to total inventory divided by two.[4] It should be noted that carrying costs consist of the value of the inventory tied up at any one time and the costs associated with these particular goods.

In the first instance, Smith can take these data and construct the total costs asso-ciated with each of a number of reorder levels. Table 9–2 shows the results of this trial-and-error process.

The Table 9–2 data indicate that Smith would be best off by placing 6 orders of 833 blenders each throughout the year. However, two points should be noted. First, Smith does not know that 6 is the ideal number of times to reorder. He merely knows that of the Table 9–2 alternatives, it is the best. But what about the other reorder pos-sibilities: 4, 5, 7, 8, 9, and 11 to 19? A second difficulty is that many inventory problems are much too sophisticated to be solved by such a simple approach. For this reason, the EOQ formula is often employed:

---

[4] This is so because average inventory is always going to be equal to half of total inventory, given a constant depletion rate. For example, if a firm orders 1,000 widgets and sells them at the rate of 20 a day for 50 days, no widgets will be left at the end of 10 weeks. However, the amount on hand at the midpoint of each week will be as follows: 950, 850, 750, 650, 550, 450, 350, 250, 150, 50. Adding these figures and dividing the total by 10 produces 500. Thus in the EOQ formula the average inventory is determined to be

$$\frac{\text{Total inventory}}{2}.$$

$$EOQ = \sqrt{\frac{2DA}{vr}},$$

where:

$D =$ *Expected annual demand*

$A =$ *Administrative costs per order*

$v =$ *Value per item*

$r =$ *Estimate for taxes, insurance, and other expenses.*

When the data are placed in the formula, it appears as follows:

$$
\begin{aligned}
EOQ &= \sqrt{\frac{2(5,000)\,(\$100)}{(\$20) \times (0.05)}} \\
&= \sqrt{\frac{\$1,000,000}{\$1}} \\
&= \sqrt{1,000,000} \\
&= 1,000.
\end{aligned}
$$

The manager's best decision will therefore be to reorder in quantities of 1,000. This will require the placement of 5 orders throughout the year, an alternative Smith has not yet pursued. The answer can be further verified through hand calculation. Five orders will result in total order costs of $500. The carrying costs will equal 1,000 ÷ 2 × ($20 × 0.05), or $500 more. Thus, by ordering 5 rather than 6 times a year, Smith can improve his total cost by $16.50 ($1,016.50 − $1,000). Figure 9–8 provides a graphic illustration of this solution.

The EOQ is only one of many mathematical techniques that have been developed to help the manager make decisions. Another is game theory.

GAME THEORY

Game theory has not been widely used in solving business problems, but it has provided important insights into the elements of competition. The manager's job is to choose the best strategy available, taking into account his or her own actions and those of the competition. Thus, an understanding and appreciation of strategy can prove very useful.

Game theory involves what are termed conflict of interest situations. One individual or organization has goals that conflict with those of other individuals or organizations. In addition, in game theory two or more alternative courses of action are always available, even though the manager never has full control over any of them. Commenting on the aspect of conflict, John McDonald, in his book *Strategy in Poker, Business and War*, has written:

The economic order quantity involves conflict of interest situations.

> *The strategical situation in game theory lies in the interaction between two or more persons, each of whose actions is based on an expectation concerning the actions of others over whom he has no control. The outcome is dependent upon the personal moves of the participants. The policy followed in making these moves is strategy. Both the military strategist and the business man act continuously in this state of suspended animation. And regardless of the amount of information given them —short of the ideal of perfect information —they generally act in the final analysis on hunch; that is, they gamble without being able to calculate the risk.* [5]

[5] John McDonald, *Strategy in Poker, Business and War* (New York: W. W. Norton, 1950), p. 16.

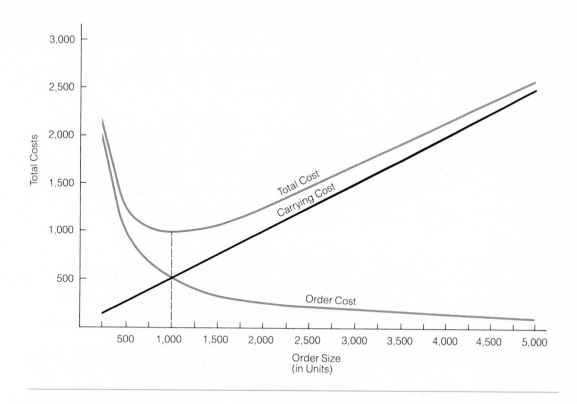

Figure 9–8 Order, Carrying, and Total Cost Relationships

Saddle Point Zero-sum Games

Most analysis conducted in the area of game theory has involved two-party *zero-sum games*. In these games are two competitors, one of whose gain is always the other's loss. This concept can be seen more clearly through the construction of a payoff matrix that shows what each competitor stands to win or lose. Before the matrix is drawn, however, it should be noted that a basic assumption of game theory is that neither side is any smarter than the other; both sides, therefore, know the payoffs in the matrix. The question, in light of these payoffs, is what each side should do.

In a zero-sum game, one competitor's loss is the other's gain.

Consider, for example, two companies (Y and Z) with the following four alternative strategies:

Company Y
A = Lower price.
B = Improve product quality.

Company Z
C = Increase advertising.
D = Hire more people in sales.

The payoff matrix for these respective strategies, in terms of gains and losses for Company Y, is seen in Figure 9–9.

Figure 9–9 *Company Y Payoff Matrix*

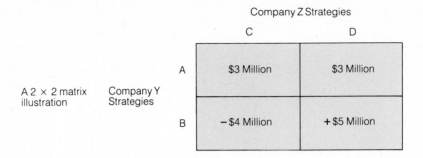

Company Z Strategies

		C	D
		C	**D**
Company Y Strategies	A	$3 Million	$3 Million
	B	−$4 Million	+$5 Million

A 2 × 2 matrix illustration

Figure 9–10 *Determining Whether a Saddle Point Exists*

Company Z Strategies

		C	D	Row Minima
Company Y Strategies	A	$3 Million	$4 Million	3 Million
	B	−$4 Million	$5 Million	−4 Million
Column Maxima		3 Million	5 Million	

Figure 9–11 *Company Y Payoff Matrix*

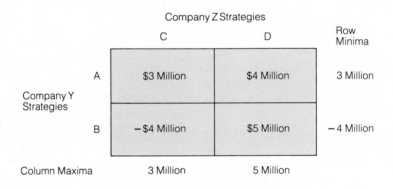

Company Z Strategies

		D	E	F
	A	$2 Million	$6 Million	$12 Million
Company Y Strategies	B	$14 Million	$8 Million	$10 Million
	C	−$4 Million	$4 Million	−$6 Million

A 3 × 3 matrix illustration.

In light of this, which strategy is most desirable to Company Y? The answer would appear to be Strategy A, for the company stands to gain $3 million, regardless. Conversely, Strategy C seems most desirable to Company Z, which stands to lose no more than $3 million and which might gain $4 million. Thus the best strategy appears to be A,C.

The logic can be verified by employing two of the most useful ideas developed in decision theory, the concepts of minimax and maximin. Minimax involves minimizing the maximum loss, and maximin involves maximizing the minimum gain. Both concepts can be applied to the payoff matrix in Figure 9–10 to determine whether there is a *saddle point,* or ideal strategy. One determines the existence of a saddle point first by identifying the smallest number in each row (Row Minima) and then ascertaining the largest number in each column (Column Maxima). If the largest number in Row Minima equals the smallest number in Column Maxima, a saddle point exists.

Using the minimax and maximin concepts allows the saddle point (ideal strategy) to be determined.

Since the largest number in Row Minima is indeed equal to the smallest number in Column Maxima, there is a saddle point or ideal strategy. This occurs at Point A,C. Thus it has been possible to identify the ideal strategy by means of a visual analysis.

The saddle point is found.

The basic concept of game theory can be expanded into even larger matrixes. For example, consider the effect of the following six strategies:

Company Y
A = Lower price.
B = Improve product quality.
C = Increase advertising.

Company Z
D = Open more distribution centers.
E = Provide easier credit terms.
F = Hire more people in sales.

When these six strategies are placed in a matrix, the payoffs, from the standpoint of Company Y, are as shown in Figure 9–11.

A visual analysis of Figure 9–11 shows that Strategy B is most favorable to Company Y. The least the firm will gain with this strategy is $8 million, and it can possibly gain $14 million. Conversely, Strategy E appears most favorable to Company Z, since the most it can lose is $8 million; this is in contrast to Strategies D and F, by which it can lose $14 million and $12 million respectively. However, because this matrix is a little more difficult to analyze than the previous one, it is desirable first to ascertain whether or not there is a saddle point. Figure 9–12 shows how this can be done.

There is a saddle point in the figure, the ideal strategy being B,E. Thus Company Y should initiate Strategy B, and Company Z should opt for Strategy E. It is important to remember that it pays neither side to opt for any other strategy if there is a saddle point. For example, according to the Figure 9–12 matrix, if Company Y maintains Strategy B, Company Z stands to lose much more than $8 million if it switches to either of the other strategies, whether D or F. Likewise, if Company Y changes to Strategy A or Strategy C while Company Z stays with Strategy E, Company Y will not gain as much as before.

Here the saddle point is calculated.

Non-zero-sum Mixed Strategy Games

The game theory illustrations to this point have all been examples of zero-sum games, but in realistic business settings zero-sum conditions rarely occur. Assume, for example, that profit per unit is $1, demand is 1,000 units, and total profit in the market is $1,000. Firms A and B both wish to obtain profits of $750 but, based on current

Figure 9–12 Saddle Point Calculation

	Company Z Strategies			Row Minima
	D	E	F	
A	$2 Million	$6 Million	$12 Million	2 Million
B	$14 Million	$8 Million	$10 Million	8 Million
C	– $4 Million	$4 Million	– $6 Million	– 6 Million
Column Maxima	14 Million	8 Million	12 Million	

Company Y Strategies

information, they know this to be impossible; the combined profits of the two cannot exceed $1,000. Thus, only the firm capturing 75 percent of the market will succeed. On the other hand, if the demand were to increase from 1,000 to 2,000 units, both companies could capture equal shares of the market and more than attain their respective goals. Because there are increases in demand, most businesses face conditions characteristic of non-zero-sum games when dealing with sales volume because most decisions are not made at the direct expense of the competition. They are thus non-zero-sum in nature.

Most situations are non-zero-sum in nature.

Likewise, most strategy situations do not have saddle points. For example, consider the matrix in Figure 9–13, which is a slight adaptation of Figure 9–12, with its accompanying Row Minima and Column Maxima calculations.

There is no saddle point in the figure, for the maxima of Row Minima is $6 million, whereas the minima of Column Maxima is $8 million. When there is no saddle point, it becomes necessary to design a mixed strategy. For example, if Company Y chose Strategy B, Company Z would go to Strategy E, choosing to lose $6 million. However, if Y knew what Z was going to do, it would opt for Strategy C, thereby increasing its payoff from $6 million to $16 million. In turn, if Company Z knew this, it would choose Strategy F, thereby gaining $6 million. And so it goes, with each company second guessing the other. The only possible way to take advantage of the situation is to determine some combination or mixed strategy. The method of calculating this will not be discussed here, but it should be noted that this mixed approach is far more realistic than the ideal, or saddle-point, strategy. If one firm found itself in an unfavorable saddle-point situation, it would alter its strategies drastically, thereby upsetting the old payoff matrix and establishing one more favorable to itself. Another way in which this discussion has been somewhat unrealistic is that the examination of game theory has dealt with only two competitive sides. In a business setting, however, a firm is generally competing against many companies. Nevertheless, the concept of game theory has proved very useful in providing an understanding of the elements of competition. Its basic ideas have been experi-

In most strategy situations there is no saddle point.

Figure 9–13 Mixed Strategy

Company Z Strategies

Company Y Strategies		D	E	F	Row Minima
	A	$2 Million	$14 Million	$10 Million	2 Million
	B	$8 Million	$6 Million	$12 Million	6 Million
	C	− $4 Million	$16 Million	− $6 Million	− 6 Million
Column Maxima		8 Million	16 Million	12 Million	

mentally expanded into bargaining and negotiating interactions and, for about twenty years now, have been employed in general management simulation games to train managers in strategy formulation and implementation.

QUEUING THEORY

Another OR technique is that of *queuing theory,* often called waiting-line theory, which employs a mathematical technique for balancing waiting lines and service. These lines occur whenever there is an irregular demand, and the manager must decide how to handle the situation. If the lines become too long and the waiting time proves excessive, customers will go elsewhere with their business. Conversely, if there is too much service, customers will be very happy but the costs will outrun the revenues. If, for example, one goes grocery shopping on Saturday morning, every cash register may have an attendant and an average waiting time of fifteen minutes. Since these conditions exist all over town, the manager must be concerned only with keeping the registers open. However, what should be done during slack periods, such as Tuesday morning? If the manager assigns only two people to the registers, there may be a sudden influx of customers, who suddenly create long lines. On the other hand, if the manager keeps all the registers going and only a few customers show up, most of the clerks will just be standing around drawing their paychecks.

Queuing theory helps the manager balance waiting lines and service.

The supermarket manager presents a very simple illustration because it takes little thought or effort to move people from the stockroom to the cash register and back. As long as a sufficient number of employees are on hand, they can be transferred around the store; and waiting lines are simply not an insurmountable problem. However, the concept can be applied to a business firm faced, for example, with a problem of plant layout. How many loading docks and fork trucks will be needed to keep the company delivery trucks' waiting time at an acceptable level? If there are too many docks and fork trucks, there will be no waiting time for loading and unloading, but the expense of building the facilities will be great. Conversely, too few docks and fork trucks entail a great deal of expensive waiting time. By means of mathematical equations, queuing theory can provide an answer to this particular problem. Sometimes, however, when arrival and service rates are not controllable, it becomes difficult to evaluate alternatives by means of equations alone. When this occurs, a Monte Carlo approach can often prove useful.

MONTE CARLO TECHNIQUE

The *Monte Carlo technique* uses a simulation approach for the purpose of creating an artificial environment and then evaluating the effect of decisions within these surroundings. A simple illustration of a simulation is found in the case of aerodynamic testing conducted on model airplanes in a wind tunnel. By simulating the effect of air currents and gale winds on the craft, engineers can evaluate the proposed design and construction.

The Monte Carlo technique allows the manager to simulate various conditions and determine the best answer from the results.

Monte Carlo is another type of simulation that attempts, via a random number generator or table, to simulate a particular environment and the effect of various decisions made within this artificial setting. For example, if a plant manager wants to determine the optimum number of trucks for the firm's delivery fleet, the problem is basically one of discrimination: If there are too many, capital investment in the trucks, coupled with excessive idle time, will prove too high. The optimum number can be determined by using the Monte Carlo technique. First, the number of shipments arriving at the loading dock must be determined; next, the time it takes to make deliveries must be ascertained. Then the expenses of owning and operating the fleet have to be computed. Finally, the costs associated with being unable to make all deliveries on time must be calculated. Employing this basic information plus some other supplemental data and some random numbers, it is possible to simulate results based on different fleet sizes. The process can be continued until the manager finds the optimum number of trucks. However, the technique is not restricted merely to determining fleet sizes. It has been successfully used in many diverse activities, from simulating machine breakdowns to determining arrivals and departures at airports.

DECISION TREES

Another OR tool is the decision tree. Many managers weigh alternatives on the basis of their immediate or short-run results, but a decision-tree format permits a more dynamic approach because it makes explicit some elements that are generally only implicit in other analyses. A *decision tree* is a graphic method that a manager can use in identifying the various courses of action that can be taken in solving a problem, assigning probability estimates to events associated with these alternatives, and calculating the payoffs corresponding to each act-event combination.

For example, consider the case of a firm that has expansion funds and must decide what to do with them. After careful analysis, the firm identifies three alternatives: (a) use the money to buy a new company, (b) expand the facilities of the current firm, or (c) put the money in a savings account. In deciding which alternative is best, the company has gathered all the available information and constructed the decision tree that is Figure 9–14.

This figure has four important components, common to all decision trees. First is the decision point, which is represented by a square that indicates where the decision maker must choose a course of action. Second is a chance point, represented by a circle, which indicates where a chance event, over which the firm has no control, is expected;

Figure 9–14   Decision Tree for Investing Expansion Funds

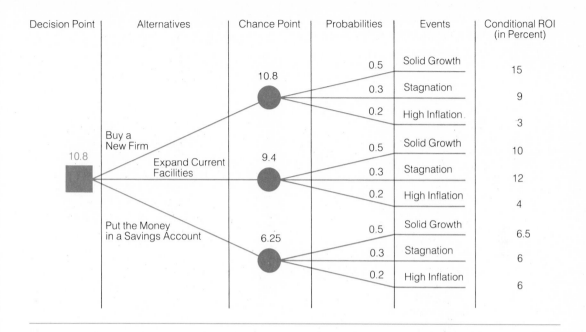

Decision Point	Alternatives	Chance Point	Probabilities	Events	Conditional ROI (in Percent)
		10.8	0.5	Solid Growth	15
			0.3	Stagnation	9
			0.2	High Inflation	3
10.8	Buy a New Firm				
	Expand Current Facilities	9.4	0.5	Solid Growth	10
			0.3	Stagnation	12
			0.2	High Inflation	4
	Put the Money in a Savings Account	6.25	0.5	Solid Growth	6.5
			0.3	Stagnation	6
			0.2	High Inflation	6

some examples of chance events are solid economic growth, stagnation, and high inflation. Third is a branch, which is represented by a line that flows from the chance points to indicate events and their likelihood—for example, 0.5 for solid growth, 0.3 for stagnation, or 0.2 for high inflation. Finally, at the far right, a payoff is associated with each branch. The payoffs are called conditional payoffs since their occurrence depends on certain conditions. For example, in Figure 9–14 the conditional return on investment (ROI) associated with buying a new firm and having solid economic growth is 15 percent, but this return depends on both of the two preceding factors—buying the firm and having solid growth.

In building a decision tree, the company starts by identifying the three alternatives, the probabilities and events associated with each, and the amount of return that can be expected from each. Having then constructed the tree, the firm is said to roll it back; proceeding from right to left, the analyst begins the decision-tree interpretation.

This analysis begins when the analyst multiplies the conditional ROIs at the far right of the tree by the probability of their occurrence. For example, if the company buys a new firm and there is solid growth in the economy, as in Figure 9–14, it will obtain a 15 percent ROI. However, the probability of such an occurrence is 0.5. Likewise, the probabilities associated with stagnant growth, where the return will be 9 percent, and high inflation, where the return will be 3 percent, are 0.3 and 0.2 respectively. To determine the expected return associated with buying a new firm, the analyst multiplies each of the conditional ROIs by its respective probability and then totals the products. For the first alternative, buying the firm, the calculation is:

Conditional ROI	Probability	Expected Return
15.0	0.5	7.5
9.0	0.3	2.7
3.0	0.2	0.6
		10.8

For the second alternative, expanding current facilities, the calculation is:

Conditional ROI	Probability	Expected Return
10.0	0.5	5.0
12.0	0.3	3.6
4.0	0.2	0.8
		9.4

For the third alternative, investing the money, the calculation is:

Conditional ROI	Probability	Expected Return
6.5	0.5	3.25
6.0	0.3	1.80
6.0	0.2	1.20
		6.25

These expected returns are often placed over the chance points on the decision tree. But they can be determined only after the tree has been drawn and the analysis of the branches has been conducted.

As can be seen in the figure, the first alternative is the best because it offers the greatest expected return. Decision trees help the manager evaluate alternatives because they identify both what can happen and the likelihood of the events' occurrences. To be able to do both, the decision tree builder moves from left to right, but the decision tree analyst moves from right to left.

In recent years many companies have frequently used decision trees to handle situations that span two or more years. For example, consider the case of a company that must decide whether to buy a new machine or use overtime in handling current demand. The new machine will cost $30,000, whereas the overtime will cost $5,000. Whichever decision is made, the company will stay with it for one year and then make a follow-up decision. If it has installed a new machine in the first year, it may install a second machine, institute overtime, or use the existing facilities to the fullest. If it has opted for overtime in the first year, it may then install a new machine, install the machine and use overtime as well, or simply institute overtime. Figure 9–15 illustrates the decision tree for this two-year period. The conditional profit is, of course, shown on the right side of the decision tree.

Figure 9–15 *Decision Tree for a Two-Year Plan of Action*

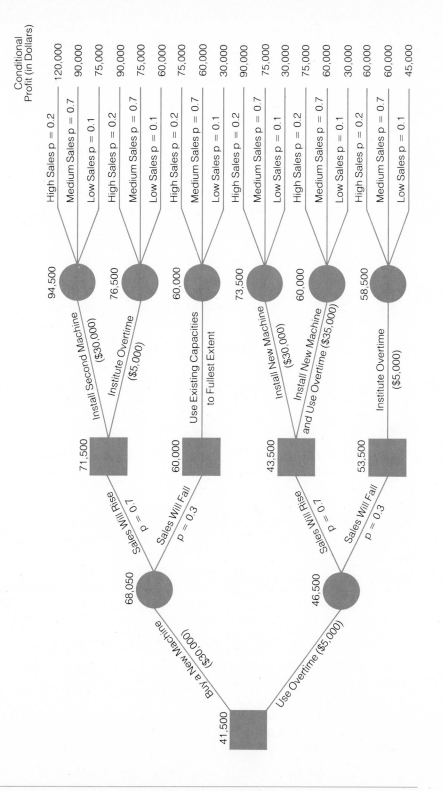

Conditional
Profit (in Dollars)

High Sales p = 0.2	120,000
Medium Sales p = 0.7	90,000
Low Sales p = 0.1	75,000
High Sales p = 0.2	90,000
Medium Sales p = 0.7	75,000
Low Sales p = 0.1	60,000
High Sales p = 0.2	75,000
Medium Sales p = 0.7	60,000
Low Sales p = 0.1	30,000
High Sales p = 0.2	90,000
Medium Sales p = 0.7	75,000
Low Sales p = 0.1	30,000
High Sales p = 0.2	75,000
Medium Sales p = 0.7	60,000
Low Sales p = 0.1	30,000
High Sales p = 0.2	60,000
Medium Sales p = 0.7	60,000
Low Sales p = 0.1	45,000

94,500 — Install Second Machine ($30,000)
76,500 — Institute Overtime ($5,000)
60,000 — Use Existing Capacities to Fullest Extent
73,500 — Install New Machine ($30,000)
60,000 — Install New Machine and Use Overtime ($35,000)
58,500 — Institute Overtime ($5,000)

71,500
60,000
43,500
53,500

Sales Will Rise p = 0.7
Sales Will Fall p = 0.3
Sales Will Rise p = 0.7
Sales Will Fall p = 0.3

68,050
46,500

Buy a New Machine ($30,000)
Use Overtime ($5,000)

41,500

Second Year

First Year

In order to determine the best initial decision—buying a new machine or using overtime—it is necessary to start by rolling the tree back from the right. First, the conditional profits must be multiplied by their probabilities. For example, starting at the top of the tree, to determine the expected values of installing the second machine, the calculation is $120,000 × 0.2 + 90,000 × 0.7 + 75,000 × 0.1 = $94,500. The same calculations for each of the other branches give expected values of $76,500, $60,000, $73,500, $60,000, and $58,500, respectively. These numbers have all been entered in the figure over their respective chance points.

Next, again starting at the top of the tree, the cost of installing a second machine must be compared with the cost of instituting overtime. When the costs of each are subtracted from their expected values of $94,500 and $76,500, the results are $64,500 and $71,500, respectively. Since the latter is greater, the firm will choose it.

The next alternative down the tree calls for using existing facilities to the fullest extent. Since this alternative has no additional costs associated with it, the $60,000 is carried back intact. Next is the cost of installing a new machine ($73,500 − $30,000 = $43,500) versus installing the machine and using overtime ($60,000 − $35,000 = $25,000). Since the former is less expensive, it is chosen. Then, on the lowest branch, there is the $58,500 expected value minus the $5,000 overtime, resulting in a new expected value of $53,500.

At this point, the analysis has run through the second year decisions; it is necessary to roll the branches back only one more year. Again starting at the top, a 0.7 probability is associated with the $71,500 expected value and a 0.3 probability is associated with the $60,000 expected value. From the sum of these answers $30,000, the cost of buying a new machine, is subtracted. The calculation follows:

$$\begin{aligned}
\$71{,}500 \times 0.7 &= \$50{,}050 \\
\$60{,}000 \times 0.3 &= \underline{18{,}000} \\
&\ \$68{,}050 \\
&\ \underline{-30{,}000} \quad \text{(new machine cost)} \\
&\ \$38{,}050
\end{aligned}$$

This is the expected value of buying the new machine immediately. The expected value of using overtime in the first year is:

$$\begin{aligned}
\$43{,}500 \times 0.7 &= \$30{,}450 \\
\$53{,}500 \times 0.3 &= \underline{16{,}050} \\
&\ \$46{,}500 \\
&\ \underline{-5{,}000} \quad \text{(use of overtime)} \\
&\ \$41{,}500
\end{aligned}$$

Since the latter expected value, $41,500, is greater than the former, $38,050, the company should first opt for overtime rather than a new machine. If sales rise, it should install a new machine the second year. Close examination of Figure 9–14 shows that if sales rise in the first year, the company is better off just installing a new machine rather than installing the machine *and* using overtime ($73,500 versus $60,000). Finally, if sales fall in the first year, the company should continue using overtime.

The decision tree does not provide definitive answers. However, it does allow the manager to weigh benefits against costs by assigning probabilities to specific events and ascertaining the respective payoffs. As Efraim Turban and Jack R. Meredith note:

The unique feature of decision trees is that they allow management to view the logical order of a sequence of decisions. They show a clear graphical presentation of the various alternative courses of action and their possible consequences. Using the decision tree, management can also examine the impact of a series of decisions (multiperiod decisions) on the objectives of the organization. The graphical presentation helps in understanding the interactions among alternative courses of action, uncertain events, and future consequences.[6]

HEURISTIC PROGRAMMING

Not all operations research approaches rely upon sophisticated mathematics. *Heuristic programming,* generally called heuristic problem-solving, is on the opposite end of the spectrum from the rigorous methodology used in some of the already examined OR techniques. Some problems are too large or too complex to be solved by a computer. Others are too unstructured; they leave a quantitative approach out of the question. In cases such as these, heuristic programming is often employed.

Heuristic means "serving to discover." Such an approach to problem solving is subjective as well as objective in nature, relying upon experience, judgment, intuition, and advice. Two of the most common heuristic approaches to problem solving are rules of thumb and trial and error.

Problems are often nothing more than brain twisters that force the manager to think. Consider the following example. An epidemic has broken out in a city. All twelve local hospitals have called a nearby pharmaceutical manufacturer and asked to have a particular serum delivered immediately. It generally takes three weeks to manufacture this serum, but the pharmaceutical company just happens to have a quantity of it on hand. Accordingly, the serum is placed in vials, wrapped in twelve individual packages, and rushed to the shipping dock. By this time, the crisis in the city has become so great that if each hospital does not have its allotted serum within the hour, patients will begin dying. Just as the manager of the pharmaceuticals shipping dock rushes the packages to the waiting delivery truck, a call comes: The worker who wrapped the packages reports that one of them is missing a five-ounce vial of serum. The vial is being sent down immediately, and in the two minutes the delivery will take, the manager's job is to ascertain which hospital has been shorted on its serum. The only available tool for the shipping dock manager is a balance scale. The problem, then, is how to isolate the package that is missing the vial of serum.

Heuristic programming employs rules of thumb and trial and error.

There are a number of ways to solve the problem. One is to place six packages on each side of the scale. The side with the light package will not go down so far as the side with the fully-packed allotments. By making this measurement, the manager reduces the number of possibilities to six. Then, by placing three on each side of the scale, it is possible to reduce the possibilities by half again. Three packages are left. There is time for only one more weighing. How should it be done? The answer is simpler than it seems. If the manager puts one package on each side of the scale, the answer is clear: Either the light package will not be able to balance the heavier or the two heavy packages will balance, thus showing that the short package is the one left off the scales.[7]

As another illustration, consider the following case. A supervisor is in the process of assigning work to a machinist. On this particular day, the machinist must do four jobs, and the supervisor wants to keep setup time to a minimum. The individual's machine is currently empty and needs to be set up for the first of the four jobs. The setup times from job to job are stated in Figure 9–16.

---

[6] Efraim Turban and Jack R. Meredith, *Fundamentals of Management Science,* 2d ed. (Dallas, Texas: Business Publications, 1981), p. 94.

[7] Adapted from Paul J. Gordon, "Heuristic Problem Solving: You Can Do It," *Business Horizons,* Spring 1962, pp. 43–53.

Figure 9–16 Setup Time in Minutes

From Job \ To Job	1	2	3	4
Empty	30	40	50	60
1	0	35	15	25
2	45	0	40	35
3	10	20	0	10
4	25	40	30	0

With the machine empty, as shown in the figure, it will take thirty minutes to set up Job 1, forty to set up Job 2, fifty to set up Job 3, and sixty to set up Job 4. Once the first job is complete, the machinist can go on to the second. In order to read Figure 9–16, assume that the supervisor chooses to have Job 3 done first; it will take fifty minutes to set up. From the figure, reading across from Job 3 on the left, it is known that the setup times for moving from Job 3 to Jobs 1, 2, and 4 are ten, twenty, and ten minutes respectively. If the supervisor should choose Job 2 second, the setup will take twenty minutes. Continuing on, suppose that the supervisor selects Job 4 for the third one: setting it up will take thirty-five minutes. Finally, reading down Figure 9–16 to Job 4 and across to Job 1, one can determine that the last job setup will take twenty-five minutes. Recapitulating the order and the times of the jobs gives the following summary:

Jobs	Setup Time (in minutes)
3	50
2	20
4	35
1	25
	130

The four jobs will take 130 minutes of setup time. Was the 3–2–4–1 sequence the one with the lowest setup time?

Table 9–3 presents the twenty-four different sequences for the four jobs. Note that the lowest time sequence is 1–3–4–2. Was this the sequence you chose? Most people do choose this one by following a simple rule. In moving from empty to the first job, they opt for the one with the lowest setup time and employ this same rule in moving from the first to the second job, second to the third, and third to the fourth. Depending on the setup

Table 9–3 Enumeration Results

Sequence Job Numbers	Setup Times	Total Minutes
1–2–3–4	30 + 35 + 40 + 10	115
1–2–4–3	30 + 35 + 30 + 30	125
1–3–2–4	30 + 15 + 20 + 35	100
1–3–4–2	30 + 15 + 10 + 40	95 Minimum
1–4–2–3	30 + 25 + 40 + 40	135
1–4–3–2	30 + 25 + 30 + 20	105
2–1–3–4	40 + 45 + 15 + 10	120
2–1–4–3	40 + 45 + 25 + 30	140
2–3–1–2	40 + 40 + 10 + 35	125
2–3–2–1	40 + 40 + 20 + 45	145
2–4–2–3	35 + 30 + 40 + 40	145
2–4–3–2	35 + 30 + 30 + 20	115
3–1–2–4	50 + 10 + 35 + 35	130
3–1–4–2	50 + 10 + 25 + 40	125
3–2–1–4	50 + 20 + 45 + 25	140
3–2–4–1	50 + 20 + 35 + 25	130
3–4–1–2	50 + 40 + 25 + 35	150
3–4–2–1	50 + 40 + 40 + 45	135
4–1–2–3	60 + 25 + 35 + 40	160
4–1–3–2	60 + 25 + 15 + 20	120
4–2–1–3	60 + 40 + 45 + 15	160
4–2–3–1	60 + 40 + 40 + 10	150
4–3–2–1	60 + 30 + 20 + 45	155
4–3–1–2	60 + 30 + 10 + 35	135

times, such a heuristic rule can provide the best answer. A heuristic approach will not always give the best answer, but heuristics can often help the manager arrive at good answers to work problems. For example, this supervisor's solution was better than twelve of the other sequences. However, a more careful analysis of the information in Table 9–3 would have led to another thirty-five minutes of reduced setup time.

These kinds of problems do not warrant sophisticated techniques, and they are far more common than those requiring linear programming and Monte Carlo simulation. Resource allocation, inventory control, plant layout, and job shop scheduling are all problems that can sometimes be solved through heuristic programming.

SUMMARY

This chapter introduced operations management (OR) and some of its distinguishing characteristics. It then presented five of the main areas of concern for operations management personnel. The chapter next examined some of the modern quantitative decision-making tools and processes, most of them falling under the heading of operations research. These varied in complexity and mathematical rigor, but all are of value to managers in the decision-making process.

Linear programming assists the manager in determining price-volume relationships for effective utilization of the organization's resources. The example used in this chapter illustrated how the technique could be employed to allocate scarce resources while simultaneously maximizing profit. The second technique discussed, the economic order quantity formula, helps the decision maker determine at what point and in what quantities inventory should be replenished. The third technique discussed, game theory, is useful in providing the manager with important insights into the elements of competition. Sometimes this competition is best represented as a zero-sum game with a saddle point, but more often it is typified by a non-zero-sum game without a saddle point, in which case it is necessary to use a mixed strategy in solving the problem. A fourth quantitative technique is queuing (waiting line) theory, which employs mathematical equations in balancing waiting lines and service. When it becomes difficult to evaluate alternatives by means of equations alone, many managers turn to the Monte Carlo technique, which uses a simulation approach and provides the decision maker with an opportunity to evaluate the effect of numerous decisions within the simulated environment. On the basis of simulation results, the manager is in a position to make the decision that best attains the objective.

Still another OR tool, and one that has been receiving increased attention in recent years, is the decision tree. This technique, which is less mathematical than those already mentioned, helps the manager weigh alternatives based on immediate and long-run results by encouraging the individual to: (a) identify the available courses of action; (b) assign probability estimates to the events associated with these alternatives; and (c) calculate the payoffs corresponding to each act-event combination. Heuristic programming, which was examined last, is the least mathematical of all OR techniques. Yet it is used far more often by the manager in every-day decision making (through rules of thumb and the use of trial and error) than any of the other OR tools.

REVIEW AND STUDY QUESTIONS

1. What are the distinguishing characteristics of operations management? What are some of the primary areas of concern for operations management personnel? Explain.
2. What is meant by the term *operations research?*
3. In your own words, define linear programming. What are its advantages to the manager in the decision-making process? What are its drawbacks?
4. What is the graphic technique?
5. Of what value is game theory to the manager?
6. What are the variables involved in the economic order quantity formula? Of what value is the formula to the manager? Explain.
7. In game theory, what is meant by the term zero-sum game? Non-zero-sum game? Saddle point?
8. Explain this statement: Most decisions made by the manager are non-zero-sum in nature.
9. What is meant by a mixed strategy?
10. What is meant by queuing theory?
11. Of what decision-making value is the Monte Carlo method to the manager? Explain.
12. How do decision trees help the manager in making long-run decisions? Short-run decisions?
13. What is heuristic programming?
14. Explain this statement: Many of the daily problems faced by managers are solved by means of heuristic programming.

SELECTED REFERENCES

Brown, R. V. "Do Managers Find Decision Theory Useful?" *Harvard Business Review,* May–June 1970, pp. 78–79.

Buffa, Elwood S. *Operations Management: The Management of Productive Systems.* New York: Wiley, 1976.

Chase, R. B., and Aquilano, J. J. *Production and Operations Management.* Homewood, Ill.: Richard D. Irwin, 1977.

Churchman, C. W.; Ackoff, R. L.; and Arnoff, E. L. *Introduction to Operations Research.* New York: Wiley, 1957.

Cook, R. M., and Russell, R. A. *Contemporary Operations Management: Text and Cases.* Englewood Cliffs, N.J.: Prentice-Hall, 1980.

Daellenbach, H. G., and Bell, E. J. *User's Guide to Linear Programming.* Englewood Cliffs, N.J.: Prentice-Hall, 1970.

Ferguson, Robert O., and Sargent, Lauren F. *Linear Programming.* New York: McGraw-Hill, 1968.

McDonald, John. *Strategy in Poker, Business and War.* New York: W. W. Norton, 1950.

Magee, J. F. "Decision Trees for Decision Making." *Harvard Business Review,* July–August 1964, pp. 126–138.

Moore, F. *Production Management.* Homewood, Ill.: Richard D. Irwin, 1973.

Moore, J. M. *Plant Layout and Design.* New York: Macmillan, 1962.

Paranka, S. "Competitive Bidding Strategy." *Business Horizons,* June 1971, pp. 39–43.

Pollay, R. "The Structure of Executive Decisions and Decision Times." *Administrative Science Quarterly,* December 1970, pp. 459–471.

Simon, Herbert A. *The New Science of Management Decision.* New York: Harper & Bros., 1960.

Trueman, R. E. *An Introduction to Quantitative Methods for Decision Making.* New York: Holt, Rinehart and Winston, 1977.

Turban, Efraim N., and Meredith, Jack R. *Fundamentals of Management Science,* 2d ed. Dallas, Texas: Business Publications, 1981, chaps. 4 and 14.

Vandell, R. F. "Management Evolution in the Quantitative World." *Harvard Business Review,* January–February 1970, pp. 83–92.

Virtis, R. J., and Garrett, R. W. "Weighing Risk in Capacity Expansion." *Harvard Business Review,* May–June 1970, pp. 132–140.

CASE: A Little of This and a Little of That

The Willowby Company had lost quite a bit of money in the previous year. As a result, its president, Norma Thurber, was determined to maximize profits as quickly as possible and show good first-quarter results. In attempting to carry out this objective, James Rogers, production manager at Willowby, found himself confronted with a resource allocation problem. The company was manufacturing two kinds of industrial machines, Type A and Type B. After examining the resources available to him, Rogers determined that he could solve the problem by means of the graphic method of linear programming. An analysis of the situation revealed that the following combinations and constraints for the two products were present:

Constraints	Type A	Type B
Assembly time	120 machines	240 machines
Available paint	150 machines	150 machines
Special casing for Type A	100 machines	—
Special casing for Type B	—	120 machines
Engines	180 machines	180 machines

After plotting these constraints on a graph, Rogers determined that there were five points within the feasibility area, permitting the following combinations of Type A and Type B to be manufactured:

1. 100 A and   0 B
2. 100 A and   40 B
3.   90 A and   60 B
4.   30 A and 120 B
5.   0 A and 120 B

In addition, each unit of A would result in a $300 profit to the firm and each unit of B would bring in $200 in profit.

Questions

1. Verify the accuracy of the above five points by drawing a graphic representation of the constraints.

2. Which of the above five alternatives is most profitable to Willowby? Show your work.

3. What other types of problems could Rogers solve by means of the graphic method? Give an illustration.

CASE: *An Economic Approach*

Ed Sharp, local manager of a radio and television retail store, used to reorder merchandise on the basis of gut feel. As he explained to one of his friends, "I don't know *exactly* when to reorder merchandise; I just use my best judgment." However, one day Robin Steele, his niece and a student in the Business College at State University, dropped by the store for a visit. When Steele learned of her uncle's unscientific approach to reordering inventory, she was shocked. "You should take a more refined approach to things, Uncle Ed," she said. "There are lots of decision-making tools and techniques you could use. For example, there's the economic order quantity formula. It can pinpoint exactly how many units you should order at any one time."

Sharp was impressed and decided to try his niece's suggestion. Together the two chose one of the most popular items in the store, a small AM-FM radio. After examining past sales records, they were able to obtain the following information: (a) the expected annual demand for the radio was 750 units; (b) the administrative costs associated with placing an order were $20; (c) the value of each radio was $30; and (d) the estimate for taxes, insurance, and other expenses was 10 percent.

Questions

1. Using a trial-and-error approach, construct a table showing the size of each order, the order cost associated with this size, the carrying cost, and the total cost if Sharp reorders inventory 1, 2, 3, 4, 5, 10, and 20 times per year.

2. Using the EOQ formula in this chapter, determine the most economic reorder quantity.

3. How much money has Steele saved her uncle's store if Sharp uses the EOQ formula rather than trial and error, assuming that he now reorders five times a year? Explain.

CASE: *Half and Half*

A group of high school seniors were touring the facilities of a large bakery not long ago. The students were impressed with the mechanization of the operations, but they were even more interested in finding out how the firm decided how much bread or how many cakes to bake. When the tour was over, the students were taken to the cafeteria for pastries and questions. One of the seniors asked, "How do you know how many and what types of cookies to bake? Or scones or anything? I'd just like to understand how you know that today is the day for 12,000 gingersnaps and 7,500 cream horns."

The tour guide smiled. "I'll tell you what," he said. "Let me call one of our staff specialists in here to give you an answer to that." A few minutes later the specialist showed up with a portable blackboard and some papers containing production statistics.

He said: "I understand you're interested in finding out how we go about deciding how much of everything to bake. Actually, we use a mathematical approach whenever we can. There's a lot less guesswork in the business than there was twenty years ago. As I explain, I'll be using baked cookies as an illustration.

"Earlier in the day we took an inventory to see how much cookie mix, molasses, labor, and oven space we had available for making both sugar cookies and gingersnaps, the only kinds we bake. Our calculations showed that we had enough cookie mix to bake, in dozens, either 2,000 sugar or 1,200 ginger cookies. In addition, we had enough labor time to bake 1,500 sugar or 1,000 ginger cookies, enough molasses for 800 ginger cookies, and enough oven space for 1,200 sugar or ginger cookies. Now I'll write those numbers on the blackboard along with the profit per dozen, which is 15 cents in the case of sugar cookies and 20 cents in the case of gingersnaps."

The speaker then put the following data on the blackboard:

	Sugar Cookies	*Gingersnaps*
Cookie Mix	1,200 dozen	1,200 dozen
Labor	1,500 dozen	1,000 dozen
Molasses	—	800 dozen
Oven Space	1,200 dozen	1,200 dozen
Profit	15¢ a dozen	20¢ a dozen

"Now, given this information plus the fact that we know we can sell everything we make, how many of each type should we bake?"

The students looked at the numbers but were confused. One pointed out that the firm could bake no more than 1,200 dozen sugar and 800 dozen gingersnaps, but no one seemed to know how to calculate the best combination of the two. After pondering the problem for five minutes, the seniors admitted defeat.

"Don't feel bad," said the speaker. "Just by looking at the data it is impossible to say. However, we have a mathematical technique by which we can prove that the best combination to bake is 600 dozen sugar and 600 dozen ginger. At this point profit is maximized."

The students were impressed. On the way out of the building one of them remarked, "I never realized baking was such a science. At my house it is still an art."

Questions

1. How much profit will the firm make if it bakes 600 dozen sugar and 600 dozen gingersnaps? Show your calculations.
2. How is this company suboptimizing its resources? Optimizing its production? Maximizing its profit?
3. How important are mathematical tools and techniques to the modern manager?

CASE: *The Big Payoff*

Gloria Adler, science editor of a large publishing house, is about ready to release a new basic biology textbook. She intends to obtain a large share of the basic biology text market. Although there are many competitors, one in particular is also coming out with a new biology book. Therefore, Adler must formulate her strategy very carefully. For this reason, instead of just designing her own plan of action, she has decided to ask herself what the opposition is going to do. She has come up with six basic strategies. Adler intends to use the first three; the second three are those that she has heard will be employed by the competition. Adler's strategy is:

1. Price the book lower than any other on the market.
2. Provide 10,000 complimentary copies to university professors.
3. Hire more salespeople to call on university professors and explain the strong points of the text.

The opposition's strategy is:

4. Give large quantity discounts to the bookstores.
5. Substantially increase the advertising budget.
6. Print the text on extremely high quality paper so as to enhance its aesthetic value.

After giving the matter a great deal of thought, Adler has concluded that the following payoff matrix represents the outcomes in thousands of textbooks that will occur under each of the above strategies:

		D	E	F
	A	6	4	9
Adler	B	9	3	2
	C	7	1	5

Questions

1. After determining the numbers in Row Minima and Column Maxima, can you find a saddle point? If so, what strategic advice would you give Adler? If not, of what value is the above information to Adler?

2. If the competition is aware of the above payoff matrix and concludes it is an accurate representation of reality, what will the other company do? Explain, bringing the concept of mixed strategy into your discussion.

CHAPTER 10

INFORMATION SYSTEMS AND DECISION MAKING

GOALS OF THE CHAPTER

In addition to helping identify and evaluate alternative courses of action, quantitative school advocates are concerned with getting this information to those who need it. When this activity is added to those described in Chapters 8 and 9, it becomes obvious that, just like the process school, the quantitative school can be viewed as a closed-loop of interrelated activities. Figure 3–2 showed that the process school consists of planning, organizing, and controlling. Figure 10–1 shows how the quantitative school can be diagrammed.

The part of the figure that has not yet been examined is the "convey the results" section. This transmittal of results is done through the use of information systems, which are studied in this chapter. The first goal of the chapter is to examine such systems. The second goal is to explore the role of computers in them. The third goal is to study links connecting the quantitative school to the process and behavioral schools.

When you have finished this chapter, you should be able to:

1. Explain how an information system can help improve a manager's decision-making ability.
2. Describe how an information system is designed.
3. State some of the major uses of computers in modern organizations.
4. Discuss some of the shortcomings of computers.
5. Illustrate some of the behavioral impacts that information systems can have on organizational personnel.
6. Discuss the links that exist between the quantitative and process schools and the quantitative and behavioral schools.

INFORMATION SYSTEMS DESIGN

Managers have many functions. They are strategists who formulate objectives, disseminators of information who communicate these goals to other organizational members, and company spokespersons who provide information to outsiders. Managers can, therefore, be thought of as nerve centers, responsible for obtaining external and internal information and passing it on to various groups. This managerial information processing system can be depicted as in Figure 10–2.

Perhaps the major problem faced by modern managers is that of receiving more information than they really need. In recent years many firms have dealt with this problem by developing their own information systems. An *information system* is:

> *an organized method of providing past, present, and projection information relating to internal operations and external intelligence. It supports the planning, control and operational functions of an organization by furnishing uniform information in the proper time-frame to assist the decision-making process.*[1]

Designing an Information System

Information systems have one primary goal: providing managers with the data necessary for making intelligent decisions. Since there are three basic levels in the managerial organization (upper, middle, and lower management), each with different interests and viewpoints, it is evident that much of this decision-making information will have to be tailor-made to meet the needs of the respective levels. The way to do this becomes clear with the recognition that two basic inputs are necessary in any effective information system. The first can be called major determinants, factors that play a role in structuring the type of information that management will be receiving. According to William M. Zani, they consist of opportunities and risks, company strategy, company structure, management and decision-making processes, available technology, and available information sources.[2] The roles of these determinants will become more evident in the next section, where an information system blueprint is examined.

There are major determinants in information system design.

The second input consists of key success variables, the factors and tasks that determine success or failure. They will differ, of course, from company to company and from industry to industry:

> *For a consumer goods company manufacturing nondifferentiated products, the key success areas might be product promotion and understanding customer responses to product, marketing, and competitive changes. . . . For a manufacturer of commodity products, manufacturing and distribution cost control and efficiency might be the major determinants of success.*[3]

These critical success factors will then be translated into primary measures which are monitored to ensure that everything goes well. For example, in the case of one microwave company, the critical success factors and primary measures in Table 10–1 were identified.

Blueprints bring key success variables together.

The Blueprint Itself The well-designed management information system blueprint brings together the determinants and key success variables cited in Table 10–1, since all these factors are interrelated. For example, the general business environment (opportunities and risks) and the company resources (personnel, money, machines, material, and

---

[1] Walter J. Kennevan, "MIS Universe," *Data Management,* September 1970, p. 63.
[2] William M. Zani, "Blueprint for MIS," *Harvard Business Review,* November–December, 1970, p. 96.
[3] Ibid., p. 98.

Figure 10–1 Quantitative School Functions

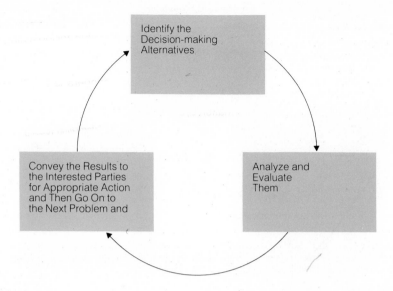

Figure 10–2 The Manager as an Information Processor

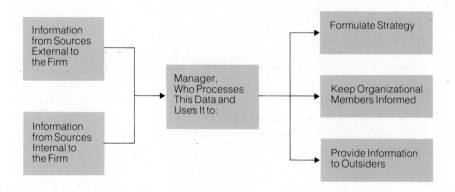

information) help establish overall strategy. In turn, this strategy serves as a basis for development of the organization structure. All four of these factors are related to the organization's key success variables. This interrelationship is schematically illustrated in Figure 10–3.

As just noted, the organization is structured to include three levels of managers, all of whom need vital information for decision making. Top management is greatly interested in major developments in the external and internal arenas that will have an impact on the organization's strategic plan. Middle-level managers need information that will help them coordinate the activities of upper and lower levels. Individuals at the lower

Table 10-1 *Critical Success Factors and Primary Measures in a Microwave Company*

Critical Success Factor	Primary Measure
Image in financial markets	Price/earnings ratio
Technological reputation with customers	Orders/bid ratio
	Customer "perception" results
Market success	Change in market share for each product
	Growth rates of the company's markets
Risk recognition in major bids and contracts	The firm's years of experience with similar products
	"New" or "old" customers
	Prior customer relationships
Profit margin on jobs	The bid profit margin as a ratio of profit on similar jobs in this product line
Company morale	Absenteeism and turnover
	Informal feedback
Performance to budget on major jobs	Job cost budgeted as a percentage of the actual cost

Source: Adapted from John F. Rockart, "Chief Executives Define Their Own Data Needs," *Harvard Business Review*, March–April 1979, p. 89. Copyright ©1979 by the President and Fellows of Harvard College; all rights reserved.

Figure 10-3 *A Partial Information Systems Blueprint*

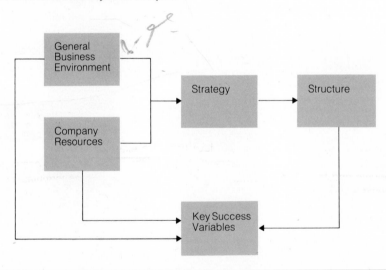

Source: Adapted from William M. Zani, "Blueprint for MIS," *Harvard Business Review*, November–December 1970, pp. 96–97. Copyright © 1970 by the President and Fellows of Harvard College; all rights reserved.

managerial levels require data related to the production of goods and services. In designing the information-decision system for each level, developers must focus primary attention on the relevance of the data to decision making.

The information required at the top levels tends to be more encompassing in nature, forming the basis for strategic planning decisions. Setting objectives, designing the

Figure 10–4 Total Information System Blueprint

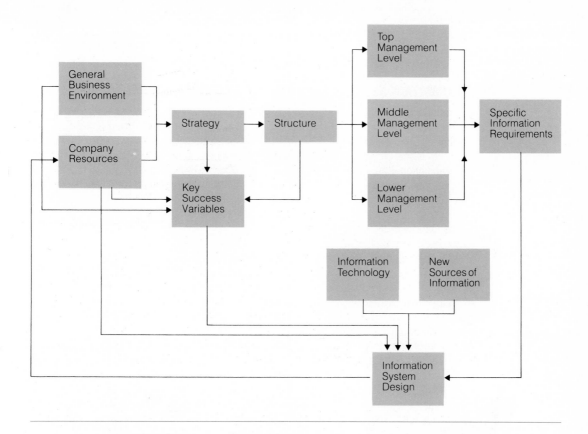

organization structure, and choosing new product lines are examples of the types of subjects that would be included. At the intermediate levels the data need to be somewhat more specific and to include information useful for activities such as formulating budgets, planning working capital, and measuring, appraising, and improving management performance. At the lower levels the data have to be very specific; they might even be programmed through the use of mathematical models and techniques. Here, the information would include such items as information on production scheduling, inventory control, and the measurement, appraisal, and improvement of worker efficiency.

Decision-making information will differ by level.

Working with these information requirements, the organization can develop an overall information system design, which will remain in operation for as long as it is useful. However, with new sources of information constantly developing, with new information requirements and with information technology continually changing, the system will have to be periodically revamped. Nevertheless, employing just the information in this section, the student of management can extend Figure 10–3 and develop a total information system blueprint as seen in Figure 10–4.

The design not only gives primary emphasis to information system determinants and key success variables but is also structured with the needs of management in mind. It follows a from-the-top-down philosophy. This is important, for as Zani notes:

If the design of management information systems begins on a high conceptual level and on a high managerial level as well, a company can avoid the unfortunate "bottom up" design phenomenon of recent history and begin to develop the real, and very great, potential of MIS as a tool for modern management.[4]

In recent years many firms have instituted and employed management information systems. The benefits these systems offer make them very valuable management tools.

INFORMATION SYSTEMS AND THE QUANTITATIVE SCHOOL

A cursory analysis of information systems might puzzle the uninitiated person, who might well wonder why the quantitative school advocates get involved in designing them. So far, this text has described their interests as resting heavily in the area of mathematical formulas. In the last two decades, however, computers have begun to play a major role in organizational life. The initial interest of the quantitative theorists in the computer was for calculation purposes. Many of the quantitative decision-making tools discussed in the previous chapter are used in conjunction with the computer. By developing prepackaged computer programs for handling EOQ, linear programming, queuing theory, and Monte Carlo simulation problems, the quantitative theorists can often save themselves hundreds of hours of work time.

As computers became more commonplace in industry, individuals who were trained to program these machines and provide management with the output started to emerge. In addition to computer programmers, systems analysts also arrived on the scene. Although their emphasis is not as quantitative as is the mathematicians', these computer people share a number of common characteristics with today's management scientists, including: (a) the application of scientific analysis to managerial problems, (b) the goal of improving the manager's decision-making ability, (c) a high regard for economic effectiveness criteria, (d) a reliance on mathematical models, and (e) the use of electronic computers.

Computer and quantitative people have much in common.

Of course, the computer-oriented employees are far less quantitative than their mathematical counterparts. In fact, in recent years some of them have contended that they are actually members of a fourth school of management—a systems school. (The validity of this type of claim will be addressed in greater detail in Chapter 15. It is first necessary to see what these systems people do.) It has already been noted that some of them help design information systems. Others work directly with the computer, a work area to be investigated now. A person about to delve into this topic, however, must keep in mind two facts: First, not all information systems are computerized. Second, the computer can do a lot more than merely solve mathematical equations and provide information for management decision making. However, as Boehm has so well noted:

The uncertainties of these times have forced a shot-gun marriage between the executive decision maker and the systems analyst. This blending of human intuition, broad and nimble, with mathematical precision backed by the power of the computer, has brought the planning and conduct of business to a high plateau of rationality.

Today more than half the companies in the Fortune "500" list have access to computer programs that model the national and world economies as integrated systems and that can be manipulated mathematically, thereby relating company policy and performance to many important economic factors. Many other companies, large and small, subscribe to such systems analysis models through their bankers or consultants.[5]

---

[4] Ibid., p. 100.
[5] George A. W. Boehm, "Shaping Decisions with Systems Analysis," *Harvard Business Review,* September–October 1976, p. 91.

INFORMATION SYSTEMS AND COMPUTERS

The past three decades have seen the entry of automation into business enterprises. Webster defines *automation* as "the technique of making an apparatus (as a calculating machine), a process (as of manufacturing) or a system (as of bookkeeping) operate automatically."[6] In broad terms, there have been four main areas of automation development: (1) automatic machinery, (2) integrated materials handling and processing equipment, (3) control mechanisms, and (4) electronic computers and data-processing machines. The fourth category—computers in particular—will be the center of focus here because of the role computers play in the area of information systems.

Modern Computers

Modern computers are of two general types: analog and digital. The *analog computer* is a measuring machine used principally by engineers in solving job-related problems. The *digital computer* is a counting machine which, by electrical impulses, can perform arithmetic calculations at a speed far in excess of human capacity; for this reason it is of great value to business firms.

Computers are of two types: analog and digital.

The basic concept of the digital computer dates back hundreds of years. However, Charles Babbage, the nineteenth-century English mathematician and mechanician, is regarded as the originator of the modern automatic computer. In 1834 Babbage conceived the principle of the analytical engine, which was similar to the modern-day computer in that it would handle a large number of variables that could be fed into the machine on punched cards.

Today, of course, with the advent of the electronic computer, Babbage's concept has been developed to far greater depth than he ever imagined. Over the last thirty years, four generations of electronic computers have emerged, and a fifth is on the horizon. The first relied on vacuum tubes and magnetic drums, the second on solid state devices and drum or magnetic cores, and the third on solid logic technology and monolithic integrated circuits. Fourth-generation computers, often referred to as "information handlers," are more versatile and powerful than any of their predecessors, as computer expert Elias M. Awad has described:

Computer power has increased dramatically.

> With fourth generation computers, the user can now access files directly, schedule various production and other problems, and acquire authorized data, when needed. They constitute a step toward a truly user-oriented, interactive computer system.
>
> One significant outcome of the evolutionary computers of the 1970s is a revolutionary effort to pack tremendous data processing power into minicomputers at a relatively low cost. As a result, minicomputers facilitate the decentralization of data processing, giving the system responsibility back to users. Users are more familiar with their particular problems and requirements than a remote data processing department that serves all company users. Thus the computer is getting back in line with the business at hand and cutting the escalating costs of business.[7]

In addition, the time-sharing concept, whereby a number of people can use the computer at the same time and encounter no delay in receiving results, has been introduced.

The future promises even more dramatic breakthroughs. For example, Awad reports that fifth generation computers "are expected to fully operationalize forecasting and

---

[6] *Webster's Third New International Dictionary*, vol. 1, s. v. "automation."

[7] Elias M. Awad, *Business Data Processing*, 5th ed. (Englewood Cliffs, N.J.: Prentice-Hall, 1980), p. 62.

---

other predictive models and make it possible for systems to interact among themselves for efficiency of data exchange."[8]

Such computers will also be able to provide electronic funds transfer systems between financial institutions, so that, for example, money can be automatically removed from one bank and deposited in another.

Additionally, middle managers will find themselves able to use these computers in planning and analyzing relevant problem areas. The wait for upper-level clearance, so common to middle management in the past, will be virtually eliminated by the efficiency of the fifth generation computers, which will feed information to the various managerial levels and control its dispersal as top management has it programmed. The result of all this is that the computer holds great promise as a management decision-making tool.

The fundamental elements of the computer have remained the same.

Despite the development of new features, the fundamental elements of the computer have remained basically the same: input, processing, and output. First the data are fed into the computer, generally as punched cards, magnetic tape, or some kind of printed document. Then the material is processed; that is, the computer coordinates material, makes computations on data, or works out logical decisions. Finally, the computer translates material into output, which often takes the form of printed paper, punched cards, or a picture displayed on a screen. Since the computer can perform these operations in a fraction of the time it would take to complete them manually, it has become an important management tool. However, a computer will only do what it is programmed to do.

Computer Programming

The *computer program* provides the machine with the step-by-step directions it is to follow. This program is usually fed into the computer on punched cards or, if it is going to be used over and over again, stored on tape or disk and called into action by the operator. Programs are generally written in computer language, and in many cases they can be purchased from computer firms. However, for a problem or assignment that is unique to the firm, a special program has to be written or a current one modified.

When a program is bought, it is often useful to first construct a flow chart of the operation to ensure that the program will be executed properly. This chart can then be translated into computer language. Figure 10–5 illustrates the flow diagram used by an investor who is pondering the purchase of a new stock. The individual has certain prerequisites which all new stocks must meet. First, they must be listed on the New York Stock Exchange. Second, their price/earnings ratio must be under ten. Third, their current prices must not be within 80 percent of their annual highs. If these three conditions are met and if sufficient funds are available in the bank or brokerage accounts, the investor will buy the stock. If not, the individual will evaluate the wisdom of taking a bank loan to buy the stock. Otherwise, the investor will compare the new stock with those in his or her present portfolio. If it appears to be a better buy than any of those currently there, the individual will sell the less profitable issues and purchase as many shares of the new stock as the proceeds make possible.

A flow diagram helps the programmer see the logic of the instructions. Anyone who has ever done any programming can attest to the fact that the machine operates with no brain of its own. The programmer should expect to take almost nothing for granted (although the latest computers have some flexibility along these lines). The computer will reject a program that lacks explicit instructions. Furthermore, a program deck that

---

[8] Elias M. Awad, *Introduction to Computers in Business* (Englewood Cliffs, N.J.: Prentice-Hall, 1977), p. 77.

Figure 10 –5   Stock Investor's Flow Diagram

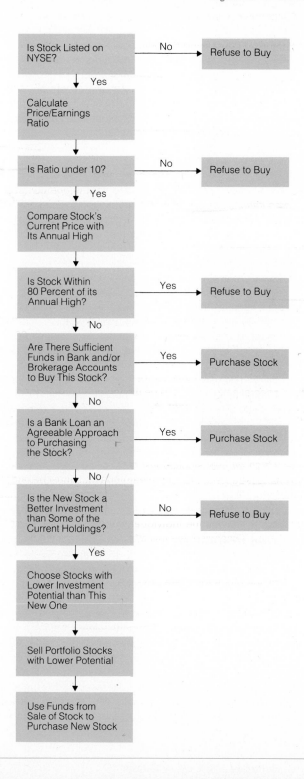

has run countless times will occasionally be rejected as erroneous because one of the cards is worn and cannot be read properly. This can result in hours of work and frustration as one searches for the error only to realize that a card merely has to be duplicated.

On the positive side, however, computer programming teaches logic. Since the computer has no mind of its own, the programmer must proceed slowly and accurately. When the machine rejects a program as illogical, the programmer, despite all the work put into the program, knows that the flow diagram is erroneous; something has been omitted or one part of the diagram is nonsensical. There are times, of course, when the computer will miss a card, and if the program is fed in again, the desired output will be obtained. However, these are exceptional cases. When the machine rejects a program, it is almost always the programmer's error.

Computer programming teaches logic.

Computer Uses

The computer has many uses, from handling routine paperwork to providing information for top-level decision making. The most common uses are the routine ones. Most companies employ the computer to perform arithmetic and bookkeeping functions, such as processing the payroll, computing customer account balances, or processing stockholder lists. In the 1980s it is highly likely that much of this routine paperwork still being handled by clerks will also be computerized.

One type of paperwork seriously being considered for computerization is that of handling stock certificates. Today, the stock purchaser is issued a certificate. When the person sells the security, the certificate must be turned over to the new buyer. However, since some stockholders will buy and sell a stock in the same day, there may be a time lag before the certificate ever gets to its rightful owner. Eliminating the use of certificates and putting all this information on a computer could result in far more accurate record keeping.

One of the widest uses of the computer is for inventory control. In retail stores, for example, it is common to find small coded tickets attached to all merchandise. When the items are sold, the tickets are torn off and sent to a central locale where the data are either placed on punched cards or read directly into the computer. In this way, the number of units on hand can be determined on a day-to-day basis, and more inventory can be ordered at the appropriate time. In recent years, large retail firms have automated their operations even further and, via machines on the sales floor, can report transactions directly to the computer. These point-of-sale systems are making it easier to control inventory.

One computer use is inventory control.

Another major application of the computer is in airline reservations, the making of which provides an illustration of what is known as "real time," which is, simply, time when the computer is relating what is going on as it is happening. In the case of reservations, the airline clerk feeds the information into a central computer via a console. The computer in turn scans its memory, reports whether seats are available on the desired flight, and automatically sends back a confirmation while simultaneously reducing the number of available seats.

Airlines reservations processing is another computer use.

The data bank is another approach that is gaining in popularity. Information on a subject is fed into the computer memory, thereby creating a bank of data from which individuals with questions on this subject can obtain ready answers. Airlines use this concept in regard to scheduled flights and departure times. For example, a man in San Francisco has business in Chicago on Friday. He then wants to go on to New York. What is the earliest flight he can catch after 6:00 P.M. on Friday that will take him to Kennedy International? The agent in San Francisco will probably not know, since the person seldom handles Chicago to New York requests; but the airline will have stored this

Data banks are a third computer use.

standard information in the computer so that the agent can readily get it for the passenger. Some insurance companies deposit all insurance policies in the data bank. Agents seeking answers to policyholder questions can obtain, through telecommunications, up-to-date responses. Other firms feed personnel information into the data bank, including statistics such as salaries, work experience, educational background, and performance appraisals. In this way, they can obtain an immediate profile of an individual being considered for promotion or a list of personnel with a particular skill or training. In the case of IBM, managers can obtain information on business activities in their own particular regions:

> A marketing manager, for example, addresses the computer with a code number that identifies him and his responsibilities. When he inquires about the state of his business, the system displays on a screen a pre-analyzed report on marketing activities in his particular region. Thus the user gets the information he needs but nothing more.[9]

Another computer application that is gaining acceptance is the automatic bank teller. In most parts of the country today, an individual can obtain money from a bank-teller machine after hours or on weekends by means of a special credit card. By placing this card in the machine, which is hooked up to a computer, and entering through a keyboard a personal identification code number and the amount to be withdrawn, the customer will automatically receive a packet of money and a coded receipt.[10] Furthermore, if the supply of funds allocated to the automatic teller begins to run low because of excessive withdrawals, the computer will alert a bank manager, who can come down and make more money available. In addition, the computer-run machine is capable of receiving deposits, transferring funds from checking to savings (and vice versa), and accepting time-credit loan payments.

Automatic bank tellers are another computer use.

Simulation In recent years, computer *simulation* has also been employed to handle "what if" questions. By simulating a situation, the manager can plug in different decisions and evaluate the outcome of each:

> If, say, the manager enters the price, the expected volume, and certain budgetary decisions, the computer will provide a pro forma profit and loss statement for that item. The judgment of the manager is used to suggest alternatives for consideration. The power of the computer is used to carry out the manager's understanding of the quantitative relationships between inputs and outputs—e.g., prices, volumes, and annual profits. The judgment of the manager is . . . called on to determine if the answer is acceptable or if further trials should be made to secure data or judgments which may produce a more acceptable output.[11]

The key to the successful use of the computer in this instance is determined by how well the company has been able to simulate actual conditions. If the model is accurate, the information being fed back to the manager is reliable; if not, the data upon which the individual is basing the decision is worthless.

Computer simulations must be accurate.

A number of firms have recently moved toward the use of computer simulation in helping their managers make decisions. In addition to the effect of price on quantity, other typical "what if" questions include:

> If a proposed new item of equipment is purchased or leased, what will be the effects on profits and cash flow of alternative financing methods?

---

[9] Boehm, "Shaping Decisions with Systems Analysis," p. 96.

[10] Currently, in most places, withdrawals are limited to a maximum of $150 a day.

[11] Curtis H. Jones, "At Last: Real Computer Power for Decision Makers," *Harvard Business Review,* September–October 1970, p. 79.

Figure 10–6 *Simulation of a Purchase versus Lease Strategy*

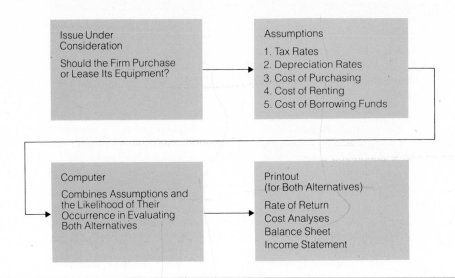

Issue Under Consideration Should the Firm Purchase or Lease Its Equipment?	**Assumptions** 1. Tax Rates 2. Depreciation Rates 3. Cost of Purchasing 4. Cost of Renting 5. Cost of Borrowing Funds
Computer Combines Assumptions and the Likelihood of Their Occurrence in Evaluating Both Alternatives	**Printout** **(for Both Alternatives)** Rate of Return Cost Analyses Balance Sheet Income Statement

If a wage increase is granted, what will be the effect on production rates, use of overtime, risk of seasonal inventory, and so on, for a production program?[12]

The questions, along with the assumptions made by the simulation designer and/or manager, are fed into the computer and evaluated according to the probability of their occurrence. The answer is then printed out in whatever form is desired; rate of return, cost analysis, balance sheet, and income statement are all possible examples. Figure 10–6 provides a general illustration.

In addition, some firms have developed models that help them make decisions when some particular problem develops. Consider the following:

At 9:32 A.M., a blowout! A blast furnace breaks down in the steel plant. Cold iron will have to be heated to produce the molten iron normally supplied to the refining process from this furnace. Processing time will be almost doubled, reducing the shop's production capacity by 60%. The cost per ton of steel will certainly rise sharply as a result of the increased processing time. But how much will it rise?

Using a remote time-shared computer terminal in his office, a manager at Island Steel Company defines the new conditions resulting from the equipment failure and enters them in a set of models which simulate the steelmaking process and the costs involved. At 11:26 A.M.—less than two hours later, the same morning—he estimates the new cost figures and prepares a revised corporate profit projection . . . the computer has vastly enhanced his decision-making capability.[13]

Thus, the computer has proved to be a valuable tool for management decision making. However, there are some very important drawbacks which also merit consideration.

---

[12] James B. Boulden and Elwood S. Buffa, "Corporate Models: On-line, Real-time Systems," *Harvard Business Review,* July–August 1970, p. 67.
[13] Ibid., p. 65.

Drawbacks to Computers

The most common argument raised against computers is that they are expensive investments which are never fully utilized. However, many managers, determined to have the latest, most sophisticated equipment, allow themselves to be sold more hardware (that is, computer machine) than they really need. As *Business Week* has noted: "Perhaps only members of the Flat Earth Society would deny that data-processing technology has revolutionized almost every aspect of the operation of a business. Yet even the strongest proponents of that revolution concede that the computer equipment in place at most companies has grown in sophistication much faster than the managerial capability for directing its use."[14]

Some companies buy expensive toys instead of the hardware they really need.

A second problem is that managers have a habit of overrating computer results, failing to remember that the output is only as valid as the input. Fred Luthans and Robert Koester, for example, conducted an experiment in which they determined that individuals with no computer training are more willing to abide by information presented in computer printout form than in noncomputer printout form. In short, people who lack a computer background are often awed by computer results and assign to them a validity and reliability that is not actually justified.[15]

Computer information can be overrated.

Managers also tend to overrate the capabilities of the computer, creating a third kind of problem. In reality the limitations of the machines are severe, but many decision makers see the machines as characterized by HAL, the on-board computer in *2001: A Space Odyssey*.[16] Highly sophisticated, HAL was capable of phenomenal feats. In fact, he could virtually think like a human. Unfortunately, there was an error in his program. But, being humanlike, he fought for survival and killed most of the crew before he was finally deprogrammed and rendered harmless. In reality, HAL is still very much a concept. For example, digital computers cannot replicate fringe consciousness (an awareness of cues in the environment), conduct essence-accident discrimination (the ability to separate necessary from incidental characteristics), or handle ambiguity tolerance (a willingness to deal with imprecisely defined variables that are nonetheless useful to the problems at hand).[17] These attributes are essential to decision making, and they continue to remain outside the realm of current computer capability.

Computer capability can be overrated too.

In fact, many of the promises made about the computer, outside the sphere of computational work, have simply not materialized. Curtis H. Jones reports that, with the possible exception of logistics, the current trend is actually away from computerized management decision making. Companies such as Western Electric, Hughes Aircraft, and Fairfield Manufacturing have all, to varying degrees, followed this retrenchment approach, shifting all or part of the decision-making functions from the computer to staff members. Of course, other companies are moving in the opposite direction, but the point is that the computer is only a management tool. It is not a replacement for the human decision maker. Along these lines, Steven L. Alter has observed:

My findings show what other researchers have reported: applications are being developed and used to support the manager responsible for making and implementing decisions, rather than to replace him. In

---

[14] "Solving a Computer Mismatch in Management," *Business Week,* April 2, 1979, p. 73.

[15] Fred Luthans and Robert Koester, "The Impact of Computer Generated Information on the Choice Activities of Decision Makers," *Academy of Management Journal,* June 1976, pp. 328–332.

[16] Arthur C. Clarke, *2001: A Space Odyssey* (New York: New American Library, 1968).

[17] Jones, "At Last: Real Computer Power for Decision Makers," p. 78. For a brief discussion of some of these computer developments, see "How Smart Can Computers Get?" *Newsweek,* June 30, 1980, pp. 52–53.

other words, people in a growing number of organizations are using what are often called decision support systems to improve their managerial effectiveness. [18]

As long as managers are aware of what the computer cannot do, they are in a good position to evaluate and maximize its usefulness in the decision-making process.

INFORMATION SYSTEMS AND PEOPLE

A well-designed information system can provide the manager with all the information necessary to make effective decisions. However, since this decision process takes place at every level of the organization, it is inevitable that information systems will have an impact on the people who work within it. Before discussing the effects of such systems on organization members, it is important to note how the quantitative school overlaps that of the management process and behavioral areas. The quantitative people provide information useful in planning and controlling operations, two areas of key importance to the process school. However, the quantitative people do sometimes create behavioral problems in the organization's employees, who often feel threatened by new information systems and the introduction of computer facilities. The following sections examine the link between the quantitative and behavioral schools by studying the impact of change brought on by information systems.

INFORMATION SYSTEMS AND THE IMPACT OF CHANGE

How is the introduction of a new information system received by organization personnel? Whenever change is introduced into an organization, there is a chance that it will result in some dysfunctional behavior. Quite simply, change tends to frighten people; and the greater the change, the more likely it is that people will resist it or react to it by way of defense mechanisms of one form or another.

Change in information systems is often viewed by employees simply as a more efficient information tool; in such cases it is welcomed. However, change brings uncertainty and is therefore sometimes viewed by employees as a threat; in such cases it can result in the development of frustration or anxiety. The response, of course, will depend on the situation and the individuals affected. What must be realized is that, like all other changes introduced into the system, information systems can cause behavioral problems.

Factors Causing Dysfunctional Behavior

Research indicates that when an information system is introduced into the organization, five major factors can cause dysfunctional behavior. [19]

New information systems can cause dysfunctional behavior.

First, the new system often necessitates redefinition of departmental boundaries. Some people are transferred to other departments; others stay in their present unit but are given new or expanded duties. In either case these changes, even though they may bring about greater organizational operating efficiency, can cause employee resistance because they upset the status quo in the formal organization structure.

---

[18] Steven L. Alter, "How Effective Managers Use Information Systems," *Harvard Business Review,* November–December 1976, p. 97.

[19] G. W. Dickson and John K. Simmons, "The Behavioral Side of MIS," *Business Horizons,* August 1970, pp. 59–71.

Figure 10–7 Frustration Created by a New Information System

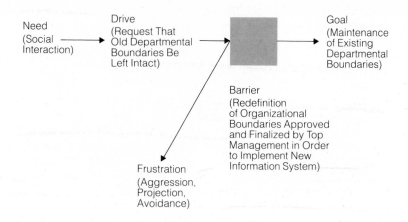

Second, there may be an accompanying effect on the informal structure: "An organization tends to develop a system of values, ethical codes, taboos, special working relations. . . . The impact of a new system on the informal structure can be as serious in terms of creating behavioral disturbances as the impact on the formal structure."[20]

Third, some people, especially older ones with many years of company service, often see the development as threatening. They believe the new system will replace them.

Fourth, in many organizations change is introduced without proper consideration of the opinions, fears, or anxieties of the employees. When this error occurs, the management information system faces trouble from the very start.

Fifth, and closely related to the above factor, is the method of introducing change. Douglas McGregor, the noted behaviorist, has written: "A fair amount of research has pointed up the fact that resistance to change is a reaction primarily to certain methods of instituting change rather than an inherent human characteristic."[21] Of course, these are not the only factors that may lead to dysfunctional behavior. They are, however, the most common and can result in a host of frustration reactions.

Frustration Reactions When one or more of the above factors is present, organizational personnel may encounter frustration. This frustration can manifest itself in many ways. The three general patterns most often associated with the introduction of a new information system are aggression, projection, and avoidance. To bring all of this together, consider the case of a company that installs a new system and, in the process, redefines departmental boundaries and breaks up an informal organization. How do the members of the informal group respond to the situation? Using a needs-satisfaction approach, Figure 10–7 provides an illustration.

Aggression is an attack (physical or nonphysical) against the object believed to be

Common frustration reactions include aggression, projection, and avoidance.

---

[20] Ibid., p. 61.

[21] Douglas McGregor, "The Scanlon Plan through a Psychologist's Eyes," in *Technology, Industry and Man,* ed. C. A. Walker (New York: McGraw-Hill, 1968), p. 124.

---

causing the problem. Sometimes this takes the form of sabotage. More commonly it occurs when people try to beat the system, as in the following example:

> The setting was an information system in a complex organization designed to collect man-hours in different work stations on a daily basis. Workers were frequently rotating from one work station to another during the day, and were supposed to clock in and out each time they moved from one station to another. During the course of an interview, one worker indicated that there had been some "ganging up" on an unpopular foreman. Workers would not punch out of a particular area when leaving for another work station or would punch in at the unpopular foreman's area and then work in a different area. [22]

Projection occurs when people blame something (or someone) for their own shortcomings. For example, if incompetent managers claim that the new information systems are feeding them insufficient information for making effective decisions, they are projecting blame for their own shortcomings onto a setup victim.

Avoidance takes place when people withdraw from a situation because it is too frustrating for them. With an information system this can occur, for example, if managers find they can receive the same information in less time from a different source and so react by ignoring the system's output. Richard L. Daft and Norman B. MacIntosh made this particularly clear when they noted that many information systems are simply too sophisticated and costly for the firms using them. The result is that people do not use them; instead they find ways to circumvent them. The best rule of the road is: When in doubt, use a simple system. Daft and MacIntosh have said it this way:

> Organizations should simply try to avoid the big, costly information system errors: don't waste time and money imposing an elaborate information system upon craft activities; don't expect technical-professional tasks to struggle along without adequate information system support; don't use precise, voluminous information in a basic research setting; and don't provide massive reports and information to people engaged in routine work. [23]

The Organization and Information Systems

Thus far the negative effects of information systems on the organization have been examined in general terms. In order to make a more specific analysis, it is necessary to consider the impact of such systems on four distinct subgroups in the organizational hierarchy. The four are operating personnel, operating management, technical staff, and top management. [24] Each will respond differently.

Operating personnel consist of two basic groups, nonclerical and clerical. The nonclerical people perform such functions as filling out forms or entering prepunched cards in a source recorder. When an organization computerizes or puts in a new information system, these people often feel threatened. Although some turn to minor sabotage, such as "forgetting" to do certain things or making deliberate mistakes, most employ projection, blaming the system for everything that goes wrong in the office.

Clerical workers mainly process input and convert it into output, and they are considered part of the information system itself. Changes in their work patterns may entail moving them from a manual to an *electronic data processing (EDP) system,* for example. Although some clerical people may be displaced, most are maintained in greatly upgraded jobs which require more education and formal training. Even so, these workers tend to have negative initial reactions because they believe they are going to be re-

Organization subgroups respond differently.

---

[22] Dickson and Simmons, "The Behavioral Side of MIS," p. 62.
[23] Richard L. Daft and Norman B. MacIntosh, "A New Approach to Design and Use of Management Information," *California Management Review,* Fall 1978, p. 91.
[24] Ibid., pp. 63–67.

Table 10-2 Causes for Resistance to Information Systems (by Working Groups)

	Operating (Nonclerical)	Operating (Clerical)	Operating Management	Top Management
Threats to economic security		X	X	
Threats to status or power		X	X*	
Increased job complexity	X		X	X
Uncertainty or unfamiliarity	X	X	X	X
Changed interpersonal relations or work patterns		X*	X	
Changed superior-subordinate relationships		X*	X	
Increased rigidity or time pressure	X	X	X	
Role ambiguity		X	X*	X
Feelings of insecurity		X	X*	X*

X = The reason is possibly the cause of resistance to information system development.
X* = The reason has a strong possibility of being the cause of resistance.
Source: G. W. Dickson and John K. Simmons, "The Behavioral Side of the MIS," *Business Horizons,* August 1970, p. 68. Copyright 1970 by the Foundation for the School of Business at Indiana University. Reprinted with permission.

placed. Like their nonclerical counterparts, they adopt projection behaviors and start blaming the new system for any mistakes that occur.

Operating managers are all management personnel from first-line supervisors up to and including middle management. These individuals receive much of the output from information systems. However, the systems also tend to centralize decision making and increase the control of higher-level managers over their subordinates. As a result, when operating managers fight the system, they do so by providing inadequate support to it and by failing to use the decision-making information provided by it. In so doing, they employ aggression, avoidance, and projection.

The technical staff, which consists of programmers and systems designers, is most involved with the information system. For this reason, it exhibits none of the common dysfunctional behavior patterns. On the other hand, the technical staff does not get along well with the operating managers. There seems to be a natural clash between the system designers (technical staff) and the system users (operating managers).

Top management is little affected by new information systems. Research shows that many top executives just do not get involved in designing the corporate information system. Some may attend short computer courses in order to obtain background information in the area, and many pay lip service to the value of such systems in effective decision making. Most executives, however, are unconcerned with the area.[25] The reasons for resistance are explained in greater depth in Table 10-2.

This section has examined the behavioral effects of information systems, with primary emphasis on some of the dysfunctional aspects. Although the problems de-

[25] For more on how modern organizations can go about managing this problem, see Fred R. McFadden and James D. Suver, "Costs and Benefits of a Data Base System," *Harvard Business Review,* January–February 1978, pp. 131–139; and Richard L. Nolan, "Managing the Crises in Data Processing," *Harvard Business Review,* March–April 1979, pp. 115–126.

scribed are common, not every change leads to them. The situation does not have to be this way. Many frustration reactions can be prevented if management: (a) works closely with the affected units, training them to understand and accept the new system by pointing out the benefits to the company while ensuring that any displaced employees are given jobs elsewhere in the organization, (b) designs the system with cogent inputs from all affected groups so that information from the system is both timely and useful, and (c) attains top management support from the very beginning. There are many advantages to be gained from a management information system and a firm can obtain them if it is aware of the potential problems and pitfalls associated with the establishment of such a system.

SUMMARY

This chapter has examined two topics: information systems and the computer. Many information systems are computerized, but this is not universal. Nevertheless, the two areas have one common characteristic: They help relate the departments and units of the organization into a harmonious system.

The primary goal of any information system is to provide decision-making information to the manager. For this reason, a well-designed system must be planned with the needs of management in mind and must follow a from-the-top-down philosophy. In addition, the system must discriminate by organization level, providing the right kinds of information to each. For example, top management will need general information from which to formulate strategic plans. Middle management will need more specific data for drawing up budgets and measuring and appraising managerial performance. Lower-level management will need very specific data for use in areas such as production scheduling and inventory control.

The modern computer is often employed as part of an information system, providing necessary information to managers throughout the hierarchy. In addition to performing bookkeeping and arithmetic functions, it is also being used for such functions as inventory control and airline reservations processing. Another one of its latest applications is answering "what if" questions through simulation.

Despite their great value, computers have some important drawbacks, of which management must be aware. First, many companies tend to buy more complex computers than they need. Second, many managers place too much faith in computer print-out results. Third, many managers tend to overrate the capabilities of the computer. There are a large number of things people still do much better than any machine and qualitative decision making is one of them.

The introduction of an information system into an organization can bring about dysfunctional behavior such as aggression, projection, and avoidance. In order to overcome these problems, management must be willing to adopt a participative decision-making approach that introduces the new system, relates its advantages to the personnel, and assures that any persons replaced because of it, will have employment secured for them elsewhere.

This chapter has also noted how management information and computer systems help managers do better planning and controlling, thereby establishing the fact that there is a link between the quantitative and process schools. Likewise, it has been noted that information systems can bring about dysfunctional behavior, thus illustrating that any advocate of the quantitative school must also be aware of the behavioral side of enterprise; there is thus a link between the quantitative and behavioral schools.

REVIEW AND STUDY QUESTIONS

1. What is a management information system? Explain.

2. What is the primary objective in the design of an effective information system?

3. What role should information system determinants and key success variables play in an information system design?

4. How does the modern computer differ from its early counterpart? What technological changes have occurred? What new ones can be expected in the next decade?

5. Why are computer programs so important to the processing of computerized data?

6. What are four common uses of the computer? Explain.

7. How is the computer being employed in answering "what if" questions? Give an illustration.

8. What are the basic drawbacks to the use of computers?

9. What are the three common dysfunctional forms of behavior often associated with the introduction of a new management information system? Explain each.

10. According to recent research, how do operating personnel tend to oppose the introduction of an information system? Operating management? Technical staff? Top management?

11. In what ways do information systems provide a bridge between the quantitative school and the process school? The quantitative school and the behavioral school?

SELECTED REFERENCES

Alter, Steven L. "How Effective Managers Use Information Systems." *Harvard Business Review,* November–December 1976, pp. 97–104.

Awad, Elias M. *Introduction to Computers in Business.* Englewood Cliffs, N.J.: Prentice-Hall, 1977.

Boehm, George A. W. "Shaping Decisions with Systems Analysis." *Harvard Business Review,* September–October 1976, pp. 91–99.

Boulden, James B., and Buffa, Elwood S. "Corporate Models: On-Line, Real-Time Systems." *Harvard Business Review,* July–August 1970, pp. 65–83.

Clarke, Arthur C. *2001: A Space Odyssey.* New York: New American Library, 1968.

Daft, Richard L., and MacIntosh, Norman B. "A New Approach to Design and Use of Management Information." *California Management Review,* Fall 1978, pp. 82–92.

Dickson, G. W., and Simmons, John K. "The Behavioral Side of MIS." *Business Horizons,* August 1970, pp. 59–71.

Field, G. A. "Behavioral Aspects of the Computer." *MSU Business Topics,* Autumn 1970, pp. 27–33.

Gallagher, G. A. "Perceptions of the Value of a Management Information System." *Academy of Management Journal,* March 1974, pp. 46–55.

Hay, L. E. "What Is an Information System?" *Business Horizons,* February 1971, pp. 65–72.

Heenan, D. A., and Addleman, R. B. "Quantitative Techniques for Today's Decision Makers." *Harvard Business Review,* May–June 1976, pp. 32–33.

Jones, Curtis H. "At Last: Real Computer Power for Decision Makers." *Harvard Business Review,* September–October, 1970, pp. 75–89.

Luthans, Fred, and Koester, Robert N. "The Impact of Computer Generated Information on the Choice Activities of Decision Makers." *Academy of Management Journal,* June 1976, pp. 328–332.

McFadden, Fred R., and Suver, James D. "Costs and Benefits of a Data Base System," *Harvard Business Review,* January–February 1978, pp. 131–139.

Mintzberg, Henry "The Myths of MIS." *California Management Review,* Fall 1972, pp. 92–97.

Nolan, Richard L. "Managing the Crisis in Data Processing." *Harvard Business Review,* March–April 1979, pp. 115–126.

Rockart, John F. "Chief Executives Define Their Own Data Needs." *Harvard Business Review,* March–April 1979, pp. 81–93.

"Solving a Computer Mismatch in Management," *Business Week,* April 2, 1979, pp. 73–74, 76.

Zani, William M. "Blueprint for MIS." *Harvard Business Review.* November–December 1970, pp. 95–100.

CASE: *Somebody Goofed*

Computers often help organizations by processing information quickly—but, unfortunately, not always efficiently. Sometimes the computer is programmed incorrectly; sometimes it is not given the latest information. The result can be frustrating, as seen by the following incidents:

—The Social Security Administration notified a woman that because her husband had died, his monthly benefits were cut off. It took the man four months to get the local benefits office to recognize that he was still alive and that it was all a computer error.

—A woman received a credit card bill for $00.00. Ignoring it, she soon began to receive weekly notices regarding her "unpaid balance." Finally, she sent the firm a check for $00.00 and the notices stopped—but she then received a charge for late payment of the bill.

—A large hotel sent its past customers a letter thanking them for their patronage and telling them of the hotel's new modernization plan. Unfortunately, the computer programmer requested the wrong mailing list, and the hotel was deluged with phone calls from husbands demanding an explanation for their wives, who were themselves demanding explanations, some threatening divorce.

In an effort to prevent such computer goofs, Shell Oil has set up a toll-free telephone line for customers who call about their computerized bills. Corning Glass Works has installed a computer to deal with complaints about the quality and durability of its products. The computer types an individualized letter in response to a consumer's gripe and, if necessary, triggers an order to a warehouse for a replacement part. In view of the tremendous computerization of business and considering how computers are being relied on to respond to computer-related errors, most Americans admit that they never expect to return to an era when most business dealings are on a person-to-person basis. Rather, they believe they will have to live with computer-generated problems.

Questions

1. What are some of the advantages of using computers? Do they outweigh the disadvantages? Explain.

2. What does this case suggest about the fallibility of computers and computer programmers?

3. Since computers are apparently here to stay, what steps can managers take to prevent incidents such as those described in this case?

CASE: The Old Ways Are Best

When the Savonarola Corporation brought in an outside management consulting firm, it asked the firm to examine company operations from top to bottom. Return on investment had not risen above 6 percent in three years, and top management felt something had to be done. The company was relying on the consultants to tell it what this should be.

Six weeks later, the consultants submitted their list of recommendations. One called for the design of a new management information system. "Savonarola managers at the present time are relying too heavily on an outdated and ineffective reporting system," read part of the report. "This system should be scrapped and a new one designed from the top down, with major emphasis given to providing up-to-date, relevant data useful for decision making."

The idea sounded fine to the top-level staff, who ordered the DP (data processing) department to design a new information system. After talking to people at all levels of the hierarchy and evaluating the current reporting system, the DP people submitted their proposal. The plan looked fine on paper, and the corporate president ordered it implemented.

Over the next twelve months, however, the company's return on investment failed to reflect any great changes in efficiency. As before, ROI stood below 6 percent. When top management decided to find out why, one of the areas it examined was the new information system. In essence, the executives discovered that managers at all levels of the organization were still relying on their old reporting systems. Virtually no one was using any of the data provided by the new system. When one of the managers was asked why he was not utilizing the new system, he replied, "Why should I? I have my own reporting system, and it tells me all I need to know. If you ask me, this whole new information system design was just a waste of money, and I could have told you that a long time ago."

Questions

1. What kinds of information should a manager receive from a well-designed information system? Explain, incorporating the term *key success variables* into your answer.

2. What error did Savonarola make in this case?

3. What recommendations are now in order? Explain your answer.

CASE: Simulation Programs

Ed Stoner, president of a medium-size firm, has come to realize that in the manufacturing business one always has to expect the unexpected. For example, two months ago one of the large machines in his company's Plant 3 went down, and it took almost two days to repair it. A few weeks later Stoner learned that the company had lost 14 percent of its total weekly output because of the machine's downtime. This cost the firm $87,000 in sales and $12,500 in profit before taxes. These data were determined by the accounting department and were based on previous cost and revenue figures.

Yesterday Stoner had a visit from a software computer salesperson who wanted to develop a "what if" software package for Stoner's firm. The package would be designed to help Stoner and his managers determine the overall effects of machine downtime, work stoppages, increases in the cost of goods sold, and a host of other key operational factors.

The computer firm would begin by analyzing Stoner's business operations, determining the relationships between critical operating factors and financial results. It would then write a computer simulation that could be used in determining the overall effect of a host of production problems. Additionally, the simulation would be useful later for anticipating problems and making early decisions, thereby reducing the overall negative effect should one or more problems occur. The salesperson explained it this way:

By feeding a potential problem into the simulation we will develop for you, your managers can determine the overall effect of that problem on their operations. An income statement for the next three, six, and twelve months can also be determined after allowing for the problem. Finally, working backward, your people can devote their energies to preventing the most serious problems from occurring. For example, if a delay in the delivery of vital raw materials has the greatest effect on your firm's income, a second supplier can be found and used as a backup whenever the first one cannot deliver the needed materials on time.

Of course, this is only one way the simulation can help. However, it illustrates how potential problems can be resolved through decision making today. And if something unanticipated does happen, the program will provide your people with assistance in analyzing the overall effects on operations and profitability, and it will help you pinpoint key decision areas that have to be addressed.

Stoner liked the basic idea of a "what if" program, although he felt overwhelmed by its many ramifications. He was also concerned that by relying on a computer program, he might be taking too much decision-making power out of the hands of his own people. "And," he worried aloud, "what if something goes wrong with the computer? What if the program is incorrect or fails to address some major problem? What will I do then?" Stoner told the salesperson to come back in a month. He planned in the interim to discuss the matter with his top managers.

Questions

1. How valuable can these "what if" simulation programs be in providing information for managerial decision making?

2. What are the drawbacks to using them? Explain.

3. What should Stoner do? Why?

CASE: *Don't Say It's in the Mail*

Over the last twenty years banks have been relying more and more on computers to handle their backroom operations, but recently, bank customers have also come in contact with these electronic devices. In 1981 nearly four thousand banks provided their customers with access to funds through more than six thousand automatic tellers. Additionally, the United States Treasury has for several years electronically deposited millions of checks monthly in the bank accounts of social security recipients and active and retired federal employees who get regular government payments.

Some people predict that this move toward electronic funds transfer (EFT) systems will eventually result in a cashless society, since EFT makes it possible for deposits to be made electronically and for bills to be paid this way as well. For example, it is likely that a working couple in the 1980s, once their pay has been electronically deposited in their bank account, will be able to sit down at their telephone with the monthly stack of bills and type the electronic equivalent of a check at a keyboard attached to the phone, dial a number, and have their bill-paying chores completed in a few minutes. The couple will also be able to pay their bills at the supermarket in a similar fashion. They will be able to insert a bank card in a machine and, by electronic signal, have their account charged for the amount of the weekly grocery bill.

One of the big problems with the EFT system, however, is that from now on people will have to have money in their account. No longer will they be able to tell their creditors that their check is "in the mail."

Questions

1. Is the computer really helpful to banking? Or, by making transactions easier, does it encourage individuals to spend more money than they ordinarily would? Explain.

2. Do you think the move toward EFT will result in unemployment? Does it not seem evident that the computer will replace some bank tellers and other bank workers? Explain.

3. What other areas do you think computers will revolutionize during the 1980s? Explain your ideas.

COMPREHENSIVE CASE: Exxon's Plan for the Eighties

Mention the Exxon Corporation, and people immediately think of a giant oil company that has diversified into still other energy sources, from coal to nuclear power. And those are the facts. The largest firm in terms of sales of *Fortune*'s 500 industrials, Exxon produced revenues in 1979 of almost $85 billion, a figure that at that time approached the gross national product of Mexico. However, Exxon does not intend to remain exclusively in the energy business. It has its eyes fixed firmly on entering the information processing industry.

In 1979 the company sold nearly $200 million worth of office equipment—not a great amount, given the huge sales volume generated by its other areas of operation. However, it does appear to be a sign of things to come; for Exxon has now created a cohesive organization out of the fiteen independent entrepreneurial companies that make up what is called Exxon Information Systems (EIS). These companies, described in Exhibit 1, have the resources of the parent company behind them, which can give them the ability to develop or acquire virtually any type of technology that is relevant to Exxon's goals. Do these developments have the other office equipment giants, like IBM and Xerox, worried? They say no, but consider the following facts. In 1979 IBM had $23 billion in sales and $3 billion in profits. Xerox had $7 billion in sales and net profits of $563 million. On its sales of $84.8 billion Exxon had net profits of $4.3 billion.

Why would Exxon be interested in getting into the information processing industry? A number of reasons can be cited. First, the return on investment is higher there than it is in many other industries. Consider the fact that Exxon's sales in 1979 were more than 3.5 times IBM's 1979 sales while its profits were only 50 percent greater than IBM's.

Second, getting into the information-processing industry and staying there long enough to make it profitable requires a sizable bankroll. Exxon has this and so is unlikely to have to retreat, as did RCA and GE. Third, by the end of the 1980s the information processing industry is expected to be generating annual sales of between $150 and $200 billion. If Exxon can capture a 10 to 15 percent share of the market, this would give the company a strong foothold in an area other than energy. Fourth, Exxon looks for two things in an industry: technology that will be around in ten to twenty years and a product that is capable of generating $100 million in annual sales. The information processing industry meets these criteria.

At the present time Exxon has invested around $500 million in the fifteen ventures it has brought together as EIS. Most of these companies have products already on the market, although a number are still in the research and development stage. (Again see Exhibit 1, which provides a breakdown and description of the companies and products that make up EIS.)

All the products and technologies provided by the firms in Exhibit 1 fit into the office of the future. This office will combine data and word processing into one overall office system. Instead of the typical typewriters, paper files, and separate telecommunications equipment that now exist apart from each other this future office will be a communications network that connects word processors, telephones, data processing terminals, and shared electronic files. While this development will not arrive on the scene within the next couple of years, it should exist by the end of the 1980s; and it is expected to offer a larger market than today's data processing market.

Analysts see Exxon's strategy as similar to that of Xerox, which is committed to providing customers with everything they need for office automation products. Under this arrangement, the typical office could begin by purchasing one of Exxon's Intelligent Typewriters, then move up to advanced work stations, backing them up with fast printers, facsimile receivers, and electronic files. This collection of office equipment could then be hooked together locally by an Exxon computer-controlled network.

All of this is, of course, planned for the future. For the moment, Exxon has to organize all the businesses under the EIS banner and get them operating profitably. None of them turned a profit in 1979, and EIS may have to generate sales as high as $1 billion before the group as a whole becomes profitable. However, Exxon believes that it has time to get organized and create an effective integrated system company. No one else is any closer than Exxon to putting together a total system for the office, claim EIS managers. However, they may be wrong. While IBM and Xerox have taken longer to move in this direction than many experts had expected, several smaller companies are growing rapidly. Wang, Datapoint Corporation, and others are moving in this direction—fast! Also, some competitors believe EIS moves too slowly. Because it has a controlling parent company and therefore has to wait on clearance from higher management, it could lose the ballgame.

Yet Exxon has made some decisions that are certain to help EIS. One is that all research and development will now be centralized. Prior to this decision, all of the firms did their own R&D, independent of each other. Now they will share their work at EIS R&D centers. The research and development centers will focus on EIS's four basic areas of business: office products, computer systems, communications, and components. The objective is to develop products along more similar lines than has been the case in the past. Compatibility, the ability to use one piece of equipment with another and share the same software and memories, will become essential as computer-like stations begin to proliferate in the business office. The compatibility concept is old hat to firms like IBM, but it is something that Exxon still has to learn about. For example, some of the disks currently turned out by EIS firms are not interchangeable, a mistake that should not be repeated.

One of the most important areas of interest for Exxon's competition is that of R&D expenditures. In 1979 only $47 million of Exxon's research and development expenditures were not directly related to its energy, chemical, and mining businesses. Rival firm Xerox put almost $380 million into R&D in the same year, with most of it going for office products, and IBM spent $1.4 billion for its office product development. Exxon's $47 million was, thus, a small amount for the office equipment business. At these low rates of investment, it is unlikely that Exxon can be very competitive. However, if it soon starts to make massive cash outlays for research and development, the picture will change radically. The competition is keeping a close eye on Exxon's R&D decisions.

In 1981 Exxon's intention was to put its energies into organizing the EIS companies. The aim was to build a firm that would closely parallel the overall corporation's decentralized management structure. Exxon's hope was that the operating companies would have a sense of entrepreneurial spirit that would encourage creativity and hard work; they would also still be closely tied to the major firm under this type of arrangement. Unfortunately for Exxon, some of the individuals who staffed the EIS companies have left, claiming that the organizational climate was poor and that Exxon had failed to handle the situation properly. On the other hand, Exxon has been raiding the competition. For example, during the early part of 1980 it hired fifty managers away from IBM; among them was the former vice-president of plans and requirements for the IBM Office Products Division, who many thought was in line for the top spot in that division. The situation is a critical one because no company in this high-technology industry can afford to lose highly skilled managers, if for no other reason than that these individuals often take people with them. One manager may leave with five subordinates, creating a problem for the previous employer.

As the 1980s began, it was unclear how successful Exxon would be. Critics believed the firm did not yet have a handle on the office system market. In particular, they felt it did not understand the merchandising task and therefore lacked a distribution system.

On the other hand, many people are unwilling to count Exxon out of anything. Regardless of the expertise it might currently lack, they feel it has the resources to go out and purchase whatever is necessary, from machines to labor to minds. Exxon's biggest strength is cash. Its energy sales, particularly in oil, have filled its coffers to the brim, a situation that must sound like a dream in the office equipment industry, where cash reserves are a major problem for most. For example, IBM had to go into the financial market in 1979 to look for over $1 billion. If it had wanted to, Exxon could probably have lent IBM the money. In any event, if Exxon decides to put serious financial backing behind this new office equipment venture, it is likely that IBM and Xerox are both going to find themselves in for the fight of their lives.

Questions

1. What kinds of problems discussed in Chapters 8 and 9 will the Exxon products in this case help solve?

2. How will the kind of information in Chapter 10 be of value to the modern manager who intends to use Exxon office equipment products?

3. Should managers be aware of any drawbacks to the use of this new technology? If you believe so, identify and explain three of them.

Exhibit 1 Exxon Information Systems (EIS)

Currently in Operation

Delphi Communications has a redundant-computer system and a telephone answering-switching system. This firm is expected to use its computer system to transmit and deliver synthesized voice messages.

Dialog Systems developed a unique system for translating spoken words into data transmittable over normal telephone lines.

Intecom has developed a switching network for both voice and data to connect all of the Exxon office products.

Optical Information Systems builds semiconductor lasers for transmitting data over optical fiber networks.

Periphonics builds voice response systems that store a vocabulary in code and make it possible for a computer to respond to users.

Qwip Systems makes telephone facsimile units and is currently aiming one unit, more expensive but easier to use, for the executive's desk.

Qyx offers a number of different products, from electronic typewriters to a communicating word processor.

Vydec turns out a word processor coupled to a display screen.

Zilog manufactures microprocessors.

Currently in the Research and Development Stage

Danbury Systems is developing a high resolution ink-jet printer capable of receiving facsimile transmission.

EPID is working on a low cost, flat-panel display to replace cathode-ray tubes.

Magnex is planning to turn out thin-film recording heads which will allow much more data to be stored more cheaply on such devices as magnetic disks.

Star Systems has developed new devices for storing data.

Summit is developing microcomputer systems.

Xonex is working on an advanced, multiple-capacity work station, capable of both word and data processing, accessing a data base, and carrying out electronic filing and mailing functions.

PART 4

The goal of this section is to familiarize the reader with some of the basic ideas and concepts of the behavioral school. Of course, to assign behavioral concepts to this school exclusively is erroneous, for the management process and management science people also value the importance of human behavior at work. Nevertheless, much of the latest, and most interesting, research conducted in management has been done by behaviorists.

Chapter 11 examines the communication process, with major attention to both interpersonal and organizational communication. Unless managers can communicate with their subordinates, they have no basis for either motivating or leading them. In particular, this chapter focuses on the communication process, some of the common barriers to effective communication, steps for overcoming these barriers, and the need to establish understanding between superiors and subordinates.

Chapter 12 examines the subject of motivation. Initial attention is devoted to the importance of understanding why people act as they do. In addition, the chapter reviews some of the basic assumptions managers have about their employees. The

THE BEHAVIORAL SCHOOL OF MANAGEMENT

chapter also presents current research findings designed to help managers understand workers in general and individuals in particular.

Next, Chapter 13 examines the area of leadership effectiveness. How does a manager prevail on subordinates to devote their efforts to attaining organizational goals? By way of answering this question, one-, two- and three-dimensional leadership models are reviewed, and emphasis is placed on the importance of contingency leadership styles.

Chapter 14 is a study of the area of human resource development. It was noted earlier that the process school uses the control process to identify problems and take corrective action. The quantitative school uses information feedback systems for the same purpose: namely, identifying problems in the decision-making process and determining the types of information needed to improve the process. Behaviorists rely on human resource development programs to control the quality of personnel output. If faulty communication, poor motivation, or ineffective leadership occur, the behaviorists introduce behaviorally oriented programs to overcome these problems.

CHAPTER 11

INTERPERSONAL AND ORGANIZATIONAL COMMUNICATION

GOALS OF THE CHAPTER

If management is the process of getting things done through people, communication is the essence of it, for without effective communication no one would know what anyone was supposed to be doing. Nor would there be any basis for answering questions, solving problems, obtaining feedback, or measuring results. The goals of this chapter are to examine interpersonal and organizational communication.

When you have finished this chapter, you should be able to:

1. *Describe the steps in the communication process.*
2. *Note some of the major barriers to effective communication.*
3. *Discuss the reason that perception is considered to be the overriding cause of poor communication.*
4. *Identify the two basic types of communication channels available to the manager.*
5. *Relate the role of the grapevine in informal organizational communication.*
6. *Discuss the advantages and limitations of both written and oral communication.*
7. *Explain how managers can protect their credibility through the use of balance theory.*
8. *Note some of the major bad listening habits.*
9. *Illustrate how the ten commandments of good communication can result in more effective management practices.*

INTERPERSONAL COMMUNICATION

One of the most important forms of communication is interpersonal communication, which entails the transmission of meaning from one person to another.

Communication Process

In the *communication process,* the sender constructs a message and passes it to the receiver. This individual interprets the message and takes action in a manner satisfactory to the sender.[1]

Many models have been developed to explain the communication process. One of these, formulated by communication theorist Raymond Ross and presented in Figure 11–1, illustrates the process in complete yet understandable terms. The basic ideas contained in the figure will be developed throughout this chapter.

Steps in the Communication Process The important thing to note is that effective communication requires both information and understanding. Unfortunately, too many managers overlook the importance of understanding and subscribe to what is known as the conveyor theory of communication. They see communication as a conveyor that carries messages from one person to another. No real consideration is given to whether the receiver understands or accepts the communiqué. This one-way type of communication is ineffective. Effective communication consists of four steps: attention, understanding, acceptance, and action.

Many managers use the conveyor theory of communication.

Attention entails getting the receiver to listen to what is being communicated. Quite often this requires overcoming message competition, which occurs when the receiver has other things on his or her mind. For example, assume that the listener, Daniel Jones, has three pressing problems out on the assembly line. In this case, the manager, Harriett Smith, who is trying to communicate with him, faces message competition because she must get Jones to put aside his problems and listen to her for the moment. If the sender does not secure the attention of the receiver, the communication process can go no further.

Attention involves getting the receiver to listen.

Understanding means that the receiver grasps the essentials of the message. Many managers find that their attempts to communicate break down at this stage because the receiver does not really know what is expected after the manager's statement. Some executives try to surmount this problem by asking the subordinates whether they understand the message. Such attempts are generally useless because the pressure is entirely on the subordinates, who feel they should say yes. Instead, the manager should ask subordinates to say what they understand. It becomes clear when the individuals repeat the message whether accurate understanding has been achieved.

Understanding means that the receiver comprehends the message.

Acceptance implies a willingness on the part of the receiver to comply with the message. As noted earlier, in the discussion of the acceptance theory of authority, feelings and attitudes of subordinates often dictate whether something will get done. In this phase of the process it is sometimes necessary for the manager to sell the subordinate on the idea. For example, employees in a particular company may have a habit of taking turns clocking in their fellow workers. Management, upon learning of this, may order the supervisors to halt the practice. However, the lower level managers may be opposed to enforcing the directive, believing it will lead to a confrontation with their own sub-

Acceptance requires a willingness to comply.

---

[1] For an excellent discussion of this topic, see David K. Berlo, *The Process of Communication* (New York: Holt, Rinehart and Winston, 1960).

Figure 11–1 The Communication Process

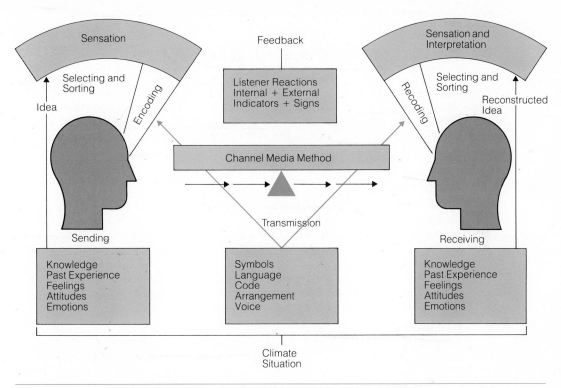

Figure 11–1 The Communication Process

Source: Raymond S. Ross, *Speech Communication: Fundamentals and Practice,* 4th edition, © 1977, p. 15. Reprinted with permission of Prentice-Hall, Inc., Englewood Cliffs, N.J.

ordinates. The department manager may have to point out that the practice is in violation of company rules. In addition, some of the workers may be arriving late because they know they are being clocked in on time. Once the supervisors realize that management is asking for no more than an equitable solution, they may prove more willing to go along with the directive.

The *action* phase entails implementation of the communication. The challenge facing the manager in this stage is seeing that things are done in the agreed upon manner. Sometimes unforeseen delays will occur; other times expediency will require a change in the initial agreement. Unless the manager puts aside time to check on the progress, communication may falter at this point. For example, Joe Brown calls in his expediter and asks him to check on a particular order and see that it is sent out by the end of the day. The expediter traces the order, finds it, has it filled, packaged, stamped, and sent down to the mail room by 4:00 P.M. However, unless the manager checks, it may occur to no one that the last daily mail pickup is at 3:30 P.M., and the order will sit in the mail room until the next day. By making themselves available for assistance and ensuring that proper action is taken on directives, managers can help their own communication to reach this fourth and final phase.

Action entails implementation of the communiqué.

Since managers spend approximately 70 percent of their time receiving and transmitting information, it is vital that they be able to communicate effectively. This calls for a knowledge and understanding of the four steps in the communication process.

COMMON BARRIERS TO EFFECTIVE COMMUNICATION

Numerous barriers to effective communication exist. Some managers may be inadequate; some subordinates may be unreceptive. More commonly, however, both groups are competent in their jobs and are trying to communicate with each other. Why, then, does communication break down? One barrier has already been examined, namely, message competition. Some of the others include perception, language, status, and resistance to change.

Perception

The overriding cause of most communication problems is *perception,* which can be defined as a person's view of reality. Since no two people have had the same training and experiences in life, no two see things exactly alike. The sender's meaning and the receiver's interpretation are not always identical, but it is not necessary that they be so; it is sufficient if the receiver understands the essence of what is being transmitted. In short, from the sender's point of view, the receiver's comprehension must be satisfactory. To some managers this means that subordinates should be "in the ball park," while to others it means "doing it the way I would have done it."

Perception can be defined as a person's view of reality.

Sensory and Normative Reality The differences in perception can be attributed to the differences in one's conception of reality. *Sensory reality* is physical reality. A chair, a horse, and a car all represent physical reality. When managers and subordinates communicate about physical reality, there are few communication problems. Both individuals know what is meant by a chair, a horse, and a car. However, there are times when meanings are not so clear-cut, and the receiver of the message may interpret the communiqué differently from its sender. This is known as *normative reality;* it is sometimes also called interpretive reality. Whenever two individuals discuss matters of personal opinion, for example, the chance of communication breakdown is high.

Sensory reality is physical reality.

Normative reality is interpretive reality.

Sensory and normative reality can be placed on a continuum such as this:

Sensory Reality ————————————————————————— Normative Reality

As one moves from sensory to normative reality, interpretations become increasingly relative. There is no longer any single right answer; instead there are a lot of right answers. Figures 11–2, 11–3, 11–4, 11–5, and 11–6 illustrate this idea. Before reading on, look at the five figures and answer the question accompanying each.

Figures 11–2, 11–3, and 11–4 have one right answer. In the first, Alternative "a" is correct. It can be verified by placing a piece of paper along the lower line. In the next two, none of the lines running across the diagrams bend in or out; all the lines are parallel. However, the background design makes it appear as if the lines in the first are bending out (Figure 11–3) and the lines in the second are bending in (Figure 11–4).

Figure 11–5 receives three common answers. Most people see a bird or a duck with a big beak; they think the fowl is looking to the left. The second most common response is that a body of water is surrounded by land with an island in the middle. The "spots" north and south of the island are clouds in this interpretation. The third most frequent

Figure 11–2 *Using just your eyes, if the line at the bottom of this diagram were drawn through it and emerged at the top, which of these answers would be correct? (a) it would run right into the shorter, lower line at the top; (b) it would run right between the two lines; (c) it would run right into the longer, upper line at the top.*

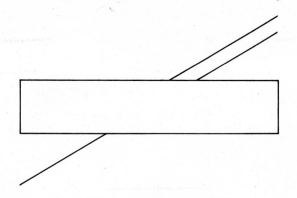

Figure 11–3 *Do the two horizontal lines bend in or bend out at the ends?*

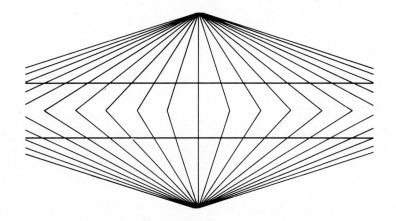

Figure 11–4 *Do the two horizontal lines bend in or bend out at the ends?*

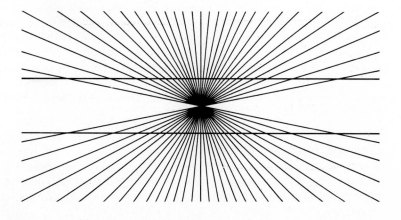

Figure 11–5 What do you see here?

response is that it is a picture of a rabbit looking to the right; in this view, the bird's beak becomes the rabbit's ears. The author has found that most people fifty years old or more opt for the lake and the island interpretation. People from twenty to fifty years old see a bird or a duck. Grammar and high school students tend to agree that it is a rabbit. Naturally, any of these three could be right because the picture is intentionally designed to allow more than one interpretation.

The final figure (Figure 11–6) receives many different interpretations. Some people see a mask; others believe it is an elephant; still others claim it is burned toast. Another common answer is that it is part of a dock, the ruffles in the upper part representing the rope used in tying up a boat. Still another interpretation is a silhouette of a woman with her hands over her head. Once again, there is no single right answer. Whatever the person sees is what is there. The point to be extracted from this is that some of the messages sent by managers to subordinates are similar to these last two figures. What the managers believe they said and what the subordinates interpret may be two different things. Too often superiors think their messages fall within the realm of sensory reality, that they are crystal clear, when the messages are actually interpretive and fall within the realm of normative reality. Figure 11–7 illustrates the different interpretations that are possible from one supposedly crystal clear message.

Language, Logic, and Abstraction

Managers use language as the method of representing their ideas. Language is the basis for most communications. Of course, astute managers gear their communiqués to the level of their audience through careful word selection and sentence construction. In

Figure 11–6 What do you see here?

Figure 11–7 A Perception Problem

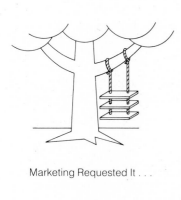

Marketing Requested It . . .

As Sales Ordered It . . .

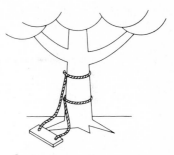

As Engineering Designed It . . .

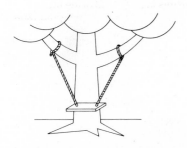

As We Manufactured It . . .

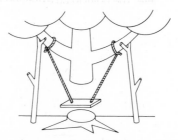

As Plant Installed It . . .

What the Customer Wanted

addition, they employ certain laws of logic, such as those advocated by Aristotle. First is the law of identity—a house is a house. Second is the law of the excluded middle—the object is either a house, or it is not a house. Third is the law of noncontradiction—something cannot be a house and not a house at the same time. These apparently simple laws of logic relate to communication because they help managers construct and convey messages in an understandable manner. Laws of logic reduce confusion.

Here are basic
Aristotelian
laws of logic.

Although these laws are helpful, managers still face the problem of abstraction. Abstraction occurs any time something is left out of the message. Yet if managers allowed for no abstraction, they would spend all their time obsessively and expensively spelling out their communiqués. This, of course, is impossible. Managers must assume that if they take care in formulating their messages, subordinates will interpret them the way they were intended. Yet this is not always the case, as the subject of inference shows.

Inference An *inference* is an assumption made by the listener that may or may not be accurate. Any time a message requires interpretation of the facts, inference enters the picture. The speaker implies and the listener infers. For example, many restaurants have a policy of establishing waiting lists when all their tables are filled. Yet, unknown to many customers, sometimes preferred clientele are moved to the front of the list and seated almost immediately. Professional people, such as clergymen and doctors, often qualify. Whenever faced with such a waiting list, a colleague of the author makes it a habit not only to use the title "Dr." in front of his name but also to ask that he be paged immediately should he receive a call from either neurosurgery or the cardiovascular unit at the nearby hospital. Then he writes his name and car license number on a piece of paper so the parking lot attendant can bring his car around in a hurry should a call come for him. Because of inferences drawn by the head waiter, this gimmick serves to drastically reduce the "doctor's" waiting time. It should be noted that although the professor makes several implications, he never states that he is an M.D. or that he will receive a call from the hospital. As a Ph.D., he is entitled to be called "Dr.," and there is always a chance that the nearby hospital will call him, no matter how remote the possibility. The communication problem rests with the head waiter, who reads facts into the message. In this case, of course, inference proves helpful to the professor because the receiver responds the way the sender wishes him to.

An inference is
an assumption
made by
a listener
or reader.

However, inferences are often stumbling blocks to effective communication because the receiver misinterprets the message, even one which, unlike the misuse of ambiguity above, is intended to be facilitative or straightforward. For example, a company is having problems in getting its product out and management begins stressing production efficiency. Things go well for the first couple of weeks. Then, suddenly, the production line again starts to have some problems. The general manager calls in one of the company's troubleshooters, explains the situation, and tells him to go down to the line, find out what is causing the trouble, and get rid of it. The man goes down, finds the automatic control unit is causing the problems, pulls it off, and replaces it. In turn, the general manager calls him in and chews him out for stopping the line to put in a new unit. "You don't pull out perfectly good equipment," the manager tells the trouble-shooter. "You fix it." What really caused the communication problem? It was inference. In going down to the line the troubleshooter followed the manager's instructions to the letter. He found the trouble, and he got rid of it. Unfortunately, the manager said more than he had in mind. By "get rid of it," the manager meant to convey an order to fix the present unit and only pull it out if absolutely necessary. The manager was operating under the conveyor theory of communication, and it got him into trouble. He thought his message was clear, and it was—to him. As communication theorists like to say, "What's clear to you is clear—to you."

Status

Status is "the totality of attributes that rank and relate individuals in an organization."[2] It affects communication because listeners tend to judge the sender as well as the message. Union representatives may feel directives from management are deliberately designed to undermine or weaken their relationship with the work force, and they regard such communiqués as troublesome. On the other hand, complaints from the workers are seen by these people as accurate descriptions of problems and firm bases from which to file charges against management. The union representatives and the membership may have high regard for each other but hold the management in low esteem.

A person's status affects the way messages are received.

The reverse, of course, is also possible. Management often discounts complaints made against its people as "union rhetoric." However, very few managers regard communiqués from higher echelons as anything but authoritative. Furthermore, the higher in the hierarchy the message originates, the more likely it is to be accepted by managers, because such executives have a great deal of status among the lower-level managers. In short, a person who has status with the listener is regarded as accurate or credible. The messages of lower status people are discounted accordingly.

Many people, all too aware of this fact, try to improve their status and credibility at the expense of others. For example, John Dean, the president's lawyer and executive legal counsel in the early 1970s, reported that in the Nixon White House changes in status occurred constantly:

> Everyone jockeyed for a position close to the President's ear, and even an unseasoned observer could sense minute changes in status. Success and failure could be seen in the size, decor, and location of offices. Anyone who moved to a smaller office was on the way down. If a carpenter or wallpaper hanger was busy in someone's office, this was a sure sign he was on the rise. Every day, workmen crawled over the White House complex like ants. Movers busied themselves with the continuous shuffling of furniture from one office to another as people moved in, up, down, or out. We learned to read office changes as an index of the internal bureaucratic power struggles.[3]

Resistance to Change

Basically, people resist change. And the greater the proposed change, the stronger the resistance. For this reason, one of the principles of communication is that the greater the change, the farther in advance must notice be given. A company planning to change work procedures may find it necessary to announce the upcoming changes four weeks prior to their enactment. The same firm planning to move the company plant from Brooklyn to Staten Island may find it necessary to announce the move eighteen months beforehand.

---

[2] Henry H. Albers, *Principles of Management: A Modern Approach,* 4th ed. (New York: Wiley, 1974), p. 172.
[3] John W. Dean III, *Blind Ambition* (New York: Simon & Schuster, 1977), p. 29.

Table 11–1   Do Superiors Tell Subordinates in Advance about Change?

	Top Staff Say about Themselves	Supervisors Say about Top Staff	Supervisors Say about Themselves	Line Workers Say about Supervisors
Always	70%	27%	40%	22%
Nearly always	30	36	52	25
More often than not		18	2	13
Occasionally		15	5	28
Seldom		4	1	12

Source: Adapted from Rensis Likert, *New Patterns of Management* (New York: McGraw-Hill, 1961), p. 52.

People cope with change in various ways, including avoidance, rejection, and distortion.

Since change and resistance are inevitable, various techniques for coping with change have been developed. For example, consider the case of the company that announces its intentions of hiring the hardcore unemployed. How do people already working there cope with this policy change? One way is avoidance, in which they pretend no policy changes have been announced; they simply ignore the directive. A second common approach is rejection. "Oh, I know what they said, but that's just talk to improve our community image." The third, and most common, is distortion, in which the receiver interprets the message through personal judgment. Those opposing the policy might say the company will bring in one or two token employees, but that is all. Those favoring the policy might claim that virtually all new hiring will be of the hardcore unemployed.

The manager's job is to overcome resistance to change.[4] One way of accomplishing this is to explain how new ideas can be beneficial to subordinates as well as to management. The difficulty of the task is clearly shown in Table 11–1. Research shows that although superiors believe they communicate information about impending changes, subordinates do not agree. Furthermore, careful scrutinization of the table indicates that this communication breakdown increases as the observer moves down the hierarchy. The problem is severe between the top staff and first-line supervisors, but it is even more severe between the supervisors and the workers.

COMMUNICATION CHANNELS

Two types of communication channels are available to the manager: formal and informal. Each can be useful in carrying information to and receiving feedback from other parts of the hierarchy.

Formal Channels

Formal channels are those established by the organization's structure. An organization chart, such as the one in Figure 11–8, provides a simple illustration of what is meant by the expression "going through channels." This is true whether the communication is

---

[4] Richard C. Huseman, Elmore R. Alexander III, Charles L. Henry, Jr., and Fred A. Denson, "Managing Change through Communication," *Personnel Journal,* January 1978, pp. 20–25.

Figure 11—8   Formal Channels of Communication

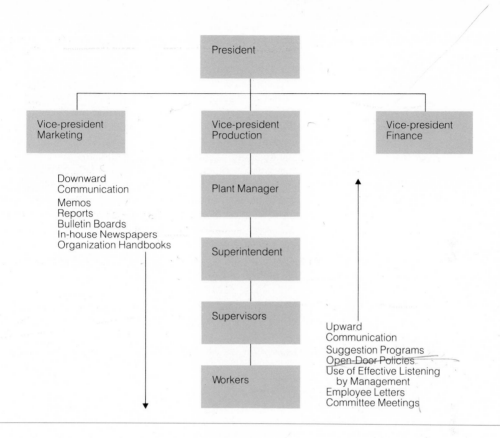

going down the chain or coming up. The following discussion examines these channels, with major attention devoted to downward and upward communication and the problems associated with each.

Downward Communication *Downward communication* is used to convey directives from superior to subordinate. The classical theorists placed prime attention on this form of communication, and many organizations today continue to do so. Daniel Katz and Robert L. Kahn have identified the five basic purposes of such communication as being: to give specific job instructions; to bring about understanding of the work and its relationship to other organizational tasks; to provide information about procedures and practices; to provide subordinates with feedback on their performance; and to provide a sense of mission by indoctrinating the workers as to organizational goals.[5] A downward orientation also helps link the levels of the hierarchy by coordinating activities among them.

Downward communication has five basic purposes.

There are, however, drawbacks associated with such an orientation. First, it tends to promote an authoritative atmosphere, which can be detrimental to morale. Second, it places a heavy burden on subordinates because much of the information coming down the organizational hierarchy will be expanded, affecting an increasing number of organizational personnel. Third, because of distortion, misinterpretation, or ignorance, information is often lost as it comes down the line. For example, Ralph G. Nichols, studying communication efficiency in 100 business and industrial firms, recorded the following loss of information among six hierarchical levels:

Certain drawbacks are associated with downward communication.

Level	Percentage of Information Received[6]
Board	100
Vice presidents	63
General supervisors	56
Plant managers	40
General foremen	30
Workers	20

This communication problem is brought on by the number of links in the chain. The greater the number of people involved, the more likely it is that information loss will occur. One way of overcoming these problems is to supplement downward orientation with an upward emphasis.

Upward Communication *Upward communication* provides subordinates with a route for conveying information to their superiors. Research indicates that it does not receive adequate attention from management; therefore, this channel is somewhat damaged by neglect. For example, Rensis Likert has reported that when he and his colleagues at the Institute for Social Research asked managers to think of the most important and difficult communication problem they had faced during the previous six months, approximately 80 percent said it dealt with downward communication. Only 10 percent indicated that it had involved upward communication.[7]

Upward communication channels carry information from subordinates to superiors.

In achieving accurate feedback from their subordinates, many managers rely upon

---

[5] Daniel Katz and Robert L. Kahn, *The Social Psychology of Organizations,* 2d ed. (New York: Wiley, 1978), p. 440.

[6] Ralph G. Nichols, "Listening Is Good Business," *Management of Personnel Quarterly,* Winter 1962, p. 4.

[7] Rensis Likert, *New Patterns of Management* (New York: McGraw-Hill, 1961), p. 46.

Table 11–2 How Free Do Subordinates Feel to Discuss Important Job Matters with Their Superior?

	Top Staff Say about Supervisors	Supervisors Say about Themselves	Supervisors Say about the Workers	Workers Say about Themselves
Very free	90%	67%	85%	51%
Fairly free	10	23	15	29
Not very free		10		14
Not free at all				6

Source: Adapted from Rensis Likert, *New Patterns of Management* (New York: McGraw-Hill, 1961), p. 47.

Table 11–3 What Do Workers Want from Their Jobs?

	Responses, as Ranked by:	
	Supervisors	Workers
Good wages	1	5
Job security	2	4
Promotion and growth with company	3	7
Good working conditions	4	9
Interesting work	5	6
Management loyalty to workers	6	8
Tactful disciplining	7	10
Full appreciation for work done	8	1
Sympathetic understanding of personal problems	9	3
Feeling "in on things"	10	2

Source: Reported in Paul Hersey and Kenneth H. Blanchard, *Management of Organizational Behavior, Utilizing Human Resources*, 3d ed. (Englewood Cliffs, N.J.: Prentice-Hall, 1977), p. 47. Reprinted by permission of Prentice-Hall, Inc.

techniques such as suggestion boxes and the so-called open door policies. However, as seen in Table 11–2, research data show that these approaches are often ineffective.

Subordinates do not feel as free to discuss their views as their superiors believe. Furthermore, upward communication is so poor in many firms that studies have consistently revealed managers as incapable of placing themselves in their subordinates' shoes and accurately responding objectively and realistically to the question, what do the workers want from their jobs? Table 11–3 clearly illustrates this, showing that upward organizational channels need to receive a great deal more attention from the manager. At present, Figure 11–9 seems to represent accurately the frequency and intensity of superior-subordinate communication.

Upward communication is poor in many firms.

Lateral and Diagonal Communication *Lateral communication,* also called horizontal, takes place among departments or people on the same level of the hierarchy. Such an interchange of information often serves to coordinate activities. For example, at the upper levels of a manufacturing firm the vice-presidents of marketing, production, and finance will coordinate their efforts in arriving at an integrated master plan. Lateral com-

Lateral communication occurs among people on the same level of the hierarchy.

Downward Communication

Upward Communication

munication also occurs between line and staff departments for the purpose of transmitting technical information necessary to carry out some particular function. As seen earlier, Henri Fayol recommended the use of lateral communication in his famous gangplank theory.

Diagonal communication involves the flow of information among departments or individuals on different levels of the hierarchy. This often occurs in the case of line and staff departments, in which the staff has functional authority. It is also common to find diagonal communication among line departments, again in which one of them has functional authority.

Diagonal communication occurs among people not on the same hierarchical level.

Informal Channels

Since formal communication channels represent only a portion of those channels that exist within the structure, much of the communication taking place is informal in nature; it is not planned by superiors. The term most often used to identify these informal channels is the grapevine.

The Grapevine The *grapevine* can be a source of factual data, although the term carries the connotation of inaccurate information. One reason for this is that anyone can start a rumor or a half-truth circulating through the organization. Since the channel is informal in nature, it is virtually impossible to determine its precise source in order to authenticate or refute its validity. Nevertheless, the grapevine is very useful in supplementing formal channels. Often it is not only a source of factual information; it provides people with an outlet for their imaginations and apprehensions as well. For example, a male supervisor, realizing that he may be beaten out for the upcoming promotion by his female counterpart who has a better production record, may start a rumor that management is putting emphasis on female promotions. This story can benefit the man for two reasons. First, it may cause management to bend over backward to give him the promotion; some firms are still under the apprehension that they must protect themselves from unfair and observably invalid claims of promoting women on the basis of sex alone. Second, if he does not get the promotion, the man can claim blatant discrimination and possibly save face among his peers. It is therefore easy to see the importance of informal communication channels to organizational members, although it should be noted that the manager must not allow the grapevine to serve as a substitute for formal channels.

The expression "the grapevine" carries the connotation of inaccurate information.

Figure 11–10 Types of Informal Communication

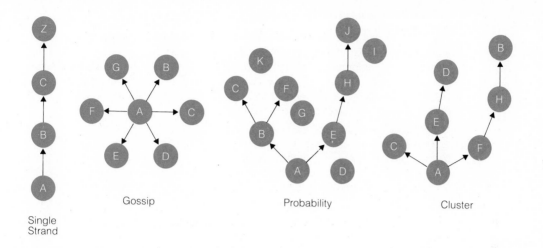

Single
Strand

Gossip

Probability

Cluster

Cluster Chains Everyone in an organization participates in the grapevine. Some people initiate or pass on information given to them by others; other people stimulate talk by their own silences. For this reason, the channel is very similar to its formal counterpart, carrying messages in four directions: up, down, horizontally, and diagonally. However, since this channel is strictly verbal in nature, it can be formed and disbanded very quickly. Its spontaneity prevents it from having permanent membership.

The cluster chain is characterized by selective communication.

Nevertheless, there is a logical pattern to informal channels of communication. There are certain individuals to whom messages will be deliberately passed and others who will be deliberately bypassed. This is often known as the *cluster chain channel;* it is characterized by selective communication. For example, Morgan Bay, vice-president of finance, has just been called into the president's office, where he was informed that the "old man" has decided to announce his retirement at the upcoming Christmas party. Several individuals, including Bay, have been in the running for some time. The president has determined that Bay will get the job, but he intends that this remain a secret until the Christmas party in four weeks. When Bay leaves the office, he is elated. He wants to tell someone the news, but on whom can he rely? Finally, he thinks of his best friend Tom Land. Bay tells Land, who does indeed keep the secret. Bay has been highly selective in his informal communication.

There are also times when individuals want to get news around quickly while maintaining the appearance of its being a secret. For example, Frances Power has decided to quit her job if she cannot get a 15 percent raise, even though she knows the average for the firm is going to be 9 percent. Rather than call her boss directly, she decides to go through the informal chain, telling the boss's secretary "in secret." It is not long before Power's superior comes by to visit with her about her upcoming raise.

The cluster chain is not the only type of chain used in informal communications. Keith Davis, famous for his writings in the behavioral area, has noted that there are three others, as seen in Figure 11–10. There is the *single strand,* in which information is passed through a long line of recipients, for example, from A to Z. There is the *gossip chain,* in

Other informal communication channels exist.

which one person tells everyone else, thereby serving as the prime source of information. Finally, there is the *probability chain,* in which information is passed on randomly. The cluster chain, however, is predominant, indicating that people are selective in choosing their informal communication channel links.

The Manager and Informal Channels It was noted in Chapter 5 that the manager must attempt to use the informal organization to help attain organizational objectives. The same is true of informal channels of communication. One of the greatest advantages of the grapevine is the rapidity with which it can disseminate information. Another is its potential for supplementing formal channels. A third is the predictable pattern of informal communication, which Davis has noted in this way:

1. People talk most when the news is recent.
2. People talk about things that affect their work.
3. People talk about people they know.
4. People working near each other are likely to be on the same grapevine.
5. People who contact each other in the chain of procedure tend to be on the same grapevine.[8]

Although the informal organization is not controlled by the manager, it can certainly be employed in helping communicate management's point of view. Of course, success will depend to a great degree on the compatibility of the formal with the the informal organization. Still, management must recognize that informal communication networks are an inevitable part of the organization and should endeavor to use them in attaining formal objectives.

COMMUNICATION MEDIA

Media transmission can take the form of words, pictures, or actions. Words are the most commonly used, as evidenced by both oral and written communication. It is therefore essential for the manager to employ them effectively. Pictures are useful aids. The fact that businesses employ them in posters, charts, and blueprints is clear evidence of their value. Action is an important communication medium, as noted by the adage that actions speak louder than words. A grimace, a handshake, a wink, and even silence, have meaning; people will attach significance to them.

Written Communication

Written communication takes a myriad of forms. Some of the more common ones in business are memos, reports, posters, bulletin-board items, inhouse newspapers, and organization handbooks. There are a number of advantages to be gleaned from written communications. One of these is the relative permanence of the communiqué, which provides a record of what was transmitted. Another is the fact that an unclear message can be reread and studied. Moreover, written messages are often more carefully constructed than oral ones because the page gives less opportunity for explanation. Another asset of writing is that a message that must go through many people is protected against continuous reinterpretation. In fact, written communications are often used when a directive contains detailed instructions that are too lengthy to be trusted to oral communication. Still another reason for favoring written messages is that they carry a degree of formality that their verbal counterparts simply do not have.

Written communication has advantages.

---

[8] Keith Davis, "Communication within Management," *Personnel,* November 1954, p. 217.

On the other hand, written communication has its drawbacks. One is that it is difficult to keep some forms of written communication up to date—for example, job descriptions and policy manuals. Things change so fast that these are often in need of revision. In addition, some written communiqués are so lengthy that superiors refuse to read them. An example is seen in the case of reports coming up the line. It is not uncommon for a subordinate to submit a long report and then spend ten minutes briefing the superior on the content. The superior does not have time to wade through the paper, so the oral report by the subordinate becomes necessary.

Written communication also has drawbacks.

Oral Communication

Most executives regard oral communication as superior to written. Not only does it save time. It also provides a basis for achieving better understanding. Some of the more common forms are face-to-face verbal orders, telephones, public address systems, speeches, and meetings.

Of these, face-to-face communication is the most effective mode. As with other forms of oral communication, it gives each party an opportunity to respond directly to the other. Disagreement, dissension, fear, tension, and anger can often be eliminated by solving the problem on the spot. This give-and-take gives the participants a basis for clarifying their own position and getting a firsthand view of that held by others. In addition, face-to-face communication provides the sender with an opportunity to note body language, such as gestures and facial responses; the sender can thereby obtain more complete feedback than is available with any other form of oral communication. How a person says something is often as important as what is said.

Face-to-face communication is the most effective.

Unfortunately, effective face-to-face communication cannot occur in large groups. With them the manager must rely on such modes of communication as meetings, speeches, and public addresses. A good understanding can often be achieved with these methods, but there is little opportunity for immediate feedback. If some people do not understand the logic behind a particular statement, they must wait until later. Most managers, if they are able to see the group, can recapitulate or reword part of the message if it becomes evident they are not conveying their ideas properly. They will usually do this only if they feel that much of the audience is confused. If it seems that almost everyone understands, the managers may well continue, leaving the one or two confused listeners to work out the meaning for themselves. There is also the case in which managers speak from a company-prepared text, a combination of written and oral communication. Many firms require that managers stay with the text, thereby limiting their freedom and preventing them from clarifying points they feel are not clear to the audience.

Large groups impose limitations on communication.

Since there are advantages and disadvantages to both written and oral communication, managers must be aware of the problems and pitfalls that prevent a message from being properly interpreted by receivers. Then, by carefully planning their own communications, they can surmount or sidestep these problems.

TOWARD EFFECTIVE COMMUNICATION

Numerous techniques are available for improving communication. Some of these help managers convey their message; others are designed to provide them with feedback. Yet all are important because managers need to know whether the receiver understands, accepts, and is willing to take the required action. Managers must also know how successful the receiver is in carrying out the directive. Following are some of the most useful techniques for obtaining effective communication.

Developing Sensitivity

The foremost way for a manager to improve communication is to be sensitive to the needs and feelings of the subordinates. Although most superiors think they are sensitive, research shows they are neither as perceptive nor as sensitive as they believe. The data in Tables 11–1 and 11–2 have illustrated this. If managers were made aware of and, more difficult, made to seriously consider these findings, it would be a start toward sensitizing them. So would the development of an awareness of nonverbal communication cues. These cues can take many forms. A listener who begins staring out the window may be telling the manager that he is either bored or unwilling to continue listening. A manager who frowns or shakes his head no is telling the speaker that he disagrees. Yet it is not necessary to confine oneself to such obvious nonverbal cues. Consider the manager who pulls a chair around the desk and sits close to a subordinate while discussing a major memo that has just been sent down from top management. This physical closeness indicates that the manager trusts the subordinate, wants the person's input on how to deal with the situation, and is going to communicate openly and freely. This is in direct contrast to the superior who stands up and leans across the desk to reprimand a nervously cringing subordinate whose only wish is to sink through the chair.

All the above are examples of nonverbal communication, and there are many more. In fact, we learn something about people by the ways they walk, stand, move their eyes, or gesture. A manager who is to develop sensitivity must learn to pick up these nonverbal cues and interpret them properly.

A second useful approach is that of *two-way communication.* By allowing subordinates to speak openly and freely, managers can assure themselves of a more accurate upward flow of information. However, since most do not like to hear unfavorable reports, subordinates tend to screen their comments. Some executives will try to overcome such resistance by telling their staff that they want accurate reporting: Bad news as well as good is to be communicated. If managers really mean this and are able to make people believe it, upward communication can become a reality. However, if they become flustered and angry on hearing bad news, subordinates will again begin paring their reports and removing all unfavorable information. The further up the hierarchy this occurs, the greater the danger to the organization. For example, failure to encourage feedback was one of World War II Nazi leader Adolf Hitler's greatest failings as an administrator. As Walter C. Langer, a psychiatrist, noted in a secret wartime report, Hitler burst into a rage whenever bad news was conveyed to him:

> It must not be supposed, however, that these rages occur only when he is crossed on major issues. On the contrary, very insignificant matters might call out this reaction. In general they are brought on whenever anyone contradicts him, when there is unpleasant news about which he might feel responsible, when there is any skepticism concerning his judgment, or when a situation arises in which his infallibility might be challenged or belittled. . . . among his staff there is a tacit understanding: "For God's sake don't excite the Fuehrer—which means do not tell him bad news—do not mention things which are not as he conceives them to be."[9]

Such an attitude discourages the free flow of ideas and impedes any development of sensitivity to the feelings of others.

Two-way communication is important.

---

[9] Walter C. Langer, *The Mind of Adolf Hitler* (New York: Basic Books, 1972), p. 76.

Table 11–4   Federal Government English versus Plain English

In Federal Government Bureaucratic Language:
We respectfully petition, request, and entreat that due and adequate provision be made, this day and the date hereinafter subscribed, for the satisfying of these petitioners' nutritional requirements and for the organizing of such methods of allocation and distribution as may be deemed necessary and proper to assure the reception by and for said petitioners of such quantities of baked cereal products as shall, in the judgment of the aforesaid petitioners, constitute a sufficient supply thereof.

In Plain English:
Give us this day our daily bread.

Source: "Turning Federalese into 'Plain English,' " *Business Week,* May 9, 1977, p. 58.

Employing Understandable, Repetitive Language

Technical terminology and multisyllabic words may be impressive, but they can also be troublesome to the listener, as Table 11–4 shows. The manager should try to use understandable language. A supervisor talking to production line workers must communicate appropriately; so too, of course, must the executive making a report to the board of directors. Effective communication will differ according to the receiver, but it must always be understandable. One way of accomplishing this is to use repetitive language. Sometimes a message will not be fully grasped the first time, and a rephrasing or recapitulation is in order. Another guideline is to convey information gradually, building the essence of the message as one goes along. This is especially helpful in conveying technical or sophisticated data.

Understandable, repetitive language will improve communication.

Protecting Credibility

One criterion for managerial effectiveness is credibility, the quality of seeming believable. When Barbara Anderson, the manager, communicates with her subordinates, they listen to and obey her because she has demonstrated through her competence, drive, character, and past performance that she is worthy of their trust. However, the astute manager knows that credibility must not be merely sought; once gained, it must be protected. Every time a manager communicates an order or issues a directive, there is a chance for credibility to be damaged. One way of illustrating the problem and a method for successfully coping with it is through the use of what is called *balance theory.*

Consider the following situation. A manager, Kathleen Fairlane, just told her subordinate that the company has decided to introduce new work procedures. In this instance there are three relevant relationships: (a) the attitude of the receiver toward the sender, (b) the attitude of the receiver toward the new changes, and (c) the receiver's perception of the sender's own attitude toward the changes. Based on the receiver's perception, either a balanced or an unbalanced triad will result. If the receiver has a positive attitude toward both the changes and the sender and, further, believes the latter also favors the new work procedures, there is a balanced triad, as in Figure 11–11. However, if the situation is unbalanced, say because the receiver does not like the new procedures, the situation becomes what is shown in Figure 11–12.

Three relationships are significant in balance theory.

Once the triad is unbalanced, how can balance be restored? There are a number

Figure 11–11   Balanced Triad

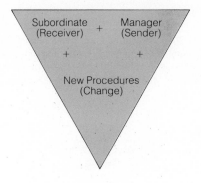

Figure 11–12   Unbalanced Triad

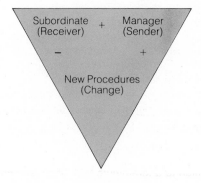

of ways, but the important thing to realize is that the triad must be all pluses or two minuses and a plus. Otherwise, it cannot be balanced.

Thus the manager has three options, as illustrated in Figure 11–13: tell the subordinate that she also opposes the new procedures (Triad A); allow the subordinate to develop a negative attitude toward her (Triad B); or persuade the subordinate to accept the new changes (Triad C).

Since the manager's job is to communicate and support directives coming down the line, it is vital that she choose alternative C. This will not only establish balance and protect the manager's credibility with her own subordinates, but it will also prevent alternative A from occurring. One way an effective manager can do this is by empathizing with the subordinate and demonstrating belief in and positive orientation toward many of the same values and ideals held by the subordinate—for example, good working conditions, a challenging job, a chance for advancement, and recognition. In this way, the manager can personally ensure the subordinate's continuing reliance and trust. Then, credibility protected, the manager can direct attention toward showing the subordinate how the new work procedures will be beneficial in attaining these values and ideals. This will lead in turn to a time for the subordinate to alter the initial, troublesome percep-

Figure 11–13 Balanced Triads

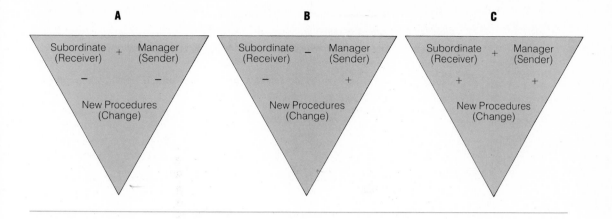

tion and view the work changes positively. The result is a balanced triad. By employing balance theory, the effective manager is able to assess communication situations, determine when credibility is threatened, and take necessary steps to protect it.

Avoiding Bad Listening Habits

The manager spends approximately 70 percent of the day communicating. Ralph Nichols, in breaking down the subfunctions of managers' communication, has estimated that 9 percent is spent in writing, 16 percent in reading, 30 percent in speaking, and 45 percent in listening.[10] Yet research shows that managers are not good listeners. Nichols has estimated that when people listen to a ten-minute talk, they operate at only 25 percent efficiency. This is unfortunate because listening to the individual employee is one of the most important methods a manager can use in learning about or evaluating the people in the firm.

Becoming a more effective listener requires an understanding of the ten most common bad habits of listening, which Nichols has defined as follows:

1. ***Calling the subject uninteresting.*** Instead of tuning in first and seeing if the speaker has something worthwhile to say, the listener assumes from the start that the topic will be boring.

2. ***Tuning the speaker out because of his delivery.*** The listener allows delivery to take precedence over content.

3. ***Getting overstimulated.*** The minute the listener hears something with which he or she disagrees the person stops listening and starts fuming, thereby missing the rest of the message.

4. ***Concentrating only on facts, to the exclusion of principles or generalizations.*** Facts do not always present the whole picture. Principles and generalizations are often necessary to put everything in its proper perspective.

These are the ten most common bad habits of listening.

---

[10] Ralph G. Nichols, "Listening: What Price Inefficiency?" *Office Executive,* April 1959, pp. 15–22.

5. **Trying to outline everything.** Some speakers are less organized than others, and until the individual gets into the presentation, it can be difficult to follow him or her via an outline. Good listeners are flexible in their note taking.

6. **Faking attentiveness.**

7. **Allowing distractions to creep in.**

8. **Tuning out difficult or technical presentations.** This often occurs when managers are listening to financial or quantitatively-oriented reports.

9. **Letting emotional words disrupt the listening process.** Any time a word evokes emotion, there is a good chance that listening will be interrupted.

10. **Wasting thought power.** Most people speak at the rate of 125 words per minute. However, the brain is capable of handing almost five times that number. If the speaker goes on for more than a few minutes, it presents a temptation to the listener to wander, mentally, returning only periodically to check in and see where the speaker is."[11]

Managers who make a concerted effort to avoid these common pitfalls find that they can improve their level of efficiency far above the 25 percent average.

Employing the Commandments of Good Communication

Although many guidelines have been put forth to improve communication, one of the most extensive compilations is that constructed by the American Management Association. Often known as the ten commandments of good communication, they are the following:

1. **Clarify ideas before communicating.** By systematically thinking through the message and considering who will be receiving and/or affected by it, the manager overcomes one of the basic pitfalls of communication—failure to properly plan the communiqué. The more systematically a message is analyzed, the more clearly it can be communicated.

2. **Examine the true purpose of communication.** The manager has to determine what he or she *really* wants to accomplish with the message. Once this objective is identified, the communiqué can be properly designed.

3. **Take the entire environment, physical and human, into consideration.** Questions such as what is said, to whom, and when will all affect the success of the communication. The physical setting, the social climate, and past communication practices should be examined in adapting the message to the environment.

4. **When valuable, obtain advice from others in planning communiqués.** Consulting with others can be a useful method of obtaining additional insights regarding how to handle the communication. In addition, those who help formulate it usually give it active support.

5. **Be aware of the overtones as well as the basic content of the message.** The listener will be affected by not only what is said but also how it is said. Voice tone, facial expression, and choice of language all influence the listener's reaction to the communiqué.

6. **When possible, convey useful information.** People remember things that are beneficial to them. If the manager wants subordinates to retain the message, he or she should phrase it so that it takes into consideration *their* interests and needs as well as the company's.

7. **Follow up on communication.** The manager must solicit feedback in ascertaining

The American Management Association has provided the ten commandments of good communication.

---

[11] Adapted from Ibid.

whether the subordinate understands the communiqué, is willing to comply with it, and then takes the appropriate action.

8. **Communicate with the future, as well as the present, in mind.** Most communications are designed to meet the demands of the current situation. However, they should be in accord with the long-range goals as well. For example, communiqués designed to improve performance or morale are valuable in handling present problems. Yet they also serve a useful future purpose by promoting long-run organizational efficiency.

9. **Support words with deeds.** When managers contradict themselves by saying one thing and doing another, they undermine their own directives. For example, the executive who issues a notice reminding everyone to be in the building by 8:30 A.M. while he or she continues to show up at 9:15 A.M. should not expect anyone to take the notice seriously. Subordinates are always cognizant of such managerial behavior and quickly discount such directives.

10. **Be a good listener.** By concentrating on the speaker's explicit and implicit meanings, the manager can obtain a much better understanding of what is being said.[12]

SUMMARY

This chapter has examined interpersonal and organizational communication. It noted that the communication process entails four steps: attention, understanding, acceptance, and action and that implementation of the process occurs in two basic channels: the formal and the informal. The astute manager uses both to advantage, keeping in mind that there tends to be an overemphasis on downward communication and an underemphasis on upward. This is unfortunate, for without some form of upward communication the manager suffers from a lack of feedback. Many managers overlook the need for this feedback, tending to follow the old conveyor theory of communication. They send their subordinates a message and expect them to act accordingly. However, communication does not work that way. People do not always interpret messages in the same way. There are many reasons for this, and all constitute barriers to effective communication. Some of the more important are perception, language, abstraction, inference, status, and resistance to change. In order to overcome these barriers, the manager must take steps to establish lines of feedback. Some of the more effective techniques are sensitivity; understandable, repetitive language; credibility; the avoidance of bad listening habits; and a general adherence to the commandments of good communication. Although many people may think these ideas appear obvious, it is really quite difficult to practice an adherence to them.[13]

REVIEW AND STUDY QUESTIONS

1. What is the communication process? Explain.
2. What is the conveyor theory of communication?
3. Describe the four steps for implementing effective communication.
4. What are some of the common barriers to effective communication?

---

[12] Adapted from American Management Association, "Ten Commandments of Good Communication," as reported in Max D. Richards and William A. Nielander, eds., *Readings in Management* (Cincinnati, Ohio: South-Western Publishing, 1958), pp. 141–143.

[13] For an excellent follow-up to the ideas contained in this chapter, see Stewart L. Tubbs and Sylvia Moss, *Human Communication,* 2d ed. (New York: Random House, 1977).

5. How does perception affect communication?

6. How can inference bring about communication breakdown? Give an illustration.

7. Why do people resist change? Is change really inevitable? Is resistance? Explain.

8. What is meant by the expression *going through channels?*

9. What are informal communication channels?

10. What are the advantages to the use of written communication? Oral communica-cation? Identify and describe two of each.

11. How can a manager promote sensitivity? Be complete in your answer.

12. How is balance theory useful to managers who need to protect their credibility? Explain.

13. What are some of the most common bad listening habits?

14. How can a manager obtain feedback for effective communication?

SELECTED REFERENCES

Athanassiades, J. C. "The Distortion of Upward Communication in Hierarchical Orga-nizations." *Academy of Management Journal,* June 1973, pp. 207–226.

Backarach, S. B., and Aiken, M. "Communication in Administrative Bureaucracies," *Academy of Management Journal,* September 1977, pp. 365–377.

Berlo, David K. *The Process of Communication.* New York: Holt, Rinehart and Winston, 1960.

Cross, G. P. "How to Overcome Defensive Communications." *Personnel Journal,* August 1978, pp. 441–443, 456.

Foltz, R. F. "Communication: Not an Art, a Necessity." *Personnel,* May–June 1972, pp. 60–64.

Greenbaum, H. H. "The Audit of Organizational Communication." *Academy of Manage-ment Journal,* December 1974, pp. 739–754.

Hall, J. "Communication Revisited." *California Management Review,* Spring 1973, pp. 56–67.

Hersey, P., and Kleity, J. W. "One-on-one OD Communication Skills," *Training and Development Journal,* April 1980, pp. 56–60.

Huseman, Richard C.; Alexander, Elmore R. III; Henry, Charles L., Jr.; and Denson, Fred A. "Managing through Communication." *Personnel Journal,* January 1978, pp. 20–25.

King, C. P. "Keep Your Communication Climate Healthy." *Personnel Journal,* April 1978, pp. 204–206.

McCaskey, M. B., and O'Reilley, C. A. III. "The Hidden Messages Managers Send," *Harvard Business Review,* November–December 1979, pp. 135–148.

Newman, R. G. "Case of the Questionable Communiqués." *Harvard Business Review,* November–December 1975, pp. 26–28.

Nichols, Ralph G. "Listening Is Good Business." *Management of Personnel Quarterly,* Winter 1962, pp. 2–9.

Roberts, K. H., and O'Reilley C. A. III. "Some Correlations of Communications Roles in Organizations." *Academy of Management Journal,* March 1979, pp. 42–57.

Shannon, W. C. "One-person Communications." *Training and Development Journal,* May 1978, pp. 20–24.

Tubbs, Stewart L., and Moss, Sylvia. *Human Communication,* 2d ed. New York: Random House, 1977.

Table 11–5 Do You Tell Your Subordinates When They Do a Good Job?

	Top Management Says of Itself	Middle Management Says of Top Management	Middle Management Says of Itself	Lower-level Management Says of Middle Management	Lower-level Management Says of Itself	Workers Say of Lower-level Management
Always	93%	82%	95%	63%	98%	39%
Often	7	14	5	15	2	23
Sometimes		4		12		18
Seldom				6		11
Never				4		9

CASE: Good Work Is Expected

An eastern pharmaceutical company hired an outside management consulting firm to analyze its operations. After five weeks, the consultants made their report to management. One of the areas they had investigated was communication between superiors and subordinates. To its dismay, management learned that there were numerous discrepancies between what superiors said they did and what their subordinates said their superiors did. For example, the consultants conducted a confidential questionnaire survey of 20 percent of the managers and workers; the responses to the question, "Do you tell your subordinates when they do a good job?" are tabulated in Table 11–5.

Management was quite distraught with the findings. As a result, at its next board of directors meeting the chairperson proposed that the firm bring back the consultants to advise and counsel them on how they could deal with this problem. The resolution was passed unanimously.

When the middle and lower level managers learned of the action, they expressed surprise. One of them said, "Just because the data indicate poor communication is no need to get excited. After all, the workers say lots of things that aren't accurate." A colleague explained, "Look, I expect subordinates to do a good job. I only tell them when they are doing a poor one. If I praised them every time they did something right, they'd all have swelled heads. My approach is to say nothing."

Questions

1. What do the data in Table 11–5 show? Explain your findings.

2. What do you think of the comments from the two managers? Do the two hold valid points of view on the practice of feedback?

3. What types of recommendations would you expect from the consultants? Explain.

CASE: Managers Don't Listen

How important is communication in the modern organization? Many management experts believe that the primary fault with top managers is that, even in the large corporations, they do not get out of their offices and find out what employees have to say. Following this lead, very few other managers spend time listening to workers. This inaction leads to all sorts of problems; and as the firm expands, the problems magnify. How can they be dealt with? One of the most effective ways is through the use of an open door policy, which encourages employees to discuss their problems with managers. In fact, many experts believe that every worker should feel free to see the boss at any time about job-related matters. However, an open door policy does not mean that individuals who fail to get satisfaction from the boss are invited to go farther up the hierarchy. Head jumping is wrong and should not be tolerated.

Another important thing for managers to remember is that communication ought to be used to prevent problems rather than to resolve them after they have come up. Unless managers work this way, they will find subordinates continually coming to them with problems, either in an effort to win recognition or out of the basic need to know how to handle the uncharted problem areas.

What, then, is the basic function of manager/worker communication? It is to help create the right climate for job satisfaction. If the climate is right, people will motivate themselves. A large part of the manager's job is the development of effective listening skills. If this is done, the rest of the pieces of the management puzzle will fall into place.

Questions

1. How common do you think it is to find managers not listening to their employees?

2. Do you agree with the comments in the case about an open door policy? Explain.

3. In addition to using the information in this case, what else would you recommend that managers do to improve communication with subordinates? Make your answer complete.

CASE: A Two-way Experiment

To emphasize the importance of communication, Maria Fontana, director of in-house training of a large western retail chain, decided to conduct an experiment during an upcoming session with a group of middle managers. When they were all settled in the room, she began by asking the value of two-way communication. All agreed it was of prime importance for effective management. Fontana then asked them how they went about obtaining feedback from subordinates. Although some of the managers contributed ideas, it was evident that the group was unsettled by the question. Finally one of the managers, Milford Graves, spoke up. "Ms. Fontana, two-way communication is great if you have a problem, but most of us really believe we can achieve our goals with successful downward communication. We really don't have trouble getting our meanings across to the workers."

By the hum in the room, Fontana realized that the rest of the managers basically agreed. "Do you mean to tell me that you are all such good communicators that your subordinates know exactly what you are talking about? They never have to ask a question?"

Figure 11–14 The First Set of Drawings

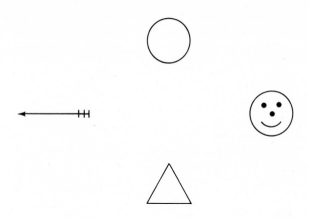

"Well, I'm not saying we're perfect," said Graves, "but speaking personally, I can make myself understood if I really have to. When I make a concerted effort, there is no real need for questions. And I'm not kidding or bragging. I've worked at it a long time, and I'm just that good."

With that Fontana asked Graves to come to the front of the room and read a piece of paper on the podium. While he was thus occupied, she said to the group, "Mr. Graves is looking at the piece of paper I have on the podium. I would like the rest of you to get ready to draw. Mr. Graves is going to describe some diagrams to you, and he is going to tell you how to draw these diagrams. You are to do exactly what he tells you. You are not to ask any questions, make any noise, or provide him with any kind of feedback indicating whether or not you are able to follow the logic of his directives."

Figure 11–14 shows the diagrams Graves was asked to describe to the group. The instructions that accompanied the diagrams told Graves to use no geometric terms. Instead, he was to get the other people in the room to draw these figures by merely using lines, dots, and geographic directions. In addition, he was to keep his head down throughout the experiment so that he could not see the group.

Graves began. By the time he finished it was evident to Fontana that many of the group members were failing to follow some of the directions. "All right, show and tell," she said. "How many of you feel you got all four diagrams right?" Four of the twenty-four raised their hands. Then Fontana held up the diagrams for all to see. It turned out that everyone had at least one of them right, but no one had all four correct. Only seven had three of the four right.

Fontana then ran the experiment again, using the diagrams in Figure 11–15. This time she told Graves to look out at the group and answer any questions they had. In addition, if he felt that he had lost the group at any point, he could go back and repeat the directions. At the end of this experiment everyone in the room had at least two of the diagrams right, and twelve had all four correct. "Well, Mr. Graves," said Fontana with a smiling nod, "you seem to have improved markedly over your first performance."

"I know," he replied, "but I never really realized how much can be lost if you don't allow people to ask questions. What surprised me even more was how much feedback I was getting just by looking at their faces and their body movements. I guess your point is

Figure 11–15 The Second Set of Drawings

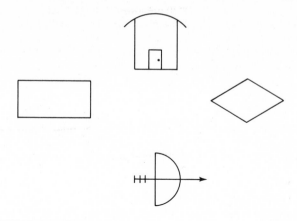

that there is a tremendous increase in understanding between one- and two-way communication. Right?''

Questions

1. Can this experiment and two-way communication on the job be correlated? Explain.
2. What are some of the most effective ways to promote two-way communication? Explain.

CASE: *Speed and Comprehension*

One of the greatest communication problems is that of getting people to increase their reading speed and comprehension. Take out a clean piece of paper before continuing with this case. Then read the following assignment. Each of the twenty-four items asks you to execute a prescribed activity.

The items vary in complexity, but you should be able to cope easily with them all. This is not an intelligence test. The exercise is designed to measure only how well you read and carry out instructions with accuracy. You have three minutes to complete the exercise. So be sure to time yourself and remain within the constraint. Enter all your answers on the piece of paper.

Read everything before doing anything.

1. Write your name in the upper right corner of the piece of paper.
2. Multiply 23 by 68 and place the result under your name.
3. Draw a square on the reverse side of the paper.
4. Draw a circle inside the square.
5. Draw a diamond inside the circle.
6. Write the month and date in the upper left corner.
7. Multiply the square root of 9 by the square of 16.

8. Subtract 1,462 from 2,221 and place the result in the lower left corner.

9. Underline your answer to Question 2.

10. If a farmer has 17 pigs, and all but 12 die, how many pigs are left alive?

11. Add 14,421 to 27,969 and place the result in the lower right corner.

12. Now subtract 14,421 from 27,969 and place the answer under the result for Question 11.

13. Square the number seven and put your answer immediately below.

14. Compute the square root of 169 and add this to the answer you worked out in Question 13.

15. Write down the name of the sixteenth President of the U.S.

16. Write Ronald Reagan's middle name on the bottom of the page.

17. If Dr. Joyce Brothers married comedian Dickie Smothers, what would her new name be?

18. Which space project was the one that got America to the moon: Gemini, Apollo, or Mercury?

19. Who won the last National League Pennant?

20. Who won the last American League Pennant?

21. Who won the first Super Bowl?

22. Take a number from 1 to 10. Add 10. Subtract 5. Multiply by 7. Square the number. What is your answer?

23. Write down the year you graduated from grammar school as a four digit number—for example, 1979. Add to this your present age. Then write down how long you have been out of grammar school. Finally, write down the year you were born. Add all four numbers together.

24. Carry out the instructions in Question 1 only and ignore all the rest.

Questions

1. What is the purpose of this exercise? What does it relate about communication problems?

2. How can these problems be overcome? Explain.

modern
winter
Thing

MODERN MOTIVATION THEORY

GOALS OF THE CHAPTER

One of the greatest challenges the manager faces is that of motivating the workers. It is a challenge that many supervisors feel they need to learn more about. For example, a recent survey among managers found that of all the areas in which they felt training could be helpful to them, motivation headed the list.[1]

This chapter will examine modern motivation theory. Much of the chapter will deal with what are called substantive or content theories. These are concerned with what it is within the individual or environment that stimulates or sustains behavior—that is, what specific things motivate people. The last part of the chapter examines three mechanical, or process, theories, which are concerned with explaining how behavior is initiated, directed, sustained, and halted. The goals of this chapter are to acquaint the reader with modern motivation theory and to indicate its relevance to management.

When you have finished this chapter, you should be able to:

1. Explain the relationship between needs and behavior.
2. Identify and describe the five basic needs in Maslow's needs hierarchy.
3. Compare and contrast the tenets of management theories X and Y.
4. Discuss the value of money, status, working conditions, increased responsibility, and challenging work in motivating people.
5. Describe some of the new process theories of motivation that emphasize individual stimulation, rather than mass motivation.

---

[1] Katherine Culbertson and Mark Thompson, "An Analysis of Supervisory Training Needs," *Training and Development Journal,* February 1980, pp. 58–62.

NEEDS AND BEHAVIORS

If managers are to be successful in getting workers to attain organizational objectives, they must understand the fundamentals of motivation. This is not an easy job, for motivation is an intervening variable—an internal, psychological process that the manager cannot see. Rather, the manager can only assume its presence (or absence) based on observance of worker behavior. If the workers are busy at their tasks, the manager may well infer that they are motivated. If they are standing around talking, the manager may conclude that they are not motivated to work.

However, this superficial approach fails to answer a key question: Why do people behave as they do? Although there are various answers, one approach is a need-satisfaction explanation. It is assumed that everyone has needs that require satisfaction. In turn, these needs cause the person to undertake some form of goal-oriented behavior, which is intended to satisfy the need. For example, hunger pangs may lead a person to go into a nearby cafe and eat. Using just this information, it is possible to design a simple diagram of motivation, shown as Figure 12–1. Every individual, of course, has many needs, but it is the need with the greatest strength that tends to dictate current behavior.

Once the need has been satisfied, it declines in importance and another need becomes dominant. The need theory of motivation has been formulated and explained in detail by Abraham Maslow, a psychologist.

MASLOW'S NEED HIERARCHY

According to Maslow, each of us is a wanting being; there is always some need to satisfy. Once one need satisfaction is accomplished, that particular need no longer motivates the person, who is free then to turn to another need, again seeking satisfaction. Maslow has represented the needs in hierarchical form, with those at the lower levels requiring basic satisfaction before the individual can move on to the next level. Figure 12–2 illustrates Maslow's *need hierarchy* of physiological, safety, social, esteem, and self-actualization needs. However, before discussion begins, it should be noted that Maslow never contended that a need must be 100 percent satisfied before the next level becomes important. As he has explained:

> In actual fact, most members of our society who are normal are partially satisfied in all their basic needs and partially unsatisfied in all their basic needs at the same time. A more realistic description of the hierarchy would be in terms of decreasing percentages of satisfaction as we go up the hierarchy of pre-potency. For instance, if I may assign arbitrary figures . . . it is as if the average citizen is satisfied perhaps 85 per cent in his physiological needs, 70 per cent in his safety needs, 50 per cent in his love needs, 40 per cent in his self-esteem needs, and 10 per cent in his self-actualization needs.[2]

Physiological Needs

At the base of the hierarchy are *physiological needs,* those necessary to sustain life. They include food, water, clothing, and shelter. An individual who lacks the basic necessities in life will probably be motivated primarily by physiological needs. As Maslow put it, "A person who is lacking food, safety, love, and esteem would most probably hunger for

---

[2] Abraham H. Maslow, "A Theory of Human Motivation," *Psychological Review,* July 1943, pp. 388–389.

Motivation is an internal, psychological process.

One way of examining motivation is through a need-satisfaction approach.

The most basic needs are physiological.

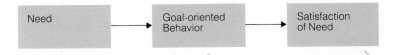

Figure 12–1 Simple Motivation Process

| Need | → | Goal-oriented Behavior | → | Satisfaction of Need |

Figure 12–2 Maslow's Hierarchy of Needs

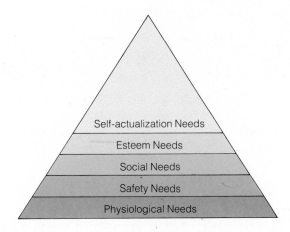

Self-actualization Needs
Esteem Needs
Social Needs
Safety Needs
Physiological Needs

food more strongly than for anything else."[3] When this is so, Figure 12–3 accurately depicts the need hierarchy.

Research indicates that satisfaction of physiological needs is usually associated with money—not the money itself in this case, but what it can buy. Although one could look at Figure 12–2 and argue that other needs could also be satisfied with money, it seems clear that the value of this factor diminishes as one goes up the hierarchy. Self-respect, for example, cannot be bought.

Safety Needs

When physiological needs are basically fulfilled, safety needs begin to manifest themselves. One of the most common is protection from physical dangers, such as fire or accident. In an industrial setting, signs such as "No Smoking in This Area" and "Beyond This Point Safety Glasses Must Be Worn" provide illustrations of how management attempts to satisfy this need.

Then come safety needs, which take many forms.

A second safety need is economic security. On the job, fringe benefits such as accident, health, and life insurance programs help fulfill this need.

A third common safety need is the desire for an orderly, predictable environment.

---

[3] Abraham H. Maslow, *Motivation and Personality,* 2d ed. (New York: Harper & Row, 1954), p. 37.

Figure 12–3 *Need Hierarchy Showing Physiological Needs Dominant*

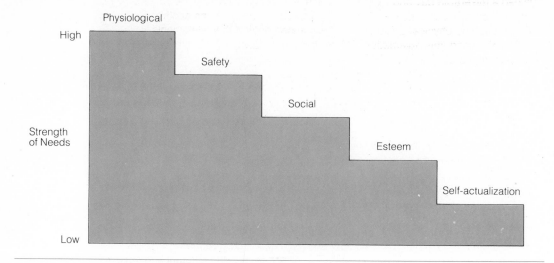

If this is difficult to understand, one must realize that people often feel threatened by work changes; similarly, they are afraid to voice their opinions on some matters for fear of losing their jobs. In cases like these, safety needs are clearly significant.

Research indicates that some individuals place great emphasis on the safety need—for example those whose parents were heavily security-minded. The parents, often having suffered economic crises, regard themselves as past and potential victims of the environment and pass this strong lack of security on to their children. The offspring, in turn, seek secure, nonthreatening positions in, for example, major corporations or federal bureaucracies, where they can carve out a stable, protected niche for themselves.

Another common source of the security-minded employee is overprotective parents. Continually sheltering their child from disappointment, they paint an unrealistic view of the world. A young person from this kind of family, once out and suffering one of the world's setbacks, is thrown for a loss and is unable to cope with the accompanying frustration, tension, and anxiety. Subconscious security motives developed through interaction with the parents have not prepared the person for this new experience. Safety needs become important to the individual, who is likely to seek a noncompetitive, sheltered environment.

Social Needs

When physiological and safety needs are basically satisfied, *social needs* become important motivators. The individual wants to receive and give acceptance, friendship, and affection. People need to feel needed. Medical research has proved that a child who is not held, cuddled, and stroked can actually die. This is not, of course, a certain event. Many unloved babies survive and grow. But the discovery is important, and it is relevant to the currently popular concept of "stroking." People seek strokes—loving and admiring physical and psychological gestures—from others and, in turn, wish to recip-

Individuals need to feel needed.

rocate. An example of a psychological stroke is a situation in which George says to his mother, "You look so pretty in that wedding picture," and the mother responds, "George, I've had a miserable day and I haven't even looked at that picture for weeks. You always do know how to make people feel good." The people here give one another a nice little touch, though no physical gestures may have accompanied their statements.

People need this interaction. When it is withdrawn, they suffer. This perhaps accounts for the use by prisons of solitary confinement, which deprives prisoners of the fulfillment of their social needs. The psychological punishment of isolation is perhaps the severest mode of inflicting hurt. The person who is excluded from normal human contact is certainly prevented from giving or receiving strokes. Some people would say that isolation, even more importantly, is a means of removing people from their own humanness.

The concept of stroking explains why Stanley Schachter has found that people with similar beliefs tend to group together.[4] They share a common bond and can reinforce each other's feelings and convictions through stroking. This is especially true when things are not going well, for misery does love company.

Esteem Needs

When physiological, safety, and social needs are essentially satisfied, *esteem needs* become dominant. These needs are twofold: The person must feel important and must also receive recognition from others, as that recognition supports the feelings of personal worth. Recognition is invaluable; without it, many people would conclude that they are greatly overrating themselves. When those around them, however, make it clear that they are indeed important, feelings of self-esteem, self-confidence, prestige, and power are produced. Full satisfaction of these needs, however, must finally rest with the individual. For instance, some people believe that they are overrated, that the world would be shocked to learn of their basic inadequacies. No external force can entirely remove that belief. The individual must somehow gain self-confidence in order to value the respect and support of those who offer it.

Feelings of self-esteem and self-confidence are important.

Research indicates that as the United States moves toward becoming a middle-class society, esteem-related needs such as prestige assume increased importance. People want to keep up with the Joneses and be viewed as important. Vance Packard's sociological book, *The Status Seekers,* portrays this kind of urge.[5] Joining the right country club, obtaining a reputation as a hard worker, and earning advanced degrees are some ways of securing prestige. Some teachers who hold doctoral degrees like to be called "Doctor," feeling that it conveys more of a sense of advancement and importance than "Professor," which is, in fact, the academically superior of the two titles.

Power is another esteem-related need. The power drive begins in early life, when babies realize that their own crying influences their parents' behavior. The famed psychiatrist Alfred Adler contended that this ability to manipulate others is inherently pleasurable to the child.[6] Of course, during the early years, the infant must have this power, being helpless without adults and in need of some method for ensuring their assistance. Later in life, when people can fend for themselves, this physical motive for power changes to one of winning respect and recognition from others. When esteem needs are basically satisfied, self-actualization needs become important.

---

[4] Stanley Schachter, *The Psychology of Affiliation* (Stanford, Calif.: Stanford University Press, 1959).

[5] Vance Packard, *The Status Seekers* (New York: David McKay, 1959).

[6] Alfred Adler, *Social Interest* (London: Faber & Faber, 1938).

Self-actualization Need

Maslow defined the *self-actualization need* as the "desire to become more and more what one idiosyncratically is, to become everything that one is capable of becoming."[7] At this level of the hierarchy, an individual attempts to realize full personal potential. The person is interested in self-fulfillment, self-development, and creativity in the broadest sense of the word.

The realization of one's full potential is also important.

Of all five of the needs Maslow identified, the least is known about self-actualization. People satisfy the need in so many different ways that it is difficult to pin down and identify. However as Paul Hersey and Kenneth H. Blanchard note, competence and achievement are closely related motives, and extensive research has been conducted on them.[8]

Competence provides people with a form of control over their environment.

Robert W. White has concluded that human beings desire competence because it gives them a form of control over their environment.[9] As they mature, people learn their limitations and capabilities from experience, and they work within these confines. For example, it is rare to find intelligent adults seriously overrating their abilities. They basically know what they can do and will remain within these parameters, choosing an objective that is attainable, such as job mastery. People pit themselves against their work as a goal that is challenging but not beyond attainment. This competence desire is related to the self-actualization need identified by Maslow.

Some individuals have a high need to achieve.

Another such related need is achievement. Some individuals will accomplish more than others because their need to achieve is greater. The noted psychologist, David C. McClelland, and his associates at Harvard have been studying this need for over twenty-five years.[10] McClelland's highly regarded studies have found that high achievers are neither low nor high risk takers. Rather, they set moderately difficult but potentially achievable goals for themselves. They like a challenge, but they want some influence over the outcome. They are aggressive realists. In addition, they are motivated more by the accomplishment of a particular objective than by the rewards associated with it. They use money, for example, merely as a means of measuring or assessing progress. High achievers also have a strong desire for feedback on how well they are doing. They want to know the score.

The Individual and the Hierarchy

Maslow's theory has general application for the manager, but several points merit specific attention. First, the hierarchy must not be viewed as a rigid structure. Levels are not clear-cut; they tend to overlap. When the intensity of one need is on the decline, the next one may be on the rise, as seen in Figure 12–4. For instance, when the safety need passes the peak of the physiological need, it assumes the dominant role and holds it until the social need rises above it.

Hierarchical levels are not clear-cut.

Second, some individuals remain primarily at the lower levels of the hierarchy, continually concerned with physiological and safety needs. This often occurs among people

---

[7] Maslow, *Motivation and Personality,* p. 46.

[8] Paul Hersey and Kenneth H. Blanchard, *Management of Organizational Behavior: Utilizing Human Resources,* 3d ed. (Englewood Cliffs, N.J.: Prentice-Hall, 1977), p. 42.

[9] Robert W. White, "Motivation Reconsidered: The Concept of Competence," *Psychological Review,* September 1959, pp. 297–333.

[10] David C. McClelland, J. W. Atkinson, R. A. Cook, and E. L. Lawler, *The Achievement Motive* (Appleton-Century-Crofts, 1953); David C. McClelland, *The Achieving Society* (Princeton, N.J.: Van Nostrand, 1961); and David C. McClelland and David H. Burnham, "Power Is the Great Motivator," *Harvard Business Review,* March–April 1976, pp. 100–110.

Figure 12–4   Changing Needs

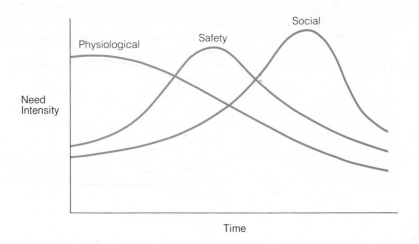

in underdeveloped areas. Conversely, others may spend a great deal of their time at the upper levels of the hierarchy. If middle-class parents have the best chance of producing high achievers and if the United States is a middle-class society, it follows that Americans probably spend a good deal of their time trying to satisfy social, esteem, and self-actualization needs.

Third, the specific order of needs suggested by Maslow may not apply to everyone; there is certainly no empirical support that it does. For example, for some people esteem needs may be more basic than safety needs.

Fourth, the same type of behavior from two different people does not necessarily represent the same need. One person may speak in a cocky manner because of feeling certain of the subject and more qualified to speak on it than anyone else, while another person may use the exact same approach to hide feelings of insecurity. The former may be fulfilling either esteem or self-actualization needs while the latter is fulfilling the safety need.

Maslow's concept is useful for indicating that individuals have needs. However, in order to motivate workers, the manager must know which needs require satisfaction at which times. Whatever approach the manager takes, it will be based on assumptions about individual workers and their need satisfactions.

Some people may remain at certain levels of the hierarchy.

Maslow's hierarchy lacks empirical evidence.

People respond differently to identical needs.

McGREGOR'S ASSUMPTIONS

Douglas McGregor provided some important insights into the area of managerial assumptions in his book *The Human Side of Enterprise*.[11] It was McGregor's thesis that "the theoretical assumptions management holds about controlling its human resources determine the whole character of the enterprise. They determine also the quality of its successive generations of management."[12] McGregor's point here was that every man-

---

[11] Douglas McGregor, *The Human Side of Enterprise* (New York: McGraw-Hill, 1960).
[12] Ibid., pp. vi–vii.

agement has a philosophy or set of assumptions it uses in handling its workers. In essence, McGregor divided these assumptions into two groups: Theory X assumptions and Theory Y assumptions. Theory X assumptions may be placed on one end of a continuum and Theory Y assumptions on the other.

McGregor found Theory X assumptions implicit in much of the literature about organization and in many of the current management practices. The assumptions that underlie *Theory X* are:

1. Management is responsible for organizing the elements of productive enterprise—money, materials, equipment, people—in the interest of economic ends.
2. With respect to people, management is a process of directing their efforts, motivating them, controlling their actions, and modifying their behavior to fit the needs of the organization.
3. Without this active intervention by management, people would be passive about—or even resistant to—organizational needs. They must, therefore, be persuaded, rewarded, punished, controlled—their activities must be directed. This is management's task—in managing subordinate managers or workers. We often sum it up by saying that management consists of getting things done through other people.

Theory X assumptions are listed.

Behind this conventional theory there are several additional beliefs—less explicit, but widespread:

4. The average person is by nature indolent and works as little as possible.
5. The individual lacks ambition, dislikes responsibility, prefers to be led.
6. The average person is inherently self-centered, indifferent to organizational needs.
7. The average person is by nature resistant to change.
8. The average person is gullible, not very bright, the ready dupe of the charlatan and the demagogue.[13]

It might appear at first glance that McGregor was constructing a straw man. But he vehemently disagreed with that notion, observing that Theory X assumptions are actually subscribed to by many managers in United States industry. Furthermore, he noted, "the principles of organization which comprise the bulk of the literature of management *could only have been derived from assumptions such as those of Theory X.* Other beliefs about human nature would have led inevitably to quite different organizational principles."[14]

The result of Theory X assumptions, according to McGregor, is that many managers give prime consideration to the satisfactions of physiological and safety needs. However, it is quite easy to see that these needs cannot be satisfied while one is on the job. Money, for example, which can purchase food, clothing, and shelter, can only be spent when the worker has left the workplace. Likewise, safety needs, as reflected in fringe benefits such as vacations, profit-sharing plans, and health and medical coverage, yield satisfaction only outside one's place of work. Nevertheless, many managers seem to feel these low-level physiological need satisfiers are of major importance. Why? In the case of money, one answer is found in the simple fact that it is an easy variable to manipulate; managers rely upon it as a motivational tool, giving or withholding financial rewards in an effort to stimulate production. Another reason is the attitude of many managers:

Prime emphasis is placed on satisfying low-level needs.

Most . . . . are highly achievement-oriented; in the psychologist's terms, they are "high in n Ach." We know that such men attach special significance to money rewards. They are strong believers in steeply increas-

---

13 Adapted from ibid., pp. 33–34.
14 Ibid., p. 35.

ing financial rewards for greater accomplishment. Because they themselves are particularly interested in some concrete measure that will sensitively reflect how well they have done, it is easy and natural for them to mistake this idea for a related one—namely, that the more money you offer someone the harder he will work.[15]

However, as noted earlier, once the employee's physiological and safety needs are taken care of, attention is focused on higher-level needs, and this is where the problem begins. Management has made no provisions for satisfying these needs, so it offers workers more physiological and safety rewards. If the workers balk at this, management brings out the threat of punishment, which is in accord with the third-listed Theory X tenet. The use of punishment seems to be a logical method of solving the issue; either the workers do the job or management will get tough. However, the problem rests with the fact that management mistakes causes for effects, the result being a self-fulfilling prophecy. Believing punishment is a necessary tool for effective management, the company introduces it the minute the workers start offering resistance, with mental notes: "See, it's just like we said. You have to get tough with these people if you want any performance." Yet it is very often management's fault that the workers are discontent in the first place.

Why do managers have trouble motivating their workers? The answer is that they hold erroneous assumptions about human nature. Management believes it should treat people like children, providing low-level need-satisfaction rewards if work is done well and withholding these benefits if it is done poorly. This carrot-and-stick theory may be useful in getting a donkey to pull a cart, but it seldom works effectively in motivating human beings. A more realistic set of assumptions is contained in Theory Y.

A carrot-and-stick approach is used.

An Age-old Phenomenon Before examining Theory Y, however, it should be realized that the basic assumptions of Theory X have existed for years. The philosophy of the early business managers was very similar to that of modern Theory X advocates. Henry P. Knowles and Borje O. Saxburg have identified the assumptions employed by these early managers in this way:

Theory X is not new.

1. The employee is a "constant" in the production equation. The implication here is that man has a fixed nature.
2. The employee is an inert adjunct of the machine, prone to inefficiency and waste unless properly programmed.
3. The employee is by nature lazy; only managers honor the "hard work" creed of the Protestant Ethic.
4. The employee's main concern is self-interest. At work, this is always expressed in economic values.
5. Given appropriate expression, these values will make man fiercely competitive among his peers as an accumulator of financial rewards.
6. Man (at least the working man) must therefore be tightly controlled and externally motivated in order to overcome his natural desire to avoid work unless the material gains available to him are worth his effort.[16]

Theory X, then, is certainly not a new phenomenon; it has been in existence for years. The only notable change is that management has been able to reduce economic hard-

---

[15] David C. McClelland, "Money as a Motivator: Some Research Insights," in *Organizational Behavior and the Practice of Management,* ed. David R. Hampton, Charles E. Summer, and Ross A. Webber (Glenview, Ill.: Scott, Foresman, 1973), p. 641.

[16] Henry P. Knowles and Borje O. Saxburg, "Human Relations and the Nature of Man," *Harvard Business Review,* March–April 1967, p. 32.

---

ship and improve working conditions among the employees since the time of Frederick Taylor and his associates. This has all been done, however, without any change in their fundamental theory of management.

Theory Y

Human behavior research has provided the basis for a new theory of management, which McGregor called *Theory Y.* Its assumptions follow:

1. Management is responsible for organizing the elements of productive enterprise —money, materials, equipment, people—in the interest of economic ends.
2. People are not by nature passive or resistant to organizational needs. They have become so as a result of experience in organizations.
3. The motivation, the potential for development, the capacity for assuming responsibility, the readiness to direct behavior toward organizational goals are all present in people. Management does not put them there. It is a responsibility of management to make it possible for people to recognize and develop these human characteristics for themselves.
4. The essential task of management is to arrange organizational conditions and methods of operation so that people can achieve their own goals best by directing their own efforts toward organizational objectives.[17]

Theory Y assumptions are listed.

In contrast to Theory X, Theory Y presents a dynamic view of man. The individual is seen as having growth and development capacities, and the problem of motivation is now placed directly in the lap of management. Since the worker has potential, management must decide how to tap it. No longer can management hide behind old Theory X assumptions. Management must re-evaluate its thinking and begin focusing attention on ways of allowing the workers to attain their upper-level needs.

Theory Y Criticism Many individuals think of Theory X as an outmoded set of ideas, believing Theory Y is a modern, superior view of the worker; but Theory Y also has its critics. Some point out that Theory Y is unreasonably idealistic. Not everyone is self-directed and self-controlled; many workers seem to like security and shun responsibility. As the popular psychoanalyst, Erich Fromm has noted, people want freedom, but only within defined limits.[18] George Strauss, the well-known industrial relationist, supports this finding, pointing out that individuals who accept complete freedom in certain areas will demand restrictions in many others.[19] Maslow also echoed the sentiment, stating that gratification of basic needs is important but that it was also the case that unrestricted indulgence could lead to irresponsibility, psychopathology, and inability to bear stress.[20]

Theory Y may be overly idealistic.

A second criticism of Theory Y is that its advocates tend to believe that the primary place of need satisfaction is on the job. However, many workers satisfy their needs off the job. This is particularly apparent in light of the trend toward a shorter work week; people are seeking satisfaction during their leisure time. Theory Y may thus overemphasize the importance of satisfying higher-level needs in the workplace.

Need satisfaction may not occur on the job.

A third common criticism involves the issue of whether a personality-organization

---

[17] Adapted from McGregor, *The Human Side of Enterprise,* pp. 47–48.
[18] Erich Fromm, *The Sane Society* (New York: Holt, Rinehart and Winston, 1955), p. 318.
[19] George Strauss, "Some Notes on Power-Equalization," in *The Social Science of Organizations,* ed. Harold J. Leavitt (Englewood Cliffs, N.J.: Prentice-Hall, 1963), p. 50.
[20] Abraham H. Maslow, *Toward a Psychology of Being* (Princeton, N.J.: Van Nostrand, 1962), pp. 153–154.

conflict does exist as a characteristic of large-scale mass-production industries. Critics contend that Theory Y assumes that such concepts as work simplification and standardization have reduced job satisfaction, though this may be only one cause of organization conflict and may be exaggerated by advocates of Theory Y.

The individual and the organization are not always in conflict.

Fourth, many managers can demonstrate good results with a Theory X philosophy. For example, research on management styles among NFL coaches reveals that most of them subscribe to a basic Theory X philosophy as represented by these beliefs:

1. The threat of being cut, benched, or traded will cause a player to perform better.
2. For the most part, players are incapable of motivating themselves.
3. Players should not have much input into the establishment of rules and policies that govern them off the field.[21]

Which of the two theories is correct? The answer probably depends on the situation and almost always represents some combination of the two. One thing appears certain, however. Most managers tend to underrate the workers, subscribing more heavily to Theory X than to Theory Y. This has been made very clear by Chris Argyris.

ARGYRIS'S IMMATURITY-MATURITY THEORY

Chris Argyris, while on the Yale faculty, studied industrial organizations to determine the effect of management practices on individual behavior and personal growth within the organization.[22] According to him, as an individual moves from infancy (immaturity) to adulthood (maturity) seven changes take place. First, the passive state of the infant gives way to the increasingly active state of the child and adult. Second, the maturing child becomes relatively independent. Third, an infant is capable of behaving in only a few ways, whereas an adult has learned to behave in many ways. Fourth, a child tends to have casual, short-term interests; an adult sometimes develops deep, strong interests. Fifth, a child's time perspective is very short. An adult's is longer, encompassing the past, present, and future. Sixth, an infant is subordinate to everyone, whereas an adult is equal or superior to others. Seventh, children lack an awareness of "self," whereas adults are aware of and able to control "self." These seven stages can be viewed as stages in a continuum:

Argyris lists seven stages of maturity development.

Immaturity ———————————————————————————————— Maturity

Argyris contends that most organizations keep their employees in a state of immaturity. Position descriptions, work assignments, and task specialization lead to routine, unchallenging jobs. They also minimize the amount of control workers have over their environment. This, in turn, encourages them to be passive, dependent, and submissive. Argyris would say that keeping people in this state is one of the formal organization's goals. Management likes to control everything and views workers as small cogs in a big machine. This type of thinking is obviously incompatible with the development of a mature personality. The result is incongruity between the mature individual and the formal organization, with its paternalistic interests. Argyris's findings echo McGregor's Theory X assumptions, indicating that management's view of the worker may be the

He believes that organizations are structured to keep employees in an immature state.

---

[21] Kelly Kerin and Charles N. Waldo, "NFL Coaches and Motivation Theory," *MSU Business Topics,* Autumn 1978, pp. 15–18.

[22] Chris Argyris, *Personality and Organization* (New York: Harper & Bros., 1957); *Interpersonal Competence and Organizational Effectiveness* (Homewood, Ill.: Dorsey Press, 1962); and *Integrating the Individual and the Organization* (New York: Wiley, 1964).

major stumbling block in the motivation process. Unaware of what really motivates non-managerial people, management is unable to come up with a viable theory of motivation. One individual who has attempted to shed light on this problem by extending Maslow's hierarchical concept and applying it to the job is Frederick Herzberg.

HERZBERG'S TWO-FACTOR THEORY OF MOTIVATION

In the late 1950s, Frederick Herzberg and his associates at the Psychological Service of Pittsburgh conducted extensive interviews with two hundred engineers and accountants from eleven industries in the Pittsburgh area.[23]

The interview subjects were asked to identify the elements of their job that made them happy or unhappy. Analysis of the findings revealed that when people were dissatisfied, their negative feelings were generally associated with the environment in which they were working. When people felt good about their jobs, they generally associated their feeling with the work itself. Herzberg labeled the factors that prevent dissatisfaction as hygiene factors and those that bring about satisfaction as motivators.

Hygiene Factors

Herzberg called the factors that prevent dissatisfaction *hygiene factors* because their effect on the worker resembles that of physical hygiene on the body. Consider, for example, the case of Art Barney, who slips on an icy path and suffers superficial hand cuts. At home Barney washes his hand and puts iodine on the wound. Two weeks later the hand is back to its normal state. The iodine did not make the hand any better than it was previous to the injury, but it prevented further deterioration, such as gangrene, and helped the hand return to its original state.

"I am a robber—my name is Dick.
Dick wants all your money. . . ."

---

[23] Frederick Herzberg, Bernard Mausner, and Barbara Bloch Snyderman, *The Motivation to Work,* 2d ed. (New York: Wiley, 1959).

Table 12–1 Hygiene and Motivators

Hygiene Factors (Environment)	Motivators (Work Itself)
Money	Work itself
Supervision	Recognition
Status	Advancement
Security	Possibility of growth
Working conditions	Responsibility
Policies and administration	Achievement
Interpersonal relations	

This is the function of hygiene. It takes a negative condition (cut hand) and brings it back to its original position (uncut hand). Conversely, if hygienic intervention is withheld, things can go from bad to worse. For example, Nancy Blair, who is in excellent health, will not become any healthier by eating food. But if she does not eat, Blair will eventually become sick and die. Likewise, breathing will not make her any healthier but total inability to breathe will kill her. Hygiene will not improve health beyond one's original state, but it prevents deterioration by returning the person to an original state, which can be called condition zero.

Herzberg found that the workplace contains many hygiene factors. These include money, supervision, status, security, working conditions, policies and administration, and interpersonal relations (see Table 12–1). These factors do not motivate people; they merely prevent dissatisfaction. They produce no growth in worker output, but they prevent loss in performance caused by work restriction. They maintain motivation at zero-level, preventing a negative type of motivation from occurring. This is why they are often referred to as maintenance factors.

Hygiene factors prevent dissatisfaction.

Motivators

Herzberg found that factors relating to the job itself can have a positive effect on job satisfaction and result in increased output. He called these *motivational factors,* or satisfiers, and identified them as the work itself, recognition, advancement, the possibility of growth, responsibility, and achievement.

Motivators have a positive effect on job satisfaction.

Motivation-Hygiene under Attack

Herzberg's two-factor theory presents some interesting ideas, but so do its critics. First, the original population studied consisted only of accountants and engineers. The study is therefore considered unrepresentative of the work force in general. Second, although Herzberg has cited replication of the results of his study amoung groups such as manufacturing supervisors, hospital maintenance personnel, nurses, military officers, and professional women,[24] other researchers have uncovered different results.[25] In some

---

[24] Frederick Herzberg, *Work and the Nature of Man* (Cleveland, Ohio: World Publishing, 1966); Valerie M. Bockman, "The Herzberg Controversy," *Personnel Psychology,* Summer 1971, pp. 155–189; and Benedict S. Grigaliunas and Frederick Herzberg, "Relevancy in the Test of Motivation-Hygiene Theory," *Journal of Applied Psychology,* February 1971, pp. 73–79.

[25] For an interesting summary of some of this work, see Alan C. Filley, Robert J. House, and Steven Kerr, *Managerial Process and Organizational Behavior,* 2d ed. (Glenview, Ill.: Scott, Foresman, 1976), pp. 197–200.

cases, hygiene or maintenance factors, such as wages or job security, were found to be viewed as motivators among blue-collar workers. In addition, what one person might call a motivator, another person in the same department might term a hygiene factor. In one study conducted among both managerial and professional workers, Donald P. Schwab, H. William DeVitt, and Larry L. Cummings found that Herzberg's hygiene factors were as useful in motivating employees as were his motivators.[26] Third, Victor H. Vroom contends that Herzberg's findings are debatable because his two-factor conclusion was only one of many that could have been drawn from the research.[27] Vroom argues that people are more likely to assign satisfaction to their own achievements and attribute dissatisfaction to company policies. Thus, the Herzberg findings are interpretive at best.

The criticism indicates that the two-factor theory is certainly not universally accepted and that more research is needed before definitive conclusions about it can be drawn. As M. Scott Myers noted, "Motivation-maintenance theory, like any theory of management, is at the mercy of its practitioners and will remain intact and find effective utilization only to the extent that it serves as a mechanism for harnessing constructive motives."[28] Nevertheless, Herzberg's theory of job satisfaction has helped extend and apply Maslow's need hierarchy to work motivation.

The Need Hierarchy and Motivation-Hygiene

Herzberg's framework is compatible with Maslow's need hierarchy. Maslow's lower-level needs are analogous to Herzberg's hygiene factors, and his upper-level needs correspond to Herzberg's motivators. The comparison between the two is shown in Figure 12–5. As the figure indicates, Herzberg's hygiene factors encompass Maslow's physiological, safety, social, and, to some degree, esteem needs. The reason for placing status in the hygiene category and advancement and recognition in the motivator group is that status is not always a reflection of personal achievement or earned recognition. For example, an individual could achieve status through family ties such as inheritance or marriage. Conversely, advancement and recognition are more often reflections of personal achievement.

However, it must be realized that Maslow and Herzberg both tend to oversimplify the motivational process. Although Herzberg makes an interesting extension of Maslow's theory, neither of their models provides an adequate link between individual need satisfaction and the achievement of organizational objectives. Nor does either of their theories really handle the problem of individual differences in motivation. For this one must turn to process or mechanical theories.

Before doing this, however, two key concepts of modern motivation theory will be examined: expectancy theory and learned behavior.

EXPECTANCY THEORY AND LEARNED BEHAVIOR

Some of the most important modern process theories rely on what is called *expectancy theory*. This concept relates to motivation as follows:

---

[26] Donald P. Schwab, H. William DeVitt, and Larry L. Cummings, "A Test of the Adequacy of the Two-factor Theory as a Predictor of Self-report Performance Effects," *Personnel Psychology,* Summer 1971, pp. 293–303.

[27] Victor H. Vroom, *Work and Motivation* (New York: Wiley, 1964), pp. 128–129.

[28] M. Scott Myers, "Who Are Your Motivated Workers?" *Harvard Business Review,* January–February 1964, p. 88.

Figure 12–5 *Comparison of Maslow and Herzberg Models*

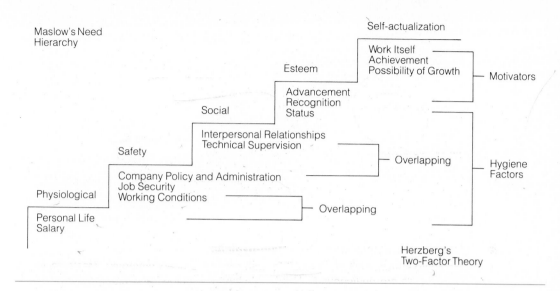

Expectancy theory predicts that an individual will generally be a high performer when he: (1) sees a high probability that his efforts will lead to high performance, (2) sees a high probability that high performance will lead to outcomes, and (3) views these outcomes to be, on balance, positively attractive to himself.[29]

In comparing Maslow's concept of needs with this idea of expectancy, it becomes evident that there are two ways of studying motivational intensity. One can examine need deficiencies, as in Maslow's hierarchy, which promote a particular form of behavior, or one can examine the goals the individual has chosen, in which case motivation is seen as a force pulling the person toward the desired objective. Furthermore, in the case of need deprivation, the emphasis is on internal deficiencies; in the case of expectancy, the focus is on external goals that help alleviate these deficiencies. In essence, although the two ideas are different, they are related. However, motivation researchers today tend to favor the expectancy theory approach. Two of the leading researchers in this field, Lyman Porter and Edward Lawler, cite the following reasons for choosing this approach:

Need-deprivation and expectancy theory approach are related.

Basically, the terminology and concepts involved seem to us to be more applicable to consideration of the complexities of human motivation and behavior, and, therefore, more applicable to understanding the attitudes and performance of managers in organizations. The emphasis in expectancy theory on rationality and expectations seems to us to describe best the kinds of conditions that influence managerial performance. . . .

Expectancy theory also greatly facilitates the incorporation of motives like status, achievement, and power into a theory of attitudes and performance. There is a considerable amount of evidence that the cen-

[29] L. L. Cummings and Donald P. Schwab, *Performance in Organizations: Determinants and Appraisal* (Glenview, Ill.: Scott, Foresman, 1973), p. 31.

tral motives for most managers are those for achievement, self-actualization, power and status, *and* income and advancement.[30]

In addition, studies employing expectancy theory have been conducted in both private and public organizations, among employees ranging from production line operators to managerial personnel. These studies have proved very successful in providing insights into this area of motivation.

If individuals are indeed motivated by expectations, they must have established some relationship between present action and future reward. For example, a person might think, "If I work hard, I will be promoted." This causal relationship is formulated through *learned behavior.* Through either direct or indirect experience, individuals learn to establish cause-effect relationships, which predict how people will respond in a given situation.

One of the key factors in learned behavior is reinforcement. If an individual does something right and the manager wants to reinforce this behavior, the manager must respond in a way which the subordinate finds satisfying—for example, by giving the person a pat on the back or a raise. This response, which is positive reinforcement, will increase the chances that the individual will repeat the behavior in the future. Conversely, if the manager wants to extinguish a given behavior, punishment or negative reinforcement, such as a reprimand or a demotion, will be effective.[31]

When the concept of expectancy theory is combined with that of learned behavior, one has the basis for understanding some of the most important modern motivation theories. One of these is Victor Vroom's expectancy-valence theory.

VROOM'S THEORY

Victor Vroom's motivation theory is complex, but nonetheless it is viewed with great favor. His basic concept can be expressed in the following equation:

$$\text{Motivation} = \Sigma \text{ valence} \times \text{expectancy.}[32]$$

Motivation is equal to the summation of valence times expectancy. To understand Vroom's theory, three concepts must be grasped: instrumentality, valence, and expectancy.

An individual's motivation is a result of the actual or perceived rewards available upon the accomplishment of some goal. For example, the company wants a man to be productive. But what is in it for him? This will, of course, depend upon the worker's perception of available rewards. Suppose for a moment that the man believes there is a direct correlation between productivity and promotion—that is, that promotion depends on productivity. Then, given this assumption, there are two outcomes to consider. There is the *first-level outcome,* which in this case is productivity, and there is the *second-level outcome,* which, again in this case, is promotion. This introduces the first of Vroom's three concepts, namely, instrumentality. *Instrumentality* is the relationship perceived by an individual between a first-level outcome and a second-level outcome.

Next, one has to consider the man's *valence,* or preference for the first-level outcome

Reinforcement is one of the key factors in learned behavior.

Instrumentality is the relationship an individual perceives between a first- and a second-level outcome.

---

[30] Lyman W. Porter and Edward E. Lawler III, *Managerial Attitudes and Performance* (Homewood, Ill.: Dorsey Press, 1968), pp. 12–13.

[31] See, for example, Fred Luthans and Robert Kreitner, "The Role of Punishment in Organizational Behavior Modification (O.B. Mod.)," *Public Personnel Management,* May–June 1973, pp. 156–161; and Fred Luthans and Robert Kreitner, *Organizational Behavior Modification* (Glenview, Ill.: Scott, Foresman, 1975).

[32] Vroom, *Work and Motivation,* chap. 2.

(productivity). To make it more meaningful, three variations of productivity will be used: high, average, and low. What is this man's valence for high productivity? This will depend on his desire for promotion. If it is very high, his valence will be positive. If he is indifferent to promotion, it will be zero. If he does not want a promotion, it will be negative. The same logic can be used in determining his valence for average and low productivity. Thus, valence and instrumentality can be brought together in the following way:

Valence or preference ⟶ Instrumentality ⟶ Second-level
for first-level   (Perceived relationships   outcome
outcome   between first- and second-   (Promotion)
(Productivity)   level outcomes)

Valence is a person's preference for a particular outcome.

In grasping Vroom's theory, one must work backward from instrumentality to valence. An individual's preference for a first-level outcome is dictated by the extent to which he or she believes this will lead to the attainment of a second-level outcome.

Vroom's third concept, expectancy, is the probability that a specific action will be followed by a particular first-level outcome. For example, what is the probability that if the man works hard he can attain high productivity? This objective probability will range from zero (no chance) to one (certainty). If the worker is convinced that with hard work he can attain high productivity, his expectancy will be equal to one. These three concepts, instrumentality, valence, and expectancy, are incorporated in Figure 12–6.

Expectancy is the probability that a specific action will yield a particular first-level outcome.

Motivation is thus in Vroom's *expectancy-valence theory* equal to the algebraic sum of the products of the valences of all first-level outcomes (the person's preference for each of the first-level outcomes) times the strength of the expectancy that the action will be followed by the attainment of these outcomes (the probability of attaining the respective first-level outcome). This formula helps the manager understand what motivates the individual worker.

It cannot be denied that Vroom's theory is difficult to comprehend. Because of the complexity of his motivation formula, this text does not apply it to a specific situation; an understanding of the basic ideas is sufficient. But it should be kept in mind that current researchers have higher regard for Vroom's theory than for most of the other motivation theories. As J. G. Hunt and J. W. Hill note:

> More work must be done before we can make any statements concerning the overall validity of Vroom's model. But the rigor of his formulation, the relative ease of making the concepts operational, and the model's emphasis on individual differences show considerable promise. We are also encouraged by the results of relatively sophisticated studies testing the theory. We believe it is time for those interested in organizational behavior to take a more thoroughly scientific look at this very complex subject of industrial motivation, and Vroom's model seems a big step in that direction.[33]

PORTER AND LAWLER'S MODEL

Another modern process theory is that proposed by Lyman Porter and Edward Lawler.[34] Porter and Lawler's model, also based on the expectancy theory of motivation, implies that individuals are motivated by future expectations based on previous experiences. In

---

[33] J. G. Hunt and J. W. Hill, "The New Look in Motivation Theory for Organizational Research," *Human Organization,* Summer 1969, p. 108.
[34] Porter and Lawler, *Managerial Attitudes and Performance.*

Figure 12–6   An Example of Vroom's Expectancy-Valence Model

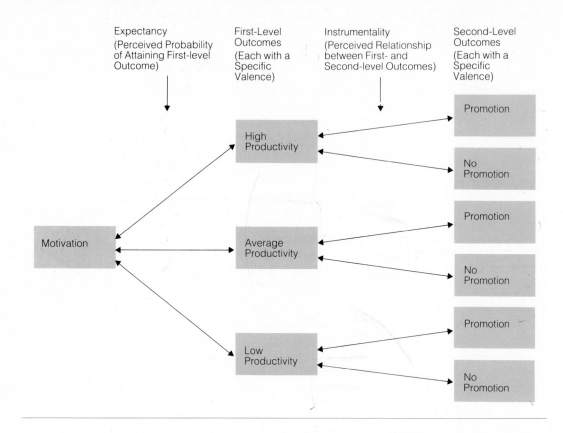

essence, their model contains a number of key variables, including effort, performance, reward, and satisfaction. Figure 12–7 illustrates the relationship among these variables.

It is important to note that Porter and Lawler use a semi-wavy line between performance and intrinsic rewards to indicate that a direct relationship exists if the job has been designed in such a way that a person who has performed well can be rewarded with an internally generated payoff, such as a feeling of accomplishment. The wavy line between performance and extrinsic rewards in the figure shows such rewards are often not directly related to performance—for example, an externally generated payoff such as a pay increase. The arrow between performance and perceived equitable rewards depicts the fact that people's performance influences their perception of what they should receive. To put it experientially, if a woman does not get the level of rewards she believes she should, satisfaction will be negatively affected.

Lawler has made several refinements of his own, presented in the model in Figure 12–7. In particular, he believes that there are two types of expectancies: E→P (effort leads to performance) and P→O (performance leads to a specific outcome).

A person's effort or motivation is influenced by his or her perception of the relationship between effort and performance (if I work hard, will I obtain the desired performance?) and the perception of the relationship between performance and a specific

Figure 12–7 Porter and Lawler's Motivation Model

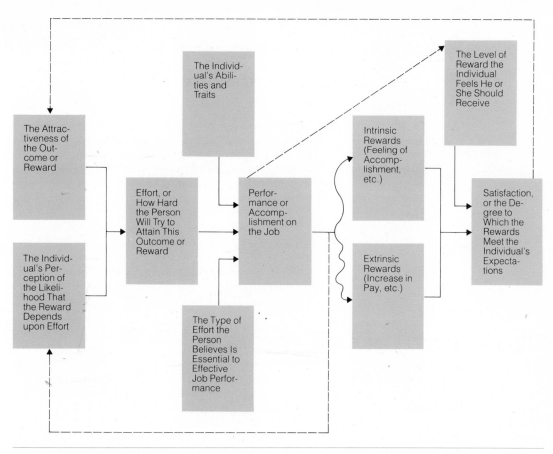

Source: Adapted from Lyman W. Porter and Edward E. Lawler III, *Managerial Attitudes and Performance* (Homewood, Ill.: Richard D. Irwin, 1968), p. 165.

outcome (if I have high performance, will I get a promotion?). Finally, the person's valence for the promotion must be considered. Some people have suggested a simple way of integrating all three ideas into a formula for determining an effort or motivation index, which is stated this way:

$$\underset{\text{(0 to 1.0)}}{E{\to}P} \times \underset{\text{(0 to 1.0)}}{P{\to}O} \times \underset{\text{(0 to 1.0)}}{\text{Valence}} = \frac{\text{Effort}}{\text{Index}}$$

Employing this formula, consider the case of Steven Acres, who believes that effort is directly related to performance (1.0); that high performance is very likely to bring about the desired outcome of promotion (0.8); and he has a high valence for the promotion (0.9). In this case, Steven's effort or motivation index is: $1.0 \times 0.8 \times 0.9 = 0.72$.

In contrast, consider the case of Ruth Schule, who believes effort is directly related to performance (1.0); but high performance is not likely to bring about a promotion (0.4), although she does have a high valence for the promotion (0.9). In this case Schule's effort or motivation index is: $1.0 \times 0.4 \times 0.9 = 0.36$. Note that if one of the three factors in the effort index is low, motivation suffers greatly.[35]

Returning to the Vroom model and comparing it with the one in Figure 12–7, it is evident that the latter is more comprehensive. It also proposes the relationship between rewards and performance, concluding that an individual's satisfaction is a function of the rewards received. In turn, these rewards are brought about by performance. Thus:

$$\text{Performance} \xrightarrow[\text{to}]{\text{Leads}} \text{Rewards} \xrightarrow[\text{Bring about}]{\text{Which}} \text{Satisfaction.}$$

This is a rather interesting finding since many managers feel that a happy worker is a productive worker—in other words, that satisfaction leads to performance. However, Porter and Lawler report just the opposite; performance causes satisfaction.

The performance-satisfaction controversy still rages.

Today the performance-satisfaction controversy continues. Which is the cause? Which is the effect? To further confuse the issue, it should be noted that there are some individuals who contend that both performance and satisfaction are caused by the reward system.[36]

Although research is still being conducted in an attempt to resolve the issue, one fact is indisputable. Rewards are important in the motivation process and the level of these rewards must be commensurate with what the individual believes they should be. This concept is known as equity theory, and although it was treated in Porter and Lawler's model, it will be considered separately now.

EQUITY OR SOCIAL COMPARISON THEORY

Equity theory, also called *social comparison theory,* is an extension of Chester Barnard's concept about the worker's weighing what he or she is getting from the company against what he or she is giving to the company. However, equity theory goes further, contending that the individual evaluates not only his or her personal position, but that of others as well.

People compare their rewards with those received by others.

People are motivated not only by what they get but also by what they see, or believe, others are getting. They make a social comparison of inputs (education, effort, time spent on the job) and rewards (money, working conditions, recognition) for themselves and others in the organization. For example, Rogers feels that he is entitled to a raise of $1,000 for the upcoming year. His superior calls him and tells him he is going to get $1,750. Rogers is elated. However, later in the day he discovers that Linz, his archrival, has received $2,300. Now Rogers is angry because he feels he is giving as much to the company as Linz, but he is receiving less. Initially, he was happy with the "extra" $750 but now he is not, because social comparison has shown that Linz is getting a bigger reward than he. Figure 12–8 shows how this social comparison works.

When people feel they are not being properly treated, tension results. This tension can bring about absenteeism and turnover. In fact, some research studies have found

---

[35] For more on this subject see Richard M. Steers and Lyman W. Porter, *Motivation and Work Behavior* (New York: McGraw-Hill, 1975), chap. 6.

[36] Charles N. Greene, "The Satisfaction-Performance Controversy," *Business Horizons,* October 1972, pp. 31–41; John M. Ivancevich, "The Performance to Satisfaction Relationship: A Causal Analysis of Stimulating and Nonstimulating Jobs," *Organizational Behavior and Human Performance,* December 1979, pp. 350–365.

Figure 12–8   Social Comparison

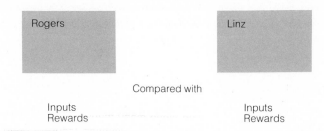

that an employee's perception of equitable treatment is a stronger prediction of absence and turnover than are variables related to job satisfaction.[37]

A number of alternatives are available to relieve this tension. For example, Rogers may quit his job. Or he may go to his boss and demand more money, thereby establishing equality with Linz. Or he may stop comparing himself with his rival because he cannot hope to keep up. If he feels the need, he can find a different rival. Or he can do less work. However, the most likely alternative is that he will change his perception of Linz's input-reward ratio. For example, "Linz has three kids and I only have one, so my $1,750 will go a lot further than his $2,300."

It is also interesting to note that some research shows that people who feel overpaid, at least initially, tend to do more work. In this way the individuals justify the higher salaries. However, in time people usually reevaluate their skills and position and conclude that they are indeed worth their pay. At this time, their output drops back to its former level. This accounts for the belief of some researchers that money is a short-run motivator at best, and only one tool among many that the manager can use in the motivation process. As McClelland has pointed out:

> [Money] is a treacherous tool because it is deceptively concrete, tempting many managers to neglect variables in the work situation and climate that really affect productivity. In the near future, there will be less and less excuse for neglecting these variables, as the behavioral sciences begin to define them and explain to management how they can be manipulated just as one might change a financial compensation plan.[38]

Perhaps the greatest shortcoming of equity theory is that not enough empirical research has yet been conducted. The theory is intuitively appealing and it can certainly be tied in to the Porter-Lawler model. However, too much of the research to date has been conducted in laboratory rather than real-world settings. The researchers must go out into the world of work. Summing up their review of the literature in this area, Michael R. Carrell and John E. Dittrich come to this conclusion:

> Equity field research can be directed at the expectancy-performance or reward-satisfaction-valence linkages in the Porter-Lawler expectancy motivation model. This model and the general proposition derived from it offer several potential areas of field research. But there is a primary need for further development,

---

[37] John E. Dittrich and Michael R. Carrell, "Organizational Equity Perceptions, Employee Job Satisfaction, and Departmental Absence and Turnover Rates," *Organizational Behavior and Human Performance,* August 1979, pp. 29–40.

[38] McClelland, "Money as a Motivator," p. 649.

measurement, and testing of employees' internal dimensions of perceived equity. The relationship of perceived equity to other criterion variables such as grievance rates, absence, turnover and safety performance also should be examined in the field.

Finally, further field research is needed to determine if the laboratory based relationships between equity perceptions and demographic characteristics, reward allocation, and quality of performance also exist in actual organizations.[39]

SUMMARY

This chapter has examined modern motivation theory. The relationship between needs and behavior was first shown through the use of Maslow's hierarchy. These ideas were then refined and applied to the workplace through Herzberg's model.

Both theories provide important general insights into workers' behavior because they stress the importance of examining the causes of human activity and help answer the question of what specific things motivate people.

However, managers must also be concerned with explaining how behavior is initiated, directed, sustained, or halted. To do this they must understand process, or mechanical, theories. This chapter examined three of these theories: Vroom's expectancy-valence theory, Porter and Lawler's motivation model, and equity or social comparison theory. All three place great emphasis on individual motivation.

In the past few years, increased attention has been given to these process theories because of their value in applying general motivation theory to specific situations. Yet, whatever approach managers use, one question must remain foremost—what will motivate the workers to attain organizational objectives? Once this is answered, managers are in a position to examine the area of leadership. When people who manage know what will motivate the people they manage, they can focus attention on leading them.

REVIEW AND STUDY QUESTIONS

1. Is there any relationship between needs and behavior? Explain.
2. What are the five needs in Maslow's hierarchy? What relevance do they have to the study of motivation?
3. How do the assumptions of Theory X differ from those of Theory Y?
4. What is Argyris's immaturity-maturity theory? Do you agree or disagree with his findings?
5. What does Herzberg mean by hygiene factors? Identify some of them.
6. What does Herzberg mean by motivators? Identify some of them.
7. What relationship do Herzberg's and Maslow's theories bear to one another in general and specifically to motivation? Explain.
8. In your own words, explain what Vroom means by instrumentality? Valence? Expectancy? Explain each.
9. Of what value is Vroom's theory to the practicing manager?
10. How does Porter and Lawler's model expand the ideas presented by Vroom?
11. Of what value is the Porter-Lawler model to the practicing manager?

---

[39] Michael R. Carrell and John E. Dittrich, "Equity Theory: The Recent Literature, Methodological Considerations, and New Directions," *Academy of Management Review*, April 1978, p. 208.

12. What is meant by equity or social comparison theory? Give an illustration. What is its relevance to motivation theory?

13. In your own words, state the steps to effective motivation. What should every manager know about the process?

SELECTED REFERENCES

Annas, J. W. "Profiles of Motivation." *Personnel Journal,* March 1973, pp. 205–208.

Argyris, Chris. *Integrating the Individual and the Organization.* New York: Wiley, 1964.

———. *Interpersonal Competence and Organizational Effectiveness.* Homewood, Ill.: Dorsey Press, 1962.

———. *Personality and Organization.* New York: Harper & Bros., 1959.

Bockman, Valerie M. "The Herzberg Controversy." *Personnel Psychology,* Summer 1971, pp. 155–189.

Carrell, Michael R., and Dittrich, John E. "Equity Theory: The Recent Literature, Methodological Considerations, and New Directions." *Academy of Management Review,* April 1978, pp. 202–210.

Cook, C. W. "Guidelines for Managing Motivation," *Business Horizons,* April 1980, pp. 61–69.

Culbertson, Katherine, and Thompson, Mark. "An Analysis of Supervisory Training Needs," *Training and Development Journal,* February 1980, pp. 58–62.

Dittrich, John E., and Carrell, Michael R. "Organizational Equity Perceptions, Employee Job Satisfaction, and Departmental Absence and Turnover Rates." *Organizational Behavior and Human Performance,* August 1979, pp. 29–40.

Gellerman, S. W. *Management by Motivation.* New York: American Management Association, 1968.

Greene, Charles N. "The Satisfaction-Performance Controversy." *Business Horizons,* October 1972, pp. 31–41.

Herzberg, Frederick. *Work and the Nature of Man.* Cleveland: World Publishing, 1966.

Herzberg, Frederick; Mausner, Bernard; and Snyderman, Barbara Block. *The Motivation to Work.* New York: Wiley, 1959.

Hulin, C. L., and Smith, P. C. "An Empirical Investigation of Two Implications of the Two-Factor Theory of Job Satisfaction." *Journal of Applied Psychology,* October 1967, pp. 396–402.

Ivancevich, John M. "The Performance to Satisfaction Relationship: A Causal Analysis of Stimulating and Nonstimulating Jobs." *Organizational Behavior and Human Performance,* December 1978, pp. 350–365.

Kerin, Kelly, and Waldo, Charles N. "NFL Coaches and Motivation Theory." *MSU Business Topics,* Autumn 1978, pp. 15–18.

Lindsay, C. A.; Marks, E.; and Gorlow, L. "The Herzberg Theory: A Critique and Reformulation." *Journal of Applied Psychology,* August 1967, pp. 330–339.

McClelland, David; Atkinson, J. W.; Cook, R. A.; and Lawler, E. L. *The Achievement Motive.* New York: Appleton-Century-Crofts, 1953.

McGregor, Douglas. *The Human Side of Enterprise.* New York: McGraw-Hill, 1960.

Maslow, Abraham H. *Eupsychian Management.* Homewood, Ill.: Dorsey Press, 1965.

———. *Motivation and Personality.* New York: Harper & Bros., 1954.

Millard, C. W.; Lockwood, D. L.; and Luthans, F. "The Impact of a Four-Day Workweek on Employees." *MSU Business Topics,* Spring 1980, pp. 31–37.

Organ, D. W. "A Reappraisal and Reinterpretation of the Satisfaction-Causes-Performance Hypothesis." *Academy of Management Review,* January 1977, pp. 46–53.

Paul, R. J. "Workers' Compensation—An Adequate Employee Benefit?" *Academy of Management Review,* October 1976, pp. 112–123.

Pinder, C. C. "Concerning the Application of Human Motivation Theories in Organizational Settings." *Academy of Management Review,* July 1977, pp. 384–397.

Porter, Lyman W., and Lawler, Edward E. III. *Managerial Attitudes and Performance.* Homewood, Ill.: Richard D. Irwin, 1968.

Steers, Richard M., and Porter, Lyman W. *Motivation and Work Behavior.* New York: McGraw-Hill, 1975.

Vroom, Victor H. *Work and Motivation.* New York: Wiley, 1964.

Weaver, C. N. "Job Preferences of White Collar and Blue Collar Workers." *Academy of Management Journal,* March 1975, pp. 167–175.

CASE: *Money and Motivation*

Is money a motivator? Some people say it always is; others believe that it depends on the situation. For example, someone earning $10,000 a year will probably be more motivated by a raise of $1,000 than someone earning $100,000 a year. Still other people believe that every raise must be separated into two parts: that which is given for cost of living (no motivation potential) and that which is given for merit (high motivation potential). Certainly that is the feeling of the union at the Waderford Corporation.

Last month the union went on strike after being unable to obtain a "cost of living plus 3 percent" contract from the management. The latter was willing to give cost of living but no more. The union refused. "Why," asked the president of the union, "should we settle for a mere cost of living? This leaves us no better off than we were last year. We want to start getting ahead of inflation. The management staff certainly does not settle for just the cost of living. Why should we?"

An arbitrator has been called in to help resolve the dispute. However, it appears as if the strike will be a long one. The union has built up a rather large strike fund and seems unwilling to settle for anything less than an "above cost of living" contract. Management, for its part, has expressed its refusal to go any higher than the cost of living. As one of the managers put it, "Now we both know the other guy's position, so it will now boil down to who's going to give in first."

Questions

1. How important is money as a motivator? Explain your answer.

2. In addition to money, what else motivates people to work hard? Cite some illustrations.

3. When is money likely to be one of the most important motivators (if not *the* most important), and when is it likely to finish way down the list? Based on your answer, what conclusions can be drawn regarding the use of money as a motivator?

CASE: *A New Philosophy*

When Andrew Anderson was laid off from his production job at a textile mill, he immediately found work at another firm in a nearby town. This new job pays $100 less a week. Yet, when he was recalled to the mill last month, Anderson chose to stay at this new job. Why? Because he finds that the new firm is much less regimented than the old one.

In particular, what Anderson likes is his new company's philosophy of labor-management relations. Blue-collar workers are treated basically the same as white-collar employees. They get weekly salaries instead of hourly wages, participate in the company pension program, and get paid for absences caused by illness. In addition, the supervisors use loose, as opposed to close, control. The result, Anderson feels, is a more meaningful work environment.

In fact, one of the things that Anderson noticed as soon as he took his new job was that the supervisor did not recite a long list of disciplinary rules. Instead, the manager simply said that the company relied on the workers to do things properly. There was no formal system of rules and penalties that would be applied when a mistake was made. Anderson liked this and felt it motivated him to do a better job.

Apparently he is not alone. Company officials reported last week that this approach to motivating employees is working extremely well. Product output in the plant is 35 percent higher than that of other plants in the industry. Also, absenteeism is running at a 3 percent level, as compared to 6 percent for the competition, and turnover as a result of voluntary resignations is only 4 percent. This compares to an average of 16 percent in the industry.

Questions

1. What particular needs in Maslow's hierarchy does this new philosophy help Anderson satisfy?

2. Are these new conditions an illustration of hygiene factors or motivators?

3. Using Porter and Lawler's model of motivation, how can you explain the increases in output in this plant, where this philosophy has been adopted, as compared to plants of the competitors?

CASE: *Looking for Practical Value*

Sally Brendshaw is a new department manager in a bank. She is also pursuing a master's degree in business. Last Tuesday, in her organizational behavior class, she learned about expectancy theory. Brendshaw finds the theory interesting, although she wonders how it can be of practical value to her.

At her bank everyone has a semiannual review, at which time raises are given out. Typically, an individual can expect to receive 3 to 5 percent each time. In rare cases a manager will recommend more than 5 percent, but Brendshaw knows of no instance where a person received less than 3 percent. This review schedule, in her opinion, is a good one because just as the motivational effect of the first semiannual raise is wearing off, the person is given a second one. However, she does realize that the difference between average performers (6 percent annually) and high achievers (10 percent annually) is only 4 percent and feels that this does not greatly motivate the latter.

The other motivational tool is promotion. Brendshaw has averaged a promotion every two years during her six-year tenure with the bank. However, she is painfully aware that this pace cannot last. Most managers are getting promotions once every five years, and some of those above her in the hierarchy have not been promoted since Brendshaw has worked at the bank. Therefore, it is clear to her that promotions from within are not very motivational because they come too infrequently. To really move up, one has to jump to another bank.

In addition to money and recommendations for promotion, Brendshaw feels she can motivate her people by praising them and keeping them informed about what is going on. However, all of this is really part of content theory, while expectancy theory is part of process theory. It seems to Brendshaw that she really knows all she has to know about motivation; she also cannot believe that expectancy theory is of any practical value to her.

Questions

1. What is the difference between content theory and process theory? Compare and contrast the two.

2. Could expectancy theory have any practical use for Brendshaw? Explain how she could use it.

3. In addition to the above answer, what other recommendations would you make to help Brendshaw motivate her subordinates? Be specific.

CASE: It's up to the Manager[40]

Historically, the United States has been an achievement-oriented culture. The national archives are bursting with tales of rugged people with purpose who tamed the frontier, moved mountains so trains could run, and built industrial empires. Yet we know from industrial research that not all managers are successful in their efforts to get subordinates to accomplish their goals.

One well-known study reveals that there are some marked differences between successful and unsuccessful managers. The former are commonly high achievers while the latter are often low achievers. Those in the middle are known as average achievers. In contrasting them, one researcher employed the following description:

> High Achievers place major emphasis on the actualization, belonging and ego-status needs composing the motivator package, paying only average attention to the hygiene factors. Low Achievers, on the other hand, virtually ignore motivators while stressing the importance of creature comfort and, particularly, safety and security issues having hygiene significance. Average Achievers stress ego-status, giving adequate attention to the actualization needs of their subordinates, essentially promoting motivation seeking among those they manage. As . . . expected, managerial achievement is linked to the motivational climate one creates for . . . subordinates as well as to personal striving.

Additionally, recent research shows that subordinates' behavior tends to reflect the attitudes of bosses. Low achievers are most interested in hygiene factors, and so are their subordinates. High achievers are more interested in self-actualization than in mere

---

[40] The data in this case can be found in: Jay Hall, "To Achieve or Not: The Manager's Choice," *California Management Review*, Summer 1975, pp. 5–18.

comfort, and so are their subordinates. Finally, average achievers tend to place highest concern on belongingness and ego-status, and so do their subordinates. In putting this all in perspective, management theorist Jay Hall has noted:

Thus are motivational prophecies fulfilled. Not only does personal motivation affect a manager's achievement level, so does his perception of the motivational process and his consequent practices in the management of motives. Indeed, in what appears to be causal fashion, a manager's achievement is directly linked to the motivational profile of his subordinates. A sobering thought is inferred: the needs and quality of motivation characterizing a manager's subordinates may say more about the manager than about his subordinates.

Questions

1. Why are high achievement-oriented managers more successful in motivating their subordinates than are low achievement-oriented managers?

2. Explain exactly what the statement that "the needs and quality of motivation characterizing a manager's subordinates may say more about the manager than about his subordinates" means.

3. How can findings such as those reported in this case help companies to motivate their employees? Explain.

CHAPTER 13

LEADERSHIP EFFECTIVENESS

GOALS OF THE CHAPTER

What makes the effective leader different from the ineffective leader? Perhaps the answer rests in the very definition of management, namely, getting things done through people. In any event, there are some managers who are successful at their jobs and others who are not. The goals of this chapter are to investigate the nature of leadership and to examine some of the current theories of leadership. The central theme will be leadership effectiveness.

When you have finished this chapter, you should be able to:

1. *Define the term leadership.*
2. *Discuss the revelevance of trait theory to the study of leadership.*
3. *Explain what is meant by situational theory and why it is so highly regarded today.*
4. *Relate the value of continuum models to the understanding of leadership.*
5. *Describe the importance of two-dimensional models in the study of leadership.*
6. *Relate the value of contingency leadership theory to the modern manager, with particular attention to Fred Fiedler's contingency model, William Reddin's 3-D theory, Paul Hersey and Kenneth Blanchard's life cycle theory, and Robert House's path-goal theory.*
7. *Discuss the importance to the modern manager of adaptive leadership styles.*

THE NATURE OF LEADERSHIP

Management theorists have defined *leadership* in many different ways. For example, Dalton E. McFarland calls it "the ability of an individual to influence others to work beyond ordinary levels to achieve goals."[1] Edgar F. Huse sees it as "the ability to persuade others to get something done."[2] Theo Haimann, William G. Scott, and Patrick E. Connor see it as a "process by which people are directed, guided, and influenced in choosing and achieving goals."[3] William F. Glueck defines it as "a set of interpersonal behaviors designed to influence employees to cooperate in the achievement of objectives."[4] Synthesizing current views, one can accurately say that most writers in the field of management feel leadership is a process of influencing people to direct their efforts toward the achievement of some particular goal or goals. As such, leadership is a part of management. Of course, managers must do more than merely lead, but if they fail to influence people to accomplish assigned goals, they fail as managers.

There are many definitions of leadership.

Every organization needs leaders, but what is it that distinguishes these individuals from others? For years, many people have sought to answer this question; in the course of the study, people have tried many methods, some sheer quackery. The analysis of handwriting (graphology), the study of skull shapes (phrenology), and the investigation of the position of the stars and other celestial elements upon human affairs (astrology) have all been employed. The two most scientific approaches that have been used are trait theory and situational theory.

Trait Theory

Trait theory examines successful leadership from the standpoint of the individual's personal characteristics; that is, what is it about this particular person that indicates a good leader? In 1940, Charles Byrd examined twenty lists of traits that were attributed to leaders in various surveys but discovered that not even one item appeared on all lists.[5] Later in the decade, William O. Jenkins, after reviewing a wide spectrum of studies encompassing such diverse groups as children, and business, professional, and military personnel, categorically stated that, "No single trait or group of characteristics has been isolated which sets off the leader from the members of his group."[6] This undoubtedly accounts for the decline in the importance of trait theory. Clear-cut results have just not been forthcoming, the reason being that the method fails to consider the entire leadership environment. Traits are important, but they are only one part of the leadership picture. The members of the work group and the situation itself (task, technology, goals, structure) are also major variables, for leadership is a function of the leader, the follower, and the situation; that is, L = f(l, f, s).

Clear-cut findings have not been obtained.

Yet, despite its failures, one must not discard trait theory too hastily, for it has made some contributions toward clarifying the nature of leadership. For example, some of the commonly listed traits of effective leaders include intelligence, understanding, percep-

---

[1] Dalton E. McFarland, *Management: Foundations and Practices,* 5th ed. (New York: Macmillan, 1979), pp. 214–215.
[2] Edgar F. Huse, *The Modern Manager* (St. Paul, Minn.: West Publishing, 1978), p. 227.
[3] Theo Haimann, William G. Scott, and Patrick E. Connor, *Managing the Modern Organization,* 3d ed. (Boston: Houghton Mifflin, 1978), p. 410.
[4] William F. Glueck, *Management,* rev. ed. (Hinsdale, Ill.: Dryden Press, 1980), p. 460.
[5] Charles Byrd, *Social Psychology* (New York: Appleton-Century-Crofts, 1940), p. 378.
[6] William O. Jenkins, "A Review of Leadership Studies with Particular Reference to Military Problems," *Psychological Bulletin,* January 1947, pp. 74–75.

---

tion, high motivation, and a possession of human relations attitudes.[7] On the other hand, trait theory tends to be more descriptive than analytical; therefore its value in predicting success has been, at best, limited. As a result, trait theory has been replaced to a large degree by situational theory.

Situational Theory

Situational theory, which has been more empirical and exhaustive in defining leadership characteristics, is now more commonly accepted than trait theory. According to this theory, a finite number of situational factors or dimensions that vary according to the leader's personality, the requirements of the task, the expectations, needs, and attitudes of the followers, and the environment in which all are operating have to do with the definition of the leader. For example, management researchers Alan C. Filley, Robert J. House, and Steven Kerr, after conducting a review of the literature, found that the following factors tend to have an impact on leadership effectiveness:

1. History of the organization.
2. Age of the previous incumbent in the leader's position.
3. Age of the leader and his or her previous experience.
4. Community in which the organization operates.
5. Particular work requirements of the group.
6. Psychological climate of the group being led.
7. Kind of job the leader holds.
8. Size of the group led.
9. Degree to which group-member cooperation is required.
10. Cultural expectations of subordinates.
11. Group-member personalities.
12. Time required and allowed for decision making.[8]

The situational studies all tend, unfortunately, to focus on widely differing variables. Although they are not contradictory, neither do they support one another. What they do illustrate is that certain types of leadership behavior are effective in certain kinds of situations.

LEADERSHIP BEHAVIOR

Since the nature of leadership has been discussed, attention will now be focused on the various types of leadership behavior—that is, how leaders act with their groups.

A Leadership Continuum

The most common approach is to view leadership behavior on a continuum, such as the one illustrated in Figure 13–1. Moving from the left to the right in the figure, the reader sees the manager exercising less authority and the subordinates receiving greater freedom.

---

[7] For more on trait theory, see Richard M. Hodgetts and Steven Altman, *Organizational Behavior* (Philadelphia: W. B. Saunders, 1979), pp. 184–185.

[8] Alan C. Filley, Robert J. House, and Steven Kerr, *Managerial Process and Organizational Behavior,* 2d ed. (Glenview, Ill.: Scott, Foresman, 1976), pp. 241–242. See also Fred E. Fiedler and Martin M. Chemers, *Leadership and Effective Management* (Glenview, Ill.: Scott, Foresman, 1974), pp. 28–31.

Figure 13-1 Continuum of Leadership Behavior

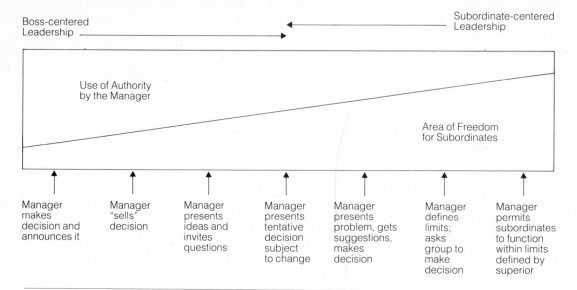

Boss-centered Leadership ————————————→ ←———————— Subordinate-centered Leadership

Use of Authority by the Manager

Area of Freedom for Subordinates

| Manager makes decision and announces it | Manager "sells" decision | Manager presents ideas and invites questions | Manager presents tentative decision subject to change | Manager presents problem, gets suggestions, makes decision | Manager defines limits; asks group to make decision | Manager permits subordinates to function within limits defined by superior |

Leadership characteristics vary.

The manager who stays on the left side of the continuum operates with an *authoritarian leadership style.* This person tends to determine all policy, maintain close control of the subordinates, and tell people only what they need to know to get the work done. Conversely, the manager on the right side of the continuum is known as a democratic leader. This person allows employees to have a say in what goes on, uses less control, and encourages feedback from subordinates. The behavior continuum illustrates that various options are available to the manager. Figure 13-1 also indicates that there are two general types of leadership style. One emphasizes the work to be done (boss-centered leader) and the other gives attention to the people who are doing this work (employee-centered leader).

This model has been criticized as too descriptive and not sufficiently helpful to the practicing manager. However, in recent years Robert Tannenbaum and Warren H. Schmidt have updated a well-known article they wrote in 1958, pointing out the importance of the external environment and the interdependence between the organization and its people.[9] Today, these researchers' approach is more sophisticated and encompassing than it was earlier.

Likert's Management Systems

Another approach, similar to the leadership continuum, has been developed by Rensis Likert and his associates at the Institute for Social Research of the University of Michigan. After conducting leadership research in hundreds of organizations, Likert discovered

---

[9] Robert Tannenbaum and Warren H. Schmidt, "How to Choose a Leadership Pattern," *Harvard Business Review,* May–June 1973, pp. 162–175, 178–180.

Figure 13–2 Likert's Systems

SYSTEM 1	SYSTEM 2	SYSTEM 3	SYSTEM 4
Exploitive-Authoritative	*Benevolent-Authoritative*	*Consultative-Democratic*	*Participative-Democratic*

four basic *management systems,* which can be depicted on a System 1 to System 4 continuum, shown in Figure 13–2.

Likert's systems can be discussed very much as he did in his 1967 book, *The Human Organization:*

System 1. Management has little confidence in the subordinates as seen by the fact that they are seldom involved in the decision-making process. Management makes most decisions and passes them down the line, employing threats and coercion when necessary to get things done. Superiors and subordinates deal with each other in an atmosphere of distrust. If an informal organization develops, it generally opposes the goals of the formal organization. *(Exploitive-authoritative.)*

System 2. Management acts in a condescending manner toward the subordinates. Although there is some decision-making at the lower levels, it occurs within a prescribed framework. Rewards and some actual punishment are used to motivate the workers. In superior-subordinate interaction, the management acts condescendingly and the subordinates appear cautious and fearful. Although an informal organization usually develops, it does not always oppose the goals of the formal organization. *(Benevolent-authoritative.)*

System 3. Management has quite a bit of confidence and trust in the subordinates. Although major important decisions are made at the top, subordinates make specific decisions at the lower levels. Two-way communication is in evidence, and there is some confidence and trust between superiors and subordinates. If an informal organization develops, it will either support or offer only a slight resistance to the goals of the formal organization. *(Consultative-democratic.)*

Likert discovered these four basic systems of leadership.

System 4. Management has complete confidence and trust in the subordinates. Decision making is highly decentralized. Communication not only flows up and down the organization but among peers as well. Superior-subordinate interaction takes place in a friendly environment and is characterized by mutual confidence and trust. The formal and informal organizations are often one and the same *(Participative-democratic.)*[10]

Systems 1 and 4 approximate the Theory X and Theory Y assumptions discussed in Chapter 12. System 1 managers are highly job-centered and authoritarian; System 4 managers are highly employee-centered and democratic.

In evaluating an organization's leadership style, Likert's group has developed a measuring instrument, a sample of which is illustrated in Figure 13–3. The instrument uses fifty-one items to encompass variables related to leadership, motivation, com-

---

[10] Adapted from Rensis Likert, *The Human Organization* (New York: McGraw-Hill, 1967), pp. 4–10.

Figure 13–3 Likert's Instrument for Measuring Management Systems

Organizational Variable	System 1	System 2	System 3	System 4
Leadership Processes Used Extent to which superiors have confidence and trust in subordinates	Have no confidence and trust in subordinates	Have condescending confidence and trust, such as master has in servant	Substantial but not complete confidence and trust, still wish to keep control of decisions	Complete confidence and trust in all matters
Character of Motivational Forces Underlying motives tapped	Physical security, economic needs, and some use of the desire for status	Economic needs and moderate use of ego motives, e.g., desire for status, affiliation, and achievement	Economic needs and considerable use of ego and other major motives, e.g., desire for new experiences	Full use of economic, ego, and other major motives such as motivational forces arising from group goals
Character of Communication Process Amount of interaction and communication aimed at achieving organization's objectives	Very little	Little	Quite a bit	Much with both individuals and groups
Character of interaction influence process Amount and character of interaction	Little interaction and always with fear and distrust	Little interaction and usually with some condescension by superiors; fear and caution by subordinates	Moderate interaction, often with fair amount of confidence and trust	Extensive friendly interaction with high degree of confidence and trust
Character of decision-making process At what level in organization are decisions formally made?	Bulk of decisions at top of organization	Policy at top, many decisions within prescribed framework made at lower levels but usually checked with top before action is taken	Broad policy decisions at top, more specific decisions at lower levels	Decision-making widely done throughout organization, although well integrated through linking process provided by overlapping groups
Character of goal setting or ordering Manner in which usually done	Orders issued	Orders issued, opportunity to comment may or may not exist	Goals are set or orders issued after discussion with subordinates of problems and planned action	Except in emergencies, goals are usually established by means of group participation

Source: Adapted from Rensis Likert, *The Human Organization* (New York: McGraw-Hill, 1967.)

Figure 13–4   Supervision and Production

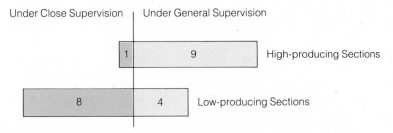

Number of Supervisors:

Under Close Supervision | Under General Supervision

Source: Reported in Rensis Likert, *New Patterns of Management* (New York: McGraw-Hill, 1961), p. 9.

Figure 13–5   Foreman's Reaction to a Poor Job (in the Opinion of the Workers)

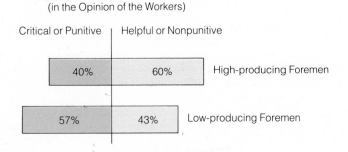

Foreman's Reaction to a Poor Job
(in the Opinion of the Workers)

Critical or Punitive | Helpful or Nonpunitive

Source: Reported in Rensis Likert, *New Patterns of Management* (New York: McGraw-Hill, 1961), p. 11.

munication, interaction-influence, decision making, goal setting, control, and performance goals. By evaluating a manager in each of these areas, the manager or analyst can compile a profile. For example, an individual may be basically a System 2 manager, essentially a benevolent-authoritative leader (see Figure 13–2). The same type of profile can be constructed for the organization as a whole as well as for individuals.

Research Results and Management Systems Likert reports that most managers feel high-producing departments are on the right of the continuum (System 4), whereas low-producing ones are on the left (System 1). Some research results seem to support this pattern. For example, Figure 13–4 shows the results of a study of clerical supervisors. Those section heads who were closely supervised tended to have lower-producing units than those who were under general supervision.

A study of railroad maintenance-of-way crews provided the results in Figure 13–5. Supervisors who ignored mistakes or tried to use them as educational experiences in showing their crews how to do the job correctly had higher-producing sections than their critical-punitive counterparts.

Figure 13–6 *Relationship between Freedom to Set Own Pace and Department Productivity*

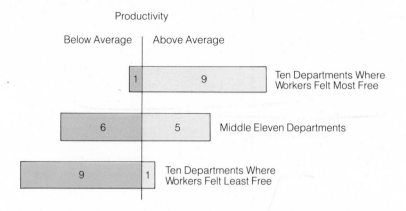

Source: Reported in Rensis Likert, *New Patterns of Management* (New York: McGraw-Hill, 1961), p. 8.

When workers in a service operation were asked how free they felt to set their own pace, the general pattern of responses was similar to that of the previous two studies, as Figure 13–6 shows.

Likert has found that "supervisors with the best records of performance focus their primary attention on the human aspects of their subordinates' problems and on endeavoring to build effective work groups with high performance goals."[11] In short, they are the employee-centered managers.

There is a problem, of course, with this approach to leadership. Simply put, it seems to argue that a System 4 style is always superior. In recent years, however, it has become evident that these management systems are less useful for telling people the style to employ than they are in identifying the style a manager is using currently. With both sets of information, a comparison can be made between present style and current performance in judging the effectiveness of the manager's approach. Therefore, Likert's systems are now employed more for evaluation purposes than anything else.[12]

Two-dimensional Leadership

An extension of Likert's leadership continuum is found in two-dimensional leadership models, as reflected in the work of the Ohio State University researchers and Robert Blake and Jane Mouton's managerial grid.

Ohio State Leadership Research In 1945, researchers in the Bureau of Business Research at Ohio State University began an extensive inquiry into the area of leadership. Eventually, they narrowed down leader behavior into two dimensions: initiating structure and consideration. *Initiating structure* referred to "the leader's behavior in delineating the relationship between himself and members of the work-group and endeavoring to establish well-

---

[11] Rensis Likert, *New Patterns of Management* (New York: McGraw-Hill, 1961), p. 7.
[12] This concept will be discussed in greater detail in chap. 14.

Figure 13–7 An Initiating Structure-Consideration Continuum

Initiating
Structure _____ Consideration

defined patterns of organization, channels of communication, and methods of procedure," and *consideration* referred to "behavior indicative of friendship, mutual trust, respect,
and warmth in the relationship between the leader and the members of his staff."[13]

In gathering information about the behavior of leaders, the Ohio State researchers
developed the now-famous *Leader Behavior Description Questionnaire (LBDQ)*. The LBDQ contains
items relating to both initiating structure and consideration and is designed to describe
how a leader carries out activities. Items related to initiating structure encompass such
areas as the rules and regulations the leader asks people to follow, the degree to which
the leader tells the followers what is expected of them, and the assignment of members
to particular tasks. Items relating to consideration deal with such topics as the amount of
time the leader finds to listen to group members, the leader's willingness to undertake
changes, and the degree to which the leader is friendly and approachable.

From their work, the researchers found that initiating structure and consideration
were separate and distinct dimensions. A person could rank high on one dimension
without ranking low on the other. Thus, instead of being on a continuum, such as the one
shown in Figure 13–7, the leader could prove to be a combination of both dimensions.
On the basis of these findings, the researchers were able to develop the leadership
quadrants shown in Figure 13–8.

Initiating structure and consideration are separate dimensions.

A leader who is high on structure but low on consideration is greatly interested in the
work the job involves, such as planning the activites and communicating information
necessary to get the tasks done on time. Conversely, a leader who is high on consideration but low on structure tends to encourage superior-subordinate cooperation and works
within an atmosphere of mutual respect and trust. The leader who is high on both dimensions is interested in both the work and the people that the job entails. The leader who
is low on both dimensions tends to stand back and let the workers do their jobs without
interference or interaction; there is very little overt leading from this person. Which of the
four is best? The answer is going to vary. In some situations the individual who is high
on structure is superior; in other cases the manager who is high on consideration is most
effective; other times the leader who is high on both dimensions does the best job; still
other times the leader who is low on both dimensions is most desirable.

The quadrant approach to examining leadership behavior is more realistic than a
continuum because it permits simultaneous consideration of two factors. This undoubtedly accounts for the fact that those who used to view leadership on a continuum
are now modifying their views.

Managerial Grid Another two-dimensional approach is the *managerial grid* developed by
Blake and Mouton. After undertaking research of their own, they rejected the Ohio State

---

[13] Andrew W. Halpin, *The Leadership Behavior of School Superintendents* (Chicago: Midwest
Administration Center, University of Chicago, 1959), p. 4.

Figure 13—8 Ohio State Leadership Quadrants

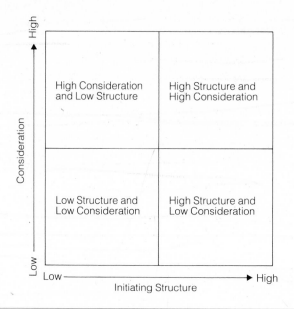

four-quadrant paradigm and developed their own now-famous Grid®.[14] Along the vertical axis they placed the term "Concern for People" and along the horizontal axis, the term "Concern for Production." In addition, they placed a scale, ranging from 1 to 9, on each axis; its purpose was to measure degree of concern.

As Figure 13—9 shows, Blake and Mouton identified five basic leadership styles. The person who is a 1,1 manager has little concern for either people or production. The 1,9 manager has great concern for people but little concern for production. The 9,1 manager has a great concern for production but little concern for people. The 5,5 manager balances the concern for people and production although neither is maximum concern. The 9,9 manager demonstrates maximum interest for both people and production.

Unlike much of the research done on leadership, Blake and Mouton's managerial grid has proved to be a useful tool for developing effective managers. Many companies have found such training helpful to their people in terms of redirecting their orientation, for example, getting a 1,9 manager more interested in the production side of the job or a 9,1 manager more interested in the personal aspect.

Six-phase Program Blake and Mouton propose a six-phase program to attain these objectives. The two initial phases involve management development and the last four help the manager work toward more complex goals of organizational development. Briefly outlined, these are:

Blake and Mouton identified five basic leadership styles.

---

[14] Robert R. Blake, Jane S. Mouton, and Benjamin Fruchter, "A Factor Analysis of Training Group Behavior," *Journal of Social Psychology,* October 1962, pp. 121–130.

Figure 13–9 Managerial Grid

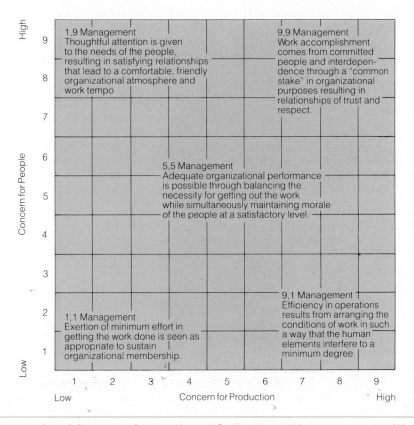

High

9 1,9 Management
Thoughtful attention is given
to the needs of the people,
resulting in satisfying relationships
that lead to a comfortable, friendly
organizational atmosphere and
work tempo

9,9 Management
Work accomplishment
comes from committed
people and interdepen-
dence through a "common
stake" in organizational
purposes resulting in
relationships of trust and
respect.

5,5 Management
Adequate organizational performance
is possible through balancing the
necessity for getting out the work
while simultaneously maintaining morale
of the people at a satisfactory level.

1,1 Management
Exertion of minimum effort in
getting the work done is seen as
appropriate to sustain
organizational membership.

9,1 Management
Efficiency in operations
results from arranging the
conditions of work in such
a way that the human
elements interfere to a
minimum degree.

Concern for People

Low

1   2   3   4   5   6   7   8   9

Low   Concern for Production   High

Source: Adapted from Robert R. Blake and Jane S. Mouton, "Managerial Facades," *Advanced Management Journal,* July 1966, p. 31.

Phase 1: Laboratory-Seminar Training. Conducted by line managers who have already taken the seminar, the purpose of this phase is to introduce the managerial grid concept. During this period managers analyze and assess their own leadership style.

Phase 2: Team Development. The concepts from Phase 1 are transferred to the job situation, and each work group or department decides its own 9,9 ground rules and relationships.

Phase 3: Intergroup Development. Focus is placed on building 9,9 ground rules and norms between groups in the work unit. Tensions between the groups are identified and examined in way of eliminating them.

They also proposed an implementation program.

Phase 4: Organizational Goal Setting. Attention is now focused on overall organizational goals. In addition, the identification of broad problems, e.g. cost control, overall profit improvement, and union-management relations, requiring commitments from all levels, is undertaken.

Phase 5: Goal Attainment. The goals and problems identified in Phase 4 are studied in greater depth and appropriate actions formulated and implemented.

Phase 6: Stabilization. Changes brought about during the first five phases are evaluated and reinforced to prevent any pressure toward "slipping back."[15]

Which of the managerial grid styles is best? Based on their seminars, Blake and Mouton report that 99.5 percent of the participants say that a 9,9 style is the soundest way to manage. Furthermore, after taking a reading two to three years after the Grid® has been used in a company, they have found many managers still holding to their 9,9 position. More importantly, Blake and Mouton themselves believe that the 9,9 style is best and argue that empirical research supports their position. They state part of their argument against a situational or contingency approach in this way:

> Contingency theorists reject the concept of one best style of leadership on at least four points. These are related to insufficient time, lack of subordinates' competence to participate, wastefulness of involving others, and the mistaken notion that a 9,9 orientation is a static as contrasted with a dynamic approach to supervision. We know that each of these is subject to management and is therefore no basic justification for shifting behavior to make it "fit" the status quo.
> Shifting from an "it all depends" to a "one best way" concept of leadership is what supervisory effectiveness training is —or should be —about.[16]

Contingency theorists, who argue that a leadership style that depends on the situation is superior to a universal 9,9 style, have probably made the most significant attack against this position. Fred Fiedler's is perhaps the most widely known contingency approach.

Fiedler's Contingency Model

After years of empirical research, Fiedler has developed what is commonly called a *contingency model of leadership effectiveness.*[17]

The essence of Fiedler's research is that any leadership style can be effective, depending on the situation. The manager must therefore be an adaptive individual. Employing Blake and Mouton's terminology, sometimes the leader should be a 9,9 manager, other times a 5,5, and still other times a 1,1 manager. According to Fiedler, three major situational variables determine the leader's effectiveness:

Fiedler deals with three major situational variables.

1. **Leader-member relations**—how well the leader is accepted by subordinates.

2. **Task structure**—the degree to which subordinates' jobs are routine and spelled out in contrast to being vague and undefined.

3. **Position power**—the formal authority provided for in the position the leader occupies.

Figure 13–10 shows that it is possible to derive eight combinations or conditions through these three dimensions.

Note that above the eight conditions in the figure there is a schematic representation of the performance of relationship- and task-motivated leaders in different situational conditions. The vertical axis in the figure shows the group's or organization's performance. The horizontal axis indicates the favorableness of the situation—that is, the degree to which the situation provides the leader with control and influence. The dotted line illustrates the performance of relationship-motivated leaders. It is best when their

---

[15] Robert R. Blake, Jane S. Mouton, Louis B. Barnes, and Larry E. Greiner, "Breakthrough in Organization Development," *Harvard Business Review,* November–December 1964, pp. 137–138.

[16] Robert R. Blake and Jane S. Mouton, "What's New with the Grid?" *Training and Development Journal,* May 1978, p. 7.

[17] Fred E. Fiedler, *A Theory of Leadership Effectiveness* (New York: McGraw-Hill, 1967).

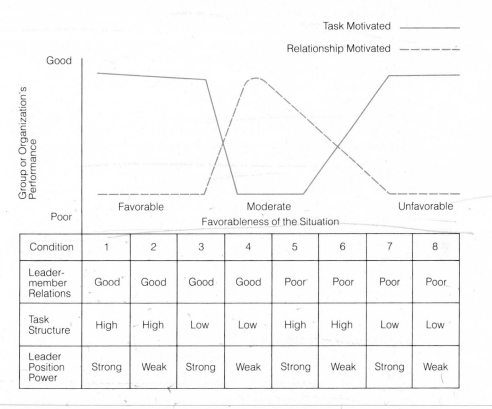

Figure 13–10 Leadership Performance in Different Situational Favorableness Conditions

Condition	1	2	3	4	5	6	7	8
Leader-member Relations	Good	Good	Good	Good	Poor	Poor	Poor	Poor
Task Structure	High	High	Low	Low	High	High	Low	Low
Leader Position Power	Strong	Weak	Strong	Weak	Strong	Weak	Strong	Weak

Source: Adapted, by permission of the publisher, from "The Leadership Game: Matching the Man to the Situation," by Fred E. Fiedler, *Organizational Dynamics,* Winter 1976, © 1976 by AMACOM, a division of American Management Associations, p. 11. All rights reserved.

relations with the subordinates are good but task structure and position power are low. They also perform well when subordinate relations are poor but task structure and position power are high. Both of these are situations of moderate favorableness.

Task-motivated leaders perform best when all three of the factors defining control and influence are either high or low. Thus task-motivated leaders do best in either highly favorable or highly unfavorable situations. Commenting on the data in the figure, Fiedler has noted:

> We can improve group performance either by changing the leader's motivational structure—that is, the basic goals he pursues in life—or else by modifying his leadership situation. While it is possible, of course, to change personality and the motivational structure that is a part of personality, this is clearly a difficult and uncertain process. It is, however, relatively easy to modify the leadership situation. We can select a person for certain kinds of jobs and not others, we can assign him certain tasks, give him more or less responsibility, or we can give him leadership training in order to increase his power and influence. . . .
> We will be better served by training our leaders in how to change their leadership situations than in how to change their personalities. Our recent studies of contingency model training show that leaders can recognize the situations in which they tend to be most successful and they can modify their situations so that

they perform more effectively. We have reason to believe that this approach holds considerable promise for the future of leadership training. [18]

Fiedler's model is important for three reasons. First, it places prime emphasis on effectiveness. Second, it illustrates that no one leadership style is best; the manager must adapt to the situation. Third, it encourages management to match the leader and the situation. If the situation is very favorable or very unfavorable, appoint a task-oriented manager; otherwise, use an employee-centered manager. Although these findings may appear to conflict with those of Likert, they actually do not. Most situations are going to be of intermediate favorableness or unfavorableness, requiring an employee-centered manager. This is why Likert found such good results occurring among groups with employee-centered leaders (Systems 3 and 4). The challenge for management is recognizing that effective leadership is contingent upon the three variables described by Fiedler: leader-member relations, task structure, and position power.

One of the main arguments made against Fiedler is that he has not identified all of the major situational variables. For example, Steven Kerr, Chester A. Schriesheim, Charles J. Murphy, and Ralph M. Stogdill have identified other such variables, including the ability of the leader to influence the subordinate and the role of subordinate expectations on leader behavior. [19]

Another criticism is that Fiedler's model does not explain how situational favorableness affects the relationship between leader behavior and subordinate performance. But Fiedler is continuing his research and will address these shortcomings and try to strengthen the applicability of the theory. [20]

Three-dimensional Leadership

In recent years, William Reddin has combined Blake and Mouton's managerial grid with Fiedler's contingency leadership style theory into a *Three-Dimension (3-D) theory of management.* [21] In essence, Reddin employs the same basic grid as Blake and Mouton but changes "concern for production" to task orientation (TO) and "concern for people" to relationships orientation (RO). Figure 13–11 depicts the four basic styles of his 3-D theory.

The separated style is the one with low task orientation and low relationships orientation; the behavior is separated from both TO and RO. The dedicated style describes managerial behavior with a high task orientation but low relationships orientation; the behavior is dedicated to the job. Conversely, the related style describes managerial behavior with high relationships orientation but low task orientation; the behavior is related to subordinates. The integrated style has high task and relationships orientation. It describes managerial behavior which combines high TO and high RO.

Reddin has done more than merely redescribe the Blake-Mouton grid in his own words. He has also introduced effectiveness, the third element that turns this two-dimensional grid into a three-dimensional one, as "the extent to which a manager achieves

---

Fiedler's model is important.

Effectiveness is important.

---

[18] Fred E. Fiedler, "The Leadership Game: Matching the Man to the Situation," *Organizational Dynamics,* Winter 1976, pp. 12, 15–16.

[19] Steven Kerr, Chester A. Schriesheim, Charles J. Murphy, and Ralph M. Stogdill, "Toward a Contingency Theory of Leadership Based upon the Consideration and Initiating Structure Literature," *Organizational Behavior and Human Performance,* August 1974, pp. 62–82.

[20] Fred E. Fiedler and Linda Mahar, "The Effectiveness of Contingency Model Training: A Review of the Validation of Leader Match," *Personnel Psychology,* Spring 1979, pp. 45–62.

[21] William J. Reddin, *Managerial Effectiveness* (New York: McGraw-Hill, 1970).

Figure 13–11 *Reddin's Basic 3-D Management Styles*

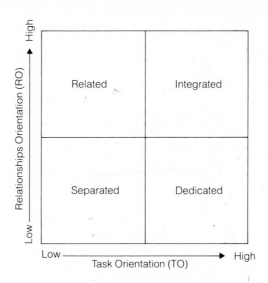

the output requirements of his position."[22] Reddin's theory not only goes one step beyond the Blake-Mouton grid but also reiterates Fiedler's main theme: Effectiveness depends on the situation. Some leadership styles are appropriate to a given situation, others are not. Figure 13–12 depicts Reddin's 3-D model. Reddin has described the eight styles in the model in this way:

More Effective Leadership Styles:

Bureaucrat: A manager who uses a low task orientation and low relationships orientation where such behavior is appropriate. This person is primarily interested in rules and procedures for their own sake and is seen as wanting to maintain and control the situation personally. This individual is also very conscientious.

Benevolent Autocrat: A manager who uses a high task orientation and low relationships orientation where such behavior is appropriate. This person knows what he or she wants and knows how to go about getting it without creating resentment.

Developer: A manager who uses a high relationships orientation and a low task orientation where such behavior is appropriate. This individual has implicit trust in people and is concerned with developing them as people.

Executive: A manager who uses a high task orientation and high relationships orientation where such behavior is appropriate. This person is a good motivator who sets high standards, treats everyone somewhat differently and prefers team management.

Less Effective Leadership Styles:

Deserter: A manager who uses a low task orientation and low relationships orientation where such behavior is inappropriate. This individual is uninvolved and passive.

---

[22] Ibid., p. 3.

Figure 13–12 Reddin's 3-D Leader Effectiveness Model

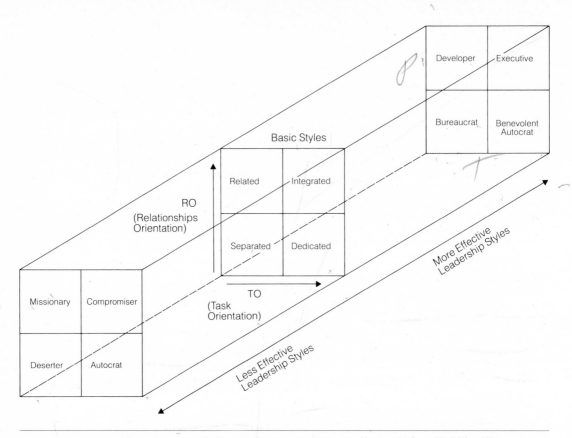

Source: Adapted from William J. Reddin, *Managerial Effectiveness* (New York: McGraw-Hill, 1970), p. 230.

Autocrat: A manager who uses a high task orientation and a low relationships orientation where such behavior is inappropriate. This person has no confidence in others, is unpleasant, and is interested only in the immediate job.

Missionary: A manager who employs a high relationships orientation and a low task orientation where such behavior is inappropriate. This individual is primarily interested in harmony.

Compromiser: A manager who uses a high task orientation and a high relationships orientation in a situation that requires high emphasis on either one or neither. This person is a poor decision maker, and attempts to minimize immediate pressures and problems rather than maximizing long-term production.[23]

The grid in the center of Figure 13–12, illustrating the four combinations of RO and TO, represents the basic styles. A manager whose behavior is appropriate to the situation

---

[23] William J. Reddin, "Managing Organizational Change," *Personnel Journal,* July 1969, p. 503.

will be more effective; the style of this kind of manager can be found on the back grid in the figure. For example, if the individual's behavior is highly oriented toward both relationships and tasks, this manager will adopt what Reddin calls "executive" style. Conversely, less effective behavior will be found on the front grid in the "compromiser" box.

Two main points should be extracted from this three-dimensional theory. First, every manager will employ some combination of TO and RO in dealing with situations. This behavior will be either appropriate (more effective) or inappropriate (less effective). Second, one must not view effectiveness as an either-or condition. Rather, it is a continuum that ranges from very effective to very ineffective. Effectiveness is a matter of degree, and the style that was effective in one situation may not be effective in another.

Effectiveness is a matter of degree.

Three-dimension theory is useful because it does three significant things: (a) brings together the concepts of task and relationship orientation, which are proven dimensions of leadership; (b) stresses that effective leadership depends on the situation; and (c) encourages leaders to be aware that no single style is always right. Just as a nightclub entertainer constantly facing a new audience must pitch an act in accordance with the changing environment (the audience), so too is an adaptive style important to managers, who also confront many changes.

Of course, the theory is descriptive rather than prescriptive. It helps leaders identify where they are but does not tell them how to change. For this reason, it must be used in conjunction with other theories discussed here.

Life Cycle Theory of Leadership

In recent years, Reddin's 3-D leader effectiveness model has been used as the basis for the formulation, at the Center for Leadership Research at Ohio University, of a *life cycle theory of leadership*. This theory, first stated by management researchers Paul Hersey and Kenneth Blanchard, has as its basic theme that as the maturity of the followers increases, appropriate leadership behavior requires varying degrees of task and relationship orientation.[24] A four-stage illustration should make this clear: When a boy is very young, his parents initiate all structure, from dressing him to feeding him; their behavior is basically task-oriented. As he gets older, the parents also begin increasing their relationship behavior by showing trust and respect for him. Now there are both a high task orientation and a high relationship orientation. As the boy begins moving into high school and college, he starts accepting responsibility for his own behavior. At this point his parents begin employing low task and high relationship behaviors. Finally, when the yong man achieves independence (takes a job, forms lasting relationships, ceases to be reliant), his parents exercise a minimum of task and relationship orientation with him.

As this boy progresses from a state of immaturity to maturity, he requires different kinds of behavior from his parents. This is also true in a work situation. If the management allows the employee to mature, changing leadership behavior will be needed. This is seen in Figure 13–13, where the four basic leadership styles have been designated with the notations Q1 (Quadrant 1, representing high task, low relationship behavior), Q2 (high task, high relationship behavior), Q3 (high relationship, low task behavior), and Q4 (low task and low relationship behavior). Beneath the grid is a continuum representing the maturity of the followers: M1 is low maturity, M2 is low to moderate maturity, M3 is moderate to high maturity, and M4 is high maturity. Bringing together the quadrants and

How mature is the worker?

---

[24] Paul Hersey and Kenneth H. Blanchard, "Life Cycle Theory of Leadership," *Training and Development Journal,* May 1969, pp. 26–34.

Figure 13–13 Life Cycle Theory of Leadership

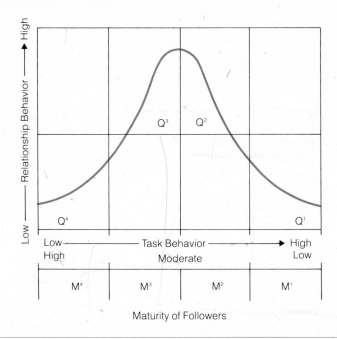

Source: Adapted from Paul Hersey and Kenneth H. Blanchard, *Management of Organizational Behavior: Utilizing Human Resources,* 3d ed. (Englewood Cliffs, N.J.: Prentice-Hall 1977), p. 167. Reprint by permission of Prentice-Hall, Inc.

the maturity of the followers, the life cycle theory or, as it has been recently renamed, the situational leadership theory, contends that:

> in working with people who are low in maturity in terms of accomplishing a specific task, a high task/low relationship style (Q1) has the highest probability of success; in dealing with people who are of low to moderate maturity (M2), a high task/high relationship style (Q2) appears to be most appropriate; in working with people who are of moderate to high maturity (M3) in terms of accomplishing a specific task, a high relationship/low task style (Q3) has the highest probability of success; and a low relationship/low task style (Q4) has the greatest probability of success with people of high task-relevant maturity (M4).[25]

Hersey and Blanchard also postulate probabilities of success or the order of preference the manager should have for each of the maturity levels, as seen in the table on the following page.[26]

The life cycle theory complements Fiedler's contingency and Reddin's three-dimensional models because it encourages the leader to evaluate the subordinates in determining an effective style.

However, because it is difficult to measure the maturity level of each subordinate, the approach can be difficult to employ. Also, some researchers feel that more work

---

[25] Paul Hersey and Kenneth H. Blanchard, *Management of Organizational Behavior: Utilizing Human Resources,* 3d ed. (Englewood Cliffs, N.J.: Prentice-Hall, 1977), p. 168.
[26] Ibid.

If Maturity Level Is	Order of Preference of Leadership Styles Is			
	1st	2nd	3rd	4th
M1	Q1	Q2	Q3	Q4
M2	Q2	Q1	Q3	Q4
M3	Q3	Q2	Q4	Q1
M4	Q4	Q3	Q2	Q1

needs to be done on the theory to substantiate many of its recommendations. For example, one recurring question is how the order of preference of leadership styles that Hersey and Blanchard describe was actually arrived at. Hersey and Blanchard continue to expand their theory, and it is likely that many current criticisms will eventually be addressed.

Path-Goal Theory of Leadership

A recent contingency theory of leadership, proposed by Robert J. House and advanced by House and Terence R. Mitchell, is the *path-goal theory.*[27] This theory is rather simple, holding that the leader's job is: (a) to help the subordinates by increasing their personal satisfactions in work-goal attainment, and (b) to make the path to these satisfactions easier to obtain. Leaders achieve this by clarifying the nature of the work, reducing the road blocks from successful task completion, and increasing the opportunities for the subordinates to obtain personal satisfactions. Subordinate motivation will increase to the degree that the leader succeeds. The specific leadership style that will work best is determined by two situational variables: the characteristics of the subordinates and the task itself.

The leader should reduce roadblocks and increase the chances for personal satisfaction.

If the subordinates are working on highly unstructured jobs and their tasks are unclear, they will welcome leader direction. If they receive it, ambiguity will be reduced and individual job satisfaction will increase. Conversely, if the individuals are working on structured tasks and they know what they should be doing, the leader should use less directiveness if he or she wants highly satisfied subordinates. Gary A. Dessler, who has helped House refine the theory, explains these points:

> Ambiguous, uncertain situations have the potential for being frustrating and . . . in such situations the structure provided by the leader will be viewed as legitimate and satisfactory by subordinates. On the other hand, in routine situations, such as might be encountered on assembly-line tasks, the additional structure provided by a production-oriented manager might be viewed as illegitimate and redundant by the subordinates, who might therefore become dissatisfied.[28]

Figure 13–14 shows how these ideas can be pulled together.

The path-goal theory is actually based on Victor Vroom's theory of motivation, which was examined in Chapter 12. Although such terms as instrumentality, valence, and expectancy are not used directly, their meanings are readily evident in the theory.

Currently, many leadership researchers have high regard for the path-goal theory. One reason is that the model does not indicate the "one best way" to lead but suggests

---

[27] Robert J. House, "A Path-Goal Theory of Leader Effectiveness," *Administrative Science Quarterly,* September 1971, pp. 321–338; and Robert J. House and Terence R. Mitchell, "Path-Goal Theory of Leadership," *Journal of Contemporary Business,* Autumn 1974, pp. 81–97.

[28] Gary A. Dessler, *Organization and Management: A Contingency Approach* (Englewood Cliffs, N.J.: Prentice-Hall, 1976), p. 172.

Figure 13–14 The Path-Goal Theory of Leadership

	High Leader Direction	Low Leader Direction
Clear Task	Low Satisfaction	High Satisfaction
Unclear Task	High Satisfaction	Low Satisfaction

instead that a leader select the style that is most appropriate to the particular situation. Of course, its full value will not be known before more research is conducted, but it does hold promise in helping explain leadership effectiveness, and it is the subject of rigorous and plentiful study.[29]

The student should keep in mind, however, that the theory has some problems. For example, research does not fully support the data in Figure 13–14. It has been found that high leader direction on unclear tasks does not always bring about high satisfaction. Also, the theory has its greatest value at the supervisory levels of management; it has not been equally effective at the upper levels.[30]

THE ADAPTIVE LEADER

The personal behavior theories examined in this chapter illustrate that there is no such thing as "one best leadership style." The effective manager must be an adaptive individual. Some people contend that an employee-centered manager is more effective than a job-centered manager. Likert's research certainly seems to indicate that this is a valid statement as does the research of the other writers. In fact, pulling together much of

---

[29] Andrew D. Szilagyi and Henry P. Sims, Jr., "An Exploration of Path-Goal Theory of Leadership in a Health Care Environment," *Academy of Management Journal,* December 1974, pp. 622–634; H. Kirk Downey, John E. Sheridan, and John W. Slocum, Jr., "Analysis of Relationships among Leader Behavior, Subordinate Job Performance and Satisfaction: A Path-Goal Approach," *Academy of Management Journal,* June 1975, pp. 242–252; Thomas C. Mawhinney and Jeffrey D. Ford, "The Path Goal Theory of Leader Effectiveness: An Operant Interpretation," *Academy of Management Review,* July 1977, pp. 398–411; and Chester Schriesheim and Mary Von Glinow, "The Path-Goal Theory of Leadership: A Theoretical and Empirical Analysis," *Academy of Management Journal,* September 1977, pp. 398–405.

[30] Hodgetts and Altman, *Organizational Behavior,* pp. 195–197.

---

the current writing in the field, it is fair to say that from a general standpoint, high positive, participative, and employee-centered styles are considered desirable.

However, the wise manager will keep in mind that arguments can be made either way. For example, after reviewing a half-dozen experimental studies related to supervisory leadership, Stephen Sales found that, in terms of productivity, no single style was consistently superior. Of six studies he reviewed, for which objective production data were available, one reported democratic supervision to be more effective, one reported authoritarian supervision to be more effective, and the other four noted no differences of consequence between the two styles.[31] Thus, because there is so much variation, careful consideration of the concepts contained in the Blake-Mouton grid, Fiedler's contingency theory, Reddin's 3-D theory, Hersey and Blanchard's life cycle theory of leadership, and House's path-goal theory will continue to be of great value to the practicing manager. The leader must evaluate each situation on its own merits.

No single leadership style is always "best."

The major problem most managers face is that of sizing up the situation. If a System 4 style were always best, the leader would have no trouble determining effective behavior; the challenge would be one of implementing the style properly. However, the issue is never this easy. Furthermore, since effective behavior in one situation may be ineffective in another, as Reddin noted, the challenge becomes even greater. Leadership research has provided a wealth of information about effective behavior, and the latest findings all point to the need for a flexible, adaptive style.

SUMMARY

This chapter has defined leadership as the process of influencing people to direct their efforts toward the attainment of some particular goal or goals. What makes an individual an effective leader? Some people feel the answer rests with personal traits and, to some degree, they are right. However, situational theory is more commonly accepted today—that is, some leadership styles are more effective than others; "best" depends on the situation.

One way of studying leadership is by placing the elements of leadership on a continuum. Rensis Likert's research, for example, shows that an employee-centered manager is more effective than a job-centered manager. But in recent years scholars and practitioners alike have found a two-dimensional model more realistic, since it sidesteps an either-or approach and allows consideration of two factors. The Ohio State leadership research and the Blake-Mouton grid are illustrations of the two-dimensional approach.

The most widely accepted approach now is probably Fred Fiedler's contingency model, which places prime emphasis on three major situational variables: leader-member relations, task structure, and position power. Fiedler's model is important because it stresses effectiveness, illustrates that no one leadership style is best, and encourages management to match the leader with the situation.

In recent years, William Reddin has combined Robert Blake and Jane Mouton's managerial grid with Fiedler's contingency model and has arrived at a three-dimensional theory of leadership. Meanwhile, at the Center for Leadership Research at Ohio University, a life cycle theory of leadership has been formulated. More recently, Robert House has postulated the path-goal theory. All three of these theories emphasize the importance of the adaptive leader who can rise to the demands of the situation. In short, the emphasis today is on a flexible style that achieves results.

---

[31] Stephen M. Sales, "Supervisory Style and Productivity: Review and Theory," *Personnel Psychology*, Autumn 1966, pp. 275–286.

REVIEW AND STUDY QUESTIONS

1. How is trait theory related to the study of leadership?
2. Why is situational theory so well accepted today? Explain, incorporating the word *adaptive* into your discussion.
3. What does Rensis Likert mean by Systems 1, 2, 3, and 4? Which is the best? Why?
4. How do two-dimensional leadership models differ from leader continuum theories? Which is more accurate? Why?
5. What is the managerial grid? What leadership dimensions does it measure?
6. According to managerial grid advocates, what leadership style is most effective? Is this right or wrong? Explain.
7. What is the theme of Fred Fiedler's contingency model of leadership effectiveness?
8. What are the three major situational variables in Fiedler's model? Explain, giving some illustrations of practical applications of the model.
9. How does William Reddin's three-dimensional leadership theory supplement Fiedler's work?
10. How can the life cycle theory of leadership be of value to the manager?
11. In your view, how valuable is the path-goal theory to the modern manager?
12. What is an adaptive leader? Explain the term, incorporating in your discussion any empirical illustrations that you may be aware of.

SELECTED REFERENCES

Barrow, J. C. "The Variables of Leadership: A Review and Conceptual Framework." *Academy of Management Review,* April 1977, pp. 231–251.

Berlew, David E. "Leadership and Organizational Excitement." *California Management Review,* Winter 1974, pp. 21–30.

Blake, Robert R., and Mouton, Jane S. "Managerial Façades." *Advanced Management Journal,* July 1966, pp. 30–37.

———. "What's New with the Grid?" *Training and Development Journal,* May 1978, pp. 3–8.

Davis, T. R. V., and Luthans, Fred. "Leadership Reexamined: A Behavioral Approach." *Academy of Management Review,* April 1979, pp. 237–248.

Fiedler, Fred E. "The Leadership Game: Matching the Man to the Situation." *Organizational Dynamics,* Winter 1976, pp. 6–16.

———. *A Theory of Leadership Effectiveness.* New York: McGraw-Hill, 1967.

Fiedler, Fred E., and Chemers, Martin M. *Leadership and Effective Management.* Glenview, Ill.: Scott, Foresman, 1974.

Fiedler, Fred, and Mahar, Linda. "The Effectiveness of Contingency Model Training: A Review of the Validation of Leader Match." *Personnel Psychology,* Spring 1979, pp. 45–62.

Flowers, V. S., and Hughes, C. L. "Choosing a Leadership Style." *Personnel,* January–February 1978, pp. 48–59.

Gellerman, S. W. "Supervision: Substance and Style." *Harvard Business Review,* March–April 1976, pp. 89–99.

Hersey, Paul, and Blanchard, Kenneth H. *Management of Organizational Behavior: Utilizing Human Resources.* 3d ed. Englewood Cliffs, N.J.: Prentice-Hall, 1977.

Hovey, D. E. "The Low-Powered Leader Confronts a Messy Problem: A Test of Fiedler's Theory." *Academy of Management Journal,* June 1974, pp. 358–362.

Justis, R. T. "Leadership Effectiveness: A Contingency Approach." *Academy of Management Journal,* March 1975, pp. 160–167.

Likert, Rensis. *New Patterns of Management.* New York: McGraw-Hill, 1961.

———. *The Human Organization.* New York: McGraw-Hill, 1967.

McClelland, David C. and Burnham, D. H. "Power Is the Great Motivator." *Harvard Business Review,* March–April 1976, pp. 100–110.

Peters, T. J. "Leadership: Sad Facts and Silver Linings." *Harvard Business Review,* November–December 1979, pp. 164–172.

Reddin, William J. *Managerial Effectiveness.* New York: McGraw-Hill, 1970.

Scanlan, B. K. "Managerial Leadership in Perspective: Getting Back to Basics." *Personnel Journal,* March 1979, pp. 168–171, 183–184.

Schriesheim, C. A.; Tolliver, J. M.; and Behling, O. C. "Leadership Theory: Some Implications for Management." *MSU Business Topics,* Summer 1978, pp. 34–40.

Skinner, W., and Sasser, W. Earl. "Managers with Impact: Versatile and Inconsistent." *Harvard Business Review,* November–December 1977, pp. 140–148.

Tannenbaum, Robert, and Schmidt, Warren H. "How to Choose a Leadership Pattern." *Harvard Business Review,* May–June 1973, pp. 162–175, 178–180.

Tosi, Henry H. "The Effect of the Interaction of Leader Behavior and Subordinate Authoritarianism." *Personnel Psychology,* Autumn 1973, pp. 339–350.

Vroom, Victor H. "Can Leaders Learn to Lead?" *Organizational Dynamics,* Winter 1976, pp. 17–28.

Zaleznik, Abraham. "Managers and Leaders: Are They Different?" *Harvard Business Review,* May–June 1977, pp. 67–78.

CASE: *A Matter of Style*

Whisk Insurance, a medium-sized insurance company located in New England, had been taking steps to improve its management effectiveness. As a result, it contracted with a private consulting company for some management training. Some of the sessions involved familiarization with and use of the managerial grid technique. The Whisk managers were asked to rate themselves, and their subordinates were given an opportunity to comment on the leadership ability of their superiors. Daniel Momaday, one of the seminar participants, had been rated as a 7,7 manager by his subordinates. Patricia Franzen, another participant, had been rated as a 1,9.

When this phase of the consultation was complete, the trainers took these basic styles and tried to explain why a 9,9 style was the most desirable by stressing the importance of placing maximum emphasis on both the production and the people aspects of the job. However, both Momaday and Franzen disagreed with this, and both used the same reasoning. Each had excellent efficiency ratings and had been told that they would be promoted within the next six months. Therefore, their argument was that their current styles were effective. Why should they worry about becoming 9,9 managers? Their 7,7 and 1,9 styles were apparently good enough. They referred to the 9,9 concept as pie in the sky.

Questions

1. Is the 9,9 concept pie in the sky, or does it have value? Explain.

2. What answer would you give to both Momaday and Franzen if you were the trainer?

3. Is the trainer right or wrong in advocating a 9,9 style? Explain your answer.

CASE: _Old Habits_

Joe Chila was known around the company as a tough cookie, definitely a System 1 man. However, he was also a good manager. He seemed to get his work out on time, his subordinates appeared to respect him, and he showed promise as a manager. Chila's superior, Frank Dunbar, decided to send him to a week-long training program entitled "Developing an Effective Leadership Style." Dunbar believed the training would help improve Chila's style.

During the program, Chila was introduced to many different concepts, from Rensis Likert's four systems to the Blake-Mouton grid, from Reddin's three-dimensional theory to Fred Fiedler's contingency model. When it was all over, Chila returned to work and began to practice much of what he had learned. "If employee-centered managers are often more effective than job-centered managers, maybe I should try to change my style," he reasoned. Following up, Chila took two steps. First, he called a meeting of his staff to discuss work assignments and get their opinions. Second, he told them that from that point on there was going to be less checking on their work. He was going to employ loose control and rely on them to do their jobs correctly.

For the next three months things went along smoothly. At first the workers were puzzled by Chila's sudden change in style. However, after they realized that he really intended to be more employee-oriented than before, they increased their output and began to establish lines of communication with him. Chila liked the new approach, and so did the employees he supervised. However, as the end of the year approached, the usual push for increased productivity began to be felt. First, a memo came down from top management to all supervisors urging greater output. Then Dunbar called Chila in to tell him to keep things going at as fast a clip as possible. The pressure began to build up. Overtime work was assigned to the production crews, and the company went to Saturday and Sunday shifts. Chila found himself working a twelve-hour day and a six-day week.

With the increased pressure, he started making more and more decisions without consulting his crew. He assigned jobs as he saw fit and spent more time than usual out on the line checking up on things. By the middle of October, he had reverted to his old style. This continued until the beginning of the year when things got back to normal. During the first week of January Chila called the men together:

"Listen, Mr. Dunbar has just talked to me and he says we did a real good job during that end-of-the-year rush. Now that we're back on an even keel, let's start talking about job assignments and how we're going to handle things for the next three months. I'd like to show you what Mr. Dunbar wants us to do and perhaps some of you have ideas on how we can handle these things."

One of the workers spoke up: "Hey, Joe, before we get into that, let me ask you a question. Why didn't you ask us to help you draw up some work plans during that big end-of-the-year push?"

"Well, I don't know. I guess I was just too busy getting things done to think about it. You know how it is when you get pushed. You find yourself going back to your old way of doing things. Listen, you guys, if you find me doing that again, let me know."

The workers promised to do so.

1. According to his new style, in which would you place Chila: System 1, 2, 3, or 4? Explain.

2. Why were his subordinates skeptical when Chila switched from being a work-oriented manager to an employee-oriented manager?

3. Suggest some methods that managers might use to avoid slipping back to old, undesirable leadership styles, and explain how they should work.

CASE: The Fast Gun

Hank Sidney has been president of his company for seven years, and initially things had gone very well. Sales increased an average of 17 percent a year, and return on investment during Sidney's term had never been lower than 15.3 percent. However, a problem developed as other firms gradually began to realize the kind of profits that could be attained in the industry and started moving in. As they did, competition increased and Sidney's big profit margins began to shrink. Prices dropped as each company tried to capture and retain large market shares. Within a few years, Sidney's firm was barely able to keep its head above water. It was then that the board of directors decided that he had to go.

This was not an easy choice for the directors to make. Everyone liked Sidney. He was a pleasant, easygoing, friendly individual. The management respected him, and the workers seemed to hold him in the highest regard. Nevertheless, the board felt that the president was unable to turn the company around, and the members would have to get someone who could.

The eventual choice was Fred Hightower, a general manager who worked for one of the company's competitors. Hightower told the board that he would take the job only if he were allowed to do things his way. In turn, he promised results. The board agreed.

Within six months of his appointment, the new president had fired over half of the old management team and one-third of the workers. In addition, he refused to hire any new personnel. If someone quit or was fired, those who were left had to pick up that additional work. When asked about this procedure, Hightower gave the following explanation:

> When I came in here, the company was going broke. There were too many people in management positions who were doing nothing. I got rid of them. The workers were having a field day with an average guy putting in only a five-hour day. Well, I changed all that by tightening things up. Now everyone around here has to pull his own weight. There's no room for fat when a company is in trouble. So I got rid of it.

It was difficult to argue with Hightower since his leadership style seemed to get results. For example, in the first eighteen months of his tenure, the company had as large a share of the market as ever; and return on investment had risen to over 16 percent.

Some of the directors, however, felt that his style was too rough. They believed that the company was going to get in trouble if it thought a System 1, task-oriented manager could continue to achieve such results in the long run. These directors acknowledged the fact that Hightower had been very successful, but they wondered if there would not be a backlash. "Doesn't the task-centered manager run the risk of driving off his best workers and irreparably damaging morale?" they asked. One of the directors compared Hightower with a fast gun in the Old West. "You know," he said, "a fast gun would be brought in to save the town. But once he had done his job, the mayor would have to get rid of him because he was bad for the town's reputation. I think Hightower falls into this category." The chairman of the board disagreed. "We were elected by the stockholders to protect their interests. When we brought Hightower in, we told him he could do things his way. Besides, we have to evaluate a man's leadership style by how effective it is. And he sure has been effective." On this point no one had any disagreement. But few of the directors felt entirely comfortable with the discussion.

Questions

1. Why was Sidney ineffective in turning the company around?

2. How do you account for such results? An employee-centered leader is supposed to be superior to a task-centered leader. What happened?

3. Do you think Hightower should be replaced or retained? Explain.

CASE: Contingency Chaos

Jennifer Kendehl, who held a doctorate in mathematics and was a university administrator of a large eastern statewide system, had just returned from a week-long training program on leadership styles and techniques. Before going back to her office, she dropped in to visit with her immediate superior, Henry Allen, who held a doctorate in education.

"Well, Jennifer, how did you like that seminar?"

"Oh, fine. Fine, Henry, just fine."

"I hoped you would think so. I sent you there because I think you have real potential as a manager around this old vine-covered place. I went to that same seminar last year and thought it was great. You know, easy money for higher education is going to run out. We have to be more efficient with our resources, and this means placing a greater stress on effective management. Now tell me, did you learn anything we should be doing around here?"

"Well, to be frank, Henry, I'm not quite sure."

Allen looked puzzled. "Well, Jennifer, I don't understand. What do you mean?"

"Well, we spent a lot of time looking at various leadership theories. You know— Likert's management systems, Blake and Mouton's managerial grid, Fiedler's contingency theory, Reddin's three-dimensional theory. Same stuff you hear about at every one of those seminars."

"But those are great ideas! What was the problem?"

"Basically, implementation, Henry. I don't know how to apply this stuff around here."

"Why not?"

"Well, the trainers this year seem to believe that Fred Fiedler's contingency model has a great deal of value for effective leadership. But this contingency idea is what throws me. If effectiveness depends on the situation, then the manager has to size up each one on its own merits. But I think there must be an easier way. For example, the trainers never really proved to me that a System 4 manager was not better than a System 1 manager. Therefore, why not be a System 4 manager and worry about exceptions when they crop up? Why spend time worrying about each individual situation? Why not develop an effective style and stick with it? You can always deal with exceptions when they manifest themselves."

Allen pondered. "That certainly is the way most managers do it. But isn't it too general an approach? You don't really deal with the individual situations; you're just playing the odds and assuming that your basic style will help you through any situation."

"Sure, Henry. But at least I have a basic style to get me through most situations. I think if you try to be too 'contingent' a manager, you'll never to able to develop any particular style to a really effective degree. I'd rather try to be a System 4 manager instead of subscribing to Fiedler's contingency theory. To me, the contingency people lead us to an overly flexible, chaotic style. I didn't get my Phi Beta Kappa key to sit around sizing up situations. We're supposed to be reasonable people here in the university. Well-educated, cool thinkers. Just like Woodrow Wilson. Why not rely on our *real* training?"

Questions

1. Evaluate Kendehl's comments. What do you think of her point of view?

2. How should Allen respond? Make your answer explicit, bringing into your discussion Fiedler's contingency model and Reddin's 3-D theory.

CHAPTER 14

HUMAN RESOURCE DEVELOPMENT

GOALS OF THE CHAPTER

Adherents of the behavioral school believe strongly in the importance of communication, motivation, and leadership. They also realize that, at times, communication will break down, motivation will be poor, and leadership will be less than effective. They believe that the way to prevent or minimize the negative impact of such factors is to develop the organization's human resources through the use of the latest behavioral techniques.

Human resource development serves as a control loop that feeds back into the original behavioral effort. For example, using just three behavioral areas—communication, motivation, and leadership—one can tie them together by noting that the manager must first communicate with the subordinates, for this is the basis of effective motivation and leadership. Second, the individual must try to motivate the people toward attaining organizational objectives. Finally, the manager has to adapt the leadership style that will be most effective in each particular situation. In carrying out each of these three functions (communicating, motivating, and leading), the manager must constantly be aware of the fact that the people in the organization are its most important assets and must be treated accordingly. One way of ensuring that they are is through a human resource development philosophy, which is usually implemented through human resource programs. It is thus possible to develop the initial conceptual framework for the behavioral school that Figure 14–1 shows.

This human resource effort actually begins when a person is first hired and continues throughout the employee's tenure with the organization. The goal of this chapter is to examine some of the tools and techniques that modern organizations are using for developing and improving human resource effectiveness.

When you have finished this chapter, you should be able to:

1. Describe the staffing function.
2. Distinguish between manipulation and motivation.
3. Explain how the change process works.

Figure 14–1 *Behavioral School Functions*

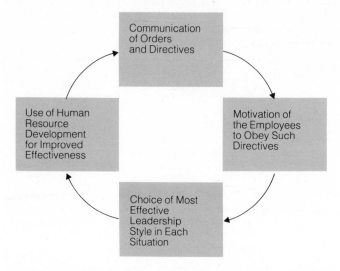

4. *Describe what job enrichment is and explain the major arguments both for and against this human resource development tool.*
5. *Tell how the job characteristics model can be of value to the modern manager.*
6. *Explain the value to modern managers of management by objectives and of sensitivity training.*
7. *State the benefits of transactional analysis in understanding and communicating with subordinates.*
8. *Explain behavior modification and how modern organizations use it to manage their human resources.*
9. *Describe human resources accounting and how organizations can make periodic evaluations of these assets.*

STAFFING

Managerial concern for an individual employee's human resource development begins when the individual is hired and does not end until the person's employment is terminated. Many organizations point to the attention they give to training and developing people's human resource potential; but in fact this effort really starts with the staffing function. *Staffing* involves the recruiting, selecting, training, and developing of individuals for organizational purposes.

Human Resource Forecasting

First comes a human resource forecast.

The first step in the staffing process is that of human resource forecasting. The organization must determine how many people it will need to manage operations over the next six to twelve months, how many it has currently, and how any gap will be handled. If more people must be hired, the firm must recruit and select. If some people must be let go, layoffs and firings must be addressed.

The human resource forecast is heavily influenced by external and internal considerations. External considerations include legal-political and economic constraints, to name only two. Such events as changes in equal opportunity legislation and upturns or downturns in the economy affect the number of people that a firm will hire, lay off, or fire. Internal considerations have to do with the number and qualifications of employees already on board. These employees constitute a labor pool which often can be tapped in filling job vacancies.

Recruiting and Selecting

Recruiting is naturally connected to human resources planning. Once an organization realizes that it needs more employees, it has to identify sources for locating and recruiting them. One of the most common sources is the internal pool of candidates. Is anyone currently working for the organization who could fill one or more of the vacancies? In answering this question, some firms have developed manager replacement charts, an example of which is provided in Figure 14–2.

Then internal personnel sources are tapped.

If internal sources do not produce enough acceptable candidates for the job openings, external sources can be tapped. Some of the most common are high schools, junior colleges, four-year colleges and universities, employment agencies, and temporary help suppliers. Firms commonly use newspapers and other media in seeking job applicants from external sources.

External sources are explored next.

Trade and competitive sources are a third source of job applicants. Trade associations often have newsletters or magazines that contain job ads. An organization will often pick up an applicant after learning through unofficial sources that some individual is unhappy with a current employer.

Having obtained a group of potential employees, the organization must choose those it wishes to hire. The selection process is sometimes quite simple, while in other cases it is very involved. The larger the organization, the more likely that the process will contain a series of formal, detailed steps. Regardless of firm size, some of the common steps in the selection process are: (a) a preliminary application screening in which the individual fills out an application blank; (b) a preliminary interview to screen out the obviously unsuitable or uninterested applicant; (c) employment tests designed to find out how well an individual can do a job; (d) a checking of reference sources; (e) a physical exam to ensure that the individual is in good health; and (f) a decision to hire.

Then a selection decision is made.

Training and Development

After it has hired a person, an organization must determine the training and development deficiencies the individual has and the types of training that may be indicated. Among lower-level employees, the most common is on-the-job training, in which the supervisor or another co-worker shows the individual how to do the job. Another is off-the-job training, in which case the individual is sent to a vocational school or institute where training is provided. Finally, coaching and counseling by the new employee's immediate manager are often useful. The purpose of these types of training is to familiarize the individual with the new job and, in turn, to encourage maximum efficiency in the new employee's performance.

Workers are given practical training.

Training and development for managers is often more involved. Some of the

Figure 14-2 Part of a Manager Replacement Chart

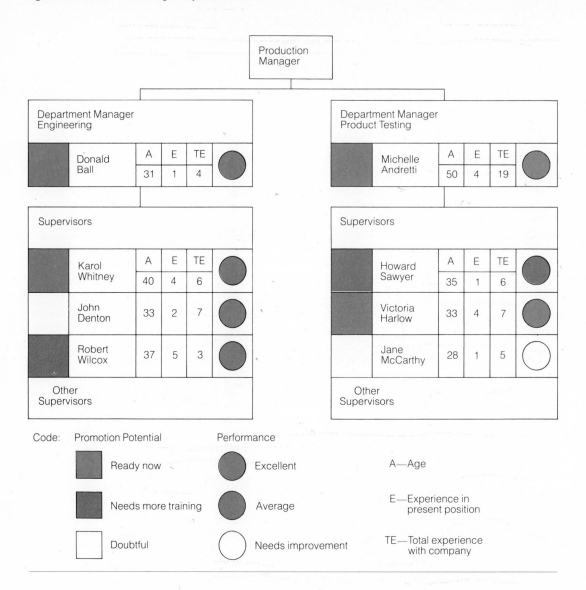

Production Manager		

Department Manager Engineering

Donald Ball	A	E	TE	
	31	1	4	

Department Manager Product Testing

Michelle Andretti	A	E	TE	
	50	4	19	

Supervisors

Karol Whitney	A	E	TE	
	40	4	6	
John Denton	33	2	7	
Robert Wilcox	37	5	3	

Other Supervisors

Supervisors

Howard Sawyer	A	E	TE	
	35	1	6	
Victoria Harlow	33	4	7	
Jane McCarthy	28	1	5	

Other Supervisors

Code: Promotion Potential   Performance

◼ Ready now   ⬤ Excellent   A—Age

◼ Needs more training   ⬤ Average   E—Experience in present position

☐ Doubtful   ◯ Needs improvement   TE—Total experience with company

Managers are given practical and theoretical training.

common approaches are: (a) rotating the individual from one job to another to broaden the person's managerial experience; (b) having the new manager do role playing in a classroom setting, with problems or situations that are commonly encountered on the job designed into the exercises; and (c) coaching and counseling by the superior. Unlike lower-level training and development, managerial training is oriented toward both theory and practice.

On-the-job Follow-up

In large organizations the staffing functions, except for coaching and counseling, are often performed by the personnel department. However, once this department has finished, further training and development are the responsibility of the manager; this is why the manager must understand what human resource development is and how it works.

THE GREAT JACKASS FALLACY

Many chief executives seem to realize that they are not as effective as they could be in handling their people. Some of them, for example, when asked to describe the effect they have on their subordinates, replied:

I believe that a real business leader is incapable of generating a climate where people can grow.
Hell, none of us would work for people like ourselves!
A real executive under any one of us would leave because he couldn't stand it.
We couldn't work for dominant characters such as ourselves. We are leaders.[1]

Most companies realize that they must take steps to combat the above problems. It is important to note, however, that some managers will adopt the newest approaches for their subordinates but still fail, because under the guise of motivating people, they actually attempt to manipulate them. This is what Harry Levinson, a well-known management writer, calls the "great jackass fallacy."[2] Workers know the difference between motivation and manipulation; it *is* impossible to fool all the people all the time. As a result, the best technique or tool in the world is useless in the hands of an insincere manager. The ultimate success of the method discussed in this chapter rests solely with management.

Workers know the difference between motivation and manipulation.

This chapter will examine a handful of the human resource development (HRD) programs used by modern organizations. In recent years these programs have been getting more attention in many firms, especially those with the following five common characteristics: (a) large size and location well up in *Fortune*'s 500 list; (b) conspicuous good management and consistently high past performance and earnings; (c) high proportion of social psychologists, usually trained in organizational development, on HRD staffs and consultant teams; (d) top management decision to push an HRD effort, which tends to work its way down into the organization; and (e) HRD staffs that are less concerned with traditional personnel and employee relations areas (recruiting, training, compensation, benefits, labor relations) and more concerned with organizing (or reorganizing), designing (or redesigning), and structuring (or restructuring) of line functions and the people and machines performing them.[3] Perhaps the simplest place to start in examining these HRD programs is with the work of those at the lowest levels of the organization, by investigating how modern organizations are attempting to implement job enrichment; but it is necessary first to briefly view the change process.

---

[1] Chris Argyris, "The CEO's Behavior: Key to Organizational Development," *Harvard Business Review,* March–April 1973, p. 57.

[2] Harry Levinson, "Asinine Attitudes toward Motivation," *Harvard Business Review,* January–February 1973, pp. 70–76.

[3] Ted Mills, "Human Resources—Why the New Concept?" *Harvard Business Review,* March–April 1975, pp. 124–125.

THE CHANGE PROCESS

Most human resource development efforts are designed to change things. Numerous examples can be cited: redesigning the work, reformulating objectives, teaching a manager how to interact more effectively with subordinates. Whatever the specific effort, the *change process* has three phases: (a) unfreezing the old ways, (b) introducing new behaviors, and (c) refreezing this new equilibrium.

First, the old situation is examined.

In unfreezing a situation, the manager has to examine why the proposed change might be opposed. For various reasons, people support the status quo. One of the most common is that people like things the way they are. After analyzing the situation, the manager should be in a position to determine how best to introduce the change. In particular, the manager should have developed arguments supporting the change over the comfortable status quo.

Next, the change is introduced.

Then the manager will introduce the change. In so doing, the individual will need to help the workers deal with it. For example, if a new reporting system is being implemented, the manager will show the subordinates how to use the system so that it helps them get work done quickly and easily. If new safety requirements are to be enforced, the manager will explain how the requirements are going to benefit the workers.

Then the new situation is refrozen.

After the change has been successfully introduced, the manager will then work on refreezing the situation. One of the best ways of doing so is to praise the workers for adopting the new changes and encourage them to continue doing so. Although many changes will take place in the observation and experience of any individual manager, all of them will begin with these three parts of the change process.

JOB ENRICHMENT

In 1973 a government report entitled *Work in America* revealed the accuracy of a suspicion many people had long held.[4] Most workers were dissatisfied with their jobs:

> *The principal sources of worker discontent . . . are to be found in the confines of the individual workplace itself. The central villains of the piece are (1) the process of work breakdown and specialization associated with the pernicious influence of Frederick W. Taylor and his industrial engineer disciples, and (2) the diminished opportunities for work autonomy, resulting from the shift in focus of jobs from self-employment or small scale enterprise to large interpersonal corporate and government bureaucracies.[5]*

While these trends have been recognized for many decades, the 1973 report found a revolutionary change in attitudes and values among many members of the work force, including youth, minority members, and women. With higher expectations generated by increased educational achievement, these groups—and the majority of workers in general—are placing greater emphasis on the intrinsic aspects of work and less on the strictly material rewards. As an attempt to overcome these problems and increase employee motivation, many firms today are adopting an approach known as job enrichment.

---

[4] W. E. Upjohn Institute for Employment Research, *Work in America: Report to the Secretary of Health, Education, and Welfare* (Cambridge, Mass.: M.I.T. Press, 1973).

[5] Harold Wool, "What's Wrong with Work in America? A Review Essay," *Monthly Labor Review*, March 1973, p. 38.

Meaningful Work

Job enrichment is an extension of job enlargement. But where *job enlargement* just gives the person more work, job enrichment provides the opportunity for increased recognition, advancement, growth, and responsibility. The technique is a direct extension of Herzberg's two-factor theory of motivation and has been highly popularized by M. Scott Myers, formerly of Texas Instruments (TI), and Robert N. Ford of the American Telephone and Telegraph Company (AT&T).

Enrichment can take many forms. Myers has encouraged making "every employee a manager"; employees help plan their own work and control the pace and quality of output.[6] Within this framework, individual workers know the deadlines they must meet and the standards they must maintain. In some cases they are even given the authority to check the quality of the output. In short, management relies on workers to get the job done right. No one looks over their shoulders; they are on their own. Myers has described one of these situations as follows:

> Assemblers on a radar assembly line are given information on customer contract commitments in terms of price, quality specifications, delivery schedules, and company data on material and personnel costs, break-even performance, and potential profit margins. Assemblers and engineers work together in methods and design improvements. Assemblers inspect, adjust and repair their own work, help test completed units, and receive copies of customer inspection reports.[7]

At AT&T, Ford has reported that after job enrichment was initiated in the shareholder relations department, there was a 27 percent reduction in the termination rate and, over a twelve-month period, an estimated cost saving of $558,000.[8] Other firms have introduced the approach on their assembly lines. For example, Motorola has workers who put together and test an entire unit by themselves.[9] Cadillac has abandoned some of its small assembly lines in favor of each worker building one complete part.[10]

Nor is job enrichment working only in the United States. Volvo, the Swedish automaker, has found that work teams can be more effective than assembly lines. Its Kalmar factory in southern Sweden is completely different from the factories of U.S. automakers:

> The design for Kalmar incorporated pleasant, quiet surroundings, arranged for group working, with each group having its own individual rest and meeting areas. The work itself is organized so that each group is responsible for a particular, identifiable portion of the car—electrical systems, interiors, doors, and so on. Individual cars are built up on self-propelling "carriers" that run around the factory following a movable conductive tape on the floor. Computers normally direct the carriers, but manual controls can override the taped route. If someone notices a scratch in the paint on the car, he or she can immediately turn the carrier back to the painting station. Under computer control again, the car will return later to the production process wherever it left off.[11]

Each work group at the Kalmar plant has its own areas for incoming and outgoing carriers and can pace itself as it wishes, organizing work inside its own areas, with the

Job enrichment is an extension of job enlargement.

Positive results have been obtained.

---

[6] M. Scott Myers, *Every Employee a Manager: More Meaningful Work through Job Enrichment* (New York: McGraw-Hill, 1970).

[7] M. Scott Myers, "Every Employee a Manager," *California Management Review,* Spring 1968, p. 10.

[8] Robert Janson, "Job Enrichment: Challenge of the 70's," *Training and Development Journal,* June 1970, p. 7.

[9] "Motorola Creates a More Demanding Job," *Business Week,* September 4, 1971, p. 32.

[10] "G.M.: The Price of Being 'Responsible,'" *Fortune,* January 1972, p. 172.

[11] Pehr G. Gyllenhammar, "How Volvo Adapts Work to People," *Harvard Business Review,* July–August 1977, p. 107.

Table 14–1 *Characteristics of Traditional and Modern Management Styles*

Traditional Style	Modern Style
1. Management dictates the goals and standards to the subordinates.	1. Management and the subordinates participate in setting goals and standards.
2. The manager checks worker performance and evaluates it as either an achievement or a failure.	2. The manager encourages the subordinates to check their own performance and counsels them on how to capitalize on their mistakes.
3. The manager works out all the shortcuts and does all the innovating.	3. The manager encourages the subordinates to develop their own new methods and induces them to innovate.
4. The manager is basically a Theory X individual.	4. The manager is basically a Theory Y individual.

members working individually or in subgroups to suit themselves. Additionally, to gain a sense of identification with the work, each team does its own inspecting.

The Volvo management admits that it costs a little bit more money to build a nontraditional plant. However, the plant has begun to show increased productivity over its traditional assembly plants. More important, perhaps, is the fact that a recent union survey of Kalmar employees revealed that almost all of them were in favor of the new work arrangements. This has led Volvo to increase its focus on working groups at other plants.[12]

Job enrichment research in the United States also reveals that it can be a useful technique in overcoming several previously mentioned causes of worker alienation, because it shifts the emphasis from the traditional management style to a more modern one. Table 14–1 illustrates this finding. The key, of course, rests with structuring the job correctly.[13] As Robert Ford points out, "When the work is right, employee attitudes are right. That is the job enrichment strategy—get the work right."[14]

Recent research shows that one place in which a restructuring of the work and an increase in autonomy and quality of work life, sometimes referred to as QWL, has helped is at the General Motors plant in Tarrytown, New York. Commenting on the results to date, Robert H. Guest, who has been writing on the quality of work life for more than twenty-five years, has reported:

> By May 1979 the Tarrytown plant, with the production of a radically new line of cars, had come through one of the most difficult times in its history. Considering all the complex technical difficulties, the changeover was successful. Production was up to projected line speed. The relationship among

---

[12] Ibid., p. 108.

[13] Richard C. Grote, "Implementing Job Enrichment," *California Management Review,* Fall 1972, pp. 16–21.

[14] Robert N. Ford, "Job Enrichment Lessons from AT&T," *Harvard Business Review,* January–February 1973, p. 106.

management, union, and the workers remained positive in spite of unusual stress conditions generated by such change.

As the production manager puts it, "Under these conditions, we used to fight the union, the worker, and the car itself. Now we've all joined together to fight the car." Not only were the hourly employees substantially involved in working out thousands of "bugs" in the operations, but plans were already underway to start up QWL orientation sessions with more than 400 new workers hired to meet increased production requirements.

Tarrytown, in short, has proved to itself at least that QWL works.[15]

Job Enrichment under Attack

Despite such successes, not everyone has found that job enrichment pays off. Although individuals such as Herzberg, Myers, and Ford[16] sing its praises, others have raised doubts about the technique.[17] M. D. Kilbridge, for example, discovered that assembly-line workers in a television plant did not necessarily regard the repetitive work as either frustrating or dissatisfying.[18] In another study, William E. Reif and Peter P. Schoderbek found that some workers actually liked routine jobs because the daily routine gave them time to daydream or socialize without impairing their productivity.[19]

It is not necessary to seek out new companies using the technique if one wishes to uncover shortcomings of job enrichment. Findings at Texas Instruments and AT&T illustrate that many of the early promises just have not materialized. Mitchell Fein, for example, has assessed TI's program as follows:

Texas Instruments' management was probably more dedicated to job enrichment than any other company in the world. They earnestly backed their managing philosophies with millions of dollars of efforts. After 15 years of unrelenting diligence, management announced in its 1968 report to the stockholders its program for "increasing human effectiveness," with the objective: "Our goal is to have approximately 10,000 TI men and women involved in team improvement efforts by the end of 1968 or 1969." Since TI employed 60,000, the program envisioned involving only 16 percent of its work force. The total involved was actually closer to 10 percent.[20]

In the case of AT&T, Robert Ford himself has reported that "of the nineteen studies, nine were rated 'outstandingly successful,' one was a complete 'flop,' and the remaining nine were 'moderately successful.'"[21] One reason for such cases may well be, as found by a recent study, that firms using job enrichment "seem to have a

Job enrichment has shortcomings.

---

[15] Robert H. Guest, "Quality of Work Life—Learning from Tarrytown," *Harvard Business Review,* July–August 1979, p. 85.

[16] William J. Paul, Jr., Keith B. Robertson, and Frederick Herzberg, "Job Enrichment Pays Off," *Harvard Business Review,* March–April 1969, pp. 61–78; M. Scott Myers, "Overcoming Union Opposition to Job Enrichment," *Harvard Business Review,* May–June 1971, pp. 37–49; and Robert N. Ford, *Motivation through the Work Itself* (New York: American Management Association, 1969).

[17] For an excellent summary of these criticisms, see William E. Reif and Fred Luthans, "Does Job Enrichment Really Pay Off?" *California Management Review,* Fall 1972, pp. 30–37; and Fred Luthans and William E. Reif, "Job Enrichment: Long on Theory, Short on Practice," *Organizational Dynamics,* Winter 1974, pp. 30–49.

[18] M. D. Kilbridge, "Do Workers Prefer Larger Jobs?" *Personnel,* September–October 1960, pp. 45–48.

[19] William E. Reif and Peter P. Schoderbek, "Job Enlargement: Antidote to Apathy," *Management of Personnel Quarterly,* Spring 1966, pp. 16–23.

[20] Mitchell Fein, "Approaches to Motivation" (Hillsdale, N.J., 1970), p. 20.

[21] Ford, *Motivation through the Work Itself,* p. 188.

Figure 14–3 Job Characteristics Model

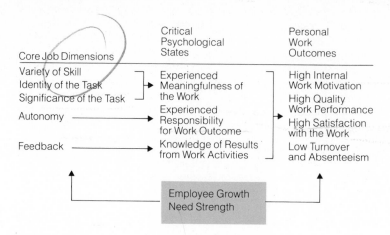

limited understanding of the concept, are unsure of how or where to apply it, and have only a vague notion of what to expect from it or how to evaluate it."[22]

In short, job enrichment has not been an overwhelming success. Why not? Reif and Luthans have proposed three reasons: Some workers do not find satisfaction in the work place, so job enrichment has no value for them; some workers prefer boring or unpleasant jobs with good social interaction to enriched jobs that reduce the opportunity for such interaction; and some workers react to the technique with feelings of inadequacy and fears of failure.[23] Additionally, Reif, this time working with David N. Ferazzi and Robert J. Evans, Jr., found that some workers have great difficulty adjusting to enriched jobs.[24] This is not to say that job enrichment is worthless; many benefits can be gained from it. But it must not be viewed as an organizational panacea for managing human assets. It has benefits and drawbacks, and management must be aware of both.[25]

JOB REDESIGN

Despite the arguments against job enrichment, behavioral scientists continue to study ways of building motivational potential into work. One of the outcomes has been the *job characteristics model,* which is presented in Figure 14–3. The model consists of three

[22] Luthans and Reif, "Job Enrichment: Long on Theory, Short on Practice," p. 33.

[23] Reif and Luthans, "Does Job Enrichment Really Pay Off?" p. 36.

[24] William E. Reif, David N. Ferruzzi, and Robert J. Evans, Jr., "Job Enrichment: Who Uses It and Why?" *Business Horizons,* February 1974, p. 76.

[25] Steven D. Norton, Douglas Massengill, and Harold L. Schneider, "Is Job Enrichment a Success or a Failure?" *Human Resource Management,* Winter 1979, pp. 28–37; and Antone F. Alber, "The Real Cost of Job Enrichment," *Business Horizons,* February 1979, pp. 60–72.

parts: core job dimensions, critical psychological states, and personal and work outcomes. In studying the model, it is easiest to move from the work outcomes back to the core job dimensions.[26]

Job Design

Personal and work outcomes are the end results the organization can achieve when work is designed properly. These outcomes are a result of the critical psychological states that Figure 14–3 identifies. If these psychological states are created, the outcomes will occur. At the heart of the model are the core job dimensions. If the organization can design these five dimensions into the job, there is a good chance that the personal and work outcomes identified will be attained. Definitions of the core job dimensions follow:

Variety of skill The degree to which the job calls for activities involving different talents and skills.

Identity of the task The degree to which the job allows for completion of a whole and identifiable piece of work.

Significance of the task The degree to which the job has an impact on the lives or work of other people.

Autonomy The degree of control the worker has over the job.

Feedback The amount of information the worker receives in regard to how well the work is being performed.

These are the core job dimensions.

Research shows that if a job has autonomy, feedback, and at least one of the other three core job dimensions, chances of motivating the worker are good. But it should also be kept in mind that the employee must have a need for such a job. If the person's growth need strength is low, redesigning the work will not increase motivation.

At the present time, research is continuing into the ways of redesigning jobs so that they contain higher degrees of these core job dimensions. Research attention is also going toward the determination of the conditions under which greatest motivation can be achieved.

MANAGEMENT BY OBJECTIVES

Another approach that has gained in popularity is *management by objectives (MBO)*. Filley, House, and Kerr report that it is perhaps the most widely employed organizational dynamics effort.[27] Like job enrichment, MBO gives the subordinate a voice in what goes on. Although first advocated by Peter Drucker, in his 1954 book, *The Practice of Management,* MBO has been made famous by George S. Odiorne, who describes it as:

> a process whereby the superior and subordinate managers of an organization jointly identify its common goals, define each individual's major areas of responsibility in terms of the results expected of him, and use these measures as guides for operating the unit and assessing the contribution of each of its members.[28]

---

[26] For more on this, see J. Richard Hackman, Greg Oldham, Robert Janson, and Kenneth Purdy, "A New Strategy for Job Enrichment," *California Management Review,* Summer 1975, pp. 57–71.

[27] Alan C. Filley, Robert J. House, and Steven Kerr, *Managerial Process and Organizational Behavior,* 2d ed. (Glenview, Ill.: Scott, Foresman, 1976), pp. 489–503.

[28] George S. Odiorne, *Management by Objectives* (New York: Pitman Publishing, 1965), pp. 55–56.

Figure 14–4 MBO in Action

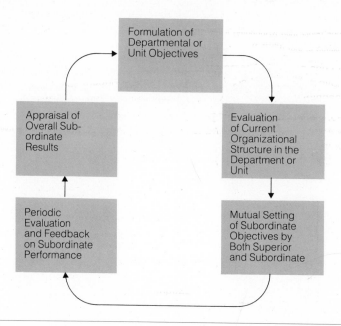

The MBO process is described.

In essence, the MBO process entails a meeting between superior and subordinate for the purpose of setting goals for the latter that are in line with overall company objectives. The two individuals jointly establish: (a) what the subordinate will do, (b) the time in which the work will be done, and (c) the method for performance evaluation. Finally, when the allotted time is over, they meet again to review the results and set further goals. Figure 14–4 provides a view of the MBO process in action.

One of the greatest benefits of MBO is the participation it allows the subordinate in the goal-setting process. A second is the clear statement of what is to be done and how performance will be measured; this clarity appears to reduce ambiguity and employee anxiety. A third benefit is the fact that MBO can be used by virtually any organization, public or private.[29]

Here are some MBO benefits.

Other commonly cited benefits include the evidence that the process: (a) encourages commitment rather than rote compliance, (2) leads to mutual respect between superior and subordinate, (3) encourages intergroup communication and teamwork, and (4) provides a rational basis for review and feedback on progress toward objectives.[30] In giving his overall evaluation of MBO, Odiorne has written:

> *It is apparent, from its history, that MBO is much more than a set of procedural rules for managing a business. As a philosophy it is consistent with the temper of our times. It responds to the restlessness*

---

[29] See, for example, Rodney H. Brady, "MBO Goes to Work in the Public Sector," *Harvard Business Review,* March–April 1973, pp. 65–74.

[30] George L. Morrisey, "Making MBO Work—The Missing Link," *Training and Development Journal,* February 1976, pp. 3–11.

which people feel toward the bureaucracy—the sense of powerlessness and alienation from the remote leadership of the large organization. It is at once functional in terms of what top management demands and developmental in terms of the people at work. It calls for human commitment rather than simply assuming that orders from the top will be self-executing. It compels forward planning and living life in an anticipatory mode rather than responding to events. It isn't based upon the prediction of the future but rather upon the creation of that future.[31]

However, MBO has presented some problems. Harold Koontz has noted that practicing managers have encountered some serious systems shortcomings and pitfalls in actual use of the technique. Some of the primary weaknesses of MBO follow:

1. Despite the fact that the logic of management by objectives is simple, many people have difficulty learning and/or adjusting to the system. The shift from planning work to planning for the accomplishment of specific objectives is quite difficult.

2. Many organizations have attempted to install an MBO system by issuing instructions and providing the necessary forms. However, such a procedure has not always ensured that the basic philosophy behind the program was explained well enough to achieve maximum results.

3. Often, managers are neither taught how to set objectives nor familiarized with the results for which they are to be held accountable. As a result, the basic MBO process is never implemented.

Here are some MBO weaknesses.

4. Sometimes the objectives of one department are not in harmony with those of another. In these cases, each department ends up going its own way, and the results are counterproductive to the overall organization.

5. Sometimes the attempt to quantify objectives results in an overreliance on numbers. Unfortunately, some objectives cannot be easily or accurately quantified, and efforts to do so prove meaningless.

6. In many cases, progress toward goal accomplishment is not adequately monitored by the superior. That individual simply sits back and forgets that periodic review, counseling, and control are mandatory to the program's success. The subordinate, lacking such direction, often turns in a mediocre performance.[32]

Despite such experiences and possibly other potential problems, MBO is still very popular in industry today. Perhaps the greatest potential of this technique is that it provides the basis for effective decision making, communication, and control through its emphasis on participative decision making and two-way communication. To date there is little empirical research to validate the effectiveness of MBO as an overall management system, but the technique is widely used and holds a great deal of promise for the future. Another such technique is sensitivity training.

SENSITIVITY TRAINING

One of the reasons that many managers handle workers ineffectively is that they simply do not understand them. Since the late 1940s, a technique known as *sensitivity training* has gained acceptance in business organizations as a method for overcoming this deficiency.

The general approach used in this training is that of group discussion. With a leader

---

[31] George S. Odiorne, "MBO: A Backward Glance," *Business Horizons,* October 1978, pp. 14–24.

[32] Harold Koontz, "Making MBO Effective," *California Management Review,* Fall 1977, pp. 5–13.

who is skilled in the technique, the group decides what it wants to talk about or do. Since the group and the content are unstructured, many of the participants feel frustrated. As Keith Davis notes:

> Basically, sensitivity training is small-group interaction under stress in an unstructured encounter group which requires people to become sensitive to one another's feelings in order to develop reasonable group activity. . . .
>
> In this environment they are encouraged to examine their own self-concepts and to become more receptive to what others say and feel. In addition, they begin to perceive how a group interacts, recognize how culture affects it, and develop skills in working with others. In summary, therefore, the goals of sensitivity training are understanding of self, understanding of others, insight into group process, understanding the influence of culture, and developing behavioral skills.[33]

After attending one of these sessions, the participant is supposed to be more open with subordinates, more willing to communicate with them, and more determined to use a leadership style to which they can favorably and comfortably respond. In many cases this is precisely what happens, and the manager is better off for having participated in the training or, as it is often called, the T-group session. However, not everyone would agree. Sensitivity training also has its opponents who argue that sensitivity training is of little, if any, value. For example, William J. Kearney and Desmond D. Martin sent a mail questionnaire to 300 business firms employing 1,000 or more people throughout the United States.[34] Two hundred twenty-five of the questionnaires were returned and used in describing the responses. Of these, 40.4 percent of the respondents said that their firm believed that sensitivity training had improved the performance of the managers. However, 43.4 percent said it had not. Additionally, while 26.2 percent of the respondents said that they would personally recommend to other firms that they emphasize sensitivity training in their management development programs, 48.9 percent said they would not.

Who is right, then—the supporters or the opponents?[35] This is a difficult question to answer. John B. Miner, for example, reports that a considerable amount of research has been directed at finding out whether the T-group approach really does change people. His answer is that it does. "Thus, potentially at least it can alter value structures on a broad basis and pave the way for widespread reorganization. Managers appear to become more sensitive, more open in their communication, more flexible, and more understanding of others."[36] On the other hand, surprisingly, there are many important aspects of sensitivity training on which virtually no research has been conducted. Marvin D. Dunnette and John P. Campbell, for example, after conducting a comprehensive review of the literature, found little research into the effects of sensitivity training on an individual's ability to face up to and resolve personal conflict, analyze information, or implement solutions to organizational problems.[37]

Nevertheless, there is currently such enthusiasm and confidence in this technique that it will undoubtedly continue to be a major organizational development tool for a long time to come.

Sensitivity training has great potential value.

---

[33] Keith Davis, *Human Behavior at Work,* 5th ed. (New York: McGraw-Hill, 1977), pp. 183–184.

[34] William J. Kearney and Desmond D. Martin, "Sensitivity Training: An Established Management Development Tool?" *Academy of Management Journal,* December 1974, pp. 755–760.

[35] For further views of the pros and cons of sensitivity training, see Filley, House, and Kerr, *Managerial Process and Organizational Behavior,* pp. 498–503.

[36] John B. Miner, *The Management Process: Theory, Research, and Practice,* 2d ed. (New York: Macmillan, 1978), p. 346.

[37] Marvin D. Dunnette and John P. Campbell, "Laboratory Education: Impact on People and Organizations," *Industrial Relations,* October 1968, p. 23.

TRANSACTIONAL ANALYSIS

Transactional analysis (TA) is a technique described by Eric Berne, a California social psychiatrist, in his 1964 best seller, *Games People Play.*[38] Although Berne died almost simultaneously with the publication of his book, the TA approach has been further popularized by Thomas A. Harris in his own best seller, *I'm OK—You're OK* (1969) and by Muriel James and Dorothy Jongeward in their two very successful co-authored books, *Born to Win* (1971) and *Winning with People* (1973). The transactional approach has also been used in popular psychology books on a number of subjects of interest to managers, among them alcoholism and inappropriate language use. In essence, TA helps the manager communicate with and understand people through an analysis of both the manager's and the subordinates' behaviors, especially including their communications.

Ego States

At the heart of TA is the concept of ego states. Everyone has three ego states: the parent, the adult, and the child.

The *parent ego state* contains the attitudes and behavior that a child receives, sometimes only through the perceptions and interpretations of childhood, from his or her parents. For better or worse, parents leave an indelible mark on the child by communicating to the latter their beliefs, their prejudices, and their fears. A person acting in a manner uncritically absorbed from the parents is said to be in the parent ego state. Generally this occurs when the individual acts in an officious way or assumes a dominant role. (This is the way it is to be done.)

The *adult ego state* is characterized by attention to fact gathering and objective analysis. No matter what prejudices or emotions were communicated by the parents, a person who is in the adult state deals with reality from an objective standpoint and analyzes the situation as dispassionately or realistically as possible. (Let's look at the facts.)

At the heart of TA is the concept of ego states.

The *child ego state* contains all impulses learned as an infant. A person in this ego state can be described in terms such as curious, impulsive, sensuous, affectionate, or uncensored. The individual is acting just the way a child acts. A common illustration is people at a football game who are rooting and cheering. They are uncensored and impulsive. (We want a touchdown!)

These three ego states are often described by one-word adjectives. The parent state is referred to as *taught,* the adult state as *thought,* and the child state as *felt.* In addition, for purposes of analysis, the three are often diagrammed as in Figure 14–5.

Types of Transactions

Throughout a normal day, people will move from one ego state to another. The manager's job is one of discerning which ego state the person is in and then responding appropriately. To do so requires that the manager, presumably in an adult state, be aware of the three basic types of transactions: complementary, crossed, and ulterior.

---

[38] Eric Berne, *Games People Play* (New York: Grove Press, 1964). Berne, a medical doctor, had made a formal presentation of the transactional theory in *Transactional Analysis in Psychotherapy* (New York: Grove Press, 1961).

Figure 14–5 *Simplified Ego State Structure*

Figure 14–6 *A Complementary Transaction*

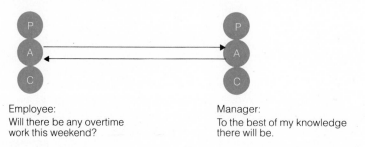

Employee:
Will there be any overtime
work this weekend?

Manager:
To the best of my knowledge
there will be.

Figure 14–7 *A Complementary Transaction*

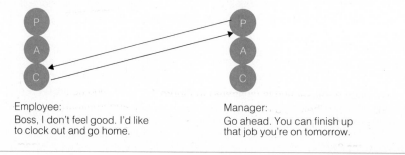

Employee:
Boss, I don't feel good. I'd like
to clock out and go home.

Manager:
Go ahead. You can finish up
that job you're on tomorrow.

Complementary transactions are appropriate and expected.

Complementary Transactions Berne defines a *complementary transaction* as one that is "appropriate and expected and follows the natural order of healthy human relationships."[39] Sometimes an employee will ask the manager a simple question (adult ego state) and expect a truthful response (adult ego state). Figure 14–6 illustrates the transaction.

It is not necessary, however, that people remain in the adult state at all times. For example, a worker may feel sick and ask to go home. In this case, the worker's act, although it is appropriate, may be compared to that of a child requesting a favor from a parent (please, Mommy, may I?). In turn, the manager assumes the parent role (you

---

[39] Berne, *Games People Play*, p. 29.

Figure 14–8   A Crossed Transaction

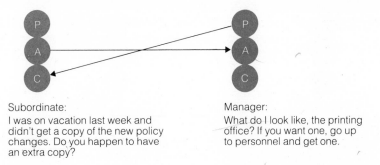

Subordinate:
I was on vacation last week and didn't get a copy of the new policy changes. Do you happen to have an extra copy?

Manager:
What do I look like, the printing office? If you want one, go up to personnel and get one.

Figure 14–9   A Crossed Transaction

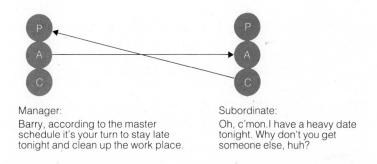

Manager:
Barry, according to the master schedule it's your turn to stay late tonight and clean up the work place.

Subordinate:
Oh, c'mon. I have a heavy date tonight. Why don't you get someone else, huh?

certainly may). Such a transaction is illustrated in Figure 14–7. As long as the manager responds appropriately, there is a complementary transaction, and communication and understanding are achieved.

Crossed Transactions *Crossed transactions* occur when there is *not* an appropriate or expected response. A diagram of the transaction can show this most clearly. Figures 14–8 and 14–9 are two examples, the first being one in which the manager errs, the second being one in which the subordinate creates the problem.

Crossed transactions are inappropriate or unexpected.

Ulterior Transactions *Ulterior transactions* are the most complex because they *always* involve more than two ego states. Usually, the real message is disguised under a socially acceptable transaction. For example, the manager wants one of the subordinates to take a job in a branch office, believing the individual needs this experience in order to succeed with the firm. However, the manager also believes the subordinate is unwilling to make the change. The manager therefore sends the person two messages, which can be seen in Figure 14–10. The verbal one is represented by a solid arrow, the ulterior one by a dotted arrow.

Ulterior transactions always involve more than two ego states.

The manager appears to be stating a fact but in reality is appealing to the subordinate's child state by throwing out a challenge and hoping the subordinate will respond

Figure 14–10   An Ulterior Transaction

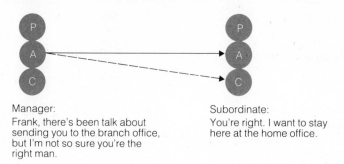

Manager:
Frank, there's been talk about
sending you to the branch office,
but I'm not so sure you're the
right man.

Subordinate:
You're right. I want to stay
here at the home office.

appropriately. If the subordinate says, "You're right, I want to stay here at the home office," the manager has failed, for the individual has answered the overt message only and responded on an adult-to-adult basis. On the other hand, if the manager injures the subordinate's pride (which is intended in this particular transaction), the worker might say, "I think I can handle the job; I'd like to try it." In so doing, the subordinate responds as a child. (I can too do it. Just you watch!) The point to remember is that when there are disguised messages, the transaction is ulterior.

TA and the Manager

Transactional analysis is currently being used by a number of firms, including American Airlines, to help managers understand and deal with their subordinates. As long as managers realize that both they and their employees have ego states and operate within them, they are in a position to analyze what is being said and how they should respond. One of the things TA emphasizes is building a strong adult ego state and encouraging others to do the same. The manager who can do this will deal with subordinates in a forthright and objective manner. Occasions naturally occur when subordinates are justified in adopting other ego states. For example, an employee may sulk upon failing to get a promotion (child state); the manager offers encouraging words (parent state). However, it is important to refrain from using ulterior transactions or treating subordinates as if they have no place in the decision-making process. If the manager can do this, the workers will respond more effectively. In explaining how TA can help managers communicate change, reduce resistance, and encourage participative decision making, American Airlines offers the following advice:

> What can you do to minimize your own as well as others' resistance to change and to improve efforts to improve? Remember that resistance to change comes from the Parent or the Child. Sometimes resistance can be reduced by providing or obtaining more data about the change. Involving people in some aspect of the decision-making (thereby requiring the use of their Adult) will help to get them unhooked from their Parent or Child reactions.
>
> The method you use in trying to improve something is also extremely important. Telling people they should or must (Parent initiated "oughtmanship") improve something will probably hook their Child (and therefore generate resistance.) For example, telling a group of employees, "You must improve your customer service and also reduce costs" will likely generate only anger, anxiety, guilt or fear (Child reaction).

Similarly, telling people that they should worry (thereby hooking their Child) about this same problem will probably not lead to improvement or change. On the other hand, the more relevant data you give employees about service and cost performance problems, the more likely you will engage their Adults in problem-solving.[40]

ORGANIZATIONAL BEHAVIOR MODIFICATION

Another technique that is currently receiving a great deal of attention is *organizational behavior modification* or, as it is commonly called today, B. Mod. In essence, the technique attempts to modify behavior by rewarding correct conduct and punishing or ignoring incorrect conduct. In this way, the individual learns to do what is expected. Quite simply, the technique uses learning theory to train (or retrain) people to do things the way the manager wants them to be done.

Behavior modification employs learning theory.

In its essence, B. Mod uses an A-B-C approach. The A stands for antecedent, the B for behavior, and the C for consequence. B. Mod specialists point out that every behavior has an antecedent and a consequence. For example, a middle manager is turning in incomplete reports. This is the behavior. Assume that she is doing this because she does not know how to properly fill out the reports (antecedent); further assume that her boss has not said anything to her, leading her to believe she is doing a good job and should keep it up (consequence). B. Mod people believe that the best way to change behavior is to look at what precedes it (the antecedent) and what follows (the consequence). For example, if this middle manager's superior calls her in and explains to her how to fill out the report more completely (a new consequence), she will have new information to use (and a new antecedent) in completing the next one. By breaking into the A–B–C chain of events, the manager can modify the subordinate's behavior.[41]

Behavior Modification in Practice

Behavior modification has been used by many organizations. One area in which it has been very widely employed is in handling mental patients and autistic children. A common approach has been to give the mental patients tokens for performing certain functions, such as work in their immediate environment, whether hospital, day treatment center, or home. These tokens can then be cashed in as payment for allowing them to engage in an activity they like—for example, watching an hour of television. This token economy modifies behavior because it gets people in treatment to carry out certain tasks they would not otherwise perform.

Behavior modification is not restricted to mental patients. The same basic approach has been used in training the hard-core unemployed. In one case, report Richard Beatty and Craig E. Schneier, the trainer starts off by giving instructions to the recruits prior to the time they actually start the job. In this phase the trainer teaches

Behavior modification is not confined to hospitals and clinics.

the skills required on the job by breaking the task into its component behaviors, using verbal instruction to demonstrate correct behaviors, and reinforcing correct behaviors. For example, consider a task requiring the trainee to procure materials from the proper place and in the proper amounts, then to arrange those materials, then to feed them to a machine, then to place the finished product on a tray or rack. In such a job, the trainee would be reinforced first for successfully procuring the materials, then reinforced for both procuring the materials correctly and arranging them correctly beside the machine, and finally reinforced

---

[40] Lyman Randall, *P-A-C at Work* (Dallas, Texas: American Airlines, 1971), p. 46.
[41] For more on this, see Fred Luthans and Robert Kreitner, *Organizational Behavior Modification* (Glenview, Ill.: Scott, Foresman, 1975).

---

for procuring, arranging, feeding, and placing correctly. Eventually, the reinforcement schedule would only reinforce completion of the entire task several times in succession.

By reinforcing each consecutive part of a task, we can "shape" behavior toward correctly performing the entire task.[42]

As the training continues, the reinforcement (money, praise) can be varied. The individual may be rewarded only upon completing the task correctly five times in a row or on a random basis. This reinforcement schedule depends, of course, on the individual and the job. However, remember that this positive reinforcement only occurs if the job is done right. If it is done incorrectly, the person is reinstructed on the proper way, for the goal is to train the individual correctly. If the worker continues to make errors, the manager will turn either to punishment (reprimanding or threatening the person with dismissal) or to extinction (ignoring the person, who, seeing the behavior is having no good consequences, may elect to learn the desired behavior, thus extinguishing the erroneous choices). Neither of these two techniques will guarantee that the trainee will perform correctly, but they may prevent the individual from doing it incorrectly. The trainer increases the probability that the individual will start seeking positive reinforcement rather than punishment or extinction by doing the job right.

The technique can be used for reducing tardiness.

Another objective for which behavior modification is being used is reducing tardiness. A hardware company in St. Louis, for example, has set up a lottery system for this purpose. If an individual is on time for work and takes only the allotted period for work breaks, this employee is eligible for a drawing at the end of the month. A prize, worth about $25, is awarded for every twenty-five eligible employees. Furthermore, at the end of six months, people with perfect attendance are eligible for a color television set drawing. In addition, the names of all winners, as well as those who were eligible, are printed in the company paper. Within sixteen months of the program's installation, the firm's sick leave costs dropped by 62 percent and the number of employees eligible for the monthly drawing rose from 151 (out of 530) in the first month to 219 in the sixteenth month.

It can also be used in modifying organizational behavior.

Luthans and Kreitner, meanwhile, have reported a number of successes with B. Mod in changing specific on-the-job behavior. In one case, a disruptive female machine operator was chosen as the subject of an experiment. Her supervisor decided to use a strategy known as extinction/positive reinforcement. Every time the woman had satisfactory production or constructive suggestions, the supervisor reinforced her with praise. Whenever she complained, the supervisor ignored her. Within forty-five working days, the manager reduced the woman's complaint frequency from three times daily to less than once daily on the average.

In another case, the same researchers reported that a supervisor was having little success in reducing the scrap rate among his work group. Posting equipment maintenance rules and frequently reminding the workers about it had little noticeable effect. The supervisor then decided to install a feedback system to inform the group of its scrap rate and to actively solicit suggestions from the workers on how to improve it. Within ten weeks the group scrap rate declined from an average of fifty pieces per day to less than twenty.

In a third case, a supervisor decided to use behavior modification to reduce the number of rejects of assembled components by one of his assemblers. He decided that anything over two per hundred was unacceptable:

Beginning a shaping process at five or less errors, the supervisor contingently praised the assembler for any improved quality. As the reject level began to drop, the reinforcement schedule was gradually stretched.

---

[42] Richard Beatty and Craig E. Schneier, "Training the Hard-Core Unemployed through Positive Reinforcement," *Human Resource Management,* Winter 1972, p. 13.

In other words, the worker had to have four, then three, and eventually only two rejects before praise was given by the supervisor. Summarized reject statistics were charted and presented to the assembler as a form of feedback on performance. Discussions of this feedback data between the assembler and the supervisor provided the opportunity for the supervisor to reinforce desirable behavior and ignore undesirable behavior.[43]

Within two weeks the supervisor had the assembler down to an average of one reject per hundred assembled components.

B. Mod is often criticized as a manipulative technique. In behavioral terminology, this means that managers offer their subordinates contrived reinforcers that are external to the work environment. For instance, if B. Mod is used to limit tardiness, the manager thinks up gimmicky approaches—for example, cash prizes, television sets, plaques—that will induce the workers to show up on time. Although such reinforcers are useful at first, managers have to face the problem of what to offer next, when the initial approach proves ineffective. For this reason, B. Mod adherents attempt to arrange the work environment more efficiently, using reinforcers that are internal to the job, such as praising a person for work well done and ignoring a person whose work is poor.[44]

Today the technique of behavior modification has been taken out of clinics and mental institutions and is being applied to the management of humans in organizations.[45] A great deal more needs to be done before B. Mod's full value for management can be determined. However, it has had a promising start and appears to be an effective technique for helping organizations manage their human assets.[46]

HUMAN RESOURCES ACCOUNTING

The ultimate objective of all the programs and techniques discussed thus far in the chapter is that of obtaining maximum efficiency. When an organization decides to review its effectiveness, it will usually examine its financial statements, such as the balance sheet, in which physical assets (cash, accounts receivable, inventory, and plant) are recorded. However, nowhere in the financial statements of most firms is there any accounting for either the productive capability of the workers or the goodwill of the customers. In the case of the work force, for example, many variables can make one firm superior to another, including:

1. Level of intelligence and aptitudes.
2. Level of training.
3. Level of performance goals and motivation to achieve organizational success.
4. Quality of leadership.
5. Capacity to use differences for purposes of innovation and improvement, rather than allowing differences to develop into bitter, irreconcilable, interpersonal conflict.
6. Quality of communicating upward, downward, and laterally.
7. Quality of decision making.

---

[43] Luthans and Kreitner, *Organizational Behavior Modification,* p. 157.

[44] For more about these on-the-job rewards, see Luthans and Kreitner, *Organizational Behavior Modification,* pp. 100–104.

[45] See, for example, Fred Luthans and Donald D. White, Jr., "Behavior Modification: Application to Manpower Management," *Personnel Administration,* July–August, 1971, pp. 41–47.

[46] For an excellent summation of this area, see Craig Eric Schneier, "Behavior Modification in Management: A Review and Critique," *Academy of Management Journal,* September 1974, pp. 528–548.

Figure 14-11   Determining Human Resource Replacement Costs

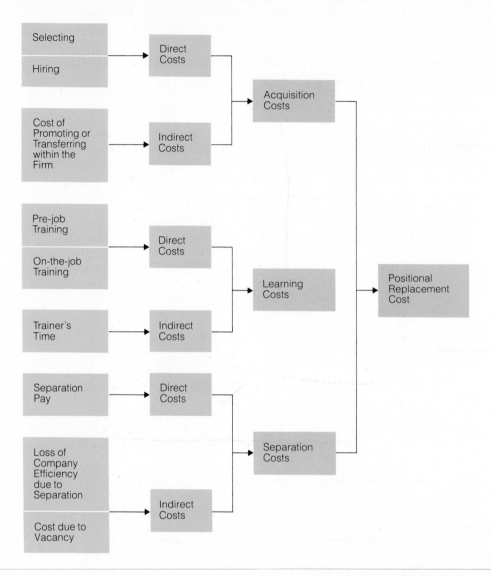

Source: Adapted by permission from Eric G. Flamholtz, "Human Resource Accounting: Measuring Positional Replacement Costs," *Human Resource Management,* Spring 1973, p. 11.   .

8. Capacity to achieve cooperative teamwork versus competitive striving for personal success at the expense of the organization.
9. Quality of the control processes of the organization and the levels of felt responsibility which exist.
10. Capacity to achieve effective coordination.

11. Capacity to use experience and measurements to guide decisions, improve operations, and introduce innovations.[47]

Nowhere on the balance sheet are these factors accounted for. In an attempt to overcome this deficiency, an area known as *human resources accounting* has developed. The method has taken two paths: viewing the acquisition and development of personnel as an investment, and obtaining a regular evaluation of these assets by measuring what are called causal and intervening variables. The following discussion will examine both of these approaches.

Personnel as an Investment

If a company is to be successful, it needs to hire and maintain competent people. How much are these people worth to the firm? This is a question human resources accounting attempts to answer. As Rensis Likert points out, this term

> refers to activity devoted to attaching dollar estimates to the value of a firm's human organization and its customer goodwill. If able, well-trained personnel leave the firm, the human organization is worth less; if they join it, the firm's human assets are increased. If bickering, distrust, and irreconcilable conflict become greater, the human enterprise is worth less; if the capacity to use differences constructively and engage in cooperative teamwork improves, the human organization is a more valuable asset.[48]

One way for the company to decide how much its human assets are worth would be to determine the amount of money it took to hire, train, and retain these people. Offsetting this figure will be such factors as retirement, transfers, separations, and obsolescence (or failure to keep up) on the part of the employees. Figure 14–11 illustrates this cost analysis. If one wished to include the customer in this analysis, the cost of maintaining goodwill could be written in and loss of customer orders (ill will) deducted.

Another method has been proposed by Philip H. Mirvis and Barry M. Macy, who developed a model for reflecting member participation in light of attendance at work and performance while on the job. Factors in the former category included absenteeism, turnover, strikes, and tardiness. In the latter were production under standard, quality under standard, grievances, accidents, unscheduled downtime, machine repair, material utilization, and inventory shrinkage. Mirvis and Macy then analyzed a firm and determined how much each of these factors was affecting it. They found that tardiness was costing the firm $56,920 a year, absenteeism was costing $286,330 annually, and losses owing to quality below standard were estimated at $663,589.[49] Human resources are thus reflected in an organization's financial statements. By managing these resources well, the organization can increase productivity and profits. Figure 14–12 shows how human resources investments can be converted into productive job behavior.

Obviously, converting human assets into dollars in the financial statements is a difficult task because the approach is very subjective. After all, how does one really decide the costs associated with the retention or loss of personnel? No definitive answer will be presented here; the entire area is still in the developmental stages. It should be

A dollar-investment approach is used.

---

[47] Rensis Likert, *The Human Organization* (New York: McGraw-Hill, 1967), p. 148.
[48] Ibid., pp. 148–149.
[49] Philip H. Mirvis and Barry M. Macy, "Human Resource Accounting: A Measurement Perspective," *Academy of Management Review,* April 1976, pp. 76–83.

Figure 14–12 Conversion of Human Resource Investments into Behavior on the Job

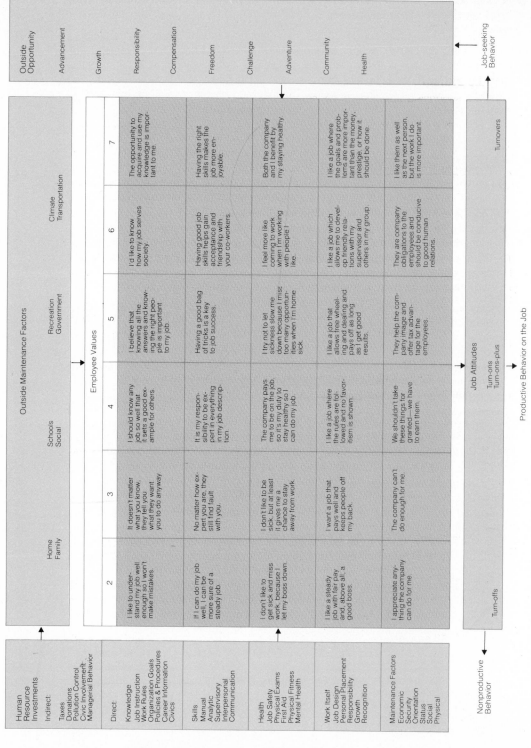

Source: M. Scott Myers and Vincent S. Flowers, "A Framework For Developing Human Assets." Copyright 1974 by the Regents of the University of California. Reprinted from *California Management Review,*

noted, however, that some companies are actually trying to reflect human resources in their financial statements.[50] If human resources accounting continues to grow at its current pace, other firms will undoubtedly be doing the same.

Periodic Evaluation of Human Resources

A second suggested approach is periodic evaluation of the state of the company's human resources. One way of doing this, in the opinion of some human resources accounting people, is to use Likert's four management systems, which were discussed in Chapter 13. By determining whether a company is operating under System 1, 2, 3, or 4, it may be possible to draw conclusions about how the human resources are being managed. The primary thesis of proponents of this theory is that the current state of a company's human resources will be reflected in future performance. If today's workers are operating under a System 3 or System 4 manager, future performance should be high. If they are working under a System 1 or System 2 manager, future performance will be lower.

When Likert's management systems are used to measure the current state of the human resources, questions such as those presented earlier (see Figure 13–3) are employed. Based on the responses, the researchers approximate a profile of the system under which the company is operating. In addition, three types of variables are examined. These are:

1. **Causal (or independent) variables,** which determine the results the company is going to achieve. Management decisions, business strategies, and leadership behavior are all illustrations.

2. **Intervening variables,** which reflect the internal state of the organization. Loyalty, attitude, and motivation are all illustrations.

3. **End-result (or dependent) variables,** which reflect the organization's achievements. Earnings, productivity, and costs are all illustrations.

According to human resources experts, a company's earnings, productivity, and costs (end-result variables) are a result of causal variables, such as business strategies and leadership behavior. However, one must do more than merely analyze cause-effect relationships. It is also necessary to examine the transformation process or intervening variables. For example, why does a particular leadership behavior result in higher earnings? The answer may well be found in such factors as loyalty, attitude, and motivation.

Intervening variables are important.

This particular concept has important implications for management because it indicates that a change in leadership style (causal variable) will result in a change in factors such as costs or earnings (end-result variables) only if there is change in factors such as loyalty, attitude, motivation, and so on (intervening variables). This particular idea is often used by human resources accounting people to illustrate what they call the *liquidation of human assets.* In essence, human resource accountants believe that a company that wishes to increase its current earnings can do so if it moves toward System 1. Figure 14–13 provides an illustration.

---

[50] William C. Pyle, "Monitoring Human Resources—On Line," *Michigan Business Review,* July 1970, pp. 19–32; D. M. C. Jones, "Accounting for Human Assets," *Management Decision,* Summer 1973, pp. 183–194; and Geoffrey M. N. Baker, "The Feasibility and Utility of Human Resource Accounting," *California Management Review,* Summer 1974, pp. 17–23.

Figure 14–13 Moving toward System 1

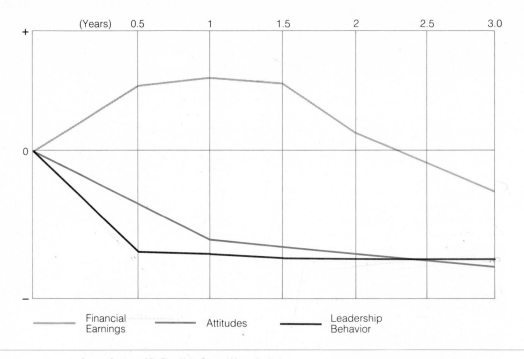

Source: Courtesy of Dr. Tony Hain, General Motors Institute.

Changes in Leadership Style As seen in Figure 14–13, by changing its strategy and leadership behavior (causal variables) the company can improve its short-run financial position (end-result variable). Of course, this lasts for only a few years and then deteriorates. However, one point to be noted from Figure 14–13 is that as the firm moves toward System 1, leadership behavior declines; managers become increasingly autocratic and start applying pressure in an attempt to improve earnings. This behavior is followed by a decline in employee attitudes and motivation. During this same period, it is also common to find some of the best workers leaving the firm. The company is thus liquidating its human resources. In a manner of speaking, it is analogous to selling machinery and equipment at a discount. On the positive side, however, the financial picture (earnings) improves and, in the above illustration, remains there for two years before finally dropping below the initial level of zero.

The same basic concepts are used by human resources people to explain what happens when a company moves toward System 4, as Figure 14–14 illustrates. First the leadership behavior (causal variable) is changed. This is followed by improvement in attitudes (intervening variable) and then improvement in earnings (end-result variable).

If the management moves toward System 1, it can milk or liquidate its human assets and achieve short-run increases in earnings. However, after a given time period the intervening variables will come into play and the earnings will decrease. Thus, in the short run, it may be advisable to change to System 1 when a critical financial situation develops, but this approach cannot be maintained indefinitely.

Figure 14–14 Moving toward System 4

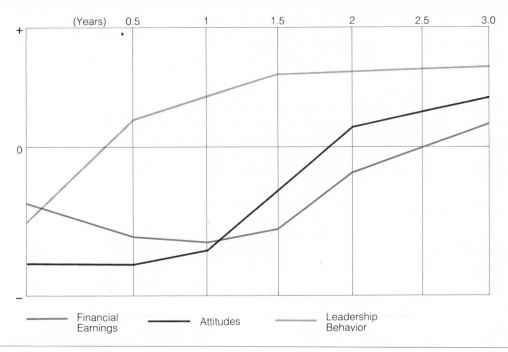

Source: Courtesy of Dr. Tony Hain, General Motors Institute.

Conversely, moving toward System 4 may not result in any increases in earnings for quite a while. As Likert points out, *"Changes in the causal variables toward System 4 apparently require an appreciable period of time before the impact of the change is fully manifest in corresponding improvement in the end-result variables."*[51] This entails a good deal of faith on the part of the management, which must be willing to continue moving toward System 4.

William M. Fox echoes Likert, noting:

> It has been found, for example, that there is a six-to-twelve-month interval between positive changes in top management behavior and positive changes in organization climate and subordinate leadership. In turn, there is a seven-to-eighteen-month lag between positive changes in subordinate leadership and group performance improvement and reduced absenteeism. Grievance rate reduction takes only about six months and changes in satisfaction take place within a matter of days or weeks.
>
> Reciprocal relationships are in evidence, also. We see that subordinate performance improvement and increased satisfaction help to cause positive changes in leadership behavior with a time lag of approximately one month.[52]

---

[51] Rensis Likert, *The Human Organization, pp. 80–81.* For more on this subject, see William F. Dowling, "At General Motors: System 4 Builds Performance and Profits," *Organizational Dynamics,* Winter 1975, pp. 23–38.

[52] William M. Fox, "Limits to the Use of Consultative-Participative Management," *California Management Review,* Winter 1977, p. 21.

Human resources researchers thus believe that the firm's current financial position may not reflect the true status of the causal and intervening variables, for these are lead factors. However, changes in these variables will be reflected in future financial statements, and this is why they are so important:

> The measurements of the causal and intervening variables should be obtained for the corporation as a whole and for each profit center or unit in the company. . . . By using appropriate statistical procedures, relationships can be computed among the causal, intervening, and such end-result variables as costs and earnings. . . . These estimates of probable subsequent productivity, costs, and earnings will reveal the earning power of the human organization at the time the causal and intervening variables were measured, even though the level of estimated subsequent earnings may not be achieved until much later. These estimates . . . provide the basis for attaching to any profit center, unit, or total corporation a statement of the present value of its human organization.[53]

The future of the firm depends on its ability to manage its human assets today.

One further point must be noted before this discussion ends. Figures 14–13 and 14–14 represent only a general pattern of results as postulated by human resources researchers. As Koontz, O'Donnell, and Weihrich note:

> To date, only a few experiments have been undertaken to measure the investment costs and losses in human resources. While it is believed that present "value" of human resources . . . can be reasonably well approached through the use of the Likert measurements, there is still little evidence that this has been done with an acceptable degree of creditability.[54]

On an overall basis, then, judgment on the value of human resources accounting must be withheld until more research has been conducted in the area.

SUMMARY

This chapter has examined some of the latest tools and techniques for managing the firm's human assets. After the chapter described the staffing process, where human resource development efforts first begin, it noted that these efforts are designed to change things. The change process has three phases: unfreezing the old ways, introducing new behaviors, and refreezing the new equilibrium.

The remainder of the chapter was devoted to the study of some of the human resource development programs currently being used in modern organizations. Job enrichment is one that has been getting a great deal of attention. It is currently employed in a number of firms, including TI, AT&T, GM's Cadillac division, and overseas in Volvo plants. In essence, job enrichment places primary emphasis on Herzberg's motivators: advancement, growth, and responsibility. Yet despite wide acceptance, the technique has a number of vociferous critics who claim that it does not always work. Three of the primary reasons cited are that some workers do not find satisfaction in the work place; some people prefer boring, unpleasant jobs with good social interaction to enriched jobs that reduce the opportunity for such interaction; and some workers react to the technique with feelings of inadequacy and fears of failure.

One of the primary ways of redesigning jobs is by building core job dimensions into them. It has been found that these dimensions are frequently correlated with such outcomes as high work motivation, high quality performance, high satisfaction, low turnover, and low absenteeism.

---

[53] Ibid., p. 150.

[54] Harold Koontz, Cyril O'Donnell, and Heinz Weihrich, *Management,* 7th ed. (New York: McGraw-Hill, 1980), p. 797.

Another technique that has also gained a great deal of popularity because of its potential for helping the manager carry out decision-making, communication, and control functions is management by objectives. In essence, MBO entails a meeting of superior and subordinate for deciding: (a) what the subordinate will do, (b) by when, and (c) how performance will be evaluated. In addition to its participative decision-making feature, subordinates like the technique because it tells them what is expected of them, thereby reducing ambiguity and anxiety.

Sensitivity training is designed to make managers more aware of their own actions and their effect on others, in addition to obtaining better insight into what makes subordinates tick. Another approach, which is less emotive but just as valuable to managers who need help communicating with their people, is transactional analysis. A number of companies, including American Airlines, are using this technique to help their managers communicate more effectively with their subordinates.

Behavior modification is another HRD approach. In essence, it attempts to get employees to do what management wants by discouraging incorrect behavior and rewarding correct behavior. Initially used by hospitals and clinics, B. Mod is today being adopted by business for handling numerous organizational challenges, from training the hard-core unemployed to reducing employee tardiness.

The last technique examined was human resources accounting. This technique suggests that the company evaluate its personnel and that this evaluation be reflected in the firm's financial statements. Well-trained, well-motivated people are an asset. Another approach is to evaluate personnel on a periodic basis by measuring causal, intervening, and end-result variables. This technique gives management a reading on the kind of performance it can expect from its people in the near future.

REVIEW AND STUDY QUESTIONS

1. What is involved in the staffing process? Identify and describe the activities that are carried out.

2. What is the "great jackass fallacy"?

3. How does the change process work? Describe its three phases.

4. What is the primary goal of job enrichment? Will we see more of it in the rest of the 1980s? Explain your answer.

5. What are some of the arguments against job enrichment?

6. What is job redesign? Incorporate the job characteristics model into your answer.

7. How does management by objectives work? Explain in some detail.

8. What are some problems associated with the use of MBO?

9. In what way can sensitivity training be of value to the manager?

10. How does TA help the manager communicate with and understand the subordinates? Bring into your discussion the three basic types of transactions: complementary, crossed, and ulterior.

11. How does behavior modification work? What are the basic steps or ideas in the process?

12. Defend or oppose this statement: "Behavior modification is nothing more than manipulation."

13. Why should a company think of its personnel as an investment? Should personnel be accounted for in financial statements?

14. What is a causal variable? An intervening variable? An end-result variable? Of what value is this information to management?

15. In general, can a company improve its short-run earnings by switching from a System 4 to a System 1 management? Explain.

16. Explain why a company moving from a System 1 to a System 4 management does not experience an immediate increase in earnings.

SELECTED REFERENCES

Baker, G. M. N. "The Feasibility and Utility of Human Resource Accounting." *California Management Review,* Summer 1974, pp. 17–23.

Barton-Dobenin, J., and Hodgetts, Richard M. "Management Training Programs: Who Uses Them and Why?" *Training and Development Journal,* March 1975, pp. 34–40.

Berne, Eric. *Games People Play.* New York: Grove Press, 1964.

Bowers, D. G. *Systems of Organization: Management of the Human Resource.* Ann Arbor, Mich.: University of Michigan Press, 1976.

Brief, A. P., and Aldag, R. J. "The Job Characteristic Inventory: An Examination." *Academy of Management Journal,* December 1978, pp. 569–670.

Bright, W. E. "How One Company Manages Its Human Resources." *Harvard Business Review,* January–February 1976, pp. 81–93.

"Business Tries Out 'Transactional Analysis,'" *Business Week,* January 12, 1974, pp. 74–75.

Ceriello, V. R. "A Guide for Building a Human Resource Data System." *Personnel Journal,* September 1978, pp. 496–503.

Cherrington, D. M., and England, J. L. "The Desire for an Enriched Job as a Moderator of the Enrichment-Satisfaction Relationship." *Organizational Behavior and Human Performance,* February 1980, pp. 139–159.

Cornwall, D. J. "Human Resource Programs: Blue Sky or Operating Priority?" *Business Horizons,* April 1980, pp. 49–54.

Dowling, W. F. "At General Motors: System 4 Builds Performance and Profits." *Organizational Dynamics,* Winter 1975, pp. 23–38.

Drucker, Peter F. *The Practice of Management.* New York: Harper & Bros., 1954.

English, J., and Marchione, A. R. "Nine Steps in Management Development." *Business Horizons,* June 1977, pp. 88–94.

Flamholtz, E. G. "Human Resources Accounting: Measuring Positional Replacement Costs." *Human Resource Management,* Spring 1973, pp. 8–16.

Ford, Robert N. *Motivation through the Work Itself.* New York: American Management Association, 1969.

Giblin, E. J., and Ornati, O. A. "Optimizing the Utilization of Human Resources." *Organizational Dynamics,* Autumn 1975, pp. 18–33.

Guest, Robert H. "Quality of Work Life—Learning from Tarrytown," *Harvard Business Review,* July–August 1979, pp. 76–87.

Harris, Thomas A. *I'm OK—You're OK.* New York: Harper & Row, 1969.

Hilton B. D. "A Human Resource System That Lives Up to Its Name." *Personnel Journal,* July 1979, pp. 460–465.

Hollmann, R. W. "Supportive Organizational Climate and Managerial Assessment of MBO Effectiveness." *Academy of Management Journal,* December 1976, pp. 560–576.

Hollmann, R. W., and Tansik, D. A. "A Life Cycle Approach to Management by Objectives." *Academy of Management Review,* October 1977, pp. 678–683.

James, Muriel, and Jongeward, Dorothy. *Born to Win,* Reading, Mass.: Addison-Wesley, 1971.

Koontz, Harold, "Making MBO Effective," *California Management Review,* Fall 1977, pp. 5–13.

Levinson, Harry. "Asinine Attitudes toward Motivation," *Harvard Business Review, January*–February 1973, pp. 70–76.

———. "The Abrasive Personality," *Harvard Business Review,* May–June 1978, pp. 86–94.

Lippitt, G. L. "Quality of Work Life: Organization Renewal in Action," *Training and Development Journal,* July 1978, pp. 4–10.

Locke, E. A. "The Myths of Behavior Mod in Organizations," *Academy of Management Review,* October 1977, pp. 543–554.

Lorsch, Jay W. "Making Behavioral Science More Useful," *Harvard Business Review,* March–April 1979, pp. 171–180.

Mahoney, T. A. "The Rearranged Work Week," *California Management Review,* Summer 1978, pp. 31–39.

Mills, Ted. "Human Resources—Why the New Concern?" *Harvard Business Review,* March–April 1975, pp. 120–134.

Mirvis, P. H., and Macy, B. A. "Human Resource Accounting: A Measurement Perspective," *Academy of Management Review,* April 1976, pp. 74–83.

Myers, M. S., and Flowers, V. S. "A Framework for Measuring Human Assets," *California Management Review,* Summer 1974, pp. 5–16.

Nemiroff, P. M., and Ford, D. L., Jr. "Task Effectiveness and Human Fulfillment in Organizations: A Review and Development of a Conceptual Contingency Model," *Academy of Management Review,* October 1976, pp. 69–82.

Neumann, S., and Segev, E. "Human Resources and Corporate Risk Management," *Personnel Journal,* February 1978, pp. 76–79.

Porter, A. L., and Rossini, F. A. "Flexiweek," *Business Horizons,* April 1978, pp. 45–51.

Puett, J. R., Jr., and Roman, D. D. "Human Resource Valuation," *Academy of Management Journal,* December 1976, pp. 656–662.

Schneier, C. E. "Behavioral Modification in Management: A Review and Critique," *Academy of Management Journal,* September 1974, pp. 528–548.

Stiner, F., Jr., and Hodgetts, Richard M. "The Social Audit and the Unit of Measurement," *Virginia Accountant,* September 1975, pp. 47–51.

Tosi, Henry, and Carroll, S. J., Jr. "Improving Management by Objective: A Diagnostic Change Program." *California Management Review,* Fall 1973, pp. 57–66.

Umstot, D. D.; Mitchell, T. F.; and Bell, C. H., Jr. "Goal Setting and Job Enrichment: An Integrated Approach to Job Design," *Academy of Management Review,* June 1978, pp. 265–274.

Walker, J. W. "Human Resource Planning: Managerial Concerns and Practices," *Business Horizons,* June 1976, pp. 55–59.

Weaver, C. N. "Sex Differences in the Determinants of Job Satisfaction," *Academy of Management Journal,* June 1978, pp. 265–274.

Ziegenfuss, J. T. "Responding to People Problems," *Business Horizons,* April 1980, pp. 73–76.

During the last five years a great deal of interest in the use of flexible work schedules has been generated. The basic idea has a number of different variations. In one the workers are allowed to come in at any time during the early to mid-morning and, depending on when they arrive, leave for home in the late afternoon or early evening. In other arrangements the employees are allowed to work thirty-two hours one week and forty-eight the next. Regardless of the specific conditions, flexitime (F-T) can be distinguished by a number of different features, including the following:

Band width   *This refers to the number of hours in the interval between the earliest possible starting time and the latest possible finishing time. A firm where the workers can start as early as 5:00 A.M. and finish as late as 8:00 P.M. has a greater band width than one where the hours are 7:00 A.M. and 7:00 P.M. respectively.*

Core hours   *These are the hours when the individual workers must be at work. In many jobs no person can arrive later than 11:00 A.M. and no one can leave before 3:00 P.M.*

Flexible hours   *These are the hours within which the individual can make choices about times to start and stop work. For example, the person may be allowed to come to work any time between 5:00 A.M. and 11:00 A.M. and go home after putting in eight hours—that is, any time between 1 P.M. and 7 P.M.*

Banking   *In some cases employees are allowed to work more than forty hours (or whatever the required number is) per week so that they can bank the surplus and use it later. In the same way people can work less than forty hours at these firms, run a deficit, and pay it back later or out of hours already in surplus.*

Do flexitime programs really improve worker performance and lead to higher morale and satisfaction? Although not all the studies indicate this, a large number report very positive results. For example, Barron H. Harvey and Fred Luthans studied three groups of workers. One was allowed to determine its work schedule on a daily basis (daily flexitime), one was allowed to determine its schedule at the beginning of each month (staggered), and the third continued to remain with the traditional schedule (fixed). The major emphasis of the Harvey-Luthans study was to compare the effect that daily flexitime and staggered hours had on employee satisfaction. They concluded that the "results support our contention that giving employees more control over jobs will have a beneficial effect. The group given daily flexitime . . . experienced improved satisfaction and seemingly less absenteeism and turnover, and better performance. The staggered hours and fixed hours groups did not experience such beneficial results."[55]

Robert T. Golembiewski and Carl W. Proehl, Jr., echo these remarks. They surveyed the empirical literature on flexible work hours and concluded that:

despite real limitations in available studies, both behavioral and attitudinal data encourage F-T applications. "Hard" data indicate that F-T is at least low-cost and may indeed imply handsome dividends on several critical organizational measures. "Soft" data strongly reinforce such a bias toward F-T applications, as seen from three organizational perspectives—that of employees, first line supervisors, and managers.[56]

Questions

1. In your own words, explain flexitime.

2. In what ways do flexitime programs help an organization develop its human resources? Make your answer complete.

---

[55] Barron H. Harvey and Fred Luthans, "Flexitime: An Empirical Analysis of Its Real Meaning and Impact." *MSU Business Topics,* Summer 1979, p. 36.

[56] Robert T. Golembiewski and Carl W. Proehl, Jr., "A Survey of the Empirical Literature on Flexible Workhours: Character and Consequences of a Major Innovation." *Academy of Management Review,* October 1978, p. 852.

3. What variations of flexitime would you expect to find being used during the 1980s? Explain.

CASE: *A Case of Eligibility*

Absenteeism at the Pallering Corporation had been staggering. Between January and June of 1980 the average employee was showing up fifteen minutes late for work three times a week. The management decided that something had to be done.

The problem was turned over to Jerry Peters of the personnel department. After pondering the situation for a few weeks, Peters suggested that the management undertake an incentive program. Every worker who was on time during the month of August would be eligible for a cash award of $100. There would be three such awards in all, and the drawing would be held on September 4. Within five days of the time the award was announced, absenteeism declined to a lower level than it had ever been in the history of the firm. Furthermore, throughout the ensuing six months, the company continued to maintain this reward system, and absenteeism remained lower than ever. In March of 1981 the firm abandoned the plan. Absenteeism soared to an all-time high but returned to its former low level in April when the award was reinstituted.

Questions

1. Has the management actually modified behavior? Explain.
2. Why did absenteeism soar when the company abandoned the plan?
3. Why did absenteeism remain so low when the incentive award was made available? After all, isn't money only a temporary motivator?

CASE: *A Liquidation of People*

When Iris Johnson became vice-president of manufacturing at the Walters Corporation in 1979, the firm had been in a downward spiral. Profits had declined from $473,000 in 1973 to just over $250,000 in fiscal 1979; return on investment during this period had dropped from 9.3 percent to 4.0 percent.

Within twenty-four months, however, Johnson turned the financial picture completely around. The accountant's report for these eight quarters revealed the following:

		Profit	*ROI*
1980	I	$290,000	4.3
	II	370,000	4.6
	III	420,000	4.9
	IV	550,000	6.1
1981	I	625,000	7.2
	II	750,000	8.1
	III	895,000	9.4
	IV	1,050,000	10.7

Then, to the president's dismay, Johnson submitted her resignation. She had been offered a job at twice her current salary, had decided to accept it, and would be leaving by the end of the month.

With only four weeks in which to find a replacement, the company quickly put out feelers to see who might fill the position. All reports seemed to indicate that Paul Robertson, factory manager for a large eastern firm, was the ideal choice. Robertson was invited in to see the facilities and financial reports. Toward the end of his visit he and the Walters president had a chance to sit down and talk.

"Paul, you've been here for three days now. Everyone is immensely impressed with your record and we'd like you to be our new vice-president of manufacturing. What do you say?"

"I appreciate the offer, Mr. Canyon. Quite frankly, though, I've decided not to accept. I just don't want to step in and spend the next two years rebuilding the firm."

"Rebuilding? Why, we have the best books in the industry."

"True, sir. On paper you look great. But what about the fact that half of your skilled work force has quit in the last eighteen months? These people are going to have to be replaced."

"Well, yes, we have lost some people. But Iris Johnson stepped into a tough position. She had to tighten things up. Before she came, we were losing money. She made everyone start to pull their own weight."

"And in the process, she alienated what sound like your best employees. She milked your human assets just about dry. I think you've gotten just about all the earnings you're going to get out of your current work force. The way I see it, you have a major rebuilding program on your hands. The woman you think you're grateful to has actually liquidated your most important asset—your people."

Questions

1. If Robertson is correct in his analysis, how has the vice-president of manufacturing liquidated the firm's human assets? Explain.

2. Why did the firm allow this to happen? Why did the president not take corrective action before this time?

3. What must the company do now? Explain.

CASE: The Abrasive Manager

Many HRD programs are designed to help managers lead their people more effectively. Sometimes, however, managers need to realize that their personal style can be most responsible for their problems. One of the most common management style problems is that of the manager with an abrasive personality. Some questions that help managers to determine whether they are abrasive follow:

When you talk to others in the organization, do you try to straighten them out?
Do you need to be in full control?
Do your personal remarks take up a large percentage of time during meetings?
Do you have a need to debate?
Do you like to acquire symbols of power and status?
Are people afraid to discuss things with you?

Do you quickly rise to attacks or challenges?

Are you reluctant to give people the same privileges as you have?

Do people think and speak of you as cold and distant?

Do you see yourself as more competent than your boss and/or your peers—and let them know it by the way you act?

Yes answers to seven or more of these indicate an abrasive personality. Attention toward identifying abrasive people and having their superiors work with them to overcome this problem has increased in recent years. If this proves ineffective, the firm or the individual might seek outside professional help.

Questions

1. How many of the questions in this case did you answer in the affirmative? What does this tell you about yourself?

2. In addition to these questions, what others would you ask in helping identify an abrasive personality?

3. Which of the HRD programs in this chapter could be helpful to a superior who is working to reduce a subordinate manager's abrasiveness? Explain your reasoning.

COMPREHENSIVE CASE: The New President's Dilemma

The Situation

Things have really been a mess at the Longworth Company. Over the last three years labor turnover has averaged 23 percent annually, and the union has filed five major grievances against the firm. A four-month strike occurred last year, and there is a dissatisfaction in the management ranks. If the present rate of turnover among these people continues, it will exceed 31 percent by year's end.

It was because of developments like this that Bedford Charles was just chosen to take over as president of Longworth. The board of directors looked Charles's record over very carefully. He had been president of a large firm in a different, but closely related, industry. While there, he had taken a firm with similar problems and turned it around and put it in the profit column within twenty-four months of his appointment as CEO. The Longworth board is hoping that he can do the same thing at Longworth.

As part of the agreement, the board agreed to allow Charles to bring his three immediate subordinates with him. "We are part of a management team," he told the board. "I would never agree to come to Longworth without them. I do not feel the company has time for me to get settled in and choose a management team, and without one there is little likelihood that the firm can be saved." The board agreed, three weeks ago, and Charles took over as Longworth's president.

His first step was to interview some of the managers in the organization. In particular, he wanted to find out exactly what the managers thought were the firm's worst problems. Charles also spent some time talking to several groups and the outgoing president. The latter had been fired by the board because his performance had been poor. Charles's logic in wanting to talk to the man was, "This will provide me with some insights regarding how *not* to manage the firm. Also, there may be some areas where he has better insight than I do. Perhaps there are some groups within the firm who are determined to prevent progress at any price. The old president could help me identify these people. Also, he might have tried to implement some ideas that should have produced good results. I would like to get an idea of what he wanted to do but did not get time to do. Likewise, would he be willing to tell me any things he did that went wrong? Whatever he tells me will give me a perspective on the company's problems."

Charles decided to talk also with the union people to get insights into labor-management problems. Why did the four-month strike take place? Charles knows what the management's explanation is, but he would like to know what the union's position is.

Charles made up his mind to talk to the workers in the production plant and to the salespeople because he feels that they, too, can provide him with useful information. The production people are unionized and could be expected to tell him a story similar to that of the union, but they might also provide some new insights as to what the overall problems are and how they can be handled. The salespeople could give him an idea of some of the problems faced by non-union employees who work at the lower levels of the organization.

Charles felt that he would be able to formulate a plan of action for resolving the situation after he had the opportunity to interview all of these people and find out what has been going on. The following is a summary of what he learned from each of the individuals and groups he interviewed in this fact-gathering mission.

Management Team

Charles was able to talk to all top managers in the firm within the first week of his arrival. He also managed to meet and have short discussions with some management team members at the middle and lower levels of the hierarchy. From the top people, he learned that the previous president apparently did not really have a plan of action. The remaining managers basically believed that the organization should be able to run itself. Therefore, instead of working with the top managers as a team, the old president had allowed each department to go off on its own. This meant that the finance department had to try to make order out of the chaos. Twice during the first year of the old president's tenure the company had a cash flow problem. In both cases this was caused by the president's approval of machinery and equipment purchases without prior approval from the finance department.

Although most of the managers felt that the former president lacked leadership ability, they agreed that he jumped in with both feet when something caught his interest. For example, there was a discussion about whether to buy a new computer. While the finance department opposed it on the grounds that it was not cost effective, the head of computer services prevailed on the president to order its purchase. The president personally supervised the acquisition and placement of the machine. Many of the managers disagreed with this leadership style, feeling that the president's job was too important to be taken up with such minor matters as worrying about the delivery of a piece of hardware.

When Charles summarized everything the managers told him about the past president, he concluded that the individual had just two leadership behaviors. The first was to be a laissez-faire manager who essentially did nothing. This seemed to be his preferred style. Second, though, he did sometimes turn on, and when he decided to take action, he assumed many of the System 1 leader characteristics. He simply pushed his way through and got those things accomplished that he wanted done.

The other major finding that came out of Charles's discussions with the managers was that the overall climate in the organization was poor. This was the result of the ex-president's continual rough manner in union negotiations. This abrasiveness had led to ill will between the two groups. In the minds of many managers, the strike resulted directly from the president's refusal to budge from his initial offer to the union. He had simply refused to come back to the bargaining table; to him, that was a matter of personal freedom. The union eventually made the firm come back to the bargaining table and hammer out an agreement by taking the company to court and getting a court ruling in its favor. In the process, the firm lost four months' productivity that year as well as $3.5 million of gross profit. The president retaliated by announcing that new machinery and equipment was going to be purchased and, therefore, some of the work force would be let go. This decision was in accord with the labor contract, in the president's interpretation, and he proceeded to implement his threat. "It soon became a battle of us versus them," said one manager, "and we were finding that they were not going to let us run all over them. If the board of directors had not stepped in and gotten rid of the president, we would have had another prolonged strike."

Some of the managers felt that the president was really a nice person but one who was unable to put up with disagreement or confrontation. "He wanted the union to go along with his proposed contract, and when they didn't, he became nasty with them. This is pretty surprising when you realize that he had a real good track record up to the time he took over here. In fact, before we hired him, we interviewed a number of candidates and did a background search on all of them. He was known by his associates as a very human relations-oriented guy. It just goes to show. Sometimes you can get fooled."

The Union

The basic problem evidenced in Charles's discussions with the union people was that the company has not lived up to the terms of its contract. They agreed that the new work procedures that had been introduced and the new machinery that had been installed during the past year were not in violation of the contract. However, the contract had a clause which said that no employee would be dismissed "except for just cause." The past president had argued that, with new machinery, there could be a cutback in the work force. In fact, he pointed out that it would be necessary to reduce the work force by fifteen people in order to meet the bank payments for the machines.

The union responded that these people should be found jobs elsewhere in the firm. However, the ex-president simply scorned their arguments and in so doing precipitated the strike. At present, the union is waiting to see what Charles will do. Ten of the fifteen people who had been terminated had been rehired after the strike, but feelings of anger and distrust are still strong among the union workers.

In addition, the union people told Charles that the management is not to be trusted. They disagree with top management's assessment that the president was responsible for all the problems that occurred. They consider top management staff to be responsible also. "They advised the president to do a lot of the things he did, and they should be replaced just like him," said one of the union officials. "Unless you begin by cleaning up your own group, you are never going to get on good working terms with the employees."

The Salespeople

The salespeople's discontent could be traced back to one specific source: disagreement over their remuneration. Five years ago all salespeople were on a combination plan of salary plus commission. However, the company decided that it would be better for both parties if the salaries were raised and the commissions dropped.

Initially, this was fine with the salespeople because the salary levels were set so high that most of them could not ever have hoped to earn this amount of money in a normal sales year. However, as inflation began to increase and the purchasing power of the dollar declined, management did not increase sales salaries accordingly. At the end of the first three years, the salespeople began to complain that they were now earning less than they would have been under the old salary-and-commission plan. In fact, while the rest of the workers, who were unionized, received an average annual increase of 8 percent during these three years, salespeople received only 4 percent. The company argued that the salespeople were given very high salaries when the old plan was scrapped and that they therefore should not be upset. The firm, management stated, was now simply allowing the other workers to catch up.

An additional problem in sales was the reorganization, during the past year, of the sales areas. Some salespeople were given much larger territories than they had previously had, while others were brought into the office and given managerial jobs. Neither group was pleased with this decision. Charles determined that only about 10 percent of the sales force planned, when he took over, to remain with the company for the next two years unless some changes were made in the current compensation policy. Also, he decided to have one of his assistants conduct a comparison study to see how well the average salaries of the salespeople compare with those of competitive firms.

The Workers

The workers themselves feel they are well represented by the union and the number of new gripes they raised, in contrast to those Charles heard from the union representatives, was minimal. However they raised two issues that he had not heard previously.

The first was related to the assembly-line people. Currently, there is an assembly-line operation that has each individual putting together one or two parts of a small hand tool and then passing it on to the next person. The line workers believe that they would be more efficient if they could each assemble the entire hand tool. Time spent in passing the work from one person to the next could be saved, and the workers feel they would like the job a lot more if they could personally finish an entire hand tool by themselves.

The second issue was that of flexitime. Many of the workers feel that since they do not work on the assembly-line operations, there is no need for them to be in the plant by 8:00 A.M. "Why not let us show up by 10:00 A.M., put in our eight hours, and then go home?" one of them said. "That way I could drop my kids at school, have a leisurely breakfast, and come in here wide awake and ready to work." Other workers echoed those sentiments.

The Past President

The past president was the last individual Charles talked with. This man had been busy interviewing with other firms for a job and had not had time to meet with him previously. In essence, the former president did not tell Charles much that coincided with what the others had said. The president felt that the workers were basically lazy and in need of constant control. "If you take your eye off them for a minute, they goof off," he told Charles. The ex-president also felt that the union was continually looking for ways to break its contract with the company. It had a large strike fund built up, and the recently-fired president believed the union representatives had called for last year's strike in order to spend some of this money as well as convince the workers that they had their best interests in mind. With understandable sarcasm, the jobless executive said, "If you don't call a strike every now and then, the membership begins to think you don't love them. And look at the results. In the recent union election every single member of their team was reelected. How do you like that? They got the workers to spend part of their strike fund and reelect them as well. If you ask me, the workers simply like to be led around like a bunch of sheep. They don't question what the union reps tell them. They simply like to believe that it is an 'us or them' situation, and they are delighted to take it out on us. To listen to the union tell it, management is directly and solely responsible for everything that has gone wrong around here since Day One."

The former president also told Charles that without his get-tough style, the union would have run the company into the ground years before: "Don't trust them for a minute. Also, keep the top management staff I put together. Believe me, those guys can be relied upon when the going gets tough." Charles promised his predecessor that he would think about it.

Making a Decison

Now the time has come for Charles to make some tough decisions. He has to decide what should be done in resolving the conflicts that exist both within and among these various organizational groups. He believes that the situation is not so basically bad that it cannot be saved. However, he also knows that it is going to take a very well-thought-out approach. The last thing Charles wants to do is to make some major decisions that turn out to be wrong. Although he would like more time to study the facts, Charles has decided that he will have a plan of action formulated within a week. With it, he is going to begin the process of trying to put the company back together again.

Questions

1. What behavioral problems have led to the present state of affairs at the Longworth Company? Make your answer complete, and refer to the text as widely as possible.

2. In order of importance, rank the problem areas at Longworth and sketch out recommendations for each. How would you suggest the president deal with each major issue?

3. What other recommendations would you make to the president to ensure that such problems do not recur? Explain.

PART 5

It is very useful to have schools of management thought as a framework in studying modern management. However, it is necessary for the student of management to understand that some topics do not fit neatly into such a framework. The subjects to be examined here in Part 5 are the current status of management theory (especially as that is related to systems theory), social responsibility, international business, and the future of management.

Chapter 15 begins with a discussion of the systems school of thought. This is followed by an examination of both general systems theory and applied systems concepts. Next, attention is focused on the general applicability of the systems approach for the practicing manager, with primary consideration given to viewing the organization as an open system. Then the three levels of management in the hierarchy are examined in systems terms. Finally, the chapter reviews the current status and future development given to a contingency theory of management.

Chapter 16 devotes attention to social responsibility. The modern business firm realizes that it must be responsible, not only to the needs of its customers and workers but also to the public at large. This chapter discusses equal opportunity, ecology, and consumerism, with major consideration given to the challenges they present to business.

THE FUTURE OF MANAGEMENT THEORY

Chapter 17 focuses on the challenges and opportunities facing those firms that decide to expand their operations into the international arena. Particular attention will be devoted to evaluating the possible advantages and disadvantages associated with going overseas; the various issues in organizing, staffing, and controlling such an undertaking; and the role of the multinational American corporation in the international economic arena.

The purpose of Chapter 18 is to draw together what has been said so far and offer predictions for the future. The chapter also focuses attention on the subject of management careers. The chapter first gives a brief review of the schools of modern management and then discusses future developments, with primary consideration being given to corporate democracy; the management of personnel; and the continuing trend toward managerial professionalism.

In discussing the subject of careers in management, Chapter 18 explores some of the necessary steps in job hunting; the initial frustrations and anxieties that young managers are likely to encounter and how they can be dealt with; and the mapping out of a career plan. Readers of this chapter will have a basic idea of where the field of management is going during the 1980s and will also be aware of some of the challenges and rewards available to successful managers in modern organizations.

CHAPTER 15

MANAGEMENT THEORY: CURRENT STATUS AND FUTURE DIRECTION

GOALS OF THE CHAPTER

The current major schools of management thought have now been presented. The question remaining is: Where does management theory go from here? The answer, of course, is that no one knows for sure. However, two major lines of thought currently have the greatest support. The first contends that the three schools—process, quantitative, and behavioral—will merge into a systems school. One group of authors has summarized the position in this way:

> Although the process, behavioral, and quantitative approaches have been widely adopted, a growing group of practitioners and academicians have felt that another approach—the systems approach—would encompass the subsystems emanating from each of the other approaches.[1]

If this is true, the development of modern management theory can be represented by Figure 15–1.

There seems to be more support, however, for the second point of view, which holds that a systems school of thought already exists and that the trend is now toward a situational, or contingency, theory of management. This thinking is represented by Figure 15–2.

If one keeps in mind that Figures 15–1 and 15–2 represent only two major points of view and that many scholars and practitioners have their own ideas, it should be evident that there is currently much disagreement about the future direction of management theory.

However, one thing does seem clear. Any examination of the current status and future direction of management theory must consider the subject of systems. Such questions as these—What is a system? How is the concept valuable in management theory? Is there a systems

---

[1] Max S. Wortman, Jr., and Fred Luthans, eds., *Emerging Concepts in Management*, 2d ed. (New York: Macmillan, 1975), p. 319.

Figure 15–1 *The Future Direction of Management Theory: One View*

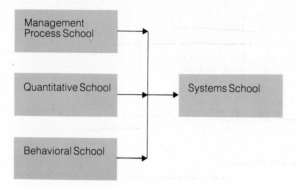

Figure 15–2 *The Future Direction of Management Theory: A Second View*

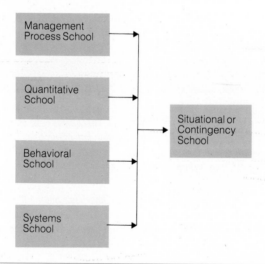

school of thought? —all merit consideration. The goal of this chapter is to deal with these questions and, in the process, to offer some general guidance about the direction management theory is likely to take in the next ten years. Attention will first be focused on what some people call the systems school and on the issues of what the basic systems philosophy is and why it has not been discussed previously. Then the general area of the application of systems to organizations will be examined, followed by a discussion of management theory in the future.

When you have finished this chapter you should be able to:

1. Discuss the systems school of management.
2. Explain why successful organizations have to function like open systems.

3. *Explain how adaptive and maintenance mechanisms are important to organizational survival.*

4. *Describe the three levels of managerial systems and the types of managers who function at each level.*

5. *Give your opinion of where management theory appears to be heading, incorporating into your answer the concept of a contingency theory of management.*

THE SYSTEMS SCHOOL

Some researchers consider that the systems school is a new school of management thought that emerged sometime in the 1960s. Although this is open to question, there are many computer and systems analysts who believe that systems theory has now developed to the stage where the formation of a systems school is justified. Whether or not they are right, it is useful for the student of management to have a general idea of what is meant by the term *systems school*. In essence, two major areas merit consideration. The first, general systems theory, contains the conceptual and philosophical bases of the systems approach.

General Systems Theory

Perhaps the key word in the vocabulary of this school is *system*. Although many definitions are available, one of the most succinct is that put forth by Fremont E. Kast and James E. Rosenzweig: A system is an organized, unitary whole composed of two or more interdependent parts, components, or subsystems and delineated by identifiable boundaries from its environmental suprasystem.[2]

Systems school advocates see all variables in the environment as mutually dependent and interactive. Before the importance of the systems concept to management is examined, some attention should be focused on what is called general systems theory. Systems theorists believe that much of systems management theory originated with general systems theory. In addition, an examination of this topic provides a basis for analyzing other important management related areas, including the movement of individuals into and out of the system; the interaction of individuals with their environment; the interaction of individuals with each other; and the general growth and stability problems of systems.[3]

Many systems management concepts originated with general systems theory.

Systems Levels Perhaps the most famous article written on systems theory is "General Systems Theory—The Skeleton of Science" by Kenneth Boulding.[4] In this article Boulding put forth a classification of the nine hierarchical levels in the universe. He described them as follows:

1. The first level can be called the level of *frameworks* and represents a static structure. Examples include geography and the anatomy of the universe.

2. The next level could be referred to as the level of *clockworks* and is characterized

---

[2] Fremont E. Kast and James E. Rosenzweig, *Organization and Management,* 3d ed. (New York: McGraw-Hill, 1979), p. 18.

[3] Kenneth E. Boulding, "General Systems Theory—The Skeleton of Science," *Management Science,* April 1956, pp. 200–202.

[4] Ibid., pp. 197–208.

by a simple, dynamic system with predetermined, necessary motions. The solar system is an illustration.

3. Next is the level of the control mechanism or cybernetic system, nicknamed the *thermostat* level. The homeostasis model, so important in physiology, is an illustration.

4. Then comes the open system of the self-maintaining structure, which can be called the level of the *cell*. At this level, life and reproduction enter the scheme.

5. The fifth level is the *genetic-societal level*. This is typified by the plant, which dominates the empirical world of the botanist.

6. Next comes the *animal* kingdom. It is characterized by teleological behavior, increased mobility and self-awareness.

7. Then comes the *human level*. In addition to possessing nearly all the characteristics of animal systems, the individual is also capable of employing language and symbols.

8. The eighth level is that of *social organizations*. At this level, concern is given to the content and meaning of messages, the nature and dimension of value systems, the transcription of images into historical records, the subtle symbolizations of art, music and poetry, and the complex gamut of human emotions.

9. The final level of the structure is *transcendental systems*. These are the ultimates, the absolutes and the inescapable unknowables, which exhibit systematic structure and relationship.[5]

Here is Boulding's system classification scheme.

A cursory review of these levels indicates that the first three are concerned with physical or mechanical systems and that they therefore have basic value for people in the physical sciences, such as astronomy and physics. The next three levels deal with biological systems and are thus of interest to biologists, botanists, and zoologists. The last three are concerned with human and social systems and are of importance to the arts, the humanities, the social sciences, and, in a more specialized way, modern management.

This classification scheme is important in understanding the systems school because it contains the basic theme of the systems approach: all phenomena, whether in the universe at large or in a business organization, are related in some way.

A second contribution of Boulding's article is the emphasis it places on integration. One of his major contentions is that specific disciplines are too narrow in their focus, whereas a general approach lacks substantive content.

> Somewhere however between the specific that has no meaning and the general that has no content there must be . . . an optimum degree of generality. It is the contention of the General Systems Theorists that this optimum degree of generality in theory is not always reached by the particular sciences.[6]

Integration of knowledge from many fields is encouraged.

In order to overcome this deficiency, Boulding recommends an integration of knowledge from many fields. "Because, in a sense, each level incorporates all those below it, much valuable information and [many] insights can be obtained by applying low-level systems to high-level subject matter."[7] The thinking of these systems theorists, however, is not confined to such an esoteric area as general systems theory. They have also put forth some concepts that have practical application.

---

[5] Ibid., pp. 202–205.
[6] Ibid., pp. 197–198.
[7] Ibid., p. 207.

"It's a simple system—I file everything under "P" for 'papers'."

Applied Systems Concepts

Proponents of a systems school like to point to useful management tools and techniques that apply the systems concept. Some of these ideas, such as operations research, simulation, PERT, and the critical path method, are directly related to management decision models.

Another set of tools and techniques can be placed under the heading of the systems approach. These are tools that help the manager choose a course of action by analyzing objectives and comparing costs, risks, and payoffs associated with the alternative strategies. By employing a big picture, or systems, approach, the manager can evaluate the interrelationships of all factors under consideration. One such approach, discussed in Chapter 6, is adaptive organization structures. Another, discussed in Chapter 7, is zero-base budgeting. A third, which will be covered in this chapter, is systems engineering.

The third set of systems tools and techniques is in the category of information systems. These are systems designed to provide managers with knowledge and task-specific data useful in carrying out their jobs. Such examples as computers, information theory, and control systems have been discussed in Chapter 10.

These three main types of tools and techniques all provide illustrations of how the systems concept has proved useful to business. They are classified in Figure 15–3.

A School or a Subsystem?

The information presented so far indicates that the systems ideas may well be sufficiently different from those of the process, quantitative, and behavioral approaches to justify the naming of a fourth school of management thought. Critics, however, argue that the systems concept is already being used by the three major schools. For example, many of the ideas in Figure 15–3 have already been examined in the preceding eleven chapters. In addition, process advocates argue that management theory consists of planning,

Several management decision models came from general systems theory.

The systems approach takes the "big picture" view.

Information systems can be valuable.

Is there a systems school of management?

Figure 15–3 A Classification of the Systems School

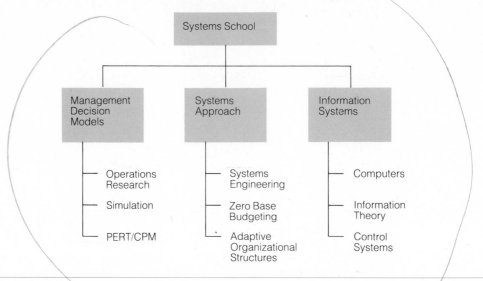

Source: Adapted from Richard Schonberger, "A Taxonomy of Systems Management," *Nebraska Journal of Economics and Business,* Spring, 1973.

organizing, and controlling processes; each is thus an interrelated subsystem of the overall management system. Behavioralists claim that for years they have been viewing the organization as a group of interrelated formal and informal systems. Quantitative school proponents feel that the systems school is really a part of their own; certainly that was how the school was presented in Chapters 3 and 10 of this text. Systems analysts, computer programmers, and so on, were all placed in the quantitative school, and there is a good reason for this. As one researcher has noted:

> Starting in about 1970, the quantitative approach turned away from emphasis on narrow operations research techniques toward a broader perspective of management science. The management science approach incorporates quantitative decision techniques and model building as in the OR approach, but it also incorporates computerized information systems and operations management. This latter emphasis in the quantitative approach marked the return toward a more broadly based management theory.[8]

The systems concept has general value for management

Is the systems approach, then, sufficiently different to justify a new school; or is it really a subsystem of one or more of the current approaches? For the purposes of this text the systems approach will be considered a part of the quantitative area.

Yet the systems concept itself is too important to be dropped without further elaboration. It contains many useful ideas for the student of management. One of these is the technique of viewing the organization as an open system.

---

[8] Fred Luthans, "The Contingency Theory of Management," *Business Horizons,* June 1973, p. 68.

Figure 15–4 An Open System

Figure 15–5 The Organization as an Open System

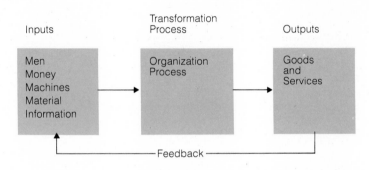

THE ORGANIZATION AS AN OPEN SYSTEM

When the planning process was discussed in Chapter 4, the areas of environmental analysis and forecasting were examined. Likewise, in Chapter 5, when the organizing process was reviewed, common forms of departmentalization were examined. However, when these processes are analyzed from a systems approach, the organization is seen as operating in an open system, constantly interacting with its external environment. These *open systems* are characterized by flexible equilibrium, as depicted in Figure 15–4. They are continually receiving external inputs, which in turn are being transformed into outputs. Information on the adequacy of the output is fed back into the system for purposes of adjustment and correction; all this is shown in the model in Figure 15–4.

Open systems constantly interact with their external environments.

One common open system, familiar to all, is the biological system. In the case of fish, for example, the input could be food, which is transformed into energy and results in a healthy and perhaps larger fish. If one wished to go further into the fish system, changes could be made in the environment. For example, one might add warm water to the tank and see how the fish adapt to the new surroundings. In both cases, external inputs are introduced into the process and transformed into some kind of outputs.

The same process can be applied to a business organization. For example, a host of economic resources serve as inputs—money, machines, material, and information. In systems theory thinking, these can be combined in some fashion (organization process) for the purpose of attaining certain output, as seen in Figure 15–5.

This basic model can be made more sophisticated by breaking down the organizational process into some preliminary design—for example, marketing, production, and

Figure 15–6   A More Refined Design of an Open System

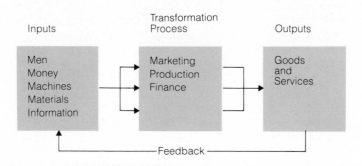

finance departments; such a process is illustrated in Figure 15–6. In this illustration, the relationships between each of the departments and (a) the external environment, (b) the other two departments, and (c) the organization at large become clearer.

Adaptive and Maintenance Mechanisms

Two other important systems concepts useful in analyzing open systems are adaptive and maintenance structures. In an open system, the organization must be able to adapt. At the same time, however, it must maintain a relative state of balance. Two mechanisms are thus in operation. The first, *adaptive mechanisms,* encourage response to the external and internal environments. The second, *maintenance mechanisms,* attempt to stop the system from changing so rapidly that it is thrown out of balance. While the two mechanisms may sometimes be in conflict, both are vital to an organization's survival. However, there are problems which arise in the use of both adaptive and maintenance mechanisms.

Adaptive forces lead to change and keep the organization viable, but they can also create tension and stress. For example, consider the case of a business firm that wishes to hire a junior accountant. The company needs the person to help handle the increase in accounts that has occurred over the last year. It turns out, however, that the starting salary for such an accountant is higher than that of some lower-level managers who have been with the firm for three years. The company must hire the accountant if it is to keep up, but doing so may create anxiety among the established management personnel. Although this may be a natural reaction, it illustrates the problems associated with adapting to environmental conditions.

Adaptive mechanisms lead to change.

Maintenance forces are conservative influences that work to prevent disequilibrium. The problem is that they may stunt an organization's growth by encouraging timidity when boldness is needed. In addition, excessive attention to maintenance factors can result in a breakdown of the open system. In Figure 15–6, this process could begin if the firm decided not to hire the new accountant. By choosing to maintain present conditions, the company would fail to adapt to its external environment. If it continued to ignore developments in the external arena, concentrating all of its attention on maintaining intracompany equilibrium, the firm would become a closed system. When this occurs, the business faces the danger of entropy.

Maintenance mechanisms are conservative influences.

Entropy and Contrived Adaptivity

One of the characteristics of a closed system is entropy. This term originated in thermodynamics, and it refers to the tendency of a closed system to move toward a chaotic, random, or inert state. Webster defines entropy as "the ultimate state reached in the degradation of the matter and energy of the universe."[9] All closed physical systems are subject to this force of entropy. Over a period of time the force increases and, ultimately, the system stops. Since a closed network has no external inputs, the system has no real hope for survival. Eventually, entropy will take its toll.

In open biological and social systems, however, entropy can be arrested and may even be transformed, through external inputs, into negative entropy. Biological systems, at least in the short run, provide a good illustration. Drawing upon the resources in their surroundings, organisms are able to survive for a period of time. For most humans, food, clothing, and shelter are the basic resources. As one ages, increased attention is given to medicine. Eventually, however, death occurs, for even biological systems are subject to deterioration.

Social systems, however, are another matter; they are not mechanical or biological, they are contrived. Human beings establish them for a particular purpose and although the founding individuals may die, others can take their place and keep the system alive. As Daniel Katz and Robert L. Kahn note:

> Social structures are essentially contrived systems. People invent the complex pattern of behavior that we call social structure, and people create social structure by enacting those patterns of behavior. Many properties of social systems derive from these essential facts. As human inventions, social systems are imperfect. They can come apart at the seams overnight, but they can also outlast by centuries the biological organisms that originally created them. The cement which holds them together is essentially psychological rather than biological. Social systems are anchored in the attitudes, perceptions, beliefs, motivations, habits, and expectations of human beings.[10]

In order for the social system to continue, however, there must be the proper balance between maintenance and adaptive forces. Maintenance forces are motivated toward maintaining stability and predictability within the organization. They work to preserve a state of equilibrium. These forces, for example, encourage the organization to make no appreciable shifts in the current pattern of activities. If the company wants to sell more goods and services, it should work toward getting current customers to buy more. In short, maintenance forces urge the organization to maintain the status quo. On the other hand are adaptive forces, which are pushing the organization to respond to external environmental factors such as changes in the marketplace. Rather than trying to sell more goods and services to the same customers, these forces encourage an expansion of market activities by offering new products and services in new market niches. Adaptive forces encourage the organization to generate appropriate responses to external conditions.[11]

These systems concepts—flexible equilibrium, adaptive mechanisms, maintenance mechanisms, entropy, and contrived adaptivity—are all useful in understanding the truly dynamic nature of the modern organization. It is important to realize, however, that an effective organization can also employ these concepts in maintaining a viable, adaptive, ongoing organization system.

Closed systems are characterized by entropy.

Social systems are contrived.

---

[9] *Webster's Third New International Dictionary*, s. v. "entropy."

[10] Daniel Katz and Robert L. Kahn, *The Social Psychology of Organizations*, 2d ed. (New York: Wiley, 1978). p. 37.

[11] Ibid., chap. 4.

Figure 15–7   A Totally Adaptive Organization System

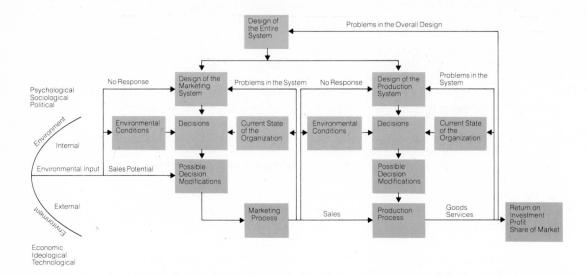

Source: Adapted from Stanley D. Young, "Organization Total System," *Proceedings of the 4th Annual Midwest Management Conference,* Carbondale, Illinois, 1966.

TOTALLY ADAPTIVE ORGANIZATION SYSTEMS

Adaptive organizations can survive indefinitely.

The organization is a man-made system, capable of indefinite survival if the proper balance between maintenance and adaptive forces can be attained. Figure 15–7 provides an illustration of a totally adaptive business organization system. The figure shows how marketing and production activities can be carried on in the attainment of organizational goals. The finance department and the rest of the enterprise are represented in the boxes entitled "Current State of the Organization," indicating that the decisions made by both marketing and production depend on conditions in the remainder of the organization. A control process is also built into the model which will, in turn, lead to a redesign of the marketing and/or production systems should disequilibrium occur. The model adapts itself to changing conditions by continuously contrasting internal and external environmental conditions and the effect of both on the goals being pursued.

Total systems design has great promise.

The concept of total systems design is not, of course, restricted to business organizations. It can be applied to such diverse activities as police work and city planning as long as the total system is examined. Any attempt to deal with the organization on a micro-level can have disastrous effects because all input factors are not being considered. For example, in police work the objective is to prevent crime. One of the best ways to do this is to concentrate resources on high-crime areas and thereby discourage potential criminals as well as apprehend those who have committed crimes. This can be done by feeding information about people and living conditions in the city into a computer which can then analyze the data and provide relevant information to the police regarding how to organize their forces.

Various cities have used this basic approach in attempts to identify trouble spots. For example, teams of mathematicians, economists, physicists, political scientists, and sociologists can be employed as "idea people," to construct a mathematical model of a city. Then, after the environment of the metropolis is simulated, a computer can be used to analyze the results and identify those sectors of the city where problems are most likely to occur. Through the use of employment data, living conditions, and other social factors, it has been possible to pinpoint such problems as high crime areas, locales where social services are required, and neighborhoods which are becoming overly crowded and in need of assistance.

Another example of the total systems approach to organizing resources is the building of new cities. After determining the site location, ad hoc task forces consisting of psychologists, sociologists, religious leaders, medical planners and care givers, and other persons with relevant knowledge work with architects and planners to determine that the social and institutional needs of the city will be met.

It is apparent by now that systems concepts are very useful in both understanding an organization and relating it to its environment. The general systems concept can also be applied within the firm in the examination of managerial systems.

MANAGERIAL SYSTEMS

The organization has been viewed as an open, adaptive system. Attention will now be focused on managerial systems. Talcott Parsons has suggested three managerial levels in the hierarchy of complex organizations: technical, organizational, and institutional.[12]

The *technical level* is concerned with the actual production and distribution of products and services. This not only entails turning out physical output but also includes the areas that support this activity—research and development, operations research, and accounting.

The *organizational level* coordinates and integrates work performance at the technical level. It is concerned with obtaining the continued flow of inputs into the system, maintaining the necessary markets for the outputs from the system, determining the nature of technical tasks, ascertaining the scale of operations, and establishing operating policies.

The *institutional level* is concerned with relating the activities of the organization to the environmental system. As Parsons notes, the organization not only has to

operate in a social environment which imposes the conditions governing the processes of disposal and procurement, it is also part of a wider social system which is the source of the "meaning," legitimation, or higher level support which makes the implementation of the organization's goals possible. Essentially, this means that just as a technical organization (at a sufficiently high level of the division of labor) is controlled and "serviced" by a managerial organization, so, in turn, is the managerial organization controlled by the "institutional" structure and agencies of the community.[13]

The managerial system spans all three levels by organizing the people, directing the technical work, and relating the organization to its environment. These three levels are illustrated as a composite system in Figure 15–8.

The technical level, or core, is concerned with turning out a product or service at a profit. In order to do this, it often attempts to set up a boundary between itself and the external environment, thereby forming a closed system. The reasoning is that if the envi-

---

[12] The middle level in Talcott Parsons's hierarchy will be referred to here as "the organizational level," since there are managers at all three levels. Parsons, though, actually called the second level "the management level."

[13] Talcott Parsons, *Structure and Process in Modern Societies* (New York: Free Press, 1960), pp. 63–64.

Figure 15–8 The Organization as a Composite System

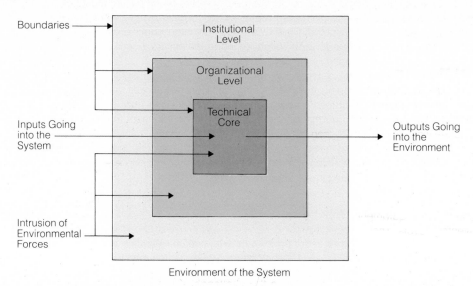

Boundaries

Institutional Level

Organizational Level

Technical Core

Inputs Going into the System

Outputs Going into the Environment

Intrusion of Environmental Forces

Environment of the System

Source: Adapted by permission from Thomas A. Petit, "A Behavioral Theory of Management," *Academy of Management Journal,* December 1967, p. 346.

ronment is too dynamic, it will never get anything done; the people in it will be continually responding to external influences. Modern technology provides an illustration of the intruding environmental force and its effect at this level. For example, companies often find that the products they are manufacturing are obsolete even before they leave the assembly line. However, at some point the design must be frozen and production begun. The technical core is subject to external influences, but it does attempt to minimize them.

Conversely, the institutional level experiences a great degree of uncertainty over environmental conditions, and the organization is unable to set up major boundaries. As a result, management at this level is by nature a very open system, and primary attention is devoted to innovation or adaptation.

The organizational level operates between these two extremes. It coordinates the technical and institutional levels, tries to straighten out irregularities and disturbances occurring in both, and serves as an all-around mediator. In a manner of speaking, it is a buffer between the maintenance (technical level) and the adaptive (institutional level) mechanisms. Thomas A. Petit has described the three levels in this way:

> The technical level has a boundary that does not seal it off entirely from the firm's environment but does have a high degree of closure. The organizational level has less closure and consequently is more susceptible to the intrusion of external elements. The institutional level has a highly permeable boundary and therefore is strongly affected by uncontrollable and unpredictable elements in the environment.[14]

Technical level is highly oriented to closed systems.

Institutional level is very open-system-oriented.

Organizational level coordinates the other two levels.

---

[14] Thomas A. Petit, "A Behavioral Theory of Management," *Academy of Management Journal,* December 1967, p. 346.

The three levels are interrelated, constituting subsystems in this overall organizational structure. Each level has individual characteristics, but coordination among them is necessary for effective performance. At the same time, however, it is possible to examine the specific requirements of each organizational level in order to classify the managers who work there.

Types of Managers

In the past, most managers were classified by organizational level (executive, middle manager, first-line supervisor) or function (sales manager, production manager, financial manager). Today, however, managers are being classified according to many criteria, including the work itself, time horizon, and decision-making strategy.

Technical Managers Because *technical managers* are concerned with producing goods and services as economically as possible, they tend to have an engineering point of view. They are also pragmatic, quick to adopt what will work for them and discard what will not. They like problems with concrete solutions, such as what criteria to employ when investing in fixed equipment or the optimal relation that should exist between production and inventory levels. They work best when confronted with quantitative (as opposed to qualitative) issues. They also tend to have a very short-run time horizon, being most interested in the operational aspects of the job.

Technical managers have engineering viewpoints.

Institutional Managers *Institutional managers* face the challenge of coping with uncertainty brought on by uncontrollable and unpredictable environmental elements. For them, major concern rests with ensuring the organization's survival. This is done in two ways. First, institutional managers continually survey the environment, noting both opportunities and threats. Second, based on the findings, they develop cooperative and competitive strategies for dealing with these elements, thereby reducing uncertainty. In order to conduct this surveillance and construct viable strategies, they need to have a long-run time perspective. They tend to be philosophical in viewpoint, capable of translating qualitative environmental changes into quantitative estimates of their impact on the organization. This requires wisdom, experience, and good judgment in the formulation of strategy.

Institutional managers have philosophical viewpoints.

Organizational Managers As already noted, *organizational managers* coordinate the efforts of the technical and institutional levels. In order to do this, the organizational manager needs to be something of a politician, capable of adopting a short- or long-run perspective, depending on the situation, and able to achieve a compromise between the technical and institutional managers. As Petit has noted in his article:

Organizational managers are mediators.

> Organizational managers use the decision-making strategy of compromise. The best interests of the firm are not served by following either the computational [technical manager] or judgmental [institutional manager] strategies exclusively. The organizational managers attempt to influence the balance between the two according to the nature of the problems facing the firm. Since these problems may be either immediate or in the future, organizational managers have both a short-run and a long-run time horizon.
>
> The viewpoint of the organizational manager is basically political. He must always be concerned with what is possible rather than ideal in mediating between technical and institutional managers.[15]

Table 15–1 shows the differences among these three types of managers.

---

[15] Ibid., p. 348.

Table 15–1 Characteristics of Managers in the Managerial System

Type of Manager	Task	Point of View	Technique	Time Perspective	Decision-Making Strategy
Technical	Technical rationality	Engineering	Quantitative	Short-run	Computational
Organizational	Coordination	Political	Mediation	Both short- and long-run	Compromise
Institutional	Deal with uncertainty and relate the organization to its environment	Philosophical and conceptual	Environmental survey; strategy formulation	Long-run	Subjective and judgmental

Source: Adapted by permission from Thomas A. Petit, "A Behavioral Theory of Management," *Academy of Management Journal,* December 1967, p. 349.

THE SYSTEMS POINT OF VIEW

The systems point of view suggests that management continually faces a dynamic environment consisting of forces that are not within its total control. Of course, some organizations have attempted to overcome this problem. The giant trusts of the early 1900s and the major conglomerates of today both represent attempts by powerful organizations to obtain major control over their environment. For the most part, however, the organization and the environment still constitute interacting forces.

The same pattern exists within the organization itself. Managers in all departments and at all levels are interdependent. Job descriptions and work assignments, for example, represent only general guidelines regarding what the managers are supposed to be doing. In actuality, as Leonard Sayles noted in his well-known book, *Managerial Behavior,* the

> systems concept emphasizes that managerial assignments do not have these neat, clearly defined boundaries; rather, the modern manager is placed in a network of mutually dependent relationships. . . . The one enduring objective is the effort to build and maintain a predictable, reciprocating system of relationships, the behavioral patterns of which stay within reasonable physical limits. But this is seeking a moving equilibrium, since the parameters of the system (the division of labor and the controls) are evolving and changing. Thus the manager endeavors to introduce regularity in a world that will never allow him to achieve the ideal. . . . Only managers who can deal with uncertainty, with ambiguity, and with battles that are never won but only fought well can hope to succeed.[16]

Organizing is a dynamic process.

This appears to be a very radical change from the organizing process that was discussed in Chapter 5 in very clear, rigid, and easy-to-grasp terms. The process may now seem to have become topsy-turvy. It must be remembered, however, that with this modern systems view the element of dynamism takes on new dimensions; and the heretofore simple concepts of planning, organizing, and controlling are viewed from a much more flexible and realistic perspective.

[16] Leonard Sayles, *Managerial Behavior* (New York: McGraw-Hill, 1964), pp. 258–259.

MANAGEMENT THEORY IN THE FUTURE

At this point no one can definitively state what will happen by 1990 in the development of management theory. However, there is a current trend toward at least a partial synthesis of these three schools of thought. This is a welcome sign, given the fact that some researchers, such as Harold Koontz, have found that the number of different groups or schools has actually increased in the last twenty years as a result of their splitting off from current ones. For example, while this text addressed researchers and theorists who have an economic or mathematical orientation as members of the quantitative school, Koontz reports that there are now three subsets of this school: mathematics, decision theory, and economic theory groups.[17] The current status of management theory is therefore more cluttered than ever—if one wants to look only at the bleak side of the picture. There is also a basis for optimism, for recent research also reveals that certain signs show the various schools beginning now to synthesize somewhat.

Signs of Synthesis

The current convergence of thinking is still in its formative stage, but a number of reported developments indicate a trend toward partial synthesis. Some of the major cited reasons include the following:

1. There is now a much greater emphasis on the distillation of fundamental management concepts than there has been at any point in the past.
2. It is now becoming increasingly clear that the systems approach to management is not unique; nor does it represent a better way of managing. Rather, it is part and parcel of the manager's job. Far from being a school of thought, it is now being recognized simply as a means of carrying out managerial tasks.
3. It is also increasingly clear that the contingency approach to management is not new. Managers have been using it for years. However, the fact that contingency research in such areas as organizing, motivating, and leading is now being actively pursued will increase our understanding of these processes and how to carry them out more effectively.
4. It is now being recognized that management theory is not as broad a topic area as is organization theory. The latter refers to almost any type of interpersonal relationship. Today's management scholars are realizing that they should be addressing management theory, a narrower field and one which is easier to research and understand.
5. There is currently more information about motivation than ever before. Of course, this provides a better understanding of how and why people act as they do. In particular, attention to organizational climate and the way in which it affects motivation is receiving productive attention.
6. A melding of motivation and leadership theory is taking place, since researchers have realized that the two are interdependent and that both are affected by organizational climate.
7. A coalescence is also taking place between studies of individual and group behavior. Researchers interested in studying one are realizing that the other cannot be ignored. In fact, writers in the field of organizational behavior are now beginning to understand that behavioral elements in group operations must be closely integrated with organization design, staffing, planning, and controlling.

---

[17] Harold Koontz, "The Management Theory Jungle Revisited," *Academy of Management Review*, April 1980, p. 182.

---

8. The impact of technology on organizational structure, behavioral patterns, and the overall management process is now being recognized and better understood.
9. Some management scientists are beginning to see that their emphasis on quantitative tools is insufficient to get things done. The manager's job is more encompassing and complex than this and there is now a move toward incorporating more nonquantitative emphases into their approaches.
10. Finally, more of an effort is being made toward clarifying management terms and thereby overcoming misapplications of semantics, one of the greatest causes of what Koontz has called the management theory jungle. Many texts in the field, including this one, contain glossaries which define key terms operatively, as they are used throughout the book.[18]

But That Is All

The ten points listed above encapsulate findings from the recent literature. Many are not at all surprising. They already have been clearly enunciated in this text. However, a final warning is in order for those who are optimistic enough to believe that the schools of management thought that were studied in the last twelve chapters will soon fade. It must be remembered that these schools are a partial result of the training, experience, and personal attitudes of the members. It is unlikely that behavioralists will soon abandon their orientation to the study of management at work in order to join ranks with management process people. Nor are the latter likely to change their minds and feel that the quantitative people or the behavioralists have better insights to the study of management than theirs. Each still has personal biases. It is thus unreasonable to expect anything more in the 1980s than a general synthesis of some interrelated areas of concern. Some progress has been made; much more is yet to come:

> Despite some signs of hope, the fact is that the management theory jungle is still with us. Although some slight progress appears to be occurring, in the interest of a far better society through improved managerial practice it is to be hoped that some means can be found to accelerate this progress.[19]

SUMMARY

This chapter has examined the so-called systems school of management. Attention was first focused on general systems theory because of the importance assigned to it by systems school advocates. Then the applied concepts of the systems approach, likewise presented from its advocates' point of view, were reviewed. Finally, the question of whether the systems approach is a new school or a subsystem of a current one was examined. Although it is difficult to deny the existence of a systems body of knowledge, it appears that the systems school is actually part of the quantitative school.

Attention was then focused on the general value of understanding the systems concept, beginning with the organization as an open, adaptive system. Since business organizations are contrived systems, they can survive the onset of entropy and, unlike their biological counterparts, exist indefinitely, depending, of course, on how well they are managed. On the one hand, they must be responsive to change (adaptive mechanisms); on the other hand, they must not change so quickly that they are seriously thrown out of equilibrium (maintenance mechanisms). Finding the right balance is one of the keys to indefinite survival.

---

[18] Koontz has written more on this subject in his April 1980 article.
[19] Koontz, "The Management Theory Jungle Revisited," p. 186.

The systems concept was next used to examine managerial systems. Three levels exist in the managerial system of a complex organization: technical, organizational, and institutional. The technical level is concerned with producing the goods or services. The organizational level coordinates and integrates the technical and institutional levels. The institutional level relates the activities of the organization to the environmental system. Within this system are three types of managers, one for each of the levels. The technical manager is a nuts-and-bolts individual; the organization manager is more like a political mediator; and the institutional manager is a conceptual-philosophical decision maker. Yet, although there are different levels and interests within the structure, all three must combine their talents and energies in the attainment of overall organizational objectives.

In order to do this, managers must plan, organize, and control. They must also make decisions and employ the latest quantitative methods where applicable; and they must understand and utilize the abilities of their subordinates through effective communication, motivation, and leadership. In short, the management process, quantitative, and behavioral schools are all still important to modern managers. In fact, managers today draw on the concepts of all three in carrying out their duties. The systems approach encourages this.

The last section of the chapter examined management theory in the future, noting that some synthesis among the schools of management thought appears to be going on. Ten specific reasons were cited. However, it was also noted that this synthesis is unlikely to result in a major change in the three schools of thought explored in this textbook. The management process school, the quantitative school, and the behavioral school of management thought will continue to endure into the indefinite future.

REVIEW AND STUDY QUESTIONS

1. Of what value is general systems theory to the systems school of management? Explain.
2. What is an open system?
3. How does a system show the impact of entropy?
4. In what way is a business organization a contrived system?
5. What are maintenance mechanisms? What are adaptive mechanisms? How do they affect the organization structure?
6. What is a totally adaptive organization?
7. Describe each of the three managerial levels in the hierarchy of complex organizations.
8. Explain how the tasks and viewpoints of the managers of these three hierarchical levels differ.
9. Of what value is the systems approach to the practicing manager?
10. Identify and describe five signs of synthesis among the schools of management.

SELECTED REFERENCES

Boulding, Kenneth E. "General Systems Theory—The Skeleton of Science." *Management Science,* April 1956, pp. 197–208.

Cleland, David I., and King, W. R. *Management: A Systems Approach.* 2d ed. New York: McGraw-Hill, 1975.

Duncan, W. J. "Transferring Management Theory to Practice." *Academy of Management Journal,* December 1974, pp. 724–738.

Greenwood, W. T. "Future Management Theory: A 'Comparative' Evolution to a General Theory." *Academy of Management Journal,* September 1974, pp. 500–513.

Kast, F. E., and Rosenzweig, J. E. "General Systems Theory: Applications for Organization and Management." *Academy of Management Journal,* December 1972, pp. 447–465.

———. *Organization and Management.* 3d ed. New York: McGraw-Hill, 1979.

Koontz, Harold. "The Management Theory Jungle." *Academy of Management Journal,* December 1961, pp. 174–188.

———. "The Management Theory Jungle Revisited." *Academy of Management Review,* April 1980, pp. 175–187.

Luthans, Fred. "The Contingency Theory of Management." *Business Horizons,* June 1973, pp. 67–72.

Luthans, Fred, and Stewart, T. "A General Contingency Theory of Management." *Academy of Management Review,* April 1977, pp. 181–195.

Mintzberg, Henry. "The Manager's Job: Folklore and Fact." *Harvard Business Review,* July–August 1975, pp. 49–61.

———. *The Nature of Managerial Work.* New York: Harper & Row, 1973.

Nehrbass, R. G. "Ideology and the Decline of Management Theory." *Academy of Management Review,* July 1979, pp. 427–431.

Petit, Thomas A. "A Behavioral Theory of Management." *Academy of Management Journal,* December 1967, pp. 341–350.

Robbins, S. P. "Reconciling Management Theory with Management Practice." *Business Horizons,* February 1977, pp. 38–47.

Von Bertalanffy, L. "The History and Status of General Systems Theory." *Academy of Management Journal,* December 1972, pp. 407–426.

Wooten, L. M. "The Mixed Blessings of Contingency Management." *Academy of Management Review,* July 1977, pp. 431–441.

Wortman, Max S., Jr., and Luthans, Fred, eds. *Emerging Concepts in Management.* 2d ed. New York: Macmillan, 1975.

CASE: *A Great Big Secret*

Jackson & Jackson, a large west coast manufacturer, instituted an in-house supervisory training program under its new president, William Hopkinson. During the initial phase, 10 percent of the managers received training related to both the technical and human relations sides of their jobs. Some critics of the program suggested that the training be suspended at this point since it was really of little value to the supervisors. An analysis of the results, however, showed that all managers participating in this initial training phase had been able to attain an increase in their units' output. The training therefore continued.

Over the next twelve months all the remaining supervisors were put through the program. During this period, productivity increased 27 percent over that of the previous year. In commenting on the value of the program, the vice-president of manufacturing said that she had noticed a number of the supervisors entering the plant earlier than usual in the morning and some staying past the closing whistle.

The results led proponents of the program to call it an unqualified success, but its opponents disagreed. Their arguments took two lines of attack. First, they pointed out that not all supervisors had been able to attain productivity increases. If the training was in fact beneficial, they should have been able to accomplish this. Second, they argued that the surge in output would be short-lived. One of them put it this way:

> What we have here is the old "Hawthorne effect." The supervisors are all excited about being part of this new program, but it won't last long. The training is now complete and the novelty is already beginning to wear thin. Everyone will soon be returning to their old way of doing things. That's the problem with training programs. The initial results are fantastic, but they soon drop off.
>
> Besides all that, we've also got another old standby, the cause-effect identification problem. Look at it this way. We have a new input—the training program. We have a new output—27 percent increase in productivity. But what causes this increase? Is it really the training program, or is it something else? What takes place in the transformation process, the black box? We all know that no one knows, so why attribute it to the training program? Maybe these productivity increases would have occurred in any event. Who knows? It's really all a great big secret.

Questions

1. Something is taking place in the transformation process that is causing a 27 percent productivity increase. What is it? Explain your answer, employing the systems concept.

2. Why does the last speaker in this case refer to the productivity increase as a "great big secret"?

CASE: Input/Output

The union at MacKelvey Incorporated had been negotiating a new contract with management for more than three months; and with only thirty days of bargaining time left, there still was no agreement. The management was willing to give an 8.4 percent increase in salary and a 6 percent increase in fringe benefits; the union was asking for 10 and 6.9 percent respectively. However, Paul Aherne, MacKelvey's vice-president of industrial relations, who had been heading the negotiations all along, reported to the president, Georgia Neffen, that he felt an agreement might be near.

"Mrs. Neffen, I think the union would settle for a 9.1 percent salary raise and a 6.3 percent increase in fringe benefits. We've done quite a bit of negotiating over the past 10 weeks, and I'm sure I understand them."

Mrs. Neffen looked noncommittal. "Actually, Mr. Aherne, the board of directors had hoped that the 8.4 and 6 percent proposals would lead to a contract."

"I see little chance of that, Mrs. Neffen. If we maintain our present position, we'll either have to hope that the union is willing to work without a contract or face the very real possibility of a strike."

"Obviously, neither of those alternatives is going to be viewed very favorably by the board. On the other hand, we certainly don't want to negotiate a contract any higher than we have to."

"Mrs. Neffen, let me be frank. I think we're almost there now. However, if we force the union to work without a contract or, heaven forbid, strike, we're going to damage one of our most important assets—union-management harmony. We have to think of the workers as inputs in the process of management. If we do something to that input, we stand the chance of seriously endangering the output, namely, our products and services. I think we should promote the goodwill that currently exists between us."

Questions

1. If you regard the workers as an input and the goods and services as an output, how would you describe the transformation process in this case?

2. How does this union contract negotiation fit into a discussion of the systems approach to management?

3. Do you think the company would be wise to follow the advice of its vice-president of industrial relations? Explain your opinion.

CASE: Modifications, Modifications

John Chilvers was angry. For the past twelve months he had been in charge of designing a new jet fighter for the United States Navy. After countless days of revising the initial design and incorporating extensive changes, his group was prepared to submit its design for approval. However, just as they were about to do this, Chilvers received a call from his boss asking him to come up to the office immediately.

The boss said: "John, I've called you in because before you submit your plan I want you to know that there's a lot of pressure on us to present the most sophisticated design possible. In addition, if there are any major flaws that result in eventual cost overruns, we're really going to be in trouble. Congress is fed up with paying for contractor mistakes."

"Mr. Adkinson, we've designed this craft five times now. I don't think there's a thing we haven't changed for the better at one time or another. I think it will be the finest plane the navy has ever had," Chilvers replied.

"I'm glad to hear that, John, because the president has really sold the big brass on this one."

"Well, believe me, sir, when we submit our design later in the week, they'll be impressed."

"Actually, John, we want you to wait a month before doing that. We still have a little time before the drawings are due, and the president has asked me to have you go over the material once more."

Chilvers bristled. "What for?"

"To see if you can't improve it a little bit. Surely there's something new you can add here and there," Adkinson said.

"Mr. Adkinson, if you gave me a year I could design an aircraft that's twice as good as this one, but I think there's a point beyond which it's not practical to go. We have a contract and a design that more than fulfills its requirements. At some point you have to quit making changes, freeze the plan, and get on with the production. If we keep delaying, we'll never get to the manufacturing stage."

"Oh, John," said a tolerant-looking Adkinson. "I understand that, of course. But the president wants to be sure that the design is as good as possible. So for the next month I want you and your team to review and make any minor modifications on the material which will improve the overall design."

Questions

1. Would you classify Chilvers as a technical, organizational, or institutional manager? Explain.

2. Is Adkinson a technical, organizational, or institutional manager? Explain. How about the president? Explain.

3. How does Chilvers's viewpoint as a manager differ from that of his superior? Be specific.

Sandra Bashion, general manager of a major food chain, met with her people once a month. She liked to regard these meetings as a chance to communicate new ideas and exchange information on any problems that had arisen in the recent month. During one of these meetings she brought up the topic of a systems approach to management. She had recently done some reading on the subject and felt it could be applied to the management of her own stores. She said to the group,

> *"You know, another thing I want all of you to start doing is to think of your department as a system. This is a new idea in management, but it's a real good one."*

One of the managers asked Bashion what she meant by a "system." She responded:

> *"A system is a host of interrelated items. Each has an effect on and can be influenced by the others. It's like the human body. An attack on any one part can influence the other parts because the body is a system. An organization is the same. If any one part of it has trouble, this can affect the other parts. You should do some reading on this topic. I'll have my secretary send all of you some references on the subject."*

With this the meeting broke up and the managers began filing out. Some of them went across the street for lunch. During the meal, the following conversation took place:

> *"You know, I'd still like to know how the organization is like a system. That part went right by me."*
> *"Don't feel bad. I doubt whether anyone understood what Bashion was talking about."*
> *"I wonder if she knew."*
> *"Well, if she did or if she didn't, if she sends us that material, we can read it and find out what it is all about. Sometimes I think Bashion throws out new ideas before she really understands them herself."*

Questions

1. What is the systems approach to management?

2. Does Bashion really understand the systems concept? Explain.

3. What should a person know to fully understand the systems approach?

CHAPTER 16

SOCIAL RESPONSIBILITY: A CONTINUING CHALLENGE

Social responsibility has been a continuing challenge to business in the 1960s and the 1970s. The term *social responsibility* is generally defined as those obligations a firm has to the society in which it operates. More specifically, businesses are realizing that this responsibility encompasses three major areas: equal opportunity, ecology, and consumerism. This chapter examines each of these issues, studying what they are and the types of responses business is making toward them.

When you have finished this chapter, you should be able to:

1. Define what is meant by the doctrine of enlightened self-interest.
2. Describe the major provisions of the Equal Pay Act of 1963 and the Civil Rights Act of 1964.
3. Relate how business is helping ensure equal opportunity for minority workers, minority capitalists, and the physically and mentally handicapped.
4. Explain the current status of women in business and what is being done to ensure equal opportunity for them.
5. Describe the major ecological challenges facing business and what is being done about them, with primary consideration given to air pollution, water pollution, and noise pollution.
6. Outline some of the major provisions of the Environmental Policy Act of 1969 and the Air Quality Standards Act of 1970.
7. Describe what consumerism is and how business firms are attempting to meet the problems associated with product safety, including some that appear to have been the result of the Consumer Product Safety Act of 1970.
8. Discuss whether social responsibility is a fad or an enduring challenge for business.

ENLIGHTENED SELF-INTEREST

By the 1960s, the United States was the most affluent nation the world had ever known. With this affluence came a social awakening, as many people started questioning conditions in this country and began to call for corrective action in such areas as equal opportunity, ecology, and consumerism. Feeling that the business community had the resources and the know-how to handle problems in these areas, and convinced that many companies had contributed to the problems' existence, the public insisted that business commit part of its efforts to *social responsibility,* the obligations a firm has to the society or community in which it operates and over which it has some economic influence. The public asked businesses to turn toward social activities as well as to its more traditional concerns.

Such action was not in direct accord with many of the traditional objectives of business: profit, survival, and growth. However, it was related by way of the doctrine of *enlightened self-interest,* which holds that business actually serves its own long-run interests when it helps out its own community. For example, since 1935, when the Internal Revenue Code permitted corporations to deduct up to 5 percent of pretax income for charitable contributions, business firms have been extremely active in their support of various charities, even though not everyone has agreed with this action. For example, some stockholders have brought suits against their companies, contending that the contributions are in no way related to the running of the business. The courts, however, have consistently ruled for the firms, holding that such donations do indeed serve the interest of the company even though they provide no direct benefits. In addition, business can contribute to higher education. This issue was settled in 1953 by the New Jersey Superior Court when it ruled that a manufacturing firm could donate funds to Princeton University. The court held that giving financial support was not only a right but a duty, because by helping society the company was actually helping itself. As it was later stated:

By helping society, business serves its own long-run interests.

> *By the same logic, expenditures to help improve community educational, health, and cultural facilities can be justified by the corporation's interest in attracting the skilled people it needs who would not move into a substandard community. Similarly, a corporation whose operations must inevitably take place in urban areas may well be justified in investing in the rehabilitation of ghetto housing and contributing to the improvement of ghetto educational, recreational, and other facilities. . . .*
>
> *Indeed, the corporate interest broadly defined by management can support involvement in helping to solve virtually any social problem, because people who have a good environment, education, and opportunity make better employees, customers and neighbors for business than those who are poor, ignorant, and oppressed.*[1]

The doctrine of enlightened self-interest extends further than merely pointing out the benefits of involvement. It is also based on the proposition that failure to assume social responsibility can jeopardize an organization's welfare. If business does not voluntarily do its share, the government will pass legislation and force it to become involved.

Statistics show that since the mid-1960s business has not only been aware of social change in the United States but has also responded with positive action. What has accounted for this? Some say it has been newly enacted legislation. Others contend that the business community is merely trying to protect its image. Still others say that busi-

---

[1] Research and Policy Committee of the Committee for Economic Development, *Social Responsibilities of Business Corporations: A Statement on National Policy* (New York: Committee for Economic Development, June 1971), pp. 27–28.

nesspeople today are more socially responsible than their predecessors. There is undoubtedly truth in all these statements. Yet, whatever the specific reason, many businesses have been developing programs to cope with the three most important social issues of the day: equal opportunity, ecology, and consumerism.[2]

EQUAL OPPORTUNITY

A number of important areas of equal opportunity action currently provide major challenges to business. In particular, they are legislation, hiring of minorities and the handicapped, support of minority capitalism, and sanctions against discrimination against females.

Legislation

One of the main reasons for the attention business has paid to the area of equal opportunity has been legislation. The two most important laws enacted thus far have been the Equal Pay Act of 1963 and the Civil Rights Act of 1964.

The *Equal Pay Act of 1963* was signed on June 10 of that year. Its purpose is to correct "the existence in industries engaged in commerce, or in the production of goods for commerce, of wage differentials based on sex."[3] Specifically, the act forbids "discrimination on the basis of sex for doing equal work on jobs requiring equal skill, effort and responsibility which are performed under similar working conditions."[4]

The *Civil Rights Act of 1964* was signed on July 2. Of its eleven major sections, Title VII is most important to business because it forbids discrimination on the basis of race, color, religion, sex, or national origin. In addition, the act established an Equal Employment Opportunity Commission (EEOC) composed of five members appointed by the U.S. president and approved by the United States Senate. The commission's job is to investigate complaints, seek to end violations through conciliation, and ask the U.S. attorney general to bring suit if such conciliation is unsuccessful.

The law forbids discrimination in employment.

These laws have been very helpful in providing equal employment, basically because people have not hesitated to use them. For example, in the first eighteen months of its existence, the EEOC received 14,000 complaints. In addition, minority group organizations such as the National Association for the Advancement of Colored People (NAACP) and the Congress on Racial Equality (CORE) have been relatively active in using these laws to bring suit against firms for discriminatory practices. Equal employment, however, has proved to be more than a legal issue. Many firms have voluntarily responded to the challenge by eliminating or reducing their barriers for employment.

Hiring Minorities and the Handicapped

For several years, business firms have made concerted efforts to hire minority group members. Specific programs can be found in literally thousands of companies throughout American industry. These programs range from recruiting and hiring minority employees to training and developing them. Some of the programs are geared more to

---

[2] Fred Luthans, Richard M. Hodgetts, and Kenneth R. Thompson *Social Issues in Business,* 3d ed. (New York: Macmillan, 1980), chaps. 4–10.

[3] U.S. Department of Labor, *Information on the Equal Pay Act of 1963* (Washington, D.C.: Government Printing Office, n.d.), p. 1.

[4] Ibid., p. 2.

the hard-core unemployed, such as black or native American ghetto youth; others extend to minorities in general. However, all have one thing in common: They are designed to provide employment opportunities to those who might otherwise have difficulty getting jobs.

Recently, more and more attention has also been focused on hiring the physically and mentally handicapped. The Vocational Rehabilitation Act of 1973 requires such affirmative action in the case of businesses that have contracts or subcontracts with the federal government. But a recent Department of Labor survey of three hundred companies revealed that 91 percent of the firms were in violation of the act.[5] This apparent noncompliance has led to lawsuits by the federal government, resulting in the prediction by two authors that "in the next several years, the employment rights of the handicapped will be a major issue as well as a focus of government attention—following the path in recent years of women's and minorities' work-related rights."[6] How can business firms rectify the situation and get back into compliance? Some of the most effective steps include the following:

1. Adopt a policy of hiring the handicapped.
2. Post equal opportunity posters in conspicuous locations in the workplace.
3. Notify the union of the company's compliance with the act.
4. Include an affirmative action clause or reference in purchase orders or contracts over $2,500.
5. Review medical questionnaires and application forms; remove any language suggesting inappropriate rejection on the basis of the medical examination.
6. Prepare an annual affirmative action program for on-site inspection by compliance officers.
7. Inform management at all levels about the firm's obligations and ask for support from these individuals.
8. Tell employees and applicants that the firm's employment and affirmative action policy statements are available for inspection.
9. Notify recruiters of the employment policy.
10. Invite handicapped employees to identify themselves and relate their status.
11. Review employment qualifications for the purpose of eliminating discrimination against handicapped employees.
12. Review facilities and equipment for reasonable accommodations to the special needs of the handicapped.

Here are twelve steps for following the Vocational Rehabilitation Act.

Minority Capitalism

Another area where business has been very active is that of promoting minority capitalism. Although some of this activity has been mandated by government, most of it is voluntary.

In 1977 the United States Congress set a precedent by writing into a $4 billion Commerce Department public works appropriation a clause requiring that 10 percent of that total be set aside for minority contractors and subcontractors. Additionally, such federal agencies as the Urban Mass Transportation Administration seek evidence before awarding grants that cities receiving these funds have set aside some of the monies for minority enterprises.

---

[5] Gopal C. Pati and John I. Adkins, Jr., "Hire the Handicapped—Compliance Is Good Business," *Harvard Business Review,* January–February 1980, p. 15.
[6] Ibid., p. 14.

Meanwhile, many business firms, acting on their own, have designated high-ranking executives to oversee special minority purchasing programs. The National Minority Purchasing Council (NMPC), a trade association, estimates that around 50 percent of *Fortune's* "500" industrial firms currently have established such programs. According to NMPC data, the *Fortune* 500's spending with minority businesses rose from $7 million in 1972 to $1.1 billion in 1977 and is targeted for over $5 billion by the middle of the 1980s. The overall results are promising, as seen by the fact that General Motors, Standard Oil of Indiana, and Borden, Inc., to name but three, have dramatically increased their spending with minority-owned companies. Other examples are:

A Chicago building maintenance concern owned by a black man is thriving, with a large contract to clean a major corporation's downtown headquarters, bringing in a great deal of revenue.

A twenty-three-year-old catering concern in the black community of another city now does $1.5 million of business annually, with a substantial increase due largely to corporate and federal contracts seeking minorities.

A small black-owned Boston electrical contractor was turned into a multimillion dollar engineering company when a large construction company seeking to conform to a municipal government set-aside requirement subcontracted more than $5 million of work to it.[7]

Recent research shows that those firms which are serious about developing minority purchasing programs are setting up formal procedures. A typical five-step approach follows:

1. Holding a meeting of division heads and profit-center managers at which the chief executive officer explains that the company is determined, as a matter of policy, to substantially increase purchases from minority-owned companies.
2. Appointing an executive to evaluate and organize the most appropriate minority purchasing program.
3. Drawing up written goals and corporate policy on minority purchases.
4. Implementing the program.
5. Making a careful review of the program in terms of both dollars spent and the names of minority businesses which have been involved.[8]

Here are five minority purchasing program procedures.

Are programs such as these helping minority capitalism? Statistics show they are. For example, referring solely to black businesses, a company with $1 million in sales in 1972 would have ranked in the top 100 U.S. firms. By the end of the decade, however, it would have taken $5.2 million in sales to make the list. Furthermore, while only thirteen black firms earned over $10 million in 1972, thirty-eight were in that category in 1979.[9] These growth figures are partially accounted for by new developments that encourage minority capitalism.

Discrimination against Women

In the first year or two of the 1980s, approximately 43 percent of the work force was made up of women, many of whom had begun to enter fields traditionally considered within the male domain. Management is one such area of work. Some of the major reasons for

---

[7] David E. Gumpert, "Seeking Minority-owned Businesses as Suppliers," *Harvard Business Review,* January–February 1979, p. 113.
[8] Ibid., p. 114.
[9] Robert J. Cole, "Cars Head Black Business List," *New York Times,* May 5, 1980, p. D5.

---

the increased number of women in the workplace are (a) the women's movement and organizations with feminist or egalitarian philosophies and orientations which supported it, (b) recent civil rights legislation prompting affirmative action programs, (c) the changing profile of the U.S. work force, and (d) the increased need for competent business managers.[10] Despite such developments, the early eighties also saw discrimination against women in the areas of salary and management promotions.

Salary Inequities Women at all levels of business organizations, according to the latest reports, make less money on the average than do their male counterparts. What accounts for this difference? The answer is often found in the interpretation of the "equal pay for equal work" doctrine of the 1963 Equal Pay Act. Many employers have contended that women do not perform equal work and so cannot receive equal salaries. Working women now file complaints, however, and the U.S. Labor Department has started filing suits. The most important early decision came in 1970, when the U.S. Circuit Court upheld a decision against the Wheaton Glass Company of Milville, New Jersey. In its ruling, the court said that the jobs did not have to be identical: If they were "substantially equal," the equal pay law applied. This ruling meant that Wheaton had to pay its female inspector-packers over $900,000 in back pay. Since then numerous firms have also lost equal-pay suits; some of the best known are RCA, American Can, and Pacific Telephone & Telegraph. Despite such legal actions, however, salary discrimination against women continues, and it is optimistic and premature to predict that such inequities will be rectified in the near future.

Women are not being paid as much as men.

Management Promotions Women at the managerial level face problems when they try for promotions. Two main areas of consideration need to be addressed when the topic of management promotions is examined: barriers to promotion and ways of overcoming these barriers.

Barriers. Three common barriers affect the promotion of women into, and up, the ranks of management. One is the perceptions and personnel approaches of women themselves. Some women are concerned with failure and opt for conservative, low-risk career strategies. Others find it difficult to work with people they do not like. Men, too, at times have these problems, but they have for so long been the primary work-force members that they have had to learn to tolerate people and work situations they may dislike. Still other women, traditionally untrained in the areas, lack an understanding of career planning and development and fail to take steps necessary for promotion or advancement. Finally, some women see luck as a dominant factor in achievement.[11] These kinds of perceptions and personal approaches constitute a major barrier to female management promotions.

Women themselves do some things that hold back their career progress.

A second barrier is hiring biases. Research has shown that in some cases, women are substantially more acceptable than men when applying for traditionally female-oriented jobs but considerably less acceptable for traditionally male-oriented jobs.[12] Additionally, there is empirical evidence that individuals applying for jobs commonly held by members of the opposite sex, have to be perceived as more qualified than applicants from the other group in order to get the job:

Some hiring biases are directed against women.

---

[10] Ellyn Mirides and Andre Cote, "Women in Management: Strategies for Removing the Barriers," *Personnel Administrator,* April 1980, p. 25.

[11] Christine D. Hay, "Women in Management: The Obstacles and Opportunities They Face," *Personnel Administrator,* April 1980, pp. 31–39.

[12] Mirides and Cote, "Women in Management," p. 26.

The implications of these findings confirm the fact that sex-role stereotyping is very prevalent at the recruiting stage and may be assumed to present a major obstacle in on-the-job conditions to those females placed in non-traditional positions. Moreover, there are indications that on-job decisions and evaluations are less favorable for equally competent women holding managerial positions than males holding those positions.[13]

A third problem is organizational barriers, which arise from policies, procedures, and systems that determine how the organization will operate. In many cases, businesses function as they have in the past, making the same kinds of promotion decisions. As a result, no woman has ever served at the upper ranks in some organizations. Therefore, when these organizations promote, the odds are against a woman moving up this high—unless, of course, she is seen as overqualified.

Organizational barriers may prevent women's rise in management.

Overcoming the Barriers. How can women overcome these barriers? How can organizations determined to ensure equality in the management ranks help reduce these barriers? There are two basic ways, and they are complementary.

One way is for women to develop specific social power strategies. Women desiring careers in management can use four traditional managerial powers in advancing themselves to and through careers in management, continuing the use of the powers so long as they work. The first of these powers is expert power, through which the woman influences people through her superior skills or business knowledge. The second is informational power, the ability to provide evaluations to others about why they should believe or behave differently. The third is referent power, by which the woman influences others because they identify with her. Fourth is coercive power, through which the woman can bring negative sanctions (poor performance rating, low recommended raise) against others.[14] Table 16–1 describes some of the ways in which these social power strategies can be employed.

Women should develop social power strategies.

A second way of overcoming sexist barriers is through the use of training programs. This approach is being given a great deal of attention today, as managements attempt to identify the specific kinds of programs to offer. Some of the most common subjects as the 1980s begin are the functions of a manager, self-awareness, dealing with conflict, leadership skills development, career development, and the uniqueness of women in management.[15]

Training programs for women use several common subjects.

Does such training really help? Joan Harley and Lois Ann Koff have found that it does, especially if given prior to the need.[16] For example, if a woman is about to be promoted into lower-level management and has had inadequate training, she should be given training in supervision. Before she is assigned to make weekly presentations to the department heads, she should possibly be given public speaking training. Such early training offers many benefits, including (1) the instilling of confidence and self-esteem, (2) prevention of poor starts, (3) ensuring that the women contribute from the start, (4) increasing women's promotability, and (5) rewarding women and giving them recognition.[17]

Additionally, academia has recently developed a role for itself in preparing women

---

[13] Ibid.

[14] Gary N. Powell, "Career Development and the Woman Manager—A Social Power Perspective," *Personnel,* May–June 1980, pp. 22–32.

[15] Hay, "Women in Management," p. 37.

[16] Joan Harley and Lois Ann Koff, "Prepare Women Now for Tomorrow's Managerial Challenges," *Personnel Administrator,* April 1980, pp. 41–42.

[17] Ibid., p. 42.

Table 16-1 Analysis of Career Development Strategies Available to Woman Managers

Strategy	Power Bases Emphasized	Advantages	Disadvantages
Use perceptions of feminine characteristics to advantage.	Expert, informational	Easily assimilated into prevailing masculine culture. Takes advantage of opportunities presently available in socially oriented functions. May be benefactor of increased importance attached to socially oriented functions.	Supports stereotyping of women as unfit for management. Leads to obtaining staff positions typically peripheral to more powerful line positions. May lead to dead-end jobs and career stagnation after initial successes.
Adopt masculine standard of behavior.	Referent.	Easily assimilated into prevailing masculine culture. Precedent established for using this strategy May succeed if adhered to rigidly.	Supports stereotyping of women as unfit for management. Initially gives up referent power Leads to conflict between sexual identity and career identity for some women.
Seek entry into informal networks.	Referent, coercive, rewarding.	More active strategy, reflects less passivity. Complementary to other strategies, may be simultaneously pursued. If successful, power held in both formal and informal systems	May find resistance to women in "old boy" networks. Results not immediately forthcoming. Maintenance of membership and particular relationship requires energy beyond that devoted to the job. If unsuccessful, may hinder career more than if entry not attempted.

Source: Reprinted, by permission of the publisher, from "Career Development and the Woman Manager—A Social Power Perspective," by Gary N. Powell, *Personnel,* May–June 1980, © by AMACOM, a division of American Management Associations, p. 26. All rights reserved.

Academia has also entered the field of training women for management development.

for management.[18] Many colleges of business are now beginning to offer course or programs dealing with the special needs of women in management. Some of the topics being covered include strategies for bringing women into management, women in leadership, corporate liberation, issues of equality, and institutional barriers faced by women.

[18] Rose K. Reha, "Preparing Women for Management Roles," *Business Horizons,* April 1979, pp. 68–71.

An emphasis is also being given to the master's in business administration (MBA). The MBA can help open many doors for today's female manager.

Of course, only time will tell whether business is really going to promote a significant number of women through the management ranks, but it is definitely in the organization's best interests to take advantage of this virtually untapped human resource; and all signs indicate that management intends to do so.

ECOLOGY

In order to grasp fully the importance of the ecological challenge facing business, the reader should understand what is meant by the word *ecology*, which Webster defines as "a branch of science concerned with the interrelationship of organisms and their environments especially as manifested by natural cycles and rhythms, community development and structure, interaction between different kinds of organisms, geographic distributions, and population alterations."[19] The key to understanding ecology rests with the word *interrelationship*. All organisms must relate in some way to their environment. If they cannot co-exist with it, change occurs; the environment is altered or the organism dies. When such changes occur in nature's ecological balance, there can be side effects in other areas. As Paul Ehrlich, a noted American biologist, has said:

The key word is interrelationship.

> If we do something to an ecological system in one place, the whole system is affected. We must learn to look at the whole world and the people in it as a single interlocking system. It's impossible to do something somewhere that has no effect anywhere else.[20]

The entire world can thus be viewed as consisting of interlocking and interrelated ecosystems. If people start making changes in these systems, havoc can result. This section of the text will examine some of the ecological challenges facing business today. Some of the current ecological legislation will then be reviewed.

Air Pollution

John Lindsay, a former mayor of New York, once commented that he liked the city's air because he enjoyed seeing what he was breathing. There is no doubt that air pollution has increased dramatically over the past few decades, especially in huge metropolitan areas like New York, Chicago, or Los Angeles. Two of the primary pollutants have been automobiles and industrial smokestacks.

Automobiles The major cause of air pollution in America is the automobile. For some time now, auto makers have been trying to control the three main automotive emissions: carbon monoxide, hydrocarbons, and nitrogen oxides. The basic approach has been engine modification. For example, in attempting to limit hydrocarbons and carbon monoxide, the major auto makers have turned to higher coolant temperatures and altered valve and retarded-spark timing. For limiting nitrogen oxides, they have given major attention to reducing peak combustion temperatures through water injection or exhaust-gas recirculation and the use of a reducing-type of catalyst for treating exhaust.

The automobile is the major cause of air pollution.

Another approach has been to reduce auto weight, thereby decreasing fuel consumption and the accompanying exhaust pollution. A third way is through the development of new auto fuels that give better mileage and lower emissions of harmful gases.

---

[19] *Webster's Third New International Dictionary,* s. v. "ecology."
[20] "Playboy Interview: Dr. Paul Ehrlich," *Playboy,* August 1970, p. 56.

Figure 16–1 *Atmospheric Improvements in the United States*

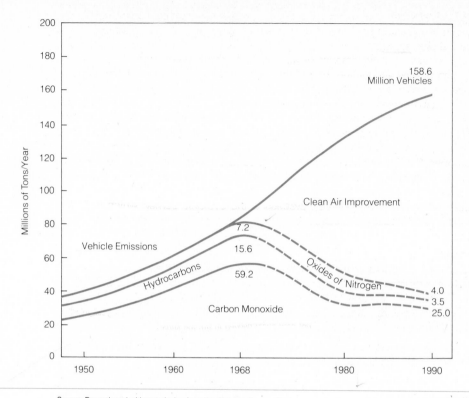

Source: Reproduced with permission from the Chrysler Corporation.

A fourth, which is being given renewed consideration, is the use of electric cars. Regard-less of what is done, however, the United States should witness a reduction in auto air pollution, at least through the 1990s, as Figure 16–1 shows. A Chrysler executive has summarized the development this way:

1. Auto emissions climbed to their peak in the atmosphere about 1968 and have been going downhill since then.

2. Emissions will continue to go down each year, even though the car population will rise and vehicle miles driven will go up. That means that the air is already cleaner today than last year or the year before. It will be cleaner year by year through the 1970's and the 1980's.

3. By the early 1980's, we will have air quality—from an automotive standpoint—nearly comparable to the 1940's. Normally, it takes between 10 to 15 years to re-place the older, high-emission cars in the vehicle population. Putting it another way, if there were no other vechicles on the road today, except the latest models, we would, overnight, breathe the same clean air we had in the 40's as far as the auto-mobile contribution is concerned. Even if we achieved the impossible by inventing and building zero-emission vehicles today, it still would take up to 15 years to replace the car population.

4. After emissions hit the low point in the air somewhere in the 1990's, they will start going up gradually as more cars keep being added to the population.[21]

Industrial Smokestacks If one drives into a big city on a cold winter day, smokestack pollution can be seen hanging over the metropolis. Among the worst of the industrial air polluters are the utilities, many of them daily hurling tons of sulphur dioxides into the air. Today experts estimate the amount of air pollutants at hundreds of millions of tons annually, with utilities accounting for a significant percentage of this. Smelting and refining firms are also major contributors.

Utilities and refineries are also big air polluters.

In an effort to decrease pollutant emission, these firms are beginning to rely on technological advances, such as power plant scrubbers and cyclonic burners. Many power plant scrubbers used today employ pulverized limestone for removing sulfur. In this process, a slurry of rock and water is sprayed into the dirty gas as it moves from the boiler to the scrubber. The limestone combines with the sulfur in the gas to form a liquid, which settles out as sludge waste. The remaining "scrubbed" gas then continues up the smokestack.

Another smokestack antipollution process is the cyclonic burner, which is being used by the lumber industry to dispose of waste products while simultaneously preserving clean air:

> The cyclonic burner is able to achieve near total combustion of solid mill wastes by "grinding them up and suspending the particles on blasts of air in the fire box. The generated heat provides a handy and economical source of energy." Because the system is virtually closed-loop, exhausts are fed back into the smokestack. Two of these systems already in operation illustrate that the heat from the burner can be used to fire kilns in the mill. As a result, it is possible for a mill cutting one million board feet a year to save $115,000 in carting costs and $85,000 on fuel previously needed to fire the kilns.[22]

Technological advances such as these are helping to reduce smokestack pollution. However, a great deal more remains to be done.

Water Pollution

Many firms have used nearby lakes or streams as drainpipes for carrying off industrial production wastes. As a result, some bodies of water, such as the Great Lakes, are said to have been very heavily polluted. In other cases companies have pumped liquid wastes into underground dumps. Unfortunately, sometimes these dumps have leaked, polluting both underground and surface water.

There is also the case of thermal, or warm-water, pollution, often brought about by hydroelectric plants. In order to generate electricity, the utility brings in cool water from a nearby lake or river. This is converted into steam to turn the plant's turbine engines. The steam is then passed through a condenser, cooled and turned back into water, and then returned to the lake or river. The problem is that often this water is returned at 5 or 10 degrees above its original temperature. The ultimate effect can be a change in the basic ecosystem of the water. The aquatic life, unaccustomed to the warmer environment, may die.

Currently, businesses receive a great deal of pressure to cease any activity that may cause water pollution. This is all part of the national goal of cleaning United States water-

---

[21] C. M. Heinen, speech before the Society of Industrial Realtors of the National Association of Real Estate Boards, Miami Beach, Florida, November 13, 1971, pp. 3–4. Heinen spoke as the executive engineer—material engineering, Chrysler Corporation.

[22] Luthans, Hodgetts, and Thompson, *Social Issues in Business,* p. 251.

---

ways so that the population is guaranteed potable water and the lesser necessities that water affords, such as nontoxic fishing streams. However, it is unlikely that "zero discharge" will become a reality because of the economic problems which that degree of pollution reduction would cause. It is too expensive to totally eliminate all water pollution. But an objective of 80 percent reduction of pollution is feasible.

Some of the major steps business has already taken to fight water pollution include the recycling of water through waste treatment systems and the development of lake restoration projects. General Motors provides a good illustration of the former:

> Water from a foundry is pumped into a large lagoon or settling basin in which the foundry solids gradually settle to the bottom. The clean water is then pumped back into the foundry for use in operations. At the present time General Motors is also looking into a new technique for purifying water to a degree suitable for reuse in any plant process. In essence the purifying process involves passing water through sand filters to remove suspended solids, through activated carbon towers to remove organics, and finally, through reverse osmosis units to reduce dissolved solids. [23]

Meanwhile, in the area of lake restoration, business firms are studying ways to restore already heavily polluted bodies of water. Union Carbide has reported success from its efforts at Lake Waccabuc in New York, the Attica, New York, reservoir, and the Ottoville, Ohio, quarry. All three suffered from oxygen deficiencies that resulted in the growth of algae. By withdrawing water from each, saturating it with oxygen and returning it to the bottom of the lake, Union Carbide eventually overcame the problem.

Noise Pollution

The amount of noise to which the average urban resident is subjected can be quite extreme. Car horns blast, pedestrians shout, and overhead aircraft roar. In the past, little was done about all this. Today, however, with the increased numbers of people and noises, steps are being taken to reduce noise pollution. One major cause of concern is medical research, which has established that people who are exposed to prolonged periods of noise at 85 decibels can suffer hearing damage. How loud is 85 decibels? The following provides a framework for answering this question:

Sound	Decibels
Whispering	30
Moderate conversation	35
Light auto traffic from 100 feet	50
Freeway from 50 feet	70
Heavy truck traffic from 50 feet	90
Power mower	95
Riveter	110
Siren	115
Commercial jet takeoff from 200 feet	120
Rocket launch	180

Today the government has established 90 decibels as an acceptable noise level for people in organized workplaces, although numerous groups, including unions, are exerting pressure to reduce this level to 85 decibels.

---

[23] Ibid.

Research also indicates that noise can prove to be a source of psychological distress, contributing to symptoms such as instability, headaches, nausea, general anxiety, and sexual impotency.[24]

Noise can also be a source of psychological distress.

Business has been taking two approaches in meeting the challenge of noise pollution. First, companies are investigating their environments to find and silence sources of noise. At some automotive plants, for example, noise suppressors are being used to reduce the noise level to 80 decibels. Ceilings and walls at these plants are covered with sound-absorbing materials, and over and around particularly noisy departments there are draft curtains—rigid, wall-like panels stuffed with noise-reducing fiberglass. Meanwhile, in factory areas where power tools are used, firms have attached hoses to the machinery to carry the noise out of the building; and to quiet conveyor systems, plants have slowed down the machines. Other types of manufacturers have used similar approaches, employing shields and padding to stifle plant noise and supplying protective ear devices to workers in areas where the noise level is over 90 decibels.

The second approach is that machine manufacturers are redesigning their equipment so that it makes less noise. For example, the hammer-type riveter is being replaced by an orbital and spin riveter. The riveter head used to be slammed into the ground; now the tool compresses the riveter head with an orbital or revolving motion instead. Attempts are also being made to stifle noise pollution from turbofan or jet engines. The most common method so far has been to redesign the engine by placing sound-absorbing materials on the walls on the inlet duct of the turbofan as well as in the exhaust duct. With these and similar developments, factory, machinery, and aircraft noise is being significantly reduced.

Of course, it is impossible to eliminate all noise pollution. However, a cutback of 10 decibels translates into a 50 percent decrease in a person's awareness of the noise. Thus, over the next decade, the United States should become a quieter place in which to work and live.

Ecological Legislation

Thus far this section has examined the ecological issues facing business. Some of these problems are being handled by means of voluntary action on the part of the business community. Also, many federal and state regulations have been enacted in recent years; these call for specific compliance. The two most important have been the Environmental Policy Act of 1969 and the National Air Quality Standards Act of 1970.

The Environmental Policy Act of 1969 established the Council on Environmental Quality. The council's basic duties are to help the U.S. president develop an annual environmental quality report, gather data on environmental trends, and develop recommendations to promote environmental quality. In addition, the act established the Environmental Protection Agency (EPA). The purpose of the agency is to coordinate all major federal pollution control programs for the purpose of achieving environmental quality.

A number of ecological laws directly affecting business have been passed.

The National Air Quality Standards Act of 1970 is one of the stiffest antipollution bills ever enacted. Some of its provisions follow:

1. All new factories must have the latest pollution control equipment.
2. Auto manufacturers must drastically reduce exhaust and nitrogen oxide emissions.
3. The federal government can set emission standards for ten major pollutants, ranging from soot to sulfur dioxide.

---

[24] Danforth W. Austin, "Factory Workers Grow Increasingly Rebellious over Noise Pollution," *Wall Street Journal,* June 14, 1972, p. 1.

In addition, each state is given the authority to set factory-emission tolerances in accord with federal standards, and if they do not, the EPA, after thirty days' notice to the respective state, can do so itself. Furthermore, the EPA can directly sue polluters; and if the agency is lax in this task, individual citizens have a right to sue both the EPA and the polluter. Finally, violators of the act are subject to maximum fines of $25,000 per day of noncompliance or one year in jail.

These are only a few of the many environmental control acts now in existence. What does the future hold? From a dollars and cents standpoint, business is going to spend increasing sums for pollution abatement. In addition, it has been predicted that the government will eventually set up a system of pollution fee assessments. The greater the amount of air and water pollution caused by a particular company, the greater penalties that company will have to pay.

CONSUMERISM

Since the late 1960s, consumerism has been a major social issue facing business. Phillip Kotler has defined *consumerism* as an organized social movement of concerned citizens and government to enhance the rights and power of buyers in relation to sellers.[25] This enhancement is taking two major forms to date: Buyers are demanding more information about the products and services they are purchasing, and they are insisting on safer products.

Consumer Information and Assistance

It is no surprise that research reveals that many people, when they lack knowledge about a product, tend to equate price with quality. After all, how does one go about deciding which of five brands of aspirin is *really* the best buy? Consumers need more than price guides, and a number of protections and aids for them have sprung up.

Legislative Protection In recent years, legislation designed to educate the consumer has been enacted. One of these laws is the Truth in Packaging Act, which sets forth the following mandatory labeling provisions:

1. The identity of the commodity shall be specified on the label.
2. The net quantity of contents shall be stated in a uniform and prominent location on the package.
3. The net quantity of contents shall be clearly expressed in ounces [only] and, if applicable, pounds [only] or in the case of liquid measures in the largest whole unit of quarts or pints.
4. The net quantity of a "serving" must be stated if the package bears a representation concerning servings.[26]

The Truth in Packaging Act sets forth mandatory labeling provisions.

A second such consumer protection is the Truth in Lending Act. This bill regulates the extension of credit to individuals and is primarily concerned with ensuring that the person know the charges, direct and indirect, associated with the loan. To give an example, open-end accounts, such as revolving charges, must provide the holder with the following information on each monthly statement:

---

[25] Phillip Kotler, *Marketing Management: Analysis, Planning, and Control,* 4th ed. (Englewood Cliffs, N.J.: Prentice-Hall, 1980), p. 693.

[26] Steward H. Rewoldt, James D. Scott, and Martin R. Warshaw, *Introduction to Marketing Management,* rev. ed. (Homewood, Ill.: Richard D. Irwin, 1973), p. 270.

1. The amount owed at the beginning of the period.
2. The amount and date of new purchases.
3. Any payments made.
4. The finance charge in dollars and cents.
5. The annual percentage rate.
6. The balance upon which the finance charge is calculated.
7. The closing date of billing and the accompanying unpaid balance.[27]

A third consumer aid is the Consumer Product Safety Act. This act is designed to:

1. Protect the public against unreasonable risk of injury from consumer products.
2. Assist consumers on evaluating the comparative safety of these products.
3. Develop uniform safety standards for consumer products while minimizing any conflicts with state or local regulations.
4. Promote research and investigation into the causes and prevention of product related injuries, illnesses, or deaths.

The Consumer Product Safety Act has four major provisions.

In order to carry out these objectives, the act established a Consumer Product Safety Commission consisting of five members appointed by the president of the United States with the advice and consent of the U.S. Senate. A primary goal of the commission is to establish and maintain product safety standards. Another is to reduce product-related accidents by demanding safer products.

Business Assistance The business community has taken action of its own to make the consumer more knowledgeable, and that effort continues. For example, General Foods and Lever Brothers have sponsored consumer clinics in which customers are taught how to use the firms' products. Sears, Roebuck is sponsoring ads designed to improve the consumer's knowledge of its products. Jewel Food Stores and Giant Foods have introduced unit pricing programs. And if something should go wrong, many firms have established departments or offices to help consumers expedite solutions to the difficulty. For example, Whirlpool offers its customers a twenty-four-hour "cool line." An individual with a complaint or question about service can call this toll-free number at any hour of the day or night from any location within the United States. Other companies have established consumer complaint departments which assign a problem to a specific individual, who stays with it until the customer is satisfied. Corning Glass has extended this idea and appointed a manager of consumer interests, whose job it is to represent the consumer and make sure the complaint does not get lost. In this way, the customer has an in-house agent.

Consumer complaint departments have been established.

Product Safety

Another major issue in consumerism is that of product safety. General product safety, and especially auto safety, have received major attention.

Auto Safety Ever since consumer advocate Ralph Nader wrote *Unsafe at Any Speed*,[28] auto safety has been an issue of concern. The 1970s were a time of dramatic increases in auto safety legislation. In all fairness to auto manufacturers, however, it must be noted that prior to this public outcry, sales indicated that people were not willing to pay for safety features. Now, of course, much of that has changed.

Many new auto safety features are being added.

---

[27] "What You Must Tell Your Customers," *Nation's Business,* June 1969, pp. 42–44.
[28] Ralph Nader, *Unsafe at Any Speed* (New York: Grossman Publishers, 1965). This book has often been cited as the book that destroyed the Chevrolet Corvair, which it criticized in some detail.

"Making them lighter every year, aren't they?"

Some of the new auto-safety features include seat belts, shoulder belts, energy-absorbing steering columns, padded dash boards, and bumpers capable of withstanding minor collisions. In addition, consideration is still being given to the air bag.

General Product Safety Many firms, spurred on by government legislation and the possibility of costly lawsuits, are placing great emphasis on product safety. Some are establishing product safety committees to evaluate current products. Others are providing safety tips, pointing out certain potentially dangerous consumer errors that should be avoided. For example, the Hoover Company makes it a practice to tell the operator not to pick up puddles of water with the vacuum. This would warn anyone who might confuse the capabilities of a household vacuum cleaner with those of the industrial-style shop vacuums.

Legal Aspects In recent years, liability laws have undergone drastic changes. Two areas of particular importance for business have been negligence and strict liability.

Privity of contract has been pushed aside.

Under old English law, businesses were liable for negligence only to the person who bought the good; this doctrine is known as privity of contract. Today the courts have pushed privity of contract aside, and an individual does not have to prove a direct contractual relationship. Persons who buy defective cars need not sue their dealers first; they can sue the auto makers directly. This means that manufacturers are now much more vulnerable to suit than before.

Most states have strict liability laws.

Strict liability means that a manufacturer can be held responsible for products that injure the buyer or user; direct negligence need not be proved. If a company places a product on the market, it must take responsibility for it.[29] Today most states have enacted strict liability laws, and it is likely that all will have them by 1990.

Safety Checklist With the courts making it easier to sue manufacturers for damages, many firms are finding it necessary to review the entire area of product safety. Carl Clark, Chief of The National Commission Task Group on Industry Self-Regulation, was quoted as suggesting that manufacturers use the following safety checklist:

[29] For more on this area, see William L. Trombetta, "Products Liability: What New Court Rulings Mean for Management," *Business Horizons,* August 1979, pp. 67–72.

1. Review working conditions and competence of key personnel.
2. Predict ways in which the product will fail and the consequences of these failures at the design stage.
3. Select raw materials that are either pretested or certified as flawless.
4. Make use of trade association research and analyses concerning product safety.
5. Insist that product safety factors be tested by an independent laboratory.
6. Document any production changes that might later affect safety problems.
7. Encourage the product safety staff to review advertising or safety aspects.
8. Inform salesmen of the product's safety features and under what conditions they will fail.
9. Provide information to the consumer on product performance.
10. Investigate every consumer complaint.[30]

Here is a manufacturer's safety checklist.

This list can be valuable to manufacturers in light of the fact that more consumers have been suing—and winning—product liability suits. The percentage of juries ruling in favor of the plaintiff and the amounts of the awards have been on the rise for some fifteen years.

THE FUTURE OF SOCIAL RESPONSIBILITY

Is the concern for social responsibility a passing fad, or is it here to stay? In this chapter, strong arguments have been made which indicate that this interest will endure. Numerous reasons in support of this view can be cited. One is that many stockholders are demanding that their businesses exhibit a greater sense of social responsibility. This has resulted in shareholder resolutions being presented to a number of boards for votes of adoption. Table 16–2 shows the results of a dozen such resolutions and how they fared: Of the 96 brought to a vote, 36 percent passed.

This stockholder influence, coupled with management initiative, has by now resulted in important steps toward the solution of social problems. Some of these follow:

Beatrice Foods and Standard Brands have adopted nutrition responsibility policies, which grew out of discussions between the companies and the shareholder groups.
Gulf Oil has agreed to adopt a policy prohibiting political contributions to South Korea.
Citibank has pledged to make no more loans to the South African government but rather to limit "its credit selectively to constructive private sector activities that create jobs which benefit all South Africans."
Chase Manhattan Bank has a policy of not making loans that will have a negative social impact.[31]

Other commonly cited reasons for business's concern with social responsibility include (a) enhanced corporate reputation and goodwill, (b) a strengthening of the social system in which the corporation functions, (c) a strengthening of the economic system in which the corporation functions, (d) greater job satisfaction among all employees, and (e) avoidance of government regulation.[32]

Finally, people today show a great deal of interest in the subject of ethics. For a long time, ethical behavior was discussed chiefly in "ideal" terms. Today it has become a practical necessity for management. The public often demands ethical consideration; the law requires it in many cases; and managers themselves think ethical practice is

---

[30] "Consumerism: The Mood Turns Mean," *Sales Management,* July 15, 1969, p. 40.
[31] Theodore V. Purcell, "Management and the 'Ethical' Investors," *Harvard Business Review,* September–October 1979, p. 30.
[32] Sandra L. Holmes, "Executive Perceptions of Corporate Social Responsibility," *Business Horizons,* June 1976, p. 38.

Table 16–2 A Dozen Shareholder Resolutions Presented to Boards of Directors

Subject	Total Presented	Total Withdrawn	Resolutions Brought to a Vote Total	Resolutions Brought to a Vote Survivors
South African issues	34	8	26	9
Trade with other repressive governments	14	2	12	4
Former government officials	16	0	16	5
Nuclear weapons and power plants	12	5	7	6
Corporate governance	11	0	11	8
Redlining and community reinvestment	8	4	4	2
Domestic political activities and contributions	7	0	7	4
Domestic labor practices and EEO	6	2	4	2
Military conversion to peacetime uses	4	1	3	1
Questionable foreign payments	4	2	2	1
Children's TV: food advertising and violence	3	2	1	0
Infant formula	3	0	3	2

good business. Furthermore, with the development of modern communication techniques, news of unethical practices can be carried via newspapers, magazines, radio, and television to virtually every corner of the globe. So it is in the best interests of business to develop specific codes of ethical behavior and to enforce sanctions against those members who violate these codes.

> In summary, a new age of instant information and public insistence on ethical behavior has transformed business ethics from an ideal condition to a reality, from a luxury to a practical necessity for the survival and success of organizations. The central instrument for making ethics operational and real in an organization is a written code of ethics which is specific . . . is based upon general ethical standards, and is enforceable by appropriate sanctions. [33]

It appears, entering the 1980s, that social responsibility will be a definite factor in future business strategy. Of course, the specific area of concern for each company may differ. For example, mining firms are more concerned with pollution abatement, conservation of resources, and other ecological issues, while wholesale and retail firms

---

[33] James Owens, "Business Ethics: Age-Old Ideal, Now Real," *Business Horizons*, February 1978, p. 30.

report heavy interest in the recruitment and managerial development of females. In the aggregate, however, businesses today are both aware of and responsive to the challenge of social responsibility.

SUMMARY

Social responsibility is a continuing challenge to modern business. Realizing that business is actually serving its own long-run interests by aiding the community, many firms today are actively meeting the three major social challenges of the day: equal opportunity, ecology, and consumerism.

Both the Equal Pay Act of 1963 and the Civil Rights Act of 1964 were landmarks in helping ensure equal opportunity in the workplace. However, business has also played a key role in helping find work for minorities and the handicapped, and many firms have also helped minority capitalists by providing them with both technical assistance and business contracts.

Yet in these areas, and particularly in the area of discrimination against women, a great deal remains to be done. Many working women today, despite the law, do not receive equal pay for equal work. Nor are their chances for management promotion as good as those of their male counterparts. Fortunately, many companies are aware of these conditions and are taking steps to rectify them.

The second major area of consideration in this chapter was ecology, with concerns ranging from air pollution to water and noise pollution. In each instance, demands on business firms have resulted in attempts to respond positively to the challenge.

Finally, today's consumers want to know what they are buying and what they are getting for their dollar. Such legislation as the Truth in Packaging Act and the Truth in Lending Act has helped provide consumers with some important information and assistance. Yet the consumer movement is more than just a need for more data. Consumers also want product safety; and when it is overlooked by manufacturers, lawsuits are likely. As a result more and more companies have begun in recent years to pay close attention to liability laws and the development of safety checklists that help ensure the requisite quality in their products.

The future of social responsibility was discussed in the last part of this chapter. Recent evidence indicates that the challenge of social responsibility is going to be here indefinitely. Further, all signs indicate that business is both willing and able to respond to it.[34]

REVIEW AND STUDY QUESTIONS

1. What is the doctrine of enlightened self-interest?
2. In what way has the Equal Pay Act of 1963 been of value in promoting equal opportunity?
3. In what way has the Civil Rights Act of 1964 been of value in promoting equal opportunity?
4. How has the Vocational Rehabilitation Act of 1973 affected business's hiring of the handicapped? Explain.
5. How has the business community helped promote minority capitalism? Give two examples, and make your answer as specific as posssible.

---

[34] For more information, see Keith Davis, "Social Responsibility Is Inevitable," *California Management Review,* Fall 1976, pp. 14–20.

6. What are the two most common forms of discrimination against working women? Explain each; give specific examples.

7. How can business help ensure equal opportunity for women in the workplace?

8. Explain the word "ecology" in your own terms.

9. What is the major cause of air pollution in America, and what is business doing about it?

10. Why is "zero discharge" considered unrealistic? Explain.

11. Does noise pollution have any effects on people? Give an example.

12. What are the major provisions of the Environmental Policy Act of 1969?

13. What are the major provisions of the National Air Quality Standards Act of 1970?

14. How does the Consumer Product Safety Act help the average consumer?

15. What is meant by the term "consumerism"?

16. What are the major provisions of the Truth in Packaging Act? The Truth in Lending Act?

17. Are any changes occurring in liability laws? What effects are they having on business? Explain.

18. Is the social responsibility of business a fad, or is it here to stay? Explain.

SELECTED REFERENCES

Alexander, G. J., and Buccholz, R. A. "Corporate Social Responsibility and Stock Market Performance." *Academy of Management Journal,* September 1978, pp. 479–486.

Andreason, A. R., and Best, A. "Consumers Complain—Does Business Respond?" *Harvard Business Review,* July–August 1977, pp. 93–101.

Barksdale, H. C., and Perreult, W. D., Jr. "Can Consumers Be Satisfied?" *MSU Business Topics,* Spring 1980, pp. 19–30.

Bhagat, R. S. "Black-White Ethnic Differences in Identification with the Work Ethic: Some Implications for Organizational Integration." *Academy of Management Review,* July 1979, pp. 381–391.

Biles, G. E., and Pryatel, H. A. "Myths, Management and Women." *Personnel Journal,* October 1978, pp. 572–577.

Bock, R. H. "Modern Values and Corporate Social Responsibility." *MSU Business Topics,* Spring 1980, pp. 5–17.

Bowman, J. S. "Business and the Environment: Corporate Attitudes, Actions in Energy-Rich States." *MSU Business Topics,* Winter 1977, pp. 37–49.

Buccholz, R. A. "An Alternative to Social Responsibility." *MSU Business Topics,* Summer 1979, pp. 12–16.

Buehler, V. M., and Shetty, Y. K. "Managerial Response to Social Responsibility Challenge." *Academy of Management Journal,* March 1976, pp. 66–78.

Burke, R. J., and Weir, T. "Readying the Sexes for Women in Management." *Business Horizons,* June 1977, pp. 30–35.

Carroll, A. B., and George, W. B. "Landmarks in the Evolution of the Social Audit." *Academy of Management Journal,* September 1975, pp. 589–599.

Carson, Rachel. *Silent Spring.* Boston: Houghton Mifflin, 1962.

Davis, Keith. "Five Propositions for Social Responsibility." *Business Horizons,* June 1975, pp. 19–24.

Edmunds, S. W. "Unifying Concepts in Social Responsibility." *Academy of Management Review,* January 1977, pp. 38–45.

Fitch, H. G. "Achieving Corporate Responsibility." *Academy of Management Review,* January 1976, pp. 38–46.

Fottler, M. D. "Retention of the Hard-core Unemployed." *Academy of Management Journal,* September 1978, pp. 366–379.

Fottler, M. D., and Bain, T. "Sex Differences in Occupational Aspirations." *Academy of Management Journal,* March 1980, pp. 144–149.

Fry, F. L. "The End of Affirmative Action." *Business Horizons,* February 1980, pp. 34–40.

Gelb, B. D., and Hunt, D. M., "Staying on the Job after Sixty-five." *Business Horizons,* February 1979, pp. 17–21.

Graham, Frank, Jr. *Since Silent Spring.* Boston: Houghton Mifflin, 1970.

Gumpert, David E. "Seeking Minority-owned Businesses as Suppliers." *Harvard Business Review,* January–February 1979, pp. 110–116.

Hay, R., and Gray, E. "Social Responsibilities of Business Managers." *Academy of Management Journal,* March 1974, pp. 135–143.

Hennig, M., and Jardim, A. *The Managerial Woman.* Garden City, N.Y.: Anchor Press, Doubleday, 1977.

Herbert, T. T., and Yost, E. B. "Women as Effective Managers: Overcoming the Barriers." *Human Resource Management,* Spring 1978, pp. 18–25.

Hise, R. T.; Gillett, P. L.; and Kelly, J. P. "The Corporate Consumer Affairs Department." *MSU Business Topics,* Summer 1978, pp. 17–26.

Holmes, Sandra L. "Adapting Corporate Structure for Social Responsiveness." *California Management Review,* Fall 1978, pp. 47–54.

———. "Corporate Social Performance: Past and Present Areas of Commitment." *Academy of Management Journal,* September 1977, pp. 433–438.

Kanter, R. M. *Men and Women of the Corporation.* New York: Basic Books, 1977.

Keim, G. D. "Corporate Social Responsibility: An Assessment of the Enlightened Self-interest Model." *Academy of Management Review,* January 1978, pp. 32–39.

———. "Managerial Behavior and the Social Responsibility Debate: Goals versus Constraints." *Academy of Management Journal,* March 1978, pp. 32–39.

Larnood, L.; Wood., M. M.; and Inderlisd, S. D. "Training Women for Management: New Problems, New Solutions." *Academy of Management Review,* July 1978, pp. 584–593.

Luthans, Fred; Hodgetts, Richard M.; and Thompson, K. R. *Social Issues in Business.* 3d ed. New York: Macmillan, 1980.

Nader, Ralph. *Unsafe at Any Speed.* New York: Grossman Publishers, 1965.

Ostlund, L. E. "Attitudes of Managers toward Corporate Social Responsibility." *California Management Review,* Summer 1977, pp. 35–49.

Owens, James. "Business Ethics: Age-old Ideal, Now Real." *Business Horizons,* February 1978, pp. 26–30.

Pati, Gopal, C., and Adkins, John I., Jr. "Hire the Handicapped—Compliance Is Good Business." *Harvard Business Review,* January–February 1980, p. 14.

Purcell, Theodore V. "Management and the 'Ethical' Investors." *Harvard Business Review,* September–October 1979, p. 24.

Reha, Rose K. "Preparing Women for Management Roles." *Business Horizons,* April 1979, pp. 68–71.

Rosen, B., and Jerdee, T. H. "Coping with Affirmative Backlash." *Business Horizons,* August 1979, pp. 15–20.

Stafford, J. E. and Enis, B. M. "Corporate Social Research." *Business Horizons,* October 1979, pp. 50–58.

Strang, W. A. "The Men of Black Business: Implications for Growth." *Business Horizons,* November 1977, pp. 62–68.

Sturdivant, F. D., and Ginter, J. L. "Corporate Social Responsiveness: Management Attitudes and Economic Performance," *California Management Review,* Spring 1977, pp. 30–39.

"The Superwoman Squeeze." *Newsweek,* May 19, 1980, pp. 72–79.

Trombetta, William L. "Products Liability: What New Court Rulings Mean for Management." *Business Horizons,* August 1979, pp. 67–72.

Veiga, J. F., and Yanouzas, J. N. "What Women in Management Want: The Ideal vs. the Real." *Academy of Management Journal,* March 1976, pp. 137–143.

Winter, R. E. "Reserve Mining Project Illustrates the Dilemma of Jobs vs. Ecology." *Wall Street Journal,* November 15, 1977, pp. 1, 29.

Zenisek, T. J. "Corporate Social Responsibility: A Conceptualization Based on Organizational Literature." *Academy of Management Review,* July 1979, pp. 359–368.

CASE: *It's Inevitable*

Is concern for social responsibility a fad, or will it be a fundamental and lasting impetus in United States business? Many people tend to believe the latter. They feel that decades ago there was only a slight difference between business's and society's life-styles. Today, however, the incongruity is quite obvious.

Financial income and security used to dominate U.S. life-style. Business, as an economic institution, helped meet the needs of the life-style and, in spite of cyclical rises and declines in public favor, its goals were compatible with those of the average person. But modern times have seen a shift toward more socially oriented desires; the pure economic mission of business is now out of step with societal values:

> The incongruence between business's lifestyle and society's lifestyle requires intelligent, creative actions to dispel differences and reduce tensions. From a practical point of view it may be assumed that the social environment is the independent variable and business is the dependent variable. The major burden for adaptation, therefore, is upon business. Eventually it must change to meet society's expectations, and not the other way around. There may be minor adaptations by society as it comes to understand business better, but the major change surely will be required of business. [35]

Finally, advocates of social responsibility envision only a limited number of options available to business. First, it can withdraw and refuse to face the issue. Second, it can take a legalistic approach by dragging its feet and fighting long, expensive legal battles against social progress. Third, it can bargain or negotiate with those pressure groups making claims on it. Fourth, it can solve the problem by making a genuine study of

---

[35] Ibid., p. 15.

society's and business's values and needs and attempt to reconcile them in constructive ways. Social responsibility advocates consider the latter the most viable strategy.

Questions

1. Is there really a growing incongruence between the lifestyles of business and society in this country? Explain.
2. Is the social responsibility factor really here to stay? Cite some illustrations to support your answer.
3. If business does choose the fourth alternative above, namely problem solving, what are some steps it should take? Be specific in your answer.

CASE: Equal Credit

Many married, divorced, and widowed women used to find that, because of their sex, they were denied credit at department stores and banks. For example, a working husband could obtain a $1,000 loan on his signature, but a working wife who wanted a similar loan had to get her husband to co-sign. Additionally, if the two divorced, it was likely that she would lose her credit rating while his would be unaffected. It has even been common for widows to find that they can no longer use credit they established in their own names but can continue to use their dead husbands' credit cards with no questions asked.

The Equal Credit Opportunity Act of 1975 has now outlawed such practices, requiring that a creditor apply the same standards of "creditworthiness" to all applicants. This is, unfortunately, not to say that a creditor cannot stall a woman on an application for credit. However, she must be notified within thirty days of any action taken on her account. If credit is denied, the notice has to be made in writing and must either cite specific reasons for the denial or indicate that such an explanation can be requested. The same right applies if a credit account is closed. Some of the most important rules of this act, as outlined by the federal government, include the following:

1. You cannot be refused credit just because you are a woman.
2. You cannot be refused credit just because you are single, married, separated, divorced, or widowed.
3. You cannot be refused credit because a creditor decides you are of childrearing age and, as a result, will not count your income.
4. You cannot be refused credit because a creditor will not count income you receive regularly from alimony or child support.
5. You can have credit in your own name if you are creditworthy.
6. When you apply for your own credit and rely on your own income, information about your spouse or his co-signature can be required only under certain circumstances.
7. You can keep your own accounts and your own credit history if your marital status changes.
8. You can build up your own credit record because accounts must now be carried in the names of husband and wife if both use the account or are liable on it.
9. If you are denied credit, you can find out why.

Questions

1. Which one of the above rules provides women the greatest protection against credit discrimination? Explain.

2. In addition to those on the list, can you think of other rules that you think should be added to ensure that women are given the same credit opportunities as men?

3. How much effect will this law have on ensuring equal credit opportunities? Explain.

CASE: *Quiet in the Home*

Conversations about noise pollution usually center around the more noticeable offenders, such as airplanes, locomotives, buses, and heavy machinery. However, a quick look around the average house or apartment is likely to uncover many other polluters, including dishwashers, blenders, garbage disposals, and vacuum cleaners. Most of the noise from these household items goes unnoticed by the average person, although recent government studies show that 16 million Americans suffer from some degree of hearing loss caused directly by noise. Since most people spend a large amount of time at home, noisy appliances quite possibly are causal factors in poor hearing.

One reason that many people are unconcerned about noise pollution from appliances is that they equate noise with power. If a machine makes a lot of noise, it is considered to be getting the job done. If it is too quiet, it is often perceived as ineffective. For example, a quiet vacuum cleaner was introduced into the marketplace in the early 1960s. It promptly flopped because consumers thought it lacked power. Similarly, when engineers at another vacuum manufacturer were bothered by a clicking sound in one of their vacuums, a consumer survey found that the noise did not disturb the users, who felt it indicated that the vacuum was working.

Nevertheless, the Environmental Protection Agency (EPA) intends to crack down on noise from home appliances. One of its proposals is to require manufacturers to label household appliances to show how much noise they emit. Another is to use a color-coding or numbering system to allow shoppers to compare noise levels of competing appliances and decide which is most tolerable for them.

EPA administrators admit that it will cost more to make appliances quieter and expect implementation to be gradual. Despite such problems, however, noise labeling is meeting with very little industry resistance.

Questions

1. List six home appliances that you believe make sufficient noise to qualify them as noise pollutants, and try to discover their decibel levels.

2. Why do people associate appliance noise with appliance power?

3. What difficulties will the EPA confront as it attempts to reduce noise in home appliances? Why?

CASE: *Suing for Damages*

When the word *consumerism* is mentioned, many people think immediately of the average person on the street who bought a defective product at the neighborhood store. However, consumerism also relates to businesses that purchase goods and supplies from other firms. One recent case very clearly illustrates this.

Ted Mark had been the president of the Xerographic Supplies Corporation. His firm was an independent outlet of the Royal Typewriter Company. It leased 193 of the Royal's dry-paper photocopy machines, which were leased in turn to doctors, lawyers, banks, schools, and so on. Soon, these customers began lodging all sorts of complaints with Mark. The machines scorched paper, jammed easily, and broke down often. Faced with frequent repairs and difficulty obtaining replacement parts, the supply company's profits never reached the level forecast by Royal Typewriter. And to make matters worse, a school employee who tried to clear one of the leased copiers suffered burns that put her in the hospital for almost three weeks.

Mark eventually recalled the leased machines and returned them to Royal. The company sold them; Mark went out of business. He then learned of a study which showed that the copiers had potential safety defects, including the possibility of fire. Contending that this showed evidence of a breach to an implied warranty that the copiers were safe, Mark sued Royal Typewriter.

The trial verdict was in Mark's favor. The federal jury agreed that Royal knowingly marketed potentially dangerous machines in an effort to cut into Xerox's corner on the copier market, and Royal was ordered to pay Mark $5 million.

Questions

1. Was the jury right in holding for Mark? Explain your thinking.

2. In what way does the concept of strict liability enter this case?

3. Are we likely to see more lawsuits of the nature discussed in this case? Why or why not?

CHAPTER 17

INTERNATIONAL MANAGEMENT: CHALLENGES AND OPPORTUNITIES

GOALS OF THE CHAPTER

For two reasons, the United States is the most important nation in the international arena. First, it does more exporting and importing than any other country in the world; there is virtually no nation with which it does not have at least some trade (see Table 17–1). Second, many of its largest business firms, including General Motors, Ford, Exxon, Mobil Oil, IBM, and ITT, earn a substantial percentage of their annual sales in the overseas market. Today's U.S. business executive is thus concerned not only with domestic management but international management as well.

This chapter will focus attention on what managers from U.S. firms need to know about managing overseas operations. The discussion draws upon and applies much of what has been presented in previous chapters; for to a large extent, the basic ideas are the same. The challenge of international business is in modifying the applications to fit the new environment.[1]

The first goal of this chapter is to examine the possible advantages and disadvantages of going international in business. The second objective is to analyze the methods used in organizing, controlling, and staffing these overseas operations. The third goal is to scrutinize the role of the multinational corporation in the international economic arena.

When you have finished this chapter, you should be able to:

1. Explain why a U.S. business firm will consider entering a foreign market.
2. Discuss the possible advantages and disadvantages of going overseas.
3. Tell how a joint venture works.

---

[1] For additional information on this process, see Richard N. Farmer and Barry M. Richman, *Comparative Management and Economic Progress* (Homewood, Ill.: Richard D. Irwin, 1965); and Harold Koontz, "A Model for Analyzing the Universality and Transferability of Management," *Academy of Management Journal,* December 1969, pp. 415–429.

	Exports			Imports		
	1976	*1977*	*1978*	*1976*	*1977*	*1978*
Canada	24,106	25,788	28,372	26,237	29,599	33,529
France	3,446	3,503	4,166	2,509	3,032	4,054
Germany	5,731	5,989	6,957	5,592	7,238	9,961
Italy	3,071	2,790	3,360	2,530	3,037	4,103
United Kingdom	4,801	5,951	7,119	4,254	5,141	6,513
Saudi Arabia	2,774	3,575	4,370	5,213	6,347	5,307
Israel	1,409	1,447	1,925	423	572	719
Japan	10,145	10,529	12,885	15,504	18,550	24,458
Phillipines	818	876	1,040	883	1,110	1,207
20 Latin American republics	15,487	16,371	20,183	13,228	16,450	18,560

Source: *The World Almanac and Book of Facts* (New York: Newspaper Enterprise Association, 1980), p. 117.

4. **Describe the various forms of organization structure used in foreign operations.**
5. **Define the degrees of control that a parent company can exercise over a subsidiary.**
6. **Explain how a business firm attempts to staff its overseas operations.**
7. **Discuss some of the incentives used in motivating employees to accept overseas assignments.**
8. **Discuss the economic power and international responsibility of the multinational corporation.**

ENTERING FOREIGN MARKETS

Why do U.S. businesses enter foreign markets? The numerous answers include: (a) a high-level executive pushes for it, (b) an outside group approaches the firm with a proposal such as an overseas joint venture, (c) a domestic competitor's expansion into certain areas abroad leads the firm to join the bandwagon, (d) strong domestic competition makes foreign expansion desirable, and (e) there is a potentially profitable overseas market for the firm's goods or services.

Identifying the Firm's Basic Mission

Regardless of the reason, the first step a firm must take before entering the international arena is to examine its operations. What kind of company is it? What is its real business? These are the same types of questions that were raised in Chapter 4 when strategic planning was examined. This time, however, the focus is on international expansion. In answering the question "How do you define your mission?" Jacques G. Maisonrouge, speaking as Chairman of the Board of IBM World Trade, has been quoted:

> We want to be in the problem-solving business — this is our mission. Our business is not to make computers. It is to help solve administrative, scientific, and even human problems. If your mission is broad enough, you do not find one day that a competitor's new product has outmoded all your equipment.[2]

What business is the firm in?

---

[2] Gene E. Bradley and Edward C. Bursk, "Multinationalism and the 29th Day," *Harvard Business Review*, January–February 1972, p. 45.

Meanwhile, Fred J. Borch, former Chairman of the General Electric Corporation, has answered the question this way:

> We no longer define it as energy, electricity, and so on. That is a limiting factor. Rather, it is those areas of opportunity where our talents (whether they are technological, manufacturing, or marketing) can make a contribution that fits both our societal objectives and our growth objectives — those we give serious consideration to. There is no limit to where our talents can take us.[3]

Both executives indicate that the firms see their missions as global in nature. Problem solving (IBM) and societal and growth objectives (GE) are not restricted to national boundaries. If a firm feels foreign expansion is within the scope of its basic mission, it can begin evaluating the possible advantages and disadvantages of going overseas.

Evaluating the Possible Advantages

Expansion into a foreign market can have many advantages, some of which are profit, stability, and a foothold in the Common Market or some similar economic union.

Profit One of the biggest attractions in going international is the possibility of increased profit. McKinsey and Company, the world-famous consulting firm, found that among a hundred major U.S. firms it examined, more than half had doubled their overseas profits during the 1950s; and the ROI of these firms was higher in the foreign than in the domestic market. During the 1960s, although the returns were somewhat lower, they were still considered quite good.[4] During the 1970s, with U.S. dollar devaluation and an increasing demand for goods and services by the general population in other countries, many overseas ventures produced very high returns; and the 1980s promise more of the same.

Profit is important.

A second profit feature is the favorable tax rate imposed by certain foreign countries; this is at times in rather great contrast to tax rates in the United States. Though the U.S. firms still must pay their U.S. taxes, the lower tax rates abroad, combined with the fact that some countries' workers accept lower wages than the U.S. firms would have to pay at home, make overseas ventures highly promising.

Stability A second major advantage of foreign expansion is stability. Many firms are capable of manufacturing far more units than they can sell domestically, and a foreign market provides a source of demand for the goods. This demand can be met through direct export to an agent abroad or through an overseas branch or subsidiary. A third common approach, brought on by rising nationalism, is to set up operations abroad and attempt to stabilize sales and production by working directly in both the foreign and domestic markets.

A foreign source of demand can aid the firm's stability.

Common Market and Other Economic Unions Foreign production, especially in some parts of Europe, can be beneficial also because it gives the company a foothold in the European Economic Community (EEC). The *Common Market,* as it is most frequently called, was created in 1957 by France, West Germany, Italy, the Netherlands, Belgium, and Luxembourg. Its goal is to reduce trade barriers among the members. By 1967 duties charged on industrial goods circulating within the Common Market were only 20 percent of their previous levels, and by mid-1968 they were entirely eliminated. During the 1970s, Great Britain, Ireland, and Denmark were granted membership in the group; and Greece entered in 1980.

---

[3] Ibid.

[4] See "Foreign Ventures Fetch More Profit for Firms Based in United States," *Wall Street Journal,* November 1, 1973, p. 1.

The EEC has helped its member countries improve their standards of living, although the last decade did not witness much progress in England, Ireland, and Italy. Nevertheless, on an overall basis, the Common Market has been a success. In addition to eliminating interior barriers, it has put a tariff wall around its members to protect them from outsiders. The result should be a united European market that can compete successfully with U.S. firms, which, in turn, can take advantage of these developments by entering the Common Market.

The basic idea of economic competition is not limited to the Common Market. Other economic unions have been formed for similar reasons, including the European Free Trade Association (Austria, Finland, Iceland, Norway, Portugal, and Switzerland), the Central American Common Market (Costa Rica, Guatemala, Nicaragua, Honduras, and El Salvador), and the Latin American Free Trade Association (most of the South American countries and Mexico). U.S. firms doing business in these countries can profit from such unions.

Evaluating the Possible Disadvantages

Some possible disadvantages are also associated with going international. They include: (a) lower-than-anticipated profits, (b) the need to understand foreign customs and culture, (c) the necessity of fostering company-government relations and unusual red tape, and (d) risk, expropriation, and the pressure, especially in underdeveloped countries, to bring in foreign partners.

Profits may not materialize.

Lower than Anticipated Profits The primary disadvantage in expanding abroad is the possibility that the expected market will not materialize, either because raw materials or workers are not available in the necessary quantities or the price for the good cannot be obtained. In either case, the result is lower than anticipated profits:

> During the 1960's, Latin America was an ideal illustration, with return on investment by American firms averaging around 13 per cent, far less than in Asia and Africa. Today, however, this may be changing as Latin countries are starting to again encourage foreign investment.[5]

Customs and culture may be major stumbling blocks.

Customs and Cultures Another disadvantage may be the unfamiliar new market itself. Precisely what does the company know about the country and its people? Does it understand the customs and the culture? What are the religious beliefs of the people, and how do they affect popular moral and ethical standards? What about the family? Is the country basically a matriarchal or patriarchal society? Are the people well educated or virtually illiterate? What are the social relationships and the value systems to which the people subscribe? If the company can answer these questions, it has a basic idea of how to interact with the people.

Yet, as John Fayerweather, an expert in international marketing, points out, still other significant attitudes among each population are left uncovered by these questions:

> Notable . . . are the artistic tastes of the people, which are important factors. . . . That these tastes differ among societies is readily apparent to anyone comparing the dance, painting, music, and other art forms found in various countries. Likewise there are temperamental differences among peoples: the Latins are given to acting on impulse, while the Germans are more solid and rational. There are also a host of specific elements in the life of each country that are significant in some way—white is for mourning in China, a cow is sacred in India, and so on.[6]

---

[5] See "Reversal of Policy: Latin America Opens the Door to Foreign Investment Again," *Business Week,* August 9, 1976, pp. 34–38.

[6] John Fayerweather, *International Marketing,* 2d ed. (Englewood Cliffs, N.J.: Prentice-Hall, 1970), p. 26.

In short, if a U.S. company is going to set up a business in another country, it needs to familiarize itself with the culture, for there are many differences between the way things are done in the United States and the way they are done elsewhere. For example, German managers commonly use a much less participative leadership style than that of the average U.S. executive. As a result, many newly arrived American managers in Germany are seen as soft or weak in dealing with their German subordinates. In Japan a new firm finds a fierce employee loyalty to the company. But it also learns that there is a quid pro quo: Virtually everyone is guaranteed lifelong employment. There is no such thing as firing the poorest workers in a department that fails to meet its production quota. These cultural norms must be understood by U.S. firms operating there.

This learning process can pose a time problem to a firm in a hurry. The last thing an entering firm wants to do is to violate local social customs or culture. But the managers of such firms are also under pressure to get action. U.S. businesspeople can find themselves frustrated in a country like Japan, where negotiations customarily move very slowly. This kind of problem is not merely an interesting point about travel and cross-cultural life-styles: Some firms have cancelled plans to expand into overseas markets because they have been unable to adapt to the norms and customs of doing business in a foreign country.

Company-government Relations In many countries, especially those in the process of developing themselves industrially, the entering company must show the government that its proposed business venture will be beneficial to both parties. If the government has a master plan (and many do) and if another business firm is already manufacturing the good or providing the proposed service, the company may not be allowed to start up. This can be true even if the firm that the government has already licensed is less efficient than the one seeking entry into the market.

Furthermore, even if an initial proposal appears feasible, the company must often fight its way through a mass of red tape. The finance minister wants to know how much money the firm will bring into the country and how operations will affect the nation's balance of payments. The minister of power wants to know how much electricity will be needed by the proposed plant. Bringing all of these government officials together and obtaining final permissions for the proposed project may take so much time that the company will simply abandon the undertaking.

Government red tape may be too great.

Risk, Expropriation, and Foreign Partners If it does proceed, the U.S. company may find that the foreign government has the authority to set the price of the good and adjust it as it sees fit, allowing the firm a "reasonable" return but no more. Many companies dislike this idea because they feel the return does not justify the risk associated with the investment and the possibility of expropriation. There are numerous illustrations of rising nationalism leading to the takeover of U.S. businesses with plants in foreign countries.

Between 1960 and 1976, expropriations of U.S. investments numbered 292. David G. Bradley has found that the greatest percentage occurred among firms with assets of less than $10 million or more than $100 million. Additionally, when he examined the firms on a regional basis, he discovered that

> . . . the Latin American countries are the greatest offenders, responsible for 49 per cent of all expropriations since 1960. Over the same decade and a half, the Arab countries of North Africa and the Middle East, plus Israel, were responsible for 27 per cent of the nationalizations, the black African states and Rhodesia for 13 per cent, and the remaining Asian nations for 11 per cent.
>
> The absolute numbers, however, are deceiving. Given the total number of U.S. investments in each region, the rate of expropriation has been considerably lower in Latin America than in the Arab states or in black Africa. In fact, only Asia appears to be a better risk than Latin America for the American investor. Since

the overthrow of the procommunist Sukarno government of Indonesia in 1966, there has been only one recorded expropriation among the noncommunist countries of Southeast Asia.[7]

To reduce the possibility of expropriation, many firms take in native partners and operate the business as a joint venture. In some countries the government actually requires such action. On the positive side, these nationals can be useful in helping cut red tape. In addition, their awareness of local customs and marketing channels can be a great advantage. On the negative side, however, most businesses dislike turning over substantial (and possibly controlling) interest to an outside party.

Nevertheless, most firms today must be willing to establish some kind of balance between their own success and the welfare of the host country if they hope to succeed in an overseas market. As Philip Cateora points out:

> *Unless the multinational investor . . . concerns himself with the host country's local economy, the growing animosity to U.S. dollars throughout the world will continue to show itself in government-initiated domestication and expropriation of U.S. investments. In order to avoid the economic pitfalls of these two policies, global investment strategies will have to include a social awareness of local needs and wants. The investment must be aimed toward becoming a fully-integrated part of the domestic economy. Such predetermined domestication seems to be the most workable policy for the coming years in light of the evolving hostile political atmosphere found in many countries around the world.*[8]

One way of attaining this goal is through a joint venture.

Joint Ventures

When a firm establishes a *joint venture,* it takes in local partners who provide money and/or managerial talent. In a number of countries where U.S. firms have been establishing themselves, nationalistic pressure, coupled with the desire of local capitalists who are eager to profit from industrial growth, has led to an increase in the use of this organizational form.

Foreign partners can be useful.

On the positive side, the joint venture combines U.S. technical expertise with nationals' understanding of how to cut government red tape and market the product. Many companies have used this approach, including Du Pont, which holds a 49 percent interest in a Mexican chemical plant, and Merck, which has a 50 percent interest in an Indian pharmaceutical operation.

However, loss of control can be dangerous.

On the negative side, however, are the issues of control and culture. Some countries insist that their people hold at least a 51 percent interest in the venture. This idea is not agreeable to many U.S. firms, including IBM, and there are some very valid reasons for opposing joint ventures. First, the local partners are sometimes more interested in their short-run profit than in the company's long-term gains. Second, the nationals may lack managerial skills necessary to particular enterprises but, as controlling partners, make decisions that may prove quite costly to the firm. Third, the partners may disagree over policy. Fourth, custom or culture may dictate that the nationals find jobs for their families in the company. Fifth, there is the problem of hammering out a jointly agreeable contract. The way Americans go about negotiating such an agreement differs markedly from, for example, the Japanese way. Americans are accustomed to trying to get the best deal and have it agreed to in writing; the Japanese, on the other hand, do not operate this way.

---

[7] David G. Bradley, "Managing against Expropriation," *Harvard Business Review,* July–August 1977, p. 78.

[8] Philip R. Cateora, "The Multinational Enterprise and Nationalism," *MSU Business Topics,* Spring 1971, p. 55.

The formal contract itself is viewed differently by the managers in these two business cultures. U.S. managers generally take the position that, given the likelihood of some misunderstanding between the two partners, the contract should provide for every conceivable contingency. Japanese managers do not believe that the contract, mere words on paper, can assure the success of the venture. In fact, the provision of a formal dispute-settling mechanism, such as binding arbitration, augurs the breakdown of mutual trust.[9] In all these instances, the firm stands to suffer. As a result, many U.S. businesses accept joint ventures only when they are forced to do so. Other firms simply stay out of countries where this form of organization is required.

Despite the disadvantages, U.S. businesses find that joint ventures are becoming more common today than ever before. Firms that are thinking of going international must be aware of the potentials and pitfalls involved in this organizational form and, especially in underdeveloped countries, be prepared to accept them.

Making the Final Decision

After evaluating the pros and cons, the company's top-level managers will make the final decision as to whether to go international and under what circumstances. Naturally, the major criterion is going to be profit, but many qualitative judgments will be reflected in the decision. First, how large is the market? Domestic consumers are very different from foreign ones. In the United States, a large percentage of the population is middle class. In England, the largest group is the working class, whose incomes would put them in the upper-lower or lower-middle levels in the U.S. In India, most people are at the lowest levels of the income scale (less than $2,000). The question of economic growth and stability is thus of obvious importance.

Size of the market affects the decision.

A major, perhaps second, consideration is whether the other country's government is stable or more disrupted by political upheavals than not. It takes time to recoup any investment, and the company must forecast such developments in the political arena. Some areas of the world are considered very risky.

Political stability is a determinant.

Third, if the market and political conditions look favorable, is the company going to export goods to the country or set up facilities there? If it is going to export, it must establish marketing channels. If it is going to set up facilities in the foreign country, it must choose a plant site by matching the needs of the firm with the locations available. Perhaps the company needs to be located near a river or a source of raw materials. In any event, one site will be more advantageous than the others, and the company will want to select it as the final choice.

Marketing channels must be advantageous.

Finally, the firm must review the market investment. How much money will this venture entail, and how long will it take to reach the break-even point? Also, if there are local partners, will they be putting up any of the money, or will the venture be financed entirely by the firm? The answers to these questions will determine the ultimate fate of the project, which will become a question of risk versus reward.

A review of market investment is the final decision-making necessity.

If the company decides to go ahead, it must then focus attention on the management of the enterprise. What type of organization structure will be best? What kind of control will the company want to exercise? How should the company go about staffing the operation?

---

[9] Richard B. Peterson and Justin Y. Shimada, "Sources of Management Problems in Japanese-American Joint Ventures," *Academy of Management Review,* October 1978, p. 799.

MANAGEMENT OF FOREIGN OPERATIONS

Organizationally, the simplest way for a company to handle its foreign operations is by exporting the goods to agents and distributors abroad. But sometimes, because of strong nationalistic feelings, import restrictions, and foreign exchange problems, the company is forced to become more deeply involved. For those wishing to keep involvement at a minimum, licensing may be the answer. Under a licensing agreement, a manufacturer will permit a product on which it holds patents or trademarks to be produced in a foreign country. In turn, the licensee will make royalty payments to the company for each unit it manufactures. To ensure that the product is made correctly, many firms will train the licensee in production methods and manufacturing management. There is thus some involvement on the part of the company.

> *The firm may decide to export or license.*

Another approach, which entails still more involvement, is to manufacture the goods at home and then ship them overseas for assembling. Many firms have used this approach, but in time it is common to find them turning more and more to foreign manufacture. In the final stage, it is likely that the entire product will be manufactured overseas and the firm will begin exporting to nearby countries.

> *Overseas assembly of U.S.-made goods is possible.*

Organization Structure

Many types of organization structure can be employed in the management of foreign operations. In essence, structure depends on the firm's degree of involvement and its desire for control.

Branch Organizations and Subsidiaries The simplest form is the *branch organization,* which is an integral part of the company structure. In essence, a branch is simply an outpost or detachment that is placed in a specific location for the purpose of accomplishing certain goals on a local level. It is quite common to find branch offices responsible primarily for selling, with the branch manager acting as a sales manager who supervises salespeople, handles orders, and resolves local problems. There is great disparity in the area of control. Some branch offices are highly autonomous and others are under close supervision of the parent company.

> *A branch organization is an integral part of the company structure.*

A *subsidiary* differs from a branch in that it is a separate company, organized under the laws of the foreign country for the purpose of carrying out tasks assigned by the parent firm. By definition, a subsidiary is controlled (at least 51 percent ownership) by the parent, although it is possible that the parent will not completely own the subsidiary.

> *A subsidiary is a separate company.*

Some subsidiaries are highly dependent on the parent for operating instructions. Subsidiary department heads, for example, might report directly to their functional counterpart in the home office, the plant manager to the vice-president of manufacturing, the head of sales to the vice-president of marketing. Although those in the home office may not be best equipped to make decisions for the subsidiary a thousand miles away, the organization structure normally is designed so that it does provide for close coordination of foreign and domestic operations.

On the other hand, many subsidiaries are highly autonomous. Some, for example, have a free hand in conducting small local operations or carrying out narrow functions in a limited market. Others are full-scale companies with a great deal of autonomy across a wide area.

Control

The key criterion in organizing foreign operations is usually that of control. How closely does the parent wish to monitor overseas activities?

There are three degrees of control a parent firm can exercise: heavy, intermediate, and light. Each has advantages and limitations.

Heavy Control When a subsidiary is required to keep the home office aware of all operations and activities and seek permission before undertaking any important actions, the parent is exercising heavy control. An advantage of heavy control is that it ensures that the subsidiary will operate in accord with home office policies. In addition, this approach makes it easier for the parent to integrate and coordinate its worldwide operations. If a problem arises, the home office is in a good position to help solve the issue because it understands, through continual monitoring of operations, what is going on.

The parent firm can exercise heavy, intermediate, or light control over the subordinate.

On the negative side, heavy control can be expensive and far less effective than the home office would like. In addition, costly delays can occur while the parent company ponders a decision. Also, the subsidiary manager and the staff may quit or ask to be transferred home, feeling that they are merely rubber stamps who are not allowed to exercise any personal initiative.

Intermediate Control When the subsidiary submits continued reports to the home office but has the freedom to make important decisions without obtaining permission in advance, the parent is exercising intermediate control. The main advantages of intermediate control are that the reporting system helps the home office monitor activities and provide assistance to the subsidiary, and the freedom to make decisions helps the subsidiary manager and the staff deal quickly with operational problems. This freedom of action can be a great morale booster for the overseas staff.

On the negative side, the manager is expected to be an operating executive and a paperwork specialist, and it may be difficult to find an individual who is qualified to fill both roles. Also, the home office may be setting the goals for the subsidiary, expecting the manager to attain them. There may be difficulty here, however, because the subsidiary is not being allowed sufficient input into the plan.

Light Control When a subsidiary is allowed virtually complete freedom, having to provide the home office with only a minimum of information, the parent is exercising light control. Light control has several advantages. First, the manager can devote full attention to running the subsidiary and making money for the firm. Second, when the paperwork is decreased, the number of employees can be cut back and the overhead cost reduced. Third, morale is likely to be high when the overseas people realize that the home office is relying on their judgment to get the job done right.

Light control also has its disadvantages. First, it may be difficult to find a manager who is qualified to handle such a demanding job. Second, the home office gives up any chance to fully coordinate and integrate worldwide operations. Third, if a problem arises, the parent company may not learn of it until a great deal of damage already has been done.

Experience shows that heavy control is often too inflexible, whereas light control is too lacking in checks and balances. For this reason, many companies use some variation of intermediate control. The manager makes decisions at the local level but continually reports to the home office on subsidiary operations. Guvence C. Alpander, after surveying sixty-four multinational corporations, reported that 17 percent used heavy control, 67 percent employed intermediate control, and 16 percent opted for light control.[10]

---

[10] Guvence C. Alpander, "Multinational Corporations: Homebase-Affiliate Relations," *California Management Review,* Spring 1978, pp. 47–56.

Staffing

In addition to organizing and controlling foreign operations, a company must concern itself with staffing the enterprise. Who should head up the subsidiary? What qualifications will the overseas employees need?

Choosing the Right People The company can answer many of the questions about staffing when it decides whether to set up a branch or a subsidiary. Other questions will be resolved when the issue of control over operations is determined. Of those questions remaining, some can be handled quite easily. For example, if the firm that has been exporting to a foreign country decides to set up a subsidiary there, the export manager may be the natural choice for subsidiary head. If the company has an operation in Venezuela and decides to open one in Colombia, it may simply transfer staff. The people at the Venezuelan site probably speak Spanish and know a great deal about South American culture and custom. Their skills are thus transferable.

Many firms that must staff subsidiaries in underdeveloped countries have formulated guidelines based on past experience. For example, many like to employ unmarried people who have learned to make quick and easy personal adjustments to transfers and who will not have families to worry about. On the other hand, one U.S. oil company operating in the Middle East considers the middle-aged men with grown children the best risks. Economic conditions of the country and the specific operations of the firm can have an effect on who is most suitable for the job. So too can the geography. Companies with desert surroundings find that people from Texas or Southern California tend to be better risks than those from New England. By employing such guidelines, the firm can often pick those most suitable for the job.[11]

However the company hires, not all staff will be Americans. Many firms realize that unless they recruit some nationals, their firms may encounter very rough going. Not only are there cultural and social problems, but there is also the issue of nationalism. Host governments may insist that the company hire local people. For both of these reasons, it is common to find multinational firms attempting to recruit local people, preferably those with good business judgment or political connections.

Monetary Incentives Once the right people have been chosen in the United States, a firm has the problem of getting them to accept overseas assignments. In addition to travel, many firms offer monetary incentives. Besides their base salary, these people may be given housing subsidies and basic allowances to keep up with the cost of living overseas. In recent years, these extras have risen dramatically.

The need to supply such incentives helps explain why many firms will hire local managers when possible. Not only can they save on these high fringe expenditures, but the pay scale for foreign managers is often much lower. For example, a French manager running a French subsidiary will receive less than an American doing the same job. Such discrepancies have long been a source of dispute with many foreign managers. The situation can become even more difficult if one considers the French student who comes to the United States, receives a degree in business administration, and then takes a job in New York City with a multinational firm. The person in this capacity will receive an equivalent U.S. salary. However, if two years later the individual is sent to France to assist the manager in running the subsidiary there, this person will leave New York earning more money than the French office superior. What should the company do?

The entire area of wages and compensation is under current examination. Multi-

---

[11] For more on this subject, see Jeffrey L. Blue and Ulric Haynes, Jr., "Preparation for the Overseas Assignment," *Business Horizons*, June 1977, pp. 61–67.

Careful staff selection is necessary.

Foreign managers are paid less.

national firms have established various schemes for resolving the problems. However, the answer still seems to depend on an individual analysis of the merits of the particular situation. Quite often, paying a competitive wage seems to be the only satisfactory solution.

Upward Mobility Another advantage in going overseas is rapid promotion. Most executives admit that the person overseas can move up the subsidiary ranks much faster than it is possible to move up the ranks at home, because although many Americans will stay overseas for two or three years, most prefer to get back to the home office, having done their job in the field. This opens up opportunities for the lower-level managers to advance. Thus, for the individual who is adaptable to other countries and who can deal with the emotional strains of going international, the promise of upward mobility is a likelihood.

Rapid promotion is possible.

However, it should be noted that such promotions will undoubtedly not come at the expense of capable local management talent. A trend toward prohibiting expatriate managers from getting such favorable treatment is currently strong. This is best seen in the United States, where a lawsuit has recently been brought against the multinational Japanese trading firm, C. Itoh. The company has been accused of systematically discriminating against American executives. The charge is that the firm's employment practices give preferential treatment to Japanese executives in its hiring, compensation, and promotion practices. Before the Itoh case came to trial, some experts in the area expected it to go all the way to the Supreme Court.[12] The 1980s will probably witness the outcome of the case.

THE MULTINATIONAL CORPORATION

A good deal of attention has recently been focused on the *multinational corporation,* or *MNC,* as it is sometimes called. The multinational corporation is the subject of some controversy, part of which is a disagreement over how to apply the term. Some people say an MNC is, quite simply, a company that operates in more than one country. Others employ more criteria. Jacques Maisonrouge of IBM, for example, has been quoted as saying that these five basic criteria must exist before a firm qualifies for multinational status:

1. The company must do business in many countries.
2. The foreign subsidiaries must be more than mere sales organizations. There must be some services, such as R&D and manufacturing, carried on.
3. Nationals should be running the local companies since they understand the people and the environment better than anyone else.
4. There must be a multinational headquarters staffed by people from many different countries.
5. The company's stock must be owned by people in many different countries.[13]

Here are five criteria for defining multinationalism.

Most people are inclined to accept far less rigid criteria and would tend to agree with the group of researchers who identified a multinational company as "any firm that has a large portion of its operations devoted to activity that is not limited to one country."[14]

---

[12] S. Prakash Sethi and Carl L. Swanson, "Hiring Alien Executives in Compliance with U.S. Civil Rights Laws," *Journal of International Business Studies,* Fall 1979, pp. 37–50.

[13] Bradley and Bursk, "Multinationalism and the 29th Day," p. 39.

[14] Richard D. Hays, Christopher M. Korth, and Manucher Roudiani, *International Business: An Introduction to the World of the Multinational Firm* (Englewood Cliffs, N.J.: Prentice-Hall, 1972), p. 260.

Figure 17–1 U.S. Direct Investment Abroad (Billions of Dollars)

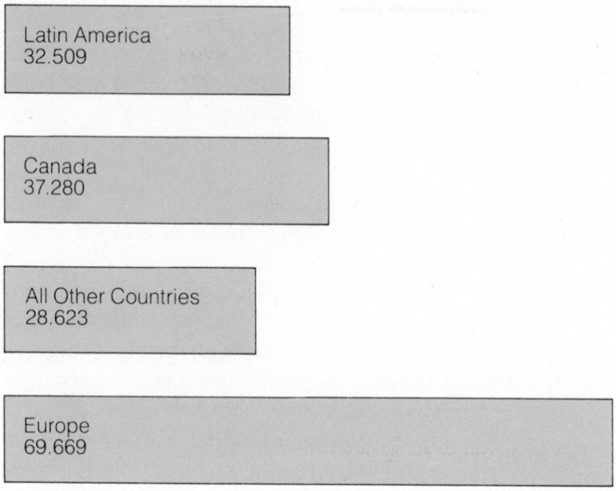

Latin America 32.509	
Canada 37.280	
All Other Countries 28.623	
Europe 69.669	

Source: *Survey of Current Business,* August 1977, p. 27.

This definition allows for various interpretations while conveying the most widely accepted meaning of the term.

U.S. firms have invested large sums in foreign lands, as Figure 17–1 shows. These investments have made the multinational U.S. firm a power in the international economic arena. Giant U.S. companies have significant economic control everywhere. In fact, more than ten years ago, U.S. MNCs in France already controlled virtually two-thirds of the country's farm machinery, telecommunications equipment, and film photographic paper production, in addition to 40 percent of the nation's petroleum market. In the whole of Europe they controlled 15 percent of all consumer goods then being manufactured, 50 percent of all semi-conductors, 80 percent of all computers, and 95 percent of the integrated circuits market. It is really no wonder that Jacques Servan-Schreiber predicted: "Fifteen years from now it is quite possible that the world's third greatest industrial power, just after the United States and Russia, will not be Europe but *American industry in Europe.*"[15]

U.S. firms have international economic power.

General Electric is a good example of U.S. success abroad. Its total and international sales picture for selected years during the 1970s is shown in Table 17–2. International sales make a significant contribution to overall sales, and in most cases this picture is not uncommon for multinational firms.

Becoming Truly International

With economic power comes responsibility.

With economic power comes responsibility. As the multinational corporations grow ever larger, they face the problem of rising nationalism. Is U.S. business trying to dominate other countries? Some people think so and believe that the challenge of the next decade

---

[15] Jacques Servan-Schreiber, *The American Challenge* (New York: Atheneum House, 1968), p. 3.

Table 17–2   General Electric Financial Data (Millions of Dollars)

	Total Sales	*International Sales*	*Net Earnings on International Sales*
1979	$22,461	$4,588	$293
1978	19,654	3,992	274
1977	17,519	3,689	245
1976	15,697	4,024	196
1974	13,918	3,218	174
1971	9,557	1,584	86

Source: General Electric 1979 Annual Report.

will be one of integrating nationals into the top ranks of these giant organizations so that management's point of view becomes international in focus. Kenneth Simmonds has stated it this way:

> Ensuring that top corporate management in the international corporation does become truly international requires planned action. There are many ways to start. Noteworthy steps include: international executive development programs that concentrate on top management problems, rotation of younger foreign executives through corporate headquarters, decentralization of staff functions to foreign sites, or adoption of policies that treat all executives as internationalists regardless of origin.[16]

Recent statistics reveal that this action is indeed beginning to occur. For example, Randolph A. Pohlman and two associates surveyed a large sample of American firms operating overseas and found the following percentage of the foreign subsidiaries' top management to be citizens of the countries in which the subsidiaries were located:

Percentage Native Born	*Percentage of Firms in Category*[17]
0–10	6
11–20	0
21–30	13
31–50	16
51–60	9
61–80	6
81–90	13
91–100	31
"Major"[a]	6

[a]"Major" is an unspecified number, considered of significance by respondents.

Pohlman, Ang, and Ali also found that most firms felt that a recruitment policy of "hiring a maximum number of nationals" was most effective. Some of these companies

---

[16] Kenneth Simmonds, "Multinational? Well, Not Quite," *Columbia Journal of World Business,* Fall 1966, p. 122.

[17] Randolph A. Pohlman, James S. Ang, and Syed I. Ali, "Policies of Multinational Firms: A Survey," *Business Horizons,* December 1976, p. 17.

said that United States citizens were used initially, but they were eventually replaced by local people. Furthermore, when Americans are used, greater care is devoted to training those individuals to fit into the host country organization.[18] It thus appears that more and more U.S. firms doing business overseas are becoming multinational in the fullest true sense of the word.

What about the charges of exploitation and imperialism that are sometimes heard? Perhaps the philosophy of U.S. multinationals is best expressed by Jacques Maisonrouge, chairman of IBM's World Trade subsidiary for Europe, the Middle East, and Africa:

> It has been our constant desire to grow, and to grow by being present in every feasible market, that has led IBM to where it is today. Wanting growth has nothing to do with imperialistic motives. Rather, it is one of the conditions necessary to remain dynamic, to remain young, and to maintain a sound level of excellence. Through time, I am sure, we will have substantial changes in the structure of the company, but one thing that will remain is our desire to grow, our desire to develop the non-U.S. markets, and to be present, as much as we can, in all the countries of the world.[19]

SUMMARY

This chapter has examined international management. U.S. firms account for a significant percentage of all international business. The student of management thus needs a working knowledge of this area.

In deciding whether or not to go international, a firm must evaluate many factors. First and foremost is its basic mission. Precisely what business is it in? If the management decides the international arena is within its sphere of operations, it can begin analyzing the possible advantages and disadvantages associated with such an undertaking. On the positive side are profit, stability, and the possibility of a foothold in an economic union, of which the European Common Market is a famous example. On the negative side are financial setbacks, unfamiliar customs and cultures, delicate company-government relations, risk, expropriation, and the possibility of having to bring in foreign partners, which, for many businesses, constitutes the biggest drawback. IBM, for one, flatly refuses to enter into a joint venture, although because of rising nationalism, such ventures are becoming a common phenomenon.

If a company decides to go ahead with a foreign operation, it must find an appropriate organization structure, which will depend, of course, on the amount of involvement it is willing to undertake. For some firms a branch organization will do; for others a subsidiary is necessary.

The next question is one of control. Which is best: heavy, intermediate, or light? Most firms opt for intermediate. Then comes staffing, which entails identifying qualified people and offering them sufficient monetary incentive and upward mobility to get them to go abroad.

The last section of this chapter examined the multinational corporation. Most multinational firms are American, and they carry a good deal of economic power in the international arena. However, with this power comes responsibility, and the challenge of the 1980s will be to continue incorporating foreign nationals into the upper ranks of management and to see that the interests of the host country, as well as the corporation, are properly served. In so doing, the multinational firms will become truly international in nature.

---

[18] Yoram Zeira and Ehud Harari, "Host-Country Organizations and Expatriate Managers in Europe," *California Management Review*, Spring 1979, pp. 40–50.

[19] Bradley and Bursk, "Multinationalism and the 29th Day," p. 45.

REVIEW AND STUDY QUESTIONS

1. Why do U.S. businesses enter foreign markets? Explain.

2. What are the advantages of going international? What are the disadvantages?

3. What is the Common Market? What are its goals?

4. How does a joint venture work?

5. How does a branch office differ from a subsidiary?

6. What are the advantages associated with heavy control of foreign subsidiaries? With loose control?

7. Why do most firms use intermediate control with their overseas subsidiaries?

8. What are some things a firm should look for in the people it chooses for overseas operations?

9. Is the chance for individual upward mobility in a foreign subsidiary better or worse than it would be in the home office?

10. What is a multinational corporation?

11. How powerful are U.S. multinational corporations in the international economic arena?

12. How international are the top management ranks of multinational corporations? Explain your answer.

SELECTED REFERENCES

Alpander, Guvence C. "Multinational Corporations: Homebase-Affiliate Relations." *California Management Review,* Spring 1978, pp. 47–56.

Apgar, M., IV. "Succeeding in Saudi Arabia." *Harvard Business Review,* January– February 1977, pp. 14–16.

Bass, B. M.; McGregor, D. W.; and Walters, J. L. "Selecting Foreign Plant Sites: Economic, Social and Political Considerations." *Academy of Management Journal,* December 1977, pp. 535–551.

Bass, B. M., and Schackleton, V. J. "Industrial Democracy and Participative Management: A Case for Synthesis." *Academy of Management Review,* July 1979, pp. 393–404.

Bernthal, W. F. "Matching German Culture and Management Style: A Book Review Essay." *Academy of Management Review,* January 1978, pp. 99–105.

Blue, Jeffrey, and Haynes, Ulric, Jr. "Preparation for the Overseas Assignment." *Business Horizons,* June 1977, pp. 61–67.

Bradley, David G. "Managing against Expropriation." *Harvard Business Review,* July– August 1977, pp. 75–83.

Bradley, Gene E., and Bursk, Edward C. "Multinationalism and the 29th Day." *Harvard Business Review,* January–February 1972, pp. 37–47.

Brandt, W. K., and Hulbert, J. N. "Headquarter Guidance in Marketing Strategy in the Multinational Subsidiary." *Columbia Journal of World Business,* Winter 1979, pp. 7–14.

Cuddy, D. M. "Planning and Control of Foreign Operations." *Managerial Planning,* November–December 1973, pp. 1–5.

Doz, Y. L., and Prahalad, C. K. "How MNC's Cope with Host Government Intervention." *Harvard Business Review,* March–April 1980, pp. 149–157.

England, G. W. "Managers and Their Value Systems: A Five-country Comparative System." *Columbia Journal of World Business,* Summer 1978, pp. 35–44.

Foote, M. R. "Controlling the Cost of International Compensation." *Harvard Business Review,* November–December 1977, pp. 123–132.

Franko, L. G. "Multinationals: The End of U.S. Dominance." *Harvard Business Review,* November–December 1978, pp. 93–101.

Heenan, D. A. "The Regional Headquarters Decision: A Comparative Analysis." *Academy of Management Journal,* July 1979, pp. 410–415.

Heenan, D. A., and Keegan, W. J. "The Rise of Third World Multinationals." *Harvard Business Review,* January–February 1979, pp. 101–109.

Horovitz, J. H. "Management Control in France, Great Britain and Germany." *Columbia Journal of World Business,* Summer 1978, pp. 16–22.

Lange, I., and Elliott, J. F. "U.S. Role in East-West Trade: An Appraisal." *Journal of International Business,* Fall–Winter 1977, pp. 5–16.

Lanier, A. R. "Selecting and Preparing Personnel for Overseas Transfers." *Personnel Journal,* March 1979, pp. 160–163.

Oh, T. K. "Japanese Management—A Critical Review." *Academy of Management Review,* January 1976, pp. 14–25.

Ouchi, W. G., and McJaeger, A. "Type Z Organization: Stability in the Midst of Mobility." *Academy of Management Review,* April 1978, pp. 306–314.

Ozawa, T. "Japanese World of Work: An Interpretive Survey." *MSU Business Topics,* Spring 1980, pp. 45–55.

Pascale, R. T. "Zen and the Art of Management." *Harvard Business Review,* March–April 1978, pp. 153–162.

Perlmutter, H. V., and Heenan, D. A. "How Multinational Should Your Top Managers Be?" *Harvard Business Review,* November–December 1974, pp. 121–132.

Peterson, Richard B., and Shimada, Justin Y. "Sources of Management Problems in Japanese-American Joint Ventures." *Academy of Management Review,* October 1978, pp. 796–804.

Reitz, H. J., and Jewell, L. "Sex, Locus of Control, and Job Involvement: A Six-country Investigation." *Academy of Management Review,* July 1979, pp. 393–404.

Robinson, R. D. *International Business Management: A Guide to Decision Making.* 2d ed. Hinsdale, Ill.: Dryden Press, 1978.

Ronen, S., and Kraut, A. I. "Similarities among Countries Based on Employee Work Values and Attitudes." *Columbia Journal of World Business,* Summer 1977, pp. 80–96.

Rummel, R. J., and Hennan, D. A. "How Multinationals Analyze Political Risk." *Harvard Business Review,* January–February 1978, pp. 67–76.

Servan-Schreiber, Jacques J. *The American Challenge.* New York: Atheneum House, 1968.

Sethi, S. Prakash, and Swanson, Carl L. "Hiring Alien Executives in Compliance with U.S. Civil Rights Laws." *Journal of International Business Studies,* Fall 1979, pp. 37–50.

Spencer, W. I. "Who Controls MNC's?" *Harvard Business Review,* November–December 1977, pp. 28–30.

Thal, N. L., and Cateora, P. R. "Opportunities for Women in International Business." *Business Horizons,* December 1979, pp. 21–27.

Weekly, J. K. "Expropriation of U.S. Multinational Investment." *MSU Business Topics,* Winter 1977, pp. 27–36.

Weigand, R. E. "International Trade without Money." *Harvard Business Review,* November–December 1977, pp. 28–30.

Widing, J. W., Jr. "Reorganizing Your Worldwide Business." *Harvard Business Review,* May–June 1973, pp. 153–160.

Zeira, Yoram, and Harari, Ehud. "Genuine Multinational Staffing Policy: Expectations and Realities." *Academy of Management Journal,* June 1977, pp. 327–333.

———. "Host-country Organizations and Expatriate Managers in Europe." *California Management Review,* Spring 1979, pp. 40–50.

———. "Managing Third-country Nationals in Multinational Corporations." *Business Horizons,* October 1977, pp. 83–88.

CASE: Twenty Questions

Before going international a business should be able to answer many questions. Some of these are:

1. Will our sales force in the new market respond best to straight salary, or to some combination of straight salary and commission?
2. How will our middleman respond to alternative policies we might employ?
3. Will the local partners be interested in long-term capital gain or exclusively in current income and prestige?
4. Will the government want to give us a maximum of elbow room in which to operate because it wants to show that it welcomes foreign investment?
5. Or will the government want to impose controls to assure, for example, that the positive-balance-of-payments effect of the investment is maximized, that the number of foreign nationals in the operation is held down to a minimum the host government will specify, and that at least a certain percentage (also to be specified by the host government) of the purchases of raw materials, components, and supplies will be from local sources?

Questions such as these are useful to the firm in developing its alternative strategies, reducing risk and uncertainty, and obtaining the greatest return on its investment.

Questions

1. In addition to the above, what other questions must be answered by a firm that is thinking about going international? Be explicit.
2. How does a firm go about getting answers to these questions?
3. Are there any questions to which a firm in this situation will not be able to obtain answers? Explain.

CASE: Getting Prepared

A large multinational corporation headquartered in the United States had been having trouble keeping its overseas staff happy. Especially when a new executive arrived, the company could always expect some critical problem. In an effort to deal with the difficulty, the company hired a consulting firm to study its overseas assignments and put together a report to help the company select and prepare people for overseas jobs.

Although it took almost six months for the consultants to compile their recommendations, the chairman of the board believes now that the corporation got its money's worth. The consulting firm made the following recommendations, which the chairman considered particularly valuable:

1. If there is time, send the executive, with spouse, to the country for an early visit. This will allow a firsthand view of the situation.

2. If English is not spoken there, give the executive couple some training in the language of the country before they leave. Even twenty to thirty hours is preferable to putting the new people through a crash course after they arrive in the new place.

3. Give arriving individuals a booklet containing information about such things as the specific culture, attitudes, religious beliefs and practices, and customs of the people of the host country. Also include in this booklet instructions on how to handle such company policy matters as travel allowances, medical plans, compensation, and vacations.

4. Where possible, have the executive visit with people in the firm who have been in the relevant country and now are stateside. These people can provide a lot of important information to the ones about to depart.

5. When new people arrive, have someone meet the plane and help them get through the first couple of weeks. If possible, have a spouse committee take care of some of this burden while the personnel office handles the rest.

Questions

1. Overall, what do you think of the consultants' suggestions?

2. Which of the five do you think are most important?

3. Would you add any other suggestions to the list? What are they? Explain your answer in detail.

CASE: ***A Foreign Invasion***

Ask anyone on the street which is the biggest nation in the international business arena, and the most likely response will be "the United States." However, other countries also are certainly interested in international business. The Japanese are a prime example. In 1970 Japanese multinational corporations invested around $2 billion overseas. By 1980 this figure was up to almost $36 billion. Forecasts put the 1985 total at just short of $80 billion; by 1990 it is expected to be in excess of $150 billion.

Where is Japan investing all this money? Practically everywhere. The following are some examples:

United States. The Nissan Motor Company, which made over $42 billion in 1979, is going to invest $300 million in the U.S. to either build or buy a production plant for turning out 120,000 units of its mini-pickup trucks. The production line is expected to be rolling by 1982.

Great Britain. A group of Japanese firms including Ishikawajima-Harima, Mitsubishi, and Kawasaki have entered into a $623-million joint venture with Rolls-Royce Ltd. The group will manufacture advanced jet engines. By the 1990s it hopes to offer stiff competition to both General Electric and United Technologies Corporation.

Australia. Three Japanese companies—Kobe Steel, Nissho-Iawai, and Mitsubishi Chemical Industries—are teaming up with the state of Victoria, Australia, in a $4-billion joint venture. The group intends to develop a coal liquefication plant that will produce over 30 million barrels of oil annually by 1989.

Saudi Arabia. Mitsubishi is looking into a $2-billion petrochemical complex that will supply Japan with almost a half-million tons of polyethylene a year. The investment will also ensure Japan additional crude oil supplies from the Saudis, who currently provide almost one-third of the country's daily oil consumption.

China. Two Japanese firms, Sanyo Electric and the Marubeni Corporation, are trying to work out a joint venture for a factory in China that will turn out almost 300,000 refrigerator compressors annually. Half of these will be exported to the United States. And in another business deal, the National Oil Company of Japan signed an agreement with the Chinese government which will allow it to drill for oil in the South China Sea.

Of course, these are only a small number of the many business deals that Japanese firms are striking worldwide. However, it is enough to convince many U.S. multinational firms that the Japanese are making serious inroads in the international arena and that they will undoubtedly present a major challenge throughout the rest of this decade and well into the 1990s.

Questions

1. Why are Japanese firms interested in investing in other nations?

2. What do you think are some of the criteria Japanese MNCs use in deciding where to invest?

3. Would the Japanese be very interested in entering into industry in the United States, or would they prefer to invest in the Far East? Explain your opinion.

CASE: Management in China

Many U.S. firms want to sell their goods in overseas markets; a new opportunity is selling the training that leads to production. Some U.S. organizations are going international by helping to train the work force of other nations. The Chinese, in particular, are interested in buying such training.

During the Cultural Revolution the government of the People's Republic of China claimed that anyone could be a manager. As a result, many business managers were sent to the country to work on farms, while people who were in political step with the government, but had not necessarily had any managerial training, took over the factories and other administrative positions.

Today China realizes that the country badly needs managerial talent. Only around 15 percent of the country's managers have had any formal managerial training. In an effort to make up lost time, the country is putting on crash courses in management for its people.

Some Chinese colleges have started offering courses in management; the government is also sending some of its young people to study management in colleges in the United States, West Germany, and Japan; and the China Business Management Association is offering short courses at branches all over the country. Topics include how to modernize factories, how to use the behavioral sciences in management, how to employ consultants, and how to conduct market forecasts. In some cases the government brings in U.S. business professors. During the summer of 1980 a U.S. government team, headed by a former dean of a business school, offered a pilot executive management program for a hundred Chinese managers and twenty college professors.

Questions

1. Are the management ideas taught in a basic management course in the United States the same as those needed by Chinese managers? Explain.

2. Can management information be marketed? Can a company offering international management programs actually succeed in the international arena? Explain.

3. Do you think China will ever have multinational corporations? Explain your answer.

CHAPTER 18

MANAGEMENT IN THE FUTURE

GOALS OF THE CHAPTER

Because past and present developments in the field of management have already been discussed, it is possible now to forecast what the future will probably hold. The first goal of this chapter, however, is to synthesize what has already been covered, for the future is at least partly determined by the past. The second goal of the chapter is to review developments in modern management theory, and the third is to examine developments on the horizon that will continue to gain importance over the next twenty years.

When you have finished this chapter, you should be able to:

1. Review the contribution of early classic management theory.
2. Recapitulate the major concepts contained in each of the three major schools of management thought.
3. Discuss current developments in management theory.
4. Describe some major trends in management today, including corporate democracy, the challenge of managing talent in a work force, and the continuing trend toward professionalism in management.

THE PAST IS PROLOGUE

In management theory, as in history, events of the past help determine events of the future; what has gone before sets the stage for what will follow. The first section of this book examined early management thought. It noted that scientific management, administrative management, and the human relations movement all made major contributions to the development of modern management theory. Although early classical theorists had their shortcomings, they did help uncover some important principles and theories that are still useful today. Alan C. Filley and Robert J. House have said this:

> In our review, many critical propositions derived from classical management theory have stood the test of research evaluation rather well. They suffer not so much from what they say as from what they fail to say. For example . . . the principle of unity of command is pragmatic convenience, not a necessity. Similarly, optimum spans of supervision do exist, but their determination depends upon a number of variables which are only now becoming clear.[1]

The classical theorists thus made lasting contributions to management.

Three distinct schools of thought have emerged.

There was, however, much more to be learned about the field. As research increased and the boundaries of management knowledge expanded, three distinct schools of thought emerged. The first, representing a continuation and expansion of Henri Fayol's work, is the management process school. Chapters 4, 5, 6, and 7, which examined planning, organizing, and controlling, established the basic framework for this school of thought. The second school, often traced directly to Frederick W. Taylor and his scientific management associates, is the quantitative school. Chapters 8, 9, and 10, which examined the fundamentals of decision making and some of the techniques being employed by the modern manager in choosing among alternatives, as well as the role of information systems, introduced the basic philosophy of this school. The third school of thought, which is concerned with applying psychosociological concepts in the workplace, is the behavioral school. Chapters 11 to 14, which examined the areas of communication, motivation, leadership, and human resources development, presented the concepts subscribed to by the advocates of this school. Management theory today can be represented as in Figure 18–1.

THE FUTURE OF MODERN MANAGEMENT THEORY

Modern management theory is advancing on a number of fronts.

Modern management theory is advancing on a number of fronts, including: (a) continued emphasis on systems theory, (b) the development of modern organization structures, (c) increased research on human behavior in organizations, and (d) greater attention to the management of change.

New developments in systems theory were examined in Chapters 6, 10, and 15. Some individuals believe that systems are a separate new school of managerial thought because a systems perspective is capable of synthesizing, from a pragmatic standpoint, the views of all other management schools. These people see systems management as the application of systems ideas to the management of organizations. Their approach calls for synthesis and pragmatism for the purpose of achieving maximum operational efficiency.

At present, however, managerial systems theory seems to be less a base for a school of management thought than an integrative concept for the manager to employ

---

[1] Alan C. Filley and Robert J. House, *Managerial Process and Organizational Behavior* (Glenview, Ill.: Scott, Foresman, 1969), p. 483.

Figure 18–1 Management Theory in the 1980s

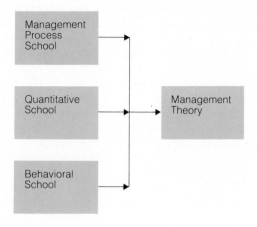

in carrying out various types of jobs. Managers today are more likely to view organizations as open systems, subject to the dynamism of the external and the internal environments; and that view is one of the ways in which systems theory has been of use in management. Another is in the way that systems work has made it possible to bring computers into broad applicability in the organization. However, the impact of the computer has not been so drastic as many writers had predicted. Rather, such external developments as changing technology and increasing competition have had more severe effects, because they have forced many organizations to abandon their mechanistic structures for more practical organic ones.

The result, as shown in Chapter 6, has been the development of modern organization structures. In contrast to their mechanistic-bureaucratic counterparts, modern organization structures are less predictable and less orderly. On the other hand, they are very well suited to meet the needs of modern businesses. In predicting what organizations of the future will look like, Fremont E. Kast and James E. Rosenzweig have offered the following descriptions:

Modern organization structures are flexible and responsive.

1. Organizations will be operating in a turbulent environment where they will have to withstand continual change and adjustment.
2. Organizations will increase in size and complexity.
3. Greater emphasis will be placed upon persuasion rather than coercion in getting employees to participate in organizational functions.
4. The influence of employees at all levels of the organization will increase, thereby resulting in power-equalization.
5. There will be an increase in the number and influence of scientists and professionals within organizations.
6. The goals of complex organizations will increase and emphasis will be given to satisficing a number of them rather than maximizing any one.[2]

[2] Fremont E. Kast and James E. Rosenzweig, *Organization and Management,* 3d ed. (New York: McGraw-Hill, 1980), pp. 605–606.

Management is also finding that, in order to manage its human assets, it has to focus increased attention on the demands of the employees for meaningful work and increased responsibility. These demands, as well as their effect on the national and international arenas, were examined in Chapters 14, 16, and 17. Today, the business organization is more than a profit-making institution, and its responsibilities cannot be limited solely to that function. It is an environment in which individuals come together and, in a give-and-take process, interact with each other and the organization itself (formal objectives, plans, policies, procedures, and rules) in producing a good or providing a service to some segment of society. In an attempt to achieve the necessary coordination and cooperation of its employees, management is trying to understand the needs and values of its people through increased research on human behavior in organizations. This research is reflected in such techniques as management by objectives, job enrichment, transactional analysis, and behavior modification. The future will hold more of the same as behaviorists attempt to answer the question of how the work force and the organization can be brought together in a harmonious, meaningful, and rewarding relationship.

Management is increasingly concerned with human behavior research.

The management of change is actually part and parcel of the three areas that have just been described. With the business environment in a continual state of flux, organizations have discovered that they have to live with change on a daily basis. As noted earlier in the book, change frightens many people. In overcoming this problem, management takes a systems approach to bringing together the people and the work.

During the 1980s, management will continue to develop techniques and tools for effectively adapting to and incorporating change. In fact, one of these adaptations, which is now beginning to emerge as a major part of many business strategies, is that of greater involvement in the political arena. A 1979 survey of *Harvard Business Review* subscribers found that executives believe that greater involvement in politics is a proper course of action for the 1980s. Specifically, the survey discovered the respondents' feeling that if business is to maintain or enchance its political position, it must:

1. Recognize that the political power now held by business is not permanent and that it will take care, skill, and effort even to maintain the current level of influence in the future.
2. Create a set of political activity guidelines that meet both the legal and moral standards of our society.
3. Establish an effective political activity control system within individual companies or industries before outside groups legislate one.
4. Train managers to work in the political arena, since this should help reduce their anxiety about political risk taking.
5. Take the general public's interest into account equally with corporate needs when formulating a political position.[3]

How will management theory integrate all these ideas? Many people feel the answer is to be found in a contingency theory of management, in which the manager draws on functional, quantitative, behavioral, and systems concepts as needed. Certainly this is the direction in which modern management theory seems to be moving. It should be realized, however, that despite what the contingency theory advocates say about a "new" school of thought, contingency is really nothing more than the formalization of very old managerial thinking. After all, Niccolo Machiavelli, in his Renaissance political treatise,

---

[3] Steven N. Brenner, "Business and Politics—An Update," *Harvard Business Review,* November–December 1979, p. 163.

The Prince, recommended pragmatism via his four principles of leadership. Is this not contingency theory? In summary, the systems and contingency schools may emerge on their own, but their basic thinking is already contained in management theory. Effective administrators are already using both systems and contingency concepts in attaining organizational objectives. Thus, a better term for this type of management theory may well be *eclectic.* The manager, having no exclusive allegiance to any of the schools, draws the best features from each and employs them pragmatically.

OTHER DEVELOPMENTS ON THE HORIZON

Although the previous section synthesizes much of what has been said in this book and provides insight into what can be expected to occur over the next few decades, three other developments, before now only alluded to in this text, merit closer examination. They are: (a) the trend toward corporate democracy, (b) the current challenge of managing personnel talent, and (c) the continuing trend toward the professionalism of management.

Corporate Democracy

One of the most pronounced trends in industry today is that of corporate democracy. Many employees, in a variety of settings, indicate their increasing desire for some code of fair play.

Current Research Findings This desire was clear in the results of a 1977 *Harvard Business Review* survey entitled "What Business Thinks about Employee Rights." A total of 7,000 *Harvard Business Review* subscribers were polled. Some of the conclusions follow:

1. Throughout industry there seems to be a steady broadening of support for methods assuring "due process" to employees who feel they have been wronged by management.
2. Among both top executives and lower management people there is increased willingness to hear employees speak out on controversial issues.
3. Strong majorities of subscribers favor advances in the right of privacy for employees.
4. A majority of HBR subscribers are well ahead of the courts in favoring protection for dissident employees, including "whistle blowers."[4]

Some of the responses in this survey were obtained through the presentation of cases and sets of alternative solutions. In one case, for example, the survey participants were told that a capable young manager in a financial service company had come back from a month's vacation with a beard and long sideburns. He also started showing up at work in bell-bottom trousers and bright sport shirts. This was a major change in dress habit for the man, and it contrasted sharply with the conservative suits worn by the other managers. The question was how the situation should be handled. The respondents answered as follows:

> *His superior should sit down with him, tell him that some people object to his appearance,*   49 percent
> *and that we'd like to have him stay with us but not if he looks like a hippy.*
>
> *How he looks is his own business unless it irritates people, in which case I would tell*   31 percent
> *him either to change his ways or begin hunting for another job.*

---

[4] David W. Ewing, "What Business Thinks about Employee Rights," *Harvard Business Review,* September–October 1977, p. 82.

In a second case the respondents were told that several top executives of a company in a large city have been disturbed by community activist organizations protesting the treatment of minority groups. The chief executive has articulated fears about the activists at local business meetings. However, a young man in the company's personnel department sympathizes with the activists and is spending a great deal of time doing unpaid volunteer work for them. When he is occasionally quoted in the newspaper, he is identified as an employee of the company. The firm's personnel director is under pressure from several top executives to warn the young man either to stop working for the activists or to resign. What should the personnel director do? The respondents answered as follows:

As along as the person keeps doing a good job, and until there is some concrete factual evidence that the company's public image is being hurt by his association with activists, I shall not interfere.   *62 percent*

People in this company and especially this department should be free to express their opinions on public problems. I'll go to bat for the young man as a matter of principle.   *19 percent*

I agree it's bad business for the chief executive to be saying one thing and a lesser official to be saying just the opposite. I'll tell the young man he's got to stop.   *8 percent*

As long as this person keeps doing a good job for the company, I shall not interfere.   *6 percent*

This is a question for the chief executive to decide, not you or me.[6]   *5 percent*

The above responses provide some interesting insights into the modern manager. The stereotype of the business executive as a conservative and oppressive individual is wide of the mark. Especially in regard to corporate democracy, today's managers indicate that they feel individual liberties and freedoms in the workplace are absolutely necessary. As expected, younger managers in the study were more liberal and tolerant than older ones. As the former begin replacing the latter, an even greater trend toward corporate democracy is likely. This study helped point this out by comparing the 1977 responses with those gathered six years earlier in a similar study by the *Harvard Business Review* editors.[7] The later poll showed that managers, on the average, were becoming increasingly concerned with corporate democracy.[8]

Specific Action If the survey is accurate and managers are becoming more interested in employee rights, what specific kinds of action are going to be necessary to meet these demands? Mack Hanan sees three necessary developments: an ombudsman's office to handle employee complaints and inquiries; an employee bill of rights; and tenure agreements tied to middle-management position descriptions.[9] All three are receiving increased attention today.

An *ombudsman* is an individual who handles complaints by investigating problem areas. Some states, for example, have appointed an ombudsman to handle complaints

---

[5] Ibid., p. 87.

[6] Ibid.

[7] David W. Ewing, "Who Wants Corporate Democracy?" *Harvard Business Review,* September–October 1971, pp. 12–28.

[8] For more on this topic, see Clyde W. Summers, "Protecting *All* Employees against Unjust Dismissal," *Harvard Business Review,* January–February 1980, pp. 132–139.

[9] Mack Hanan, "Make Way for the New Organization Man," *Harvard Business Review,* July–August 1971, pp. 135–137.

Table 18–1 Sample Corporate Bill of Rights

Article 1

Management shall in no way abridge the right of an employee to express his or her social, economic, political, or religious beliefs within or outside the confines of the organization.

Article 2

The offices, papers, and personal effects of an employee should be secure from unreasonable searches and seizures.

Article 3

No employee shall have to answer for a malfeasance or misfeasance unless management presents to him or her in writing the exact nature and cause of the accusation.

Article 4

If an employee is involved in a dispute, he or she shall be entitled to a public hearing within the organization; have a right to be confronted by those bringing in the complaint(s) against him or her; bring in witnesses favorable to his or her position; and be assisted by the company ombudsman or other counsel for his or her defense.

Article 5

No employee shall be dismissed from his or her job without due process of deliberation.

from citizens regarding corruption or inefficiency in state agencies and departments. The individual's job is to cut through red tape and initiate positive action. The same approach is being used in some corporate settings, where the ombudsman listens to complaints and acts as an impartial judge.

An ombudsman handles complaints.

> The ombudsman's domain is developing to include all grievances which adversely affect an individual or a small group of individuals. An ombudsman may function alone as a one-man office. Or he may head an Office of Management Counsel to represent individual interests before the organization. In this enlarged role, the ombudsman's office acts as an impartial tribunal of quasi-judicial review.[10]

An *employee bill of rights* spells out some of the obligations management has to the workers. It contrasts greatly with the booklets many companies give their new people which relate only what the firm expects of them. Some managers like to comment on the pamphlet they received when they first joined the company, which contained twenty-five pages of duties and obligations and one page of employee rights. As one middle manager stated it, "You learn your responsibilities as soon as you join a company. But you earn the knowledge of your rights one by one over many years. They don't exist anywhere; you have to sense them out. If you sense wrong, or if you sense too much too soon, that's it: you suddenly have another responsibility—to find a new job."[11] The bill of rights (see Table 18–1) is less a protective device and more a recognition by the company of the freedoms the employees have a right to exercise.

An employee bill of rights enumerates management's responsibilities to the workers.

[10] Ibid., p. 135.
[11] Ibid., p. 136.

Modern employees feel that corporate life obviously entails some sacrifice of personal liberty but that there is also a limit to how much the company may demand.

Tenure agreements for middle managers are, quite simply, employment contracts. They have three very important advantages. First, they acknowledge the individuality of the manager by signifying that the person has voluntarily stated a willingness to perform some service for the corporation and, in turn, will receive some reimbursement. The point to be noted is that the manager chooses to accept the contract; it is not granted through force. Second, this guarantee of employment allows the manager to begin formulating career self-development plans. Third, tenure implies accomplishment and proof of contribution. The manager no longer has to wait for years before being ensured of a permanent place in the organization but is instead rewarded on the basis of accomplishment, not seniority.

Tenure agreements are employment contracts.

The rise of corporate democracy is actually inevitable. In the late 1950s, William H. Whyte, Jr. wrote *The Organization Man,* in which he contended that corporate bureaucracies were molding people into what were most commonly called "company men."[12] The Protestant Ethic, characterized by rugged individualism and thriftiness, was being replaced by a social ethic that put primary emphasis upon conformity to group norms and the need to belong. Today, it appears that Whyte's fears will not materialize. If anything, industry is putting greater emphasis on individuality. The old organization man is being replaced by an employee who demands freedom of expression as well as personal involvement in organizational affairs.

Managing Human Talent

During the 1980s new demands will be placed on management in terms of how employees are treated. The composition of the work force is quite unlike that of previous decades. For example, in 1950 there were 23.3 million blue-collar workers and 22.4 white-collar workers. By 1975 the number of blue-collar workers had risen to 27.2 million, but the white-collar group had mushroomed to 42.1 million. By the end of the 1980s it is estimated that professional and technical jobs will increase by another 73 percent while blue-collar positions will rise only 30 percent. The United States will indeed have a white-collar work force.[13]

With this change will come increased demand for modern management styles, similar to those discussed in Chapter 13. Employees will be better educated and more knowledgeable than their predecessors, and they will demand a mature, adaptive style that allows them to pursue challenging, meaningful objectives.

At the same time, management is going to have to deal with many of the problems that have been carried over from the 1970s. These problems are best reflected in the changing values of employees, who currently report that they are discontent and that they expect more from their jobs than they have received in the past. A number of researchers have documented this shift in attitudes and values.

A recent report by M. R. Cooper and three associates, for example, shows a synthesis of employee attitudes gathered over a twenty-five-year period. The data indicate changes in employee values and increases in dissatisfaction among workers. This discontent manifests itself in ways which have major implications for management. Some findings from this study follow:

---

[12] William H. Whyte, Jr., *The Organization Man* (New York: Doubleday, Anchor Books, 1957).
[13] Edward Mandt, "Managing the Knowledge Worker of the Future," *Personnel Journal,* March 1978, pp. 138–143, 162.

1. Employees express consistent differences of opinion at many levels in the organization. In particular, managers are more content with conditions than clerical and hourly workers.
2. In the minds of most, the organization is not so good a place to work as it was in the past. In fact, the percentage of managers who perceive improvement in their companies has declined steadily over the last seventeen years.
3. Discontent among both hourly and clerical employees is growing.
4. While most employees say their rate of pay is fair, many feel dissatisfied and some, disrespected. This is particularly true at the lower levels of the hierarchy.
5. Most employees feel they are not treated equitably. Furthermore, expectations for advancement are the lowest they have ever been.
6. Employees expect their organizations to do something about their problems, but only one in four clerical and hourly employees feels the company is doing so.[14]

Attitudes and values are changing.

How can organizations deal with these problems? One way is through the use of employee attitude survey results. Many firms today have begun to realize that such surveys can serve as an important form of communication. They allow for an expression of personal feelings on the part of the employees, coupled with the input for developing relevant corrective plans by management. Second, feeding back to the employees the results of the surveys and management's plan for resolving the problems can build higher morale and establish a permanent two-way communication channel.

Another approach that seems likely to develop during the current decade is the reformulation of compensation policies. The types of rewards that will motivate people are likely to change. Numerous reasons can be cited for the decreasing value of money as a motivator; among them are the following:

1. Inflation is eroding the purchasing power of the dollar at almost as fast a rate as many organizations can replace it.
2. Giving people more money to keep up with inflation just pushes them into higher income tax brackets, further reducing the effect of their salary raises.
3. With the values of many people in the work force markedly different from those of twenty years ago, pay sometimes becomes a secondary consideration.

Compensation policies must be reformulated.

Organizations are going to have to offer more than just money. This point can be more clearly illustrated by taking a situation in which an individual is given an 8 percent annual raise (rather common today), and inflation is running at 6.5 percent (certainly a low estimate). While the employee should, on first glance, end up with a net increase in salary of 1.5 percent, the tax rate actually takes so much of the person's salary that the net effect can be negative. Table 18–2 illustrates this clearly.

A calculation of the net change after taxes and inflation computed as a percentage of the individual's adjusted gross income in Year 1 would show that the person making $15,000 a year would end up with a net increase in income of just over 1 percent. No one else would have done even this well, and the person making $60,000 in Year 1 would suffer a loss of over 2 percent in real income.

How will organizations of the 1980s deal with this problem? One way will probably be to offer more fringe, or nontaxable, benefits such as fully paid health plans, 100 percent company contributed retirement programs, and nonmonetary forms of compensation. The latter category includes such things as increased responsibility, a chance for challenging work, and an opportunity to feel important and do meaningful

---

[14] M. R. Cooper, B. S. Morgan, P. M. Foley, and L. B. Kaplan, "Changing Employee Values: Deepening Discontent?" *Harvard Business Review,* January–February 1979, pp. 117–118.

Table 18-2 Taxes and Inflation Can Seriously Erode an 8 Percent Raise

Adjusted Gross Income		Aftertax Income		Effective Tax Rate	After-tax Income	Net Change after Taxes and Inflation
Year 1	Year 2	Year 1	Year 2	Year 2	Year 2	Year 2ᵃ–Year 1
$15,000	$16,200	$13,339	$14,421	10.98%	$13,541	$ +202
20,000	21,600	17,454	18,759	13.15	17,614	+160
25,000	27,000	21,335	22,833	15.43	21,439	+104
30,000	32,400	24,990	26,744	17.46	25,112	+122
35,000	37,800	28,636	30,531	19.23	28,668	+ 32
40,000	43,200	32,237	34,252	20.71	32,162	− 75
45,000	48,600	35,850	37,743	22.34	35,439	−411
50,000	54,000	38,880	41,022	24.03	38,518	−362
55,000	59,400	41,981	44,813	24.56	42,078	+ 97
60,000	64,800	45,112	46,973	27.51	44,106	−1,006
65,000	70,200	47,382	50,738	27.72	47,641	+259
70,000	75,600	50,579	54,169	28.35	50,863	+284
75,000	81,000	53,731	57,229	29.35	53,736	+ 5

ᵃAssuming a 6.5 percent inflation in Year 2.

work. By designing compensation policies geared toward specific employee needs, management will be better able to attract and retain the kinds of employees it needs. And this will have to be done![15]

Continuing Trend Toward Professionalism

A trend toward the professionalization of management began some years ago and continues today. Although many definitions have been given to the word *profession,* the following is one of the most comprehensive:

> A profession is a vocation whose practice is founded upon an understanding of the theoretical structure of some department of learning or science, and upon the abilities accompanying such understanding. This understanding and these abilities are applied to the vital practical affairs of man. The practices of the profession are modified by knowledge of a generalized nature and by the accumulated wisdom and experience of mankind, which serve to correct the errors of specialism. The profession, serving the vital needs of man, considers its first ethical imperative to be altruistic service to the client.[16]

Five criteria are necessary for a profession.

The major criteria for a profession are knowledge, competent application, social responsibility, self-control, and community sanction.[17] It should be noted before these are discussed that management differs from many of the other professions, especially the traditional ones of theology, law, and medicine, in that one cannot rigidly apply a

---

[15] For other suggestions on approaches that management might take, see D. Quinn Mills, "Human Resources in the 1980s," *Harvard Business Review,* July–August 1979, pp. 154–162.

[16] Reported in Kenneth R. Andrews, "Toward Professionalism in Business Management," *Harvard Business Review,* March–April 1969, p. 50.

[17] Ibid., pp. 50–51.

set of conditions. With this qualification in mind, it is possible to show that management is indeed moving toward professionalism.

Management Knowledge Throughout this book, evidence of a tremendous increase in management knowledge over the last twenty-five years has appeared. As Kenneth Andrews points out, "No responsible critic . . . will deny that management practice now rests on a developing body of knowledge being systematically extended by valid research methods."[18] Thus, management meets this first criterion.

Competent Application Many professions, such as medicine and law, ensure competent application by certifying their members for practice. Although this is not the case in management, the surveillance of junior managers by higher-level executives serves the same purpose. Furthermore, "the diversity of business practice, the market mechanism rewarding successful and penalizing unsuccessful entrepreneurship, and the organization means for supervising competence in management all make it impracticable and unnecessary to erect educational requirements in imitation of the formality of law, medicine, and the ministry."[19]

Social Responsibility This topic has been discussed at greater length in Chapter 16. Today, more than ever before, business is aware of the importance of its own social role. Profit is certainly not a dirty word. Even so, business is making it increasingly clear that it is pursuing multiple objectives, with profit only one of them.

Other objectives are the provision of goods and services to the customer and the integration of the firm into the everyday life of the community. In this decade many businesses have been formulating social responsibility philosophies by way of meeting this criterion.

Emergence of Self-control Federal and state agencies have been established to regulate business and ensure compliance to prescribed norms. At the national level, for example, are the Federal Drug Administration, the Federal Trade Commission, and the Antitrust Division of the Department of Justice. It should be realized, however, that business also exercises degrees of self-control as reflected by industry codes of conduct. For example, the National Association of Purchasing Agents has an extensive code, one of its standards being "to buy and sell on the basis of value, recognizing that value represents the combination of quality, service and price which assures greatest ultimate economy to the user." The American Association of Advertising Agencies has an analogous set of standards, one of them being "Advertising shall tell the truth and shall reveal material facts, the concealment of which might mislead the public." Codes like these will undoubtedly increase in number in the foreseeable future. Why? The answer is twofold. First, the public is demanding higher ethical standards. Second, business managers not only believe that ethics are good for business but also feel that an industry code can have many additional advantages.

For example, an industry code is a useful aid when businesspeople want to refuse an unethical request impersonally. A manager who has been approached unethically may be said by the would-be influencer to be hiding behind the industry code. In fact, though, this manager is simply taking advantage of a freedom from risk that the business has provided. Such a code would also help businesspeople define the limits of accept-

---

[18] Ibid., p. 52.
[19] Ibid., p. 53.

We do care how we get results. We expect compliance with our standards of integrity throughout the organization. We will not tolerate an employee who achieves results at the cost of violation of laws or unscrupulous dealing. By the same token, we will support, and we expect you to support, an employee who passes up an opportunity or advantage which can only be secured at the sacrifice of principle.

Equally important, we expect candor from managers at all levels, and compliance with accounting rules and controls. We don't want liars for managers, whether they are lying in a mistaken effort to protect us or to make themselves look good. One of the kinds of harm which results when a manager conceals information from higher management and the auditors is that his subordinates think they are being given a signal that company policies and rules, including accounting and control rules, can be ignored whenever inconvenient. This can result in corruption and demoralization of an organization. Our system of management will not work without honesty, including honest book-keeping, honest budget proposals, and honest economic evaluation of projects.

It has been and continues to be Exxon's policy that all transactions shall be accurately reflected in its books and records. This, of course, means that falsification of its books and records and any off-the-record bank accounts are strictly prohibited.

Source: *Ethics and Responsible Behavior* (Houston, Texas: Exxon, 1979), pp. 4–5. Reprinted by permission.

able conduct and, where severe competition existed, reduce cutthroat practices. There is thus the emergence of self-control. Table 18–3 is one example of an industry code.

Community Sanction The final attribute of a profession, community sanction, also exists in management today, even though many business groups are not held in esteem by the public. Electricians who are called in to install a new outlet and then charge the home owner $67.50 do little to win community acceptance. Plumbers who fix a sink in five minutes but have a minimum house-call fee of $27.50 leave people angry and disillusioned. Fortunately, however, the management profession does not suffer from such stigmas. In fact, in many areas of social distress the public realizes that U.S. management has the technical skill and the organizational expertise to help overcome the problems; management can, for example, hire and train the hard-core unemployed, build housing of decent quality for low-income groups, and ease the problems of personal poverty and a stagnant economy by developing jobs, given sufficient capital. If anything, community sanction of management is stronger than ever.

Future Developments Despite its gains, management still has a way to go before it will fully qualify as a profession. However, significant steps have been taken, and the 1980s will see even greater progress. In particular will be the continuing development of academic management curricula, including: (a) the growth of new methods of quantitative analysis associated with the computer; (b) the study of organizational behavior; (c) better concepts for analyzing, understanding, and reacting responsibly to the social, economic, technical, and political environment of business; and (d) the study of policy formulation.[20] This, in turn, will lead to more sophisticated management practices, better self-regulation, and more attention to people problems in both the domestic and international arenas.

[20] Ibid., p. 59.

JUST A BEGINNING

The purpose of this text has been to identify, define, and place in perspective the concepts most important to the modern manager. This knowledge alone will not solve all problems for an organization, but it will provide a basis for formulating intelligent approaches to dealing with each specific situation. From here on, managers have to employ the method that they believe will work best. As J. Paul Getty, the oil billionaire, noted:

Managerial knowledge is a good beginning.

> To argue that business management is a science, in the sense that chemistry is a science, is to misunderstand the functions of management and to disregard its most significant element: people. Management — the fine art of being boss — is nothing less than the direction of human activities, obtaining results through people. Formal business education can only form a basis on which man can build. . . . But no theory in the world holds that a man with one, two or even three degrees in business administration can repair a cracking corporate structure merely because he has a collection of sheepskins hanging on his office wall. [21]

Coupling this perspective with the facts that modern organizations are in a state of flux and the environment promises to become more, not less, dynamic, management may appear to be a profession that should be pursued only by the most daring (or foolhardy). On the other hand, much information is available to the manager proceeding through the maze of modern organizational problems, and the rewards and challenges promise to make it an exciting career for those who have the potential and the desire. For example, Dalton McFarland puts it this way:

> Although management alone cannot solve the world's problems, managers and organizations will continue to play a central role in changing social institutions. Thus the field of management stands at the brink of an enormous challenge. If society's problems are centered in organizations and social institutions rather than inherent in human nature, management theory and practice can provide ample scope for the advancement of an enduring civilization. [22]

A CAREER IN MANAGEMENT

Now that the basic field of management has been examined, it is time to ask the reader a personal question: Do you think you might like a career in management? You might well feel you do not yet know enough about the overall field to be sure whether it would offer you the type of challenge you would like. However, it is not too early to examine the subject of career planning. The first place to begin is with an evaluation of yourself.

Know Thyself

No matter how much you know about management, in order to be an effective manager you must have a desire or willingness to work with others. Can you usually interact well with people, especially in a supervisory or managerial way? Or are you the type of person who prefers to work alone or with one or two people at most? Successful managers must be able to get things done through others.

Second, what kind of a job would appeal to you? Your answer to this question can help you pinpoint the type of organization where you can begin your search.

---

[21] J. Paul Getty, "The Fine Art of Being the Boss," *Playboy,* June 1972, p. 146.

[22] Dalton E. McFarland, "Management, Humanism, and Society: The Case for Macromanagement Theory," *Academy of Management Review,* October 1977, p. 622.

Third, how well do you take pressure? Are you the type of person who likes to be involved in a lot of activity and feels no pressure when time demands are placed on you? Or are you the kind of individual who likes to work at a leisurely pace and does not function well in a high pressure situation? Depending on your answer to this question, you can eliminate certain types of industries or jobs because of the amount of pressure they have or do not have. People and pressure need to be well matched.

While these are only three of the many questions that you should ask yourself in getting a personal profile, they are important because they help point out your likes and dislikes. Remember, to be effective as a manager, you are going to have to like the job. Very few people are successful doing things they do not like. So begin with an analysis of yourself.

The Interviewing Process

Once you have identified the type of job or organization in which you want to work, the next step is getting hired. Today, virtually no firm will hire you without first having interviewed you. And many people fail to get a job with the organization of their choice because they do not know how to come across well during the interview. Interviews frustrate or frighten some people for a surprising reason: There is not a great deal that one needs to do in preparing for the interview. You should dress properly, be courteous, and try to answer the recruiter's questions as accurately and completely as possible. Otherwise, there is little else you need to know, although some experts recommend that if you are interviewing with a national firm you should look through the company's annual reports and learn a little about the firm. This, they feel, helps prove to the interviewer that you are indeed interested in the job. Certainly, it helps distinguish you from most, if not all, of the individuals the person will interview that day; and it will probably create a positive image in the interviewer's mind. Be sure, though, not to try to lecture on the company.

Possibly the best way to prepare for the interview is to be aware of some of the typical questions that the individual is likely to ask you. Some people have tried role-playing with friends to simulate the situation and the questions, some of which will be:

1. Tell me a little about yourself. What is your background?
2. Why are you interested in working for our organization?
3. What did you major in at school? What are your favorite subjects? Which did you like least? Why?
4. What do you feel are your biggest strengths? Your biggest weaknesses?
5. What are your career objectives? How do you hope to achieve them?
6. Why do you feel we should hire you?

These, of course, are not the only questions the interviewer is likely to ask you; but they represent the general, most commonly used, approach.

Forewarned Is Forearmed

Once you get that all-important first job, you know that you will be expected to perform well. You should also know that there is more to this job than just performance requirements. A whole new world of work faces you, and you should be aware of some of the common pitfalls and problems that confront the new young employee embarking on a career. In this way you will be forewarned and prepared to deal with them.

One of the first things you should realize is that most young people who are starting out have very high expectations. They believe that their job will be extremely interesting, challenging, and personally rewarding. Actually, while the salary may be good, the work itself is often boring, routine, or simply monotonous. The real excitement will come later as you move up the hierarchy. Expect your enthusiasm to be replaced with the cold reality that the work will not be up to your level of expectation. Many times you will find yourself doing menial tasks that seem to have no real benefit. Nevertheless, this is part of the job.

Young managers' early expectations are very high.

Additionally, new employees, especially those on first jobs, feel a great deal of anxiety about these jobs. Many people are so anxious to be successful that they read every comment from the boss as being personal praise or admonishment. Actually, the boss will probably give you little feedback on your performance except to encourage you to keep trying hard and point out any big mistakes you have made so that you can avoid them in the future. However, you will not have such a significant job that a mistake will be catastrophic for the organization. You will, at best, make little mistakes. So relax and try to master the job as quickly as possible.

Their anxiety level is also high.

Third, maintain a positive attitude and show the boss that even when you do not know what you are supposed to be doing, or when you have done something wrong, you are prepared to keep going. At this early stage of your career, enthusiasm and drive are often as important as actual job performance because there is so little of the latter on which you can be evaluated.

A positive attitude is necessary.

Fourth, remember that every boss has an "in group" that he or she is looking after. The boss may recommend everyone in the department for a cost of living raise, but there are some who will be recommended for more. Try to get into this special group. One way of doing this is by proving to the boss that you are trustworthy and hardworking. You can be counted on. In fact, where possible, try to be not just reliable but indispensable to the boss. As soon as this individual realizes that you are an important part of the team, your status will go up; and your superior will take care of you. After all, you have shown that your boss cannot afford to be without you. Furthermore, as you begin to move up the hierarchy, try to develop a mentor, someone who will look after you and guide you a bit. Many up-and-coming managers are taken under the wing of a higher-ranking executive who makes sure that they move up the organization together. In this way, the mentor takes care of you and you, in turn, reciprocate. Today, many individuals report that part of their success can be traced directly to their mentor. It may be regrettable, but this is particularly true for women in large organizations. Without a mentor to ensure that they are given a fair deal, many of them find themselves sidetracked or shunted into dead-end jobs.

A mentor can be helpful.

Develop a Career Plan

When you first start out, it is difficult to develop a career plan. After all, you really do not know what type of career track is available to you. Nor do you have any idea of how fast the organization is going to promote you. And many other such unknowable variables will face you. However, after you have been pursuing your career for three to five years, you should consider setting long-range career objectives. Here are some illustrations:

1. By the time I am thirty, I will be making $35,000 a year.
2. I will develop a sponsor within eighteen months.
3. I will receive a promotion every two years for the next eight years or leave the firm and find employment elsewhere.
4. I will be an upper-middle manager at the end of ten more years.
5. I will be in charge of a major department or division by the time I am forty-five.

Set personal objectives.

Keep in mind that these goals are only set forth as examples of typical career objectives. They are not meant to apply to all people; nor are they intended to be inflexible. The important thing is to have a plan of action. The case entitled "Who Really Succeeds?" gives more of a perspective on this.

The Sky Is the Limit

What kinds of rewards are available to the successful manager? In a manner of speaking, the sky is the limit. For example, in recent years all types of financial arrangements have been structured to entice managers to join companies. CBS recently paid $1 million to Thomas Wyman of the Pillsbury Company before he even showed up for work, while the Chrysler Corporation made a similar financial agreement with Lee Iacocca after he had been fired by the Ford Motor Company.

In fact, in addition to salary and performance incentives, more and more firms are using these "front-end bonuses" to lure executives. Others are offering very lucrative packages that include pension benefits, insurance programs, paid personal serivces, and relocation and mortgage provisions. Sometimes these compensation contracts take months to work out, and the amounts can be staggering. In one recent case, a manager received the right to collect $290,000 a year for life, beginning seven years after the five-year contract ended. Another supplemental pension deal had an estimated value of over $8 million. In still a third, the following package was offered to a fifty-three-year-old manager who was being offered a job with a fashion-industry-related company with $650 million in sales:

1. A three-year, eight-month contract.
2. Either a $175,000 front-end bonus or a deferred payment option.
3. An annual bonus which could go as high as 50 percent of the annual salary.
4. Thirty thousand shares of stock at market value as of the closing price on the first day of work.
5. A leased Cadillac (or car of equivalent value) and membership in a luncheon or athletic club.
6. Fully paid medical insurance; group life insurance of $950,000; long-term disability of $5,000 a month; and travel insurance of $600,000.
7. Accounting and legal services up to $5,000 a year.
8. All relocation expenses.
9. Up to a $100,000 loan to help with the mortgage down payment with annual interest of 5 percent and no principal required for three years.
10. If the contract is not renewed, $50,000 a year for ten years and either pension fund vesting equal to six years or 60 percent of benefits at age sixty-five.[23]

Here is a notable executive compensation package.

This type of arrangement, of course, is offered only to top managers who have proved themselves in other firms. However, their success is partially attributable to their career planning. By setting goals for themselves and moving rapidly along their career path, they have been able to obtain lucrative financial offers. In thinking about a career in management remember that the challenges it offers are many, but for those who are highly successful, the rewards are great.

---

[23] Thomas C. Hayes, "The 'Front-End' Bonus Lure," *New York Times,* July 7, 1980, p. D1.

SUMMARY

Management has come a long way since the days of the early classical theorists. It has received contributions from many people in many fields, including psychology, sociology, and anthropology. Thus management thought has not developed in one basic direction. Rather, it has branched out into three schools: management process, quantitative, and behavioral.

What does the future hold? In one respect it will be more of the same: continued emphasis on systems theory; the development of modern organization structures; increased research on human behavior in organizations; and greater attention to the management of change. Other developments on the management horizon include corporate democracy; the management of employee talent; and the continuing trend toward professionalism.

Managers of the future will need to be aware of these developments. However, this knowledge, in and of itself, is no guarantee of success. The challenges of management are too great to be solved by simple knowledge of effective management processes and practices. On the other hand, for those who have the ability and the desire to study and to work and continue to learn, the opportunities and rewards in the field of management promise to be very great indeed.

The last part of the chapter offered some suggestions for those who feel they might like a career in management. The first step is a personal evaluation. Second, the individual should prepare for interviews by thinking of responses to questions typically asked during such meetings. Third, before taking a job, the individual should realize some of the common pitfalls and problems that confront new, young employees. Fourth, young managers should eventually develop a career plan. For the person who is very effective in this overall career planning process, all kinds of rewards are available. The sky is the limit.

REVIEW AND STUDY QUESTIONS

1. What contributions did the classical theorists make to management theory?
2. What are the three major schools of management thought? Briefly describe each.
3. What is the contingency school of thought?
4. How are the systems and contingency approaches eclectic in nature?
5. "The future will see a continued emphasis on corporate democracy." Explain this statement, incorporating into your answer the results found by the editors of the *Harvard Business Review* in their 1970s research on this subject.
6. What is a corporate ombudsman? How can this individual be useful to the employees?
7. What is an employee bill of rights? Explain.
8. In what ways will the management of executive talent prove to be a challenge to business during the 1980s? Why will this be so?
9. What does the term "profession" mean?
10. What are the major criteria for a profession? Explain.
11. Is management a profession? Give your reasoning.
12. How can a person prepare for a job interview? What are some questions the recruiter will be likely to ask?
13. What are some of the common pitfalls and problems that face individuals just starting their careers?

14. How important are career objectives? List some.

15. Explain in your own words what some of the rewards for successful managers are.

SELECTED REFERENCES

Andrews, Kenneth R. "Toward Professionalism in Business Management." *Harvard Business Review,* March–April 1969, pp. 49–60.

Boettinger, H. M. "Is Management Really an Art?" *Harvard Business Review,* January–February 1975, pp. 54–64.

Boone, Louis E., and Johnson, James C. "Profiles of the 801 Men and 1 Woman at the Top." *Business Horizons,* February 1980, pp. 47–52.

Bowman, J. S. "Managerial Ethics in Business and Government." *Business Horizons,* October 1976, pp. 48–54.

Brenner, S. N. "Business and Politics—An Update." *Harvard Business Review,* November–December 1979, pp. 149–163.

Brenner, S. N. A., and Molander, E. A. "Is the Ethics of Business Changing?" *Harvard Business Review,* January–February 1977, pp. 57–71.

Byron, W. J., S. J., "The Meaning of Ethics in Business." *Business Horizons,* December 1977, pp. 31–34.

Cohen, S. L., and Meyer, H. H. "Toward a More Comprehensive Career Planning Program." *Personnel Journal,* September 1979, pp. 611–615.

Cooper, M. R.; Morgan, B. S.; Foley, P. M.; and Kaplan, L. B. "Changing Employee Values: Deepening Discontent?" *Harvard Business Review,* January–February 1979, pp. 117–125.

Duncan, W. J. "Transferring Management Theory to Practice." *Academy of Management Journal,* December 1974, pp. 724–738.

Ewing, D. W. "What Business Thinks about Employee Rights." *Harvard Business Review,* September–October 1971, pp. 81–94.

———. "Who Wants Corporate Democracy?" *Harvard Business Review,* September–October 1971, pp. 12–28, 146–149.

———. "Who Wants Employee Rights?" *Harvard Business Review,* November–December 1971, pp. 22–35, 155–160.

Ference, T. P.; Stoner, J. A. F.; and Warren E. K. "Managing the Career Plateau." *Academy of Management Review,* October 1977, pp. 602–612.

Ford, D. H. "A Manager's View of Business Journals." *Business Horizons,* April 1978, pp. 18–22.

Hanan, Mack. "Make Way for the New Organization Man." *Harvard Business Review,* July–August 1971, pp. 22–35, 155–160.

House, Robert J. "The Quest for Relevance in Management Education: Some Second Thoughts and Undesired Consequences." *Academy of Management Journal,* June 1975, pp. 323–333.

Lazer, W. "The 1980s and Beyond: A Perspective." *MSU Business Topics,* Spring 1977, pp. 21–35.

McFarland, Dalton E. "Management, Humanism, and Society: The Case for Macromanagement Theory," *Academy of Management Review,* October 1977, pp. 613–623.

Mandt, Edward. "Managing the Knowledge Worker of the Future." *Personnel Journal,* March 1978, pp. 138–143, 162.

Martin, W. F. and Lodge, G. C. "Our Society in 1985—Business May Not Like It." *Harvard Business Review,* November–December 1975, pp. 143–152.

Maxwell, S. R. "Corporate Values and the Business School Curriculum." *California Management Review,* Fall 1975, pp. 72–77.

Mee, J. F. "The Manager of the Future." *Business Horizons,* June 1973, pp. 5–14.

Mills, D. Q. "Human Resources in the 1980s." *Harvard Business Review,* July–August 1979, pp. 154–162.

Miner, J. B. "Implications of Managerial Talent Projections for Management Education." *Academy of Management Review,* July 1977, pp. 412–420.

Steiner, G. "Invent Your Own Future." *California Management Review,* Fall 1976, pp. 29–33.

Summers, C. W. "Protecting All Employees against Unjust Dismissal." *Harvard Business Review,* January–February 1980, pp. 132–139.

Udell, J; Laczniak, G. R.; and Lusch, R. F. "The Business Environment of 1985." *Business Horizons,* June 1976, pp. 45–54.

Walters, K. D. "Your Employees' Right to Blow the Whistle." *Harvard Business Review,* July–August 1975, pp. 26–28.

Webber, R. A. "Career Problems of Young Managers." *California Management Review,* Spring 1976, pp. 19–33.

Whyte, William H., Jr. *The Organization Man.* New York: Doubleday, Anchor Books, 1957.

CASE: *The Role of the Ombudsman*

In one form or another, ombudsmen have been around for 150 years. Their goal is usually to curb abuses of government against individuals. In the early 1970s, corporations began to use ombudsmen also, Xerox and General Electric being two prime examples.

The purpose of the ombudsman is to handle complaints over such issues as salary, job performance appraisals, layoffs, and the scale of employee benefits. Some of these problems can be solved in a few hours; others take weeks. GE ombudsmen, for example, say that they each handle about 150 cases annually. In most instances, the ombudsman, with the employee's consent, goes to the boss and discusses the grievance. If the manager, the employee, and the ombudsman are unable to work out a settlement that the ombudsman feels is fair, the latter can go over the boss's head and talk to this person's supervisor. The ombudsman has no authority to overrule any managerial decision but can only call it to the attention of a higher-level manager. In the final analysis, the ombudsman does not make decisions or rulings. The individual merely tries to see that the employee gets a fair shake.

When the idea of the ombudsman started to become popular in industry, many managers expressed concern over the possibility that the men and women who took these jobs would side with the employee to the detriment of management. However, there is evidence that this has not happened. At the Xerox Corporation, for example, ombudsmen relate that their decisions favor employees about 40 percent of the time and management about 30 percent of the time and end in compromises the remaining 30 percent of the time.

One of the most important aspects of the ombudsman's job is to recommend constructive changes in organizational units which are facing a multitude of complaints. Ombudsmen, of course, cannot cure everything. However, companies using them say that feedback from the ombudsman's position helps them to recognize the effectiveness of some management policies. As one ombudsman put it, "It's a window through which management can look for a reaction to its style."

Questions

1. In what ways can the ombudsman help ensure corporate democracy?

2. Can ombudsmen really be very effective? After all, are they not merely go-betweens trying to work out settlements but possessing no authority to enforce their proposed solutions?

3. Do you think the 1980s will see an increase or decrease in the use of ombudsmen? Explain.

CASE: *Worlds Apart*

Is there a gap between management research and management practice? Many people seem to think so. For example, some management professors claim that their research is ignored by practitioners. One senior-level professor had his graduate students investigate whether recommendations from management studies in the literature were actually implemented by managers in those firms that were investigated. He found they were not. Supporting this argument, many managers admit that while their firms may subscribe to various business journals and periodicals, they seldom read the management literature.

On the other hand, practicing managers argue that there is a big gap between the way management scholars say things happen and the way in which they actually occur. Most contend that management research is simplistic, devoted to attacking nonexistent or unlikely problem areas, or that it addresses issues that simply do not warrant the manager's time.

How can this gap between research and practice be narrowed? One suggestion has been the establishment of closer rapport between individual firms and schools of business by having managers work in academia for short periods of time, while professors go off to industry for similar periods. In this way, each would gain insights into what the others do. Businesspeople would obtain new appreciation for the academic world, and professors of management would get a clearer idea of the problems facing the practicing manager and how they should be addressed.

Questions

1. How much of the research done by professors in business schools do you think is really applied by practicing managers? Give reasons for your opinion.

2. In addition to the suggestions given in this case, how else can the gap between theory and practice be reduced?

3. Realistically speaking, how much progress toward narrowing the gap between theory and practice do you believe can be expected between now and 1990? Why?

CASE: *Career Problems*

All young managers face career problems. What should they be doing to assure their future upward mobility? How can they be certain that their current career track is best for them? Assuming that a manager's goal is to move up the managerial ranks, various experts have offered the following suggestions:

1. Be a high-level performer. This is the surest road to the top.
2. Try to get into positions that offer visibility and exposure so that the chance of promotion is increased.
3. Get a sponsor who will help you move ahead. The most preferable is a mobile senior executive.
4. Learn the job as quickly as possible.
5. Train a subordinate so that you will be available to move.
6. Before taking any position, rigorously assess your strengths and weaknesses and only take the job if it draws on your strengths.
7. If you think you'll do well in a position, nominate yourself!
8. Do not stay under a boss who has not been promoted within the last three to five years.
9. Fight only necessary battles and refrain from contending with upper-level managers unless very important issues are involved.
10. If you decide to leave, do so at your own convenience and on good terms with the organization.

Questions

1. For the young manager seeking upward mobility, which of the above guidelines do you think is most important? Least important?

2. Would your answers to the first question change by industry, or are they universally applicable to all organizations? Explain.

3. In addition to the list set forth in this case, what other specific recommendations would you make to young managers seeking upward mobility?

CASE: *Who Really Succeeds?*

Career development planning is important to everyone who is interested in a working career. However, many people believe that, regardless of career planning, certain individuals have a better chance of making it to the top than do others. Two commonly cited success factors are family income and area of organizational specialization. Do these two have any real effect on career success? Research shows that the first is of limited significance, but the second does appear to be important.

For example, family background was much more important in 1900 than it is today. During this period around 12 percent of company presidents in major corporations came from poor families, 43 percent were from middle-class families, and 45 percent came from wealthy families.[24] Today the picture is quite different. While 10 percent of

---

[24] Charles G. Burck, "A Group Profile of the *Fortune* 500 Chief Executive," *Fortune,* May 1976, p. 174.

Table 18–4   *Major Areas of Emphasis of Chief Executive Officers*

Primary Career Emphasis of CEOs	Reports by Percent Responding "Primary"
Financial	19.5
Administrative/general management	16.4
Marketing	13.7
Legal	12.0
Production/operations	10.7
Banking	10.7
Technical	9.4
Owner/manager	5.2
Other	2.4

Source: Data analyzed in Louis E. Boone and James C. Johnson, "Profiles of the 801 Men and 1 Woman at the Top," *Business Horizons*, February 1980, p. 50. Originally from "How Much Does *Your* Boss Make?" *Forbes*, June 11, 1979, pp. 117–148.

chief executives of the five-hundred largest corporations in the country come from poor families, only around 7 percent are from wealthy families. The remaining 83 percent are middle-class children. These findings are in line with current research indicating that middle-income families produce the largest percentage of high achievers.

More important to those interested in career progress is the basic emphasis or area of specialization. Research shows that there are some fast tracks to the top. For example, a recent survey by Forbes reveals the major area of emphasis of chief executive officers. (See Table 18–4.)

Even in view of such findings, it should be noted that over the years the fastest route to the top has always depended on the firm. For example, some companies heavily emphasize marketing, and the presidents of such firms are always drawn from this functional area. In others, finance people hold sway, and so on. On the other hand, research also shows that in three out of four firms, new CEOs do not come from the same area of specialization as their predecessors.

It appears that today a manager who comes from a middle-income family and is in the financial area may have a slightly better overall chance of becoming a chief executive officer. However, the best chance is, as always, held by those individuals with the greatest performance records. In the final analysis, nothing succeeds like success; and when looking to promote at any level of the hierarchy, the question the search teams most often ask is: Which individual has the combination of the expertise for this job and a good track record? In short, there is no substitute for hard work and high performance.

Questions

1. In what kinds of firms would a person in the finance area have a better chance of becoming the CEO than a person in the production area?

2. Which functional area do you think would be best for an individual hoping to make it to the top if the person worked in a bank? An insurance firm? A manufacturing firm? A retail organization?

3. Why is a good track record more important than functional training? For example, why might the head of administration of a large bank be elected to the presidency rather than the head of the commercial loan department? Explain.

Exhibit 1   Operating Performance for Ten Well-managed Companies

	Sales (Millions of Dollars)	Profits (Millions of Dollars)	Return on Sales	Return on Equity
IBM	$22,863	$3,011	14.8%	21.6%
Procter & Gamble	10,081	616	5.6	19.3
3M	5,440	655	12.2	24.4
Johnson & Johnson	4,212	352	6.5	19.6
Texas Instruments	3,224	173	5.1	19.2
Dana	2,789	166	6.1	19.3
Emerson Electric	2,750	209	7.5	21.5
Hewlett-Packard	2,361	203	8.2	18.1
Digital Equipment	2,032	208	9.7	19.7
McDonald's	1,938	189	8.7	22.5

COMPREHENSIVE CASE: What Makes for Success?

As management enters the 1980s, one overriding question appears certain to continue as a major issue that executive decision makers must face: How can an organization achieve excellence in management? Many organizations have attempted to respond to this query, and a recent report by the management consulting firm of McKinsey & Company may have provided the answer.

After conducting an analysis of almost forty firms that are often pointed to as examples of well-run organizations, the consulting group focused its attention on ten: IBM, Procter & Gamble, 3M, Johnson & Johnson, Texas Instruments, Dana, Emerson Electric, Hewlett-Packard, Digital Equipment, and McDonald's. Exhibit 1 provides a brief overview of their 1979 performance.

None of these organizations is a holding company; all are operating firms. And all of them succeed because their management adheres closely to the eight characteristics which this case will discuss. Interestingly, none of these characteristics requires the use of sophisticated management tools or gimmicks. None calls for the specific expenditure of funds. Rather, all that is needed is a commitment on the part of management to devote the necessary time and effort to ensuring that these eight characteristics exist within the firm.

First: Be Prepared to Move to Action

Successful firms do not spend a great deal of time analyzing and reanalyzing problem areas or marketing opportunities. They look the situation over, determine the best course of action, and get on with the process of implementing the plan. Sometimes, of course, the plan does not work well. When that happens, this kind of company sets about adjusting the plan and trying it again.

In particular, successful companies avoid long or complicated procedures for developing new ideas. They realize that their plans may not be perfect; but plans can always be fixed up. Furthermore, as these firms begin to develop this philosophy of action, they become better and better at avoiding typical pitfalls into which other, more hesitant, firms fall.

The 3M Company, which demands that proposals for new product ideas be written in five pages or less, is a good example of these firms' action orientation. Procter & Gamble is another such company, with a one-page memo more the rule than the exception there.

Furthermore, in order to keep their action plans simple, many of these organizations set forth only one or two objectives. For example, in getting an advertising program off the ground, a company manager would pursue a goal of "Have the entire advertising program implemented by June 30." The statement of the goal is simple and to the point, though a timid manager probably would find its latitude frightening.

When it comes to dealing with problems, the action orientation of these firms is basically the same. Once a problem is identified, someone is put in charge of attaining a solution. If a task-force approach is used, a time period is set; and an answer must be forthcoming by this date.

Second: Keep the Organization Structure Simple

All of these successful firms believe one thing—a small structure is better than a big one. Even though all of these corporations are quite large, they get around typical bureaucratic problems by breaking the company into small entrepreneurial units. For example, Hewlett-Packard keeps its division size at no more than 1,000 people. And where possible, each is autonomous, functioning independently of the others in all possible ways. Texas Instruments, where there are 90 product customer centers, each functioning independently of the others, is another such example.

TI uses this same basic approach within each of the units. Small, manageable groups are formed and, to the extent possible, work independently of the others. This, in turn, helps keep the overall corporate bureaucracy to a minimum.

Third: Stay Close to the Customer

Technology is important to many successful firms. However, they examine technology in terms of the customer. How will new developments help the purchaser? What is in it for the buyer? By concentrating on these types of questions, the firms keep their emphasis on the marketing side of the business equation.

One way in which they do this is by soliciting ideas from customers. Instead of working out new product ideas in the lab, believing that the product is really very interesting and a sure customer appeal, these firms go out and ask the purchaser: What modifications would you like to see in our products? What other types of products would help you do your work more easily or more efficiently?

McKinsey & Company found that some firms have their top managers in the field as many as thirty days a year for the purpose of talking to customers and getting new product ideas. Companies like IBM, for example, believe that this hands-on approach is important; and in most cases, they do not leave people in staff positions for more than three years. They want these people out in the mainstream where they can interact regularly with customers. In fact, regular staff, such as individuals in R&D or finance, are sent out to the field on occasion to get a feel for the customer's perspective on the product line and to assess how the firm can be more effective in improving customer relationships.

Another way of getting market information is through customer-satisfaction surveys. Also, some of these firms hire individuals in "assistant to" positions to senior executives, with the assistant's sole responsibility being the handling of customer complaints within twenty-four hours of the time they are received.

Four: Improve Productivity through Increased Motivation

One of the easiest ways to improve productivity is to bring in new machinery. However, this method is limited by the fact that the competition can do the same thing and offset any real edge the firm is hoping to gain. McKinsey & Company found that the companies in its study tried to improve productivity simultaneously with motivation. One of the primary ways of doing this was to give the individuals increased autonomy. In production settings, shop floor teams set their own pace for production, the only stipulation being that they meet the agreed upon output target. Managers report that this approach often leads workers to setting ambitious but attainable objectives.

In firms where new product development is the name of the game, it is common to find a product group. In this group will be individuals from all of the necessary areas: marketing, technology, finance, and production. The group then operates on a self-sufficient basis and remains intact from the inception of the new product until its national introduction. The team spirit and morale that develop with this approach more than offset any costs associated with its use.

Finally, while many behavioral theorists frown upon such hygiene factors as recognition awards like plaques, badges, pins, and medals, these well-managed firms use them with success. However, monetary rewards are not the only form of recognition. In some companies a successful production team would be given an intrinsic reward, such as an invitation to describe its success to the board of directors.

Fifth: Use Autonomy to Encourage Entrepreneurship

Autonomy fosters independence and creative thinking. Firms of the sort under discussion find that individuals respond better when they work in a loose-control environment. This is why the organization encourages its managers to act like entrepreneurs. In plants, the head managers are free to make purchasing decisions and start productivity programs as they see fit. Does this approach really pay off? McKinsey & Company has found that it does, reporting that among such groups the grievance rate tends to be lower than the average for similar firms in the industry.

Furthermore, while the top staff may offer general direction, it does not force lower-level managers to make decisions that are not in accord with their personal judgment. Certainly, marketing analysis is used to help pinpoint target areas and develop product promotion campaigns; but these firms also realize that the manager is the one who must be sold on the success of the campaign. If this individual thinks the whole thing is a bad idea, or that it is a good idea but poorly timed, the firm usually listens to this manager.

Additionally, while many managers like to develop large numbers of successful products and make their organizational divisions ever larger, it is common in successful companies to find the product being pushed out of the division to stand on its own, while rewarding the manager for the product's success. Entrepreneurship is encouraged and nurtured. TI, for example, charges special groups with assessing new product ideas. IBM has a Fellows Program that serves essentially the same purpose.

Sixth: Emphasize Key Business Factors

One or two business factors in each of these firms are the keys to success. Keeping the emphasis on these factors, the company improves its chances for growth and profitability. For example, Dana's top management focus was on cost reduction and productivity improvement; in seven years the firm doubled its productivity. At TI, where the focus is on product development, the chairman of the firm made it a point every evening on the way home to drop in at a development laboratory. At IBM, even after his retirement, Thomas Watson, Jr., continued to write memos to the staff on the topic of calling on customers, even going so far as to discuss the proper way to dress for such calls.

As the firm begins to emphasize key business factors, they become a basis for daily action. For example, at Hewlett-Packard the operational review is focused on new products, while a minimal amount of time is devoted to financial projections or results. The company is convinced that if new product plans are properly implemented, finances will take care of themselves.

As managers who have been shaped in these experiences move up the line, they serve as role models for those who take their place. In this way, a firm ensures that these key business values permeate the organization. Everyone eventually begins to stress the same key business factors, with the result being an increase in efficiency, teamwork, and profits.

Seventh: Lead from Strength

All of these firms adhere to one basic principle—they stick to what they know best. They never acquire a business that they do not know how to run. They have identified their particular strengths, and they try to develop strategy around them. Some of the strengths possessed by the group McKinsey & Company studied follow: (a) IBM—customer service; (b) Dana—productivity improvement; (c) Hewlett-Packard and 3M—new product development; (4) Procter & Gamble—product quality; and (5) McDonald's—customer service, including value, quality, and cleanliness.

Eighth: Employ the Proper Combination of Tight and Loose Controls

Some controls have to be tightly applied. The rest can be used flexibly and loosely. For example, at the 3M Company return on sales is one of the tight controls. Management watches this statistic closely. In most other things, such as control of day-to-day operations, however, the lower-level manager has a lot of leeway. At Dana all divisions report costs and revenues on a daily basis, while other controls are used flexibly.

These eight characteristics have enabled the firms in Exhibit 1 to achieve better-than-average growth. One reason for this is that following these eight basic rules allows the companies to concentrate their attention on the external environment—the competition, industry changes, and customer needs. Internal considerations, such as profit and loss, efficiency, cost reduction, and staffing, are taken care of in the process. The external focus helps ensure internal effectiveness at the same time that it helps the firm succeed in its external environment.

Successful firms during the 1980s will find that their progress can be attributed less to sophisticated control techniques and more to the basics of effective management. Succinctly stated, these are service to the customer, productivity improvement, innovation, low-cost manufacturing, and risk taking. Current research indicates that these criteria will continue to separate well-run organizations from their mediocre counterparts.

Questions

1. How difficult is it to follow the eight guidelines in this case? Why is it that more firms do not follow them?

2. During the 1980s, which of the eight guidelines will be hardest for most firms to implement? Why?

3. How can the material in this book help the management practitioner become more effective in implementing these eight guidelines? Explain, using specific applications where possible.

GLOSSARY

This glossary contains definitions of many of the concepts and terms used in the book. For the most part, the terms correspond to those given in the text, and their definitions are followed by the numbers of the chapters in which they appear. A few definitions not included in the book have been added to provide the most comprehensive and useful glossary possible.

Absoluteness of responsibility   The concept that managers cannot avoid responsibility for the activities of their subordinates. They may delegate authority to their people, but they cannot delegate all responsibility. (Chapter 3)

Acceptance   The third step in the communication process, implying a willingness on the part of the receiver to comply with the message. (Chapter 11)

Acceptance theory of authority   Popularized through the writings of Chester I. Barnard, this theory states that the ultimate source of authority is the subordinate, who chooses either to accept or to reject orders issued by a superior. (Chapter 2)

Action   The last step in the communication process, entailing the implementation of the communication. (Chapter 11)

Activity   An operation required to accomplish a particular event in a PERT network. (Chapter 7)

Adaptive mechanism   A mechanism that, through its acceptance of dynamism, encourages responses to external and internal environments. (Chapter 15)

Ad hoc committee   A committee that is appointed for a specific purpose and disbanded upon completion of the job. (Chapter 5)

Administrative costs   Expenses associated with ordering inventory. *See* Clerical costs. (Chapter 9)

Adult ego state   In transactional analysis, an ego state characterized by attention to reasonable fact gathering and objective analysis. (Chapter 14)

Aggression   A frustration reaction that consists of attacking, either physically or symbolically, whatever barriers may prevent goal attainment. (Chapter 10)

Alternative budget   A budgetary approach in which budgets are set up on the basis of the level of operations: high, medium, or low. (Chapter 7)

Analog computer   A measuring machine used principally by engineers in solving job-related problems. (Chapter 10)

Attention   The first step in the communication process; it involves getting the receiver to listen to whatever is being communicated. (Chapter 11)

Authority   The right to command and the power to make oneself obeyed. (Chapter 2)

Authority of knowledge   The right to command that is held by the person who knows the most about the situation and is therefore put in charge of its operation. (Chapter 5)

Authority of the situation   The right to command that is held by a person on the basis of the need for immediate action, as in a crisis in which a leader emerges. (Chapter 5)

Automation   The technique of making an apparatus, a process, or a system operate automatically. (Chapter 10)

Autonomy   The degree of control a worker has over a job. (Chapter 14)

Avoidance   A frustration reaction that consists of withdrawal from a situation that the individual considers too personally thwarting to endure. (Chapter 10)

Balance theory   A theory used in the study of communication to explain how people react to change. The theory places primary attention on the consideration of three relationships: (a) the attitude of the receiver toward the sender, (b) the attitude of the receiver toward the change, and (c) the receiver's perception of the sender's own attitude toward the change. (Chapter 11)

Basic socioeconomic purpose   The reason for an organization's existence. (Chapter 4)

Basic decisions   Long-range decisions, often involving large expenditures of funds and carrying a high degree of importance. (Chapter 8)

Behavioral school   A modern school of management thought propounded by those persons who view management as a psychosociological process. Advocates of this school are particularly concerned with such topics as needs, drives, motivation, leadership, personality, behavior, work groups, and the management of change. (Chapter 3)

Benevolent-authoritative leadership style   A basic leadership style in which management acts in a condescending manner toward subordinates and decision making at the lower levels occurs only within a prescribed framework. (Chapter 13)

Black box concept   The inner workings that take place between input and output. As applied to human behavior, the concept may involve such things as the introduction of a new wage incentive payment scheme (input) and a 10 percent increase in productivity (output). The reason for the change may be the wage plan, but it may also be something else. The black box, or transformation process between input and output, is said to contain the answer. (Chapter 2)

B. mod   *See* Organizational behavior modification.

Branch organization Often employed in a firm's operations in other countries, it is simply an overseas office set up by the parent company. (Chapter 17)

Break-even point The volume of sales sufficient to cover all fixed and variable expenses but providing no profit. (Chapter 7)

Budget A plan that specifies anticipated results in numerical terms and serves as a control device for feedback, evaluation, and follow-up. (Chapter 7)

Bureaucracy A highly structured organization which has a clear-cut division of labor, a hierarchy of offices, a consistent system of abstract rules and standards, a spirit of impersonality, and employment based on technical qualifications and protected from arbitrary dismissal. (Chapter 6)

Carrying costs Costs associated with keeping inventory on hand, including sundry expenses, such as storage space, taxes, and obsolescence. (Chapter 9)

Causal variables Independent variables that determine the results that will be attained. Examples include management decisions, business strategies, and leadership behavior. (Chapter 14)

Centralization A system of management in which major decisions are made at the upper levels of the hierarchy.

Certainty decisions Decision situations in which the manager knows all possible alternatives and the outcome of each. (Chapter 8)

Change process A three-step process entailing the unfreezing of old ways, the introduction of new behaviors, and the refreezing of a resulting new equilibrium. (Chapter 14)

Child ego state In transactional analysis, an ego state that is made up of all the impulses learned in infancy and early childhood. (Chapter 14)

Civil Rights Act of 1964 Federal legislation that forbids discrimination against individuals or groups when the discrimination is based on race, color, religion, sex, or national origin. The act provides an agency, the Equal Employment Opportunity Commission, for dealing with employment-related discrimination complaints and charges.

Clerical and administrative costs Expenses associated with ordering inventory. *See* Administrative costs. (Chapter 9)

Closed system A system that does not interact with its external environment. (Chapter 7)

Closed-loop system A system that does not receive inputs from the external environment. (Chapter 7)

Cluster chain An informal communication chain in which information is passed on a selective basis. (Chapter 11)

Commanding The art of leadership coupled with the goal of putting an organization into motion. (Chapter 2)

Common Market A European economic community formed in 1957 by France, West Germany, Italy, Holland, Belgium, and Luxembourg. Today Great Britain, Denmark, Ireland, and Greece are also members. (Chapter 17)

Communication process The conveying of meaning from sender to receiver. (Chapter 11)

Complementary transaction In transactional analysis, a transaction that is appropriate and expected; it follows the natural order of healthy human relationships. (Chapter 14)

Completed staff work Staff work whose completed recommendation or solution can either be approved or disapproved by a line executive without the necessity for any further investigation. (Chapter 5)

Comprehensive budgeting A budgeting process that covers all phases of operations. (Chapter 7)

Comprehensive planning Planning that incorporates all levels of the organization: top, middle, and lower. (Chapter 4)

Compulsory staff service A concept developed centuries ago by the Roman Catholic Church, requiring superiors to solicit the advice of specified subordinates before making any decisions. (Chapter 2)

Computer program A set of instructions that tells a computer what to do. (Chapter 10)

Conditional value The payoff that occurs if a particular strategy proves successful. (Chapter 8)

Consideration Behavior indicative of friendship, mutual trust, respect, and warmth in the leader-staff relationship. (Chapter 13)

Consultative-democratic leadership style A basic leadership style in which management has confidence and trust in subordinates and a great deal of decision making is carried out at the lower levels. (Chapter 13)

Consumer Product Safety Act of 1970 A federal law designed to develop uniform safety standards for consumer products and to protect the public against unreasonable risk of injury from such products. (Chapter 16)

Consumerism Attempts by concerned citizens and government units to enhance the rights and power of buyers in relation to sellers. (Chapter 16)

Contingency model of leadership effectiveness A leadership model, developed by Fred Fiedler, that postulates that a leader's effectiveness is determined by three variables: (a) how well the leader is accepted by subordinates, (b) the degree to which subordinates' jobs are routine and spelled out (in contrast to vague and undefined), and (c) the formal authority provided for in the position the leader holds. (Chapter 13)

Contingency organization design Organization structures that are fixed after taking forces in the task, the managers, the subordinates, and the environment into consideration. (Chapter 14)

Controlling The managerial function of seeing that everything is done in accord with adopted plans. (Chapter 2)

Controlling process The process of determining that everything is going according to plan. In essence, the process consists of three steps: (a) the establishment of standards, (b) the comparison of performance against standards, and (c) the correction of any deviations that occur. (Chapter 7)

Coordinating The managerial function used in attaining the necessary unity and harmony to attain organizational goals. (Chapter 2)

Critical path The longest path in a PERT network; it begins with the first event and ends with the last one. *See* Event and Program evaluation, and review techniques. (Chapter 7)

Crossed transaction In transactional analysis, a transaction that occurs when a response is not appropriate or expected. (Chapter 14)

Decentralization   A system of management in which a great deal of decision-making authority rests at the lower levels of the hierarchy. (Chapter 5)

Decision making   The process of choosing from among alternatives. (Chapter 8)

Decision tree   An operations research tool that permits: (a) the identification of alternative courses of action in solving a problem, (b) the assignment of probability estimates to the events associated with these alternatives, and (c) the calculation of the payoffs corresponding to each act-event combination. (Chapter 9)

Delegation of authority   The managerial process used to distribute work to subordinates. (Chapter 5)

Delphi technique   A method of forecasting future developments, especially technological discoveries. (Chapter 8)

Departmentalization   The process of grouping jobs on the basis of some common characteristic—for example, function, product, territory, customer, process. (Chapter 5)

Departmentalization by equipment or process   The organization of employees on the basis of the equipment they operate or the process they perform. (Chapter 5)

Departmentalization by simple numbers   The organization of employees on the basis of numbers of people working. (Chapter 5)

Departmentalization by time   The organization of employees on the basis of work time schedules (for example, day, swing, and graveyard shifts). (Chapter 5)

Derivative departments   Departments formed through the subdivision of major departments. For example, derivative production departments could include manufacturing and purchasing. (Chapter 5)

Diagonal communication   Communication that involves the flow of information across departments or people on different levels of the hierarchy. It allows for messages to be transmitted directly instead of emanating from the bottom up to the top and down again. (Chapter 11)

Differential piece-rate system   An incentive wage system, formulated by Frederick W. Taylor, that paid a fixed rate per piece for all production up to standard and a higher rate for all pieces if the standard was met.

Digital computer   A counting machine which, by use of electrical impulses, can perform arithmetic calculations far in excess of human capacity. This was one of the most widely used of the early computers in business. (Chapter 10)

Division of work   Breaking down a job into simple, routine tasks so that each worker becomes a specialist in handling one particular phase of an operation. Often results in increased production efficiency. (Chapter 2)

Domestic system   The stage of a materially productive civilization in which individuals, assured of their own survival, begin to specialize in areas (for example, fabricating textiles) in order to sell the goods at local fairs for whatever price they will bring. Predominant system in England in the early eighteenth century. (Chapter 2)

Downward communication   Communications used to convey directives from superiors to subordinates. (Chapter 11)

Ecology   A scientific study area concerned with the interrelationships of organisms and other environments, especially as manifested by natural cycles and rhythms, community development and structure, interaction between different kinds of organisms, geographic distributions, and population alterations. (Chapter 16)

Econometrics   A mathematical approach used in economic forecasting. (Chapter 4)

Economic order formula   An economic order quantity model useful to the manager in the determination of how many units to order in replenishing inventory. (Chapter 9)

Economic man   A term used to identify someone who makes decisions that maximize the person's economic objectives. (Chapter 2)

Electronic data processing (EDP)   The processing of information through the use of electronic equipment such as computers and calculators. (Chapter 10)

Employee bill of rights   A list of some of management's obligations to employees. (Chapter 18)

End-result variables   Outcomes brought about by causal variables (for example, earnings, productivity, and costs). (Chapter 14)

Enlightened self-interest   A doctrine that business actually serves its own long-run interests by helping out its community. (Chapter 16)

Entropy   The tendency of a closed system to move toward a chaotic random, or inert state. (Chapter 15)

EOQ formula   *See* Economic order formula.

Equal Pay Act of 1963   Federal legislation designed to correct the existence of wage differentials based on sex; applies to industries engaged in commerce or in the production of goods for commerce. (Chapter 16)

Equity or social comparison theory   The contention that people are motivated not only by what they receive but also by what they see, or believe, others receive. According to this theory, individuals compare their rewards with those of others in judging whether their own remuneration is equitable. (Chapter 12)

Esteem needs   A person's need to feel important and receive recognition from others that supports feelings of personal worth; fourth level in Maslow's hierarchy. (Chapter 12)

Event   A point in time when an activity starts or ends. *See also* Activity; Program evaluation and review technique. (Chapter 7)

Expected time   A time estimate for each activity in a PERT network; it is calculated by means of the following formula:

$$t_E = \frac{t_o + 4t_m + t_p}{6}$$

where:

$$t_E = \text{Expected time}$$
$$t_o = \text{Optimistic time}$$
$$t_m = \text{Most likely time}$$
$$t_p = \text{Pessimistic time.}$$

(Chapter 7)

Expected value   The result of the multiplication of a conditional value by its success probability. (Chapter 8)

Exploitative-authoritative leadership style   A basic leadership style in which management has little confidence in its subordinates. Decision making tends, therefore, to be highly centralized. (Chapter 13)

Exploratory forecast   A technological forecasting technique that assumes that future technological progress will continue at its present rate. This technique moves from the present to the future and considers technical factors more heavily than other variables. (Chapter 4)

External audit   An audit conducted by an outside accounting firm. (Chapter 7)

Extrapolation   The simplest form of economic forecast, consisting of the straightforward projection of current trends into the future. (Chapter 4)

Exception principle   The belief that managers should concern themselves with exceptional, not routine, cases and results. (Chapter 7)

Expectancy   The probability that a specific action will be followed by a particular first-level outcome. (Chapter 12)

Expectancy theory   A theory of motivation that holds that individuals will be high-level performers when they: (a) see a high likelihood that their efforts will lead to high performance, (b) see a high probability that high-level performance will lead to specific outcomes, and (c) view these outcomes as personally desirable. (Chapter 12)

Expectancy-valence theory   A motivation theory, formulated by Victor Vroom, that states that motivation is equal to the summation of valence times expectancy. *See also* Instrumentality; Expectancy; Valence. (Chapter 12)

Factory system   The final stage in the evolution of a materially productive civilization; characterized by the introduction of power-driven machinery. Workers come to one central site, where the machinery is located (that is, the factory) rather than working at home. *See also* Domestic system; Putting-out system. (Chapter 2)

Feedback   The amount of information that an individual receives in regard to how well the work is being performed. (Chapter 14)

First-level outcome   A factor that brings about a second-level outcome; for example, productivity (first-level outcome) leads to promotion (second-level outcome) in many companies. (Chapter 12)

First wave of change   Changes that occurred as a result of the agricultural revolution. (Chapter 1)

Fixed costs   Costs that will remain constant, at least in the short run, regardless of operations (for example, property taxes and administrative salaries). (Chapter 7)

Flat organization structure   A unit structure characterized by a wide span of control, with only a small number of levels in the hierarchy. *See also* Tall organization structure.

Flexitime   A work schedule that management makes flexible enough to allow employees some decision-making authority over when they begin and end their workdays. (Chapter 14)

Forecasting   A method of projecting future business conditions for the purpose of establishing goals and budgets. (Chapter 4)

Formal organization   The officially designated jobs and relationships in an organization as seen on the organization chart and in the job descriptions. (Chapter 5)

Free-form organization structure   *See* Organic organization structure.

Functional authority   Authority in a department other than one's own, as in the case of a comptroller who can order production workers to provide cost-per-unit data directly to the finance department. (Chapter 5)

Functional departmentalization   Organization of a department along the lines of major activities. In a manufacturing firm so organized, it is not uncommon to find marketing, production, and finance departments reporting directly to the president. (Chapter 5)

Fusion process   The process by which an individual and an organization, when they come together, tend to influence each other's objectives. (Chapter 5)

Game theory   Theory used in operations research to study conflict-of-interest situations. (Chapter 9)

Gangplank principle   Developed by Henri Fayol, a principle holding that individuals at the same hierarchical level should be allowed to communicate directly, provided that they have permission from their superiors to do so and that they tell their respective chiefs afterward what they have agreed to do. The purpose of the principle is to cut red tape while maintaining hierarchical integrity. (Chapter 2)

Gantt chart   A chart on which progress on various parts of an undertaking is compared with time. (Chapter 7)

GNP   *See* Gross national product.

Gossip chain   An informal communication chain in which one person passes information along to the rest. (Chapter 11)

Grapevine   The informal communication channel in an organization. (Chapter 11)

Grass-roots method   A sales forecasting method that relies on input from salespeople in the field. (Chapter 4)

Gross national product (GNP)   The value of goods and services produced within a country in a year. (Chapter 4)

Group behaivor branch   A branch of the behavioral school that is interested in the study of groups and organizational behavior. (Chapter 3)

Hawthorne effect   Behavior that is differentiated by people's awareness of being under observation. Named after this phenomenon as first described by the Hawthorne researchers. (Chapter 2)

Hawthorne studies   Studies conducted at the Western Electric plant in Cicero, Illinois, that provided the impetus for the human relations movement. The research had four major phases: (a) illumination experiments, (b) relay assembly test room experiments, (c) massive interviewing program, and (d) the bank wiring observation room study. (Chapter 2)

Heuristic programming   An operations research technique that employs both rules of thumb and the use of trial and error.

Hierarchy of objectives   The interrelationship of objectives within an organization; short-term objectives are related to intermediate-range objectives, which are in turn related to long-range objectives. (Chapter 4)

Human relations philosophy   A philosophy that holds that the business organization is a social system and that employees are largely motivated and controlled by the human relationships in that system. (Chapter 2)

Human resources accounting   A recent development in management whose purpose is: (a) to view the acquisition of organizational employees as an investment of the firm and (b) to obtain a regular evaluation of these assets. (Chapter 14)

Human resources philosophy   A philosophy that holds that individuals want not only to be treated well but to be able to contribute creatively to organizational solutions to problems. For contrast, *see* Human relations philosophy. *See also* Theory Y. (Chapter 2)

Hygiene factors   Factors, identified by Frederick Herzberg in his two-factor theory of motivation, that will motivate people by their absence but not by their presence (for example, money, security, and good working conditions). (Chapter 12)

Identity of the task   The degree to which a job allows for completion of a whole or identifiable piece of work. (Chapter 14)

Industrial psychology   A subfield of psychology concerned with applying psychological knowledge to the selection, training, and development of an organization's employees.

Inference   A view of reality held by a person in response to implied data. (Chapter 11)

Informal group norms   Sentiments to which individuals must adhere in order to win acceptance and maintain membership in a group. Observed in the Hawthorne bank wiring observation room, for example, they included these dicta: (a) you should not turn out too much work; (b) you should not turn out too little work; (c) you should not tell a superior anything to the detriment of an associate; (d) you should not attempt to maintain social distance or act officious; and (e) you should not be noisy, self-advancing, or anxious for leadership. (Chapter 2)

Informal organization   The unofficially designated relationships in an organization; not shown on organization charts and often not reflected in job descriptions. (Chapter 5)

Information design   A process of filtering the number and kinds of reports and other data being sent to managers; the purpose is to prevent managers from being inundated with irrelevant reading. (Chapter 7)

Information system   An organized method of providing past, present, and projected information related to internal operations and external intelligence. (Chapter 10)

Initiating structure   The leader's behavior in delineating the relationship between leader and work group and the leader's work toward establishing well-defined patterns of organization, channels of communication, and procedural methods. (Chapter 13)

Institutional level   Upper level of the organization; concerned with relating the overall organization to its environment. (Chapter 15)

Institutional managers   Top-level managers whose concern is surveying the environment and developing cooperative and competitive strategies that will ensure the organization's survival. Such managers tend to adopt philosophical viewpoints. (Chapter 15)

Instrumentality   The relationship an individual perceives between a first-level and second-level outcome. *See also* Expectancy-valence theory; First-level outcome; Second-level outcome. (Chapter 12)

Intermediate-range planning   The setting of subobjectives and substrategies that are in accord with the long-run objectives and strategies of the overall plan. (Chapter 4)

Internal audit   An audit conducted by the organization's own staff specialists. (Chapter 7)

Interpersonal behavior branch   A behavioralist school that is heavily oriented toward the individual, especially in regard to motivations. (Chapter 3)

Intervening variables   Internal, unobservable, psychological processes that account for human behavior. These variables cannot be measured directly but instead must be inferred; motivation is one example of such a variable. (Chapter 14)

Job characteristics model   A model that helps explain how jobs can be redesigned so as to become more motivational in nature. (Chapter 14)

Job description   Description of the authority and responsibilities that accompany a job.

Job enlargement   An attempt to make work more psychologically rewarding; consists of increasing the number of tasks being performed by a given worker. (Chapter 14)

Job enrichment   An attempt to make work more psychologically rewarding; consists of building motivators into jobs in order that the worker can satisfy some personal higher-level needs. Popularized by M. Scott Myers. *See also* Motivational factors. (Chapter 14)

Joint venture   An enterprise undertaken by two or more parties. In international trade, it often consists of a foreign corporation, such as a U.S. business firm, and a host-country partner. (Chapter 17)

Jury of executive opinion   A sales forecasting method that relies on input from the organization's executives. (Chapter 4)

Key area control   A control technique by which a firm measures its performance in a number of vital areas. At General Electric, for example, key areas include profitability, market position, productivity, product leadership, personnel development, employee attitudes, public responsibility, and integration of short-range and long-range objectives. (Chapter 7)

Lag indicators   Series of economic indicators that often follow changes in the economic cycle. (Chapter 4)

Laplace criterion   A basis for decision making; using it, the manager applies equal probabilities to all states of nature. (Chapter 8)

Lateral communication   Communication that takes place among departments or people on the same hierarchical level. (Chapter 11)

LBDQ   *See* Leader behavior description questionnaire.

Law of triviality   Formulated by C. Northcote Parkinson, a law stating that the time spent on any agenda item will be in inverse proportion to the monetary sum involved. (Chapter 5)

Lead indicators   Series of economic indicators which often precede changes in the economic cycle. (Chapter 4)

Leader behavior description questionnaire (LBDQ)   A questionnaire designed for gathering information on how a leader carries out leadership activities. (Chapter 13)

Leadership   A process of influencing people to direct their efforts toward the achievement of some particular goal or goals. (Chapter 13)

Leading from strength   A rule of strategy holding that an organization should draw on its strong points in fashioning its strategy. (Chapter 4)

Learned behavior   Behavior based on some form of reinforcement or its lack. (Chapter 12)

Life cycle theory of leadership   A leadership theory, developed by Paul Hersey and Kenneth Blanchard, that contends that appropriate leadership behavior requires varying degrees of task and relationship orientation as the maturity of the followers increases. Chapter 13)

Line authority   Direct authority, as in the case of a superior who can give orders directly to a subordinate. (Chapter 5)

Line department   A department concerned with attaining the basic objectives of the organization. In a manufacturing firm, production, marketing, and finance would be line departments. (Chapter 5)

Linear programming   A mathematical technique for determining optimum answers in cases in which a linear relationship exists among the variables. (Chapter 9)

Maintenance mechanism   A mechanism that attempts to stop a system from changing so rapidly that it is thrown out of balance. (Chapter 15)

Management   The process of setting objectives, organizing resources to attain them, and then evaluating the results for the purpose of determining future action. (Chapter 1)

Management audit   An evaluation of the management's success in operating the organization. Criteria often employed in this evaluation include production efficiency, health of earnings, fairness to stockholders, and executive ability. (Chapter 7)

Management by objectives (MBO)   A process in which superior and subordinate jointly identify common goals, define the subordinate's areas of responsibility in terms of expected results, and then use these measures as guides in operating the unit and in evaluating the subordinate's contribution. (Chapter 14)

Management functions   The activities managers perform in carrying out their jobs. Planning, organizing, and controlling are the most commonly accepted ones. (Chapter 3)

Management information system (MIS)   An organized method of gathering and providing information to managers for use in decision making. (Chapter 10)

Management process school   Modern school of management thought whose adherents believe that the way to study management is through a systematic analysis of the managerial function, i.e., planning, organizing, and controlling.

Management science   *See* Operations research.

Management systems   Basic leadership styles identified by Rensis Likert. In essence, there are four: exploitive-authoritative, benevolent-authoritative, consultative-democratic, and participative-democratic. (Chapter 13)

Managerial grid   A two-dimensional leadership model that permits simultaneous consideration of concern for production and concern for people. (Chapter 13)

Marginal analysis   Analysis that concerns the extra output attainable by adding an extra unit of input. (Chapter 8)

Marginal cost   The costs incurred by selling one more unit of output. (Chapter 8)

Marginal physical product   The extra output obtained by adding one unit of input while all other factors are held constant (for example, the extra output obtained by adding one unit of labor while holding all other inputs constant). (Chapter 8)

Marginal revenue The additional revenue obtained by selling one more unit of output. (Chapter 8)

Matrix structure A hybrid form of organization containing characteristics of both project and functional structures. (Chapter 6)

Maximax criterion A decision-making basis. The manager determines the greatest pay-off for each strategy and then chooses the one that is most favorable, thus maximizing the maximum gain. (Chapter 8)

Maximin criterion A decision-making basis. The manager determines the most negative payoff for each strategy and then chooses the one that is most favorable, thus maximizing the minimum gain. (Chapter 8)

Mechanistic organization structure An organization structure that is often effective in a stable environment where technology is not very significant. (Chapter 6)

Microchronometer A clock with a large sweeping hand capable of recording time to 1/2000 of a minute. Developed by Frank and Lillian Gilbreth, the clock is still of use today in photographing time and motion patterns. (Chapter 2)

Milestone scheduling A scheduling and controlling procedure that employs bar charts to monitor progress. In essence, it is very similar to a Gantt chart, but its use is not restricted to production activities. (Chapter 7)

MIS *See* Management information system.

MNC *See* Multinational corporation.

Monte Carlo technique An operations research technique that makes use of simulation and random numbers in arriving at optimal solutions. (Chapter 9)

Motion study The process of analyzing work in order to determine the preferred motions for completing the job most efficiently. (Chapter 2)

Motivational factors Identified by Frederick Herzberg in his two-factor theory of motivation, the term refers to those factors that will build high levels of motivation and job satisfaction. Some of the motivational factors Herzberg identified are recognition, advancement, and achievement. (Chapter 12).

Multinational corporation (MNC) Any firm that has a large percentage of its operations devoted to activities in more than one country. (Chapter 17)

Need hierarchy A widely accepted framework of motivation, developed by Abraham H. Maslow. In essence, the theory makes three major statements: (a) The five levels of needs, in order of importance, are physiological, safety, social, esteem, and self-actualization. (b) Only those needs not yet satisfied influence behavior. (c) When one level of needs has been satisfied, the next higher level emerges as dominant and influential. (Chapter 12)

Net present value (NPV) The statement of future cash flows in terms of current dollars. (Chapter 8)

Nonprogrammed decisions Important decisions, novel and unstructured in nature. (Chapter 8)

Non-zero-sum games   Games in which gains by one side do not automatically result in equal losses to the other side. (Chapter 9)

Normative forecasting   A technological forecasting technique that begins with the identification of some future technological objective and works back to the present, identifying problem areas that will have to be surmounted along the way. Although it is a technological technique, normative forecasting considers both technological and nontechnological factors. (Chapter 4)

NPV   *See* Net present value.

Ombudsman   An individual who handles complaints by making inquiries and investigating problem areas. (Chapter 18)

Open system   A system that is in constant interaction with its external environment. (Chapter 15)

Open-loop system   A system that receives inputs from the outside environment. (Chapter 7)

Operational planning   The setting of short-run goals and targets that are in accord with the subobjectives and substrategies of the intermediate-range plan. (Chapter 4)

Operations management   An area that takes into account the design, operations, and control of organizational systems; it is heavily concerned with such functions as work flow, production planning, purchasing, materials requirements, inventory control, and quality control. (Chapter 9)

Operations research (OR)   The application of mathematical tools and techniques to the decision-making process. (Chapter 9)

Optimistic time   *See* Expected time.

Optimization   The combining of elements in just the right balance, often to secure maximum profit. (Chapter 3)

OR   *See* Operations research.

Organic functions   Activities that the organization must carry out to remain in existence (examples in a manufacturing firm are marketing, production, and finance). (Chapter 5)

Organic organization structure   Structure that is most effective in a dynamic environment especially where technology plays a significant role; since the structure can take any design, it is also known as free-form structure. (Chapter 6)

Organization chart   A diagram of an organization's departments and their relationships to each other. (Chapter 5)

Organizational behavior modification (B. mod)   A behavioral technique designed to modify behavior by rewarding correct conduct and punishing or ignoring incorrect conduct. (Chapter 14)

Organizational decisions   Decisions made by executives in their role as managers. (Chapter 8)

Organizational level   Middle level of a company, concerned with coordinating and integrating work performance at the technical level. (Chapter 15)

Organizational managers   Middle managers whose goal is to coordinate the technical and institutional levels of the firm in some harmonious fashion and who tend to assume a political or mediating viewpoint. (Chapter 15)

Organizing   The structuring of activities, materials, and employees for accomplishing assigned tasks. (Chapter 2)

Organizing function   The assignment of duties and coordination of efforts among all employees to ensure maximum efficiency in the attainment of predetermined objectives. (Chapter 5)

Parent ego state   An ego state containing the supervisory attitudes and behaviors that children perceive in their parents and later replicate in supervisory situations. (Chapter 14)

Participative-democratic leadership style   A basic leadership style in which management has complete confidence and trust in the subordinates and in which decision making is highly decentralized. (Chapter 13)

Path-goal theory of leadership   A theory which holds that the leader's job is: (a) to help the subordinates by increasing their personal satisfactions in work-goal attainment and (b) to make the path to these satisfactions easier. (Chapter 13)

Payback period   The time it takes for an investment to pay for itself. (Chapter 8)

Perception   A person's view of reality. (Chapter 11)

Personal decisions   Decisions that relate to the manager as an individual, not as a member of the organization. (Chapter 8)

Personal power   Informal authority that is created or sustained by such factors as experience, drive, association with the right groups, and education. (Chapter 5)

PERT   *See* Program evaluation and review technique.

Pessimistic time   *See* Expected time.

Physiological needs   Physical needs (for example, food, clothing, and shelter); the first level in Maslow's hierarchy. (Chapter 12)

Planning   A forecast of events and, based on the forecast, the construction of an operating program; one of the three most basic managerial functions. (Chapter 2)

Planning function   The formulation of objectives and the steps that are employed in attaining them. (Chapter 4)

Planning organization   An organization specifically designed to help a company develop a comprehensive and logical approach to planning at all the hierarchical levels. (Chapter 4)

Plural executives   Committees having the authority to order that their recommendations be implemented. (Chapter 5)

Policy   A general guide to thinking and action. (Chapter 8)

Primacy of planning   The principle that, at least initially, planning precedes all the other managerial functions. (Chapter 3)

Principles of management   General guidelines (in the case of the classical theorists, they were basically inflexible) useful to the manager in carrying out the practice of management. (Chapter 3)

Principles of scientific management Set forth by Frederick W. Taylor, principles that include the following four points: (a) Develop a science for each element of an employee's work, thus replacing the old rule-of-thumb method. (b) Scientifically select and then train, teach, and develop the employee, as contrasted with the earlier practices of letting a worker individually pick up whatever knowledge was available. (c) Heartily cooperate with the workers to ensure that all work is being done is in accord with the principles of scientific management. (d) Divide work almost equally between management and employees, with the difference from the past being that managers take over managerial tasks, whereas these formerly fell generally on the employees. (Chapter 2)

Probability The likelihood that a particular outcome will occur. (Chapter 8)

Probability chain An informal communication chain in which information is passed on a random basis. (Chapter 11)

Procedure A guide to action that relates the chronological steps entailed in attaining some objective, such as allowing a person to return faulty merchandise. (Chapter 8)

Product departmentalization The organization of a department, particularly one belonging to a large corporation, along product lines. (Chapter 5)

Productivity Output divided by input. (Chapter 2)

Profession A vocation whose practice is founded on an understanding of some department of learning or science or upon the abilities accompanying such understanding (for example, physician, attorney, professor, priest). Major criteria include: (a) knowledge, (b) competent application, (c) social responsibility, (d) self-control, and (e) community sanction. (Chapter 18)

Profit The remainder after expenses are deducted from revenues. (Chapter 7)

Program evaluation and review technique (PERT) A sophisticated time-event network series that permits a manager to evaluate and control the progress of a complex undertaking. *See also* Activity; Event. (Chapter 7)

Programmed decisions Routine decisions often handled in the implementation of predetermined policies. (Chapter 8)

Project authority Authority exercised by project managers over personnel assigned to them for a project. This authority, which flows horizontally, contrasts with functional authority. (Chapter 6)

Project organization An organization that is created for the attainment of a particular objective and disbanded on its completion. (Chapter 6)

Projection A frustration reaction that involves blaming others for one's own shortcomings. (Chapter 10)

Psychology The study of human behavior.

Putting-out system The second stage in the evolution of a materially productive civilization initially characterized by an entrepreneur's agreement to take all the output an individual (or family) can produce at a fixed price. This stage eventually progressed to the stage where the entrepreneur provided the workers with the raw materials and paid them on a piece-rate basis for finished goods. *See also* Domestic system; Factory system. (Chapter 2)

Quantitative school A modern school of management thought consisting of theories on management as a system of mathematical models and processes. Advocates of this school are greatly concerned with decision making. The genesis of the school is scientific management. (Chapter 3)

Queuing theory   An operations research technique used for balancing waiting lines and service. (Chapter 9)

Rabble hypothesis   The belief that the workers are a disorganized group of individuals, each acting out of personal interest.

Responsibility   The obligation of a subordinate to perform assigned tasks. (Chapter 2)

Return on investment (ROI)   A control technique used to determine how well a firm is managing its assets. In essence, the ROI computation is:

$$\frac{\text{Earnings}}{\text{Sales}} \times \frac{\text{Sales}}{\text{Total investment}}.$$

(Chapter 7)

Revery   Used by Elton D. Mayo to refer generally to an individual's entire outlook on life. (Chapter 2)

Risk decisions   Decision situations in which the manager has some information on the outcomes of each alternative and can formulate probability estimates based on the knowledge. (Chapter 8)

Routine decisions   Decisions that are often repetitive in nature and have only a minor impact on the firm. (Chapter 8)

Saddle point   A term used in game theory to identify an ideal strategy. (Chapter 9)

Safety needs   The need for such things as economic security, job security, and an orderly environment; second level in Maslow's hierarchy. (Chapter 12)

Sales forecast   A method of projecting future sales. Some common techniques include survey of current sales information, the jury of executive opinion, the grass-roots method, and user expectation. (Chapter 4)

Satisficing   Striving for a level that is good enough, or satisfactory; it will not necessarily be maximally achieving to satisfice.

SBU   *See* Strategic business unit.

Scalar chain   The chain of command that runs from the top of an organization to its lowest ranks. (Chapter 2)

Scientific management   A system of management popularized by Frederick W. Taylor and others in the early twentieth century that sought to develop: (a) ways of increasing productivity by making work easier to perform and (b) methods for motivating workers to take advantages of these labor-saving devices and techniques. (Chapter 2)

Scientific method   A logical problem-solving process used in identifying the problem, diagnosing the situation, gathering preliminary data, classifying the information, stating a tentative answer to the problem, and testing the answer. (Chapter 2)

Second-level outcome   The effect brought about by a first-level outcome—for example, a promotion (second-level outcome) brought about by productivity (first-level outcome). (Chapter 12)

Second wave of change   Changes that occurred as a result of the Industrial Revolution. (Chapter 1)

Self-actualization needs   The need to realize one's full potential; highest level in Maslow's hierarchy. (Chapter 7)

Self-audit   An evaluation of organizational performance which is carried out by individuals working in the enterprise. (Chapter 7)

Sensitivity training   A form of training designed to make managers more aware of their own feelings and those of others. (Chapter 14)

Sensory reality   Physical reality, such as a house or a chair. (Chapter 11)

Significance of the task   The degree to which a job has an impact on the lives or work of other people. (Chapter 14)

Simulation   As used in a business setting, mathematical models designed to provide answers to "what if" questions. (Chapter 10)

Single strand   An informal communication chain in which information is passed from one person to another, through a line of recipients. (Chapter 11)

Situational theory   View of leadership as multidimensional, consisting of the leader's personality; the requirements of the task; the expectations, needs, and attitudes of the followers; and the environment in which they operate. (Chapter 13)

Slack   The time difference between scheduled completion and each of the paths in a PERT network. (Chapter 7)

Social needs   The need for acceptance, friendship, and affection; third level in Maslow's hierarchy. (Chapter 12)

Social responsibility   The obligations of business to society, especially in the areas of equal opportunity, ecology, and consumerism. (Chapter 16)

Sociology   The study of group behavior.

Span of control   The number of subordinates who report to a given superior. (Chapter 5)

Staff authority   Auxiliary authority as seen in the case of individuals who advise, assist, recommend, or facilitate organizational activities (for example, the company lawyer who advises the chief executive officer on the legality of contract matters). (Chapter 5)

Staff department   A department that provides assistance and support to line departments in attaining basic objectives of the organization. In a manufacturing firm, purchasing and accounting would be staff departments. (Chapter 5)

Staff independence   A concept developed centuries ago by the Roman Catholic Church whereby advisors are neither appointed by the person they advise nor removable by that person; the yes-man pitfall is avoided by this concept. (Chapter 2)

Staffing   The recruiting, selecting, training, and developing of individuals for organizational purposes. (Chapter 14)

Standing committee   A committee, often advisory in nature, that exists for an indefinite period of time. (Chapter 5)

Status   Attributes that rank and relate individuals in an organization. (Chapter 11)

Strategic business unit (SBU)   A unit within the overall organization which has a single business, a distinct mission, competitors, and a responsible manager. (Chapter 4)

Strategic planning   The determination of an organization's major objectives and the policies and strategies that will govern the acquisition, use, and disposition of resources in achieving these objectives. (Chapter 4)

Suboptimization   Using less than the total of each input in order to maximize the total output or profit. (Chapter 3)

Subsidiary   A company that is owned in part or fully by another firm. (Chapter 17)

Supplemental monthly budget   A budgetary approach in which the firm determines a minimum operational budget and prior to the beginning of each month provides the units with additional funds to supplement this minimum. (Chapter 7)

TA   *See* Transactional analysis.

Tall organization structure   An organization structure in which there is a narrow span of control with a large number of levels in the hierarchy. *See also* Flat organization structure. (Chapter 5)

Technical level   Low organizational level concerned primarily with the production and distribution of goods and services. (Chapter 15)

Technical managers   Low-level managers concerned with turning out goods and services as economically as possible. These managers tend to have an engineering point of view. (Chapter 15)

Tenure agreements   Employment contracts. (Chapter 18)

Territorial departmentalization   Organization of a department along the lines of geographic location. An example is found in a company with four major divisions: eastern, midwestern, western, and foreign. (Chapter 5)

Theory X   A set of assumptions that holds that people: (a) dislike work, (b) have little ambition, (c) want security above all else, and (d) must be coerced, controlled, and threatened with punishment in order for them to produce. (Chapter 12)

Theory Y   A set of assumptions that holds that: (a) if conditions are favorable, people will not only accept responsibility but will seek it; (b) if people are committed to organizational objectives, they will exercise self-direction and self-control; and (c) commitment is a function of the rewards associated with goal attainment. (Chapter 12)

Therblig   A term used in time and motion study to identify a basic hand motion (for example, "grasp" or "hold"). The word is formed by spelling Gilbreth backward, transposing the *t* and *h*. (Chapter 2)

Three-dimension leadership model   A leadership model, developed by William J. Reddin, that stresses the importance of three factors: (a) task orientation, (b) relationships orientation, and (c) effectiveness. (Chapter 13)

Third wave of change   Changes that are now occurring as a result of recent developments in such areas as technology, information handling, the world of work, organizational loyalty, organizational structures, redefinition of organizational purpose, and multinational corporations. (Chapter 1)

Time study   A method of determining the time it takes to perform a particular task. The procedure often involves the use of a stopwatch for timing all the various elements associated with the task (for example, the time for picking up a piece of material, positioning it, or inserting it into the machine). Time study was widely used by the scientific managers in determining a fair day's work and is still employed in industrial settings. (Chapter 2)

Time-event analyses   Control techniques that permit the manager to monitor and evaluate elapsed time and attained progress on an undertaking. (Chapter 7)

Trait theory   A theory of leadership that attempts to relate success to an individual's personal characteristics or traits. (Chapter 13)

Transactional analysis (TA)   A technique designed to help managers communicate with and understand their people through an analysis of their own behavior as well as that of the subordinates. (Chapter 14)

Transformation process   *See* Black box concept.

Two-dimensional leadership model   A leadership model that addresses the importance of two factors: (a) task orientation and (b) relationship orientation. (Chapter 13)

Two-way communication   Transmission of information and ideas both up and down the hierarchy. (Chapter 11)

Ulterior transaction   A complex transaction involving more than two ego states with the real message often disguised under a socially acceptable transaction. (Chapter 14)

Uncertainty decisions   Decision situations in which managers feel they cannot develop probability estimates because they have no way of gauging the likelihood of the various alternatives. (Chapter 8)

Understanding   The second step in the communication process; it involves ensuring that the receiver grasps the essentials of the message. (Chapter 11)

Unity of command   A management principle that states that a subordinate should report to only one superior. (Chapter 2)

Unity of direction   *See* Unity of management.

Unity of management   One of Henri Fayol's classical principles, calling for one manager and one plan for all operations having the same objective. Also called unity of direction. (Chapter 2)

Upward communication   Communications channels which provide a route for subordinates to convey information to superiors. (Chapter 11)

User expectation   A sales forecast that is constructed after conducting a consumer survey or some other form of consumer research. (Chapter 4)

Valence   A person's preference for a first-level outcome. *See also* Expectancy; Expectancy-valence theory; First-level outcome; Instrumentality. (Chapter 12)

Variable costs   Costs that change in relation to output (for example, salaries and cost of materials). (Chapter 7)

Variable expense budget   A budget in which expenses and allowances are computed for different levels of activity, then adjusted following the budget period in accord with a predetermined formula. (Chapter 7)

Variety of skill   The degree to which a job calls for activities involving different talents and skills. (Chapter 14)

Vocational Rehabilitation Act of 1973 A federal law that requires businesses with contracts or subcontracts with the federal government to hire the handicapped. (Chapter 16)

Zero-base budgeting A budgeting technique in which all organizational activities or projects are broken into decision packages, then cost estimated, and finally ranked by priority; no unit is assumed to automatically receive any sum above $0 in the initial process. (Chapter 7)

Zero-sum games Games in which gains by one side are offset by losses to the other side. (Chapter 9)

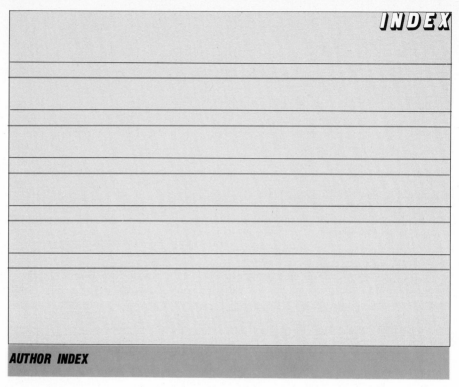

INDEX

AUTHOR INDEX

Bernthal, W. F., 473
Best, A., 452
Bhagat, R. S., 452
Biles, G. E., 452
Blake, R. R., 350, 351, 352, 362
Blanchard, K. H., 295, 318, 357, 358, 362
Blau, P. M., 38, 132
Blue, J. L., 468, 473
Bock, R. H., 452
Bockman, V. M., 325, 335
Boehm, G. A. W., 258, 263, 271
Boettinger, H. M., 133, 158, 496
Bonoma, T. V., 215
Boone, L., 496, 500
Borch, F. J., 46
Boulden, J. B., 264, 271
Boulding, K. E., 413, 414, 427
Bowers, D. G., 398
Bowman, J. S., 452, 496
Bracker, J., 94
Bradley, D. G., 463, 464, 473
Bradley, G. E., 460, 461, 469
Bradspies, R. W., 182
Brady, R. H., 380
Brandt, W. K., 473
Brenner, S. N., 496
Brief, A. P., 398
Bright, J. R., 211
Bright, W. E., 398
Brown, R. L., 169, 182
Brown, R. V., 247
Buccholz, R. A., 452
Buchele, R. B., 181
Buehler, V. M., 452
Buffa, E. S., 247, 264, 271
Burack, E. H., 95
Burck, G. C., 499
Burke, R. J., 452
Burnham, D. H., 318, 363
Burns, T., 135, 158
Bursk, E. C., 460, 461, 469
Butler, A. G., Jr., 158
Byrd, C., 342
Byron, W. J., S. J., 496

C

Campbell, J. P., 382
Carlisle, H. M., 153, 154, 159
Carrell, M. R., 333, 334, 335
Carroll, A. B., 452
Carroll, S. J., Jr., 399
Carson, R., 452
Carzo, R., Jr., 111
Cateora, P. R., 464, 474
Ceriello, V. R., 398
Chandler, A. D., Jr., 102, 125, 139
Chase, R. B., 247
Chemers, M. M., 343, 362
Cherrington, D. M., 398
Child, J., 153, 158
Churchman, C. W., 247

Clarke, A. C., 265, 271
Clarke, D. G., 95
Clark, P. A., 125
Clarkson, S., 15
Cleland, D. I., 141, 147, 158, 427
Cohen, K. H., 94
Cohen, S. L., 496
Cole, R. J., 437
Connor, P. E., 50, 342
Cook, C. W., 335
Cook, R. A., 318, 335
Cook, R. M., 247
Cooper, M. R., 487, 496
Cornwall, D. J., 398
Cote, A., 438, 439
Coubrough, J. A., 27, 28
Cowen, S. S., 168, 181
Cross, G. P., 306
Cuddy, D. M., 473
Culbertson, K., 313, 335
Cummings, L. L., 326, 327
Cyert, R. M., 94

D

Daellenbach, H. G., 247
Daft, R. L., 268, 271
Dale, E., 109, 118, 119, 120, 125
Dalton, D. R., 111, 125
Davis, K., 297, 298, 382, 451, 452
Davis, S. M., 15, 147, 148, 158
Davis, T. R. V., 362
Day, G. S., 83
Dean, B. V., 168, 181
Dean, J. W., III, 291
Denson, F. A., 292, 306
Dessler, G., 50, 359
Devitt, H. W., 326
Dickson, G. G., 266, 268, 269, 271
Dickson, W. J., 34, 45
Dirsmith, M. W., 169, 181
Dittrich, J. E., 333, 334, 335
Donovan, N. B., 95
Dory, J. P., 213
Dowling, W. F., 395, 398
Downey, H. K., 360
Doz, Y. L., 473
Drucker, P. F., 16, 81, 94, 111, 125, 181, 215, 379, 398
Duncan, W. J., 58, 94, 427, 496
Dunne, E. J., Jr., 145, 158
Dunnette, M. D., 382
Durant, W., 22

E

Edmonds, C. P., III, 530
Edmunds, S. W., 453
Ehrlich, P., 441
Elliott, J. F., 474
England, J. L., 398
England, G. W., 473

English, J., 398
Evans, R. J., Jr., 378
Ewing, D. W., 483, 484, 496

F

Farmer, R. N., 459
Farney, D., 181
Fayerweather, J., 462, 473
Fayol, H., 26–30, 40, 44, 50, 62, 164, 481
Fein, M., 377
Ference, T. P., 496
Ferguson, R. D., 224, 247
Ferruzzi, D. N., 378
Fiedler, F., 343, 352, 353, 354, 362
Field, G. A., 271
Fielding, G. J., 111, 125
Filley, A. C., 325, 343, 379, 382, 480
Fitch, H. G., 453
Flamholtz, E. G., 390, 398
Flowers, V. S., 362, 392, 399
Foley, P. M., 487, 496
Foltz, R. F., 306
Foote, M. R., 474
Ford, D. H., 496
Ford, D. L., Jr., 399
Ford, H., 73
Ford, J. D., 360
Ford, R. N., 376, 377, 398
Foster, R. N., 211
Fottler, M. D., 453
Fox, W. M., 395, 396
Franko, L. G., 474
Fraser, L. B., III, 181
Fromm, E., 322
Fruchter, B., 350
Fry, L., 453
Fusfeld, A. R., 211

G

Gallagher, G. A., 271
Gantt, H. L., 44, 172
Garrett, R. W., 247
Gelb, B. D., 453
Gellerman, S. W., 335, 362
George, C. S., Jr., 35
George, W. B., 452
George, W. W., 152, 158
Gerald, A., 83
Gerwin, D., 158
Getty, J. P., 491
Gibbons, C. C., 181
Giblin, E. J., 398
Giglioni, G. B., 181
Gilbreth, F., 25–26, 44
Gilbreth, L., 25–26, 44
Gillett, P. L., 453
Glueck, W. F., 94, 153, 342
Goetz, B., 179
Golembiewski, R. T., 400
Gordon, P. J., 62, 243

Gordon, T. J., 211
Gorlow, L., 335
Graham, F., Jr., 453
Graham, M. B. W., 213, 216
Gray, E., 453
Greenbaum, H. H., 306
Greene, C. N., 332, 335
Greenwood, W. T., 180, 428
Grigaliunas, B. S., 325
Gross, A. C., 158
Grote, R. C., 376
Guest, R. H., 377, 398
Gulick, L., 39
Gumpert, D. E., 437, 453
Guth, W. D., 195, 196, 215
Gyllenhammar, P. G., 375

H

Hackman, J. R., 379
Haimann, T., 50, 342
Hain, T., 394, 395
Hall, J., 306
Hall, R. H., 59
Hall, W. K., 94
Halpin, A. W., 349
Hampton, D., 50, 321
Hanan, M., 484, 485
Hand, J. H., 197
Harari, E., 472
Harley, J., 439
Harrell, T., 125, 129
Harris, T. A., 383, 398
Harvey, B. H., 400
Harvey, E., 139
Hathaway, H. K., 26
Hay, C. D., 438
Hay, L. E., 271
Hay, R., 453
Hayes, T. C., 494
Haynes, V., Jr., 468, 473
Hays, R. D., 469
Heenan, D. A., 271, 474
Heinen, C. M., 443
Henderson, H., 16
Hennig, M., 453
Henry, C. L., Jr., 292, 306
Herbert, T. T., 453
Hersey, P., 295, 306, 318, 357, 358, 362
Herzberg, F., 324, 325, 327, 335, 377
Hickson, D. J., 139, 158
Hill, J. W., 329
Hilton, B. D., 398
Hise, R. T., 453
Hobbs, J. M., 94
Hodgetts, R. M., 16, 123, 140, 144, 145, 156,
    158, 196, 210, 212, 215, 343, 360, 398, 399,
    435, 443, 444, 453
Hofer, C. W., 83
Hollmann, R. W., 398
Holmes, S. L., 449, 453
Homans, G. C., 34

Hopeman, R. J., 175
Horovitz, J. H., 474
House, R. J., 111, 125, 325, 343, 359, 379, 382, 480, 496
Hovey, D. E., 363
Hughes, C. L., 362
Hulbert, J. H., 473
Hulin, C. L., 335
Hunt, D. M., 453
Hunt, J. G., 329
Hunt, R. G., 158
Huse, E. F., 342
Huseman, R. C., 292, 306

I

Inderlisd, S. D., 453
Ivancevich, J. M., 332, 335
Ives, B. D., 215

J

Jablonsky, S. F., 169, 181
James, M., 399
Janger, A. R., 16
Janson, R., 375, 379
Jardim, A., 453
Jay, A., 44
Jenkins, W. O., 342
Jewell, L., 474
Johnson, J. C., 496, 500
Johnson, L. B., 113
Jones, C. H., 263, 265, 271
Jones, D. M. C., 393
Jongeward, D., 399
Justis, R. T., 363

K

Kabus, I., 216
Kahn, R. L., 294, 419
Kakar, S., 44
Kanter, R. M., 123, 125, 453
Kaplan, L. B., 487, 496
Kast, F. E., 158, 413, 428, 481
Katz, D., 294, 419
Kearney, W. J., 382
Keegan, W. J., 474
Keim, G. D., 453
Kelley, R. E., 179, 182
Kelly, J., 62
Kelly, J. P., 453
Kennedy, J. F., 113, 211
Kennell, J. D., 95
Kennevan, W. J., 254
Kerin, K., 323, 335
Kerlinger, F. N., 42
Kerr, S., 325, 343, 354, 379, 382
Kilbridge, M. D., 377
King, C. P., 306
King, W. R., 141, 147, 158, 427
Kinnunen, R. M., 95

Kleity, J. W., 306
Knowles, H. P., 321
Koester, R., 265, 272
Koff, L. A., 439
Kolodny, H. F., 158
Koontz, H., 50, 57, 58, 62, 95, 182, 224, 381, 396, 399, 425, 426, 428, 459
Korda, M., 16
Korth, C. M., 469
Kotter, P., 74, 81, 95, 446
Krasner, D. J., 95
Kraut, A. I., 474
Kreitner, R., 328, 387, 388, 389

L

Laczniak, G. R., 497
Landsberger, H. A., 40, 44
Lange, I., 474
Langer, W. C., 300
Lanier, A. R., 474
Larnood, L., 453
Lawler, E. E., 10, 318, 328, 329, 331, 335, 336
Lawrence, P. R., 15, 138, 147, 148, 153, 158
Lazer, W., 496
Lebell, D., 95
Leitch, D. C., 215
Levinson, H., 373, 399
Lewin, K., 35
Likert, R., 158, 292, 294, 295, 345, 346, 347, 348, 363, 391, 393, 394, 395
Lindsay, C. A., 335
Linneman, R. E., 95
Lippitt, G. L., 399
Lippitt, R., 35
Locke, E. A., 399
Lockwood, D. L., 335
Lodge, G. C., 497
Loebl, E., 16
Lohrasbi, A., 181
Lorange, P., 95
Lord, R. J., 213
Lorsch, J. W., 138, 153, 156, 158, 399
Lusch, R. F., 497
Luthans, F., 16, 58, 63, 123, 196, 265, 272, 328, 335, 362, 377, 378, 387, 388, 389, 400, 411, 416, 428, 435, 443, 444, 453

M

Machiavelli, N., 482, 483
Macintosh, N. B., 268, 271
Mackinnon, N. L., 376
Macy, B. M., 391, 399
Magee, J. F., 247
Mahar, L., 354, 362
Mahoney, T. A., 399
Maisonrouge, J. G., 460, 472
Mandt, E., 486, 496
Mann, F. C., 135
Marchione, A. R., 398
Marcus, S., 182

Marks, E., 335
Martin, D. D., 382
Martin, W. F., 497
Martindell, J., 180, 182
Maslow, A. H., 314, 315, 318, 319, 323, 327, 335
Mason, R. H., 89, 90, 91, 95
Massengill, D., 378
Mawhinney, T. C., 360
Maxwell, S. R., 497
Mayo, E., 30–31, 39, 40, 45
McCaskey, M. B., 95, 306
McClelland, D. C., 318, 321, 332, 335, 363
McDonald, J., 232, 247
McFadden, F. R., 269, 272
McFarland, D. E., 158, 342, 491, 496
McGregor, D., 267, 319, 320, 323, 335
McGregor, D. W., 473
McJaeger, A., 474
Mee, J. F., 45, 497
Melhart, L. J., Jr., 145, 158
Meredith, J. R., 243, 247
Merrill, C. F., 45
Meyer, H. H., 496
Meyer, M. W., 139
Miles, R. E., 41
Millard, C. W., 335
Mills, D. Q., 488, 497
Mills, T., 373, 399
Milner, B., 45
Miner, J. B., 58, 59, 60, 62, 63, 111, 125, 382, 497
Mintzberg, H., 272, 428
Mirides, E., 438, 439
Mirvis, P. H., 391, 399
Mitchell, T. F., 399
Mitchell, T. R., 359
Molander, E. A., 496
Moore, F., 247
Moore, J. M., 247
Mooney, J. D., 22, 45
Morgan, B. S., 487, 496
Morrissey, G. L., 380
Morse, J. J., 156, 158
Moss, S., 305, 307
Most, K. S., 95
Mouton, J. S., 350, 351, 352, 362
Munsterberg, H., 45
Murphy, C. J., 354
Myers, M. S., 326, 375, 392, 399

N

Nader, R., 447, 453
Nehrbass, R. G., 428
Nemiroff, P. M., 399
Neumann, S., 216, 399
Newman, R. G., 306
Newman, W. H., 121
Nichols, R. G., 294, 303, 304, 306
Nielander, W. A., 305
Nixon, R. M., 211

Nolan, R. L., 269, 272
Norton, S. D., 378

O

Odiorne, G. S., 379, 381
O'Donnell, C., 50, 58, 62, 224, 396
Oh, T. K., 474
Oldham, G., 379
O'Reilley, C. A., III, 306
Organ, D. W., 336
Ornati, O. A., 398
Ostlund, L. E., 453
Ouchi, W. G., 474
Owens, J., 450, 453
Ozawa, T., 474

P

Packard, V., 317
Paranka, S., 247
Parkinson, C. N., 108, 125
Parsons, T., 421
Pascale, R. T., 474
Pascucci, J. H., 150
Pati, G. C., 436, 453
Paul, R. J., 336
Paul, R. N., 95
Paul, W. J., Jr., 377
Pekar, P. P., Jr., 95
Perlmutter, H. V., 474
Perreult, W. D., Jr., 452
Perroni, A. G., 45
Person, H. S., 23
Peters, T. J., 159, 363
Peterson, R. B., 465, 474
Petit, T. A., 422, 423, 424, 428
Pheysey, D. C., 139, 158
Pinder, C. C., 336
Pohlman, R. A., 471
Pollay, R., 247
Porter, L. W., 328, 329, 331, 332, 336
Porter, A. L., 399
Porter, L. W., 111, 125
Powell, G. N., 439, 440
Prahalad, C. K., 473
Proehl, C. W., Jr., 400
Pryatel, H. A., 452
Puett, J. A., Jr., 399
Pugh, D. S., 139, 158
Purcell, T. V., 449, 450, 453
Purdy, K., 379
Pyle, W. C., 393

R

Randall, L., 387
Reddin, W. J., 354, 355, 356, 363
Reha, R. K., 440, 453
Reif, W. E., 377, 378
Reiley, A. C., 22, 45
Reitz, H. J., 474

Voich, D., Jr., 50
von Bertalanffy, L., 428
von Glinow, M., 360
Vroom, V. H., 326, 328, 330, 336, 363

W

Waldo, C. N., 323, 335
Walker, J. W., 123, 399
Walters, J. L., 473
Walters, K. D., 182, 497
Ware, W. W., 158
Warren, E. K., 121, 496
Warshaw, M. R., 446
Weaver, C. N., 336, 399
Webber, R., 321, 497
Weber, M., 132
Weekly, J. K., 474
Weigand, R. E., 474
Weihrich, H., 50, 62, 224, 396
Werner, J. B., 151
Weir, T., 452
Wheelright, S. C., 95
White, D. D., Jr., 389
White, G. R., 213, 216
White, R. K., 35
White, R. W., 318

Whyte, W. H., Jr., 488, 497
Widing, J. W., Jr., 475
Williams, L. K., 135, 216
Willis, R., 94
Wood, M. M., 453
Woodward, H. N., 95
Woodward, J., 135–137, 139
Wool, H., 374
Woolf, D. A., 63
Wooten, L. M., 428
Worthy, J. C., 109, 110
Wortman, M. S., Jr., 58, 63, 411, 429
Wrege, C. D., 45
Wren, D. A., 31, 45, 50

Y

Yanouzas, J. N., 111
Yost, E. B., 453

Z

Zaleznik, A., 363
Zani, W. M., 254, 256, 258, 272
Zeira, Y., 472, 474
Ziegenfuss, J. T., 399
Zwerman, W. L., 138

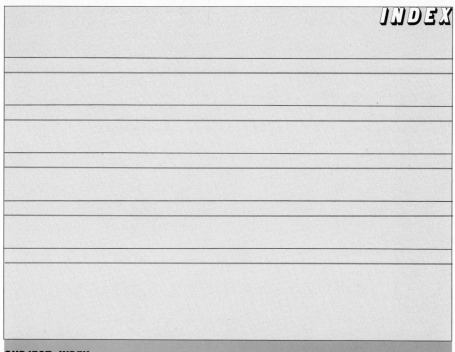

INDEX

SUBJECT INDEX